Experiencing Russia's Civil War

Experiencing Russia's Civil War

POLITICS, SOCIETY, AND

REVOLUTIONARY CULTURE

IN SARATOV, 1917–1922

Donald J. Raleigh

PRINCETON UNIVERSITY PRESS   PRINCETON AND OXFORD

Copyright © 2002 by Princeton University Press
Published by Princeton University Press, 41 William Street, Princeton, New Jersey 08540
In the United Kingdom: Princeton University Press, 3 Market Place,
Woodstock, Oxfordshire OX20 1SY
All Rights Reserved

Library of Congress Cataloging-in-Publication Data

Raleigh, Donald J.
    Experiencing Russia's civil war : politics, society, and revolutionary culture in
    Saratov, 1917–1922 / Donald J. Raleigh.
        p.   cm.
    Includes bibliographical references and index.
    ISBN 0-691-03433-8 (alk. paper) — ISBN 0-691-11320-3 (pbk. : alk. paper)
    1. Saratov Region (Russia) — History.   2. Soviet Union — History — Revolution,
    1917–1921.   I. Title.

DK265.8.S37 R338 2002
947'.460841 — dc21   2002025291

British Library Cataloging-in-Publication Data is available

This book has been composed in Sabon with Helvetica Compress Display

Printed on acid-free paper. ∞

www.pupress.princeton.edu

Printed in the United States of America

1   3   5   7   9   10   8   6   4   2

10   9   8   7   6   5   4   3   2   1

To my son, Adam Sanders Raleigh

Contents

The Bibliography for this book can be found in its entirety on the
Princeton University Press website, www.pupress.princeton.edu/biblios/raleigh

Illustrations

Figures

Maps

Tables

Acknowledgments

I TAKE GREAT pleasure in thanking those many organizations and individuals who contributed to the researching and writing of this book. A study that necessitated more than a dozen trips to the Soviet Union and Russia could not have been completed without generous financial backing. Fulbright-Hays and International Research and Exchanges Board (IREX) fellowships enabled me to launch this project in 1986. With monies provided by the National Endowment for the Humanities and the United States Information Agency, IREX supported additional research trips in 1988, 1990, and 1992. A fellowship from the Hoover Institution, funded by the U.S. Department of State's discretionary grant program, based on the "Soviet-Eastern European Research & Training Act of 1983, Public Law 98–164, Title VIII, 97 Stat. 1047–50," permitted me to spend a summer working in the Bay Area. Fellowships during the 1991–92 academic year from the National Humanities Center, the National Endowment for the Humanities, and the American Council of Learned Societies made it possible for me to start the project over once the Gorbachev Revolution made available heretofore off-limit Russian archives. A University of North Carolina Kenan Competitive Leave, an Institute for Arts and Humanities Fellowship, and a research and study leave from the Department of History freed me from my teaching responsibilities so that I could draft and revise this book, while several awards from the University Research Council and funds from my Pardue professorship subsidized annual summer visits to Saratov.

I am grateful for the opportunity to acknowledge the archives, libraries, and museums where I conducted my research, and those individuals who made important contributions to it. In the United States I carried out research at the Hoover Institution on War, Revolution, and Peace, the Library of Congress, the New York Public Library, the University of Hawai'i's Hamilton Library, the University of Illinois at Champaign-Urbana Library, the University of North Carolina's Davis Library, and Columbia University's Butler Library. In Russia, I re-

searched this book at the Russian State (Lenin) Library and Fundamental
Library of the Social Sciences (INION) in Moscow, at the Library of the
Academy of Sciences and the Saltykov-Shchedrin (Public) Library in St.
Petersburg, and at the Research Library of Saratov University, where I
was aided enormously by the late Vera Aleksandrovna Artisevich. I also
located valuable materials at the Central Historical Museum (Moscow),
and at the Saratov, Balashov, and Khvalynsk Local Studies Museums.

I wish to record my appreciation to the staffs of the State Archive of
the Russian Federation (GA RF) and the Russian State Archive of Socio-
Political History (RGASPI, the former Communist Party Archive) in
Moscow. I am especially indebted to the truly exceptional archivists
at the State Archive of Saratov Oblast (GASO), particularly to Z. E.
Gusakova and her coworkers (G. A. Dziakovich, G. P. Koreykova, H. I.
Shirova, A. S. Maiorova, N. V. Samokhvalova, G. B. Kuliavtseva, and
others), who extended to me (and my students) not only every professional courtesy, but also sincere human warmth and concern. Their at-
tentiveness, quality research assistance, genuine interest in my project,
and friendship made it difficult for me to work in other repositories!
Thanks too to the archivists at the Center for the Documentation of
Modern History of Saratov Oblast (TsDNISO, the former oblast Communist Party archive), and to the branch of GASO in the city of
Balashov.

I wish to express my personal and professional gratitude to those
Saratov colleagues and friends who supported my first trip to the banks
of the Volga: V. S. Semenov, V. I. Nikolaeva, A. V. Rodionov, I. R. Pleve,
the late I. D. Parfenov, and the late S. V. Katkov. The wisdom, friendship, irreproachable professionalism, and unfaltering support of N. I.
Deviataikina sustained me throughout the research and writing of this
book. So did the close companionship and ready assistance of A. A.
Kreder, whose untimely death in 2000 deprived those of us who be-
friended him of a dignified, generous colleague. A. A. German, A. I.
Avrus, V. S. Mirzekhanov, and D. I. Trubetskov provided regular doses
of encouragement. I also thank E. A. Abrosimova, R. M. Bazyleva, O. V.
Kachaeva, I. V. Gorfinkel, V. A. Dines, S. V. Sushchenko, A. V. Vor-
onezhtsev, E. R. Iarskaia-Smirnova, P. V. Romanov, G. N. Koloiarskii,
O. Iu. Abakumov, S. M. Levin, V. A. Mitrokhin, A. G. Riabkov, Iu.
A. Safronov, S. Iu. Shenin, F. A. Rashitov, and V. M. Zakharov. V. V.
Gleizer, G. A. Mishin, and V. A. Solomonov kindly shared materials
with me held in their private collections. David E. Barclay, Peter Holquist, Edward Kasinec, Patricia Polansky, and Nadia Zilper brought
sources to my attention that otherwise might have eluded me.

I have been especially fortunate to have received invaluable help at
the writing stage. A sympathetic but critical colleague and friend, Louise

McReynolds, read the first draft of the book, pushed me to clarify my ideas and develop my arguments, and provided stimulating intellectual companionship over the years. Jonathan Wallace applied his expert editorial skills to the same draft. Alexander Rabinowitch, whose encouragement and support have been unwavering, carefully critiqued a revised version of the manuscript, making numerous suggestions for improving it. Betsy Jones Hemenway, Paula Michaels, Beth Holmgren, and Barbara Harris offered sound advice on individual chapters. Peter Holquist's generous and meticulous reading of the penultimate draft helped me sharpen the final version. I also acknowledge the ideas for improving the manuscript of the anonymous readers at Princeton University Press, and of my editor, Brigitta van Rheinberg, who convinced me that a shorter manuscript would make a better book. My copy editor, Jodi Beder, edited the volume with great care. Sharon Kowalsky ably prepared the index. It goes without saying that none of these individuals is responsible for the views expressed in the study, or for any remaining errors.

In incorporating into this book modified forms of previously published material, I wish to thank the relevant journals and publishers for permission to do so. A modified version of my article, "Languages of Power: How the Saratov Bolsheviks Imagined Their Enemies," *Slavic Review* 57, no. 2 (1998): 320–49, is reprinted in chapter 2 with permission from the American Association for the Advancement of Slavic Studies, the publisher and copyright holder of *Slavic Review*. An expanded version of "Co-optation *amid* Repression: The Revolutionary Communists in Saratov Province, 1918–1920," *Cahiers du Monde russe* 40, no. 4 (1999): 625–56, appears in chapter 5 and is reprinted with permission from the journal. A shorter version of chapter 12, "A Provincial Kronstadt: Popular Unrest in Saratov at the End of the Civil War," was published in *Provincial Landscapes: Local Dimensions of Soviet Power, 1917–1953* (Pittsburgh, 2001), and is reprinted with permission of the University of Pittsburgh Press. Bruce Cornelison prepared the maps, earlier versions of which are found in *A Russian Civil War Diary: Alexis Babine in Saratov* (Durham, 1988), published by Duke University Press.

The sustained support and love of my wife Karen and son Adam nurtured me throughout the process of researching and writing this study, particularly during my frequent absences from home. Both have let Russia — and Saratov — become a bigger part of their lives than they probably care to admit.

I dedicate this book to my son, Adam Sanders Raleigh, a great teenager and aspiring marine biologist, who knows as much about sharks as I know about Saratov, and who helped me get, and keep, my priorities straight. Thanks, buddy!

Glossary and Abbreviations
Used in Archival Citations

glavki, chief industrial branch administrations
gorispolkom, city executive committee
gorkom, city party committee
gubispolkom, provincial executive committee
gubkom, provincial party committee
Gubprodkom, Provincial Food Supply Commissariat
Gubprofsovet, Saratov Trade Union Council
Gubsovnarkhoz, Provincial Economic Council (GSNKh)
ispolkom, (soviet) executive committee
kombedy, committees of the village poor
Narkomprod, Food Commmissariat
prodnalog, tax in kind, instituted in March 1921
Rabkrin, Workers'-Peasants' Inspectorate (WPI)
raikom, neighborhood party committee
razverstka, obligatory grain quota assessment
revkom, military revolutionary committee
samogon, illicit alcohol
Sarrabsoiuz, Workers' Cooperative Council
Sovnarkhoz, Supreme Economic Council
sovnarkhozy, economic councils
Sovnarkom, Council of People's Commissars
tovaroobmen, the commodity exchange
uispolkom, uezd executive committee

Abbreviations in Archival Citations

op., *opis'* (inventory)
l., ll., *list, listy* (folio, folios, basically sheets or pages)
f., *fond* (collection)

d. dd., *delo, dela* (files, files)*
ob, *oborot* (back side)

*For the sake of convenience, I have also used d. (*delo*) to designate *edinitsa khraneniia* (ed. khr., best translated as storage unit encountered in some older collections in the State Archive of Saratov Oblast [GASO]).

Experiencing Russia's Civil War

Introduction

Experiencing Russia's Civil War

As SELF-PROCLAIMED heir to the French Revolution, the Russian Revolution also had universal aspirations. One of the great defining events of the twentieth century, it aroused desires to overthrow exploitation, injustice, and colonial domination. Although it failed to live up to its expectations, the Revolution forced a reconfiguration of politics in Europe and the United States by presenting itself as an inevitable alternative to Western socioeconomic and political practices. The Revolution likewise fired the imaginations of intellectuals and nationalists in the developing world, who sought to liberate themselves from the confident global empires. Supplanting the "Marseillaise" as the anthem of the downtrodden, the "International" echoed throughout the century and reverberates *sotto voce* even today.

Given its singular significance, it is not surprising that no other topic in Soviet history has been as politically charged and so often retold as the story of the Revolution of 1917. This is not true, however, of its most decisive chapter, the Civil War, the historiography of which remains remarkably underdeveloped,[1] considering the conflict's relation-

---

[1] John Keep, "Social Aspects of the Russian Revolutionary Era (1917–1923) in Recent English-Language Historiography," *East European Quarterly* 24, no. 2 (1990): 159–60. Other thoughtful essays that survey the general contours of the debates in the recent past are Ronald G. Suny, "Toward a Social History of the October Revolution," *American Historical Review* 88, no. 1 (1983): 31–52; idem., "Revision and Retreat in the Historiography of 1917: Social History and Its Critics," *Russian Review* 53, no. 2 (1994): 165–82; and Steve Smith, "Writing the History of the Russian Revolution after the Fall of Communism," *Europe-Asia Studies* 46, no. 4 (1994): 563–78.

ship to the subsequent course of Soviet history. Before researching this book I subscribed to the view that Stalinism marked a departure from Leninism and that the fledgling Soviet system entering the 1920s sustained less authoritarian alternatives to the path that Russian history ultimately took with the launching of Joseph Stalin's grandiose industrialization drive at the end of the 1920s. I no longer am so sure. For one thing, as the "matrix of the contemporary world," World War I inaugurated a century "of revolution and ideological politics" and "international and social violence par excellence,"[2] marking a watershed in the methods the European states used to govern their populations. As Peter Holquist persuasively shows, many of the features we tend to associate with the Civil War period, such as militarization, centralization, and the concept of the internal enemy, first emerged during the Great War, while practices we associate with the Bolsheviks — surveillance, state control of food supply, and the application of violence for political ends — were also widely employed by other belligerent powers.[3] Then there is the unanticipated and contingent. In his comparative study of the French and Russian Revolutions, Arno J. Mayer insists that "the Furies of revolution are fueled above all else by the resistance of the forces and ideas opposed to it." In emphasizing that the by-no-means innocent opposition to revolution helped nurture a spiral of terror, Mayer poignantly demonstrates how violence overwhelmed the revolutionaries who had come to power.[4] Although I see great merit in Mayer's bold argument, I believe he undervalues the extent to which the Bolsheviks and other elements of the country's radical Left actually promoted a climate of violence, owing to Russian political culture, ideology, and the broader wartime practices referred to earlier. Their determination to rule as a minority party in order to reorder society resulted in the militarization of public life, which bequeathed a traumatic legacy by ordaining how the Bolsheviks would, in subsequent years, realize their plans for social engineering: many of the practices we associate with the Stalinist era were experimented with and even became an integral part of the new order already during the Civil War, as did the population's strategies of accommodation and resistance.

[2] Martin Malia, *Russia under Western Eyes: From the Bronze Horseman to the Lenin Mausoleum* (Cambridge, Mass., 1999), 235, 293.

[3] Peter I. Holquist, "'Information Is the *Alpha* and *Omega* of Our Work': Bolshevik Surveillance in Its Pan-European Context," *Journal of Modern History* 69 (September 1997): 443–46. See also his forthcoming book, *Making War, Forging Revolution: Russia's Don Territory during Total War and Revolution, 1914–21,* to be published by Harvard University Press.

[4] Arno J. Mayer, *The Furies: Violence and Terror in the French and Russian Revolutions* (Princeton, 2000), 23, also 4, 7, 17.

Despite the crucial long-term consequences of the experiential and social aspects of the Russian Civil War, Western scholarship on the topic has focused on military operations, diplomacy, and politics at the top, due to the nature of the available sources as well as to dominant paradigms in the historical profession.[5] Since the 1980s, however, heightened awareness on the part of Western historians of the importance of the years 1918–21 as a formative experience for the Soviet state has resulted in a shift to heretofore neglected questions of social history and Bolshevik cultural experimentation,[6] stimulating publication of new academic and popular overviews of the Civil War.[7] Nevertheless, the traditional emphasis on military and political aspects of the conflict has not abated.[8] While some 1920s Soviet publications on the subject that appeared before the imposition of Stalinist orthodoxy on intellectual life still appeal to contemporary readers, nearly all later historiography in the USSR on the 1918–21 period suffers from the general shortcomings common to Soviet historical writing. True, Soviet historians who studied 1917 often produced results that were not entirely invalidated by ideological content, but this is much less the case in regard to the Civil War years. In fact, my research indicates the enormous extent to which Soviet historians patently falsified the history of the Civil War in their

[5] This is not because those of us who wrote on 1917 did not want to expose the dark side of the Bolsheviks' social experiment by extending our narratives beyond the confines of that year. Indeed, the social history of the Russian Revolution, and of the Soviet Union for that matter, was still in its infancy a mere twenty-five years ago, and it was only natural that historians first applied the research strategies of the then new social history to 1917 itself. More importantly, the sources available for many topics on the post-1917 period were simply inadequate. Despite the lack of access to Russian archives before the mid-1980s, historians exploring the social dimensions of the Revolution could at least rely on the rich Russian press. Yet once the Bolsheviks imposed censorship — almost immediately after October 1917 — they silenced opposition voices or drove them into the underground.

[6] See Peter Kenez, "Western Historiography of the Russian Civil War," in *Essays in Russian and East European History: Festschrift in Honor of Edward C. Thaden*, ed. by Leo Schelbert and Nick Ceh (Boulder, 1995), 199–205.

[7] I have in mind works such as Evan Mawdsley's *The Russian Civil War* (Boston, 1987); Vladimir N. Brovkin, *Behind the Front Lines of the Civil War: Political Parties and Social Movements in Russia, 1918–1922* (Princeton, 1994); and W. Bruce Lincoln's *Red Victory* (New York, 1989).

[8] See, for instance, Jonathan Smele, *Civil War in Siberia: The Anti-Bolshevik Government of Admiral Kolchak, 1918–1920* (New York, 1996); Norman G. O. Pereira, *White Siberia: The Politics of Civil War* (Montreal, 1996); and the publications of Susan Z. Rupp: "Conflict and Crippled Compromise: Civil-War Politics in the East and the Ufa State Conference," *Russian Review* 56, no. 2 (1997): 249–64; idem., "The Struggle in the East: Opposition Politics in Siberia, 1918," *Carl Beck Papers in Russian and East European Studies*, no. 1304 (Pittsburgh, 1998).

attempts to employ the "science" of Marxist history as an instrument to fight émigré and Western accounts of the Revolution.

My book, the aim of which is to bring to life the diverse experiences of the Russian Civil War in the city and province of Saratov, thus marks a major departure in the historiography for which a local or case study of a Russian province during the hostilities is virtual terra incognita.[9] Because Russia is a vast country with a diverse and dispersed population, a local study can tell us a tremendous amount about momentous events and arguably is the only way to learn about them, for the approach allows the researcher to probe complex interrelationships that are difficult to ascertain on a national level and to attack questions that previously were either considered in isolation or ignored. Instead of stressing the "typicality" of Saratov, I wish to show that while the particular events presented in this study are unique — as they would be in any setting — they have condensed within them more general experiences that are larger than the local. As Allan R. Pred argues, "it is through their intersection with the locally peculiar, the locally sedimented and contingent, the locally configured context, that more global structuring processes are given their forms and become perpetuated or transformed."[10]

Saratov proved to be an ideal choice for my study as well as for my earlier book on the Revolution of 1917, when I specifically sought out an administrative, trade, and cultural center that had some, but limited, industrial development, making it more representative of provincial Russian towns than a major industrial city with a sizable working class. For a variety of objective and fortuitous reasons, sources on Saratov were more plentiful and diverse than those available for other urban areas. Furthermore, the peasant problem loomed so large in Saratov Province that its capital city became a center of Russian populism and of Russia's most popular party, the Socialist Revolutionaries. Saratov similarly affords a suitable setting in which to explore Bolshevik efforts during the Civil War to construct Soviet power both politically and lin-

---

[9] An exception to this generalization is Igor' Narskii's *Zhizn' v katastrofe: Budni naseleniia Urala v 1917–1922 gg.* (Moscow, 2001), which appeared while my book was in production. I was pleased to see that many of Narskii's conclusions about the consequences of the Civil War agree with my own. My work also complements studies on Russia's capitals, but differs in its methodology and in that I had access to archival materials. See Mary McAuley, *Bread and Justice: State and Society in Petrograd, 1917–1922* (Oxford, 1991), and Richard Sakwa, *Soviet Communists in Power: A Study of Moscow during the Civil War, 1918–21* (London, 1988).

[10] *Making Histories and Constructing Human Geographies: The Local Transformation of Practice, Power Relations, and Consciousness* (Boulder, 1990), 15.

guistically, because it remained in Bolshevik hands throughout the tortuous ordeal that lasted locally from 1917 until 1922.

Interested in how different groups lived their lives in particular surroundings and circumstances, I situate my research around the experiences of revolutionaries and of key social groups affected by Bolshevik policies, and use each as an illuminating foil to reflect broader tendencies. I complicate our understanding of the period by considering the languages that represented the divergent experiences and interests of distinct social and political elements, reading certain actions as symbols of political attitudes embedded in social and cultural matrixes that defy easy categorization. While the conceptual ground admittedly is treacherous here, I seek to show how Russian political culture (which I define as the subjective aspects of social life that distinguish one society from another), Bolshevik practices, and the circumstances of civil war molded diverse elements of society into an organic experiential whole. Because those living through the Civil War saw no logic or structure to it, no "center" or generally accepted integrating myth or narrative (despite Bolshevik efforts to craft one), a strict chronological approach would impose a false order on a chaotic chapter in the country's history. Although I observe chronological boundaries, I therefore proceed synchronically, linking a disparate cast of social actors who, at various times, adopted, contested, and/or manipulated to their own advantage the Bolsheviks' attempts at cultural creation.

The major problems my project investigates include the social and political relations and divisions created by revolutionaries; the discursive battle the Bolsheviks and their opponents fought in presenting rival versions of the revolutionary tale; manifestations of "localism," and Saratov leaders' troubled relationship with Moscow and with Bolsheviks in the province's backwaters; the largely unknown role of the left populist movement in helping to keep Soviet power afloat; the development of new rituals of power and attempts to create a "proletarian" culture and to establish cultural hegemony; local economic policies and their effects on daily life; how Saratov peasants, workers, and members of the much despised — but needed — bourgeoisie, responded to Bolshevik rule; and the far-reaching crisis erupting in 1921 that heretofore has been neglected in the scholarly literature. By focusing on the vital, even explosive, interaction between social context and ideologically inspired politics, I seek to comprehend how the experiences of revolution and civil war transformed people and structures.[11]

---

[11] Although my work is informed by recent historical writing on the French Revolution and the cultural turn, I part ways with François Furet and others, who argue in favor of

The great advantage of the approach I am taking is that it brings a new dimension to our understanding of the period by providing insight into how millions of people who lived in the provinces experienced the essential events and issues that confronted the new Soviet regime. Until now, we knew relatively little about the dynamics of civil war at the local level, about daily life in Soviet Russia at this time, about mass attitudes toward social and political experimentation, about center-periphery relations, and about the long-term impact of this extended period of disruption and brutalization on the continuities of social life. By showing how the Bolsheviks were able to stay in power in Saratov Province, I deepen our knowledge of why they survived the Civil War, of the price they paid to do so, and of what this meant for the new type of state they created. My detailed account of what I call the total experience of civil war between 1917 and 1922 permits me to demonstrate how the powerful legacy of the struggle portended social and political clashes to come. In many respects, the ideologically justified devaluation of human life at the time represents the first inkling that the consequences of World War I would reverberate throughout the century.

During the conflict the Bolsheviks or Reds, renamed Communists in 1918,[12] found themselves pitted against the Whites, many of whom represented the country's business and landowning elite. Opposing social (and socialist) revolution, the Whites were a more diverse group than the Bolshevik label of "counterrevolution" would suggest: some sought to set up a conservative government and to restore the old order, but others harbored reformist ideas. Much more complicated were the Bolsheviks' relations with Russia's moderate socialists, the Mensheviks and Socialist Revolutionaries (SRs), who wished to establish a government that would, at the least, include all socialist parties. Often subsumed within the wider conflict of Reds and Whites, the internecine struggle within the socialist camp in fact prevailed during much of 1918, persisted throughout the Civil War, and flared up once again after the Bolsheviks routed the Whites in 1920. Moreover, left-wing SRs and Mensheviks sided with the Bolsheviks against the Whites during the initial phase of the Civil War. Despite their increasingly difficult relationship with the Bolsheviks as the Civil War progressed, these groups tended to accept a semi-legal status during the struggle, backing the Communists at critical junctures or remaining neutral.

Because opposition to revolution was every bit as deeply anchored in

---

an exclusive focus on revolutionary discourse. François Furet, *Interpreting the French Revolution* (New York and London, 1981).

[12] I use both terms interchangeably throughout this study.

Russian political life as the fashion for revolution, armed opposition to the Bolsheviks arose immediately after the events of October 1917, when officers of the Imperial Army, Lavr Kornilov, Anton Denikin, Aleksei Kaledin, and others, formed the first White force known as the Volunteer Army, based in southern Russia. Political opposition to the Bolsheviks became more resolved after they closed down the Constituent Assembly in January 1918, elected in November to decide the country's political future. The period between November 1917 and mid-1918 remained one of great uncertainty that ended with a spate of armed conflicts in Russian towns along the Volga between Bolshevik-run soviets and Czechoslovak legionnaires (former prisoners of war from the Austro-Hungarian armies who were to be transported back to the Western front, where they were to join the Allies in the fight to defeat the Central Powers). These skirmishes emboldened the SR opposition to set up an anti-Bolshevik government in the Volga city of Samara. Many delegates elected to the Constituent Assembly congregated there before the city fell to the Bolsheviks that fall.

Determined to sweep the Bolsheviks from power, the Whites posed a more serious threat to the Red republic after the Allies defeated Germany and decided to back the Whites' cause. The Allies had dispatched troops to Russia in order to secure war materiel for World War I, which they feared would fall into the wrong hands. But their hostility to Bolshevism's call for world revolution and to Russia's withdrawal from the war in March 1918 turned them into supporters of the Whites, who soon fought the Reds along four fronts: southern Russia, western Siberia, northern Russia, and the Baltic region. Until their defeat in 1920, White forces controlled much of Siberia and southern Russia, while the Reds, who moved their capital to Moscow, clung desperately to the Russian heartland, including agriculturally rich Saratov. Emerging in the fall of 1918 as official leader of the White movement, Admiral Kolchak maintained his headquarters in Siberia until major defeats forced him to resign in early 1920.

The Whites' launching of a three-pronged attack against Moscow in March 1919 greatly imperiled the Soviet state. Despite their initial success, the Whites eventually went down in defeat in November, after which their routed forces replaced General Denikin with General Petr Wrangel, usually regarded as the most competent of all of the White commanders. The Whites opened one final offensive in the spring of 1920, which coincided with an invasion of Russia by forces of the newly resurrected Polish state. Red forces overcame Wrangel's army in November, after which he and his troops evacuated Russia by sea from the Crimea. In the meantime, the Bolsheviks' conflict with the Poles ended in stalemate when the belligerent parties signed an armistice in October 1920.

Apart from their military encounters with the Whites, the Bolsheviks also had to contend with a front behind their own lines because party economic policies alienated much of the working class and drove the peasantry to rise up against the requisitioning of grain and related measures. Known as Greens, peasant bands comprised of deserters and others first surfaced in 1919 during the White offensive. They presented an even more pressing danger in mid-1920, triggering uprisings in many Volga provinces, especially Tambov and Saratov. By early 1921, mass unrest, including worker discontent, had convinced the Bolshevik Party to replace their unpopular economic policies known as War Communism, characterized by economic centralization, nationalization of industry and land, and compulsory requisitioning of grain, with the New Economic Policy (NEP), which promised to replace the hated grain requisitioning with a tax in kind and to restore some legal private economic activity. The soundness of this shift in policy from stick to carrot was made clear when, in early March, sailors of the Kronstadt naval fortress, the "pride and glory" of the Revolution, rose up against the Bolsheviks whom they had helped bring to power. Historians traditionally view this episode and the introduction of the NEP as the last acts of the Civil War, after which the party mopped up remaining pockets of opposition, mainly in the borderlands that had gone their separate ways during the ordeal. They depict the ruinous famine that first made itself felt in the winter of 1920–21 and hit hard the next year as one of the Civil War's consequences.

Although Saratov remained Red throughout the period, it came dangerously close to falling to the Whites. Opposition to the Bolshevik takeover in Saratov first found expression in boycotts by the majority of the city's officials and professionals, who hoped to undermine Soviet power by refusing to cooperate with it. Financial collapse, turmoil among the once pro-Bolshevik soldiers, and sporadic peasant disturbances also threatened Saratov's new leaders. Moreover, a full-scale revolt in the local garrison in May 1918 forced the party to introduce martial law in Saratov and revealed that the Bolsheviks lacked a popular mandate. The revolt of Czechoslovakian troops and formation of an anti-Bolshevik government in Samara also drove the Bolsheviks to harden their policies. In addition, by summer the eastern and southern fronts had converged on Saratov as the armies of the White generals seized nearby towns. In August, strategically important Tsaritsyn fell under siege; in September, Moscow placed Saratov under martial law once again. Local authorities now directed all of their energies at warding off the military threat, made more difficult when food brigades sought to wrest grain from the countryside, thereby turning many elements within the local peasantry against Soviet power.

Galvanized into action by their belief in world revolution — and by Moscow's neglect — Saratov Bolshevik leaders in 1918 took steps to create new institutions of Soviet power as the country descended into anarchy and chaos. Following an independent course with their Left SR allies, they declared Saratov a "republic," an action that gave rise to Moscow's charges of "localism." This first heady phase in the local civil war ended with the Center's recall of Saratov's most prominent local Bolshevik leaders at the close of 1918. Their departure amounted to a turning point in the local civil war, for it ushered in a new period for Saratov as it became run like an armed camp by outsiders who had few ties if any locally. Moscow's interference likewise signified the beginning of state centralization. Meanwhile, lack of raw materials and fuel and the disruption of transportation wreaked further havoc on the local economy, which was already in shambles owing to a severe lack of revenue. Scarcities of all sorts forced people to reorient their priorities, restrained the Bolsheviks' efforts at cultural creation, and made it easier for them to justify their use of coercion.

The White offensive of 1919 represented another crucial turning point for Saratov, which had not only strategic significance, but economic and logistical importance as well, for it had become a main source of bread for the hungry cities of central Russia. Placed for the third time under martial law, Soviet power in Saratov teetered between collapse and surrender. Desertions from the Red Army reached alarming levels as Saratov was transformed into an armed camp, its party rulers became isolated from the population, and civilian life and administration became militarized. Relations with the peasantry deteriorated because the party used force to requisition grain.

From a military perspective the tide of events had shifted in favor of the Bolsheviks by 1920, yet keeping oneself fed, and poorly at that, remained a Sisyphean labor. Deeming the economic front every bit as important as the military one, the regime took desperate and unpopular measures to avert total economic collapse, which gave credence to the claims of anarchists and Mensheviks that the Bolshevik usurpers had brought Russia nothing but ruin. That summer Greens burst into Saratov, igniting uprisings in several districts, and resulting in the imposition of martial law yet again. The uprisings quickly spread throughout much of the province, serving as an ominous backdrop to burgeoning worker unrest. In early March 1921, angry worker rallies developed into a general strike, which the Bolsheviks put down by force and intimidation. Repression and the introduction of the NEP kept the Bolsheviks afloat as famine, the consequence of Bolshevik policies and climate, claimed its first victims. This horrific concluding chapter of the local civil war lasted well into 1924, largely negating any of the positive developments normally associated with the NEP.

I have divided my study of Saratov into two parts. Part One makes a case for the centrality of politics to the period. Chapter 1 sketches Saratov's historical development, throwing light on the peculiar features of the local revolution and civil war. Chapter 2 examines how the languages of Bolshevism attempted to understand, represent, and manipulate the flood of resistance to the party's assumption of power during this liminal period in the definition of socialism. Chapter 3 offers a case study of the fate of the Saratov Soviet and of soviets at the district (*uezd*) and county (*volost*) level, emphasizing the defining nature of war and geopolitics in the process of state formation. Through the prism of the dialectical relationship between ideologically inspired attempts to restructure society and general cultural patterns, chapter 4 analyzes the local Communist Party organization. Chapter 5 retrieves from the dustbin of history the so-called Revolutionary Communist Party, without whose support the Bolsheviks would have lost Saratov, and assesses the Leninists' strategy of co-option amid repression in dealing with their radical populist allies as well as with other socialist parties.

My goal in Part Two is to scrutinize the processes that invest social life with meaning, including the consequences of the Bolsheviks' understanding of class. Chapter 6 documents the physical impact of civil war on Saratov as a community or set of social relations, underscoring the extent to which Saratov during the Civil War was not only a community in disarray, but also a community in the making. Chapter 7 canvasses the cultural practices of provincial Communists, demonstrating that their need to employ the coercive power of the state made cultural hegemony an elusive goal. Although it has been suggested that Marxist class analysis became useless for analytical purposes because the Russian class structure disintegrated during the Civil War, class is not just the consequence of social and economic change, but also of reconfigurations of discourse in which class can serve as an organizing principle for constructing social reality.[13] Indeed, given Bolshevik efforts to reify the proletariat and to strike the bourgeoisie as close to home as possible — in their identity, class, as the Bolsheviks politically defined it, remains a useful, even essential concept in my effort to weigh the impact of the Civil War on specific social groups. Thus, chapter 8 draws on provincial diaries and memoirs to furnish elements of concreteness and individu-

---

[13] Sheila Fitzpatrick, "The Bolsheviks' Dilemma: Class, Culture, and Politics in Early Soviet Years," *Slavic Review* 47, no. 4 (1988): 599–613. See also Smith, "Writing," 571.

ality to the experiences of Saratov's ascribed class "other," the bourgeoisie, the target of Bolshevik discriminatory policies. Investigating the Red Guard assault on capital, chapter 9 is as much about the new economic order the Bolsheviks instituted, as it is about the significance of how they attempted to create it. The chapter supplies the background necessary to understand the foci of chapters 10 and 11, which depict the experiences of Saratov peasants and workers, respectively. These chapters chronicle how a consciousness of interpreted experience gave workers and peasants collective identities outside those the Bolsheviks fabricated for them in their narratives of revolution. Chapter 12 probes mass discontent with Bolshevik rule in the spring of 1921 and explains the role of the famine, the last chapter of the local civil war, in keeping the Bolsheviks in power. The conclusion pulls together my findings but also lets the evidence that I have assembled speak for itself.

Dates used in this book before January 1918 are given according to the Julian calendar, which was thirteen days behind the Gregorian calendar of the West; all later dates are given according to the Gregorian calendar. Transliteration from Russian is based on the Library of Congress system. For stylistic considerations, however, I have dropped the soft sign from place names (Volsk, not Vol'sk), proper nouns (Zhest metalworks, not Zhest'), and surnames (Vasiliev, not Vasil'ev). Moreover, in some surnames "ii" is rendered "y" to conform to common usage: Kerensky, Chernyshevsky, and Trotsky.

Part One

POLITICS

One

Revolution on the Volga

REVOLUTIONS always have several histories. The Russian Revolution of 1917 has Bolshevik and non-Bolshevik ones, all of which can be told in several ways, depending upon when one takes up a position in the historiography and from which political or personal vantage point. Soviet practitioners of local history made study of the Revolution thematically dependent on a larger national narrative. By providing in this chapter a thumbnail sketch of Saratov's historical development and a summary and analysis of the local events of 1917, I proceed from the premise that the Center (St. Petersburg, later Moscow) does not determine the periphery, but the periphery determines the Center. I explain the Revolution in terms of local contexts, calling attention to Saratov's socioeconomic structure and political life, and to the dynamic and symbiotic relationship between local and national politics. The correspondence between the two should not detract from Saratov's distinctive texture, but should instead call attention to the enormity of Russia's political and social crises that brought revolution in 1905 and again in 1917. In casting the Revolution as a political event, I suggest that it was also a cultural creation. I determine the impact of the Great War on the revolutionary events of 1917, especially on growing social polarization, economic breakdown, and mounting anarchy. In analyzing the nature of local political power, I throw light on the peculiar features of the October Revolution that made civil war inevitable, and on the fragile foundation on which the Bolsheviks "established" Soviet power in Saratov Province.

15

From Frontier Outpost to Provincial Center

Founded in 1590 as one of a chain of fortresses to protect Muscovy's vulnerable Volga frontier, Saratov is located in the eastern tip of the fertile black-earth (*chernozem*) zone, where forest and steppe converge. As a military settlement guarding Muscovy's eastern holdings, Saratov repeatedly fell under siege in the seventeenth century to marauders and peasant rebels who laid waste to and torched the stronghold. For more than a century Saratov remained a sparsely settled, vulnerable frontier outpost. When the expansion of Russia's frontiers beyond the Volga in the eighteenth century reduced Saratov's military importance, the fortress began to acquire new commercial significance, connected to fishing communities that arose along the Volga and later to the extraction of salt from local mines. As part of the administrative reforms implemented during the reign of Catherine the Great (1762–96), Saratov was designated the administrative center of newly created Saratov Province. By 1917, the province was the thirteenth largest in the Russian empire. Occupying 84,640 square kilometers and comprising ten districts (*uezdy*)—Atkarsk, Balashov, Kamyshin, Khvalynsk, Kuznetsk, Petrovsk, Saratov, Serdobsk, Tsaritsyn, and Volsk—it was roughly the size of South Carolina or Portugal.[1]

During the nineteenth century, the town became vitally linked to the rich black earth of the northern part of the province and to the processing and shipping of grain and agricultural products. Emerging as a commercial anchor for the Lower Volga region, Saratov registered dramatic population growth during the boom years of industrialization in the 1890s and once again after 1910. By 1897 the city's population had reached 137,147 (92 percent of whom were ethnic Russians). Industrial expansion had pushed it to 202,848 by 1904 (a stunning growth of almost 50 percent in seven years) and to 242,425 in 1913, making it the eleventh largest city in the Russian empire (figure 1.1). Saratov was not, however, a major industrial town; in 1914 only about 25,000 of its workers were classified as members of the industrial proletariat, employed in approximately 150 small and medium-sized factories. The rest of the working class—about 55,000 strong—consisted of artisans, dockhands, domestics, and unskilled workers.

Far from being the woefully provincial town of Russian belletristic writing, Saratov boasted the third music conservatory to open in all of Russia, the first provincial art museum to welcome the unscrubbed

[1] See James G. Hart, "From Frontier Outpost to Provincial Capital," in *Politics and Society in Provincial Russia: Saratov, 1590–1917*, ed. Rex A. Wade and Scott J. Seregny (Columbus, Ohio, 1989), 10–27; and I. V. Porokh et al., *Ocherki istorii Saratovskogo Povolzh'ia (1855–1894)*, vol. 2, pt. 1 (Saratov, 1995), 101.

1.1 Saratov in the early twentieth century. Courtesy Gosudarstvennyi Arkhiv Saratovskoi Oblasti (GASO).

masses free of charge, a university founded in 1909 and named after Nicholas II (figure 1.2), a progressive local government, and a broad range of newspapers and publishing houses meeting the needs of an increasingly literate reading public. To be sure, another Saratov of workers' tenements thrown up indiscriminately straggled off along the riverfront, the town's outer perimeter, and its two ravines, Glebuchev and Beloglinskii, which ran through the city perpendicular to the Volga, dividing it, in effect, into three distinct regions. Few of the amenities of modern urban life could be found in these densely populated, largely working-class districts decried for their poor sanitation and harsh and desperate conditions.

Saratov's ethnic makeup revealed the territory's frontier origin as well as the long reach of the state. Freebooters, fugitives, religious dissenters, disgruntled peasants, and others fled to the undergoverned Volga from central Russia during Saratov's fortress days, as a result of which Slavic peasants soon composed the bulk of the population, diversified by pockets of indigenous Mordva, Tatars, Chuvash, and Kalmyks. Administrative assimilation of the area during the eighteenth century resulted in state-sponsored colonization and economic development of the province. In addition to recruiting peasants from Voronezh Province and the Ukraine to work the local salt mines, the government invited Germans and other foreigners and Old Believers to relocate to the area. Settling along the right bank of the Volga in Kamyshin, Saratov, Tsaritsyn, and Atkarsk Districts, and on the left bank in Samara Province, the Volga

1.2 Founded in 1909, Saratov University's first home was in this building, which earlier housed the local feldsher's school. Photo property of author.

German element became a distinct feature of Saratov Province, while the city of Saratov functioned as the major commercial center and informal capital of the Volga German community. The Saratov region likewise served as a magnet for peasant migrants from central Russia until the second half of the nineteenth century, when out-migration — reflecting the stagnant nature of local agriculture, overpopulation, and unemployment — reversed earlier trends.[2]

[2] V. M. Kabuzan, *Izmeneniia v razmeshchenii naseleniia Rossii v XVIII-pervoi polovine*

As Saratov Province entered the twentieth century, its population was predominantly rural and Slavic; its ethnic minorities lived in relative isolation, linked to the Slavic majority largely by economic interaction. The 1897 census put the province's population at 2,405,829, of whom 76.75 percent were Russians (all Slavs combined made up 83.1 percent of the total). The German minority, living primarily in Kamyshin and Saratov Districts, made up 6.92 percent of the population. The Mordva minority, accounting for 5.15 percent of the population, inhabited Petrovsk, Kuznetsk, and Khvalynsk Districts. Comprising 3.94 percent of the population, the Tatars were also concentrated in these same three uezds. In the province's ten districts the percentage of Russians varied from Serdobsk, where they accounted for 99.7 percent of the total population, to Kamyshin, where they made up only 44.46 percent of the inhabitants. The 1897 census data demonstrate that few non-Slavs had been assimilated into the Russian population with the exception of those residing in the cities of Saratov and Tsaritsyn. For example, in Kamyshin the Volga Germans, who constituted 40 percent of the uezd's population, lived in distinct ethnic communities. So did the Mordva, Tatars, Chuvash, and Kalmyks, most of whom were also separated from the Slavic elements by language and religion (map 1).

World War I altered Saratov's social makeup, creating conditions that left an imprint on the political events of 1917. Roughly 25 percent of the indigenous workforce was conscripted. Polish and Latvian workers evacuated from the front as well as other refugees, including students from Kiev University, soon flooded the city. By early 1916 an estimated 41,000 refugees made up the second largest social group in Saratov, amounting to 17.9 percent of the city's total population. Moreover, after Kazan, Saratov housed the largest garrison in the Kazan Military District. In 1917, the local garrison fluctuated in size between 30,000 and 70,000 soldiers. All of the district centers except Khvalynsk, inaccessible by rail, also housed garrisons, which in some instances were more populous than the towns themselves.[3]

The Revolutionary Tradition

Although Saratov's revolutionary past cast a heavy shadow over 1917, Soviet historians minimized the provinces' distinctive features and distorted the role of the Bolsheviks' rivals, whose contributions to provincial life have yet to be fully appreciated. Provincial Russia provided the

---

XIX v. (Moscow, 1971), 28, 31–32, and A. A. Mal'kov, *Estestvennoe dvizhenie naseleniia Saratovskoi gubernii* (Saratov, 1926), 3, 5.

[3] See my *Revolution on the Volga: 1917 in Saratov* (Ithaca, 1986), 17–30.

1. Saratov Province in 1917.

country with most of its prominent revolutionary leaders, including V. I. Lenin, and much of Russia's powerful non-Bolshevik, populist and socialist tradition that went down in defeat during the Civil War was, at heart, provincial-based. In Saratov, local conditions reflecting the overall political health of the country had created a favorable climate for the development of a unique radical tradition. Serfdom had come late to the province, aggravating agrarian relations in the northwestern black-earth districts and to a lesser extent in the less fertile uezds in the southeast. Popular violence had a long pedigree: the local peasantry's collective memory included intense images of past rebellion, especially of Stenka Razin's campaign of 1670 and Emelian Pugachev's furious uprising in the 1770s. Social discontent racing ahead of government reform expressed itself in an eruption of public initiative during the heady days of reform in the 1860s. Mistaking a critical civil society for conspiracy, the government set in motion its arbitrary police and administrative mechanisms, which guaranteed a conspiratorial opposition movement.[4]

By this time the inherently dynamic and symbiotic relationship between town and country, and between the capital and the provinces, had already manifested itself. The plight of the rural masses, in particular, brought about by acute land shortage and overpopulation, had exalted the peasants in the eyes of the local intelligentsia. Saratov Province emerged as a hotbed of Russian populism in the 1870s and again in the 1890s, when it became a center of the Socialist Revolutionary (SR) Party, the country's most popular political party in 1917. A constant influx of political exiles into the city promoted the development and diversification of the radical movement, and by the second half of the 1890s the first hesitant Marxist circles had taken root in town. Further, the wide-reaching activities of Saratov's vigorous and progressive *zemstvos* (organs of local administration) made the province a center of Russian liberalism. A liberal-radical alliance and a tradition of cooperation between moderates and extremists became characteristics of the local opposition movement. So did the lack of clearly drawn lines within the revolutionary camp.[5]

On the eve of the Revolution of 1905, the upsurge of professional and political activism within local society, which linked the sharply etched socioeconomic conflicts with the government's intransigence, had exerted great influence on Saratov's intelligentsia even in rural areas.

[4] See Alan Kimball, "Conspiracy and Circumstance in Saratov, 1859–1864," in Wade and Seregny, *Politics and Society*, 28–48.

[5] Michael Melancon, "Athens or Babylon? The Birth of the Socialist Revolutionary and Social Democratic Parties in Saratov, 1890–1905," in Wade and Seregny, *Politics and Society*, 73–112.

Revolution came to Saratov in 1905 with a vengeance, as the peasant movement became one of the most intense in the country. Many liberals committed to reform cooperated with radicals to create a formidable challenge to Governor P. A. Stolypin, which later affected his tenure as Russia's prime minister between 1906 and 1911, by helping to convince him of the need to initiate sweeping agrarian reform.[6]

The vicissitudes of the Saratov revolutionary movement and of liberal politics after 1905 follow the pattern for the country at large as fixed in the generally accepted historical literature subscribed to by most historians but undoubtedly in need of revision. Because the period ended in revolution, historians naturally have highlighted its origins rather than identifying alternative strains within Russia's historical development: police repression between 1907 and 1910; a rise in working-class activism beginning in 1910 and coming into its own in 1912; confusion in the socialist movement caused by World War I; and growing economic unrest during the war itself, resulting in a revival of the strike movement and a rejuvenation of revolutionary activities by the autumn of 1915. Early the next year, however, police infiltration of the underground movement led to a spate of arrests, preventing worker activists and the intelligentsia from forging a united front.[7] As the February Revolution of 1917 approached, a small group of Social Democratic (Bolshevik and Menshevik) worker activists, in cooperation with other elements of the opposition, sought to restore ties with metalworkers, lumberyard workers, Latvian workers relocated to Saratov from Riga during the war, and other strata of the proletariat. In the meantime, the socioeconomic strains of war had created deep anxieties among townspeople as food shortages coinciding with an energy and transportation crisis forced factories to close.

We need to seek the origins of the Russian Revolution in the peculiarities of the country's political development before 1917, rather than in the chaos brought about by Russia's involvement in World War I. In the mid-1960s Leopold Haimson argued that dangerous polarizations threatened Russian society's stability already on the eve of war, as the elite became alienated from the autocracy and as industrial workers pulled away from the intelligentsia, the moderate socialist parties (Mensheviks and mainstream Socialist Revolutionaries), and the State Duma.

---

[6] See Thomas Fallows, "Governor Stolypin and the Revolution of 1905 in Saratov," in Wade and Seregny, *Politics and Society*, 160–90; and Timothy Mixter, "Collective Action in Saratov Province, 1902–1906," ibid., 191–232.

[7] Gosudarstvennyi Arkhiv Saratovskoi Oblasti, hereafter GASO, f. 3586, op. 1, d. 8, l. 73. For a discussion of the local student movement in the decade before 1917 see V. A. Solomonov, *Revoliutsionnoe studencheskoe dvizhenie v Saratove, 1910–1917 godov* (Saratov, 1991).

Most recent studies, including those that disagree with Haimson, confirm that the fault lines in society ran deep before 1914, and that the impulse for social programs had shifted from the government to the growing private sector as Russia's budding civil society pressed for a greater role in public life.[8]

Indeed, the broad legacy of the past quarter century determined political relationships after the fall of the tsarist autocracy in February 1917. Changes in the structural relations between classes, between the tsarist government and social groups, and between Russia and the European states had made the autocratic system ever more precarious in the early twentieth century. Under siege, the traditional ideology of the Old Regime had made room for an ideology of revolution. Representing an anonymous, transpersonal force that both constrained and enabled, this ideology of revolution encompassed myriad groups and actors who pressed partisan political agendas—both democratic and authoritarian ones. As a counterpoint to the ideology of autocracy, this ideology of revolution was what the various opposition forces had in common.[9] The "creation" of the autocracy by the opposition marked the conceptual space in which revolution was invented in Russia, providing symbolic coherence, structure, and meaning to the very disparate actions of 1905 and of February and October 1917.[10] In other words, the ideological origin of the Russian Revolution was less a matter of imagining a brave new world—although it was that, too—than it was of delegitimating the autocratic system. Revolution became a tradition in Russia before it was a fact. In few countries was popular belief in the likelihood of some sort of revolutionary explosion as broadly held as in early twentieth-century Russia. Generations of malcontents had made expectations of revolutionary change the prevailing moral language of much of society; "the 'fashion for socialism' had already spread widely before the February Revolution."[11]

---

[8] The literature is vast. See, for example, Joan Neuberger, *Hooliganism: Crime, Culture, and Power in St. Petersburg, 1900–1914* (Berkeley, 1993), 277, and Louise McReynolds, *The News under Russia's Old Regime: The Development of a Mass-Circulation Press* (Princeton, 1991), 283. For the growing involvement of the private sector see Adele Lindenmeyr, *Poverty Is Not a Vice: Charity, Society, and the State in Imperial Russia* (Princeton, 1996).

[9] I borrow this anthropological view of ideology from William H. Sewell, Jr., "Ideologies and Social Revolutions: Reflections on the French Case," *Journal of Modern History* 57, no. 1 (1985): 58–61. See also Anthony Giddens, *New Rules of Sociological Method* (London, 1976).

[10] Here I draw on Keith Michael Baker, *Inventing the French Revolution: Essays on French Political Culture in the Eighteenth Century* (New York, 1990), 4.

[11] Boris I. Kolonitskii, "Antibourgeois Propaganda and Anti-'Burzhui' Consciousness in 1917," *Russian Review* 53, no. 2 (1994): 187.

If the origins of the Revolution — and of Bolshevism — lie in the peculiarities of Russia's political development before 1917, the origins of the
Bolshevik victory are found in the wrenching changes brought about by
war, which poet Anna Akhmatova called the beginning of "the real
twentieth century" of revolution and ideological politics.[12] While a
broadly based socialist government probably could have been established in Russia even without war, the Bolsheviks would have been unable to create a one-party system had Russia somehow withdrawn from
the conflict or avoided it altogether. Splitting apart Russian socialism,
the war redefined and aggravated serious social grievances and political
issues that had been manifest for over a generation, thereby contributing to the outbreak of revolution and strongly determining its outcome.
War also gave rise to rampant rumors of moral corruption and treason
at court and of an emasculated tsar who had been cuckolded by the
sinister Rasputin. These rumors desacralized the monarchy by making it
patriotic to oppose the Romanovs.[13] Further, without war there would
have been no crowded garrisons in the Russian heartland, and the embittered soldiers played an enormous role in establishing Soviet power.[14]
Finally, the war marked a watershed in the methods the European states
used to govern their populations. In Russia, the idea that state planning
and regulation needed to be applied to the economy on the model of the
German *Kriegssozialismus* had already gained currency among socialists
and non-socialists alike before 1917.[15]

The February Revolution and the Peculiarities of Dual Power

The conflicts and conditions that brought about the Revolution were
systemic. The tsarist political system, with all of its shortcomings, had
provided rich soil for the growth of a local opposition movement. The
autocracy had alienated much of the country's professional middle
class. It had failed to satisfy the peasants' land hunger. It had hampered
workers' attempts to alleviate the social ills of industrialization and the
arbitrariness of authority relations at the workplace. Then came war.
The socioeconomic disequilibrium and the extraordinary movement of
people that it caused, and the government's suspicion of public initiative

---

[12] Cited in Malia, *Russia*, 293.

[13] Orlando Figes and Boris Kolonitskii, *Interpreting the Russian Revolution: The Language and Symbols of 1917* (New Haven, 1999), 10–29.

[14] See my "The Impact of World War I on Saratov and Its Revolutionary Movement," in
Wade and Seregny, *Politics and Society*, 255–76.

[15] Francis King, "The Russian Revolution and the Idea of a Single Economic Plan,
1917–28," *Revolutionary Russia* 12, no. 1 (1999): 69–72.

as it progressed, furthered discontent, exacerbating antigovernment feelings even within official circles.

The resultant February Revolution that swept away the tsarist autocracy dealt a deathblow to centralized state authority, making all power relationships largely voluntary, and inaugurating the direct participation in politics of the heretofore disenfranchised Russian masses. The ideology of revolution now became the dominant idiom of government; revolutionary ideology itself became an important historical actor.[16] In Saratov, as elsewhere, the Revolution unfolded without detailed directives from the capital, and in a few days a new political apparatus arose locally. By the evening of March 2, 1917, the election of a workers' soviet and the formation of a military committee in the garrison, as well as the arrest of more than three hundred tsarist officials by soldiers and workers, prompted the city *duma* (town council) to create a Public Executive Committee (*Obshchestvennyi ispolnitel'nyi komitet*) (hereafter PEC) empowered to serve as an impartial government and to work with the army "for a decisive victory over the enemy." The PEC included representatives from the duma, the Saratov Soviet, the city's organization of lawyers, the zemstvo, and the cooperatives, and was chaired by a lawyer and former State Duma deputy who belonged to Russia's premiere liberal party, the Constitutional Democrats or Kadets, A. A. Tokarskii.

From Saratov the Revolution spread quickly to the district towns and from there to the countryside, as newly elected executive committees and soviets replaced the old administrations in all of the province's district centers. For the most part, their populations were involved in trade and handicraft activities, and there were few industrial workers. Populism, and to a much lesser extent liberalism, represented the most consequential political currents among the educated strata. Factors such as the record of local progressive elements before 1917 and proximity to Saratov, to the city of Tsaritsyn, and to major railroad arteries also shaped the way the Revolution unfolded at the district level. Yet in virtually every instance the army emerged as the truly decisive element in shifting the balance of forces against the old administrations. Without exception, garrison troops, at times joined by workers, arrested the old tsarist police, gendarmes, unpopular garrison commanders, and officers.

Expressing few regrets over the collapse of the old order, the villages displayed the same penchant for independent initiative as the urban population. Peasants elected their own county (*volost*) executive committees to work toward what the Revolution had signified to them: an end to the exploitative system of rents and the transfer of land to those

---

[16] See Furet's *Interpreting the French Revolution.*

who tilled it. On March 19 the Provisional Government, set up to govern Russia until a constituent assembly determined the country's political future, recognized the legitimacy of the volost executive committees, turning over to them the responsibilities of the old volost administrations until the zemstvos were reelected along democratic lines.[17]

In Saratov and other provinces the alignment of political forces differed from the situation in the capital where, with the exception of Alexander F. Kerensky, soviet leaders did not join the government. In provincial Russia, besides soviets, variously titled executive committees were set up by city dumas, zemstvos, representatives of wartime public committees, cooperatives, and industrial enterprises, and by revolutionary activists, soldiers, officers, and workers. The majority of soviets not only cooperated with these new executive committees, but took part in them and sometimes even formed them, creating broadly representative coalition organs. Local conditions and experiences in each case determined the specific strength of the propertied strata of society vis-à-vis the elements of the so-called "democracy" (*demokratiia*), a term that soon assumed an exclusive usage, dividing the laboring people from the bourgeoisie.[18]

The overriding strength of the socialist parties within the PEC in Saratov, however, compelled political developments to follow a logic of their own. By late spring 1917 the PEC began fading away, its leadership undermined from the start by its inclusion of socialists and representatives from the Saratov Soviet. It bears repeating that socialist leaders did not perceive the soviets as an alternative form of government, but as organs for watching over the bourgeoisie and for defending the gains of the Revolution. Many socialists considered the February Revolution "bourgeois" and hence did not look upon the soviets as the focus of political power. Moreover, the Petrograd Soviet instructed local soviets to work in conjunction with other organizations, and under no circumstances to assume governmental functions. Be that as it may, in Saratov a small number of socialist activists dominated the soviet, provided leadership for the nonbourgeois political parties, edited their respective party newspapers, participated in the PEC, and gained control over the city duma. When these same individuals began to ignore the PEC, it simply stopped meeting. In effect, a situation bordering on the single power (*edinovlastie*) of the local soviet was taking shape, which

---

[17] Donald J. Raleigh, "The Revolution of 1917 and the Establishment of Soviet Power in Saratov," in Wade and Seregny, *Politics and Society,* 278–79.

[18] See Boris I. Kolonitskii, "'Democracy' in the Political Consciousness of the February Revolution," *Slavic Review* 57, no. 1 (1998): 95–106; also Figes and Kolonitskii, *Interpreting,* 122–25.

meant that by late spring 1917 the real question of political power in Saratov concerned not so much the transfer of power to the soviet as the outcome of the intrasoviet party fighting—barely felt in March, but quite noticeable by April.

Two developments in April profoundly affected Saratov politics and led to the situation described above. The first was Lenin's return to Russia and the Bolshevik Party's eventual adoption of his April Theses, which advocated an end to the war and an immediate struggle for a transfer of power to the soviets. The other development, the April crisis, brought about the collapse of the Provisional Government and its replacement by the First Coalition Government on May 5, which included representatives from the socialist parties, with the notable exception of the Bolsheviks. Besides Kerensky, five other socialists accepted cabinet portfolios. Even though dissatisfaction with the previous government's stance on the war had led to its downfall, the First Coalition Government, while paying lip service to the Petrograd Soviet's peace declarations, also failed to take any serious measures toward securing peace. In the following months the Bolsheviks' refusal to serve in a government with the bourgeoisie and their increasingly vocal support for Lenin's theses contributed to the drawing of hard party and class lines in political institutions everywhere in the country.[19]

The Saratov Bolsheviks' adoption of Lenin's April Theses and the public outcry over the April crisis undermined the concept of coalition along the Volga. Local socialists consolidated their position at the expense of the liberal parties and the Right, which were too weak to pick up the reins of power in the spring of 1917. At the same time, however, a critical split developed between moderate and radical socialists. As a result of elections to the soviet in May, Socialist Revolutionaries and Mensheviks came to dominate the council. Having joined the non-socialist parties in a coalition government at the national level, the moderate socialists sought to make the local organs of government work, too. They argued against Soviet power, maintaining that the councils of workers and soldiers, as class institutions, would strengthen centrifugal tendencies and that the prosecution of the war required unity. Such attitudes affected their determination to curb the powers of the local soviet. The ambiguous behavior of their leaders confused some workers and soldiers, led to their dissatisfaction with the political status quo, and tied the fate of the soviets to the Bolsheviks and radical offshoots of the SRs and Mensheviks.

The rapid collapse of the organs of the Provisional Government at the

---

[19] For the impact of Lenin's theses and the April crisis see chapter 3 of my *Revolution on the Volga*.

local level and the administrative paralysis resulting from the weakness of the PEC must be emphasized in any assessment of the Revolution in provincial Russia because the inherent incongruities of coalition were exposed earlier in the provinces than in Petrograd. In Saratov the soviet filled the political vacuum and soon generated vast political power, dealing a psychological deathblow to the city duma by forcing the mayor's resignation and new elections. Until these were held, early in July, many duma members stopped attending the infrequent meetings, which were usually canceled anyway for lack of a quorum. At the same time, as described above, the soviet won the upper hand over the PEC, which experienced increasing difficulty in reaching a consensus on pressing business. The PEC's decline was broadly recognized, prompting the editors of *Saratovskii vestnik* (Saratov Herald) to complain that "lately power not only in the city but throughout the province has actually passed to the [city] soviet of workers' and soldiers' deputies."[20] Significantly, the withdrawal of the Saratov Bolsheviks from the PEC in May marked the end of their willingness to cooperate with the nonsocialist elements and the beginning of their as yet restrained advocacy of an all-socialist soviet government.

Representations of Power and Social Polarization

How did the Saratov Soviet come to amass so much power? To a certain extent, a straight line of development connects the soviets of 1905, the first freely elected workers' mass organizations, with the revolutionary councils of 1917. Moreover, the lower classes' implicit recognition of the need for some sort of institution that would articulate their revolutionary energies and project their sheer numerical strength gave rise to the formation of soviets and the myriad of other mass organizations in 1917. Throughout the year, the socialist parties combined captured large majorities of the popular vote in elections to city dumas, food-supply assemblies, and the Constituent Assembly. For instance, the socialist parties won 82.3 percent of the popular vote in the July duma elections, and approximately the same percentage in elections to the Constituent Assembly in Saratov Province in November.

The power of the soviets had other sources as well. The very revolutionary origin of these councils, chosen in free elections, made them instantly popular, for elections were deemed essential as a bulwark against privilege. Another reason for the leading position of the Saratov

---

[20] *Saratovskii vestnik*, no. 138, June 28, 1917, 3, and *Saratovskii listok*, no. 136, June 24, 1917, 3.

Soviet was that it developed independently of the political parties and initially remained neutral toward partisan politics. Further, the Revolution had given rise to expectations that many problems facing the people could be resolved in a short time. The soviet's apparent success in dealing with the threat to public order and with dwindling food supplies seemed to justify such expectations, at least in the period immediately after February. Concrete steps taken by the soviet to democratize all organs of local government and to improve the economic situation of its constituency likewise justified its claim to speak for the previously disenfranchised. This was particularly the case in view of the collapse of local organs of the government, a development that turned the soviets into governing bodies in which the economic and political struggles were fused. Not surprisingly, once the soviets appropriated authority, the public held them accountable too. As a result, they soon became political battlegrounds; their radicalization reflected the radicalization of the masses.

The Saratov Soviet also emerged as a popular institution because, in Furet's formulation, revolutionary ideology itself became a political actor. The immediate experience of revolution itself forged new values and expectations, shaped, to be sure, by the alienation of the socialist intelligentsia from the old state structure and by faith in the regenerative power of revolution. As a marketplace for revolutionary ideas, the soviet served as a distribution point for revolutionary language (the "privileged bourgeoisie" and the "revolutionary democracy"), for revolutionary symbols (red bunting and ribbons, workers' caps and soldiers' greatcoats), and for revolutionary practices (the soviet proposed the renaming of streets and presided over revolutionary celebrations and rituals such as May Day, a "socialist" holiday formerly observed discretely but now celebrated with fanfare). What one did for a living, what one wore, what one ate, and where one lived, took on new significance. Political authority requires some sort of "cultural frame" with a "center" commanding sacred status. In Saratov the soviet—at least temporarily—gave those formerly excluded from the corridors of power their sense of place in society, "the place where culture, society, and politics come together."[21]

Social polarization made language an expression of power, too, as ideas, social relations, politics, and social psychologies collided. The unprecedented proliferation of revolutionary party newspapers whose circulations quickly surpassed that of the established press, the mass printings of party programs and pamphlets written in a popular style, and

[21] Cited in Lynn Hunt, *Politics, Culture, and Class in the French Revolution* (Berkeley, 1984), 87.

the public singing of revolutionary songs such as the "Marseillaise" served both to demonstrate and to prop up power. The ideology of revolution, however, was not monolithic but contested — comprising scenarios for a democratic republic, agrarian-based socialism, and Marxist socialism. As the various political groups came to see how linguistic authority bolstered political authority, they arrogated for themselves the right to speak for those social groups they privileged. Russia's mass circulation press functioned as heavy artillery on the rhetorical battlefield. The propaganda of the Bolsheviks and moderate socialists certainly shared common features, particularly its anticapitalist, antibourgeois tone.[22] Yet while Russia's moderate socialists in 1917 invoked "coalition," "unity," and "democracy," the Bolsheviks highlighted "class struggle," emphasizing that they represented the only socialist party willing to make a complete break with the bourgeoisie. "[The] very fact that several political languages were functioning simultaneously," concludes Kolonitskii, "objectively impeded the country's democratic development."[23]

At the same time, the unprecedented level of mass participation in all aspects of public affairs created an environment in which various social groups worked to effect their own diverse goals. For the ruling circles and Western-oriented political leaders of the country, the Revolution had swept away all of the frustrating impediments that had made a scandal of the war effort under Nicholas II. To many ordinary citizens, however, the Revolution had created conditions that would bring about a better life and end the war. The deeply rooted feelings of injustice and suspicion they harbored toward the old order now carried over to those in the post-February administration who sought to curb popular initiative. Among the overlapping network of popular organizations created in the first half of 1917, those elected directly by the people commanded the most authority: factory committees and soviets, soldier committees, volost and village executive committees. These lower-level bodies tried to establish some means of control over the "middle-class" government and its institutions. The practices of the popular institutions often had little in common with Western notions of representative political democracy, which the common people may not have understood at all, or viewed with suspicion.[24]

Social polarization complicated the tactical dilemma of the moderate

---

[22] Kolonitskii, "Antibourgeois Propaganda," 184, 187. For the role the press played in shaping Russian public opinion at this time, see McReynolds, *The News under Russia's Old Regime*.

[23] Kolonitskii, "'Democracy,'" 106.

[24] See Michael Melancon, "The Syntax of Soviet Power: The Resolutions of Local Soviets and Other Institutions, March–October 1917," *Russian Review* 52, no. 4 (1993): 504.

socialists who entered the government in May by bringing problems within the parties to the foreground. Many Saratov SR and Menshevik leaders had rightly feared that joining with the liberal Kadets and other nonsocialist parties would compromise their programs and beliefs. This was particularly true of the SRs, who enjoyed tremendous influence in Saratov Province. While the fate of some SRs became linked to that of the coalition government, others more directly involved with the peasantry undertook to carry out programs advocated by the party even before 1905, encouraging the local peasantry to disregard the Provisional Government's successive agrarian programs. The moderate leaders of the SR Party were hard put to deal with "our Bolsheviks," as they called their impatient comrades. Meanwhile, the Bolsheviks' call for Soviet power and their rejection of the coalition government sharply distinguished their program from that of the other parties. Their vocal antiwar stand also came to distance them from the majority socialists. By late June the illusion of socialist solidarity had been shattered, and the leaders of the moderate socialist parties sought to apply the brakes to a social revolution that threatened to speed past them.

The moderate socialist parties fared better in the district towns, where local executive committees, dumas led by socialists, or soviets had amassed considerable power by early summer. Although soviets had not been formed in the district towns during the 1905 Revolution, they were elected in most uezd centers by the end of March 1917. Soviets of soldiers' deputies usually appeared first, and they in turn assisted in the election of workers' soviets. Most district soviets had nonpartisan memberships, but the SRs dominated local politics as they had since 1905. Toward summer, a few soviets became involved in disputes with the old dumas or with commanding officers. More often than not, the dumas lacked the authority to challenge soviets and executive committees, and consequently submitted to reelection along democratic lines.

In the summer of 1917 local and national political attitudes underwent profound changes owing to the abortive July days uprising in Petrograd, which threatened to topple the government, and to the Kornilov affair at the end of August, which sought to establish a conservative dictatorship in Russia.[25] The July days further complicated the question of political power in provincial Russia, because Saratov's moderate socialists now strove to revive the authority of the city dumas. In a sense, a resurgence of the city duma, elected in the aftermath of the July crisis when Bolshevik fortunes were at their lowest, could be seen as being to the moderates' advantage, for it was a representative rather than a class

---

[25] For a discussion of the two episodes, see Alexander Rabinowitch, *Prelude to Revolution: The Petrograd Bolsheviks and the July 1917 Uprising* (Bloomington, 1968), and *The Bolsheviks Come to Power: The Revolution of 1917 in Petrograd* (New York, 1976).

organ (that excluded the bourgeoisie), and the Bolsheviks made up only 12 percent of its membership. Restoring the authority of the duma also appealed to some moderate socialist leaders' belief that cooperation with the bourgeoisie remained essential. Besides, the Provisional Government had instructed local communities to reelect dumas to replace PECs. The moderate socialist leaders, however, did not foresee that the class-oriented soviet would continue to muster more authority than a democratically elected duma, and that the working class and soldiers in Saratov were beginning to listen more attentively to what the Bolsheviks had to say. But this should not cloud the fact that a real paradox had emerged, for workers and soldiers were growing indifferent to the soviet as well. Plenums were called less frequently and decision making was left to the executive bodies—a phenomenon that appears to have been common in much of urban Russia at the time. The reason for the indifference toward the soviet may well have been that the advances of the Revolution were coming to a halt, partly because of the visible deterioration of the economy. All in all, by the summer of 1917 the impulse toward localism, followed by an emerging organizational malaise, had actually contributed to a further breakdown of the state apparatus and of law and order in general. The seriousness of the administrative crisis facing the country reveals how close Russia had come to civil war already by the summer of 1917.[26]

The attempt by the political Right to seize state power during the Kornilov affair at the end of August and the blatant snubbing of popular organs by military authorities in neighboring Tsaritsyn[27] radicalized politics along the Volga, for these events convinced many workers and soldiers that the Bolsheviks' version of the revolution in process was the correct one. Workers and soldiers in Saratov responded to Kornilov as if they themselves were fighting surrogate Kornilovs, and in this respect the effort at a conservative restoration in the summer of 1917 served as a dress rehearsal for October. The Bolsheviks in the city now capitalized on the fact that new elections to the soviet had given them a majority. To the dismay of the burghers of Saratov, armed workers expressed their willingness to fight against "counterrevolutionaries," while soldiers in the garrison enthusiastically echoed Bolshevik slogans. Compromised by their support of the coalition government, the local SR and Menshevik organizations split apart as their left-leaning members sided

---

[26] Donald J. Raleigh, "Political Power in the Russian Revolution: A Case Study of Saratov," in *Revolution in Russia: Reassessments of 1917*, ed. by Edith R. Frankel, Jonathan Frankel, and Baruch Knei-Paz (Cambridge, Eng., 1992), 40–43, 47–48.

[27] See my "Revolutionary Politics in Provincial Russia: The Tsaritsyn 'Republic' in 1917," *Slavic Review* 40, no. 2 (1981): 194–209.

with the Bolsheviks against further coalition with propertied Russia and as the centrist elements refused to repudiate policies they had pursued since February, still hoping that civil war could be staved off.

No easy, or perhaps peaceful, solution to Russia's political crisis presented itself after the Kornilov affair. A Bolshevik majority in the soviet did not resolve the political impasse facing Saratov but compounded it. The mood of provincial Russia now had a synergistic effect on Lenin and other Bolshevik militants and helped convince them that the country was ripe for a transfer of power to the soviets. Reacting to the popular mood, leftist elements among the SRs and Mensheviks joined with the Bolsheviks in urging the exclusion of the propertied elements from the new government. The moderate socialists, fearing even greater social tension and civil war, continued to shore up the coalition with the liberal Kadets, in spite of their concern over the party leadership's willingness to accommodate Kornilov.[28]

Economic dislocation and war-weariness go far to explain the burgeoning militancy of the local working class and soldiers and show the degree to which a new set of revolutionary processes, reflected in the rising visibility of extremist groups, now determined political outcomes. As Russia broke up into local economic units, officials at each administrative level first took measures to ward off local hunger and to cope with swollen crime rates. The food crisis worsened in Saratov as the agrarian movement gained momentum. Right-wing as well as anarchist agitation reached new heights. In September and October the strike movement became more militant than at any other time during the year.[29] Further, no authority could control the war-weary soldiers, who emerged from the Kornilov affair radicalized and susceptible to extremist agitation, but not as stalwart Bolsheviks. As October approached, the city found itself at the soldiers' mercy. Confiscating public buildings, they began moving into town to avoid another winter in their dilapidated barracks. Local newspapers linked the alarming crime rate to those "in soldier's garb." This situation prevailed throughout the province and the Volga region.[30]

Moreover, in late summer the rural revolution converged with the urban one, marking the failure of the Provisional Government to establish authority through the printed word and to develop a "national discourse of civic rights and duties." Instead, peasant notions of citizenship

[28] See Rex A. Wade, *The Russian Revolution, 1917* (Cambridge, Eng., 2000), 170–232.

[29] See Raleigh, *Revolution on the Volga*, 245–46.

[30] Robert F. Browder and Alexander F. Kerensky, eds., *The Russian Provisional Government, 1917: Documents* (Stanford, 1961), 3:1644–45; *Izvestiia Kazanskogo Voenno-okruzhnogo komiteta*, no. 93, Sept. 16, 1917, 4; no. 94, Sept. 17, 1917, 3, and no. 102, Sept. 30, 1917, 4.

and their construction of power inverted state structures to suit their own goals. As Figes notes, "the new language of citizenship was reinterpreted to suit the peasants' own revolutionary and social needs."[31] Having seized lands and repudiated rental agreements during planting season, the peasants now turned to taking equipment and livestock, felling trees, and mowing grass for haymaking. After the harvest was in, the number of confiscations of estates and the use of force shot up markedly. The proceedings of a local peasant congress in September reveal that self-demobilized, armed soldiers and outside agitators pushed the situation to the left: the mood in the villages had become more militant than that of the urban-based populist party committees. Despite real hostility to the Bolsheviks, the delegates passed Left SR resolutions virtually identical to Bolshevik ones. The congress adopted the SR land program, voicing its opposition to further coalition with the bourgeoisie. In the following weeks, an emboldened peasant movement broke out in Serdobsk, Balashov, and Atkarsk, all of which had been centers of rural revolt in 1905. As the Bolshevik press clamored for a transfer of power to the soviets, the headlines of Saratov's (liberal) *Saratovskii vestnik* (Saratov Herald) flashed: "Russia experiences complete anarchy and demoralization."[32]

Saratov's October

The October Revolution in Saratov came as no surprise: conflicting but persistent rumors that the Bolsheviks were planning an armed uprising against the government in conjunction with the opening of the Second Congress of Soviets slated to convene in Petrograd on October 24 had broad currency. They shaped popular attitudes at this time, for moderate socialists continued to fear the anarchistic temperament of the masses, who had been brutalized by poverty, ignorance, and years of suffering from the war. The lawlessness of everyday life and the readiness with which the people seemed to fall victim to opportunistic slogans of the radical left merely reinforced the moderates' conviction that Russia was ill-prepared for social revolution. This especially seemed to be the case when the Bolshevik and Left SR majority at a regional congress of soviets in mid-October endorsed a call for Soviet power.[33]

Afterward, tensions mounted in Saratov between the Bolsheviks and moderate socialists. The Bolsheviks, who politically stood for Soviet

[31] Orlando Figes, "The Russian Revolution and Its Language in the Village," *Russian Review* 56, no. 3 (1997): 324, 335–38, 344.

[32] *Saratovskii vestnik*, no. 222, Oct. 8, 1917, 3.

[33] *Proletarii Povolzh'ia*, no. 115, Oct. 17, 1917, 3–4.

power and an end to the war, competed against the moderate socialists and liberals. In terms of national politics, the contest revolved around support for the Second Congress of Soviets (the Bolsheviks and left-wing factions of the other socialist parties) or for the Constituent Assembly (moderate socialists, liberals, and some conservatives). On October 7 a soviet plenum adopted a resolution expressing mistrust of the new government formed a few days before, which included Kadet ministers, despite their collusion with Kornilov back in August. When Kerensky threatened to order a punitive expedition to Saratov, the soviet announced that local soldiers would answer with bayonets and bullets. Days later, the Saratov Soviet carried a defiant resolution affirming that it no longer recognized the government's authority. When the SRs withdrew from all executive organs of the soviet, it approved a plan to be implemented in the event an armed uprising broke out in Saratov. The local Bolshevik committee, meanwhile, turned to Petrograd for directives, but none came.

Once news of the October insurrection in the capital reached Saratov, the duma formed a Committee to Save the Revolution, as both sides prepared themselves for a possible showdown and simultaneously stalled for time. The Bolsheviks waited for directives from their Central Committee; the moderates pinned their hopes on a speedy rescue by nearby Cossack forces. The standoff ended when the soviet's Bolshevik-led executive committee formed a Military Revolutionary Committee, announcing to the population that the latter had assumed power on behalf of the soviet. The committee issued a decree on land (of local provenance) based on the SR program, replaced the provincial commissar, appointed emissaries to assume the responsibilities of former district commissars, and prepared for an attack on the soviet.[34] These measures provoked the duma to declare itself the legitimate organ of power in the province. Its appeal to all able-bodied persons to appear at the duma building drew about three thousand people, including leaders of the moderate socialist parties, duma members, officer trainees, officials, office workers, students, and shop owners. But as the likelihood of bloodshed increased, the duma forces began to thin because those inside feared the unruly soldiers. So did the Bolshevik leaders, who sought to keep the troops in their barracks and to rely instead on armed worker units formed during the Kornilov crisis and known as Red Guardsmen, whom the Bolsheviks ordered to surround the duma. Shots broke out on the evening of October 28 and continued all night. When the duma forces capitulated in the morning, there were several dead and wounded

[34] For a detailed discussion of the October Revolution in Saratov see chapter 7 of my *Revolution on the Volga*.

on each side. As the defeated were led away, a hostile crowd, some ten thousand strong, pressed against them, demanding that they be shot or thrown into the Volga. One young Cossack officer remembered how a crowd of angry women "threw themselves upon us, scratching our faces with their dirty hands. Murderers! [they yelled]."[35]

Opening Shots of the Local Civil War

The Saratov Soviet's "victory" over the duma represented the opening shots of the local civil war. The possibility of direct Cossack intervention bolstered the anti-Soviet opposition, while news of conflict within the Bolshevik top leadership kept hopes burning locally that Soviet power would collapse. The debate among socialists became more polarized after October, when SR and Menshevik newspapers decried the Bolsheviks' "senseless" and "reckless adventurism" that took the country to the brink of civil war. To discredit the Bolsheviks, the SRs and Mensheviks—who now depicted themselves as victims—insisted that the Bolsheviks had stolen their programs. In turn, the Bolsheviks underscored the "hypocrisy and treachery" of the not truly socialist, but petit-bourgeois parties, equating their opposition with "counterrevolution." These rhetorical skirmishes at both the national and local levels served to frame Saratov Bolshevik efforts to understand and explain subsequent events.[36] As anti-Bolshevik groups called upon townspeople "to protest the Bolsheviks' crude use of force," a strike by telegraph and postal workers cut off Saratov from Petrograd for almost two months, guaranteeing the circulation of rumors that also left their mark upon local developments. Sustained opposition to the new regime, a lack of directives from Petrograd or contradictory ones, and an even more frightful level of lawlessness characterized the first months of "Soviet power" in Saratov.[37]

Nevertheless, the rupture of the Bolsheviks' most formidable rival, the SR Party, and the entrance of its radical wing into the new government, the Council of People's Commissars (*Sovnarkom*), contributed

---

[35] M. A. Golubov, "Saratov v 1917 g.: Vospominaniia pomoshchnika Kursovogo ofitsera Saratovskoi shkoly praporshchikov," unpublished manuscript dated Innsbruck, Austria, 1955 (Columbia University, Butler Library), 47–48.

[36] Elizabeth J. Hemenway, "A Revolution of Words: Socialist Rhetoric, Newspapers, and October" (seminar paper, University of North Carolina, December 13, 1991). Saratov newspapers make similar claims. See the Bolsheviks' *Sotsial-demokrat*, the Mensheviks' *Proletarii Povolzh'ia*, and the SRs' *Zemlia i volia*, as well as *Saratovskii vestnik* and *Saratovskii listok*.

[37] See my *Revolution on the Volga*, 292–97.

immensely to strengthening the Bolsheviks' hand. In Saratov, the Left SRs' joining the soviet's executive committee helped to turn the tide in the Bolsheviks' favor. Although united in their hostility toward the Bolsheviks, the moderate socialists and Kadets simply lacked a broader base for cooperation — and would continue to do so during the Civil War. Moreover, some moderate socialists now voiced their willingness to break with the bourgeoisie if certain conditions were met, but these were not to the Bolsheviks' liking. When the soviet invited city employees to a meeting in November, an estimated ten thousand people held a counterdemonstration inspired by the SRs to condemn one-party rule and to demand freedom of speech and the press. Emphasizing the legitimacy of the upcoming Constituent Assembly, the meeting called for the creation of a new national government that excluded the bourgeoisie.

As the storm clouds of civil war hovered over Saratov, the soviet adopted a more militant attitude toward its opponents, who refused to recognize or to serve the new authorities. Apart from slamming shut the doors of the city duma in late November, the Bolshevik-Left SR soviet sequestered local banks, extended the duties of worker control groups, organized workers who had not taken part in unions earlier, took over the railroads, created a new militia, and assumed responsibility for Saratov's economic survival. The more power it wielded, the more impassioned the voices of opposition became. "Down with the autocracy of Lenin and Trotsky!" was answered with the soviet's decision in December to close down the non-Bolshevik press.

During the second week of November the people of Russia elected deputies to the Constituent Assembly, which had become the rallying point of all those opposed to Bolshevism or to that party's break with the concept of soviet democracy. Within the city of Saratov, civilians cast 47,522 votes and soldiers, 12,600 votes. The Bolsheviks captured the most support of any party, polling 22,712 votes or 37.7 percent of the total. The Kadets came in second, with 11,971 votes, or 19.9 percent. Since July, both Bolshevik and Kadet support had roughly doubled, while the SRs and Mensheviks had hemorrhaged support to both the Right and the Left. According to *Saratovskii vestnik*, 15,000 voters had switched from the SR-Menshevik bloc to the Bolsheviks, while 10,000 former socialists had moved into the liberal camp. Consideration of the garrison vote makes the nature of Bolshevik strength stand out more clearly: the Bolsheviks won 70.6 percent of the 12,660 votes cast by soldiers.

In Tsaritsyn, the other large city in the province, the results were similar to those in Saratov and also followed class lines. The collapse of the political center in Saratov and Tsaritsyn thus paralleled developments in Petrograd and Moscow, where the Kadets also polled more votes than the SRs. The cities had become Bolshevik strongholds as well as centers of the Bolsheviks' class enemies. Although election results for the remaining districts of Saratov Province are incomplete, soldiers sustained Bolshevism in the district towns in what was an otherwise indifferent or even hostile environment. In Serdobsk, where the Bolsheviks polled 33 percent of the garrison vote, Left SRs guaranteed an early consolidation of Soviet power. Left SRs also boasted a strong organization in Balashov, Kamyshin, and Kuznetsk. At the district level, the same strengthening of the political extremes at the expense of the center had occurred, but not to the same degree as in Saratov or Tsaritsyn (table 1.1).

The Saratov election results reinforce Oliver H. Radkey's conclusions about voter behavior in the country at large.[38] Across the country, ethnically Russian rural communities voted heavily for the SRs. The formal split within the party's ranks came shortly after the elections, and the peasants thus cast ballots for an organizationally defunct party. It is impossible to say how they would have voted had the elections been postponed and the peasants had the option of voting for the Left SRs. It must be remembered that many had not yet heard of the October events, or of the Second Congress of Soviets' endorsement of Lenin's land decree (to be discussed below). Still, the national pattern held true for Saratov, where the SRs won 56 percent of the votes cast in the province, and the second-place Bolsheviks, 24 percent. Combined, the two socialist parties won 80 percent of the votes, and the liberal Kadets a mere 2.5 percent, capturing a paltry 27,226 votes out of a total of over one million.

The Spread of Soviet Power

News of the consolidation of Soviet power in Saratov spread unevenly throughout the province, because ties between Saratov and the district and volost centers had been interrupted. The process of "recognizing" the new political order began when the Saratov and Tsaritsyn Soviets assumed power, and ended in January 1918, when soviets in the remaining districts carried pro-Bolshevik resolutions. These anemic declarations of Soviet power, however, often marked the start of stubborn opposition to the radical Left. Since there were few Bolsheviks in the

---

[38] Oliver H. Radkey, *Russia Goes to the Polls: The Election to the All-Russian Constituent Assembly*, foreword by Sheila Fitzpatrick (Ithaca, 1990).

TABLE 1.1

Valid Votes Cast for Delegates to Constituent Assembly in Saratov Province, by Party

Ballot Number and Party	Votes	Percent
1. Kadet	22,226	2.5
2. Menshevik	15,152	1.4
3. Union of Ukrainian and Tatar SR Peasant Organizations	53,445	4.9
4. Old Believers	13,956	1.3
5. Orthodox People's	17,414	1.6
6. Union of Landowners	13,804	1.3
7. Volga German	50,025	4.6
8. Popular Socialist	10,243	0.9
9. Society for Faith and Order	6,600	0.6
10. Bolshevik	261,308	24.0
11. Peasants of Petrovsk Uezd and Mordva	6,379	0.6
12. Socialist Revolutionary	612,094	56.3
All parties	1,087,646	100.0

Source: *Saratovskaia zemskaia nedelia*, no. 1, Feb. 5 (18), 1918, 17.

district towns, Soviet power rested on soldiers' bayonets, the popularity of Left SRs and SR Maximalists (another radical offshoot of the SR Party), at times on armed detachments from Saratov or elsewhere, and in a few instances on agitated peasants who instinctively may have been looking for support from the towns to legitimize their own seizures of land. Moderate SRs and Kadets, ensconced in dumas or zemstvos, tended to compete against radical elements, although the presence of Cossack divisions in some districts cooled the revolutionaries' fervor. The power struggles also entailed passive resistance of all sorts, which tended to induce fiscal crises and food shortages. Perhaps the most telling statement about the vitality of Soviet power is that anti-Bolshevik uprisings broke out in the majority of district towns in 1918.[39]

The militancy of the local peasant movement on the eve of the October days helped to shape the revolution in the villages. Snatching up

[39] For a discussion of the revolution at the district level see my *Revolution on the Volga*, 302–11. See also GASO, f. 521, op. 1, d. 14, l. 15; f. 521, op. 1, d. 14, l. 29; Gosudarstvennyi Arkhiv Rossiiskoi Federatsii, hereafter, GA RF, f. 393, op. 3, d. 335, ll. 1–1 ob, 3–4, 5–6; f. 393, op. 2, d. 80, l. 103–3 ob; f. 393, op. 2, d. 80, ll. 289–94, 298, 299, 301–2, 320, 330; and *Otchet Novouzenskogo Soveta soldatskikh, rabochikh i krest'ianskikh deputatov* (Novouzensk, 1918), 1, 3, 5, 8–10, 17, 19, 22, 29–33, 52.

inventory, equipment, grain, livestock, and manor houses, peasants increasingly resorted to terror against landowners and so-called Stolypin peasants who remained outside the commune.[40] After the insurrection, Bolshevik agitators from Saratov and Petrograd sought to win over the peasants by informing them of the Saratov Soviet's land decree, while SRs entrenched in the zemstvos agitated on behalf of elections to the Constituent Assembly. The more remote villages often learned of the Revolution only after the balloting had ended. In this volatile environment, the peasant soldier played the decisive role in establishing Soviet power in many district centers as well as in the villages. Owing to severe food shortages, local authorities carried out demobilization quickly. But this did not keep many impatient soldiers from deserting. Returning home, they implemented the soviet's land decree, which placed all landowner, church, and privately owned land at the disposal of peasant committees. Despite prevailing anti-Bolshevik feelings in the countryside, the flood of soldiers back into the rural areas shifted the balance of forces in favor of the new regime, even where opposition to the Bolsheviks remained spirited. Soviet power, though, rested on a shaky foundation that had to be bolstered by armed force or intimidation; moreover, *Soviet* power had been "recognized," *not* Bolshevik power.

Ironically, on the day shooting broke out in Saratov between the forces of the soviet and city duma, the so-called Peasant Soviet and related bodies finally agreed to transfer all land to land committees. The Peasant Soviet, which had emerged as the focal point of SR activities, then issued stinging denunciations of Bolshevik power, demanding the creation of an all-socialist government that would exclude the liberals *and* Bolsheviks. Similar to the one issued by the Saratov Soviet, Lenin's land decree, calling for an end to private ownership, confiscation of landowners' estates, and a halt to the much-hated terms of renting and buying, undermined the appeal of the Peasant Soviet, and with its neutralization the SRs temporarily lost the villages. Saratov SRs attacked Lenin's decree, instead offering peasants a rival one,[41] but this political

---

[40] A state-sponsored attempt on the eve of World War I to reshape the social structure of the countryside, the Stolypin reforms facilitated the release of peasants from the confines of the commune. Although a significant number of local peasants took advantage of the legislation, most rejoined the collective fold in 1917. For peasant radicalism see G. A. Gerasimenko, *Nizovye krest'ianskie organizatsii v 1917-pervoi polovine 1918 godov (Na materialakh Nizhnego Povolzh'ia)* (Saratov, 1974), 172–75. The figure for estate seizures is found in V. P. Antonov-Saratovskii, *Pod stiagom proletarskoi bor'by: Otryvki iz vospominanii o rabote v Saratove* (Moscow and Leningrad, 1925), 143, and in *Saratovskaia zemskaia nedelia*, no. 2, Oct. 7, 1917, 1.

[41] M. O. Sagrad'ian, *Osushchestvlenie Leninskogo dekreta o zemle v Saratovskoi gubernii* (Saratov, 1966), 22.

squabbling was lost on the peasants, who interpreted both decrees to suit their own needs.

Frustrated, the SRs scrambled to convene a provincial peasant congress before one called by the Bolsheviks met.[42] The left-wing majority within the local SR organization, however, remained committed to cooperating with the Bolsheviks in order to avoid civil war. Such dissent within SR ranks undermined the party's peasant congress.[43] Desperate SR leaders next tried unsuccessfully to convince delegates to the Bolshevik-sponsored peasant congress that they had been deceived. Although no clear answer emerges regarding how representative the congress was or the extent of the use of force and intimidation during this impassioned time,[44] the gathering's adoption of Bolshevik resolutions contributed to the consolidation of Soviet power locally because peasant delegates returning to their villages spearheaded the election of soviets and the calling of district congresses. Sources show that most young peasants who had served in the army voiced Left SR or Bolshevik sentiments. After the peasant congress closed, a provincial congress of soviets that opened in Saratov under somewhat dubious circumstances also voiced approval of the new government.[45] Representing about half of the district soviets, the congress adjourned in the wake of the Left SRs' entry into the national government and the local committee's joining with the Saratov Soviet's Executive Committee.

Thus, Soviet power became recognized in much of rural Saratov Province at the start of the brief coalition between Bolsheviks and Left SRs both at the national level and locally, that is, between December 1917 and March 1918. It found reflection in the liquidation of volost zemstvos and their replacement by soviets. Most soviets in the province, as elsewhere in Russia, were set up in January and February 1918.[46] To

---

[42] F. A. Rashitov, "Osnovnye etapy Sovetskogo stroitel'stva v Saratovskoi gubernii v pervoi polovine 1918 goda," *Materialy k nauchnoi konferentsii aspirantov i molodykh nauchnykh sotrudnikov*, no. 1 (Saratov, 1965): 9.

[43] *Saratovskii vestnik*, no. 252, Nov. 24, 1917, 3. See also V. P. Antonov-Saratovskii, ed., *Saratovskii Sovet rabochikh deputatov, 1917–1918: Sbornik dokumentov* (Moscow and Leningrad, 1931) (hereafter *Saratovskii Sovet*), 265, and Z. Petrov, "Saratovskii proletariat v bor'be za vlast'," in *1917 god v Saratove* (Saratov, 1927), 26–27.

[44] G. A. Gerasimenko, "Ustanovlenie Sovetskoi vlasti v uezdakh Nizhnego Povolzh'ia," in *Iz istorii Saratovskogo Povolzh'ia* (Saratov, 1968), 81; and G. A. Gerasimenko and V. P. Sem'ianinov, *Sovetskaia vlast' v derevne na pervom etape Oktiabria* (Saratov, 1980), 45.

[45] *Izvestiia Saratovskogo Soveta* (hereafter *ISS*), no. 107, Dec. 12, 1917, 3. The Mensheviks considered the congress illegal not only because of the absence of delegates from many districts, but also because the Bolsheviks secretly opened the gathering early. See *Proletarii Povolzh'ia*, no. 142, Dec. 9, 1917, 4.

[46] G. A. Gerasimenko and D. S. Tochenyi, *Sovety Povolzh'ia v 1917 godu: Bor'ba par-

be sure, some peasants voiced reservations about their readiness to assume the zemstvos' responsibilities, lamenting the rift between the better-off peasants and the poorer elements.[47] Great confusion reigned in the countryside at this time. As one peasant put it, "we know nothing . . . about what's going on in Russia."[48]

Postscript

The ideology of revolution had delegitimated the autocratic system and provided symbolic coherence in the battle against the autocratic order, but it provided no popular alternative, thereby greatly increasing the chances of civil war. So, too, did the Bolsheviks' commandeering of power on the eve of the opening of the Second Congress of Soviets, which demonstrates the party leadership's willingness to break with the idea of Soviet democracy. More importantly, the readiness with which the Bolshevik elite soon resorted to the use of force when they lacked the necessary support reveals their belief that they had the moral authority to rule. This precluded the possibility of a genuine coalition government, guaranteeing that the Civil War would be savage.

Although the October Revolution represented the triumph of all radical groups that had broken with the camp supporting further coalition with the bourgeoisie, Bolshevik attitudes, civil war circumstances, Russian political practices, and the impact of war on state formation ultimately resulted in the rise of a one-party dictatorship, creation of a centralized party-state, and the eruption of vengeance and violence. The Russian experience proved once again that revolutions bring about unintended consequences as the struggle to uproot injustice and inequality gave rise to new grievances and disparities. To understand why, it is necessary to consider not only the transformative power of revolution, but also how people endured the experience of civil war, which gave rise to new Communist Party foundation myths that defined criteria for membership and also for exclusion from the emerging Soviet polity.

---

tii, bol'shevizatsiia sovetov, oktiabr'skie dni (Saratov, 1977), 291–94, and G. A. Gerasimenko, "Vozniknovenie Sovetskoi vlasti v volostiakh Saratovskoi gubernii," *Povolzhskii krai*, no. 1 (1972): 70–75.

[47] GASO, f. 521, op. 1, d. 59, ll. 1–8.

[48] GA RF, f. 393, op. 2, d. 80, l. 244.

Two

Languages of Power

How the Saratov Bolsheviks Imagined Their Enemies

LIKE THE FRENCH revolutionaries of the eighteenth century, the Bolsheviks created new political and social relations as well as divisions through their use of language, symbols, images, and everyday practices.[1] This was particularly true of language, for Bolshevik authorities drew heavily on linguistic authority[2] as they constructed a heroic narrative of the revolutionary present, which was in constant flux owing to the changing policies, initiatives, and alliances brought about by civil war.[3] Uncertain how to interpret October 1917, and confused by the rupture within the socialist camp, the Bolsheviks found meaning — and unity — in the immediate appearance of an opposition.

In this chapter I examine the Saratov Bolsheviks' attempts to understand, represent, and manipulate the flood of resistance triggered by their assumption of power through mid-1919, by which time all of the party's rhetorical strategies used during the Civil War — and perhaps later as well — were in place. I do so with an eye toward showing how

[1] William A. Gamson, "Political Discourse and Collective Action," *International Social Movement Research: A Research Annual* 1 (Greenwich, Conn., 1988): 221; Hunt, *Politics, Culture, and Class*, 12.

[2] As Keith Baker argues, "a revolution can be defined as a transformation of the discursive practice of the community, a moment in which social relations are reconstituted and the discourse defining the political relations between individuals and groups is radically recast." See *Inventing the French Revolution*, 18.

[3] See Hunt's discussion of the "mythic" present during the French Revolution in *Politics, Culture, and Class*, 27–28.

the Bolsheviks' "social vocabulary of everyday politics"[4] interpreted events from an ideological and class perspective, justifying the ruling powers' growing use of coercion as they imposed censorship in territories under their control and began the difficult processes of centralizing the state and of snuffing out factionalism within the party. Apart from a set of ideas and symbols used to define political relations between social groups, Bolshevik discourse comprised two main *emerging* and potentially contradictory languages. (By language I mean not only fields of vocabulary and syntax, but also content or what was permissible to write about.) Simplifying things greatly, I call one of them the party's external language, essentially that of party newspapers, public meetings, agitational literature, and propaganda, which presented the revolution in process in heroic and at times solicitous tones. I dub the second one the party's internal language, the language of classified and confidential reports and closed meetings and other private forums that were not intended for mass consumption. A "hidden" or "backstage transcript" of the powerful, this internal language consisted of "the practices and claims of their rule" that could not be "openly avowed."[5]

I purposefully overlook the complicating fact that party members knew several external and internal languages depending upon whom they were addressing.[6] Instead, I emphasize the *heuristic* value of demonstrating how the Bolsheviks spoke in two registers at once. It goes without saying that both languages were contested, that the boundaries between them were porous, and that they were interpenetrable. But this became less true as the Civil War unfolded. Those wishing to use them successfully had to observe their forms and formalities, which were shaped by ideology and by the immediate social context within which party members acted. Certainly "leaks" frequently occurred, and the external language could be critical of central policies. Yet as the Communists banned factionalism and outlawed other political parties, forbade local newspapers from criticizing party committees, and carried out a "linguistic cleansing"[7] in their wholesale exile of dissident intellectuals at civil war's end, party members learned the price for not observing the rules of how to "speak Bolshevik."[8]

[4] This is the formulation of Thomas Childers. See "The Social Language of Politics in Germany: The Sociology of Political Discourse in the Weimar Republic," *American Historical Review* 95, no. 2 (1990): 335.

[5] James C. Scott, *Domination and the Arts of Resistance: Hidden Transcripts* (New Haven, 1990), xii.

[6] Ibid., 14.

[7] The term is Carol Emerson's. See "New Words, New Epochs, Old Thoughts," *Russian Review* 55, no. 3 (1996): 357.

[8] Stephen Kotkin uses this phrase. See "Coercion and Identity: Workers' Lives in Stalin's

In illuminating how the Bolsheviks used the two languages to help survive the Civil War and to establish ideological dominance, I analyze how each depicted the two gravest military threats to Soviet power locally during the Civil War: the uprising that broke out in the local garrison in May 1918, and the siege by White forces in the spring and summer of 1919. While considering the common ideological value system linking the two languages, I offer some thoughts about the significance of their differences, and complicate our understanding of the Bolshevik sources used for viewing this critical period. I spotlight the events the languages of Bolshevism sought to depict and their immediate, short-term features in order to suggest how they became structuring elements.

Surviving the First Threats to Soviet Power

The belief that Bolshevik power would collapse or that the party would be forced to broaden the ruling coalition encouraged many Saratovites to go out on strike or otherwise subvert the functioning of the administrative machinery in the weeks following the Revolution. A strike originating in Petrograd that spread to Saratov's postal and telegraph workers made information hard to come by, while bank officials diverted much-needed funds from the soviet.[9] Such acts, which Bolshevik leaders interpreted as "sabotage," thereby giving legitimacy to their own behavior, became more unrestrained. A potent demonstration against the soviet on December 31, 1917, organized by the Bolsheviks' socialist opponents and resulting in casualties, proved to be an ominous portent of the new year, as did a resolution carried that same day by the local Bolshevik committee that the "Constituent Assembly, which does not recognize Soviet power, must not be allowed to exist for a single day."[10] A similar scenario unfolded in Tsaritsyn, and actually in much of Russia, as a result of which the Bolshevik government established the Vecheka (Cheka) or political police in December 1917.[11]

Showcase City," in Lewis H. Siegelbaum and Ronald G. Suny, eds., *Making Workers Soviet: Power, Class, and Identity* (Ithaca, 1994), 302.

[9] Tsentral'nyi muzei revoliutsii, GIK 30244/200, "Avtobiografiia V. P. Antonova (Saratovskogo)." See Antonov's speech of Oct. 3, 1918.

[10] *ISS*, no. 1, Jan. 3, 1918, 1, 4.

[11] The "sabotage" on the part of the bureaucracy is discussed in T. H. Rigby, *Lenin's Government: Sovnarkom, 1917–1922* (Cambridge, Eng., 1979), 44–46. For the Saratov events see *ISS*, no. 7, Jan. 11, 1918, 2; no. 14, Jan. 19, 1918, 3; *Saratovskii Sovet*, 307–12, 330–35; V. P. Antonov-Saratovskii, "Politika Saratovskogo Soveta," in *Godovshchina sotsial'noi revoliutsii v Saratove* (hereafter cited as *Godovshchina*), ed. by V. P. Antonov-Saratovskii (Saratov, 1918), 32; and *Ocherki istorii Saratovskoi organizatsii KPSS*, vol. 2,

Although the Constituent Assembly had already become the rallying cry of those contesting the events of October, its image acquired greater symbolic importance as the Civil War unfolded and opposition to the Bolsheviks increased. Initially, indifference, perhaps linked to the belief that the Bolshevik regime would collapse, diluted the appeal of dumas, zemstvos, and other social organizations that rejected the Bolshevik order. Paradoxically, the victory of the mainstream SRs in the elections also enhanced the Bolsheviks' position in the countryside because the land decree that they issued immediately upon coming to power enabled them to take credit for land reform.[12] Peasants in the settlement of Romanovka, Balashov Uezd, for instance, demanded new elections to the Constituent Assembly, insisting that they had voted for the SRs under pressure, but now wished "to vote for the Bolshevik-democrats," because of the party's land decree. To be sure, later in the Civil War the countryside rose in revolt against the Soviet regime; however, at this time rural Russia contributed in its own way to keeping the Bolsheviks in power.[13]

At the end of January 1918, a religious procession involving thousands of participants turned into a demonstration against Soviet power after the Bolsheviks decreed the separation of church and state. The recent appearance of a group of anarchists in Saratov complicated the public's reaction to the decree. Hailing the world socialist revolution and "anarchistic communism," they issued a leaflet that denounced all governments, private property, state power, and religion. Another decree also ascribed to the anarchists circulated at this time, announcing the "abolition of private ownership of women." According to the soviet, local Black Hundred elements had proposed to the anarchists that they join them in an alliance against the soviet, and the anarchists' refusal triggered disturbances. Whatever sparked the turmoil, a furious mob of mostly women smashed the anarchists' headquarters. As an example of how the social vocabulary of everyday politics was changing, the soviet pinned the blame for the turmoil on provocateurs "backed by priests, capitalists, and landowners," and outlawed all street gatherings, meetings, and the carrying of weapons.[14]

1918–1937 (Saratov, 1965), 50–51. For Tsaritsyn, see V. I. Tomarev, "Bol'sheviki Tsaritsyna v bor'be za ustanovlenie i uprochenie Sovetskoi vlasti (mart 1917–iiun' 1918 gg.)" (candidate diss., Moscow State University, 1961), 167–72.

[12] Malvin M. Helgesen, "The Origins of the Party-State Monolith in Soviet Russia: Relations Between the Soviets and Party Committees in the Central Provinces, October 1917–March 1921" (Ph.D. diss., SUNY, Stony Brook, 1980), 46.

[13] GA RF, f. 393, op. 3, d. 331, l. 164. For similar attitudes in Volsk see *ISS*, no. 10, Jan. 14, 1918, 3.

[14] GASO, f. 1280, d. 2919; *ISS*, no. 24, Jan. 31, 1918, 1, 3; and *Saratovskii Sovet*, 359–60.

The activities of Cossack forces in the Volga vicinity also helped give rise to a siege mentality among Saratov's Bolshevik leaders, instilling hope in those opposed to Bolshevik rule that military might would sweep the party from power. Cossack units maneuvering in the Volga basin had threatened to disband local soviets during the Kornilov affair of August 1917, and supporters of the city duma had turned to Orenburg Cossacks in October to come to their rescue. Now, Cossack armies in the Don region emerged as the focal point of resistance to Soviet power. Fearing the consequences of the Ural, Astrakhan, and Don Cossacks joining forces and assisting "anti-Bolshevik elements," the Bolshevik-controlled Saratov Soviet cobbled together the so-called Eastern Army of several thousand volunteers from the Saratov garrison and worker Red Guardsmen under the command of S. I. Zagumennyi in response to the Orenburg and Astrakhan Soviets' appeals for help when Cossacks rose against them in January 1918. Aided in part by dissent within Cossack ranks, the Eastern Army prevented the Cossacks from uniting into a powerful anti-Bolshevik force. But Ural Cossacks approached Saratov after the departure of the Eastern Army, forcing the soviet to declare the city "under siege."[15]

The soviet's relations with the Cossacks deteriorated in the following months, by which time the volunteer Eastern Army had already been disbanded, prompting the Saratov Soviet to organize the Osobaia (Special) Army, so designated because its special task was to clear the Volga basin of Cossack forces. Engagements with the Cossacks ended in defeat for the Special Army, however, as its demoralized units went their separate ways in response to peasant uprisings behind the lines within the province. The peasant unrest had been prompted by the Czechoslovak uprising of mid-1918 and the fall of nearby Samara to the forces of the Constituent Assembly.[16] To review, when Czechoslovak troops, formerly prisoners of war, embarked upon a journey across Russia they became entangled in skirmishes with local soviets along the Volga. Encouraging the Czechoslovaks to seize Samara in early June, the SRs formed the Committee of Members of the Constitutent Assembly (Komuch). Although the Samara events emboldened anti-Soviet forces

[15] A. A. Klempert, "Rol' Saratovskogo Soveta rabochikh, soldatskikh i krest'ianskikh deputatov v bor'be s astrakhanskimi i ural'skimi belokazakami," Saratov: Sbornik statei i materialov po voprosam narodnogo khoziaistva i kul'tury, no. 6 (Saratov, 1948): 44–46; and S. V. Terekhin, Gody ognevye: Saratovskaia organizatsiia bol'shevikov v period Oktiabr'skoi revoliutsi i grazhdanskoi voiny (Saratov, 1967), 77, 97.

[16] Godovshchina, 45–56. The Special Army included a unit under the command of V. I. Chapaev, the Civil War partisan hero whose adventures provided the material for a multimedia cultural industry following the 1923 publication of D. Furmanov's novel, Chapaev.

2.1 V. P. Antonov (Saratovskii) addressing a crowd in Revolutionary Square, 1918. Courtesy Central State Museum of Modern Russian History, Moscow.

throughout Russia, Komuch failed to win popular support and in October fell to the Bolsheviks.[17]

Another threat to Soviet power emerged when local Bolshevik leaders demobilized units of the Imperial Army, not only because demobilization left the vulnerable soviet with only a handful of armed workers to come to its defense. When the 7,000 demobilized soldiers set up a union of *frontoviki* (soldiers evacuated from the front), which demanded jobs and other preferential treatment, the soviet had no way of controlling them. An embittered Vladimir Pavlovich Antonov (Saratovskii) (figure 2.1), the city's most prominent Bolshevik leader, revealed his party's low ideological regard for the peasantry in observing that greed had turned the soldiers into "beasts" who had forgotten everything except "how to take as much public property as possible back with them to the villages."[18] In early March the frontoviki clashed with Red Guard detachments on several occasions, resulting in casualties on both sides.[19]

Within days of the showdown with the frontoviki, two incidents,

[17] Stephen M. Berk, "The Democratic Counter-revolution: Komuch and the Civil War on the Volga," *Canadian-American Slavic Studies* 7, no. 4 (1973): 443–59.

[18] *Godovshchina*, 30. See also GASO, f. 521, op. 2, d. 28, l. 8.

[19] *Godovshchina*, 50–51, and GASO, f. 3586, op. 1, d. 56, l. 2.

probably unrelated, gave the local Bolsheviks their first post-October political martyrs, magnified their sense of growing conspiracy, and suggested how crucial the battle over the printed word had become. Shots fired by unknown people during a soviet-sponsored demonstration resulted in the death of David Tsyrkin, editor of the Bolsheviks' *Krasnaia gazeta* (Red Newspaper).[20] The soviet devoted an entire issue of the publication to the fallen revolutionary's memory, replete with expressions of support from the districts.[21] Shortly afterward, an old man named Rabinovich shot and killed Commissar of the Press P. A. Alekseev, who had sought to requisition Rabinovich's printing press. Depicting Tsyrkin's and Alekseev's deaths as "the first acts in a new chain of White Guard terror," the Bolsheviks staged elaborate funerals for the revolutionary martyrs, declaring that the soviet "would answer such threats with terror."[22] These were not empty words. When Rabinovich went into hiding the Bolsheviks executed his son. As during the French Revolution, a near obsession with conspiracy, which found reflection in socialist propaganda already in 1917, began to dominate the Bolsheviks' external language. Not specific to the Bolsheviks, this sentiment represented yet another consequence of World War I.[23]

In early 1918 the Bolsheviks' rapidly deteriorating relations with the other socialist parties — as well as with local workers — underscored the party's growing sense of isolation. Although the parties shared a common revolutionary heritage, their differing blueprints for the future and present affected how they represented the latter to their supporters. After shutting down the opposition press in December, the soviet briefly allowed the moderate socialists to resume publishing newspapers. Offering an alternative revolutionary narrative to that of the Bolsheviks, *Slovo proletariia* (Word of the Proletarian), put out by the local Menshevik organization, argued that "the soviets have lost their independence, and their role has turned into that of confirming all resolutions proposed by the Bolsheviks, of approving with applause all political crimes committed by the worker-peasant government."[24] Workers at the Gantke plant, a metallurgical enterprise, agreed, voicing their concern over restrictions on freedom of speech, the Mensheviks' expulsion from the soviet, and the dispersal of the Constituent Assembly. These same

[20] *ISS*, no. 49, March 19, 1918, 3, and *Saratovskii Sovet*, 399–400.

[21] *Krasnaia gazeta* (hereafter *KG*), no. 20, March 17, 1918, 1–4.

[22] *ISS*, no. 57, March 28, 1918, 2, 3; no. 58, March 29, 1918, 1; no. 60, March 31, 1918, 1; and *Na strazhe revoliutsii (Iz istorii Saratovskogo gorodskogo soveta, 1917–1921)* (Saratov, 1921), 7.

[23] Furet, *Interpreting the French Revolution*, 67–68. See *ISS* for March and April 1918. Holquist makes this point about the war in "Information," passim.

[24] *Slovo proletariia*, no. 1, Jan. 21, 1918, 4, and no. 7, Jan. 28, 1918, 1.

workers and others called for an end to Bolshevik rule and the restoration of the assembly. Even Latvian workers who had traditionally supported the Bolsheviks expressed hostility toward the party when it banned the "opposition press" once again.[25]

The Bolsheviks' strained relations with the moderate socialists and workers likewise found expression in elections to the soviet in December 1917 and April 1918, which show that the party's support among workers had begun to erode. For example, the Bolsheviks had captured 320 seats in the Workers' Section in September, when the Mensheviks won only 76 seats and the SRs 103. At that time the Bolsheviks received 71 percent of the soldiers' vote. But in December 1917, Bolsheviks captured a suspicious 201 of 400 seats in the Workers' Section, and the Mensheviks, 52 seats. The Bolsheviks fared better in the Soldiers' Section, to which 167 Bolsheviks and 32 Left SRs were elected, but the garrison broke up shortly afterward and the section was liquidated.[26] During the April elections, about two-thirds of the 157 industrial enterprises for which there is information chose representatives by secret ballot. Wherever both pro-soviet and pro-Constituent Assembly support was found in the same enterprise, the elections were carried out with difficulty and with intimidation.[27] The Menshevik platform made inroads among Saratov's railroad workers, who gave them 644 votes versus the Bolsheviks' 838, and among printers, who supported the Menshevik mandate. Those who backed the Mensheviks or Right SRs called for the restoration of the Constituent Assembly, while anarcho-syndicalist elements supported the Bolshevik platform[28] (table 2.1).

The Bolshevik press's failure to publish final election results at the time suggests that they did not please the party.[29] Only later, in Septem-

---

[25] GASO, f. 521, op. 1, d. 207, l. 118; M. Shchepakin, "Saratovskie gruzchiki na zashchite zavoevanii oktiabria," in *V boiakh za diktatury proletariata (Sbornik vospominanii uchastnikov Oktiabria i grazhdanskoi voiny v Nizhnem Povolzh'e)* (Saratov, 1933), 19–20; and G. L. Semenov, "Saratovskie gruzchiki v dni velikikh sobytii," in *Za vlast' sovetov: Vospominaniia uchastnikov revoliutsionnykh sobytii 1917 goda v Saratovskoi gubernii*, ed. by G. Sukharev et al. (Saratov, 1957), 142.

[26] It is hard to account for the large bloc of unaffiliated deputies. Later, the rubric cloaked what was the Bolsheviks' socialist opposition. At this early stage it may have reflected workers' dissatisfaction with partisan politics. GA RF, f. 7471, op. 1, d. 89, ll. 12–13.

[27] *ISS*, no. 73, April 16, 1918, 3; no. 74, April 17, 1918, 3; no. 75, April 18, 1918, 3; and *KG*, no. 46, April 17, 1918, 3. Also see *KG*, no. 49, April 20, 1918, 4; *ISS*, no. 76, April 19, 1918, 3; and G. A. Gerasimenko, et al., eds., *Khronika revoliutsionnykh sobytii v Saratovskom Povolzh'e* (Saratov, 1968), 255.

[28] *KG*, no. 52, April 24, 1918, 4; Rashitov, "Sovety," 213–16; idem., "Osnovnye etapy," 43–44; and *ISS*, no. 77, April 20, 1918, 3.

[29] The rise of Menshevik fortunes at this time has not gone unnoticed. See V. I. Lebedeff, *The Russian Democracy in Its Struggle against the Bolshevist Tyranny* (New

TABLE 2.1
Results of the April 1918 Elections to the Saratov Soviet

Party	No. of Deputies Elected
1. Communists	386
2. Nonparty	190
3. Communist sympathizers	128
4. Mensheviks and Right SRs	116
5. Left SRs	66
6. SR Maximalists	20
7. Anarchists	5
Total	911

Source: Rashitov, "Osnovnye etapy Sovetskogo stroitel'stva," 43 (citing ISS, no. 200, Sept. 26, 1918, 3).

ber 1918, did *Izvestiia Saratovskogo Soveta* (News of the Saratov Soviet, hereafter *Izvestiia*) announce that the Communists had won a plurality of votes. The bitter polemics associated with the election campaign in Saratov spilled over into the first plenum meeting of the newly elected soviet, which expelled the Right SRs and Mensheviks from the council. In doing so, the Bolsheviks invoked the tautology that their enemies were "not only the bourgeoisie, but their servants-Mensheviks and Right SRs." In justifying the moderate socialists' expulsion from the soviet (before Moscow had done so), Antonov pinned responsibility for the party's difficulties on them: "*We could not be patient, we could not admit into the soviet those parties that organized uprisings against the soviet, organized Cossack attacks on Saratov, consciously organized sabotage, and so on.*"[30] At this point the separate elements composing the opposition—the bourgeoisie, Cossacks, and other socialist parties—further lost their distinctiveness in the Saratov Bolsheviks' emerging external language, which was increasingly obsessed with conspiracy. As *Izvestiia* put it, "the Russian socialist republic at present is like a camp besieged on all sides."[31]

York, 1919), 7, also available as *Bor'ba russkoi demokratii protiv bol'shevikov: Zapiski ochevidtsa i uchastnika sverzheniia bol'shevistskoi vlasti na Volge i v Sibiri* (New York, 1919). Leonard Schapiro also called attention to the phenomenon in *The Origin of the Communist Autocracy: Political Opposition in the Soviet State. First Phase, 1917–1922*, 2d ed. (Cambridge, Mass., 1977), 191. V. N. Brovkin in greater detail has examined the Mensheviks' political "comeback" in the spring of 1918. V. N. Brovkin, "The Mensheviks under Attack: The Transformation of Soviet Politics, June–Sept. 1918," *Jahrbücher für Geschichte Osteuropas* 32 (1984): 378–79. See also Brovkin, *The Mensheviks after October: Socialist Opposition and the Rise of the Bolshevik Dictatorship* (Ithaca, 1987).

[30] Emphasis added. *Godovshchina*, 27, and ISS, no. 87, May 5, 1918, 2.

[31] *ISS*, no. 69, April 11, 1918, 1, and no. 71, April 13, 1918, 1.

Making Language an Expression of Power

We need to pause for a moment to consider the many factors involved in the production of what soon would become two distinct Bolshevik (since early 1918 Communist) Party languages. The party's origins in the political underground and the vituperative exchanges between and within factions and parties at home and abroad certainly generated many of the languages' semantic features. So too did the anti-bourgeois ideology of revolution that delegitimated the autocratic system. The Bolsheviks' faith in the perfectibility of humankind through conscious action, as well as in Marxism as an instrument of understanding, likewise shaped party discourse by providing a package of values, practices, and dispositions that made them prone to act and react in certain ways: we should not underestimate their determination to transform society or their belief that history was on their side. Although the ideological assumptions of Bolshevism provided the basis for the party's understanding of political life, Russian political culture likewise legitimated autocratic practices. The widely accepted view of the state as a moving force in history, and the intelligentsia's exaggerated belief in its own historical mission were among its prominent features. The latter trait — evident across the political spectrum — exposed a large degree of condescension toward the Russian people and their indigenous culture, whose autonomy and spontaneity they mistrusted.[32] It also revealed the elite's belief that they had the moral authority to rule, a position that made it easier for the party leadership to resort to violence.

In making language an expression of political power, the Bolsheviks furthered their own political cause by claiming to speak for the social groups they privileged, especially workers. To be sure, this was part of a larger practice of Russian politics common to all of the socialist parties at the time; Bolshevik rhetorical strategies were deeply embedded in a much broader linguistic universe, but one in which the party came to predominate owing to its imposition of censorship and controls over the press. While the semantic and stylistic features of the party's external language had taken shape before and during 1917, its fundamental sce-

---

[32] I am not ignoring growing democratic strains in Russian political culture, but am emphasizing that in circumstances of civil war they had much less chance to develop. Anna Geifman and Peter Kenez make similar points regarding the intelligentsia's role. See Anna Geifman, "The Russian Intelligentsia, Terror, and Revolution," in *The Bolsheviks in Russian Society: The Revolution and the Civil War*, ed. by Vladimir N. Brovkin (New Haven, 1997), 35, and Peter Kenez, *The Birth of the Propaganda State: Soviet Methods of Mass Mobilization, 1917–1929* (Cambridge, Eng., 1985), 4–7.

narios and points of interpretation appeared during the crisis of civil war in response to the sorts of dangers to Soviet power noted earlier. Thus, while acknowledging that language has the capacity to transform human relationships and can help bring into existence that which it seeks to represent, I believe that the languages of Bolshevism were also referential and responsive.[33]

The soviet's *Izvestiia* was the most important means for disseminating the party's external language, but it was only during the first half of 1918 that it came to function in a restrictive and repressive environment. The party newspaper *Sotsial-demokrat* (Social Democrat) and the papers put out in the uezd towns served this same purpose. *Sotsial-demokrat* first went to press in March 1917, was renamed *Krasnaia gazeta* (Red Newspaper, undoubtedly to reflect a broadening sense of constituency) in early 1918, and folded in 1919 with the emergence of a party-state. After the ban on opposition papers, party newspapers, edited by leading revolutionaries—Antonov, Illarion Vissarionovich Mgeladze (Vardin), and Mikhail Ivanovich Vasiliev (Iuzhin)—became the basic source of news for both friend and foe of Soviet power.[34] Mirroring the soviet plenum's loss of power, news about the transactions of the soviet disappeared from their pages, replaced by sanitized coverage of sundry "campaigns" that reflected party priorities. These changes came about in a strained political atmosphere that included broad disagreement on fundamental issues within the party itself; they likewise constituted elements of a broader civil war culture developing at the time. As a result, *Izvestiia* experimented with many rhetorical devices, some of which would become standard features of the Soviet press. Newspaper language was studded with binary images (labor/Capital, workers/bourgeoisie, life/death, freedom/slavery, victory/defeat, bright future/dark past), and inversions (the hired slave had become master of the land and ran the factories, the humble now voted while the bourgeoisie were excluded from Soviet power). In providing readers a hereti-

---

[33] I find it problematic to come down on one side or another in the debate over whether language is defined by social situation or whether language shapes experience, and therefore consciously seek to combine the two approaches by drawing on theoretical models that, at first glance, might appear to be at odds with each other. Models suggesting that language contributes to constituting the subject help us understand Bolshevik practices, whereas models emphasizing how agents deploy language facilitate our understanding of those who do not control the dominant discourse.

[34] For the new role of the press see Kenez, *Birth*, 21–49. A paper shortage kept local press runs small—approximately 10,000. N. A. Iakorev, "Iz opyta politicheskoi raboty v massakh v gody grazhdanskoi voiny (Po materialam Saratovskoi partiinoi organizatsii)," *Uchenye zapiski Saratovskogo universiteta* 59 (1958): 239.

cal subversion of the social world, *Izvestiia* tested the capacity of Bolshevik ideas to transform human relationships.[35]

To be sure, despite a shared common mentality and the appearance of coherence and unity, Bolshevism contained internal contradictions. The circumstances in which Saratov Bolsheviks operated and the daunting tasks they faced resulted in diverse understandings of how best to rule. Declaring Saratov a "republic," local Bolshevik leaders navigated an independent course until early 1919, ignoring the Center's rulings. Manifestations of "localism" (*mestnichestvo*) frequently caused ruptures between the national Bolshevik press and its local counterpart. But this would prove too dangerous a development for a party fighting what was fast becoming a barbarous civil war. Independent-minded members of the party elite who deviated from central directives made it difficult to construct a unified public narrative of the Bolsheviks' heroic present, potentially undermining the party's claim to power. As chapter 3 shows, Moscow intervened, replacing local leaders with outsiders in early 1919. This furthered the development of a unified external language. So did the Center's efforts to coordinate the activities of local soviets' agitational departments and to purge the party of undisciplined members, and other steps taken to centralize the emerging party-state.[36]

The May 1918 Red Army Uprising

The various manifestations of opposition confronting the local Bolsheviks came to a head in mid-May 1918, when an uprising against Soviet power broke out in Saratov. In its external language the party depicted the disturbance as the outgrowth of the actions of its *collective* enemies: White Guards, tsarist officer organizations, Black Hundreds, Cossacks, Czechoslovaks, and now, unambiguously and emphatically, Right SRs and Mensheviks. But the classified report of the Extraordinary Investigative Commission charged with studying the insurrection saw it as a spontaneous, disorganized movement caused by excessive use of force that turned the city's inhabitants against Soviet power, which lacked a popular mandate.

Given the problems connected to the dissolution of the Saratov garrison and the need to mobilize military forces to ward off the Cossack

---

[35] As Pierre Bourdieu suggests, discursive strategies such as these help create the social structures they depict. See *Language and Symbolic Power*, ed. and introduced by John B. Thompson, trans. by Gino Raymond and Matthew Adamson (Cambridge, Mass., 1994), 128.

[36] For the problem of constructing a unified public narrative see Scott, *Domination*, 11, 67.

threat, the soviet's military department could not be selective in signing up volunteers to defend the red republic. It took in many individuals who had joined partisan units in Ukraine (a "disgraceful rabble" in Antonov's estimation), and who were not inclined to subordinate themselves to the soviet. Referred to in Bolshevik sources as anarchist-terrorists (some had fallen under the influence of Ukrainian anarchism), they plundered their way to Saratov from Odessa, often dispersing local soviets en route. Once they arrived in Saratov, their influence appears to have been largely disruptive. For instance, their promotion of the slogan "seize everything from the bourgeoisie" (who, as one pundit observed, had already been fleeced by the soviet) gave Bolshevik leaders grounds for seeing the newcomers as a mixed blessing. However, the Bolshevik-controlled soviet had few reliable forces at its disposal, because local workers had rejected a call to join paramilitary units back in March. As a result, the soviet defended the "anarchist-terrorists" when enraged citizens sought to disarm them following distribution of the leaflet claiming that women had been "nationalized" in Saratov.

On the eve of their would-be departure for the Ural front to engage Cossack forces, the feisty troops demanded their wages in advance, new boots, and restoration of soldier committees with their former rights. When rumors spread that the soldiers would be disarmed, agitated — and inebriated — soldiers opened fire. Former tsarist officers or cadets (*iunkera*) and Right SRs joined the disgruntled soldiers, advancing a leader named Viktorov, who appears in the various sources as both a one-time Bolshevik and a former Cossack officer. Promising to free all imprisoned soldiers and to elect a new soviet, Viktorov won adherents among artillerymen and infantry troops. Other units in the garrison declared their "neutrality." Negotiations between the soviet and insurgent soldiers broke down, as Viktorov demanded that all workers be disarmed. The soviet's uncertain fate emboldened the city's anti-Bolshevik elements, which sought to arrest party functionaries. Right SRs tried to give some direction to the movement, putting out one issue of a newspaper, which proclaimed that "the army and the frontoviki have overthrown the Bolshevik rule of force," and called for the creation of a government by all the people on the basis of free elections.[37] During the

[37] *Godovshchina*, 31–32; A. Tsekher, "Istoriia Saratovskogo Soveta," in *Piat' let proletarskoi bor'by, 1917–1922* (Saratov, 1922), 39; and V. Berdintsev, "Epizody bor'by s kontrrevoliutsiei v Saratove v 1918 godu," in *V boiakh za diktaturu proletariata: Sbornik vospominanii uchastnikov Oktiabria i grazhdanskoi voiny v Nizhnem Povolzh'e* (Saratov, 1933), 12–13. The paper issued by the SRs is *Golos trudovogo naroda*. See the report from *Svoboda Rossii*, no. 33, May 24, 1918, 3, published in James Bunyan, *Intervention, Civil War, and Communism in Russia. April–December 1918: Documents and Materials* (Baltimore, 1936), 160–61.

night of May 16–17, the two sides exchanged fire. Seizing arms ware-houses, the disgruntled soldiers launched artillery fire against the soviet, destroying its building and trapping those inside. For several days the soviet's fate hung by a thread.[38] Only with the arrival of Latvian sharp-shooters, an internationalist detachment, and units from other towns did the tide turn in favor of the soviet, which suppressed the rebellion on May 18.[39]

The complete indifference of local workers, the "neutrality" of sev-eral key military units, and the fact that non-Russian forces played a critical role in crushing the revolt made the necessary impression on the soviet's leaders, who introduced martial law in Saratov, ordering all citi-zens to turn in their firearms. Those failing to do so risked being shot. Registering former tsarist officers and officer trainees living in Saratov, the victors established a provincial military commissariat in the hopes of preventing some of the problems that had emerged in recruiting and training the Special Army.[40] They also banned outsiders from entering Saratov Province without special permission. Although the decree would prove impossible to implement, its intent is worth noting.[41] Finally, the SRs' backing of the uprising and the Mensheviks' unwillingness to come to the soviet's rescue provided grounds for justifying the earlier expul-sion of the moderate socialists from the soviet by annulling the April elections. In the following weeks, workers at mass meetings "admitting their error" in refusing to take part earlier in paramilitary training, re-called Menshevik, Right SR, and nonparty delegates from the council, and voiced their eagerness "to defend the gains of the revolution."[42]

In their external language, Bolshevik leaders represented the uprising as inspired by Right SRs and Mensheviks, suggesting a link between it and anti-Soviet disturbances in Ukraine and the Ural region. According to the procrustean public version articulated in the party press, these "false" socialist parties, "traitors of the workers' revolution," had occu-pied a "wait-and-see position" until it seemed that the insurrectionists

---

[38] The soviet explained to townspeople that a large band of rowdy troops, who called themselves terrorists, had arrived in Saratov, where they hoped to receive the support of local anarchists, but were rebuffed. Because of rumors that Soviet power was about to collapse and owing to an increase in armed attacks against townspeople, the Cheka had decided to disarm them, and this resulted in a showdown. *ISS*, no. 94, May 17, 1918, 3.

[39] *KG*, no. 69, May 24, 1918, 1; *ISS*, no. 96, May 21, 1918, 1; no. 97, May 22, 1918, 2; Berdintsev, "Epizody bor'by," 13; Rashitov, "Sovety," 50, 217; and GA RF, f. 130, op. 2, d. 627, l. 3.

[40] GA RF, f. 130, op. 2, d. 627, ll. 11–12, and *Saratovskii Sovet*, 505–15.

[41] *ISS*, no. 96, May 21, 1918, 1.

[42] Rashitov, "Sovety," 218–19; *Saratovskii Sovet*, 535–36; *Godovshchina*, 29–30; and *ISS*, no. 98, May 24, 1918, 3. Also see nos. 101–8 of *ISS* and nos. 79–81 of *KG*.

had won the upper hand, whereupon they "removed their masks" and stepped up their agitation against the soviet, which was saved by the "glorious defenders of the revolution arriving from the Ural front." Saratov's Antonov saw a connection between the rebellion and SR-Menshevik efforts that had convinced workers to reject the soviet's call for paramilitary training for all workers, an interpretation that denied the workers' agency, thereby making their indiscretion less threatening. In florid language with religious overtones, Antonov appealed to his comrades "in the name of life, through death, and to victory" to sacrifice themselves for Soviet power, while the commissar of the Ural front maintained that the peaceful period of its spread had "drawn to a close."[43]

History, according to the winners, presented the "trial of the counter-revolutionaries" as a "people's trial of the betrayers of the worker-peasant revolution," as a trial of the parties "that call themselves socialist." The Revolution was now even more deliberately depicted as a "worker-peasant" affair: a Left SR-dominated provincial peasant congress had convened in Saratov, at which local Bolsheviks hailed the "family" and "union" of workers and peasants.[44] Invoking images of the heroic Paris Commune, Antonov stressed the link between the capitalists' invasion of Ukraine, Finland, and Poland on the one hand, and the Cossacks, Black Hundreds, Mensheviks, Right SRs, Kadets, and Czechoslovaks who endangered Saratov on the other. In effect, this established a pattern of significance *retrospectively*. "As a revolutionary who has fought against the dark forces of Capitalism, I appeal to you, hurry! To arms!" Meanwhile, the public funeral of those who died during the shelling of the city was staged as a "protest against the enemies of the socialist revolution." Columns of workers, members of the provincial peasant congress then in session, and Red Army soldiers converged on Theater Square (soon to be renamed Revolutionary Square) for the mass burial. The slogans selected for the event — "death to the enemies of the revolution" and eternal remembrance of those comrades "who had fallen in the battle with the dark forces of the old world" — justified the Revolutionary Tribunal's decision to exile forty-three of those imprisoned for taking part in the uprising and to shoot sixty-two others. *Izvestiia* chided its opponents "for believing that the fate of the soviet had hung by a thread" and that the workers would not defend it. "They misun-

---

[43] *ISS*, no. 96, May 21, 1918, 1; no. 95, May 20, 1918, 1; no. 101, May 28, 1918, 1; no. 116, June 15, 1918, 2; and *Saratovskii Sovet*, 509–15.

[44] *KG*, no. 84, June 11, 1918, 4; *Protokoly Saratovskogo gubernskogo s"ezda sovetov krest'ianskikh deputatov, proiskhodivshego v g. Saratove s 25 maia po 2-e iiunia n/st. 1918 g.* (Saratov, 1918), 2, 112–13.

derstood the wavering moods among some strata of workers as opposition, as so-called nonparty opposition."[45]

In the following weeks the local press linked the May uprising in Saratov and disturbances in neighboring Tsaritsyn and Samara to the Czechoslovak uprising[46] that broke out in nearby Rtishchevo on May 25, and resulted in reversals for soviet power in the area. "Comrade workers and peasants!" flashed the headlines of *Izvestiia*. "Our enemies, the enemies of Soviet power, having endured failure in Saratov, have risen up in a host of other cities."[47] Days later Atkarsk and Kamyshin were placed under martial law. So was Moscow. An anti-Soviet uprising took place in Tambov in mid-June, followed by strikes in Tula and Sormovo. At the end of June anti-Soviet forces rose up in nearby Balakovo, up the river from Saratov.[48] Samara, Syzran, Khvalynsk, Volsk, and riparian villages south of Volsk on the road to Saratov fell to the armies of Admiral A. V. Kolchak and other "counterrevolutionary" units. As the Czechoslovak troops zigzagged across the Volga, peasant disturbances flared up in Saratov Province.[49] Rumors circulated that the intruders had arrested 2,000 Communists in Khvalynsk, loaded them onto a barge docked in the Volga, shot some, and removed others to Siberia.[50]

Although non-Bolshevik sources claim that the Right SRs instigated the Saratov uprising, an interpretation supported by their publication of a misleading newspaper informing townspeople that soldiers had overthrown Soviet power, Bolshevik external language expressed greater outrage at the behavior of local Mensheviks, undoubtedly because the two parties were competing fiercely for the loyalties of Saratov's working class.[51] Thus, when Saratov's Menshevik leaders promoted the program of the Extraordinary Assembly of Delegates from Petrograd Factories,[52] which appealed for restoring the authority of the Constituent

---

[45] *Saratovskii Sovet*, 515, 598; *ISS*, no. 98, May 24, 1918, 3; and no. 101, May 28, 1918, 1.

[46] Antonov claimed he spurned Trotsky's orders to accommodate them in Saratov and instead proposed finding lodging and food for them in the uezds, *Godovshchina*, 28–29, and *ISS*, no. 104, May 31, 1918, 3.

[47] *ISS*, no. 103, May 30, 1918, 1.

[48] I. Sorin, "Saratovskoe vosstanie 1918 g. (Po chernovym zametkam)," *Letopis' revoliutsii*, no. 5 (1923): 219; Gerasimenko, *Khronika*, 266, 271–72, 275, 278; and Terekhin, *Gody ognevye*, 96.

[49] See G. A. Malinin, "Saratovskii Sovet v gody inostrannoi voennoi interventsii i grazhdanskoi voiny," *Nauchnyi ezhegodnik SGU* (1954): 111–12; and GASO, f. 521, op. 1, d. 181, ll. 23, 141–41 ob.

[50] Levinson, "Kontrrevoliutsiia v Saratovskoi gubernii," *1917 god v Saratove* (Saratov, 1927), 87, and *Godovshchina*, 58.

[51] Sorin, "Saratovskoe vosstanie," 224.

[52] Bunyan, *Intervention, Civil War, and Communism*, 161.

Assembly and other democratic organs, and resuming the war against Germany, the Communists instructed the Cheka to take measures "to liquidate the counterrevolutionary activities of the Menshevik Party," urging Moscow to launch a frontal attack against "the counterrevolutionary acts of the Mensheviks and Right SRs."[53] Party external language also stepped up its denunciation of the "counterrevolutionary activities of lawyers without practices, and journalists without newspapers."[54] Vigorously denying accusations that they were in union with Black Hundred officers, Saratov Mensheviks demanded that the soviet's executive committee be taken to court for slander![55] But on June 9 the soviet put the entire Menshevik Party committee on trial for supporting the Extraordinary Assembly in Petrograd. The prosecutor called for "destroying the counterrevolutionary nest that sabotages and opposes the creative work of the soviets and *threatens uprisings similar to that which Saratov has already lived through.*"[56] Soldiers and workers sympathized with the accused, however, turning the trial of the Mensheviks "into a trial of the accusers." Unable to sentence the Mensheviks to hard labor, the embarrassed judges had to settle for the empty gesture of expelling them "from the ranks of the working class."[57]

The Extraordinary Investigative Commission's report of the May uprising in Saratov contrasts sharply with how the local party press represented the event, but nonetheless betrays a common ideological origin that likewise encoded a hierarchy of class. In explaining the causes for the uprising, which it too linked to "similar" events across Russia, the document underscored the "narrowness and precariousness" of Soviet power in Saratov. It regretted that the 40,000 local workers ("such an insignificant number of truly revolutionary elements") were simply "not enough" to provide a stable basis of support for Soviet power in "philistine" Saratov, where "petit-bourgeois elements drawn into the revolutionary process in large numbers could not assimilate new forms of state power quickly enough." Unlike the situation in central Russia, the Saratov Soviet had to battle against a determined opposition from the start ("more than in any other place") for the simple reason that it *"lacks moral authority."* To highlight this point the report, which can

---

[53] *ISS*, no. 111, June 8, 1918, 3. See the soviet's discussion in *Saratovskii Sovet*, 523–24, 526.

[54] *KG*, no. 83, June 9, 1918, 1.

[55] *Rabochii internatsional*, no. 4, June 2, 1918 (RSDRP, Nicolaevsky Collection, Hoover Institution, folder 5, box 4).

[56] Emphasis added. *KG*, no. 84, June 11, 1918, 2.

[57] *Nash golos*, no. 3, June 9 (22), 1918, and Vladimir N. Brovkin, ed. and trans., *Dear Comrades: Menshevik Reports on the Bolshevik Revolution and the Civil War* (Stanford, 1991), 121.

also be read as an indictment of localism, chronicles all of the manifestations of this opposition since the start of 1918. The resulting "excessive use of police measures" against the inhabitants ("the arrest of
more than 700 people") made the city's population "hostile to Soviet
power," which "lacks any significant popularity." In fact, the "quasi-
revolutionary" methods of local agents of Soviet power—senseless requisitions, unnecessary mass arrests, and police repression—"enraged the
population." The Saratov party organization had "no direct contact
with the masses," as a result of which "bureaucratism and irresponsibility were on the rise." And, because local Bolshevik leaders ignored
the party organization, "without exaggeration it can be said that the
party doesn't exist in Saratov." Although local leaders took pride in
their independence, they "in essence flow with the tide and are a toy in
the hands of adventurists." "Disorganization, dilettantism, and the need
for discipline" are the major traits of the "misinformed" local Bolshevik
leadership.[58]

Party internal language makes clear that "the attitude of the city's
population toward the events was unambiguously filled with enmity toward Soviet power." Even the long pro-Bolshevik Latvian sharpshooters
wavered before coming to the soviet's defense. Despite the external language's insistence that counterrevolutionary SRs and Mensheviks had
masterminded the insurgency, the commission found "no evidence that
systematic anti-Soviet propaganda among the soldiers had been carried
out," pinning the blame instead on the local Communist Party organization's neglect of the troops and stressing the *spontaneity* of the uprising. The report admitted that many soldiers had joined the Red Army
out of desperation merely to receive wages, concluding that the level of
political awareness of Soviet Red Army men "is very low," and that "a
very significant portion of them don't have the slightest understanding
of the events taking place, have no idea whatsoever of the meaning of
Soviet power."[59]

While the examples of the two languages adduced above suggest substantial stylistic differences and voices, they nonetheless share common
cultural and ideological references. Both make use of "ideologemes," or
words that combine descriptive and evaluative language. Thus, terms
such as "working class" and "petite bourgeoisie" refer not only to so-

[58] Emphasis added. The report is found in GASO, f. 3586, op. 1, d. 201, ll. 1–6. The
commission was made up of representatives from the Supreme Military Inspectorate and
members of the Saratov party organization, many of whom were newcomers to Saratov.
The commission's membership is found in *Saratovskii Sovet*, 508. Antonov later tried to
undermine the credibility of the commission. See *Saratovskii Sovet*, 793 n232.

[59] GASO, f. 3586, op. 1, d. 201, ll. 1–6. See also *Novaia zhizn'* no. 102 (317), May 16
(29), 1918, 4.

cial groups but also to an abstract evaluative concept. Mikhail Epstein points out that "the very usage of an ideological word frees the speaker from the necessity of logical proof."[60]

The party's external language obviously presented only a partial, partisan, and "lopsided" version of the uprising. A representation of how the Bolsheviks would like things to have been, external language was fighting talk designed "to affirm and naturalize" their power, and "to conceal or euphemize the dirty linen of their rule."[61] Inspired by its opponents' actions, Bolshevik external language often fell silent about events that contradicted it, mentioned them only so as to deny them, blamed its socialist rivals for the difficulties the party faced, and/or conflated all of its opponents. In effect, the language sought to erase the difference between ideas and the realities of which it was not a faithful reflection.

While less propagandistic, the party's internal language also contained judgments that present as natural certain characteristics of Russia's key social groups. Maintaining that the small size of the city's proletariat limited Soviet power's chances to secure a firm foothold in the city, it chided the *meshchantsvo* or philistinism of Saratov's population, a term used at the time to describe people with petty, narrow views motivated solely by personal interest and indifferent to society's needs or, in this case, those members of the city's middle strata who did not welcome Bolshevik rule. Similarly, internal language insisted that the soldiers "didn't have the slightest understanding of the events taking place," because they were peasants with "low" political awareness. In other words, if they had been members of the "conscious" proletariat they would never have behaved that way.

Contradicting party external language by rejecting its depiction of the uprising as the work of Right SRs and Mensheviks, party internal language instead underscored the event's spontaneity and denied that any systematic anti-Soviet propaganda had been carried out. It admitted the precariousness of local Soviet power, and the local party committee's (but *not* the party leadership's) lack of moral authority and of any significant popularity. And it condemned the localism of Saratov's Bolshevik leaders, rebuking their quasi-revolutionary methods and reliance on police measures (and revealing an institutional clash between the outside inspection commission and local organs). Rather than fingering

---

[60] Mikhail N. Epstein, *After the Future: The Paradoxes of Postmodernism and Contemporary Russian Culture*, trans. with an introduction by Anesa Miller-Pagacar (Amherst, Mass., 1995), 104, 107–8, 117–18.

[61] Scott, *Domination*, x, 18. Also framed by the party's external language, Bolshevik propaganda represented a more conscious and systematic effort to educate and transmit values.

counterrevolutionaries, betrayers of the Revolution, and enemies of Soviet power, it considered problems from within the local party committee that had contributed to the explosion of discontent, making plain
the extent to which internal language was contested. By classifying the
uprising as spontaneous, moreover, the commission report reduced the
political and ideological threat posed by the event, denying it the consciousness of a movement organized by rival political groups. Such reasoning turned a blind eye to the fact that, despite the uprising's im-
promptu character, it represented one of the only possible modes of
protest in a restrictive political environment. Be that as it may, in depicting the masses' behavior as spontaneous, internal language assigned
them an inferior position in the class hierarchy and justified their further domination.[62]

The Fall of Volsk and the Fate of Defeated Revolutionaries

In mid-1918 the armies of Admiral Kolchak and other "counterrevolutionary" units took Samara, Syzran, Khvalynsk, Volsk, and riparian villages south of Volsk on the road to Saratov. The fall of Saratov's third
largest city, Volsk, to the Whites — and the fate of the town's revolutionary forces — underscored the Saratov Soviet's own vulnerability and
heightened the fear of conspiracy, prompting the Saratov Soviet to end
its reliance on voluntary armed forces and to draft all eligible males
who came of age between 1913 and 1917. Soviet power in Volsk, a
town with a population of 50,000, of whom 20,000 were workers,
rested on a rickety foundation.[63] Workers at the town's celebrated cement factories eventually fell under Bolshevik influence, but they never
emerged as a bastion of radicalism. In the villages, demobilized and
armed soldiers willing to resort to intimidation stood behind the Bolsheviks. Power remained in the hands of the duma and zemstvo until
late March 1918, when outside troops arrested the two bodies' leaders
and transferred their functions to organs created by the soviet. Many
individuals staffing the imperial institutions remained at their posts, because those who spurned the Volsk Soviet's rulings were to be tried by a
revolutionary court as "counterrevolutionaries."

Apart from the hostility of its own officials, the local soviet had to
cope with lack of money, bread shortages, and a band of truculent frontoviki. Hostility toward the new government for shutting down the

[62] Ibid., 151, 36.
[63] V. Sviatogorov, "1918 god. Sovetskoe stroitel'stvo v uezde (Po gazetnym materialam)," *Kommunisticheskii put'*, no. 9 (34) (1923): 65.

Constituent Assembly, moreover, forced serious breaches within the socialist camp. Until their withdrawal from the soviet in late March, Volsk Mensheviks petitioned for the restoration of the Constituent Assembly, while delegates to local peasant congresses sought to throw open the debate on the question of political power. As the local economy collapsed, the soviet had to levy financial contributions on the bourgeoisie and wrench bread from the peasants to survive. But the latter reacted with hostility. The arrival of workers' brigades in search of bread triggered a violent uprising among German colonists across the river from Volsk and peasant disturbances across a broad swath of the uezd.[64]

On the eve of Volsk's fall to the Whites, the local executive committee comprised 30 Bolsheviks and sympathizers, 42 Left SRs, and 3 anarchists and was chaired by Left SR Sergei Ivanovich Chugunov, active in the local SR organization since 1905. His deputy chairman was Mikhail Mikhailovich Struin, a Left SR who purportedly joined the Bolsheviks days before Volsk fell (he had earlier briefly worked in Saratov as editor of *Izvestiia*). Left SRs also served as secretary of the executive committee and as editor of the Volsk newspaper. A classified report admits that "except for some workers," the townspeople "opposed Soviet power" and that in the countryside part of the peasantry approved of Soviet power while the rest were hostile to it.[65]

Taking advantage of the departure of units of the Volsk garrison to suppress anti-Soviet revolts elsewhere, local opponents of Soviet power on July 1 shelled the soviet. The masterminds behind the plot drew their support from officers and students enrolled in the military gymnasium, seminary, and high school. An enraged mob brutally dismembered Struin and others, leaving mutilated corpses of the fallen revolutionaries and Red Army soldiers in the streets to rot. The anti-Bolshevik forces held the city for six days, during which time the revolt spread across the river to Nikolaevsk, prompting uprisings in Petrovsk, Atkarsk, and in the countryside of Saratov Province. A commission charged with investigating the events concluded that Soviet power had been set up "incorrectly" in Volsk from the beginning, that is, it rested in the hands of Left SRs. While this assessment acknowledged that the Bolsheviks lacked mass support in Volsk and freed them from blame, it did little to reassure anxious leaders in Saratov, who knew from confidential reports

[64] V. Sushitskii, "Oktiabr'skaia revoliutsiia v Vol'skom i Atkarskom uezdakh," *Kommunisticheskii put'*, no. 20 (1927): 102–6; *Izvestiia Vol'skogo Soveta*, no. 4, Feb. 19, 1918, 2–4; no. 6, Feb. 21, 1918, 3; *ISS*, no. 64, April 5, 1918, 4; no. 66, April 7, 1918, 4; no. 114, June 12, 1918, 3; I. P. Nesterov, "Pered vystupleniem na Volge," *Volia Rossii*, no. 10–11 (1928): 95–98; and Sviatogorov, "1918 god," 62–65.

[65] GA RF, f. 393, op. 3, d. 332, ll. 16–18.

that Volsk's population remained hostile or indifferent[66] and that the "uezd suffers from lack of conscious and of experienced individuals who could organize, unite, and enlighten the rural masses, the foundation of our socialist Soviet power."[67]

The Militarization of Civilian Life and the Siege of 1919

An uncontested external language upon which all agree is an impossibility, but during the Civil War party external language as reflected in the local press became more sanitized — and less likely to deviate from the central press — as party members learned to observe the forms and formalities of both languages as they evolved. Once localism came under fire from the Center (see chapter 3), debates over centralization, localism, and other controversial issues were increasingly relegated to the party's internal language. Matters usually consigned to internal language, however, continued to bleed through into the external one until the end of the Civil War,[68] even though Moscow's removal of local leaders, appointment of outsiders to positions of authority in Saratov, and centralization of economic and propaganda activities made both languages more homogeneous.

Resorting more often to outright denial and to denial by means of conscious omission, external language had to counter potent new threats to Soviet power posed by the "foreign bourgeoisie and world Capitalism." For example, *Izvestiia* dismissed rumors that the Czechoslovak legionnaires had grabbed Volsk, Balakovo, Kamyshin, Tsaritsyn, and Astrakhan ("None of these rumors has any factual basis and [they are] absolutely absurd"). Yet two weeks later the paper could no longer deny that the troops had taken Khvalynsk and Volsk for a second time and that General P. N. Krasnov's Cossack army had launched an offensive.[69] External language also extolled the heroic virtues of the local working class, largely ignoring the times when workers responded with hostility to Soviet power. More and more, political allegiance determined social identity in Bolshevik external language; class was defined

---

[66] Ibid., f. 393, op. 3, d. 327, l. 67; *ISS*, no. 175, Aug. 27, 1918, 3; GA RF, f. 393, op. 2. d. 80, ll. 11–11 ob; and Sviatogorov, "1918 god," 67. The Whites briefly took Volsk again in September. See GA RF, f. 393, op. 3, d. 327, l. 82; f. 130, op. 2, d. 627, l. 27; and *Saratovskii Sovet*, 634–36.

[67] GA RF, f. 393, op. 3, d. 332, ll. 7–8.

[68] Jeffrey Brooks dates the existence of a "single overarching discourse" to the 1930s. See his "Socialist Realism in *Pravda*: Read All about It!," *Slavic Review* 53, no. 4 (1994): 975.

[69] *ISS*, no. 163, Aug. 11, 1918, 2, and no. 175, Aug. 27, 1918, 3.

in *political*, not sociological terms. The "true proletariat" backed Soviet power; those who did not were not "real workers." As Holquist writes, the party saw social movements as "political-moral" projections.[70] Assuming a more militant tone, internationalist, class-based language also became the common idiom of expression and interpretation in newspapers published in the district towns, although the sources do not reveal the process whereby this took place.[71] Further, the Bolsheviks consciously depicted their revolution as the legitimate heir to the French Revolution, an attempt to instill legitimacy in their struggle and to justify (Jacobinian) terror. The synchronous Red Terror unleashed following an assassination attempt on Lenin's life in August demonstrates how class-based public language affected specific party policies. The Cheka took the patriarchs of Saratov's wealthy families hostage and held them on a Volga barge, executed twenty people seized for "taking part in uprisings against Soviet power," and arrested many others.[72]

A deteriorating situation on the Ural and Volga fronts and Saratov's "exclusive significance" (as a source of food) brought Leon Trotsky to the Volga in September 1918 to impose martial law. The document introducing the measure appealed to all members of Soviet parties and all workers and peasants "committed to the great cause of emancipating labor" to increase tenfold their efforts in the "great, responsible work" that had befallen them, in order to assist the "great task" of the glorious Red Army. An added incentive was provided for townspeople unconvinced by the impassioned rhetoric: as *Izvestiia* made clear, "each act of negligence, carelessness, laziness, and especially sabotage of the great cause of forging our military strength is an inexcusable crime against which we will battle with all of our might."[73]

When the Whites launched their most serious effort to date to overthrow Soviet power in March 1919, desertion from the Red Army reached new levels as peasant disturbances resonated throughout the province. In Khvalynsk Uezd, peasants hid deserters, refusing orders to mobilize people and livestock. Uprisings broke out in Kuznetsk and Balashov. Armed bands in Balashov, Serdobsk, and Atkarsk torched war supplies, blew up bridges, and dispersed volost soviets. In Balashov, peasant de-

---

[70] Ibid., no. 196, Sept. 21, 1918, 1. This same strategy was used with all groups; thus, "kulaks" were all peasants who opposed Soviet power. See Peter I. Holquist, "A Russian Vendee: The Practice of Revolutionary Politics in the Don Countryside, 1917–1921" (Ph.D. diss., Columbia University, 1994), 850–51.

[71] Tsentr Dokumentatsii Noveishei Istorii Saratovskoi Oblasti, hereafter, TsDNISO, f. 151/95, op. 2, d. 1, l. 1; and GA RF, f. 393, op. 3, d. 392, ll. 315–15 ob.

[72] *ISS*, no. 181, Sept. 4, 1918, 1–2, and B. B. Lobach-Zhuchenko, "Nezabyvaemyi 1918-i god," 12, unpublished memoir.

[73] *ISS*, no. 202, Sept. 29, 1918, 1.

serters murdered the local military commissar. By May 1919 peasants refused to turn over their grain reserves.[74] Saratov Province was placed under martial law in April and the city was designated a fortified region, responsible for military operations on the Volga fronts at a time when heated dissension within the local party organization had forced the recall of Antonov and Vasiliev and the arrival of Communist leaders from the outside. The lines between civilian and military rule in external language had vanished as they presided over a series of unpopular mobilizations as well as special ones for Communist Party members. Twenty percent of Saratov's union members were drafted into the Red Army and military training was made obligatory for the others.[75] Meanwhile, troops were detained in Saratov and not dispatched to the front, owing to lack of boots, underwear, and coats (in Commissarese, "owing to technical reasons"). With bread reserves for only ten days, city leaders had to reduce rations to prevent a catastrophe.[76]

Attempts to counteract the unpopularity of these measures resulted in significant shifts in external language, which now drew selectively from the internal one. The party's new solicitousness toward the "middle peasants" following the Eighth Party Congress, discussed in chapter 10, set the tone. All representatives of the party were "obliged" to demonstrate "the most thoughtful consideration to the needs and legitimate demands of the toiling peasantry . . . in the interests of developing and strengthening the Communist revolution and also of striving to institute the friendliest relations among all toilers."[77] Saratov papers admitted that the peasantry's encounters with Soviet power *had* provided "understandable grounds for discontent," denouncing the application of the term "counterrevolutionary" and *kulak* (rich peasant) to peasants who expressed dissatisfaction with the system, making it "the personal responsibility of each agent of Soviet power" not "to confuse the middle peasant with the kulak."[78] The Communists also enlisted the support of Menshevik Internationalists and Revolutionary Communists (an offshoot of the Left SRs examined in chapter 5) who, despite their ongoing

---

[74] GASO, f. 456, op. 1, d. 218, l. 49; f. 521, op. 1, d. 444, ll. 8, 20; V. A. Radus-Zen'kovich, *Dva goda vlasti rabochikh i krest'ian* (Saratov, 1919), 18; *Izvestiia Balashovskogo Soveta*, no. 136, June 26, 1919, 2–3.

[75] GASO, f. 521, op. 1, d. 427, l. 4. See O. A. Vas'kovskii, "Sovety Saratovskoi gubernii v bor'be za organizatsiiu tyla v period pervogo i vtorogo pokhodov Antanty" (candidate diss., Saratov State University, 1953), 87, 111.

[76] TsDNISO, f. 27, op. 1, d. 87, ll. 36, 92, 144; d. 56, l. 25; and f. 27, op. 1, d. 56, l. 40.

[77] *ISS*, no. 85, April 24, 1919, 1 (also see *Izvestiia Vol'skogo Soveta* for April 1919).

[78] After a disastrous attempt to foment class war in the villages, the Soviet government began openly to court the so-called middle peasant. See *ISS*, no. 91, May 4, 1919, 3, and *KG*, no. 340, May 4, 1919, 3.

ideological dispute with the Leninists, called upon workers "to unite in the common struggle against the Whites." Insisting that world revolution was about to break out, the soviet declared war on "bureaucratism," a term coined for a variety of negative features ranging from apathy and corruption to hostile behavior. To deepen the association of the Russian Revolution with the French, an issue of *Izvestiia* commemorated the 130th anniversary of the fall of the Bastille.[79]

Kolchak's army had been dealt a serious blow back in April 1919, but now Petr Wrangel's and Anton Denikin's forces both reached the Volga; Tsaritsyn fell to their troops on July 2, after which Denikin's units and Wrangel's Caucasian Army pushed onward to Saratov. The next day, Saratov Province was placed under siege again as hostile Cossack units reinforced by peasant bands burst into Balashov. A Military Revolutionary Committee assumed power and conducted widespread agitation, ordering all male workers and young women to dig trenches and carry out other defense-related activities. A full plenum of the soviet took a solemn oath to defend Soviet power. An appeal issued to Saratov's workers personalized Denikin's threat: "Saratov workers — if you don't want Denikin's bands to thrash your wives' bellies, if you don't want them to rape your daughters, if you don't want them to smash the heads of your infants . . . then to arms! Saratov peasants! If you want to keep your land, if you don't want the landowners to return — hurry up and join the ranks of the Red Army." In addressing women, the document targeted gender in a traditional way. "In the name of the salvation of your lives and the lives of your children, persuade your brothers, husbands, sons, and fathers to fall in the ranks of the Red Army."[80] The desperate tone of external language and the obvious attempt to scare people into action can be traced to the fact that "counterrevolutionary" elements claiming they would mete out reprisals against Communists openly agitated among Saratov workers.[81] The Cheka uncovered "conspiratorial activities" of a White Guard group, plotting to form units within Saratov that would rise up in conjunction with Denikin's moves.[82]

[79] *KG*, no. 334, April 24, 1919, 2–3; no. 335, April 25, 1919, 2; *ISS*, no. 88, April 27, 1919, 2; and no. 150, July 14, 1919.

[80] Vas'kovskii, "Sovety Saratovskoi gubernii," 179–91; idem., "Rabota partiinykh i sovetskikh organizatsii Saratovskoi gubernii po sozdaniiu prochnogo tyla letom 1919 goda," *Uchenye zapiski Saratovskogo universiteta* 47 (1956): 27–29. The appeal is found in Iakorev, "Iz opyta," 240, and in TsDNISO, f. 27, d. 76, l. 12.

[81] TsDNISO, f. 2804, op. 1, d. 1, l. 2.

[82] M. I. Latsis, *Dva goda bor'by na vnutrennem fronte: Populiarnyi obzor dvukhgodichnoi deiatel'nosti Chrezvychainykh komissii po bor'be s kontrrevoliutsiei, spekuliatsiei i prestupleniiami po dolzhnosti* (Moscow, 1920), 28, and Vas'kovskii, "Sovety," 244–46.

Saratov's *Izvestiia* now took the unprecedented step of admitting Soviet power's vulnerability: "Tsaritsyn has fallen. The enemies are at the gates. Everyone to Saratov's defense! Sound the alarm! Everyone to arms!" screamed the headlines on July 5. The next day, *Izvestiia* reported: "There is much counterrevolutionary scum among the city's inhabitants that seeks to sow discord and panic in the hearts of both townspeople and Red Army men." The paper acknowledged that "local organs of power had to carry out massive arrests among Saratov's counterrevolutionary bourgeoisie."[83] Atrocities purportedly committed by the Whites likewise received extensive press coverage.

At the end of July, Denikin's forces were within seventy kilometers of Saratov. As panic gripped the city, people fled. The Cheka executed "class enemies," confiscated weapons, and removed war materiel, food reserves, and other goods, while the party drew up a secret plan to evacuate the families of local Communists and nonparty officials in Soviet institutions.[84] In Atkarsk, the Cheka took opponents of Soviet power hostage, threatening to shoot them if any attempts were made on the lives of local Communists as the entire population was mobilized to fortify the city.[85] Rumors spread elsewhere in the province that Saratov had fallen. Papers put out in the district towns affirmed the imminence of world revolution as they decried Red Russia's growing encirclement by the foreign bourgeoisie. There was also the by now familiar solicitousness. "We know that Soviet power has its faults and has incorrect views on things, but now, both at the Center and locally, these mistakes are being corrected." *Izvestiia* admitted that party newspapers had become little more than agitation organs and were unpopular.[86]

At no other point during the Civil War did the soviet's agitation department expend so much energy to popularize the party's public version of the Revolution. It prepared agitators and literature, showed short propaganda films (*agitki*), and played recordings of Lenin's speeches.[87] The department coordinated the efforts of five agitation trains and a river steamer, each equipped with a cinema, radio station, and printing press, that brought their message to provincial Russia. The most important activity of this sort involved Mikhail Ivanovich Kalinin, the party's most prominent leader of peasant origin, who traveled to the

[83] *ISS*, no. 142, July 5, 1919, 1; no. 143, July 6, 1919, 2; and no. 144, July 8, 1919, 2.

[84] TsDNISO, f. 81, op. 1, d. 5, l. 169; f. 27, op. 1, d. 57, l. 70; and *ISS*, no. 151, July 15, 1919, 3.

[85] *Izvestiia Atkarskogo Voenno-revoliutsionnogo komiteta*, no. 256, July 22, 1919, 4.

[86] *Rabochii i krest'ianin* (Volsk), no. 146, July 3, 1919, 2, and *ISS*, no. 155, July 19, 1919, 2.

[87] Iakorev, "Iz opyta," 232–36. For a discussion of propaganda methods see Kenez, *Birth*, 50–63, 95–118.

Volga five times in 1919 to convince local audiences that Soviet power would do a better job in the future of satisfying them.[88]

Party internal language explained that the "predominantly kulak composition" of the province's population made the situation grave. Without the "active involvement" of each party member in "exposing counterrevolution," a confidential circular to district party committees warned, the Cheka would not be able to cope with the "dark forces" that found "such rich soil" in Saratov Province. The military authorities agreed, noting that the majority of peasants in the province would "at the drop of a hat support any attempt to overthrow Soviet power in Saratov," and that the city's middle class and officials were "counter-revolutionary." Only a fourth of the city's 40,000 workers could be counted on "to defend the revolution in Saratov," while Red Army units, "made up of peasants and former officers," could be expected to rise up as they had done in May 1918. Acknowledging that "in the event of an uprising from within, it would be difficult to put it down with internal forces," the account urged that artillery be placed in the woods above Saratov to be turned on the city if necessary. It also de-cried the formation of units comprised of Saratov Province's Germans, who could not be supporters of Soviet power "because of their social status." Moreover, the city's defense fell into the hands of "450 poorly trained Communists and sympathizers," whose "lack of enthusiasm" angered the commander of the eastern front. The explosive situation in local garrisons could easily boil over into "full-scale rebellion," owing not only to anti-Soviet agitation, but, more important, to the "awful material conditions" in which the soldiers lived.[89]

The Saratov party committee's internal assessment of the local politi-cal mood warned of "counterrevolutionary activities," a rise in Menshe-vik and SR popularity, and the "unreliability" of the garrison.[90] The local Cheka observed widespread enmity toward Soviet power in the rail-road depot, whose workers, threatening to strike, denounced the mobil-izations and the war *within* "the democracy."[91] "Bourgeois elements" that had obtained cushy jobs in the Soviet bureaucracy fell under criti-

---

[88] See L. V. Maksakova, *Agitpoezd "Oktiabr'skaia revoliutsiia" (1919–1920)* (Moscow, 1956), 52–55, 58–61,163–64; Vas'kovskii, "Sovety," 205–21; 226, 228, 232, 234–35; M. I. Kalinin, *Rechi i besedy* (Moscow, 1919), 4–6, 8, 10–11, 22; also *Rabochii i krest'ianin* (Volsk), no. 166, July 26, 1919, 1–2; *Privolzhskii krasnyi put'*, no. 14 (1919): 4–5; and TsDNISO, f. 27, op. 1, d. 89, l. 6.

[89] TsDNISO, f. 81, op. 1, d. 5, l. 90; f. 27, op. 1, d. 56, ll. 7, 10, 35; and GASO, f. 521, op. 1, d. 431, ll. 76–82.

[90] GASO, f. 521, op. 1, d. 286, ll. 24–25.

[91] TsDNISO, f. 27, op. 1, d. 57, l. 16; d. 76, ll. 112–13, 115–16, and *Privolzhskii krasnyi put'*, no. 11–12 (1919): 1.

cism as party zealots called for sending them to concentration camps, replacing them with workers. Moreover, those caught spreading false rumors were to be "severely punished."[92] The Cheka uncovered "counterrevolutionary plots" against Soviet power across the river in Pokrovsk,[93] while in Volsk *Communists* carried out anti-Soviet agitation.[94] In neighboring Simbirsk and Samara, enraged peasant crowds brutally murdered Communists, torturing those who expressed sympathy for Soviet power.[95]

Both party languages' depiction of the siege reveals how vulnerable Soviet power had become. Implying that opposition was senseless insofar as world revolution was about to explode, the tone of external language evinced an unprecedented solicitousness toward the peasantry. It admitted that "Soviet power has its faults." It recognized that the peasantry had "understandable grounds for discontent." It denounced the broad application of the terms "kulak" and "counterrevolution" in regard to the villages. It co-opted some of its socialist rivals, who threw their support behind the party at this crucial time. It even acknowledged the potent dangers lurking inside the city. It had no choice, for it had everything to lose. Yet, ironically, if these rhetorical strategies did anything to fortify Soviet power, they did so at a price, for they also subverted external language by discounting earlier versions of the heroic present. For instance, just a few months before, external language had fomented "class war" in the villages, rejecting all peasant opposition to the party's controversial and unpopular policies as a manifestation of counterrevolution. It must have been obvious to others besides besieged party leaders that the peasantry would "at the drop of a hat" support any attempt to overthrow Soviet power in Saratov. Readers undoubtedly reacted to the press's solicitousness with understandable cynicism as they learned how to read Soviet public parlance.

Internal language once again displayed an encoded class hierarchy that reified workers, peasants, and the bourgeoisie. Thus the "kulak" nature of the province's peasantry and the "counterrevolutionary" bourgeoisie provided "rich soil" for "dark forces" and "counterrevolution." Similarly, only a quarter of Saratov's workers—in effect, those deemed members of the industrial proletariat—were "true workers" and thus potentially conscious enough to defend Soviet power. The party's internal register contained an implicit understanding that despite the unfavorable social geography for Soviet power in Saratov Province,

[92] GASO, f. 521, op. 1, d. 427, ll. 5, 8.
[93] TsDNISO, f. 27, op. 1, d. 76, ll. 76–77, and *KG*, no. 331, April 17, 1919, 4.
[94] *Izvestiia Ispolnitel'nogo komiteta Vol'skogo Soveta*, no. 66, March 25, 1919, 4.
[95] GASO, f. 521, op. 1, d. 286, l. 43.

the active involvement and selfless dedication of party members could make up for the shortcomings. This language also disclosed differences within the party, notably friction between civilian and military party leaders. For example, internal language generated by military authorities criticized local Communists for their "poor training" (incompetence?) and "lack of enthusiasm" (cowardice?). While acknowledging that awful conditions in the armed forces could trigger mutinies and peasant disorders, internal language likewise saw the Red Army's unreliability as a consequence of its class makeup: peasants (potential kulaks) and former officers (potential White Guards). The party could not rely on the province's well-off (and therefore hostile) German minority or on Soviet officialdom, comprised of "bourgeois elements" that were counterrevolutionary by definition. In expressing a willingness to turn artillery on the city, internal language disclosed the high price a besieged party elite afloat in a sea of hostility was willing to pay to stay in power.

In late August the siege of Saratov was lifted, and by the end of 1919 all enemy forces had been expelled from Saratov Province. When new threats emerged the party's external language responded in predictable fashion, providing ever-changing versions of the heroic present, even though this strategy risked discrediting earlier accounts of it. In contrast, internal language, consisting of "the practices and claims of their rule that cannot be openly avowed," retained the potential to contradict Bolshevik external language.

Conclusion

Because language reveals "entire systems of meaning and value" and how people understand the organization of their world,[96] I have sought to historicize the emergence of two distinct Communist Party languages — external and internal — during the early phases of the Civil War. As reflected in the press, party external language presented an idealized heroic present of a revolutionary dictatorship of the proletariat and, when convenient, the peasantry, under siege by conspiratorial counterrevolutionaries. Throughout the first half of 1918 and even later, external language also evinced elements of localism or provincial Bolshevism. All of this began to change as a centralized bureaucratic apparatus started to exert itself, after which opposition within the party was increasingly but not exclusively relegated to internal language. In providing a political

[96] Joan W. Scott, "On Language, Gender, and Working-Class History," *International Labor and Working-Class History* 31 (Spring 1987): 6.

myth of rule, the resulting "authoritative" external language offered a means of understanding present changes through affirmation only.[97]

Obsessed with conspiracy, the Bolsheviks raised a shrill voice against "the dark forces of the Old World," capitalists, landowners, priests, kulaks, Black Hundreds, White Guards, and the Messrs. Bourgeoisie. In responding to "real" threats from their opponents that they sought hard to comprehend, the Saratov Bolsheviks broadened their definition of the enemy to include the "false" socialists. Contradictory visions of Soviet power already had emerged during 1917, putting Bolsheviks and moderate socialists on opposite sides of the barricades in October. The "sabotage" of government officials and groups within the intelligentsia, the appearance of hostile Cossack forces, the public outcry over the dispersal of the Constituent Assembly, the disturbances caused by frontoviki, the challenge of anarchists and terrorists, worker opposition during elections to the soviet in April 1918, the May uprising that almost swept the Bolsheviks from power, the explosion of anti-Bolshevik uprisings connected with the resistance of the Czechoslovakian troops, peasant disturbances, and the brutal reprisals taken against Volsk revolutionaries after the town fell to the Whites all contributed to a growing siege mentality that provided the "real" context of the Bolsheviks' efforts to reconstitute society and social relationships rhetorically.[98]

By the time White armies made their inroads into the province in 1919, the lines between civil and military rule had vanished; the Bolsheviks were obsessed with the vileness of the opposition. Lenin's party stood virtually alone in the *great* struggle to hold on to power until the fire of world revolution was ignited in Europe, making struggle the *justification and basis for party discipline*. As Pierre Bourdieu observes, "one need only mention the real or potential struggle, or even re-kindle it more or less artificially, in order to restore the legitimacy of discipline."[99] This practice became a legacy of the Civil War. The problem was that in invoking specific themes, the Bolsheviks unwittingly made the counterthemes relevant, too.

In pinning labels on the party's opponents, external language sought to divert attention from its rivals' political claims, which had broad currency. It had other strategies as well. One was to deny (the Whites did *not* seize Volsk); another was to determine social and political identity through behavior (*real* workers supported Soviet power; *false* socialists insisted the soviets had lost their democratic nature). The party's

---

[97] M. M. Bakhtin, *The Dialogic Imagination*, ed. by Michael Holquist, trans. by Caryl Emerson and Michael Holquist (Austin, Texas, 1981).

[98] See Antonov's version of this in *Saratovskii Sovet*, 765–78.

[99] Bourdieu, *Language and Symbolic Power*, 201.

vulnerabilities were only rarely acknowledged, as when the enemies were at the gate and all available resources had to be mobilized to defeat them during the siege of Saratov in mid-1919; it was precisely at such times that external language was most like its internal counterpart. The practice of frequently reinterpreting the heroic present, and the periodic need to be more forthcoming in its external language, served to undermine that language by discounting earlier versions of it. Paradoxically, then, the Bolsheviks' control of the press contributed to the party's survival during the Civil War, but practices on the rhetorical battlefield undermined the party's credibility as well.

Always a potential counter-canon to external language, internal language also was ideologically generated and authoritative. The medium of classified and confidential party documents and reports, internal language privileged the Communists themselves, especially the party elite, who were mostly members of the intelligentsia, the revolutionary vanguard swept up into a life-and-death struggle *on behalf* of backward Russia's imperfect equivalent of those social groups upon whose shoulders a new society was to be built. The party elite could admit only that the Saratov party committee, but not the party at large, lacked the "moral authority" to rule. It pinned the blame for the party's shaky base of support on what it understood as the intrinsic characteristics — in this case the shortcomings — of those over whom party leaders lorded. Although Russia's workers might not always grasp the historical role they were called upon to play, party leaders believed they did. This absolute faith in their historical mission and the cultural grid that created it enabled them to justify their use of coercion,[100] their decision to rule without mass support, and their growing intolerance of minority views within the party. As we shall see in the next chapter, those most aware of the party's vulnerabilities saw holding onto power for some higher goal no matter what the cost as a more attractive alternative to popular rule, which would have necessitated a sweeping reinterpretation — a subversion — of the party's external language.

---

[100] The Whites held similar views. See Leonid Heretz, "The Psychology of the White Movement," in Vladimir N. Brovkin, ed., *The Bolsheviks in Russian Society: The Revolution and the Civil Wars* (New Haven, 1997), 105–21.

Three

The Rise and Fall
of the Saratov "Republic"

WAR AND GEOPOLITICS play defining roles in the process of state formation.[1] Arguably itself the result of war, the October Revolution brought about civil war and the rapid devolution of power to the localities, as Russia came apart at the seams and regional, local, class, and economic interests undermined central authority. With the old administrative apparatus in disarray and the Imperial Army in shambles, the country's laws became meaningless. The frightful level of social anarchy and violence that characterized the period left an indelible imprint on state formation and on revolutionary values after 1917. As a centralized one-party state emerged from the Civil War, local interests became a casualty of the ordeal. So did the revolutionary debate organs called soviets, which became transformed into pillars of state power once their executive committees and presidiums came to govern Russia. Modern political revolutions, in other words, are not only about class struggle, but also about conflicts over the kinds of state organizations that eventually replace revolutionary regimes.

In examining the fate of the soviets, this chapter focuses on the trou-

[1] For the importance of war and geopolitics see Felix Driver, "Political Geography and State Formation: Disputed Territory," in *Progress in Human Geography* 15, no. 3 (1991): 268–80; Anthony Giddens, *A Contemporary Critique of Historical Materialism*, vol. 2, *The Nation-State and Violence* (Oxford, 1985); Michael Mann, "The Autonomous Power of the State: Its Origins, Mechanisms and Results," *States in History* (Oxford, 1986), 112; and Nicos Poulantzas, *State, Power, Socialism* (London, 1978).

bled relationship between the Saratov Soviet and the Center during the Civil War, and between the Saratov Soviet and those at the district level. Although one might be tempted to locate a more benign alternative to the Bolshevik dictatorship in the manifestations of "localism" analyzed in this chapter, I argue that they represent less the possibility of a more inclusive, "democratic" form of Bolshevism than they do a Center-periphery version, an intraparty rendition of Lenin's dictum, who-whom (*kto-kogo*), or who beats whom. Adapting to the civil war environment, the Saratov Soviet remained an instrument of political and social change, yet as a single-party institution it became estranged from many of the people in whose name it ruled. During the Civil War the "despotic" power of the state — that is, the ruling elite's willingness to govern without regular negotiation with civil society groups — *continued* to transcend its "infrastructural" power or capacity to penetrate civil society in implementing political decisions.[2] The nature of this despotic power had much to do with the tsarist autocratic legacy — after all, the tsarist government also snubbed the country's emerging civil society — as well as with political and social processes in which the state interacted, forged in the heat of world war, revolution, and civil war.

Localism and the Saratov "Republic"

A decentralization of political power throughout Russia and the growth of what Moscow called separatism or localism (*mestnichestvo*) characterized 1918, especially until the Fifth Congress of Soviets in July ratified a new constitution, but even afterward — in fact, for much of the Civil War. In many localities, including Saratov Province, revolutionary leaders responded to post-October 1917 conditions by setting up their own councils of people's commissars (*sovnarkomy*) at the provincial, uezd, and even volost level. These bodies frequently declared themselves independent republics or communes, an allusion to the Paris Commune of 1871 that figured prominently in Russian revolutionary lore. Mestnichestvo emerged because each local unit of administration, more often than not, had to rely on its own resources to establish state power, and also because provincial leaders took pride in their own revolutions. As

---

[2] Even though there is no agreement as to whether Russia had a civil society (I think one clearly was emerging), I still find Mann's formulation useful. Mann, "The Autonomous Power," 112. Gerald Easter argues that the personal networking of the party's regional leaders helped to implement policy and thus served as a form of infrastructural power. I disagree with his reading of Mann, for whom this networking would represent a barrier to infrastructural power, not a manifestation of it. See Easter, *Reconstructing the State: Personal Networks and Elite Identity in Soviet Russia* (New York, 2000).

Saratov's Vasiliev boasted, "our commune *is the beginning of a world-wide commune*. We, as the leaders, assume full responsibility and fear nothing."[3]

Reflecting the degree to which prospects for world revolution shaped political choices made at the time, Vasiliev's optimism suggests the importance local leaders attached to their own revolutions. Promoting a literal interpretation of the slogan "all power to the soviets," Saratov's aspiring Bolshevik leaders proclaimed the founding of the "Saratov republic" and formed a local economic council (*sovnarkhoz*) patterned on that of the national government. They also took steps to establish a regional "Volga republic" that would comprise nine surrounding provinces, but its implementation was never realized, ostensibly because of opposition from within the local party organization and from some of the provinces that might have joined it.[4]

In January the soviet's executive committee (*ispolkom*) assumed responsibility for provincial administration, becoming the provincial executive committee (*gubispolkom*). The soviet "governed" the province in an ad hoc fashion through various departments that reported, on occasion, to its executive committee. To a large extent, its authority outside the city limits depended upon Antonov, whose style of rule was simple: the districts did not receive funds if they ignored instructions from Saratov.[5] However, the soviet's influence rarely penetrated outside Saratov itself. For example, when Pokrovsk (located across the Volga from Saratov) refused to recognize the authority of Saratov's food supply organs in June 1918, Saratov threatened the use of armed force to extend its mandate. Not to be intimidated, the Pokrovsk Uezd Executive Committee (*uispolkom*) resolved to secede from Saratov Province and set up a separate "republic."[6] Even within the city of Saratov the soviet had difficulty subordinating a group of refugees arriving from Ukraine who sought to establish their own "republic."[7] In Saratov Province, quipped

[3] Cited in Robert Service, *The Bolshevik Party in Revolution, 1917–1923: A Study in Organisational Change* (New York, 1979), 77 (emphasis added).

[4] Rashitov, "Osnovnye etapy," 1–48; idem., "Sovety," 208–9, 383, 386; *Saratovskii Sovet*, 463–64; GASO, f. 521, op. 1, d. 153; *ISS*, no. 79, April 23, 1918, 1; Vas'kovskii, "Sovety," 15–16; *Godovshchina*, 44; and S. A. Sokolov, *Revoliutsiia i khleb: Iz istorii Sovetskoi prodovol'stvennoi politiki v 1917–1918 gg.* (Saratov, 1967), 21. For localism elsewhere in Russia see F. V. Chebaevskii, "Stroitel'stvo mestnykh Sovetov v kontse 1917 i v pervoi polovine 1918 g.," *Istoricheskie zapiski* 61 (1957): 252–55, and E. G. Gimpel'son, *Formirovanie Sovetskoi politicheskoi sistemy, 1917–1923 gg.* (Moscow, 1995), 25–26.

[5] *Godovshchina*, 44.

[6] Chebaevskii, "Stroitel'stvo," 254. For another example from Kamyshin see GA RF, f. 393, op. 3, d. 333, l. 14 ob.

[7] *KG*, no. 52, April 25, 1918, 3.

one participant, "each uezd represented an independent republic," which negotiated and bargained with others; "the uezds lived their own lives and all of the enormous task of political education and organizational work in the villages" was accomplished thanks largely to outside forces such as food brigades and workers from central Russia and the capitals.[8] Delegates from the districts did not take part in the Saratov Soviet's deliberations in 1918, except when local congresses were held, which not only served to maintain ties with Saratov but also to challenge its authority. As Service observed, "Local institutions, when they were not quarreling with Sovnarkom, were likely to be engaged in disputes among themselves."[9]

The total collapse of any broadly recognized authority represents the most striking feature of political life at this time. In Saratov, the job of governing fell on the shoulders of a handful of Old Bolsheviks who found it impossible to carry out all of their responsibilities. As one of them put it, "the tasks before us were infinitely great, and we lacked any experience."[10] Attendance at party meetings declined as party members succumbed to the burden of administrative work. The Saratov experience corresponds to a national trend; elsewhere, too, power became concentrated in the hands of a few individuals.

In Saratov the revolutionaries running the soviet were political newcomers V. P. Antonov-Saratovskii, M. I. Vasiliev-Iuzhin, I. V. Mgeladze (Vardin), and P. A. Lebedev. G. G. Telberg, who later became a minister in the Omsk (anti-Bolshevik) government, was struck by how young they were, as well as by the fact that the rank-and-file deputies enthusiastically backed their proposals.[11] Another eyewitness described Antonov (figure 3.1) as "a big man, broad shouldered, with a face that reminds you of pictures of Christ," and Vasiliev (figure 3.2) as "a smallish man, with the face of a monkey."[12] As in the French Revolution, the revolutionaries' young age and position as outsiders might have promoted the development of revolutionary rhetoric and symbols, which were essential to defining the Revolution and identifying the new political class. These same traits also predisposed them to believe in the threat of conspiracy.[13] Antonov (1884–1965) had been a party member since 1902. A lawyer by training, he graduated from Moscow Univer-

[8] GASO, f. 521, op. 3, d. 15, l. 2. See also Rashitov, "Sovety," 127–28, 166–70.

[9] Service, *The Bolshevik Party in Revolution*, 65.

[10] GASO, f. 521, op. 1, d. 108, l. 3.

[11] George Gustav Telberg, "The Papers of George Gustav Telberg," Library of Congress, Manuscript Division, Telberg Papers, box 2, chapter VII, "Snova na Volge," 28.

[12] Quoted in Donald J. Raleigh, ed., *A Russian Civil War Diary: Alexis Babine in Saratov, 1917–1922* (Durham, 1988), 84.

[13] Hunt, *Politics, Culture, and Class*, 214–15.

3.1 V. P. Antonov (*center*) with his wife and a revolutionary comrade. Courtesy Gosudarstvennyi Arkhiv Saratovskoi Oblasti (GASO).

sity in 1911. He became a leader of the Saratov Bolsheviks during the war, but his views did not always toe the party line, a fact that he unsuccessfully tried to conceal when he published his memoirs in the early 1920s, which evoked a storm of criticism. From August 1917 until the end of 1918 Antonov chaired the Saratov Soviet. He later replaced V. I. Nevskii as rector of Sverdlovsk Communist University, and in the late 1920s served as a judge in the Shakty and Promparty show trials. Antonov remained involved in the state's judiciary system, managing to survive the purges, perhaps because he supported Joseph Stalin in 1918 in the feud smoldering between him and Trotsky over the de-

3.2 M. I. Vasiliev-Iuzhin, known as a fiery revolutionary orator. Courtesy Gosudarstvennyi Arkhiv Saratovskoi Oblasti (GASO).

fense of Tsaritsyn.[14] Mikhail (Misha) I. Vasiliev (Iuzhin) (1876–1937) also spent part of his formative years in the Saratov underground before leading the local Bolshevik movement in 1917. In the 1920s he became part of a much-feared *troika* or panel of three, an organ of the political police that sentenced individuals without trial, and later served with Antonov as a member of the tribunal at the Shakty trial.[15] A former Menshevik turned Left Communist, Mgeladze enjoyed popularity among local railroad workers and remained committed to purging the party of unhealthy elements. Ironically, his one-time Menshevism

[14] For the debate over Antonov's memoirs, see my *Revolution on the Volga*, 66. Also see GA RF, f. 393, op. 3, d. 327, l. 84, and Antonov, "Avtobiografiia," 9–10.
[15] Aleksandr I. Solzhenitsyn, *The Gulag Archipelago, 1918–1956*, vol. 1–11, *An Experiment in Literary Investigation* (New York, 1973), 282, 373n, 635.

doomed him during Stalin's purges. Another lawyer by training, Pavel Lebedev, represented the voice of moderation in the local revolutionary drama.

The realities of governing soon prompted these leaders to reassess how quickly a socialist order could be constructed in Russia. Antonov, Vasiliev, and Mgeladze backed a "Red Guard assault against Capital," insisting that the old order must be swept away as soon as possible, while their less sanguine comrades, namely Lebedev, Tsyrkin, and S. Rapoport, believed in the need to build socialism gradually.[16] In its own assessment, a crisis had overtaken the party by mid-1918 as many of those who had thought the transition to socialism would be easy now admitted they had been unprepared for the trials of the transition period,[17] one of which was the angry controversy surrounding Russia's signing of the Brest-Litovsk Peace in March 1918. Ending hostilities with Germany, the treaty exacted a stiff price: Red Russia gave up approximately one-quarter of its territory and population. Supporting Central Committee member Nikolai Bukharin and a faction known as the Left Communists who favored waging a revolutionary war against Germany, most Saratov Bolsheviks "from an emotional point of view" disagreed with Sovnarkom. Linking Germany to the opposition bubbling inside Russia, local Bolsheviks damned "the ratified peace" as an "unquestionable mistake." In contact with the Moscow Oblast Party Bureau, Saratov Communists informed local soviets of its opposition, calling upon them "to immediately organize a Red Guard to fight against the German White Guard." The Saratov Soviet instructed its delegates dispatched to Moscow to vote against the treaty and urged "the Russian proletariat and peasantry to conduct a merciless struggle with all the allies of the domestic enemies of the October Revolution."[18] Saratov's Left SRs also protested against the peace.[19] Insisting the Soviet government was "obliged to subordinate itself to the decision of the overwhelming majority of soviets in Russia," local Bolsheviks pressed a party congress "to call the Ts. K. [Central Committee] to order." A Saratov Soviet plenum discussed the congress's decision only on March 23, when the city's newspapers published Lenin's justification of the treaty. Even though they eventually came to accept the peace, local

---

[16] Rashitov, "Stroitel'stvo," 149–51.

[17] *KG*, no. 76, June 1, 1918, 1.

[18] *Godovshchina*, 27; *ISS*, no. 30, Feb. 21, 1918, 1–2; no. 34, Feb. 26, 1918, 1–2; no. 40, March 5, 1918, 4; *KG*, no. 2, Feb. 21, 1918, 1; no. 7, Feb. 27, 1918, 2; *Saratovskii Sovet*, 393–94; GASO, f. 521, op. 1, d. 125, ll. 1–2; and op. 2, d. 27, ll. 15, 22–22 ob, 25.

[19] TsDNISO, f. 151/95, op. 1, d. 5, l. 18, and GASO, f. 521, op. 2, d. 27, l. 12.

leaders encouraged the party "to strain every nerve to further class war."[20]

Often turning into debates on Soviet power, discussion of the treaty in the district towns drove a wedge between them and Saratov. Although the majority of district soviets in Saratov Province, as in much of Russia, favored signing the peace, some objected and took advantage of the opportunity to criticize Lenin's government.[21] Rejecting the "criminal act of the Bolshevik authorities," SRs and SDs in Volsk called for an end to civil war, the creation of a new government drawing on all elements of the revolutionary democracy elected via universal suffrage, restoration of democratic organs of local government, and convocation of the Constituent Assembly and of a national conference of socialist parties.[22] The Balashov Soviet responded similarly, while its leader, Grigorii Solonin, angrily lashed out against Lenin and those who advocated signing the peace.[23] The debate rarely touched the newly formed volost soviets; however, when it did they tended to back the treaty. The Mikhailovskii Volost Soviet, Saratov Uezd, thus recognized the draconian nature of the German proposal, but concluded "that in view of the disintegration of our army and economic breakdown in the country it is necessary to sign" the document. As in the district towns, discussion of the peace provided opportunity to address larger political issues: some volost soviets demanded the transfer of power to the Constituent Assembly.[24]

Moscow denounced as manifestations of localism the stance Saratov Bolsheviks took on the Brest-Litovsk Peace, because this proved too dangerous a development for a party fighting what was fast becoming a brutal civil war. Independent-minded members of the party elite who deviated from central directives made it difficult to construct a unified public narrative of the Bolshevik revolution, potentially contradicting the party's claim to power. Although the process itself remains elusive,

[20] *ISS*, no. 40, March 5, 1918, 4; no. 45, March 10, 1918, 2; *KG*, no. 21, March 19, 1918, 1; *Saratovskii Sovet*, 411–12; Rashitov, "Osnovnye etapy," 35; *Stenograficheskii otchet 4-go Chrezvychainogo s"ezda sovetov rabochikh, soldatskikh, krest'ianskikh, i kazach'ikh deputatov* (Moscow, 1920), 123; and Institut marksizma-leninizma pri TsK KPSS, *Sed'moi ekstrennyi s"ezd RKP/b/mart 1918 goda: Stenograficheskii otchet* (Moscow, 1962).

[21] Some examples are found in *Otchet Novouzenskogo Soveta*, 67–68; *ISS*, no. 78, April 21, 1918, 3; V. F. Bagaev, "Bor'ba kommunisticheskoi partii za mir v period uprocheniia Sovetskoi vlasti," *Nauchnye zapiski Leningradskogo Finansovo-ekonomicheskogo instituta*, no. 17 (1957): 76–77.

[22] GA RF, f. 393, op. 3, d. 332, l. 27.

[23] Rashitov, "Sovety," 107, and Gerasimenko, *Khronika*, 237.

[24] GA RF, f. 393, op. 3, d. 338, l. 172, and Rashitov, "Sovety," 108.

mention of Lenin's justification for the peace soon crept into the local press, reflecting the beginning of state centralization.

The Decline of the Saratov Soviet Plenum

The Bolsheviks had won the political showdown in October because of their strength within the soviets and their identification with Soviet power. The Saratov Soviet, like others, had emerged as a popular institution because the immediate experience of revolution itself had forged new values and expectations. The masses' involvement in politics via elections to the soviets and participation in plenums, factory committees, trade unions, and the like carried great symbolic and practical importance, for it represented their understanding of the term "Soviet democracy." Despite a shared common mentality and the appearance of unity, however, Bolshevism remained factionalized, and this complicated the party's consolidation of power. Lenin proved willing to rule without the other parties, even though he realized the expediency of a coalition with the Left SRs. Some leading Saratov Bolsheviks felt similarly, but the majority of local Communists probably did not share this view. In addition, prominent members of Lenin's Council of People's Commissars resigned in protest in late 1917, when he broke off negotiations with the moderate socialists over forming a coalition government. Such dissent within the Bolsheviks' ranks made it easier for the opposition socialists to take the moral high ground and become intransigent in their dealings with the Bolsheviks. The fragility of the situation did not augur well for the future of Soviet democracy: the Bolsheviks would have to rely more and more on repression to survive the Civil War, and this proved incompatible with the type of popular representation in soviets that had exploded onto the scene in 1917.

Although some Saratov Bolsheviks also seemed willing to rule without the moderate socialist parties, others lamented the breakdown within the socialist camp. For instance, Mgeladze argued that without the involvement of the Mensheviks and Right SRs in the soviets, they would fail to cope with the problems the local population faced.[25] For their part, some moderate socialists decried their own parties' criticism of Soviet power. Saratov Menshevik leaders admitted that often workers and soldiers had encouraged the Soviet government's militant policies and that for this reason a handful of local Mensheviks quit the party at this time.[26] While the Bolsheviks' relationship with the Mensheviks and

[25] *ISS*, no. 27, Feb. 17, 1918, 3, and *Saratovskii Sovet*, 361.
[26] *Slovo proletariia*, no. 17, Feb. 9 (22), 1918, 1, 3–4, and *ISS*, no. 29, Feb. 20, 1918, 3.

SRs continued to deteriorate, the Bolshevik-Left SR bloc retained its dynamism. Throughout the first half of 1918 the two parties prevailed in local soviets, which more than at any time during the Civil War functioned as organs of Soviet democracy. Convenience as much as revolutionary pedigree gave this coalition its vitality. The Bolsheviks needed the Left SRs to claim majorities in local soviets; the Left SRs needed the Bolsheviks in the wake of the Constituent Assembly elections that had produced a Right SR victory, in part because the ballots had been printed before the formal split in the party had occurred. Left SRs composed 30 percent of the delegates elected in the Volga provinces to the Fourth Congress of Soviets in March; their influence grew even more afterward.[27]

Despite the Bolshevik-Left-SR alliance, the soviet plenum lost influence as the separate soldiers', workers', and peasants' sections became defunct, and as power shifted to its executive committee and then to its presidium.[28] In October 1917, the soviet had comprised approximately 800 deputies; after the December 1917 elections reduced the size to 600 deputies, soviet plenums still met frequently. By spring 1918, however, they were called less often, because the Bolsheviks' popularity among local workers already had begun to erode, and because the need to address administrative and political concerns of immense importance made evident the shortcomings of popular democracy. As a result, a small group of leaders gathered the reins of power in their hands, justifying their actions by insisting that opposition to Soviet power had made them necessary. Once power shifted to the soviet's executive committee,[29] it came into conflict with the local Communist Party organization, with Communists in the province's district towns, with rival military and economic bureaucracies, and with the Cheka. The decline of the plenum picked up momentum when local Communists expelled Mensheviks and Right SRs from the soviet in the spring of 1918. This is instructive: in the summer of 1917 Lenin had been prepared to dispense with the soviets altogether when moderates predominated in them. But they now had acquired far too much practical and symbolic importance

[27] D. S. Tochenyi, "Raspad levoeserovskikh organizatsii v Povolzh'e," *Nauchnye trudy Kuibyshevskogo gosudarstvennogo pedagogicheskogo instituta* 165 (1975), no. 2, *Nash krai*, 56–57. The soviet's gubispolkom comprised 81 members (55 Communists, 23 Left SRs, and 3 SR Maximalists). See Rashitov, "Sovety," 216, 220–22.

[28] *ISS*, no. 16, Jan. 21, 1918, 2–3; no. 35, Feb. 27, 1918, 3; no. 38, March 2, 1918, 3; and *KG*, no. 42, April 12, 1918, 4. The Workers' Section urged Moscow to convene a national congress to determine the role of such sections in the workers' movement. Moscow never responded. GA RF, f. 393, op. 3, d. 327, l. 192.

[29] F. V. Chebaevskii, ed., "K istorii organizatsii Sovetskogo gosudarstvennogo apparata (1917–1918)," *Istoricheskii arkhiv*, no. 5 (1956): 79.

to be swept aside. Instead, the party took control of the electoral process to guarantee a docile membership; as a result, its constituency's interest in participatory politics waned.

Examination of the published protocols of the Saratov Soviet for 1918 show how important the executive committee and its presidium became and reveal what issues concerned the leadership. The strikes and "sabotage" of the intelligentsia after October 1917 and the need to defend the Soviet republic from "conspiracies" receive considerable coverage. So do economic issues such as food supplies, financial breakdown, nationalization of industry, labor relations, unemployment, and wage disputes. The protocols likewise reflect concern over crime, widespread public drunkenness, the refugee problem, health and sanitation issues, a transportation breakdown, and the restructuring of schools. Yet they have little to say about relations with the uezds, the debate over the Brest-Litovsk Peace, the rift with the Center, the strained relations with the local party organization, the process by which the plenum lost ground, or the use of Red Terror. In accounting for these silences, a suspicious gaze must be cast on Antonov, who edited and published the documents in 1931. In the mid-1930s, an embittered Vasiliev denounced Antonov, insisting that in preparing the protocols for publication Antonov had taken them from Saratov, thereby making it impossible for the editorial board (which included Vasiliev) to check them. Indeed, nineteen protocols are missing from the volume.[30]

The debate over the relationship between party organizations and soviet and other governmental organs intensified in the second half of 1918 when two distinct camps formed in Saratov, the Antonovtsy and Vasilevtsy, representing the old local party organization that had come to power in 1917 and was based in Saratov, and the Dashkovtsy, representing a cohort of party members (and named after their leader) who had fled to Saratov from Ukraine. The resulting feud undermined the local party organization and grounded party work to a halt.[31] Expressing its dismay over the gubispolkom's independence and the Saratov Soviet's weak ties with the uezds, a city party conference in May charged a new city committee (*gorkom*) to address these shortcomings, but it failed to influence the soviet's leaders. In fact, during the Civil War the tension inherent in the relationship between the party (the political state) and the soviets (the civilian state) remained unresolved.[32]

In preparing for the Fifth Congress of Soviets in July, the Saratov

---

[30] See *Saratovskii Sovet*; GASO, f. 3586, op. 1, d. 78, ll. 1–26, especially l. 6; and Rashitov, "Stroitel'stvo," 140.

[31] M. Blinov, "Saratovskaia organizatsiia za 4 goda," *Vestnik Saratovskogo gubkoma RKP* (hereafter *VSG*), no. 12 (1921): 24; and *Saratovskii Sovet*, 778.

[32] Richard Sakwa makes this point in his study of Moscow during the Civil War. See his *Soviet Communists in Power*, 165.

Communist Party organization discussed the issue of separatism and the relationship between Soviet (i.e., governmental) institutions and party committees. More than those of any other local leader, Antonov's views colored the local soviet's behavior, just as they had during discussion of the Brest-Litovsk Peace. Noting that Saratov had received no directives from the Center for several months, then contradictory ones, Antonov argued that Saratov leaders had no choice but to resolve problems on their own. They lacked time to report to the Center and, for that reason, Antonov dismissed Saratov's "deviations" from norms prescribed in Moscow as immaterial.[33] Admitting the need to defer to the Center in principle, he opposed "bureaucratic centralism" and specific decrees that preserved "old forms of the capitalist order." "Decrees and instructions must be implemented by local authorities, *but only insofar as they meet local needs, and when they don't we correct the decree and inform the Center about the situation locally.*" For example, Antonov opposed Moscow's reliance on bourgeois specialists in Soviet organs and the Red Army, insisting that they sought to undermine Soviet power from within. He favored establishment of a commissarocracy (*komissaroderzhavie*), that is, rule by a group of powerful commissars, a consideration that cautions against seeing localism as a more democratic alternative to the path the party ultimately took. And he saw no merit in the Center's chiding the Saratov Soviet for expelling the moderate socialists before Moscow did, because this relationship had gone wrong back on the barricades in October 1917. Making their case public, the Dashkovtsy remained highly critical of Antonov and others. The local party newspaper, temporarily under Dashkovskii's editorship, attacked their manner of personal rule, and their freewheeling life style, decrying the demagogic spell they cast over party members. But the majority of local Communists shared Antonov's hostility to employing bourgeois specialists in state organs and his faith in decentralization.[34] When Dashkovskii's efforts to drive through a resolution on centralization failed he withdrew from the party committee, thereby taking it one step closer to splitting as it bickered over whether the city or provincial party organization — or the soviet's executive committees — represented the highest authority in the province.[35]

Saratov's potent separatist tendencies did not go unnoticed by Lenin and Trotsky or by the Commissariat of Internal Affairs (NKVD),[36] which began to purge soviet executive committees of those opposed to centralism and to turn party organizations into overseers of local so-

---

[33] *Godovshchina*, 34; Vas'kovskii, "Sovety," 19; and Rashitov, "Sovety," 381.
[34] *KG*, no. 97, June 28, 1918, 3–4.
[35] Emphasis added. Ibid., no. 100, July 2, 1918, 4.
[36] Ibid., no. 94, June 23, 1918, 3.

viets. Exacerbating relations with the Left SRs, these policies marked the beginning of the transfer of de facto power to the party committees, a process that took place in several stages. In April the NKVD instructed local soviets to set up administrative departments. Following a national congress of provincial executive committee chairmen held in July, administrative departments were formed in Saratov and in the uezds.[37] The gradual implementation of the first Soviet constitution ratified in July thus helped to transform the country's soviets into pillars of state power by more narrowly defining their functions, making them financially dependent upon the Center, and obliging local soviets to execute the decrees of higher organs of power.[38] Soviet plenums met less frequently as the soviets became "transmission belts for central policy."[39] The soviets also began to decline as mass organizations because of *how* they represented workers and soldiers. Local leaders ended secret balloting and organized Communist election victories.[40] The result was a deeper rift between the party and those social groups it claimed to privilege. The next blow to the Saratov Soviet's independence came in October 1918 from the administrative departments of uezd executive committees, which angrily complained that the Saratov Soviet's gubispolkom functioned too independently, and did not serve the entire province. Citing the Soviet constitution, leaders of uezd soviets, particularly those from Petrovsk, appealed to Moscow to dispatch a fact-finding mission to Saratov.[41] Before examining this head-on collision with the Center, it is instructive to understand why Petrovsk District came to challenge Saratov.

Revolutionary Power in Petrovsk Uezd

The case study of Petrovsk reveals how policies unleashed by political elites and outsiders determined the local civil war. Armed force had to

---

[37] Vas'kovskii, "Sovety," 24–26. Ivanov, a "separatist," headed the provincial administrative department. See GASO, f. 456, op. 1, d. 118, ll. 2–2 ob.

[38] Helgesen, "Origins," 161–65. See also Oskar Anweiler, *The Soviets: The Russian Workers, Peasants, and Soldiers Councils, 1905–1921* (New York, 1974), 223, 227, and *Piatyi Vserossiiskii s"ezd sovetov rabochikh, krest'ianskikh, soldatskikh i kazach'ikh deputatov: Stenograficheskii otchet* (Moscow, 1918).

[39] Helgesen, "Origins," 183–84. See also Vas'kovskii, "Sovety," 6–7; Rashitov, "Sovety," 354–58; and M. F. Vladimirskii, *Organizatsiia Sovetskoi vlasti na mestakh* (Moscow, 1921), 5–40.

[40] V. P. Antonov-Saratovskii, ed., *Sovety v epokhu voennogo kommunizma: Sbornik dokumentov* (Moscow, 1928, 1929), 1: 265–71.

[41] Leaders of district soviets likewise sought to curb the power of the Cheka and military commissariats. See GA RF, f. 393, op. 3, d. 327, ll. 2–26; Vas'kovskii, "Sovety," 19–21, 24; Antonov-Saratovskii, *Sovety*, 1: 135–40; and *Saratovskii Sovet*, 648, 654, 734.

be used to consolidate the Bolsheviks' tenuous hold over Petrovsk, a small town of about 2,500 located in the northcentral part of the province, with only a few industrial enterprises employing, in the party's internal language, a "backward and unorganized proletariat" that was "greatly diluted with the petit-bourgeois element."[42] The Petrovsk Soviet did not assume the functions of the town duma until March 1918, after which the local Cheka busied itself with identifying opposition and curbing widespread drunkenness and the resulting abuses of power that accompanied public intemperance on the part of Cheka members and Soviet officials alike.[43]

This new chapter in the soviet's history began with the election of an outsider, M. E. Kosterin,[44] chairman of the soviet. Under his leadership, it took increasingly uncompromising measures to consolidate its position and disable its opponents.[45] "Any, even the slightest disorder will be liquidated in the most merciless way," threatened one decree, while those resisting efforts "to establish order" would be "shot on the spot." "Provocateurs, capitalists, landowners, Right SRs, Mensheviks, and gossips" spreading rumors that Czechoslovaks and Germans had inflicted blows to Soviet power were to be offered up as sacrifice to the Revolutionary Tribunal. To be sure, the exhaustion of food supplies that had "bordered on catastrophe" assured an opposition, feeding a cycle of escalating measures to curb the general lawlessness that colored this period. Angry citizens tore down and defaced Soviet decrees; others agitated against mobilization for the Red Army. Fearing open revolt, the soviet confiscated weapons and, owing to the anti-Soviet uprising in Volsk, placed Petrovsk under martial law. The Cheka shot "Black Hundreds" and former officers for counterrevolutionary activities, and executed others that tried to arrest the soviet's leaders. Following the attempt on Lenin's life in August 1918, the soviet "nationalized" private property, confiscating gold and other valuables from the bourgeoisie. It mobilized "cultural and educational" forces, with the exception of "kulaks, merchants, speculators, and the rich," who were to be forced into "special worker departments for the most menial labor."

After the deputy chair of the soviet, D. P. Kaplan, attended a meeting in Moscow on the role of local soviets, Petrovsk's leaders became even more zealous in conforming with the Center's decrees, and this, in turn, brought it to blows with Saratov. Like Kosterin, Kaplan was a longtime

---

[42] GASO, f. 521, op. 1, d. 181, l. 4.

[43] GA RF, f. 393, op. 3, d. 336, l. 51, and op. 3, d. 335, ll. 13–13 ob.

[44] N. Poliantsev et al., eds., *Saratovskaia partiinaia organizatsiia v gody grazhdanskoi voiny: Dokumenty i materialy, 1918–1920 gg.* (Saratov, 1958), 348. For biographical information on the leadership of the Petrovsk Soviet see GA RF, f. 393, op. 3, d. 335, ll. 232–36.

[45] GA RF, f. 393, op. 3, d. 335, ll. 33–34 ob, 92–92 ob.

party member and metalworker, who had extensive experience in the revolutionary underground outside Saratov Province. Ruling with the assistance of the police and Cheka, Petrovsk's leaders carried out a methodical destruction of the Left SR organization and, unlike their Saratov counterparts, aggressively promoted the introduction of class warfare in the villages, which is discussed in chapter 10.[46] Their conflict with Saratov began in May 1918, when the Saratov Soviet added peasant representatives to its membership. Objecting to the influx of peasant deputies into the council, Kaplan lamented that "the broad proletarian strata of the population of the uezd towns do not participate at all in power at the provincial level." But the Petrovsk revolutionaries' ambition accounts for their support of centralization, as there were no industrial enterprises in Petrovsk to speak of and the town's Bolsheviks saw local workers as "backward."[47] Eager to meet Moscow's grain quotas established for the district, the gadfly Kaplan denounced the independent policies of other district executive committees. Now that Saratov played a key role in keeping the industrial heartland fed, "the question of the correct organization of Soviet power . . . had not only local, but national significance [as well]."[48] Such reasoning convinced Moscow to intervene in local political life.

The End of the Saratov "Republic"

When the Saratov Soviet assumed the role of a provincial organ its provincial executive committee (gubispolkom) found itself reporting to the city executive committee (*gorispolkom*) headed by Antonov, Vasiliev, and other local Bolsheviks. Thus, one facet of the disagreement over local governance was the conflict arising from the existence of two executive committees, in which the provincial organ found itself subordinate to the city one. Yet another conflictual power relationship was between Soviet or governmental institutions and Communist Party organizations. The city party committee or gorkom barely functioned because its leaders held key posts in the soviet's executive committee and had little time for anything else. Moreover, intoxicated by the heady atmosphere of early 1918, many of them felt that their control of the soviets had made the party itself superfluous. When outsiders revived the gorkom in mid-1918, its relationship with the provincial party committee (*gubkom*) became strained. There were grounds, then, for three potential

[46] Ibid., ll. 40 ob, 52, 70, 74, 103–4, 118, 132, 143, 159, 217–17 ob, 237–37 ob, 240–40 ob, 246–47 ob; and d. 336, ll. 34, 38–39, 42, 47, 52–53, 62, 64.

[47] See ibid., f. 393, op. 3, d. 335, l. 134, and d. 336, ll. 1, 28, 51.

[48] Ibid., f. 393, op. 2, d. 80, ll. 266–67, 271–71 ob, 273–74.

conflicts, all of which emerged in Saratov Province: (1) between the city and provincial soviet executive committees; (2) between the city and provincial Communist Party committees; and (3) between the state administration (the soviet executive committees) and the party committees. These bureaucratic and personal conflicts, it must be stressed, did not represent real alternatives to the Bolshevik dictatorship.

In late fall 1918, the Center dispatched two commissions as well as individual emissaries to Saratov, including Iakov Sverdlov, to investigate charges of localism. Their reports throw a searching light on the differing perspectives of the warring camps and on how the Central Committee understood the disagreement. Cast in the party's internal language, the first report of the Central Committee's Special Investigative Commission emphasized the weakness of local party organizations and the structure of Soviet power, noting that the provincial party committee had not convened a single meeting. The commission saw the operation of the local Cheka as totally unsatisfactory, too ("All of its members do as they please, without . . . reporting on their activities"). According to the report, since May 1918 the Saratov Soviet's two executive committees (city and provincial) had merged into a single organ dominated by the old Saratov party committee led by Antonov and Vasiliev. Apart from the "abnormal" relationship between the soviet and party committee, the latter found itself in constant conflict with the soviet's executive committee, which denied the party's right to interfere in the soviet's affairs. In this manner, the commission concluded, two warring camps had been created: *"there were no deep disagreements based on principle,"* they were *"artificial and inflated."* Decrying the lack of discipline among party members, the commission feared the situation would "lead to the breakup of the party."[49]

When the commission confirmed the existence of separatist tendencies, Moscow recalled separatists Antonov and Vasiliev from Saratov (both of whom had been elected to the All-Russian Central Executive Committee), but allowed them to stay in Saratov until mid-December because of an upcoming provincial party conference, a provincial congress of soviets, and soviet elections. On December 2, the provincial party conference considered a resolution on the role of city executive committees, which criticized the Soviet constitution for neglecting the locales. Inspired by Antonov, the document petitioned the Central Committee to permit the temporary organization of united provincial executive committees in the provincial capitals that would be answerable to soviet plenums and provincial congresses of soviets.[50] In justifying their

[49] Emphasis added. Ibid., f. 393, op. 3, d. 327, ll. 179 ob–80.
[50] Ibid., f. 1235, op. 93, d. 491, ll. 183–83 ob.

request, Saratov's leaders pointed to the lack of party cadres and the closeness of the front, but also to the province's social makeup, which was "kulak, without skilled proletarians."[51] Despite Antonov and Vasiliev's efforts, however, the provincial party conference voted to "organize a provincial executive committee that does not have any organizational ties with the Saratov City Soviet" and a separate executive committee for Saratov.[52]

The provincial congress of soviets meeting on December 5 confirmed the ruling of the party conference; however, Antonov and Vasiliev continued to oppose the creation of two executive committees, refusing to take part in the provincial executive committee to which they had been elected. They struck out at the "shortcomings" of the Soviet constitution, rejected the idea of the two separate executive committees, and argued that the district party organizations were choked with petit-bourgeois elements. Claiming to be motivated by a belief that the working class must lead the masses, Antonov insisted that a false impression was created at the Center regarding localism.[53] Days later a Saratov Soviet plenum further criticized the decisions reached by the provincial congress, while the city party organization defiantly *refused* to subordinate itself to the provincial party committee. Two points need to be emphasized: first, interregional and cross-organizational personal networks played decisive roles in revolutionary events; it is difficult to untangle the extent to which personal networks, rivalries, and/or differing views of the Revolution contributed to the factionalism. Second, each faction framed its actions in terms of what was best for the working class, but without asking workers, thereby revealing that the political beliefs of local leaders did not differ from those in Moscow.

After Antonov and Vasiliev left Saratov, their close associate F. T. Ivanov sought to discredit the new gubispolkom, turning down its requests for accommodations and for transforming *Izvestiia* into a provincial organ. Although Ivanov denied these allegations, a second Central Committee commission affirmed them. Its report rebuked the

[51] TsDNISO, f. 27, op. 1, d. 1, ll. 1, 3, 6, 22–24, 29, 33.

[52] Ibid., f. 151/95, op. 1, d. 8, l. 5.

[53] Rashitov, "Sovety," 170–71, 184–85, and *Godovshchina*, 37. See Antonov's "Avtobiografiia," in Tsentral'nyi muzei revoliutsii GIK 30244/200. A source from the early 1920s claims that the dispute in reality was also over how to relate to the peasantry, since Antonov and others, allied with the Left SRs and later with the Revolutionary Communists, demonstrated little enthusiasm for establishing kombedy. See P. G., "Saratovskaia organizatsiia RKP k 7-i godovshchine proletarskoi revoliutsii," *Kommunisticheskii put'*, no. 21 (1924): 38; and S. Kish, "Saratovskaia organizatsiia RKP(b) k 8-i godovshchine proletarskoi revoliutsii," *Kommunisticheskii put'*, no. 34 (1925): 16. See also GASO, f. 456, op. 1, d. 234, ll. 1–2, 6.

Antonov group for carrying out demagogic agitation, dismissing its argument that it was motivated by belief in the hegemony of the proletariat and fear of the petit-bourgeois danger posed by the district towns. It also blasted the Antonov faction's insistence that the gubispolkom report to the soviet plenum. In explaining the influence of the group in Saratov itself, the report pointed to the privileges extended to Communists, whose numbers had grown from 700–800 members in September to some 2,500 by mid-December. "This does not need commentary," the commission observed. Rejecting the suggestion of impropriety as "obvious slander," Antonov fired off his own missive to the NKVD.[54]

The Central Committee disbanded both party factions, reregistered all party members, and created two new executive committees;[55] however, discord accompanied these measures, as the city executive committee sought to discredit the Central Committee commission.[56] In this atmosphere a new soviet was elected at the start of 1919. The electoral commission charged with verifying the results admitted low voter turnout and the need to call electoral meetings several times; in some mysterious cases turnout was strong, yet few voted, ostensibly to protest "forced changes in the composition of soviets with the aim of guaranteeing exclusive representation of the Bolshevik Party."[57]

The Saratov experience teaches that the soviets declined as the Bolsheviks sought to reconfigure the practices of Soviet democracy by controlling participation in public life. The debate over centralization vs. localism also undermined the soviets, for the loss of local autonomy resulted in the strengthening of a party-state. Civil war conditions and the emergence of rival military and economic bureaucracies only accelerated these trends. By the time Saratov fell under siege in 1919, soviet plenums had been rechoreographed to affirm decisions already made and to mobilize support. But the Bolsheviks continued to take soviet elections seriously, in part because electoral campaigns revealed much about popular attitudes.[58] However, it could not have been reassuring

---

[54] Rossiiskii Gosudarstvennyi Arkhiv Sotsial'no-politicheskoi Istorii, hereafter, RGASPI, f. 17, op. 6, d. 278, ll. 60–60 ob. Antonov's denials are found on ll. 63–64.

[55] *Izvestiia Vol'skogo Ispolnitel'nogo komiteta*, no. 13, Jan. 18, 1919, 3. The Central Committee also disbanded party committees in Kazan and Voronezh for the same reason. See Institut marksizma-leninizma pri TsK KPSS, *Vos'maia konferentsiia RKP/b/, dekabr' 1919 goda: Protokoly* (Moscow, 1961), 29.

[56] RGASPI, f. 17, op. 6, d. 278, ll. 61–61 ob, 65–65 ob, and GA RF, f. 1235, op. 93, d. 491, ll. 210–12. See also GA RF, f. 393, op. 3, d. 327, ll. 149–50 ob; GASO, f. 521, op. 2, d. 25, ll. 1–3; and f. 521, op. 2, d. 25, l. 4.

[57] Among the 415 elected were 271 Communists, 96 sympathizers, 22 nonparty deputies, 7 Revolutionary Communists, and a handful of others. *ISS*, no. 5, Jan. 7, 1919, 2; the quote comes from Rashitov, "Sovety," 346–47.

[58] Brovkin, *Behind the Front Lines*, 284–87.

that many elements within their constituency used the controlled elections to protest the growing rupture between party rhetoric regarding Soviet democracy and real practices.

The Debate on Power Continues

The departure of Antonov and Vasiliev (and also of many of the Dashkovtsy who had sparred with them) did not resolve the problem of localism or the estrangement between Saratov and the uezd towns, because many of their supporters remained behind.[59] P. A. Lebedev became head of the reconstituted provincial executive committee, and the newly elected Saratov Soviet fell once again under the influence of Ivanov and other separatists. The provincial party committee instructed the Saratov city party organization to purge the soviet leadership of separatists, but this proved impossible, as Ivanov made no secret of his opposition to the decision to divide functions between the two executive committees. And, in fact, the committees failed to work out a *modus operandi* before Saratov fell under siege in 1919. In order to put an end to the personal rivalries and bickering, the central authorities brought in more outsiders to manage local affairs; however, this strategy further jeopardized the party's popularity when it could least afford it, and did not end the dispute over how to run the province.[60]

The government's attempts to centralize the political system gained momentum at the Eighth Party Congress in March 1919, as a result of which a principle of dual subordination was introduced: all administrative departments formed by soviet executive committees were to be subordinate to them but also to the corresponding Moscow commissariats. Although it has been argued that a monolith was now in place, exemplified by the correspondence in membership between local executive committees and party committees, the Saratov case study shows that party factionalism made the situation more complicated than this.[61] Common throughout Russia, disputes over how centralized the new Soviet state should be and over the relationship between party and soviet organs were in many cases not resolved until the end of the Civil War. Later, in December 1919, the party ruled to let each locale decide the matter on its own, in consultation with the Central Executive Committee.[62]

---

[59] GA RF, f. 393, op. 2, d. 80, ll. 273–75.

[60] See GASO, f. 521, op. 3, d. 15; f. 456, op. 1, d. 157, ll. 34–34 ob; TsDNISO, f. 27, op. 1, d. 56, l. 6; and op. 1, d. 18, l. 13.

[61] Helgesen, "Origins," 431–32, and for related information, Jonathan R. Adelman, "The Development of the Soviet Party Apparat in the Civil War: Center, Localities, and Nationality Areas," *Russian History*, 9, pt. 1 (1982): 87–89.

[62] Vladimirskii, *Organizatsiia Sovetskoi vlasti*, 45–47.

By that time the debate also revolved around the extent to which popular opposition to Communist rule, treated in later chapters, would compel the party to risk reviving the soviets by democratizing them. The Saratov party city committee backed a resolution carried at a conference of Democratic Centralists in Moscow.[63] Led by T. V. Sapronov (active in the Saratov underground during World War I) and V. V. Osinskii, the Democratic Centralists (DCs) believed that the decline in elective offices and collective decision-making caused the current malaise within the party. They maintained that a vigorous party "necessitated a balance between hierarchical coordination and discipline on the one hand and patterns of democratic accountability on the other."[64] Seeking to define the powers of the Central Committee rather than limit them, the DCs criticized "bureaucratic centralism." This term mostly referred to Moscow's insistence that its rulings be applied everywhere uniformly, regardless of circumstances, but could also mean Moscow's isolation from local affairs or interference in them. The DCs supported the integrity of the soviets vis-à-vis local party organizations and the Center, opposing Moscow's periodic redistribution of cadres, for it cut them off from their political base.[65] The DCs debated these issues before the March 1919 party congress and later led a full-scale attack against Lenin, the Central Committee, and bureaucratic centralism.[66]

Proponents of bureaucratic centralism, or constitutionalists as they were called locally, failed in their attempt to gain control over the Saratov Soviet, which remained in the hands of Democratic Centralists.[67] When the Whites converged on Saratov during their 1919 offensive, the provincial party committee, in violation of the constitution, temporarily united the two executive committees under separatist Fedor Ivanov,[68] after a mobilization of local Communists tipped the scales in favor of the separatists. Moscow had appointed an outsider named Fedorov chairman of the gubispolkom, however, and he locked horns with local Bolsheviks, including Antonov, who had returned to Saratov in order to whip up support against the Whites.[69] When the local gubkom expelled Fedorov from Saratov, the Central Committee overruled the decision,

[63] *KG*, no. 305, March 12, 1919, 2.

[64] Service, *The Bolshevik Party in Revolution*, 108. For the views of Sapronov and Osinskii see Institut marksizma-leninizma pri TsK KPSS, *Vos'moi s"ezd RKP/b/mart 1919 goda: Protokoly* (Moscow, 1959), 199–201, and the 1933 edition published in Moscow under the same title and edited by E. Iaroslavskii.

[65] Sakwa, *Soviet Communists in Power*, 186–88.

[66] See Institut marksizma-leninizma pri TsK KPSS, *Deviatyi s"ezd RPP/b/, mart-aprel' 1920 goda: Protokoly* (Moscow, 1960).

[67] TsDNISO, f. 27, op. 1, d. 46, ll. 3–4. Constitutionalists were stronger in the uezds. For example, see Antonov-Saratovskii, *Sovety*, 1: 192–94.

[68] RGASPI, f. 17, op. 6, d. 277, l. 53.

[69] TsDNISO, f. 27, op. 1, d. 18, ll. 30–31.

and instead recalled Antonov and several others once again. "It will be impossible for the remaining members to work in the Saratov organization," warned Ivanov, for the replacement of local party leaders with outsiders would breed demoralization. Eloquently defending local rights, Saratov's A. L. Bankvitser charged that "the Central Committee treats the members of the Saratov organization like scoundrels, not like Communists." He cautioned: "And the Saratov proletariat is not the Petersburg or Moscow [proletariat] — it's only half-revolutionary, and must be dealt with carefully."[70] This remark, too, suggests that localism did not represent an alternative to the establishment of a party autocracy.

The renewed conflict with the Center resulted in Moscow's removal of Fedorov, and appointment of V. A. Radus-Zenkovich, a doctor by training who became a prominent Soviet statesman and author, as chairman of the provincial executive committee. Among the many formidable tasks facing him was the need to overcome differences with local Communists, now led by Pavel Lebedev.[71] A Democratic Centralist, Lebedev maintained that a strong central authority could be established only by strengthening the power of provincial centers, a point of view that continued to evoke harsh criticism from the uezds.[72] The military danger contributed to the concentration of power in the hands of the soviet's executive committees, and this did nothing to improve relations with the district towns, whose representatives chided the gubispolkom for limiting its ties with the uezds to occasional visits and for sending "inexperienced people with a paltry suitcase of knowledge." The uneasy relationship between the party and soviet organs also continued, as the gubispolkom contended that most reproaches aimed at it needed to be redirected at the provincial party committee: only five of the twenty-five members of the gubispolkom remained at their posts, because the Saratov committee or Central Committee had reassigned the rest.[73]

Attempts to Revive the Saratov Soviet

In September 1919, Saratov's Democratic Centralists attempted the impossible: they sought to breathe life back into the city soviets without

[70] Neighborhood party organizations wanted to arrest Fedorov. RGASPI, f. 17, op. 6, d. 277, ll. 242–52. Central Committee members Rykov and Rudzutak recommended the removal of Antonov and the others. See TsDNISO, f. 27, op. 1, d. 18, ll. 45–48. Related information on the recall is found in RGASPI, f. 17, op. 3, d. 7, l. 2, and op. 6, d. 277, ll. 77–80.

[71] TsDNISO, f. 27, op. 1, d. 56, ll. 16, 18, 21, 24; GASO, f. 456, op. 1, d. 157, ll. 41–43, 45, 58, 88; and f. 521, op. 3, d. 15, l. 5.

[72] GASO, f. 521, op. 3, d. 15, l. 11; *ISS*, no. 201, Sept. 12, 1919, 1–2; no. 202, Sept. 13, 1919, 1–2; no. 203, Sept. 14, 1919, 3–4; and no. 204, Sept. 16, 1919, 1.

[73] *ISS*, no. 203, Sept. 14, 1919, 1, and no. 204, Sept. 16, 1919, 1.

restoring their democratic features, such as the ability to hold free elections that would end the Bolsheviks' monopoly on power. Joining forces with like-minded party members elsewhere, they, nonetheless, briefly appeared to influence the course the entire party was taking on this matter, providing formidable evidence for the importance of the local. Mgeladze, now back in Saratov, fought particularly hard for the creation of a single executive committee for both the city and province, which between local congresses would report to the city soviet that would not merely rubber-stamp decisions of its executive committee. His proposal carried at a city party conference.[74]

The discussion in Saratov on the role of the soviets anticipated larger debates on this matter at the Eighth Party Conference and Seventh Congress of Soviets held in December 1919, which deliberated over the future of the soviets. At the Eighth Party Conference, Mgeladze argued that although city soviets in Moscow and other cities had been reduced to nothing, that was no reason to dispense with them. "With the destruction of the city soviets the Soviet system is being destroyed." Challenging official party spokesman M. F. Vladimirskii (as well as Radus-Zenkovich), Mgeladze opposed merging city soviets with uezd soviets. The soviets were not dying out, Mgeladze insisted, "but are being killed." He likewise attacked the policy of moving local cadres around, which weakened the party's ties with the masses.[75]

Delegates passed a proposal introduced by Democratic Centralist Sapronov, defeating the rival one proposed by Vladimirskii,[76] both at the Eighth Party Conference and at the Seventh Congress of Soviets.[77] Vladimirskii (and M. Krestinskii) had posited that soviets should exist only in places where the majority of the population consisted of industrial workers, and should be limited to electing and controlling executive committees. Overruling Vladimirskii, the congress carried a proposal of the Saratov delegation that "all basic questions of local and general nature must be presented at the soviet plenum . . . so that the

---

[74] Mgeladze's views are found in *Novyi mir*, no. 1, Jan. 22, 1920, 15; *ISS*, no. 263, Nov. 26, 1919, 4, and no. 272, Dec. 6, 1919, 2. See also *Novyi mir*, no. 1, Jan. 22, 1920, 305, and no. 3, March 7, 1920, 2–4. The interinstitutional rivalry is noted in *ISS*, no. 135, June 27, 1919, 3, and no. 267, Nov. 30, 1919, 1.

[75] Institut marksizma-leninizma, *Vos'maia konferentsiia*, 116–18, also 33, 149. In Moscow no elections to the soviet were held between early 1918 and early 1920. See Sakwa, *Soviet Communists in Power*, 173. See also Arthur Ransome, *The Crisis in Russia* (New York, 1921), ix.

[76] See the protocols of *Vos'maia konferentsiia* and the editors' questionable interpretation of the fate of Sapronov's proposal (see xi).

[77] Richard Gregor, *Resolutions and Decisions of the Communist Party of the Soviet Union*, vol. 2, *The Early Soviet Period: 1917–1929* (Toronto, 1974), 90. See also L. Kamenev, *Tsentr i mesta: Doklad po sovetskomu stroitel'stvu na VII Vserossiiskom S"ezde Sovetov Deputatov* (Moscow, 1919).

situation of the city soviets would be preserved corresponding to their role and significance in the revolution."[78] Despite its adoption by the congress, Sapronov's draft "remained a dead letter."[79]

Nevertheless, freer debate briefly characterized public life thanks to the determination of Mgeladze and others to revitalize the soviets. But the local party organization sought to accomplish this revitalization by expanding the electorate rather than by allowing truly free elections because of the inherent dangers of permitting the latter, and for this reason its efforts failed. Elections in mid-1919 had resulted in a three-fold increase in the number of unaffiliated deputies.[80] In elections to the soviet in early 1920, working women and wives of Red Army men voted for the first time; however, the turnout remained low for workers (40 percent), considering that elections took place at the workplace. More to the point, as we will see in chapter 11, some workers defiantly voted for anarchists, Revolutionary Communists, or Mensheviks.[81]

Mobilizations of cadres for the war against Poland and other emergencies further circumscribed the efforts underway to redefine the practices of Soviet democracy. When elections to the soviet were held in June 1920, more than half of its membership had been sent to fight or to wrench grain from the villages. Others had simply succumbed "to lack of discipline and inertia."[82] Rival socialist parties hiding behind the "nonparty" rubric had stepped up their activities, while workers, using

---

[78] *Novyi mir*, no. 1, Jan. 22, 1920, 1–3; *ISS*, no. 283, Dec. 19, 1919, 1; no. 293, Dec. 31, 1919, 4.

[79] Schapiro, *Origin*, 223.

[80] *ISS*, no. 136, June 28, 1919, 1; no. 137, June 29, 1919, 1; no. 145, July 9, 1919, 2; and no. 146, July 10, 1919, 3.

[81] The new soviet included 513 Communists, 14 Revolutionary Communists, 71 nonparty deputies, and a handful of others. See *ISS*, no. 9, Jan. 14, 1920, 1; no. 11, Jan. 16, 1920, 2; no. 13, Jan. 18, 1920, 2; no. 18, Jan. 27, 1920, 2; and *Novyi mir*, no. 2, Feb. 14, 1920, 7–9. This more open atmosphere resulted in the creation of a single gubispolkom in May 1920, which was to report to regularly scheduled provincial congresses of soviets. M. F. Vladimirskii observed that more party activists from the uezds were showing up in provincial administrations and that few members of gubispolkomy had extensive prior experience. See *Sovety, ispolkomy i s"ezdy sovetov (Materialy k izucheniiu stroeniia i deiatel'nosti organov mestnogo upravleniia)* vol. 2, *S"ezdy sovetov v 1917–1921 g., Ispolkomy v 1920–1921 g., Gorodskie sovety v 1920–1921 g.*, (Moscow, 1921), 16. A similar structure was introduced at lower levels. See GASO, f. 456, op. 1, d. 218, ll. 223–23 ob; and *Rezoliutsii VIII s"ezda Sovetov Saratovskoi gubernii* (Saratov, 1920), 3–4, 9–10. See also A. Tsekher, "Istoriia Saratovskogo Soveta za 5 let (Kratkii ocherk)," in *Piat' let proletarskoi bor'by, 1917–1922* (Saratov, 1922), 39–40, and the Saratov Soviet's *Kratkii sbornik dekretov i rasporiazhenii Sovetskoi tsentral'noi i mestnoi vlasti* (Saratov, 1920), and *ISS*, no. 227, Oct. 8, 1920, 2. For similar developments elsewhere see Antonov-Saratovskii, *Sovety*, 2: 140–41, 143–44.

[82] *ISS*, no. 133, June 17, 1920, 1.

the language of 1917, backed the joining of all socialist parties into a united revolutionary front.[83] New elections to the soviet in September 1920 indicate that support for the Communists had waned further;[84] as before, the presidium handled most of the soviet's work.[85] By the time famine had claimed its first victims in 1921, the beleaguered gubispolkom organized itself along military lines, as the soviet's constituency vanished when demobilized Red Army soldiers fled Saratov.[86]

The Communists' conceptual space led many of them to conclude that the reason for the transformation of the soviets from revolutionary debate clubs into large and inefficient bureaucracies did not lie with the party's policies, but with the province's "kulak nature" and lack of "qualified proletarians," or, as Lenin put it, with the masses' "low cultural level." For others, however, the decline of the soviets was symptomatic of all that had gone wrong since October 1917. Not surprisingly, efforts made at the end of 1919 to rejuvenate soviet plenums actually revitalized the other socialist parties instead, stirring open debate and a distinctive revolutionary impulse reminiscent of 1917, as workers appealed for joining all socialist parties into a united front (see chapter 11). The hopes of a party minority to restore the democratic potential of the soviets thus never materialized because of the implications this had for Soviet power as practiced and because of the need to win the Civil War. The dashing of these expectations contributed to a mass rejection of Communist rule at the beginning of 1921. As popular organs, the soviets were weaker at the end of the ordeal than at the start, reflecting the extent to which participation in public life had become a casualty of civil war.

The District Soviets

This was true in the districts as well. In January 1918 the Soviet government called for the replacement of all commissars, committees, and volost bodies with soviets, transferring the funds and inventory of all dumas to them. At this time, both central and provincial party organi-

[83] Ibid., no. 144, June 30, 1920, 1, and no. 146, July 2, 1920, 2.

[84] Ibid., no. 280, Dec. 9, 1920, 3; no. 91, April 25, 1921, 2; GASO, f. 521, op. 1, d. 632, l. 2; and op. 2, d. 43, l. 5 ob.

[85] Antonov-Saratovskii, *Sovety*, 2: 82–90. See *Otchet Saratovskogo Gubernskogo Ispolnitel'nogo Komiteta S.R.K.iK.D. 9-go sozyva 10-mu Gubernskomu S"ezdu Sovetov za oktiabr' 1920 g.-iiun' 1921 g.* (Saratov, 1921), 6–7.

[86] *ISS*, no. 227, Oct. 8, 1920, 2–4; no. 253, Nov. 15, 1921, 1; no. 142, June 29, 1921, 2; *Otchet Prezidiuma Gorsoveta i Gubispolkoma* (Saratov, 1921), 1–10; and GASO, f. 456, op. 1, d. 678, l. 452.

zations indulged the localities with financial support, literature, representatives, and armed assistance. Following the initial flood of solicitousness, however, local authorities had to rely on their own resources. As a result, soviets did not replace the old administrative units throughout Saratov Province until June 1918. In political terms, a hybrid radical social democratic-populist bloc became consolidated in the district towns in 1918, where the left-wing groups of the SRs were as strong as the Communists in the executive committees[87] until the so-called Left-SR uprising in July (see chapter 5), and the assassination attempt against Lenin. Afterward, Bolsheviks in many districts tried to expel Left SR deputies from executive committees or limit their representation in local congresses.[88]

Case studies of Kuznetsk, Atkarsk, and Kamyshin will illustrate the frail foundations on which Soviet power was established. SR sympathies prevailed in Kuznetsk, a town with a population of roughly 30,000. Ardently supporting the Constituent Assembly and socialist unity, its citizens instructed their delegate to the assembly to back the formation of a democratic, federative republic and abolishment of private land ownership. Radicalized soldiers who had no base in the city and local Left SRs emerged as the champions of Soviet power; a Bolshevik organization with ties among local workers appeared only in April 1918. Challenge after challenge beset the revolutionary authorities: in March 1918 the frontoviki rose up; in April a detachment of "terrorists" from Khvalynsk launched a looting and shooting spree until Red Army units drove them out; in May townspeople turned against the revolutionaries; in June Czechoslovak forces seized Kuznetsk and executed members of its executive committee; in July panicky Red Army units in the garrison fled when reports trickled in that the front was moving in on Kuznetsk. Then White units captured the town for several days. Not until the end of the year, when fresh support arrived from Moscow and local SRs joined the Communist Party, did some semblance of stable authority temporarily seem in place.[89]

[87] Left SRs predominated in Volsk and Khvalynsk and were as strong as the Bolsheviks in Serdobsk, Balashov, and Kuznetsk and popular in the German commune and in Nikolaevsk. The uispolkomy in these seven uezds comprised 109 Bolsheviks and 106 Left SRs and Maximalists (as well as 3 anarchists and 20 nonparty representatives). See Rashitov, "Sovety," 228–29.

[88] Most party delegates elected to an uezd congress in Kamyshin came from elsewhere and were resented. *Izvestiia Kamyshinskogo uezda*, no. 84, Sept. 27, 1918, 1, and GA RF, f. 393, op. 3, d. 393, ll. 19 ob–21 ob.

[89] GASO, f. 521, op. 1, d. 181, ll. 127–29; Levinson, "Kontrrevoliutsiia," 84–85; *Serp i molot* (Kutnetsk), no. 38, Feb. 20, 1921, 1; and *Sbornik: Ves' Kuznetsk* (Kuznetsk, 1927), 76.

In Atkarsk Uezd, a traditional center of peasant rebelliousness before and during 1917, the lines of civil war ran deep. In February 1918, local merchants, former officers, and police sought to disarm the Red Guard and disband the soviet, but failed when armed workers pounded them with cannon fire.[90] As a result, the position of the Left SRs and Bolsheviks hardened,[91] and by August they demanded "civil war with the domestic bourgeoisie and with all spongers of the counterrevolutionary camp." Lest there be any doubt, the resolution identified the Revolution's enemies: "Mensheviks and Right SRs, and also village kulaks, who exploit the labor of others, and engage in trade and speculation." The resolution declared "merciless war against the Czechoslovaks and Cossacks, these shady bands of the Mssrs. Constituent Assemblyists, led by Krasnov and Dutov and all the parasites of the laboring people."[92]

The situation in Kamyshin Uezd underscores the devastating impact of economic breakdown. The executive committee selected at a local congress found itself hard put to deal with the mounting financial crisis, nagging shortages of bread and seed, and pleas for help from invalids, refugees, local schools, and factories. Responding to a swell of support from the volosts, the committee abolished fixed prices within the district. Coming into conflict with the town soviet, it resolved to disband the body comprised of "nothing but kulaks." It also turned to Saratov for help,[93] but the Saratov Soviet lacked the human and financial resources to provide it.

In most cases local leaders could barely cope with keeping the towns running in view of the collapse of market relations, chaotic population movements, and financial stress, caused by the breakdown of the tax system, which affected all public and social services. When Moscow insisted that the districts find resources on their own, the Volsk uispolkom reduced the number of volosts to curb spending.[94] After a peasant congress gave authorities in Kamyshin extensive taxation rights to meet local obligations, no one paid the taxes (the ispolkom survived on retributions paid by German colonists who had risen up against Soviet

---

[90] *ISS*, no. 36, Feb. 28, 1918, 3.

[91] GA RF, f. 393, op. 3, d. 330, ll. 14, 17 ob–18, 38 ob.

[92] *Izvestiia Atkarskogo Soveta*, no. 38, Aug. 11, 1918, 1; the resolution is also found in *ISS*, no. 163, Aug. 11, 1918, 3.

[93] See *Zhurnaly prezidiuma Ispolnitel'nogo komiteta Kamyshinskogo Soveta rabochikh, krest'ianskikh i kazach'ikh deputatov 3-go sozyva s 28 marta do 5 iiunia* (Kamyshin, 1918).

[94] GASO, f. 456, op. 1, d. 218, l. 42; f. 521, op. 1, d. 116, l. 1 ob; and Rashitov, "Sovety," 132–33.

power).[95] Left to fend for themselves, the districts fired off complaints to Saratov both for ignoring the districts and for its erratic intervention in local affairs.[96] Khvalynsk's inebriated Communists denounced the "terror" from above, announcing their intention "to ignore all orders emanating from Saratov."[97] In contrast, authorities in Volsk in early 1919 fussed that they had heard "absolutely nothing about the activities of the Saratov gubispolkom."[98] Many uezd soviets lodged similar complaints about lack of directives or financial assistance from Saratov and/ or Moscow.[99]

Because of shortages of cadres and because of their cadres' lack of know-how, the Communists needed the expertise of those they classified as class enemies, whom they co-opted in various ways. For example, although conflict accompanied attempts to liquidate the zemstvos, the structure and personnel of the zemstvo system were often utilized in setting up soviets and their departments. In Atkarsk, virtually the *entire* membership of the zemstvo reemerged as a department of the local soviet. At the volost level, in fact, some zemstvos were merely renamed soviets.[100] To be sure, revolutionaries conveniently blamed "bureaucratic suffocation" on Soviet officialdom's "class composition," and on the "paunchy bourgeoisie" who ran Soviet agencies, yet little could be done about it, for experienced, literate officials were hard to come by.[101] A multitude of reasons prompted these individuals to serve the system, but a deteriorating economic situation drove many to work as Soviet officials in order to obtain rations.[102]

Owing to the problems outlined above, soviet plenums at the district level declined much more rapidly than in Saratov, as power soon became concentrated in the hands of uezd executive committees (*uispolkomy*) and their presidiums. Before the Soviet constitution fixed the size of the committees at no more than twenty, they tended to be large and unwieldy. Afterward, most local uispolkomy had between fifteen and nineteen members. Women were conspicuously absent from the committees, 75 percent of whose membership came from the under-forty

[95] GASO, f. 456, op. 1, d. 51, l. 62.

[96] *ISS*, no. 78, April 21, 1918, 3, and GA RF, f. 393, op. 3, d. 334, l. 26.

[97] TsDNISO, f. 27, op. 1, d. 57, ll. 7–8, 20.

[98] *Izvestiia Vol'skogo Ispolnitel'nogo komiteta*, no. 38, Feb. 18, 1919, 3, and *Vol'skie izvestiia*, no. 81, April 1919, 4.

[99] See *Izvestiia Soveta Kamyshinskogo*, no. 89, Oct. 4, 1918, 2.

[100] *Saratovskaia zemskaia nedelia*, no. 1, Feb. 5 (18), 1918, 10, 12–23; Rashitov, "Sovety," 60, 72–78; and GA RF, f. 393, op. 2, d. 79, l. 46.

[101] *Golos kommunizma*, no. 116 (153), May 9, 1919, 2, and *Rezoliutsii VIII s"ezda sovetov Saratovskoi gubernii*, passim.

[102] GA RF, f. 393, op. 3, d. 330, l. 188, and GASO, f. 456, op. 1, d. 48, l. 49 ob.

age cohort, but peasant representation was greater than in Saratov and the number of worker delegates lower. By late fall 1918, two-thirds of the members were Communists or sympathizers, and almost 90 percent had joined the party in 1917 or during the Civil War.[103] The success of an office, department, or soviet often depended on a single individual.[104] Unfortunately, so could its failure. A party political instructor visiting the rail junction at Rtishchevo in 1919, for example, observed that the chairman of the local ispolkom "lives like a 'little tsar'" and was not motivated by any concern with building Soviet power, but by the desire "to stuff his pockets and leave."[105]

Another example is the situation that unfolded in Balashov, where revolutionary forces and their opponents battled it out.[106] After a member of the executive committee was killed, it declared martial law in the city and began to rule capriciously with a Left SR named Solonin at the helm (figure 3.3).[107] In mid-1918, Solonin found himself and what has come down in the literature as a "band of adventurists" the object of a special investigation for their arrogant snubbing of their comrades. Voted out of office by a local congress of soviets, Solonin threatened to shoot all the deputies. The resulting investigation revealed that the distressing rumors circulating about him were true, prompting a debate regarding his party affiliation, as populist groups denied any association with him. The state of affairs must have been unfortunate, for it led a local leader to wonder "whether there were any honest people in the Soviet republic." The Revolutionary Committee that appropriated power during the Solonin affair also had to replace the local military apparatus and overhaul the militia because of its pandemic bribe taking, drunkenness, and misconduct.[108]

To sum up, these examples demonstrate that on the eve of Saratov Province's falling under siege in 1919, political instability, a deterioration in living standards and human values, and social unrest shaped the emerging political-administrative structures at the district level. Shortages of all kinds, disease, crime, a breakdown in transportation, desertion, and the illegal distilling and consumption of alcohol characterized everyday life. The uezd soviets failed to influence the countryside, where disorders, "arbitrary rule and complete confusion" prevailed. "The vil-

[103] Vladimirskii, *Sovety,* 1: 4–7, 11, 14, 34.

[104] GASO, f. 521, op. 1, d. 360, l. 1.

[105] GA RF, f. 393, op. 3, d. 331, l. 19.

[106] GASO, f. 521, op. 1, d. 182, ll. 1–4, and d. 181, l. 108.

[107] Ibid., d. 191, and *KG,* no. 35, April 4, 1918, 4.

[108] GA RF, f. 393, op. 3, d. 331, ll. 27–28; *Izvestiia Balashovskogo Ispolnitel'nogo komiteta,* no. 173, Sept. 25, 1918, 1–2; no. 14, Jan. 21, 1919, 3; and no. 110, May 23, 1919, 4.

3.3 Left SR Grigorii Solonin is seated in the middle wearing the white cap. This photo from March 1918 depicts the members of a special investigative commission charged with resolving a conflict at the Balashov rail station. Courtesy Balashov Kraevedcheskii Museum.

lages," one confidential report concluded, "very shortly will be against Soviet power."[109] Indeed, conditions triggered disturbances as bands of peasant deserters known as Greens rose up in Balashov Uezd, striking a responsive chord throughout the province.[110]

The siege of 1919 undermined the authority of the district executive committees as military revolutionary committees (revkomy) set up in many district towns ruled autocratically. The Kuznetsk Revkom, for example, shot peasant "bandits and counterrevolutionaries," sending 200 members of the bourgeoisie and "kulaks" to concentration camps. Thanks to its "cruelty in dealing with enemies of the laboring people," Soviet power was "restored."[111] By late 1919 district soviets tended not to function at all,[112] and where they did the relationship between soviets and party committees remained rocky and a good deal depended upon personal relations.[113] Saratov complained that the executive committees and soviets, "as in the past," submitted reports only after long delays.[114] The village population complained about town administrations and Communists.[115] Local departments complained about agents sent from Moscow. Everyone complained about corruption in Soviet institutions.[116] Front-line conditions made it difficult for Saratov to call quarterly congresses of soviets, and when they did occur elections resulted in Communist minorities in Balashov, Khvalynsk, Kuznetsk, Atkarsk, and Saratov Uezds,[117] and in Atkarsk District once again in 1920. As pressure on the Revolutionary Communists increased (see chapter 5), their ranks declined at local congresses, while the number of nonparty deputies grew.[118] Most were populists in disguise, while others were supporters of Soviet power who saw party labels as something unfortunate that un-

---

[109] For examples, see TsDNISO, f. 27, op. 1, d. 186, l. 6; GASO, f. 456, op. 1, d. 48, l. 41, and d. 218, ll. 25, 87–88; GA RF, f. 393, op. 12, d. 19, l. 408; and Za dva goda, 35.

[110] GASO, f. 456, op. 1, d. 218, ll. 15, 120–20 ob; Rabochii i krest'ianin (Volsk), no. 245, Oct. 31, 1919, 1; and TsDNISO, f. 27, op. 1, d. 199, l. 23.

[111] Antonov-Saratovskii, Sovety, 1: 318–20, and E. G. Gimpel'son, Sovety v gody inostrannoi interventsii i grazhdanskoi voiny (Moscow, 1968), 140.

[112] GASO, f. 456, op. 1, d. 173, l. 7.

[113] Izvestiia Atkarskogo Voenno-revoliutsionnogo komiteta, no. 254, July 18, 1919, 3, and TsDNISO, f. 27, op. 1, d. 117, ll. 37–37 ob.

[114] Alekseev and Kul'manov, "Otchet," VSG, no. 1 (1921): 15.

[115] Izvestiia Atkarskogo Ispolnitel'nogo komiteta, no. 331, Oct. 21, 1919, 4.

[116] GA RF, f. 393, op. 12, d. 19, l. 417, and Rabochii i krest'ianin (Volsk), no. 266, Nov. 27, 1919, 2.

[117] By January 1920 the majority of delegates at an uezd congress were Communists, owing to measures taken against the radical populists. Krasnyi pakhar', no. 18, Jan. 31, 1920, 2.

[118] Izvestiia Atkarskogo Ispolnitel'nogo komiteta, no. 238, July 1, 1919, 3; no. 240, July 3, 1920, 4; no. 244, July 8, 1919, 4; no. 297, Sept. 10, 1919, 3; no. 356, Nov. 22, 1919, 3–4; and no. 30, Feb. 10, 1920, 1.

dermined unity.[119] All in all, the minority position of Communists in the districts even in a controlled political climate reveals how anemic Bolshevik power was.

According to Gimpelson's social profile of the 113 members of district executive committees of Saratov Province in 1920, 83 percent were Communists. Workers made up the largest group (38), followed by officials (33), peasants (20), members of the intelligentsia (17), and others (5). Seventy-five percent of them had only an elementary education or none at all, and only one of them was female.[120] A growing number of district executive committee members had joined the party after 1917, and their educational level had declined. While the majority of members had several years' administrative experience, a flow of new faces who had none is also discernible. Although the executive committees were to meet regularly, the presidiums, comprised of the chairmen of the uispolkom, the secretary, and the heads of important departments, tended to rule on behalf of the full committee.[121]

As the Civil War drew to a close the district executive committees remained estranged from the local populations and from Saratov. A typical report, this one from Novouzensk, admits that the uispolkom "enjoyed no popularity whatsoever," that many of its departments did not function, that "local living conditions are awful," and that the district would soon rise up.[122] Owing to worker disturbances against Soviet power and peasant uprisings in early 1921, revolutionary committees again appropriated power in the districts.[123] Local congresses of soviets continued to attract more unaffiliated delegates than Communists, who predominated in the executive committees.[124] Clinging to power in desperate circumstances, the uispolkomy frequently promulgated decrees that contradicted ones issued by Moscow and Saratov. Saratov blamed the committees for failing to file reports, but they, in what was by now a familiar pattern, took to task the gubispolkom for maintaining weak

[119] *Izvestiia Atkarskogo Ispolnitel'nogo komiteta*, no. 362, Oct. 29, 1919, 2.

[120] Gimpel'son, *Sovety*, 494–95.

[121] Vladimirskii, *Sovety*, 2: 14–16, and *Organizatsiia Sovetskoi vlasti*, 67–75, 79–90. See also *Posstanovleniia i rezoliutsii VIII Vserossiiskogo s"ezda sovetov rabochikh, krest'ianskikh, krasnoarmeiskikh, i kazach'ikh deputatov (23–29 dekabria 1920 goda)* (Moscow, 1920), 12–13.

[122] GASO, f. 521, op. 5e, d. 10, ll. 1–3. A similar situation existed in Kuznetsk, GASO, f. 456, op. 1, d. 355, l. 20.

[123] *ISS*, no. 109, May 19, 1921, 1; no. 114, May 25, 1921, 2; *Serp i molot* (Serdobsk), no. 50, May 10, 1921, 1; and no. 180, Dec. 7, 1921, 2. See also TsDNISO, f. 27, op. 2, d. 43, l. 112.

[124] Vladimirskii, *Sovety*, 2: 10, 32; idem., *Organizatsiia Sovetskoi vlasti*, 62–63; and *Serp i molot* (Serdobsk), no. 184, Dec. 11, 1921, 1.

ties with the uezds.[125] Early in this chapter I noted Pokrovsk's determination to secede from Saratov Province. Little had changed by Civil War's end: Saratov now maintained that it knew more about some of the most distant districts than it did about Pokrovsk, directly across the Volga.[126]

Conclusion

The Saratov Soviet leaders' dogged battle with Moscow might suggest that other scenarios enjoyed currency at the time and that the political outcome as of 1921 — a closed political dictatorship — while perhaps likely (especially in view of Lenin's attitudes), was not predetermined. Many leaders in Saratov backed Democratic Centralism, resenting Moscow's interference in local affairs. Indeed, it would be too convenient to understand what happened to popular power as embodied in the soviets exclusively as an outcome of Bolshevik ideology. At all levels, local revolutionaries clung stubbornly to their rights. We have seen how Petrovsk came to challenge the authority of Saratov, and how Saratov took on the Center. What stood behind the dissension was not only rival views on specific issues — and not surprisingly, given the factional debates that had rocked the party from the very start — but also conflicts and strife of a personal nature, resentment of outsiders, and a myriad of other considerations that Moscow commissions chose to dismiss, believing they represented no deep disagreements on principle. They were right. These various manifestations of "localism" did not constitute a true alternative to the Communist Party dictatorship, but rather center-periphery and personal versions of *kto-kogo* that shared a common cultural and ideological reference, particularly an absolute faith in the revolutionary intelligentsia's historical mission, which justified their holding onto power for some higher goal. Ultimately, the party's drive to cling to power at all costs gave primacy to state interests over local ones and strengthened the "despotic" power of the state, which continued to transcend the ruling elite's ability to penetrate Russia's nascent civil society. In this regard, the Bolshevik state that emerged in civil war conditions in some respects was a radical extension

---

[125] *Odinnadtsatyi gubernskii s"ezd Sovetov rabochikh, krest'ianskikh i krasnoarmeiskikh deputatov Saratovskoi gubernii, 16–17 dekabria 1921 goda: Stenograficheskii otchet* (Saratov, 1921), 27.

[126] GASO, f. 521, op. 3, d. 25, ll. 30, 41, 85, 146, 178. By this time the uispolkomy functioned like the military. See, for example, *Otchet Saratovskogo Uezdnogo Ispolnitel'nogo Komiteta 10-go sozyva 11-mu Uezdnomu S"ezdu Sovetov RKiKD za dekabr' 1921 g.–dekabr' 1922 g.* (Saratov, 1922), 4.

of the past rather than a revolutionary break with it.[127] Put somewhat differently, establishment of a democratic socialist order would have symbolized a more revolutionary rupture with the tsarist tradition than the Bolshevik party-state did.

Civil war also brought a rapid breakdown in the political administration of the district towns, triggering a descent into chaos and anarchy or the concentration of power in the hands of a small group of influential revolutionaries, often outsiders, as in Petrovsk. Swollen with war refugees, and later with workers from the Russian heartland in desperate search of food, the towns endured economic collapse, epidemics, violence, and a deterioration of all public services. In most cases Soviet power had been challenged and therefore soviet plenums were less influential than in Saratov from the very start. Power, such as it was, fell into the hands of the executive committees and eventually of their presidiums. As the Civil War drew to a close an effective provincial soviet apparatus did not exist; local soviets remained estranged from the people.

In 1917, the soviets lay at the center of a revolutionary cultural frame, but the imposition of party controls over the soviets catapulted the *party* onto center stage too, affecting how the state would function as an instrument of restructuring. Here is where ideology fits in: as later chapters will demonstrate, what was new about the despotic power of the Bolshevik state was how ideology transformed the ends to which it employed its intrusive practices. The rupture between party hyperbole regarding the soviets and the everyday practices of "Soviet democracy" already at this time blurred the distinctions between what constituted the authoritative, the authentic, and the real. To a large extent this outcome was shaped by the nexus of human agency and structure, of which Russia's political culture, as we shall see in the next chapter, constituted a decisive part.

---

[127] I agree with William G. Rosenberg and Boris I. Kolonitskii on this point. See Rosenberg, "Social Mediation and State Construction(s) in Revolutionary Russia," *Social History* 19, no. 2 (1994): 188, and Kolonitskii, "Democracy," 106.

Four

Cadres Resolve All

The Communists in Power

DESPITE THE intentions of revolutionaries, periods of radical change carry considerable baggage from the prerevolutionary period. As Robert Putnam puts it, "where you can get to depends on where you're coming from."[1] History matters. Culture — the subjective aspects of social life that are socially inherited and customary and that distinguish one society from another — counts.[2] Finding expression in a

---

[1] Robert D. Putnam, *Making Democracy Work: Civic Traditions in Modern Italy* (Princeton, 1993), 179.

[2] Harry Eckstein, "A Culturalist Theory of Political Change," *American Political Science Review* 82, no. 3 (1988): 803, and Howard J. Wiarda, "Political Culture and National Development," *The Fletcher Forum of World Affairs* 13, no. 2 (1989): 198. In Lotman and Uspenskii's formulation, culture "may be understood as a nonhereditary memory of a group, expressed in a certain system of prohibitions and commandments." Iurii M. Lotman and Boris A. Uspenskii, "Binary Models in the Dynamics of Russian Culture (to the End of the Eighteenth Century)," in *The Semiotics of Russian Cultural History: Essays by Iurii M. Lotman, Boris A. Uspenskii, Lidiia Ia. Ginsburg*, ed. by Alexander D. and Alice Stone Nakhimovsky (Ithaca, 1985), 30. Culture is akin to Bourdieu's "habitus," a set of dispositions that incline people to act in certain ways that orient, but do not determine, behavior. See Bourdieu, *Languages and Symbolic Power*. See also Frederic J. Fleron, Jr., "Post-Soviet Political Culture in Russia: An Assessment of Recent Empirical Investigations," *Europe-Asia Studies* 48, no. 2 (1996): 225–60. Historically reproduced in action, culture is "the organization of the current situation in the terms of a past." Marshall Sahlins, *Islands of History* (Chicago, 1985), vii, 155. Anthony Giddens's theory of structuration similarly underscores the recursiveness of social life in the mutual

set of competing discourses and symbolic practices, culture is not a closed or coherent system, but contains within it "potentially contestable messages, images, and actions."[3] It is what the Bolsheviks, Whites, and Greens had in common.

To be sure, the formerly disenfranchised who found themselves in power during the Civil War, as well as those who opposed them, drew their idea of what constituted acceptable civic behavior from their experiences under the Romanovs: the cultural frame that defined the parameters of Bolshevik practices was rooted in centuries of autocracy characterized by Russia's frail representative institutions; low levels of popular participation in political life; centralization; a bureaucratic, authoritarian government with broad powers; and highly personalized political attachments.[4] Not surprisingly, certain Bolshevik practices and the population's reaction to them seemed all too familiar to Lenin and other party leaders, who decried the lingering impact of these influences while they ironically succumbed to them in the battle to root them out.

Yet culture does absorb new influences from historical experience. The awful conditions of the 1914–21 period transformed civic practices, endowing them with exaggerated, even grotesque features. Gimpelson, among others, grounds the party elite's political impatience and maximalism in the circumstances of World War I. The conflict created a new political type prone to apply military methods to civilian life, which, as Holquist argues, the Bolsheviks drew from "a common European tool kit of total war measures." The ends to which they employed the practices, however, were different. Coming to power when there was a decline in the value of human life, they resented people of culture. The attitudes and skills the new leaders acquired, forged in the heat of civil war during a period of destruction, breakdown, and hunger, made them inflexible warriors and enemies of compromise who believed that anything that served the proletariat was moral. Such beliefs fed corruption, abuses of power, and arbitrary behavior, as well as a system of privileges that kept the party afloat in a sea of indifference and hostility from the people whose support

dependence of structure (culture) and human agency. Anthony Giddens, *Central Problems in Social Theory: Action, Structure and Contradiction in Social Analysis* (London, 1979), 5, 70.

[3] John and Jean Comaroff, *Ethnography and the Historical Imagination* (Boulder, 1992), 27. Nicolai N. Petro makes the case for the democratic strains in Russian political culture in his *The Rebirth of Russian Democracy: An Interpretation of Political Culture* (Cambridge, Mass., 1995), 3.

[4] Stephen White, "The USSR: Patterns of Autocracy and Industrialization," in *Political Culture and Political Change in Communist States*, 2d ed., ed. by Archie Brown and Jack Gray (New York, 1979), 25. Also see Orlando Figes, *A People's Tragedy: A History of the Russian Revolution* (New York, 1997), 808.

they lost.[5] Moreover, in promoting the use of violence in all aspects of public life, the Civil War affected the political attitudes not only of Bolsheviks: a synchronous birth of "strong power" forms of government emerged among both Reds and Whites. If the logic of civil war reactivated this phenomenon, which certainly had pre-1918 precedents, it was both sides' determination to stay in power that produced *chrezvychaishchina*, or forms of government based on mass terror, which left a deep mark on the country's political culture.[6]

The Communists certainly benefited from this broadened perspective regarding what constituted appropriate conduct on the part of those who rule. A "formative" experience for the Soviet state, the Civil War affected the mentality of Russia's leadership by resulting in the militarization of public life.[7] Dispositions that normally emerge over generations come about during periods of rapid transition only "at great costs resulting from raw power, withdrawal, and (because of withdrawal) forced mobilization and rebelliousness against it."[8] More than a scenario of accommodation and resistance, this dynamic caused the Communist Party to internalize *alien* cultural forms just as the population over whom it lorded did. Affecting the party and its civic practices in unexpected ways, the Civil War thus bequeathed a syncretic culture combining different beliefs and practices. As later chapters will show, Russia's vulnerable democratic traditions continued to coexist with Soviet power or manifest themselves as varieties of "otherness." But the Civil War experience greatly reduced the likelihood that the democratic strains in Russian public life would supplant the authoritarian ones.

The "Ascendancy" of the Party after the Siege of 1919

In light of Russia's political traditions, it is not surprising that during the Civil War the state asserted its primacy over local interests, as the party asserted its primacy over state organs. Although this transforma-

[5] See Gimpel'son, "Sovetskie upravlentsy," 45–52, and Sheila Fitzpatrick, "The Civil War as a Formative Experience," in Abbott Gleason, Peter Kenez, and Richard Stites, eds., *Bolshevik Culture: Experiment and Order in the Russian Revolution* (Bloomington, 1985), 57–76. Holquist's remark is found in the conclusion to his "Making War, Forging Revolution."

[6] See Gennadij Bordjugov, "Chrezvychainye mery i 'Chrezvychaishchina' v Sovetskoi respublike i drugikh gosudarstvennykh obrazovaniiakh na territorii Rossii v 1918–1920 gg.," *Cahiers du Monde russe* 38, no. 1–2 (1997): 29–44. V. Buldakov underscores the role of violence in his *Krasnaia smuta: Priroda i posledstviia revoliutsionnogo nasiliia* (Moscow, 1997). For a trenchant example, see N. Gromov, "Vospominaniia k 5-letnemu iubileiu soiuza zheleznodorozhnikov," *Krasnyi put'*, no. 2 (41) (1923): 7–9.

[7] See Fitzpatrick, "Civil War."

[8] Eckstein, "A Culturalist Theory," 798.

tion did not take place without opposition, the circumstances of civil war ultimately undermined localism because they compelled the party to resort to coercion in order to remain at the helm of state. And they ground to a halt "party work"—the agitation, mobilization, and political education of the population as well as of party members whose understanding of or commitment to Bolshevism remained shaky. This necessitated frequent purges and campaigns to enroll new party members.

Moscow's appointment of outsiders to rule Saratov coincided with the start of a more intense stage in the Civil War, which furthered centralization and alienated people from public life. Running the province like an armed camp, Saratov's leaders had to cope with the White offensive of 1919, food and energy crises, mobilizations, and desertion in the Red Army, which assumed pandemic proportions. In October 1919, they launched an attack on the dismal "economic front," preparing food, fuel, and transportation "campaigns." The extensive propaganda efforts bolstering these activities, however, could not hide the fact that the party's attempts to educate the population in a political sense remained at a rudimentary level.[9] Shortages of fuel and a transportation crisis made it impossible for the provincial party committee (gubkom) to convene conferences. In order to improve ties with the districts, it began to publish a party weekly, *Novyi mir* (New World), and opened party schools.[10] But mobilization of party members "reached unbelievable levels,"[11] depriving the organization of active party workers, as committees fell into disarray and work at the district level terminated.[12] Elements within the party advocated reorganizing it along military lines and establishing "iron discipline" so that party work could be directed at achieving victory on the "labor front."[13] This resulted in the introduction of a uniform system of provincial committees and departments; however, later mobilizations depleted ranks and the work fell to the gubkom's presidium,[14] which lacked the personnel to report on the activities of the province's district party committees.[15]

In 1920 the gubkom became preoccupied with monitoring the population's mood, the forays of angry peasant bands into the province, workers' strikes, and the explosive situation in the garrison, which housed unreliable units comprised of former deserters.[16] At this time,

---

[9] See the dry and formulaic gubkom protocols in TsDNISO, f. 27, op. 1, d. 487.

[10] For party schools see *Biulleten' Saratovskogo gubkoma* (hereafter BSG), no. 1, 1920, 2; TsDNISO, f. 27, op. 1, d. 487, l. 5 and d. 758, l. 7; and f. 200, op. 1, d. 57, l. 89.

[11] Blinov, "Saratovskaia organizatsiia," 24–25.

[12] TsDNISO, f. 27, op. 1, d. 489, l. 34.

[13] *ISS*, no. 88, April 22, 1920, 2.

[14] TsDNISO, f. 27, op. 1, d. 489, l. 45.

[15] RGASPI, f. 17, op. 12, d. 469, l. 1l.

[16] TsDNISO, f. 27, op. 1, d. 507, ll. 20, 3.

both national and local party officials feared the growing gap between leaders and the rank and file, as the latter voiced their hostility toward the former's privileges. Hinting at the split between the party's upper and lower ranks, the local press blamed it on the flow of "undisciplined" young people into the party and the arrogant behavior of some senior functionaries. It also owned up to the low level of political understanding among party members, to the downside of party mobilizations, and to the large number of "dead souls" on the rosters.[17] Many members who had joined during a fall 1919 recruitment drive now withdrew, claiming that illness or family circumstances motivated them. But the real reason was to have "the freedom to speculate,"[18] that is, the freedom to participate in the black market, revealing the difficulty the party had attracting new members committed to its goals.

The condition of the local party organization eroded further with the introduction of the New Economic Policy or NEP, approved at the Tenth Party Congress in March 1921, and as hunger and cholera seized hold of the province. Party "work" had simply failed to prepare cadres for what must have seemed to many like a rejection of Communist principles. Striking a "blow to the young," the NEP split organizations as factions battled over its implementation.[19] The younger party members' disaffection also found reflection in their belief that gubkom secretary F. T. Ivanov and other comrades "had sat too long."[20] Saratov Communists eventually approved the introduction of the NEP, stating that disagreements within the party were inadmissible. This reflects the party's ban on factionalism and reaffirmation of party discipline, yet it had more declarative than practical value:[21] many party members withdrew from the organization in order to take advantage of opportunities, inimical to the party's interests, which the New Economic Policy (NEP) presented.[22] Although the elliptical evidence does not clarify the issues at stake, at the end of 1921, the Central Committee rebuked two factions sparring over the Saratov gubkom's composition and methods of work.[23] Those in control of the gubkom depicted opposition to it from rank-and-file members as evidence of their political immaturity and "backwardness." A major purge rid the

[17] *Materialy 8-i Saratovskoi gubernskoi konferentsii RKP (3–4 oktiabria 1920 g.)* (Saratov, 1920), 3–4, 7, 12–16, 25–26, and *Otchet Saratovskogo Gubernskogo Ispolnitel'nogo Komiteta*, 11.

[18] *Na transport*, no. 115, Nov. 21, 1920, 2.

[19] *Otchet Saratovskogo gubkoma RKP XI gubpartkonferentsii (s 19 iiunia po 12 dekabria 1921 g.)* (Saratov, 1921), 6.

[20] RGASPI, f. 17, op. 13, d. 869, ll. 2–6.

[21] See, for example, TsDNISO, f. 110, op. 1, d. 5, ll. 3, 24; f. 81, op. 1, d. 49, l. 16; and N. Bogdanov and I. Kosatkin, "1i raion gor. Saratova," *VSG*, no. 11 (1921): 7.

[22] See S. Kish, "Desiat' let partiinogo stroitel'stva," *Kommunisticheskii put'*, no. 20 (1927): 65, and Blinov, "Saratovskaia organizatsiia," 25.

[23] RGASPI, f. 17, op. 13, d. 872, l. 73; d. 867, l. 1 ob.

organization of elements that discredited it; however, the party's determination to retain a proletarian core posed challenges, since some "politically backward" party members of proletarian background strove for "a life of luxury, for acquiring bourgeois customs and habits." Others got involved in private trade and business, or were so shaken by the NEP that they denied the possibility of a Communist future.[24]

The situation outside Saratov was even more precarious: "The first thing an outsider feels in a district organization," recalled Petrovsk's Kaplan, "is the weak pulse of public and political life . . . [and] the closer one gets to a village cell, the more one feels isolation and a narrow preoccupation with one's limited responsibilities."[25] Indeed, Communists frequently took up private farming.[26] To discourage ideological wavering when factories and government agencies downsized and party members lost their jobs, the gubkom implemented an affirmative action program for Communists.[27] Despite these measures, the provincial committee had to battle against "the striving of a *large majority* of members to leave the starving province."[28] By 1922, the party elite considered most rank-and-file members "politically illiterate." Only a handful of Communists in the provinces (1 to 3 percent) had joined the party before 1917. Numerous tsarist officials could be found in district organizations, while most rural Communists were government employees seeking to advance their careers.[29] As Rigby observes, "the break in continuity of the political elite is rarely if ever complete."[30]

Party Organizations in the City of Saratov and in the Districts

Before the siege of 1919, a ruling group of seven (*semerka*) ran the local gubkom, whose periodic meetings with representatives of the city's neighborhood party committees (*raikomy*) were considered the equivalent of a city plenum. The gubkom also met episodically with uezd representatives. It comprised nine members, five of whom belonged to the

[24] TsDNISO, f. 27, op. 2, d. 1171, l. 28; f. 1383, op. 1, d. 38, l. 17; and f. 138, op. 1, d. 36, l. 149.

[25] D. Kaplan, "K voprosu o sostoianii i metodakh partiinoi raboty v uezdakh," *VSG*, no. 10 (1921): 10–11.

[26] RGASPI, f. 17, op. 14, d. 658, l. 71 ob.

[27] *Plenum Saratovskogo gubkoma RKP (Doklady i rezoliutsii)* (Saratov, 1921), 39; TsDNISO, f. 138, op. 1, d. 33, l. 134; and f. 721, op. 1, d. 1, l. 84.

[28] Emphasis added. *Otchet Saratovskogo gubkoma*, 3; TsDNISO, f. 136, op. 1, d. 81, l. 10; and f. 138, op. 1, d. 38, l. 154.

[29] Adelman, "Development," 101–2, 106.

[30] T. H. Rigby, "The Soviet Political Elite," *British Journal of Political Science* I (1971): 415.

presidium, which directed important departments (statistical-distribution, information, organizational, and propaganda). The gubkom secretary coordinated work among them by calling erratic meetings of all department heads. From the party organization's perspective, the problem was not an unsatisfactory form of organization but "lack of experienced party workers."[31]

For much of the Civil War the gubkom also functioned as the Saratov city party committee (gorkom). Back in 1917, the latter had comprised the city, railroad yard, factory, riverfront (Volga), and military (garrison) neighborhood party committees. The party dissolved the city region in mid-1919, and the military one in mid-1921. Until 1919 the raikomy accomplished little apart from collecting dues. Afterward they intermittently convened gatherings of secretaries of party cells that existed at most factories and workplaces. Centralization clarified the functions of the neighborhood committees, but mobilizations depleted their ranks, and this meant that the committees remained inactive until a spirited drive to boost party membership in late 1919.[32] The problems associated with the large influx of raw political recruits at the time, however, soon drove observers to bemoan the need for "discipline" among party members.[33] By lack of discipline the party meant behavior that conflicted with its objectives. The party relied on education and "enlightenment" to deal with the more benign form of the problem, and purge to address the potentially more dangerous variety.

Party internal language had nothing good to say about the neighborhood committees. The "first" or railroad region committee had 603 party members, virtually all men, in September 1919 (figure 4.1). More than half were over thirty years old and had enrolled in the party in 1918, but it is impossible to determine why they had joined. Almost 20 percent had belonged to other parties (probably the Menshevik and Bund parties); 96 percent were Russian by nationality. Because of a growing tendency not to attend meetings, some cells stood on the verge of collapse.[34] As a result of the membership drive of September 1919, the organization grew to over 1,000 members. A year later, however, no cell existed at the Zhest factory and one was but recently formed at Novaia Etna, which were two of the largest mechanized enterprises in Saratov.[35] Growing economic difficulties made it hard to carry out party work, "for everyone was preoccupied with the same problem—[grub-

[31] TsDNISO, f. 27, op. 1, d. 57, l. 61.

[32] See *ISS*, no. 288, Dec. 23, 1919, 4, and TsDNISO, f. 28, op. 1, d. 3, l. 40.

[33] TsDNISO, f. 136, op. 1, d. 43, ll. 7, 16, and RGASPI, f. 17, op. 6, d. 277, l. 214 ob.

[34] TsDNISO, f. 81, op. 1, d. 10, l. 29, and d. 16, l. 82.

[35] Ibid., f. 81, op. 1, d. 31, ll. 1, 16, 24, 31, 33.

4.1 Members of the first regional or neighborhood committee (raikom) of the Saratov Communist Party Committee. Antonov is seated sixth from the left. Courtesy Saratov Kraevedcheskii Museum, photo 33170.

bing for] bread." Workers remained "indifferent toward the cells;"[36] in 1921 the organization's pulse was "weak, like that of someone who was gravely ill," as the number of cells fell by more than half. The majority expelled from the party at this time had joined in 1919 and were charged with lack of discipline or with taking advantage of new opportunities brought about by the NEP.[37] At a meeting of cells representing the police, all of the members wanted to quit the party.[38]

The factory (second) neighborhood committee in mid-1919 had no ties with party cells and did not even maintain a list of successful ones, or of party members. Observing that "counterrevolutionary" activities in the factories were mounting, leaders blamed circumstances for undermining efforts to renew party life, especially the endless forays of the Whites and mobilizations. Although most mobilized Communists came from this raikom,[39] its two-person presidium handled all of the work, leaving behind formulaic handwritten protocols that reveal little of im-

---

[36] Ibid., f. 81, op. 1, d. 58, l. 6.
[37] Bogdanov and Kosatkin, "1i raion," 6–8.
[38] TsDNISO, f. 81, op. 1, d. 58, l. 14, and d. 47, l. 15.
[39] Ibid., f. 136, op. 1, d. 9, ll. 6, 8.

portance.[40] A snapshot of the committee in mid-1920 shows that it had 1,461 members, 223 of whom were women. Eighty-two percent of its members belonged to the 24-to-40-year-old age cohort, but some were as young as 15 or even under. They were just cutting their political teeth: one-third of the total had been in the party for less than three months, and only six had belonged to other parties.[41] Reports from 1921 acknowledge "the wretchedness of direct party ties with the masses and the party's influence over them," and that some workers viewed the Communists as "enemies," while others "cursed Soviet power for all it was worth."[42]

Dockworkers and other unskilled laborers populated the riverfront (third) region, where the requirements of Communist Party membership clashed more manifestly with deeper cultural patterns. In November 1918 the district had only 154 Communists, most of whom worked in Soviet institutions and "were quite indifferent to life in the region." Sympathizing with "Christian socialism," workers invited a priest to preside over a local party meeting. Despite recruitment efforts, few barge haulers and dockhands joined the party; in fact, "there was a colossal percentage of Black Hundreds" among them. The local organization met with some success recruiting only among Red Army men and water transportation workers.[43] The membership drive of fall 1919 did not invigorate the party's efforts in this district, which "were carried out badly," owing to "a complete lack of active party workers." About 75 of the newly registered members were young teenage girls — individuals deemed the least likely to conduct party work successfully among male workers. The apathetic raikom itself was "unfit," because its members "did not display any initiative or discipline."[44]

Despite the scanty documentation on the military district committee, it is clear that the party enrolled large numbers of soldiers, who also lacked "discipline" and political consciousness.[45] Saratov had become a center for supplying units with soldiers and war materiel, as a result of which the size of the local garrison remained in flux. In mid-1920, the party registered some one hundred cells in the garrison with 8,500 Communists, suggesting the extent to which the party relied on soldiers to stay afloat.[46] More will be said about them in chapter 10.

[40] See ibid., f. 136, op. 1, d. 37, ll. 1–137.

[41] Ibid., f. 27, op. 1, d. 637, l. 22.

[42] Gorshenin, "2i raion," VSG, no. 10 (1921): 14–15, and TsDNISO, f. 136, op. 1, d. 61, l. 59 ob.

[43] TsDNISO, f. 138, op. 1, d. 2, ll. 1–2.

[44] Ibid., f. 28, op. 1, d. 18, ll. 7–8, and f. 138, op. 1, d. 73, l. 22.

[45] ISS, no. 79, April 11, 1919, 4.

[46] Ibid., no. 149, July 6, 1920, 3.

The cell was the basic building block of all party organizations; however, assessments of the condition of party cells in 1919 note that their activities slowed down or stopped with the departure of comrades to the front, making it difficult to convene meetings. In some factories cells did not exist at all, or had to compete with the semiunderground activities of rival socialist parties.[47] A campaign to revitalize cells launched in the summer of 1919 brought only cosmetic changes. The cells were to organize mandatory military training for party members, raise their political and class consciousness through attendance at weekly meetings, carry out agitational and propaganda activities among workers, report violations of Soviet power at the workplace, maintain party discipline, set a good example through hard work, and fight against coarseness and drinking.[48] Yet reports on the status of party cells at the workplace emphasize their inactivity or weakness.[49]

Consideration of party organizations outside Saratov provides telling examples of how institutions develop and adapt to their environments. Ties between the Saratov party organization and the districts remained precarious throughout the Civil War, complicated by localism, unresolved tensions between party organizations and soviets, and Bolshevism's limited appeal. Local officials often did not understand what rulings to implement—or else used this as an excuse for their objectionable policies. Saratov knew little about what went on at the district level; the district towns, in turn, often had no knowledge of what transpired in the volosts.[50] Well into 1920, Saratov maintained no regular ties with the uezds, which suffered from shortages of party activists.[51] Both Saratov and Moscow dispatched agents to the uezds to overcome these problems, but they "often do not want to work in contact with the uispolkomy, often don't want to do anything at all, and sometimes are involved in shady business."[52] Reports from the end of 1920 and later repeat the by now formulaic refrains that the districts had no or very poor ties with the villages, and that Saratov needed to "establish living ties with the uezd organizations."[53] During 1921 the party organizations continued their decline, as local soviets became "completely nonparty" in membership.[54] Efforts to purge the party in 1921 brought mixed re-

---

[47] TsDNISO, f. 27, op. 1, d. 185, l. 5.

[48] *Polozhenie o kommunisticheskikh iacheikakh* (Saratov, 1919), 2–10.

[49] See TsDNISO, f. 721, op. 1, d. 1, ll. 35, 37.

[50] Blinov, "Saratovskaia organizatsiia," 24.

[51] *ISS*, no. 18, Jan. 27, 1920, 2; see also no. 17, Jan. 25, 1920, 3.

[52] *Otchet Saratovskogo gubkoma*, 11.

[53] GASO, f. 456, op. 1, d. 337, l. 2 ob, and *ISS*, no. 46, March 1, 1921, 1.

[54] *ISS*, no. 82, April 15, 1921, 3, and RGASPI, f. 17, op. 3, d. 867, ll. 88 ob–89, and *ISS*, no. 127, June 9, 1921, 1.

sults.[55] Many Communists quit the party when enraged peasant bands appeared, while local Komsomol organizations teetered on the brink of collapse. Other party members "took advantage" of the new opportunities associated with the NEP.[56] The situation at the start of 1922 revealed the further decline of the party outside Saratov and a host of unhealthy phenomena.[57]

Shifting the blame for their own shortcomings onto higher-level agencies, party organizations at each level tended to decry the actions of lower-level bodies. Finding fault with "unhealthy tendencies" in each district except Petrovsk, one party leader alleged that in some locales the word Communist had become synonymous with the term "aggressor." Stinging criticism of this sort bled into the press whenever Soviet power was vulnerable. In March 1919, Saratov's Kirill Plaksin observed that "the illness is the same in all the districts of Saratov Province: drunkenness, irresponsibility, and a negligent attitude toward one's responsibilities."[58] These developments were by no means peculiar to Saratov. As L. S. Sosnovskii lamented, in touring the provinces his group of Central Committee representatives "lacked prison cars to transport entire executive committees and [party] committees back to Moscow."[59] In turn, local executive committees tended to dismiss volost executive committees as "inadequate," characterized by "the brewing of moonshine," while occasional reports from the volosts criticize the "blind" actions of rural cells.[60] Leaders in Saratov maintained that the majority of irresponsible political instructors "lacked objectivity," often reporting things in hyperbolic language.[61] But the latter trait proved to be fairly standard for the party at large as its members learned to speak Bolshevik. Confidential documents cast the sorry state of affairs as the consequence of the fact that most party members in the district towns were involved only in government work,[62] thinking it was the same as party work.[63]

Back in 1918 the strongest local party organizations were found in Saratov, Atkarsk, Petrovsk, and Serdobsk, and the weakest in Balashov and Kamyshin, owing to the nearness of the front. Elsewhere they re-

---

[55] TsDNISO, f. 27, op. 2, d. 814, l. 10.

[56] *Plenum Saratovskogo gubkoma*, 9–23, and RGASPI, f. 17, op. 13, d. 867, ll. 2–3.

[57] TsDNISO, f. 27, op. 2, d. 814, ll. 12, 15. See also RGASPI, f. 17, op. 13, d. 872, ll. 26, 73.

[58] *KG*, no. 310, March 21, 1919, 2, and no. 311, March 22, 1919, 3.

[59] Institut marksizma-leninizma pri TsK KPSS, *Vos'moi s"ezd*, 174.

[60] Kish, "Desiat' let," 64.

[61] GA RF, f. 1235, op. 93, d. 493, ll. 44, 48–50 ob.

[62] *ISS*, no. 122, June 12, 1919, 1.

[63] See RGASPI, f. 17, op. 6, d. 277, l. 109.

mained anemic.[64] While Atkarsk boasted the most sizable party organization (3,764), Communists had to compete for influence with Left SRs and then with the Revolutionary Communists. With a population of 12,500, Atkarsk had few industrial workers. As Saratov's Lebedev observed, "Atkarsk's inhabitants take little interest in politics . . . [but] they do not especially complain about Bolshevik power."[65] Nonetheless, "counterrevolutionary" uprisings nearby shaped political life in 1918, as did the city's appalling unsanitary conditions.[66] Although Atkarsk never fell to the Whites in 1919, it remained an anxious place, and martial law had to be introduced. Involved in government work, Communists had no time for party affairs, and many Atkarsk Communists remained ignorant of what the party stood for (figure 4.2).[67] A confidential report determined that "there are no real committed Communists, . . . it's necessary to disband all [party] cells and the uezd party committee, otherwise all will be lost."[68] Perhaps indicative of the public's mood at the time was the local press's denial of the rumor that the wife of a local Communist, Kharatonov, had given birth to the Anti-christ, horns and all.[69]

The district party executive committee (*uezdkom*) had not only replaced the soviet as the local government, but resolved not to elect a new soviet in 1920, because "in Atkarsk we have nothing but philistines (*odna obyvatel'shchina*), and the proletariat through whom we could influence the masses is very small, and of suspect quality."[70] This assessment once again reveals the party's ideological understanding of politics and its willingness to rule without popular support. A report from May 1920 reads that "thanks to the poor organization of party work from the beginning, the city organization finds itself in a stage of complete disintegration." Discipline was lacking altogether, no permanent work was carried out among women, work in the trade unions was "permeated with anti-Soviet agitation," and "no work at all" was conducted in the countryside, where the "population is hostile toward Soviet power."[71]

[64] TsDNISO, f. 27, op. 1, d. 11, ll. 13–13 ob, and Poliantsev, *Saratovskaia partiinaia organizatsiia*, 60–61.

[65] *ISS*, no. 207, Sept. 19, 1919, 2.

[66] *Protokoly i doklady VI-go Atkarskogo uezdnogo s"ezda sovetov rabochikh, krest'ianskikh, i krasno-armeiskikh deputatov* (Atkarsk, 1918), 4–5, 16–26, 41.

[67] *ISS*, no. 17, Jan. 25, 1920, 3, and *Izvestiia Atkarskogo Soveta*, no. 13, Jan. 18, 1920, 3–4.

[68] TsDNISO, f. 27, op. 1, d. 186, l. 6.

[69] See the denial in *ISS*, no. 287, Dec. 24, 1919, 2.

[70] RGASPI, f. 17, op. 12, d. 471, l. 23.

[71] Ibid., ll. 132, 155–58. See also TsDNISO, f. 200, op. 1, d. 126, ll. 1–2, 6–6 ob.

4.2 Atkarsk Communists with representatives of the *kombedy* at their first conference in 1918. Courtesy Saratov Kraevedcheskii Museum, photo 22408/87.

And Atkarsk had the largest and most "successful" district party committee.[72]

In late 1920, the Atkarsk party organization experienced "a massive exit from the party" in connection with the Green movement,[73] and growing "careerism and Bonapartism" among party members resulting in the collapse of Soviet institutions and party organizations.[74] A group of old party comrades who had made the local revolution and had done as they pleased were now reigned in as outraged citizens protested to the Cheka.[75] The uezdkom purged 10 percent of its members:[76] in October 1921 factionalism and apathy of its members continued to cripple

---

[72] TsDNISO, f. 200, op. 1, d. 126, l. 5.

[73] Ibid., f. 27, op. 2, d. 37, l. 15 ob.

[74] Ibid., f. 200, op. 1, d. 135, l. 7.

[75] RGASPI, f. 17, op. 12, d. 471, ll. 135–35 ob.

[76] *Izvestiia Atkarskogo uispolkoma*, no. 136, Sept. 30, 1920, 1, and TsDNISO, f. 200, op. 1, d. 275, ll. 1–6 ob.

the local organization.[77] A secret commission reported in 1922 that the majority of members had illegally acquired property. Estranged from the lower elements and indifferent to the plight of their constituents, they drank excessively and were seen "driving around in automobiles with women whose social position raises doubts within the party." They bickered among themselves, gathering compromising material to be used against one another.[78]

Following the Solonin affair discussed in chapter 3, the party sought to fortify its position in Balashov, but the uezdkom had trouble recovering, despite the growth in party membership (table 4.1).[79] The 1919 threat from the Whites gave rise to chaos and anarchy, as the local political department requested party agitators to pacify mutinous army units.[80] "In general," reads a report from May, "there are disorders in Balashov Uezd among the [local] population and among the local authorities."[81] One unsavory opponent of Soviet power named Shirshov, hired by the Cheka, now settled old scores. By July "party life had completely died out, and the few cells have collapsed." "There is confusion in the entire uezd," in part owing to the "enormous unrest among the peasantry, massive desertion, and so on."[82] Failing to respond to attempts to enlist them in the battle against peasant bands, workers surrendered the town.[83] The inhabitants of nearby Rtishchevo "talk about the Communists as if they were their most hated enemies," and no wonder, for a Saratov commissar arrested local Communists when he discovered 428 unburied bodies (presumably of people who died of various causes) rotting in a chapel.[84] Attempts to recruit new members increased the size of the Bolshevik organization threefold, but "cells exist only on paper."[85] Famine and peasant discontent soon put an end to hopes of recovery.[86]

Examination of the status of party organizations in the other district towns reveals that the situation there was all too reminiscent of what had taken place in Atkarsk and Balashov.[87] Soviet and government work

[77] TsDNISO, f. 200, op. 1, d. 279, ll. 25–32, and *VSG*, no. 11 (1921): 9–11.

[78] TsDNISO, f. 27, op. 2, d. 1093, l. 8.

[79] *Izvestiia Balashovskogo Soveta*, no. 168, Sept. 19, 1918, 1.

[80] TsDNISO, f. 27, op. 1, d. 199, l. 6, and f. 27, op. 1, d. 46, l. 14.

[81] GA RF, f. 393, op. 3, d. 331, l. 21 ob.

[82] TsDNISO, f. 1328, op. 1, d. 48, ll. 2, 10, 26–47; f. 27, op. 1, d. 103, l. 15; and f. 27, op. 1, d. 199, l. 23.

[83] *Krasnyi noiabr'* (Balashov), Nov. 7, 1920, 3.

[84] TsDNISO, f. 27, op. 1, d. 199, ll. 2–6, and op. 1, d. 635, l. 56.

[85] *Krasnyi pakhar'*, no. 56, March 16, 1920, 2, and RGASPI, f. 17, op. 12, d. 472, ll. 1–2, 107.

[86] See, for example, *Materialy k 9-i uezdnoi konferentsii R.K.* (Balashov, 1921).

[87] The documentation is too voluminous to include here.

TABLE 4.1
Number of Party Cells and Party Members in Saratov Province in Late 1919

Uezd	Number of Cells		No. of Party Members
	in City	in Uezd	
Saratov city	128		4,342
Atkarsk	12	75	1,137
Balashov	7	105	1,137
Volsk	26	47	936
Kamyshin	18	39	788
Kuznetsk	14	40	302
Novouzensk	12	16	308
Pokrovsk	18	27	469
Petrovsk	11	?	624
Saratov		38	413
Serdobsk	8	78	954
Dergachevsk	7	21	461
Elansk	?	?	311
Khvalynsk	7	26	255
Total	268	512	12,437

Source: TsDNISO, f. 27, op. 2, d. 867, l. 4.

lurched and party work remained neglected as its members—mainly "rumor-mongers, careerists, and those with unsavory principles"[88]— were preoccupied with their personal affairs: speculating, drinking, and terrorizing the local population. These newcomers to the party who lacked political awareness ruled autocratically and arbitrarily, ignoring the activities of party cells in the villages. As a result, several of the districts were pulsating with unrest not only owing to "White Guardists," but also to mass dissatisfaction with Communist cells, whose "criminal" elements intimidated and threatened the population.

Party Activities among Women, Youth, Ethnic Minorities, and Foreign Nationals

A handful of Saratov Bolshevik women or *Bolshevichki* played key roles in public life, in a manner not seen before October 1917. Raia Tseitlin (figure 4.3), E. N. Bogdanova, and Korneeva served as secretaries of the soviet's ispolkom, and Z. Krasilshchik and Volkovskaia worked in the

[88] *Otchet k XI*, 55.

4.3 Communist Party member Raia Tseitlin. Courtesy Saratov Kraevedcheskii Museum, 22408/25.

Cheka.[89] Despite Bolshevik efforts to involve women from the radical parties in public life, the powerful role of cultural restraints as well as civil war circumstances restricted women's participation within the top leadership and ultimately "strengthened the masculinist cast of Bolshevik political culture." Marginalizing women politically, the party became "more autocratic, hierarchical, and gendered in its division of labor and power."[90]

In February 1919 the Saratov gubkom established a bureau responsible for carrying out party work among women (*Zhenskii otdel* or *Zhenotdel*), which throughout the Civil War suffered from a shortage of competent individuals. Zhenotdel sponsored mass meetings at Saratov factories during mid-1919 to prepare for the first citywide conference of

---

[89] E. N. Bogdanova, "Uchastie zhenshchiny v stroitel'stve Sovetskoi vlasti Saratova (Iz vospominanii)," *Kommunisticheskii put'*, no. 23 (85) (1927): 45–47.

[90] Barbara E. Clements, *Bolshevik Women* (Cambridge, Eng., 1997), 189, 191.

"nonparty" women, which opened in August.[91] Following the conference, forty women joined the party, and many others began working in
various departments of provincial and city executive committees and for
the police.[92] Some did so merely to lick the struggle for survival.[93]
Zhenotdel aimed at educating women by explaining how production
was managed, how Soviet Russia unlike capitalist countries protected
female labor, and how goods were distributed. It addressed issues such
as motherhood and social services, the goals of Communism, the
women's struggle in the West, the constitutional order, the role of
unions, nationalism, and public education. Zhenotdel preached that Soviet power emancipated women from household slavery, making them
equal to men.[94] Although the Soviet Family Code of 1918 sought
to liberate women by having the state assume responsibility for child-
rearing, cooking, laundry, caring for the ill, etcetera, literature distributed among Saratov's female population reinforced traditional roles by
enlisting their support in attending to the needs of the families of soldiers, the old, invalids, and orphans.[95]

Party external language insists that female workers and peasants were
not indifferent to the party's efforts,[96] but its internal register acknowledges that work among women in the province remained "very poor"
and that the party conducted no agitation among women in most district towns until 1920, and virtually none in the villages.[97] The first
Zhenotdel party workers sent there were physically threatened. Moreover, peasant families and village and volost authorities reacted with
enmity and suspicion to female peasants chosen as delegates to conferences.[98] In general the initiative for all of Zhenotdel's activities "came
from above," admitted activist S. Liubimova. When her comrades
showed up at the workplace to sponsor meetings they were "nearly
always on themes that had no connection whatsoever with the ques-

[91] TsDNISO, f. 81, op. 1, d. 27, l. 3.

[92] *ISS*, no. 248, Nov. 7, 1919, 6, and Vas'kovskii, "Sovety," 352–53.

[93] Zateeva and Novichkova, "Rabotnitsa i krest'ianka i Oktiabr'skaia revoliutsiia," *Kommunisticheskii put'*, no. 20, 87; Vas'kovskii, "Sovety," 355; and GASO, f. 521, op 2, d. 34, l. 193.

[94] TsDNISO, f. 136, op. 1, d. 55, l. 42, and f. 138, op. 1, d. 58, l. 7.

[95] *BSG*, no. 3, July 5, 1920, 2; Poliantsev, *Saratovskaia partiinaia organizatsiia*, 232–33; *Materialy k 9-i uezdnoi konferentsii*, 5–6.

[96] See, for example, *ISS*, no. 2, Jan. 3, 1920, 3; *Serp i molot* (Serdobsk), no. 39 (323), Feb. 28, 1920, 2; no. 47 (331), March 9, 1920, 4; and *Stranichka zhenshchiny-rabotnitsy* (Atkarsk), no. 1, Dec. 12, 1920 (found in *Izvestiia Atkarskogo uispolkoma*, no. 164).

[97] RGASPI, f. 17, op. 6, d. 277, l. 8 ob; Zateeva and Novichkova, "Rabotnitsa," 85; TsDNISO, f. 27, op. 1, d. 413, ll. 3–14; and *ISS*, no. 254, Nov. 15, 1919, 4.

[98] Zateeva and Novichkova, "Rabotnitsa," 87–88; TsDNISO, f. 27, op. 1, d. 507, d. 16; and f. 136, op. 1, d. 43, l. 32.

tions that were of burning interest to the women."[99] Zhenotdel later stepped up its efforts to establish contact with the majority of Saratov women, housewives, and to shift the focus of agitational work away from military needs to restoring the economy and eliminating illiteracy.[100] Yet an activist from Atkarsk found "few women truly sympathetic" to Communism. The majority "distrust the [Bolshevik] organization," whose agitators had to avoid offending the women's religious beliefs.[101] Moreover, gatherings organized by Zhenotdel increasingly turned into forums at which women indicted the party for their awful economic conditions.[102]

The introduction of the NEP promoted a "liquidationist mood" within the local party organization concerning Zhenotdel's activities; the Atkarsk Zhenotdel was actually disbanded.[103] Ironically, the liquidationist mood came at a time when the need for a Zhenotdel had grown, for unemployment among women shot up at year's end. As a result, prostitution reached a "phenomenal level," owing to downsizing at enterprises and the demobilization of the Red Army, which resulted in a flood of men returning to the workplace and displacing female workers.[104] In 1921, only eighty-four women were elected to city soviets in Saratov Province (8.3 percent of the total); there were no women chosen to the volost executive committees and only a token handful to village soviets.[105] Nonetheless, when compared with the situation before 1917, it is clear that a critical shift had taken place in regard to women's circumscribed role in public life, especially in urban centers.

Although the party's efforts to win over the country's youth en masse also met with little success, it did manage to co-opt a steady stream of young people into its organizations. From the start, the Communist Youth League or Komsomol, founded in October 1918, sought to serve as a conduit into the party by means of political education. This is important because of youth's greater willingness to accept sweeping change, which in turn can affect broad cultural patterns. Tirado reminds us that "the Revolution was often personified as a young

---

[99] G. Liubimova, "Na fabriki i zavody," *VSG*, no. 4 (1921): 2.

[100] TsDNISO, f. 138, op. 1, d. 91, l. 1, and f. 81, op. 1, d. 50, l. 4.

[101] Ibid., f. 200, op. 1, d. 261, ll. 5, 11.

[102] For examples see ibid., f. 27, op. 1, d. 38, l. 154, and *Biulleten' Sar. ot. gub. po rab. sredi zhenshchin*, no. 1, Feb. 19, 1921, 1–2, and RGASPI, f. 17, op. 13, d. 867, ll. 87–88 ob.

[103] Zateeva and Novichkova, "Rabotnitsa," 88, and *Plenum Saratovskogo gubkoma*, 24.

[104] *Otchet Saratovskogo gubkoma*, 35–36.

[105] Zateeva and Novichkova, "Rabotnitsa," 91; Clements, *Bolshevik Women*, 189–93; TsDNISO, f. 27, op. 2, d. 814, l. 26; and *ISS*, no. 129, June 10, 1922, 2.

worker,"[106] and this was certainly contrary to regnant political culture. But the Komsomol's volatile organizational structure, and the endless mobilizations that deprived it of stable leadership, kept the Saratov organization weak. Defense of the Soviet republic became the league's justification and the focal point of its lean activities.

Students set up the first Komsomol cells in Saratov in December 1918, encouraged by the Department of Public Education (*Gubotnarob*).[107] They later sought to draw in working-class youth with the help of Proletkult, an umbrella organization for new working-class cultural groups.[108] A citywide youth conference in January 1919 elected a temporary Komsomol committee,[109] which was undermined from the start by mobilization of 20 percent of the league's membership.[110] Komsomol organizations, modeled on party committees, existed in Saratov and just a few district towns before September 1919, when the first local congress elected a provincial committee.[111] Although the league banned the formation of "national" or ethnic organizations, Jewish, Polish, and Tatar "sections" were established in Saratov. Organizers from Moscow arrived to work with the minorities, but the former often did not know the language or customs of the people they were to serve.[112] The Saratov Komsomol irregularly issued a sheet for young proletarians on the back page of *Izvestiia*; however, these efforts soon lapsed both in Saratov and in the district towns.[113]

The Komsomol never became a mass movement during the Civil War

[106] Isabel A. Tirado, *Young Guard! The Communist Youth League, Petrograd 1917–1920* (New York, 1988), 1. Soviet accounts are found in V. B. Ostrovskii, ed., *Iz istorii Leninskogo komsomola* (Saratov, 1968); V. A. Dines, *Partiinoe rukovodstvo komsomolom, 1921–1925* (Saratov, 1984); and Ia. A. El'fond et al., eds., *Saratovskii komsomol: Stranitsy istorii* (Saratov, 1989).

[107] V. G. Shido, "Iz istorii sozdaniia Saratovskoi komsomol'skoi organizatsii," *Povolzhskii krai*, no. 6 (1970): 49–51; *Partii pomoshchnik boevoi: Iz istorii Saratovskoi organizatsii VLKSM (1918–1958)* (Saratov, 1959), 29–30, 34; V. I. Rogovitskii, "Deiatel'nost' komsomol'skikh organizatsii Nizhnei Volgi v 1918–1925 godakh," *Iz istorii partiinykh i komsomol'skikh organizatsii Povolzh'ia* (Volgograd, 1972), 64–67; and S. Koblents, "Saratovskaia organizatsiia RKSM (7/XII 1918–7/XII 1921 g.)," *VSG*, no. 14 (1921): 17.

[108] TsDNISO, f. 28, op. 1, d. 2, l. 7.

[109] Ibid., f. 28, op. 1, d. 14, l. 2; op. 1, d. 2, l. 1; op. 1, d. 1, l. 1; and Koblents, "Saratovskaia organizatsiia," 17.

[110] Rogovitskii, "Deiatel'nost'," 70–71, and Beliakov, "Komsomol'skie mobilizatsii na front i ikh itogi," *Komsomol'skaia letopis'*, nos. 5–6 (1927): 144.

[111] RGASPI, f. 17, op. 6, d. 277, ll. 8 ob–9, and Rogovitskii, "Deiatel'nost'," 68–69.

[112] V. A. Samsonova, "Deiatel'nost' komsomola po organizatsionnomu splocheniiu molodezhi natsional'nykh men'shinstv v vosstanovitel'nyi period (1921–1925 gg.)," in *Iz istorii sotsialisticheskogo stroitel'stva*, no. 8 (1979): 123, 125.

[113] A. A. Galagan, "Iz istorii Saratovskoi komsomol'skoi pechati (1919–1925 gg)," *Iz istorii sotsialisticheskogo stroitel'stva*, no. 3 (1971): 68–69; see also *Krasnaia molodezh'*, published in *Izvestiia Atkarskogo Ispolnitel'nogo komiteta* in 1920.

because its political and educational activities failed to interest young people. Moreover, disappointed party leaders decried the fact that students, who were largely anti-Bolshevik, rather than workers, predominated in it, as they did elsewhere in Russia. Despite their good intentions, they proved "powerless to lead the Communist youth movement,"[114] and sometimes clashed with factory committees and workers.[115] In Turki, Balashov District, the group that created a local youth league was arrested for counterrevolutionary activity. Hamstrung by personal rivalries and by a dearth of party workers and finances, the provincial committee failed to carry out work outside Saratov.[116] Efforts to recruit new members in early 1920 doubled the size of the Saratov Komsomol, as more than one thousand new members enrolled.[117] But recruiters operated "under the nonparty flag" when they signed up new members in the hostile railroad district, where young people enrolled because agitators promised them theater tickets, musical instruments, and even revolvers. Many withdrew from the organization upon learning of its true orientation.[118]

The party succeeded in co-opting the Komsomol's leadership[119] during the period between the league's second provincial congress in February 1920 (when it registered 10,798 members)[120] and September 1920, when the league held its third congress. At this time the leadership remained in the hands of students and young officials or children of officials, but 95 percent of the delegates belonged to the Communist Party.[121] By year's end, the league's membership fell by half, probably owing to the party's encroachment on the Komsomol and the party's effort to involve the youth in rebuilding the shattered economy.[122] Efforts to for-

---

[114] *ISS*, no. 269, Dec. 3, 1919, 3; also no. 18, Jan. 27, 1920, 2.

[115] A. Petrovskii, "Iz proshlogo. 1920–21 goda (Vospominaniia)," in *Piat' let II raionnoi organizatsii Komsomola g. Saratova: Iubileinyi sbornik* (Saratov, 1924), 21; TsDNISO, f. 28, op. 1, d. 5, ll. 24–24 ob. See Tirado, *Young Guard*, 110; *Iunyi kommunist*, no. 4–5 (1920): 21–25; *ISS*, no. 201, Sept. 12, 1919, 2; and *Stranichka iunogo proletariia*, no. 2, Sept. 13, 1919, 1.

[116] *ISS*, no. 272, Dec. 6, 1919, 2; no. 271, Dec. 5, 1919, 3; no. 274, Dec. 9, 1919, 4; and no. 293, Dec. 31, 1919, 2.

[117] See *Novyi mir*, no. 2, Feb. 14, 1920, 12; *ISS*, no. 36, Feb. 15, 1920, 3; and no. 44, Feb. 24, 1920, 3.

[118] TsDNISO, f. 81, op. 1, d. 16, l. 28 ob, and Petrovskii, "Iz proshlogo," 21–22.

[119] *Iunyi kommunist*, no. 2 (1920): 15–16.

[120] *Vtoroi Saratovskii gubernskii s"ezd kommunisticheskogo soiuza molodezhi, 11–14 fevralia 1920 g. (Rezoliutsii i tezisy, priniatye s"ezdom)* (Saratov, 1920); *ISS*, no. 284, Dec. 14, 1920; *Izvestiia Atkarskogo Soveta*, no. 49, March 1920, 2; *Serp i molot*, no. 90 (374), May 6, 1920, 3; *Rabochii i krest'ianin*, no. 65, March 24, 1920, 2; and TsDNISO, f. 28, op. 1, d. 33, l. 127.

[121] TsDNISO, f. 28, op. 1, d. 16, ll. 1–2, 17–17 ob.

[122] See Katkov, "Rabota Gub. kom," *VSG*, no. 14 (1921): 18–20; TsDNISO, f. 28, op. 1, d. 20, ll. 15–17; and *Iunyi kommunist*, no. 4–5 (1921): 20.

tify the youth league's activities among factory workers and Red Army youth in 1921 resulted in clashes with unions.[123] Famine further enervated the Komsomol in the hungry Volga provinces,[124] as did personal rivalries and a decline in the number of workers in connection with the NEP.[125]

Work among the ethnic minorities proved similar to that among women and the young, yet the overall failure should not detract from the critical fact that Bolshevik practices opened the party's door to individuals excluded from public life earlier. In late 1918 the Communist Party resolved not to promote party organizations along national lines, but to create "sectors" whose purpose was to provide appropriate literature as well as speakers in the minorities' native languages. The most important were the Muslim and Mordva ones.[126] A group of Muslim Bolsheviks and sympathizers organized in Saratov in April 1918 in order to work among the roughly 150,000 Muslims in the province, mainly in Khvalynsk and Kuznetsk, whom the party considered a "dark mass" of peasants that did not know Russian and that were illiterate in their own Turkic tongues. In 1920 the Muslim sector distributed a Tatar-language newspaper (about 5 percent or 400 local Communists were Muslim).[127] The Mordva department that began functioning only in 1920 also irregularly put out a Mordva-language newspaper.[128] In 1918 the gubkom attempted to organize the Saratov Committee for Jewish Affairs, but most Jewish workers voted down a resolution to form a committee that would be the "only expression of the will of the Jewish proletariat and Jewish poor."[129]

Foreign Communists arguably played a more visible role than local minorities in fortifying Soviet power in Saratov. In October 1917, Saratov Province housed an estimated forty thousand foreign nationals, mainly prisoners of war from the Austro-Hungarian empire. In addition, several thousand Chinese workers ended up in Saratov, as well as small numbers of French and Belgian workers and 10–15,000 evacuees from Rumania. In 1918 the Communist Party began forming foreign

[123] See TsDNISO, f. 28, op. 1, d. 50, l. 11, and f. 136, op. 1, d. 65, l. 204.

[124] Ibid., f. 28, op. 1, d. 46, l. 65, and L. I. Sokol'nikova, "Partiinoe rukovodstvo komsomolom Nizhnego Povolzh'ia v period vosstanovleniia narodnogo khoziaistva (1921–1925 gg.)," *Povolzhskii krai*, no. 6 (1979): 65–66.

[125] TsDNISO, f. 136, op. 1, d. 63, l. 39, and f. 44, op. 1, d. 8, l. 1; and RGASPI, f. 17, op. 13, d. 872, ll. 4–5.

[126] A. Parre, "Godovoi obzor natsional'nykh proletarskikh organizatsii v Saratove," *Godovshchina*, 89–91, and TsDNISO, f. 27, op. 1, d. 1033, l. 8.

[127] GASO, f. 521, op. 1, d. 125, l. 11, and TsDNISO, f. 27, op. 1, d. 1033, l. 8, also d. 492, l. 29.

[128] RGASPI, f. 17, op. 12, d. 470, ll. 21, 21 ob; TsDNISO, f. 27, op. 2, d. 286, l. 101; and d. 726, l. 111.

[129] *ISS*, no. 181, Sept. 4, 1918, 3.

groups, while the gubispolkom set up national departments under the leadership of a Latvian, A. F. Parre. In early 1918 Polish radical groups formed a pro-Bolshevik Polish Revolutionary Committee chaired by Jan Mizerkiewicz, who afterward headed the gubkom's nationalities department. In March the Union of German Socialists of the Volga and German socialist prisoners of war organized. At the national level, the foreign party organizations formed the Federation of Foreign Communists (FFC) headed by Bela Kun, responsible for coordinating publication efforts, work in the Red Army, and preparing agitators. Uniting Hungarian, Rumanian, Serbian, Austrian, Polish, Korean, and Czech groups, the FFC in Saratov existed until early 1920, by which time many of the foreign nationals had left Russia for their homelands.[130] However, because of the invaluable service the foreign Communists provided, Soviet leaders were reluctant to permit them to return home.[131] For instance, Hungarian prisoners of war served in the Saratov Red Guard, joined the first Red Army units, quelled peasant disturbances, put down the May 1918 uprising in the Saratov garrison, and carried out agitation work among prisoners of war.[132]

Evaluating the gubkom's work among foreign Communists, the FFC recommended that it send couriers to Moscow to obtain literature, and open up party schools to train foreign Communists. Those needs became more essential in 1919, when "counterrevolutionaries" tried to stir up the nationalities against the Communists, forcing the Bolsheviks to abolish "bourgeois nationalist" groups such as the Saratov Province National Muslim Administration, the Polish House, and others. Further, frequent mobilizations depleted the ranks of the loyal national sectors, as a result of which many of them existed only on paper.[133]

Studies have shown that the process of reforming political culture has special appeal to the more susceptible young and socially marginal, and that political culture changes, if ever so slowly, absorbing new influences from historical experience as older elements "are eroded, meta-

---

[130] See Ia. A. El'fond, "O deiatel'nosti inostrannykh grupp rossiiskoi kommunisticheskoi partii (bol'shevikov) v gody grazhdanskoi voiny i inostrannoi interventsii (1918–20 gg.)," *Uchenye zapiski Saratovskogo universiteta* 59 (1958): 130–57, and E. I. Medvedev, "Partiino-sovetskoe stroitel'stvo v Srednem Povolzh'e v 1918 godu," *Ocherki istorii i kul'tury Povolzh'ia*, no. 1 (1976), 72.

[131] TsDNISO, f. 27, op. 1, d. 1033, ll. 10, 33–34, and op. 2, d. 726, l. 38.

[132] See Padlovich, "I-i Saratovskii kavaleriiskii polk," in *Vengerskie internatsionalisty v Velikoi Oktiabr'skoi sotsialisticheskoi revoliutsii*, comp. Jeno Gyorkei (Moscow, 1959), 273–74, and *Vilagszabadsag* (Penza, May 22, 1918, made available to the author by Mikhail Bernshtam).

[133] G. Germashev, "Osushchestvlenie leninskoi natsional'noi politiki v Povolzh'e v pervye gody Sovetskoi vlasti (1917–1922 gg.)," *Povolzhskii krai*, no. 2 (1973): 37; TsDNISO, f. 27, op. 1, d. 74, l. 14; d. 1033, l. 1; and *ISS*, no. 148, July 4, 1920, 3.

morphosed, or sloughed off."[134] Indeed, the inclusion of women, the young, and minorities in public life should not be dismissed, despite the party's own negative assessment of its efforts, precisely because it marked a break from the past and had great symbolic importance. True, these groups' involvement in public life remained restricted; however, this was as much the result of custom as it was of the fact that, paradoxically, popular participation in public life in general had become a casualty of the Civil War.

Mobilization and Membership

Although some individuals joined the party not out of any deep belief in its convictions, but in order to take advantage of its perquisites, party membership entailed a downside that undoubtedly kept the organization small: mobilizations to serve on a variety of "fronts," both military and economic. In April 1919 the Central Committee ordered a mobilization of party organizations, ranging from 10 to 50 percent of their memberships and even more in regions close to the front. The mobilization involved sympathizers, Komsomol members, Revolutionary Communists, and union members. That August the local organization mobilized all Communists and workers to defend the city in the absence of Red Army units. Both of these mobilizations gravely undermined party organizations throughout the region, removing "the last Communists from responsible positions," in Atkarsk and elsewhere.[135]

The frequent mobilizations handicapped efforts to institutionalize Soviet power, increased desertion, and depleted the party's ranks (figure 4.4). To be sure, the system allowed for corruption; influential Communists could and did save close associates from being mobilized. Some Communists refused assignments to fighting units, or failed to respond to the mobilization, as a result of which the local organization expelled them. Personal considerations determined some party members' response to mobilizations, which were hard on the families left behind. True, they were granted numerous privileges — free rent, additional food coupons, and the like — but often the resources were unavailable to make good on promises of assistance. Families of deceased Communists faced particularly awful hardships during the famine of 1921–22.[136]

Although the Bolsheviks perhaps never aimed for the party to be a

[134] Cited in Fleron, "Post-Soviet Political Culture," 166.

[135] Vas'kovskii, "Sovety," 88–95, 241–43; idem., "Bor'ba," 24–27; and TsDNISO, f. 27, op. 1, d. 117, l. 52.

[136] TsDNISO, f. 27, op. 1, d. 635, ll. 110, 113; f. 27, op. 1, d. 88, l. 68; f. 81, op. 1, d. 8, l. 4; op. 1, d. 57, l. 37; and d. 16, l. 10.

4.4 A meeting of Communists mobilized in Pugachevsk to depart for the Polish front, May 1920. Courtesy Saratov Kraevedcheskii Museum, photo 9088/44.

large organization, the Communist Party drew fewer supporters than the leadership would have liked. The fourth largest in Russia during the Civil War, the Saratov Communist Party Organization never amounted to more than 1 percent of the local population. Its size fluctuated greatly before 1921, reflecting larger trends in the party. Approximately 1.5 million people enrolled in the party's ranks between 1917 and 1920, but there were fewer than a half million members left by 1922.[137] Despite the fact that the Saratov organization did not carry out any systematic record keeping, the available data do not deviate from the national pattern. As table 4.2 shows, party membership declined in mid-1918, owing to the mobilization of Bolsheviks to defend the eastern front. It rose once again in late 1918 before the mobilization and reregistration campaigns of early 1919, as a result of which it fell sharply until the orchestrated membership drive (party week) of fall 1919. At that time an estimated 14,000 people—more than in any other locale except Moscow—joined party organizations in Saratov

[137] Adelman, "Development," 91–92.

TABLE 4.2
Size of Communist Party in Saratov Province

Date	No. of Party Members in Saratov	No. of Party Members in Province	No. of Candidate Members
Oct. 1917		5,000	
July 1918	2,000	3,600	
Dec. 1918	2,250	5,493	
March 1919	1,300	2,113	
Dec. 1919		11,679	2,530
Jan. 1920		21,146	
May 1920		20,535	2,415
Oct. 1920	5,800	16,250	
March 1921		17,064	
Sept. 1921		10,383	
Jan. 1922		8,433	

Source: ISS, no. 236, Oct. 24, 1919, 3; no. 237, Oct. 25, 1919, 2; no. 16, Jan. 24, 1920, 1; no. 49, March 4, 1921, 1; *Ocherki istorii*, 93, 111; *KG*, no. 305, March 12, 1919, 2; *Materialy k vos'moi Saratovskoi gubernskoi konferentsii*, 5; Rodionov, *Saratovskaia oblastnaia organizatsiia*, 19, 23; P.G., "Saratovskaia organizatsiia RKP," 38; and TsDNISO, f. 27, op. 2, d. 592, l. 11.

Province, bringing the total to just over 20,000.[138] A new recruit of working-class origin normally spent two months as a "candidate" member before being admitted into the party upon the recommendation of two active members. As part of a continuing recruitment campaign, the party also instituted a formal category of "sympathizers," who for various reasons were unwilling to assume the burden of membership. The party gave them broad powers, but banned them from closed meetings. The local provincial organization lost 28 percent of its membership during the reregistration drive in the fall of 1920[139] and declined to under 10,000 members following a purge and withdrawals from the party in connection with the introduction of the NEP.

Information on the social composition, nationality, age, educational level, and length of political career of Saratov party members confirms Rigby's observation that the Civil War widened access to the political elite for members of all revolutionary parties, young adults, women, national minorities, and the poorly educated, creating not a workers'

[138] Ibid., 92, and V. I. Tkachev, "K voprosu ideino-organizatsionnogo ukrepleniia partiinykh organizatsii Nizhnego Povolzh'ia (1921–1925 gg.)," in *Istoriia partiinykh organizatsii*, no. 1 (Saratov, 1973), 126; V. A. Rodionov, et al., eds., *Saratovskaia oblastnaia organizatsiia KPSS v tsifrakh, 1917–1975* (Saratov, 1977), 18–19.

[139] *Materialy 8-i Saratovskoi gubernskoi konferentsii*, 5.

party, but a *plebeian* one, run mainly by intellectuals.[140] Throughout the Civil War, workers made up roughly 40 percent of the local party organization's membership and the peasantry 20 percent. Officials and members of the intelligentsia accounted for the rest, and perhaps for this reason the party remained better educated than the population at large. About 94 percent had at least an elementary education and only 3 percent were illiterate; .6 percent had a higher education. Eighty-eight percent of the members of district committees in mid-1920 had joined the party in 1919–20.[141] Although Civil War circumstances propelled large numbers of recent converts into positions of prominence, Old Bolsheviks continued to monopolize the political leadership, which also contained a larger percentage of minority nationalities than among the rank and file.[142]

Culture, Circumstances, and Corruption

In Russia, the political and cultural elite kept a distance from the lower classes, and this held true of the Communist Party elite too.[143] Although its members came almost exclusively from the intelligentsia, they emphasized that it was their principles and behavior that distinguished them from others. Dramatizing their differences from non-Communists, the Bolsheviks cast themselves as disciplined, hard, selfless, dedicated, committed, honest, and sober. (Arguably, this prototype first emerged in the mid-nineteenth century among elements of the Russian intelligentsia that believed in their own historical mission.) The Bolsheviks embraced these traits both because they went against the grain of the regnant political culture and because they were a manifestation or valence of it. The gulf existing between Bolshevik self-representation and individual party members' personal attributes was so large, however, that party diehards mistrusted the rank and file who, in turn, came to resent the Old Bolsheviks. Party leader L. B. Krasin, for instance, opined that 90 percent of the party's members were "unscrupulous time-servers."[144] Appreciating the powerful role of cultural constraints, the party en-

[140] Rigby, "The Soviet Political Elite," 436; for Saratov city see *KG*, no. 286, Feb. 15, 1919, 3, and *ISS*, no. 40, Feb. 22, 1921, 2.

[141] G., "Saratovskaia organizatsiia," 38; N. N. Kalashnikov, "Saratovskaia organizatsiia kommunisticheskoi partii v bor'be za ukreplenie soiuza rabochikh i krest'ian pri perekhode k NEPu," *Uchenye zapiski Balashovskogo pedinstituta* 2 (1957): 24; and Rigby, "The Soviet Political Elite," 418–19, 422.

[142] *ISS*, no. 53, March 9, 1921, 2.

[143] Indeed, there are some remarkable similarities between the Communist Party in Russia and colonialism. See Comaroff and Comaroff, *Ethnography*, 42.

[144] Cited in Gimpel'son, "Sovetskie upravlentsy," 44.

rolled thousands of young recruits on probation in the hopes that they would work out, maintaining a revolving door policy, and periodically purging itself of members who compromised it. The party's critical gaze fell on its leaders too: Central Committee representatives routinely drew confidential profiles of local leaders' human qualities and suitability to perform at different levels in the party hierarchy.[145]

While corruption was an inherent feature of the tsarist bureaucracy, the Soviet government's ban on private trade and introduction of a mil-itarized economic "system" characterized by shortages, confiscation, barter, rationing, and the rise of a black market (see chapter 9) provided favorable grounds for even greater levels of corruption and other prob-lems. A negligent attitude toward one's work, red tape, excessive drink-ing, and other abuses discredited the party — virtually everywhere in the province.[146] Petrovsk's Kaplan concluded that "Soviet workers were be-coming uncontrollable and were abusing their power," thereby strength-ening counterrevolutionary elements.[147] Reports from Atkarsk in 1919 criticize rural Communist cells for "plundering" peasants and the uezd executive committee for sending punitive detachments to the villages.[148] The party dismissed the chair of the Serdobsk ispolkom for turning a blind eye to abuses and for ordering the arrest of a political instructor who dared criticize the committee's disreputable dealings.[149] An agent sent from Saratov to Atkarsk to improve the distribution of aid to war invalids was locked up for peddling the items he was supposed to dole out.[150] The Cheka jailed Balakovo Communists for the illegal brewing of alcohol.[151] Drunkenness and collective binge drinking became such a major problem that the *entire* Khvalynsk party committee was dis-banded because of drunkenness. Investigating problems in Balashov in 1920, a commission found that the local organization "represents a mob of drunks and card sharks."[152] By 1921, repressive measures had

[145] See assessments of F. I. Ivanov, TsDNISO, f. 17, op. 2, d. 1277, l. 7, and f. 27, op. 1, d. 507, l. 32. For assessments of other local leaders see f. 27, op. 1, d. 507, ll. 33–36.

[146] Ibid., f. 27, op. 1, d. 230, l. 33; *Serp i molot*, no. 19 (218), Sept. 11, 1919, 2; and *ISS*, no. 184, Aug. 15, 1920, 3.

[147] *KG*, no. 124, July 31, 1918, 3.

[148] GASO, f. 456, op. 1, d. 218, ll. 103–4 ob. See also *Rabochii i krest'ianin*, no. 199, Sept. 5, 1919, 1, and A. Berelovich and V. Danilov, eds., *Sovetskaia derevnia glazami VChK-OGPU-NKVD, 1918–1939: Dokumenty i materialy v 4 tomakh*, vol. 1, *1918–1922* (Moscow, 1998), 160.

[149] Vas'kovskii, "Sovety," 149.

[150] *Izvestiia Atkarskogo Ispolnitel'nogo komiteta*, no. 363, Nov. 30, 1919, 4.

[151] See GASO, f. 456, op. 1, d. 158, l. 49; d. 218, l. 6; and GA RF, f. 1235, op. 93, d. 493, l. 49 ob.

[152] TsDNISO, f. 27, op. 1, d. 32, l. 16, and f. 27, op. 1, d. 487, l. 8.

driven much public drinking underground, but "heavy drinking [among Communists] did not diminish."[153]

Blaming corruption within the organization for the Whites' success, the party made it a class issue by depicting it as a "dirty" form of class relationships inherited from old Russia, as bourgeois specialists and former tsarist bureaucrats, that is, "middle-class careerists," obtained administrative positions (and rations) "simply by applying for party membership the day before applying for the job itself."[154] Indeed, in 1918 the Bolsheviks began to institutionalize their political capital in the form of jobs in the state bureaucracy, recruiting heavily from among the educated strata out of necessity, even if their views were inimical to Bolshevism.[155] This phenomenon is not unique to Russia, for bureaucracies tend to survive upheavals and sometimes are strengthened by them; bureaucratic self-interest is not the same as personal self-interest.[156] Moreover, it would be wrong to see this aspect of the Civil War only as a problem for the Bolsheviks, since even when groups hostile to the ideals of Communism joined the party or served within its bureaucracy, they nonetheless were obliged, on occasion, to behave in ways that were compatible with the principles that supposedly motivated them.

Corruption even extended to the Cheka, established in late 1917 as the gubispolkom's Department for the Struggle against Counterrevolution. Undergoing a major expansion in 1919, it grew to 300 party members. Initially under the leadership of M. A. Deich, M. S. Vengerov (a Saratov worker), and I. B. Genkin, the organization later was directed by a harsh outsider and Petrograd worker, I. P. Zhukov, for part of 1918 and again in the summer of 1919. By late 1918 party leaders sought to subordinate the Cheka to local party organs, as complaints were registered that it often made illegal arrests and held prisoners without presenting formal accusations.[157] Early the next year the party temporarily abolished the Cheka at the uezd level, but in transferring the authority to issue verdicts to revolutionary tribunals it simply placed the power to repress in the hands of others.

Membership in the party did not guarantee immunity from the Cheka's arbitrary terror, and for this reason most party members feared the political police. At a meeting of the factory region in July 1919 "the ma-

---

[153] RGASPI, f. 17, op. 13, d. 872, l. 26.

[154] TsDNISO, f. 138, op. 1, d. 10, ll. 29–29 ob, and Service, *The Bolshevik Party in Revolution*, 90.

[155] Bourdieu, *Language and Symbolic Power*, 197.

[156] Eckstein, "A Culturalist Theory," 796.

[157] *Saratovskii Sovet*, 642, 759–60, 762. See also S. V. Leonov, *Rozhdenie Sovetskoi imperii: Gosudarstvo i ideologiia, 1917–1922 gg.* (Moscow, 1997), 225, 250, 254–56.

jority of speakers consider[ed] the provincial Cheka's work nasty,"[158] while the Saratov Cheka informed Lenin that "it's absolutely impossible" to find party members willing to join the organization.[159] One of its members who described the situation within the local organization as "awful" reacted in disgust to the ubiquitous bribe taking. He urged the gubkom to "replace the entire staff of this commission of scoundrels, thieves, and robbers" or else he would blow the whistle and tell Lenin.[160] The so-called State Control Commission received an "enormous" number of complaints lodged against the Cheka in the fall of 1919 "concerning arrests, confiscations, and requisitions of property."[161] Although the gubkom proposed that the Cheka no longer arrest Communists without authorization from the appropriate party organization, in 1921 Communists still protested Cheka abuses.[162]

When the Central Committee in April 1919 broadened the activities of the State Control Commission to do something about the problem of corruption, the commission found serious inadequacies in virtually *all* local Soviet institutions, filing charges of malfeasance, theft, speculation and the like against all party organs, including the Cheka and police.[163] True, party members often denounced comrades who abused their power, or voiced resentment toward those who avoided military service or mobilization. Yet control commissions regularly dismissed denunciations, suggesting that false accusations were made, that insufficient evidence was marshaled, or that the arbitrating bodies themselves were corrupt. A reregistration of party members did not curtail these abuses, nor did other steps the Central Committee took.[164] In 1920, accusations of abuses of power, negligence, and bureaucratic red tape assumed monstrous proportions, owing to the growing lawlessness and ubiquitous shortages of everything.[165]

---

[158] TsDNISO, f. 136, op. 1, d. 9, l. 6.

[159] N. I. Shabanov and N. A. Makarov, comps., *Gubcheka: Sbornik dokumentov i materialov iz istorii Saratovskoi gubernskoi chrezvychainoi komissii, 1917–1921 gg.* (Saratov, 1980), 118. This appears to have been a problem elsewhere, and throughout the Civil War. See TsDNISO, f. 27, op. 1, d. 634, l. 72, and d. 635, l. 139.

[160] TsDNISO, f. 1328, op. 1, d. 43, l. 31. This was true elsewhere too. See Leonov, *Rozhdenie*, 258–60.

[161] *Obzor deiatel'nosti Saratovskogo Otdeleniia Narodnogo Komissariata Gosudarstvennogo Kontrolia za period s sentiabria 1919 goda po fevral' 1920 goda* (Saratov, 1920), 22–23.

[162] TsDNISO, f. 151/95, op. 1, d. 89, l. 1; f. 138, op. 1, d. 33, l. 245; and f. 27, op. 1, d. 635, l. 135.

[163] *Obzor deiatel'nosti*, Saratovskogo Otdeleniia 1, 3–6, 8–16, and *Kommuna*, no. 49 (191), June 27, 1920, 3.

[164] TsDNISO, f. 27, op. 1, d. 76, ll. 144–47; f. 81, op. 1, d. 5, l. 216; and GASO, f. 456, op. 1, d. 447, l. 12.

[165] See, for example, *Iacheiki sodeistviia raboche-krest'ianskoi inspektsii, ikh organizats-*

As part of a national campaign to curb abuses of power, restore discipline, cut down on red tape, revive industry, and overcome growing worker alienation from the party by involving them in participatory practices, the party replaced the State Control Commission in 1920 with the Workers'-Peasants' Inspectorate (*Rabkrin*), or WPI, headed by Stalin. Emphasizing that rooting out corruption was impossible without involving the masses, the WPI planned to set up cells in all factories, enterprises, institutions, and villages. Party literature admonished every "honest" citizen to get involved in the program or else be considered a participant in the crimes now under fire. The Saratov Rabkrin created eleven subdepartments to oversee, among other things, food supplies, industry, agriculture, health, justice, and education, and a network of 574 cells with 1,722 members.[166] Their ultimate failure exposes the billiard-ball interaction of circumstances, ideologically fueled initiatives, rivalries, misunderstandings, and deep cultural patterns.

Some local organs of the inspectorate clashed with district executive committees and/or the local Cheka, who did not welcome independent bodies observing and reporting on their activities. Nor did volost authorities appear to have appreciated what they perceived as an intrusion into their affairs.[167] Undoubtedly, the principal reason for the hostility toward the WPI was the unbelievably awful functioning of virtually all institutions and organizations. The WPI in Volsk, for example, found that "in almost all institutions, business was carried out extremely badly," and that this problem was difficult to root out because of officials' unwillingness to subordinate themselves to the inspectorate. The Cheka conveniently blamed the "failure" of the WPI, which contained only six Communists, on the "working intelligentsia and petite bourgeoisie," who composed it, all of whom exhibited indifference to politics.[168]

Lack of competent workers owing to poor remuneration represented another important reason for the inspectorate's ultimate failure, as its staff members searched for jobs elsewhere because of low wages.[169] Famine conditions and the introduction of the NEP further exacerbated the paucity of financial incentives, making it next to impossible to attract new inspectors as old ones fled. By November 1921 only 5 percent of the WPI's former staff members still remained at their posts. Short-

---

iia i zadachi (Volsk, 1920), 3–4; *Izvestiia Atkarskogo uispolkoma*, no. 131, Sept. 17, 1920, 2.

[166] *Iacheiki sodeistviia*, 3–7; GASO, f. 521, op. 1, d. 401, ll. 1–3; and f. 338, op. 1, d. 13, ll. 2–5.

[167] GASO, f. 338, op. 1, d. 11, ll. 85 ob–87 ob; d. 19, ll. 3 ob–5 ob, 36; and d. 57, l. 12.

[168] Ibid., f. 338, op. 1, d. 11, ll. 8–10; also d. 13, l. 6; and f. 3310, op. 1, d. 1, ll. 8–9.

[169] Some examples are found in ibid., f. 338, op. 1, d. 11, 1l. 36 ob, 37 ob, 88 ob, and d. 23, l. 24 ob; d. 49, ll. 12–15 ob.

ages of instructions, overwork, the passivity of their members, and absence of monetary rewards had made the majority of cells inactive.[170]

The WPI did provide an opportunity for everyday citizens to lodge grievances, but this amounted to protest within the regime's value system. For the six-month period ending in October 1920, the WPI received 1,229 complaints, the majority of which were directed at the local housing department for wrongful confiscations. When the government collected an emergency tax from the countryside in 1920, peasants flooded the inspectorates with accusations against the military and food supply organs. An examination of charges filed in Balashov and Serdobsk Uezds shows that the largest number concerned requisitions and confiscations, followed by complaints against the housing authorities. In its deliberations, the WPI placed greater trust in plaintiffs from the "right" classes.[171]

The WPI did little to curb abuses of power, in part because of the party's unwillingness to permit public organizations to function without controls, in part because the introduction of the New Economic Policy pushed bribery and corruption to new levels. Some party members even argued that the misunderstandings and factions within the party were rooted not in ideological differences but in the material inequality among party workers resulting from the NEP.[172] Other party leaders emphasized the desirability of staffing provincial committees with Old Bolsheviks, turning to newer party members to fulfill such tasks only when absolutely necessary and when workers could vouch for them. Yet little changed, and the marker "old" often had more to do with following the rules than it did with years of service in the party.[173] Above all, this discussion of corruption suggests that while circumstances certainly contributed to the problem, Russian political culture determined how it would manifest itself.[174]

Purging the Party

During the Civil War the party carried out periodic reregistrations and purges to rid its membership of individuals who compromised Soviet

---

[170] Ibid., f. 338, op. 1, d. 43, ll. 63–64, and d. 45, ll. 7–8, 14–17 ob.

[171] The WPI examined 68 percent of them and decided in favor of 307 complainants. Ibid., f. 338, op. 1, d. 11, ll. 35–35 ob; f. 338, op. 1, d. 25, l. 14; f. 338, op. 1, d. 19, ll. 21–23; d. 25, l. 631; see also d. 56, ll. 48–50.

[172] *Serp i molot*, no. 235, Dec. 2, 1920, 1; TsDNISO, f. 27, op. 2, d. 824, l. 123; and Kaplan, "K voprosu," 11.

[173] TsDNISO, f. 81, op. 1, d. 48, l. 136, and f. 27, op. 2, d. 1171, l. 41.

[174] This discussion illustrates Bourdieu's point that particular practices should be seen "as the product of the relation between the habitus . . . and the specific social contexts or 'fields' within which individuals act." Bourdieu, *Language and Symbolic Power*, 14.

power.[175] The party ascribed great symbolic import to the act of excommunication, making those weeded out the scapegoats for its failures. Moreover, purging enabled the party to define what was acceptable public behavior for its members as it tried to reorient Russian political culture. The most serious attempts to flush the party of undesirable elements took place in the spring of 1919, when 46.8 percent of the party's total membership was expelled. During the purge of 1920, 28.6 percent of the party's members were dropped, and in 1921, 24.8 percent.[176] These are stunning figures, given the size of the party, and they correspond to national averages.[177]

Comrade or party courts irregularly considered violations of party discipline between purges, but they functioned poorly; otherwise there would have been less cause for subsequent purges. In 1919 no more than 200 cases were actually presented, and of those, more than half were dismissed or remained unresolved. The most frequently made charges concerned breaches of party discipline, malfeasance, drunkenness, counterrevolutionary activities, and desertion. The comrade courts frequently did nothing more than issue reprimands where drinking was concerned, because the party sorely needed cadres and because of deeply rooted cultural attitudes toward alcohol.[178] Here is a telling example of how attempts to change society by cleansing the party gave way to larger cultural patterns.

The party sponsored a major purge of its members in late 1921, following the introduction of the NEP, when it insisted that those who used their party membership for personal gain would be "swept away with an iron broom." *Izvestiia* made it clear that this would not be another reregistration campaign, but a "radical purge" that would rid the party of the bourgeois element that cleverly gave lip service to party programs.[179] Encouraging non-Communists to identify corrupt party members, the party sponsored public meetings for this purpose. The reasons cited for purging individuals from the party are all too familiar: succumbing to the temptations of the NEP, systematic drinking and debauchery, violation of party directives, including work-related criminal activities (theft, embezzlement, issuance of false documents), negligence,

[175] Examples are found in TsDNISO, f. 27, op. 1, d. 11, l. 5, and *Izvestiia Vol'skogo ispolkoma*, no. 49, March 2, 1919, 3.

[176] Adelman, "Development," 97.

[177] For example, *see KG*, no. 299, March 4, 1919, 1; *Golos kommunista*, no. 132, May 28, 1919, 3; Bul'in, "Stranitsy zhizni," 32–33; and *ISS*, no. 225, Oct. 11, 1919, 3. For Serdobsk see *Serp i molot*, no. 189 (473), Sept. 3, 1920, 1.

[178] TsDNISO, f. 1328, op. 1, d. 2, ll. 1–4, and f. 81, op. 1, d. 7, l. 58.

[179] *ISS*, no. 148, July 6, 1921, 1; no. 192, Aug. 27, 1921, 1; and TsDNISO f. 138, op. 1, d. 70, l. 124.

laziness and indifference, and harmful behavior (e.g., drinking, hooliganism), with observance of religious practices in last place.[180] The more "proletarian" the neighborhood committee, the higher the percentage purged. The iron broom swept through Red Army units; however, in the bureaucracy party members tended to cover up for their comrades, another cultural holdover from the past. The percentage of party members expelled from the district organizations ranged widely, reaching a high of 50 percent in Kuznetsk and Elansk.[181]

The downsizing of the party in 1921 paralleled a reduction in the number of Soviet administrative organizations and of officials on the payroll, as the departments of the provincial and city executive committees were merged and the number of volosts in each uezd reduced. While the party found Saratov bureaucracies swollen with "bourgeois elements" responsible for red tape, its internal language ironically admits the party's need for "the broadscale use of experienced and honest nonparty members." The party instructed local organizations to avoid employing those accused of discrediting Soviet power and of malfeasance, but to enlist the support of those expelled from the party for transgressions such as former membership in other parties or taking part in religious rites.[182] As noted earlier, the size of the Saratov party organization was reduced by 22–24 percent to 11,473 (the figures vary), and it fell even more precipitously in 1922 to only 8,433 members.

Conclusion

Although classified by the Central Committee at civil war's end as one of the strongest in provincial Russia,[183] the Saratov Communist Party Organization remained small, poorly organized, alienated from the population, riddled with problems, and divided over critical issues such as the meaning of the NEP, the relationship between Old Bolsheviks and newcomers, and various Bolshevik public practices. Party membership did not grant one immunity from arbitrary or justifiable arrest on the part of the Cheka, while the party leadership constantly cast a sus-

---

[180] TsDNISO, f. 138, op. 1, d. 73, ll. 1–6, 11, 21, 23–29; *ISS*, no. 236, Oct. 19, 1921, 2–3; TsDNISO, f. 721, op. 1, d. 1, l. 117; and f. 138, op. 1, d. 70, l. 92.

[181] *ISS*, no. 70 (270), Nov. 17, 1921, 4; no. 271, Nov. 30, 1921, 2; no. 238, Oct. 21, 1921, 3; V. A. Osipov et al., eds., *Saratovskaia partiinaia organizatsiia v gody vosstanovleniia narodnogo khoziaistva: Dokumenty i materialy, 1921–1925 gg.* (Saratov, 1960), 92–96.

[182] See Vas'kovskii, "Sovety," 122–24; *ISS*, Jan. 12, 1922, 2; and TsDNISO, f. 136, op. 1, d. 94, l. 7.

[183] RGASPI, f. 17, op. 11, d. 15, ll. 1–2.

picious gaze at the organization's rank-and-file Communists, who became the subject of voluminous documentation meant only for the party elite. This was not what Lenin had envisaged when he promoted civil war. To be sure, the idealized image of the selfless, dedicated, sober, tough-minded revolutionary had not vanished, nor had belief in a Communist future. The ordeal of Civil War, however, had made the ideals more elusive. As Part Two will demonstrate, the party's wielding of raw power in a depressed economic climate turned survival into a basic instinct, resulting in people's withdrawal from public life, which necessitated the application of even greater coercion. The mobilization of society and resistance to mobilization established a pattern of governing that enabled the Communists to co-opt individuals from among the formerly disenfranchised, but it also forced the Communists to make room for the hordes of opportunists who joined the party.

Thus, for the Bolsheviks, culture represented a conservative force that got in the way of their political goals. Ironically, they relied on traditional ideas and values themselves — especially on ones that had taken on exaggerated forms during the 1914–21 period — when they resorted to autocratic political practices in order to implement their ideologically fueled experiment aimed at changing the very culture that ultimately restrained them and their subjects. The striking features of their radical authoritarian rule packaged in an ideology that was open to challenge included eventual curtailment of democracy within the party, the use of force to achieve political objectives, and the reliance on a plebeian population for support, resulting in, among other things, dependence, mistrust, and exploitation. The postrevolutionary state, in other words, was more centralized, authoritarian, and bureaucratic than its predecessor; popular participation in public life remained low, while political attachments continued to be highly personalized.

The short-term effects of social transformations on the magnitude of the Civil War are, due to "sheer cultural inertia," frequently greater than the long-term ones. They helped to create a template for Soviet history because people respond to concrete situations through mediating orientations that vary among social segments within a society owing to "culturally determined learning" in which "early learning conditions later learning."[184] In viewing the Civil War through these lenses we can appreciate how the chaos and violence of the period left their imprint on party practices, characterized by apathy, red tape, opportunism, negligence, and corruption, which in turn made necessary endless campaigns and purges. Drunken commissars lording over angry, anxious populations, terror from above, denunciation, corruption, and embez-

---

[184] Eckstein, "A Culturalist Theory," 790, 792, 800.

zlement of state property became features of everyday life for many. To be sure, party leaders pinned the blame for these ills on the need to subordinate all else to the military cause, which made it impossible to elevate the cadres' overall cultural level. They failed to realize, however, that raising the cultural level would generate both support for and hostility to the system.

Five

Co-optation *amid* Repression

The Revolutionary Communists and Other Socialist Parties in Saratov Province

THIS IS A book for which the archives matter. They reveal that from late 1918 until October 1920 a populist political party called the Revolutionary Communists (RCs) participated in the ruling coalition in Saratov, attracting a considerable following in several key districts, as well as elsewhere in the Volga region and Urals. Perhaps the most important supplier of grain to the urban centers of the Communist-controlled heartland, frontline Saratov Province remained Red throughout the Civil War, owing to the hybrid form of left-socialist radicalism that emerged there, of which Revolutionary Communism constituted an essential part.

Despite the fact that Soviet power in Saratov would have collapsed had it not been for the Revolutionary Communists' support of the Bolsheviks, Western historians have totally neglected the party.[1] The few Soviet historians who acknowledged its existence dismissed the Revolu-

---

[1] In his monograph on the Volga countryside, Orlando Figes does not mention the party at all. See *Peasant Russia Civil War: The Volga Countryside in Revolution, 1917–1921* (Oxford, 1989). Neither does Brovkin in *Behind the Front Lines*, Sakwa in *Soviet Communists in Power*, or Ettore Cinnella in "The Tragedy of the Russian Revolution: Promise and Default of the Left Socialist Revolutionaries in 1918," *Cahiers du Monde russe* 38, no. 1–2 (1997): 45–82. In fact, none of the recent studies on the Civil War mentions the Revolutionary Communists, even though Schapiro devotes a page to them in his classic work on the period, *Origins*, 180–81.

tionary Communists as a group of former Left SRs who broke with the parent party in July 1918 after the murder of the German ambassador, Count Mirbach, in order to form a separate organization that September, which eventually collapsed under the weight of its own "ideological contradictions."[2] Such an interpretation offers but a crude representation of a fascinating and important political phenomenon. It is time to restore this influential but unknown party to the historical record, to clarify the Revolutionary Communist Party's contribution to the survival of Soviet power, its relationship to Bolshevism, the reasons for the party's decline in 1920, and its fate vis-à-vis that of the other socialist parties during the Civil War.[3] The RCs' merger with the Communists had considerable symbolic importance, for it foretold a bleak future for Russia's other socialist parties and for a multiparty system in general.

This case study also suggests how societies control their subjects not only by imposing constraints, but also by co-opting their subjects' strategies of dissent.[4] Indeed, because the Bolsheviks relied heavily on despotic power in order to effect the changes they believed they had the moral right to introduce into Russia, they readily resorted to repression and likewise sought to manipulate the dominant discourse in which politics were played out. In either case they often selectively co-opted their rivals' political programs. The resulting dynamic of co-optation amid repression became a characteristic Bolshevik practice during the period and a critical element of the formative experience of Civil War for all involved. Thus, examination of the party's relationship toward its populist ally and other socialist parties offers valuable insights into how the Bolsheviks exercised state power in general.

[2] The fullest discussions of the party are in the works of Iu. I. Shestak, *Bol'sheviki i levye techeniia melkoburzhuaznoi demokratii* (Moscow, 1974); *Taktika bol'shevikov po otnosheniiu k partii levykh eserov i otkolovshimsia ot nee partiiam revoliutsionnykh kommunistov i narodnikov-kommunistov* (Moscow, 1971); "Vzaimootnosheniia bol'shevikov s levymi melkoburzhuaznymi partiiami i gruppami v gody grazhdanskoi voiny," in *Bankrotstvo melkoburzhuaznykh partii Rossii, 1917–1922 gg.*, ed. I. I. Mints (Moscow, 1977), 126–36; and "Bankrotstvo partii 'Revoliutsionnykh kommunistov' v Povolzh'e," *Povolzhskii krai*, no. 4 (1975): 24–38. Brief mention of the RCs is found in M. V. Spirina, *Krakh melkoburzhuaznoi kontseptsii sotsializma eserov* (Moscow, 1987), and K. V. Gusev, *Krakh partii levykh eserov* (Moscow, 1963). For Saratov see M. Sagrad'ian, "Iz istorii vozniknoveniia odnopartiinoi sistemy v Sovetskoi respublike," in *Istoriia partiinykh organizatsii Povolzh'ia (Mezhvuzovskii nauchnyi sbornik)*, no. 1 (Saratov, 1973): 108–23. A post-Soviet attempt to illuminate the party's role is Iu. P. Suslov's, *Sotsialisticheskie partii i krest'ianstvo Povolzh'ia (oktiabr' 1917–1920)* (Saratov, 1994).

[3] For a fuller treatment of the RC Party see my "Co-optation *amid* Repression: The Revolutionary Communists in Saratov Province, 1918–20," *Cahiers du Monde russe* 40, no. 4 (1999): 625–56.

[4] Gerald Graff, "Co-optation," in H. Aram Veeser, ed., *The New Historicism* (New York, 1989), 168–69.

The Saratov Left SRs

The Revolutionary Communists emerged from the radical wing of the SR Party, the Left SRs, who broke from the parent party following the October insurrection and joined the Lenin government. The Left SR Party program — published by the Saratov Soviet — made them an essential ally of the Bolsheviks. Viewing themselves as "one of the divisions in the army of international socialism," the Left SRs considered the industrial proletariat, the toiling peasant majority, and the revolutionary-socialist intelligentsia the three component parts of the exploited population whose task was to emancipate itself through social revolution. The party advocated establishment of a dictatorship of all toiling people, the extension of voting rights only to toilers, repression of the exploiting classes, and a free federation of Soviet republics. Like Lenin, the Left SR leaders believed the Constituent Assembly should not be allowed to supplant Soviet power. Convinced they were in the best position to influence Bolshevik policies in regard to Russia's peasant majority, they accepted portfolios in Lenin's government, while in the provinces they supported the transfer of power to local soviets.[5]

Although the Left SRs' faith in the subjective forces of history, such as personality and individualism, and their belief that ethical considerations were as important as economic factors distanced them from the Marxists, they remained committed to class war, to revolution, and to Soviet power, especially as it faced growing opposition from both moderate socialists and the Whites.[6] As a result, the potent Bolshevik-Left-SR alliance in Saratov even weathered the controversy over the Brest-Litovsk Peace that poisoned relations between the two parties' central committees early in 1918, after which the Left SRs withdrew from the Sovnarkom in protest. The Left SRs, like the Bolsheviks, were similarly divided over Lenin's foreign policy: in Saratov both party organizations initially railed against the peace treaty.[7]

The common ground both local party organizations found regarding the disputed treaty strengthened the left-socialist bloc in Saratov. So did the arrival from Poltava and Kharkov of Left SR activists, who carried

[5] Partiia levykh sotsialistov-revoliutsionerov (internatsionalistov), *Programma i ustav partii levykh sotsialistov-revoliutsionerov (internatsionalistov)* (Saratov, 1918), 5–9, and *Znamia revoliutsii*, no. 4 (96), Nov. 29, 1918, 3.

[6] Partiia levykh sotsialistov-revoliutsionerov (internatsionalistov), *Materialy po peresmotru partiinoi programmy*, vol. 3, *Sbornik statei po peresmotru programmy* (Moscow, 1918).

[7] See chapter 3. Also, *Protokoly pervogo s"ezda partii levykh sotsialistov-revoliutsionerov (internatsionalistov)* (Moscow, 1918), 9. For rifts within the Left SR leadership see Cinnella, "Tragedy," 62–63.

out party work at the district and volost level, and kept the April 1918 elections to the Saratov Soviet from being a rout for the Bolsheviks.[8] However, conflict flaring up within the Left SR Party leadership over tactics, often exacerbated by personal rivalries, presaged the breakup of the party in the summer of 1918. These developments found resonance along the Volga after another influx of "outsiders" appeared in town. Comprised mainly of workers, the Saratov Left SR organization had lacked leaders of national stature until May, when M. G. Markariants, V. Chernyi, A. M. Ustinov, P. F. Sapozhnikov, and others traveled to Saratov to set up a Volga regional party center for the purpose of uniting those who opposed the Central Committee's "destructive" tactics aimed at undermining the Brest-Litovsk Peace. Saratov offered a favorable atmosphere, for the local Left SR organization, like those in Kazan, Penza, Ufa, and elsewhere in the region, had protested the "revolutionary fantasy and political emotionalism" of the party's Central Committee.[9] In their own estimation, Saratov Left SRs believed the relationship with the Leninists remained "excellent." During the anti-Bolshevik uprising that broke out in Saratov in May 1918, an armed guard of Left SRs from Kharkov rose to the soviet's defense; more than half of the delegates to a provincial peasant congress in May were Left SRs, and luminaries such as Ustinov and Sapozhnikov sat on the congress's presidium.[10] At this time Ustinov already proposed that the Left SRs rename themselves Communist-Socialists in order to link themselves more closely with the Bolsheviks and separate themselves from the parent SR Party.

Other threats to Soviet power followed hard on the heels of the May uprising, as a result of which the Saratov Soviet expelled its socialist opposition (but not the Left SRs) *before* the Central Executive Committee took similar steps. The success of local Left SRs in the Saratov countryside, however, caused growing concern within the Bolshevik organization, which, at the end of June, resolved to break off joint agitation work with the populists. Relations between the parties at the local level were thus beginning to show the first signs of strain when news of the assassination of Count Mirbach in the capital in conjunction with the start of the Fifth Congress of Soviets, generally cited as the opening salvo in the so-called Left SR uprising, reached Saratov in early July 1918. The Bolsheviks interpreted the murder and related events as a

[8] The Left SRs received as many votes as the Right SRs. See *Znamia revoliutsii*, no. 3 (95), Nov. 7, 1918, 4.

[9] Partiia levykh sotsialistov-revoliutsionerov (internatsionalistov), *Vokrug moskovskikh iiul'skikh sobytii: Sbornik statei* (Saratov, 1918).

[10] *Znamia revoliutsii*, no. 3 (95), Nov. 7, 1918, 4.

conspiracy against Soviet power—which it was in one sense—and took advantage of the situation to decapitate the Left SR Party. The Bolshevik response should come as no surprise, given the party's fixation with conspiracy and the anti-Bolshevik uprising, probably unrelated, which broke out in Yaroslavl the same day.[11]

Reactions to the Left SR "Uprising"

Study of the reaction in Saratov to the Mirbach murder reveals serious factionalism within the Left SR Party leadership and considerable hostility toward its Central Committee. It also challenges Brovkin's conclusion that "all over Russia the Left SRs . . . were arrested and expelled from the local soviets."[12] At an emergency meeting Left SRs protested against their party's Central Committee in Moscow; the Saratov Left SR organization carried a resolution distancing itself from the tactics of the party's Central Committee and calling for a national party conference to be held in Saratov on July 21. A resolution passed on July 9 at a citywide Left SR conference states unambiguously that whatever the intentions of their Moscow comrades, the "uprising" against the ruling party had turned into one against Soviet power. The resolution proclaims that the local organization would have judged its Central Committee "even more harshly" if it had not been for the deep certainty "that its stupid heroism had its source in an incorrect assessment of real facts and was the most egregious tactical mistake of a group of the most selfless revolutionaries." Arguing that the Central Committee's tactics since March "logically had to end with an uprising against the very government," it called for deepening the class struggle and forging a united front with the Bolsheviks.[13] Similarly, articles written by Rudakov, Chernyi, Sapozhnikov, and Ustinov in preparation for the Saratov conference backed the working out of a new political tactic based on the principle of class struggle, seeking to save the party that "did not die and cannot die." The authors rejected individual acts of terror, emphat-

[11] Most historians accept the notion of an uprising, while a few historians (namely G. Katkov, Iu. Fel'shtinskii, and Vladimir Brovkin) argue that the Bolsheviks had actually conspired against the Left SRs. Calling for a reassessment, Lutz Hafner maintains that the "Bolsheviks consciously and quite successfully aimed to split and thereby destroy the Left SR Party." See his "The Assassination of Count Mirbach and the 'July Uprising' of the Left Socialist Revolutionaries in Moscow, 1918," *Russian Review* 50, no. 3 (1991): 324–44 (quote found on 340).

[12] Brovkin, *Behind the Front Lines*, 20.

[13] Partiia levykh sotsialistov-revoliutsionerov (internatsionalistov), *Materialy k Vserossiiskoi konferentsii Partii levykh s.r. (internatsionalistov) v g. Saratove (iiul', 1918 g.)* (Saratov, 1918), 3–6.

ically denying that the entire party bore responsibility for its Central Committee, "which is far removed from local party organizations." The essays accent the primacy of the class struggle in a united front with the Bolsheviks against the enemies of Soviet power for the triumph of the social revolution.[14]

Another collection of essays put out by Saratov Left SRs boasts that they were the first to sound the alarm against their Central Committee, but also cautiously suggests that not all the facts surrounding the July events were known.[15] While condemning Mirbach's murder as a counterrevolutionary act, Rudakov stressed that without complete information it was impossible to say what drove the party's leadership to rise up against the ruling party,[16] and that local Left SRs must morally support their Central Committee, even if it had made a mistake. Insofar as the majority of local committees *opposed* the party's leadership, the Bolsheviks were forcing an artificial split.[17] Ustinov suggested that those who criticized the party for "wagging like the Bolsheviks' tail" may actually have prompted leaders to show the party's "real face," which *did* separate it from the Bolsheviks *and* the Right SRs. More importantly — for it demonstrates the party's belief that it could moderate Bolshevik policies — he reminded his comrades that the Bolsheviks *had* fallen under Left SR influence in "recognizing the possibility of constructing socialism in a backward country . . . the socialization of land, and the vanguard role of a minority that took the initiative, etc."[18]

Denying that their actions represented a schismatic act or one of insubordination, twenty delegates representing thirteen Left SR organizations assembled in Saratov on July 21, 1918, where the majority condemned Mirbach's murder and reiterated the need to convene a national congress to set up a new party.[19] The defenders of the party's Central Committee at the Saratov conference largely represented provincial organizations, whereas delegates from uezd centers in the same provinces "voted for a radical change in the tactics of the party and in its attitude toward Soviet practical work."[20]

The events surrounding the murder of Count Mirbach sundered the

---

[14] Ibid., 7–21.
[15] Partiia levykh sotsialistov-revoliutsionerov, *Vokrug moskovskikh sobytii*, 3.
[16] Ibid., 5–6.
[17] Ibid., 34–38.
[18] Ibid., 8–9.
[19] A development greeted warmly, incidentally, by V. I. Lenin. See *Polnoe sobranie sochinenii* (Moscow, 1963), vol. 37, 35–36, and Sagrad'ian, "Iz istorii," 109. Shestak claims that eighteen organizations sent representatives to Saratov. See *Bol'sheviki i levye techeniia*, 33.
[20] Partiia levykh sotsialistov-revoliutsionerov, *Vokrug moskovskikh sobytii*, 43.

Left SR Party as the Bolsheviks expressed their desire to continue working only with those Left SRs who condemned their Central Committee's policies. As the view took hold that the Left SRs had risen up unsuccessfully against Soviet power, an "enormous" number of Left SRs joined the Bolsheviks, suggesting the importance of the Bolsheviks' ability to control the dominant political discourse. While some radical populists continued calling themselves Left SRs, two new parties emerged as well, the Revolutionary Communists (*Revoliutsionnye kommunisty*), who participated in the ruling coalition until October 1920, and the Popular Communists (*Narodniki-kommunisty*), who merged with the Communist Party already in November 1918.[21] Saratov's Ustinov and A. L. Kolegaev emerged as the most forceful spokesmen of the Revolutionary Communists, although the latter soon joined the Communist Party, acquiring a reputation as a ruthless figure in repressing the Don rebellion on the southern front. While the two men did not see eye to eye on all tactical matters, they had nothing good to say about the Left SR Central Committee. This is particularly true of Ustinov, who emphasized that the Left SRs' withdrawal from the Fifth Congress had demonstrated that the Left SRs "were henceforth enemies of the majority of representatives of the workers and peasants." He denounced Central Committee members as a "group of madmen-*intelligenti*, thirsting for success among the petite-bourgeoisie, middle-class urban dwellers, and village kulaks."[22]

Breaking tactically with the Left SRs, former party members founded the Revolutionary Communist Party in Moscow on September 25–27, 1918. Their organ, *Volia truda* (The Will of Labor), disavowed the use of force to undermine the Brest-Litovsk Peace; acts of terrorism; open struggle against the ruling Communist Party in order to seize power by force; and any policies that weakened the class character of the Revolution, "which, through civil war, will lead to socialism." The Central Committee included "Saratovites" Ustinov and Chernyi.[23] As the Revolutionary Communists saw things, the deepening rift between the class of toilers and the bourgeoisie had driven all those not committed to the class struggle into the counterrevolutionary camp.[24] This division had

---

[21] Formed in September 1918, the Popular Communists declared that all Soviet parties have one program—the building of Communism—and one tactic—class struggle. See Gusev, *Krakh*, 226, 256.

[22] G. Ustinov, *Krushenie partii levykh "es-erov"* (Moscow, 1918), 6–7, 11–12, 16–18, 21–22.

[23] Gusev, *Krakh*, 226; resolutions from the congress are found in *Znamia revoliutsii*, no. 1 (93), Oct. 21, 1918, 3–4; Shestak, "RKP(b)," 20; and RGASPI, f. 282, op. 2, d. 3, ll. 2–5 ob.

[24] See, for instance, *Znamia revoliutsii*, no. 89, Sept. 20, 1918.

fractured the Left SR Party, whose revolutionary wing had become the Revolutionary Communists. Apart from them, only the Bolsheviks understood the class nature of the social revolution that had engulfed Russia. The RCs emphasized, however, that it was not through the dictatorship of the proletariat but through the dictatorship of *all* toiling elements that socialism would be built.[25]

With the Power of the Toilers to Socialism!

The first issue of the Saratov Revolutionary Communists' newspaper, *Znamia revoliutsii* (The Banner of Revolution), explained: "We are *Communists*, that is, we are moving toward socialism, through concrete forms of the communization of the economy. And we are *revolutionaries* . . . in a programmatic-tactical sense, insofar as we have promoted and promote . . . the creative role of personality, the role of the revolutionary minority [that shows] initiative in history." More to the point: "not through the dictatorship of the proletariat, but through the dictatorship of all toiling elements, united in a single class of labor" will socialism be brought to Russia.[26] *Vlast'iu trudiashchikhsia — k sotsializmu* (With the power of the toilers to socialism!).

Those familiar with Russian populism will recognize its legacy in the RCs' emphasis on the individual (rather than the collective), on developing all facets of a person (rather than accenting economic considerations), on local initiative (rather than centralization), on the revolutionary potential of the toiling masses (rather than of the industrial proletariat). Although party leaders disagreed over how to effect economic transformation in the countryside, they advocated the socialization, not nationalization, of land, which must belong to those who work it, and under no circumstances to the state.[27] Seeking to establish a mass party, the RCs appealed to morally righteous people to join them. Sensitive to their own opposition to the Left SR Central Committee, the RCs called for disciplined compliance with all directives issued by the party.[28]

The Revolutionary Communists' tactics can best be summed up as the application of radical populist principles and doctrine to ever-changing civil war conditions without undermining the alliance with the Communists. Dividing society into two groups, the toilers and those who exploited them, RC theorists believed the party should harness the

[25] TsDNISO, f. 151/95, op. 1, d. 15, ll. 8–11.
[26] *Znamia revoliutsii*, no. 1 (93), Oct. 21, 1918, 1.
[27] Spirina, *Krakh*, 174–76, 184, and RGASPI, f. 282, op. 2, d. 3, ll. 57–57 ob.
[28] TsDNISO, f. 151/95, op. 1, d. 14, l. 1.

creative power of the toiling masses and *broaden* the "dictatorship of the proletariat."[29] Party literature emphasized that social revolution had broken out in *peasant* Russia, and that the Bolsheviks wrongly sought to build a new socialist economy without taking the peasant majority into consideration.[30] Walking a fine line between criticizing specific Bolshevik policies and supporting Soviet power, the RCs felt compelled to reiterate their commitment to Soviet power and to a united revolutionary front with the Bolsheviks.[31]

The Revolutionary Communists' understanding of the social dynamics of the Revolution involved them in a discursive struggle with the Communists in which the populists were on the defensive from the very start. The events of October 1917 had underscored the central role of the proletariat and even of the dictatorship of the proletariat. But the RCs held that the narrow dictatorship had significance *only* during the period of the seizure of power and destruction of the bourgeois state apparatus, and that a dictatorship of *all* toiling elements was essential for building a new order. Confident of their ability to compete with the Bolsheviks on these grounds (recall Ustinov's conviction that the Bolsheviks' belief that socialism could be constructed in peasant Russia had a populist origin), the Revolutionary Communists held that they could persuade the Bolsheviks to change their tactics. Evidence of the Bolsheviks altering their policies gave the RCs their self-assurance. For instance, Saratov Bolsheviks reluctantly introduced the committees of the village poor (*kombedy*), which a regional RC Party conference condemned, lamenting that the "dictatorship of the proletariat is becoming a dictatorship of the Bolshevik Party." Although this stance exacerbated relations between the two parties at the local level, the Communist Party's subsequent decision to disband the kombedy convinced the RCs that they and other "revolution-minded elements of the population" *could* get the Bolsheviks to alter their policies and co-opt those of the populists.

The Revolutionary Communists' commitment to Soviet power prompted them (as it did many Bolsheviks) to perceive otherwise questionable Bolshevik practices as the consequences of temporary circumstances brought about by civil war. They thus recognized the need for a centralization of Russian political life in this transition period characterized by a life-and-death struggle with the Whites. Moreover, the RCs rejected cooperation with the Mensheviks and SRs, affirming that the Bolsheviks

[29] Ibid., f. 151/95, op. 1, d. 14, ll. 3, 4 ob.

[30] Ibid., f. 151/95, op. 3, d. 1, l. 13.

[31] Ibid., f. 151/95, op. 1, d. 8, l. 11. See also *Znamia revoliutsii*, no. 2 (94), Oct. 28 (Nov. 1), 1918, 2–3.

represented the "major fighting force of the social revolution."[32] When Saratov fell under siege in 1919, the chair of the provincial RC committee, Sapozhnikov, instructed all party members to join forces with the Bolsheviks, to refrain from carrying out any independent policies, particularly in regard to the Communists' detested grain policies. "In case of disagreements with Bolsheviks at the local level," he instructed RCs to "investigate the matter and disband the [party] organizations."[33]

This is not to say that the Revolutionary Communists lost sight of their goals or their constituency. Resolutions carried by the First Conference (*sovet*) of the Revolutionary Communist Party held in Saratov that difficult summer underscore the "significant withdrawal of the laboring masses from politics and from the soviets" brought about by the Communists' attempts to introduce a party dictatorship in conditions of overall economic ruin and class war. Although the RCs welcomed the new political course adopted by the Communists at their Eighth Congress in March 1919 when they embraced the middle peasant, the RCs held that the change could not win over the toiling peasantry. As the RCs saw it, the anti-Bolshevik mood that had spontaneously flared up in Russia deepened the apolitical feelings of significant strata of laborers susceptible to the forces of counterrevolution, spreading hopes that to topple Soviet power would put an end to war and hunger. Reaffirming their commitment to class struggle and to a united revolutionary front with the ruling party, the RCs believed they needed to organize the peasantry and strengthen the authority of the soviets in order to create a stable revolutionary-socialist majority. They fully intended, however, to propagate their ideas and strengthen their influence over the masses, inviting all populist groups and parties that shared its program and tactics to join them in building a new order, thereby leaving the door open to merger.[34] And it was this above all else that made the Bolsheviks leery of their allies.

It proved difficult for the Revolutionary Communists to press their own agenda while backing the Bolsheviks. The RCs reiterated the principle of lasting support for the Bolsheviks despite their methods of constructing socialism and the peasantry's "natural desire" to reject the party's rural program, because "the main task of the moment is the battle against capitalism." Maintaining that the proletariat and toiling peasantry were equal players in the revolutionary drama, the RCs called

[32] Shestak, *Bol'sheviki i levye techeniia*, 23–24.

[33] TsDNISO, f. 151/95, op. 1, d. 49, l. 25; f. 151/95, op. 1, d. 98, l. 3; f. 151/95, op. 1, d. 56, ll. 12–17; and op. 1, d. 52, ll. 7–8. See also TsDNISO, f. 151/95, op. 1, d. 46, ll. 4, 5.

[34] Ibid., f. 151/95, op. 1, d. 9, ll. 1–2 ob.

upon its members to take part in Soviet work and to strengthen the Red Army, all the while preserving friendly relations with the Bolsheviks.[35] But a resolution on tactics passed in September 1919 noted that the disagreement between the two methods of socialist construction could only be resolved by the *organic* evolution of new socioeconomic forms. And they insisted that "only revolutionary populism" represented *all* the toiling masses.

Until the very end of their existence the Revolutionary Communists continued to question specific Bolshevik strategies; however, as in the past, the RCs did not waver in their commitment to Soviet power or in their willingness to subordinate their party to the Bolsheviks when they felt the Revolution was at stake. For example, in 1920 the Revolutionary Communists spoke out against the efficacy of a policy known as labor conscription. Yet Saratov's Sapozhnikov, in a sincere if desperate attempt to make sense of it, eventually saw the temporary necessity of labor armies, labor conscription, and coercion.[36] Similarly, in early 1920 the RCs promoted the organization of a production union of workers of the land (*proizvodstvennyi soiuz rabotnikov zemli*) in order "to bring about socialism by means of the dictatorship of the proletariat." Even though the union's organizers emphasized their support for Soviet power, the Cheka arrested those who set them up,[37] because the union seemed all too similar to the SRs' Union of Toiling Peasants (*Soiuz trudovogo krest'ianstva*), whose purpose was the "overthrow of Communist-Bolshevik power."[38] And, in fact, rank-and-file RCs do not always appear to have appreciated the difference.[39] Under fire, the RCs' Central Committee instructed party members to stop organizing new unions until the disagreement with the Bolsheviks was resolved.[40]

Co-optation amid Repression: Relations with the Bolsheviks

In some district towns in Saratov Province the Moscow events of midsummer 1918 impaired relations between Left SRs and Bolsheviks, despite the conciliatory tone the Saratov Left SRs had taken. Often out-

[35] Ibid, f. 151/95, op. 1, d. 42, ll. 7–8, 10–11, 19, 22–24, and op. 1, d. 44, ll. 12, 17.

[36] Ibid., f. 151/95, op. 1, d. 85, ll. 15–22. See also GASO, f. 3310, op. 1, d. 1, l. 137.

[37] TsDNISO, f. 151/95, op. 3, d. 16, l. 15. Information on Volsk is found in ibid., l. 1, and in d. 15, ll. 34–34 ob.

[38] GASO, f. 521, op. 5, d. 11, ll. 13, 24; RGASPI, f. 282, op. 1, d. 47, l. 33; and Marc Jansen, *The Socialist-Revolutionary Party after October 1917: Documents from the S.-R. Archives* (Amsterdam, 1989), 548.

[39] GASO, f. 3310, op. 1, d. 1, ll. 124 ob–25.

[40] TsDNISO, f. 151/95, op. 3, d. 16, ll. 8–8 ob, 12.

siders sent by Moscow or Saratov, Bolshevik leaders in the locales now had grounds to undermine the influential Left SRs.[41] This hostility carried over to the RCs, in part because the Soviet government did not formally legalize the party until February 1919, and despite the Saratov Communist organization's agreeing to work with the RC Party.[42] Even though some Saratov Revolutionary Communists withdrew from the party to join the Bolsheviks,[43] and the RCs' Sapozhnikov distanced the party from the Left SRs,[44] tension colored the Saratov RCs' relations with the Bolsheviks. Balashov Bolsheviks ridiculed the new party's name, while Volsk Bolsheviks kept the RCs out of the local executive committee. In Kuznetsk the local Bolshevik organization cooperated with the RCs until the arrival of Bolsheviks from Moscow "who with all their might want to wipe us [the RCs] from the face of the earth."[45]

At this particular point during the Civil War there is little evidence of Foucauldian co-optation, and plenty of evidence of coercion. Relations between the two parties rapidly deteriorated in December 1918 over representation at a local peasant congress,[46] and then as elections took place to village and volost soviets in early 1919. Balashov Bolsheviks disbanded the RC organization in early 1919, "inviting" its members to join the Communist Party.[47] The Atkarsk Bolsheviks declared the local RC organization illegal, arrested the party's uezd committee, prevented the party from holding meetings in rural areas, and interfered in elections to rural soviets — resorting to intimidation, armed force, and arrest — all in violation of the Soviet constitution. They justified excluding RCs from a local congress by claiming that the RCs opposed organization of the kombedy and backed the unity of the entire peasantry.[48] Finally, they informed Moscow that they considered the Revolutionary Communists illegal "because the overwhelming majority of their organizations represent kulak elements."[49] In response, RCs complained that

[41] *Znamia revoliutsii*, no. 1 (93), Oct. 21, 1918, 4, and GA RF, f. 393, op. 3, d. 333, ll. 19 ob–20.

[42] GA RF, f. 393, op. 3, d. 327, l. 103.

[43] *Znamia revoliutsii*, no. 1 (93), Oct. 21, 1918, 2.

[44] GASO, f. 456, op. 1, d. 16, ll. 30–30 ob. See also *Saratovskii Sovet*, 724.

[45] *Znamia revoliutsii*, no. 4 (96), Nov. 29, 1918, 4.

[46] Sagrad'ian, "Iz istorii," 117.

[47] *Izvestiia Balashovskogo Ispolnitel'nogo komiteta*, no. 17, Jan. 25, 1919, 4.

[48] TsDNISO, f. 151/95, op. 1, d. 52, ll. 2–5, 16–17; f. 151/95, op. 2, d. 4, l. 8; op. 2, d. 16, ll. 12–13; and op. 2, d. 41, ll. 2–3. See also *Krasnaia kommuna*, no. 80, Nov. 29, 1918, 4; no. 150, Feb. 28, 1919, 3–4; *KG*, no. 301, March 6, 1919, 2; and GASO, f. 521, op. 6, d. 1, l. 116.

[49] TsDNISO, f. 27, op. 1, d. 227, l. 9, and Sagrad'ian, *Iz istorii*, 119.

the Bolsheviks often prevented them from meeting and that force was used to manipulate village elections.[50] Other RC reports from the localities read like "indictments against the Bolsheviks," for RC activists viewed them as a dirty riffraff, as political speculators seeking above all to avoid being packed off to the front.[51]

Admitting numerous cases of Bolshevik repression against RCs, the government legalized the RCs as part of the new spirit of accommodation following the November 1918 revolution in Germany and launching of a White offensive.[52] At their Eighth Party Congress in March 1919 the Bolsheviks softened their dictatorship of the proletariat by openly courting the middle peasantry (recognizing the "power of the toiling people" [*vlast' trudiashchikhsia*]?). In May Central Committee agent I. P. Flerovskii investigated abuses of power in Atkarsk and the use of force in elections to village soviets,[53] after which Saratov Bolsheviks agreed to let Revolutionary Communists take part in local government, thereby ending the period of "merciless coercion."[54] The timing says a good deal about the motivations of both parties: Denikin's troops moving against Saratov would have eagerly executed members of either. Moreover, a classified report reveals that Bolshevik power in the countryside was so disdained that without the assistance of an armed detachment to combat desertion, the party would have lost the villages. While the document criticizes the populists' opposition to Bolshevik agrarian policies, it admits that the RCs' provincial committee habitually affirmed its loyalty to Soviet power,[55] as a result of which some Communists highly valued their populist allies.[56]

An agreement reached between the two party committees in Saratov in May 1919 allowed the Revolutionary Communists to carry out party work in the villages and garrison, and to participate in soviets at all levels. RCs and Bolsheviks would collaborate in sending out agitators to the districts, and the Bolshevik Party would fund RC Party work and publications. Periodically, the two parties would hold joint meetings. Revolutionary Communists would also report any subversive activities to the Cheka.[57] Yet the initiative to normalize and improve relations

[50] TsDNISO, f. 200, op. 1, d. 90, ll. 1–1 ob.

[51] Ibid., l. 8.

[52] RGASPI, f. 282, op. 2, d. 3, ll. 22–23. For Lenin's views see *Polnoe sobranie*, vol. 41, 56–57 and vol. 50, 120.

[53] TsDNISO, f. 151/95, op. 1, d. 48, ll. 17–20. See also RGASPI, f. 282, op. 1, d. 66, ll. 5–6 ob, and d. 1, l. 31.

[54] GASO, f. 456, op. 1, d. 48, l. 103, and TsDNISO, f. 151/95, op. 1, d. 48, l. 12.

[55] See, for example, TsDNISO, f. 151/95, op. 1, d. 55, l. 87.

[56] Ibid., f. 151/95, op. 3, d. 1, l. 12.

[57] Ibid., f. 151/95, op. 1, d. 50, l. 6, and d. 77, l. 16.

always came from the RCs.[58] Saratov Bolshevik leader Ivanov cautioned
his associates in the locales to be vigilant, for the "petit-bourgeois" (i.e.,
peasant) nature of the [RC] Party would eventually reveal itself in a
manner "similar to that of the earlier uprising of the Left SRs."[59] Bolshevik organizations in Volsk and Atkarsk soon invited the RCs to join
the provincial and city executive committees; however, some local Bolsheviks ignored the new line,[60] making it difficult for the RCs to organize cells.[61]

Even during the heyday of cooperation, the Bolshevik press often portrayed the RCs as a party of kulaks opposed to Soviet policies.[62] And, in
fact, RC activists in the villages frequently sided with the peasantry
against the Bolsheviks, promoting the slogans, "Down with the Bolsheviks! Long live Soviet power!" The evidence suggests a rift between
RC leaders in the towns and party activists in the villages, whose origins
can be found in the party's opposition to the kombedy and to the food
brigades that frequented the area. Revolutionary Communist sources
even claim that the party's rural cells at times comprised "kulak and
White Guard elements." Similarly, the Volsk organization declared that
fear of arrest owing to Bolshevik opposition to the party and the fear of
having "kulak and White Guard" elements predominate in their organizations hampered party work.[63]

The RCs' concern over arrest must not be dismissed.[64] Despite (as a
result of?) the "agreement" reached between the two parties in the
spring of 1919, cooperation with the Bolsheviks began to break down
as soon as the threat posed by the Whites receded,[65] especially in those
uezds where local Bolshevik leaders took pride in their revolutionary
pedigree, such as Petrovsk.[66] During the second half of 1919 the Revolutionary Communists denounced the Communists' efforts to curb the

---

[58] Shestak, *Bol'sheviki i levye techeniia*, 24 (quote) and 40–41, and Suslov, *Sotsialisticheskie partii*, 42.

[59] Sagrad'ian, "Iz istorii," 111.

[60] TsDNISO, f. 151/95, op. 3, d. 4, l. 1. See also ibid., f. 151/95, op. 2, d. 8, l. 5. For
Volsk see *Rabochii i krest'ianin*, no. 146, July 3, 1919, 2, and TsDNISO, f. 27, op. 1, d.
236, l. 3.

[61] TsDNISO, f. 151/95, op. 3, d. 1, l. 3; f. 151/95, op. 1, d. 53, l. 6; and *Izvestiia
Balashovskogo Ispolnitel'nogo komiteta*, no. 22, Jan. 31, 1919, 4.

[62] GASO, f. 521, op. 3, d. 15, ll. 8–9. See also *Rabochii i krest'ianin* (Volsk), no. 66,
March 25, 1920, 2.

[63] TsDNISO, f. 151/95, op. 1, d. 70, l. 1.

[64] See *Izvestiia Atkarskogo uispolkoma*, no. 234, June 26, 1919, 4; TsDNISO, f.
151/95, op. 3, d. 5, ll. 14–15; and op. 2, d. 42, l. 18.

[65] TsDNISO, f. 151/95, op. 1, d. 42, ll. 1–4. Also in *Znamia revoliutsii*, no. 2, Sept. 30,
1919, 3.

[66] TsDNISO, f. 151/95, op. 1, d. 52, ll. 91–93, and op. 1, d. 50, l. 31.

party's representation at local congresses,[67] complaining that the Bolsheviks did everything possible "to keep our representation to a minimum." The Bolsheviks also denied the RCs' request for proportional representation in the provincial executive committee, offering the party only two places. "Guided by the interests of the revolution . . . our fraction was forced to accept this," lamented one RC leader.[68] Not surprisingly, RCs from the villages and district centers, who had to battle the Bolsheviks constantly, expressed concern over the Saratov city committee's unequivocal support for the Communists.

The Revolutionary Communists sought to extract a price for their commitment to Soviet power, at times exaggerating the extent of Bolshevik antipathy.[69] In Atkarsk in June 1919 they demanded almost half the seats in the presidium selected at an uezd congress. This scenario was repeated in Novouzensk and in Petrovsk.[70] Further, whenever the RCs felt secure, they took up the peasant question, the real source of conflict with the Bolsheviks. At a congress of soviets in Volsk, Revolutionary Communists blasted Bolshevik land policies, calling upon the RC Party to carry out independent work and "to end the use of force against the peasants." RCs also denounced several Bolshevik candidates nominated to the Volsk Executive Committee, while RC delegates from the villages called for the election of members "who would seize the Bolsheviks by the throat."[71] Fearing the RCs' demands to raise fixed prices for grain would undermine the state's bread campaign, local Bolsheviks attacked their rivals with great hostility.[72]

In late 1919 and early 1920 a new period of repression against the RCs set in, perhaps owing to the growing factionalism within the Bolshevik Party, and to the confidence that came with victory over the Whites. The Saratov RC committee demanded explanations regarding the Cheka's arrest of party members in certain locales.[73] Relations soured in Serdobsk over the RCs' disagreements with Bolshevik economic policies.[74] Bolsheviks in Balashov's Ivanovskaia Volost disbanded the executive committee, seized its money, and arrested its members. During the episode the head of the police raped the wife of a local RC

[67] See *Znamia revoliutsii*, no. 1, Sept. 5, 1919, 1.

[68] TsDNISO, f. 151/95, op. 1, d. 43, ll. 7, 60. See also *Znamia revoliutsii*, no. 2, Sept. 30, 1919, 4.

[69] RGASPI, f. 282, op. 1, d. 45, l. 10.

[70] TsDNISO, f. 151/95, op. 1, d. 52, ll. 66–70, 91–99.

[71] Ibid., f. 151/95, op. 1, d. 53, l. 12.

[72] Ibid., f. 151/95, op. 1, d. 91, l. 2, and Suslov, *Sotsialisticheskie partii*, 78.

[73] For example, see TsDNISO, f. 151/95, op. 1, d. 55, ll. 16, 94, and f. 1328, op. 1, d. 43, l. 1.

[74] *Serp i molot*, no. 98 (382), May 15, 1920, 2.

leader. The Volsk RC committee contended that in 1920 "terror" had been unleashed against them as reports of illegal arrests emanated from the countryside. Atkarsk RCs also protested an array of transgressions.[75] Even though the mood in the villages had again turned against Bolshevik policies, RC leaders called upon party members not to take advantage of this, and instead to explain to the peasantry why it was in their own best interests to work for the Soviet cause. Maintaining that the only way out of the situation was the joining together of both Soviet parties, the RC organization favored "a rapprochement (*sblizhenie*) within the toiling population," satisfying its greatest needs, quick socialization of land and a struggle against "the caprice of local and central agents."[76]

The Extent of the Revolutionary Communists' Influence

The Communist Party's backing away from its extreme — and ineffectual — policies in the villages (particularly in regard to the kombedy) and Saratov's falling under siege in 1919 gave the Revolutionary Communists the opportunity to function legally as a "Soviet party," but not without undue harassment. Soon Revolutionary Communist Party organizations appeared everywhere radical populist elements traditionally had been found in Saratov Province. Soviet historians argued that outside Saratov it was rare to encounter strong RC groups at the uezd level; however, new research might revise this impression.[77] Before May 1919 an active district RC committee existed only in Atkarsk,[78] but at the time that Saratov fell under siege, party organizations existed in five uezds and RCs could be found in four uezd executive committees. Moreover, the party set up an oblast bureau joining party organizations in nine neighboring provinces.[79]

The sources do not reveal the numerical strength of the Revolutionary Communists, because party enrollments remained in flux, frequent mobilizations depleted local committees, and local party cells bitterly protested Bolshevik repression, often refusing to provide information about themselves. I counted 355 and 758 members/sympathizers for

---

[75] RGASPI, f. 282, op. 2, d. 12, ll. 24 ob–26; d. 21, l. 15; TsDNISO, f. 151/95, op. 2, d. 42, l. 9; and op. 3, d. 15, ll. 11, 22.

[76] TsDNISO, f. 151/95, op. 3, d. 14, l. 12.

[77] For an incomplete list of RC organizations elsewhere in Russia, see TsDNISO, f. 151/95, op. 1, d. 21, ll. 1–1 ob.

[78] *Znamia revoliutsii*, no. 2, Sept. 30, 1919, 3.

[79] RGASPI, f. 282, op. 1, d. 45, ll. 30–30 ob.

1918 in the Volsk and Atkarsk organizations respectively,[80] figures that raise serious doubts about statistics Soviet historians adduced on the size of RC organizations.[81] In late 1919 there were 1,432 party members and sympathizers in five districts of Saratov Province. Suslov has recently challenged the notion that membership had begun to decline already in the second half of 1919, arguing that the party could still dictate its policies in these uezds.[82]

Who joined the party? At the national level, 77 percent of the party's membership consisted of peasants, and 11 percent, workers, while former Left SRs made up the party's national leadership. The Bolsheviks took advantage of such information to expose the "class" nature of the RCs, thereby dismissing their programs and actions, and justifying the Communists' own tactics in regard to their questionable allies. Military service among party members was almost universal, suggesting the extent to which the party comprised younger males and to which military service served as a school for radicalism — as it did for the Bolsheviks.[83] Data on the composition of the Saratov city organization indicate it would be a distortion to describe the RCs merely as an offshoot of the Left SRs, although this appears to have been the case in the districts.[84]

The party's strength remained in the districts, where at the end of 1919, they were well represented in the Atkarsk, Serdobsk, Balashov, and Kuznetsk executive committees. They also fared well in elections to congresses of soviets in some uezds.[85] New members continued to join the party and new cells formed (and collapsed) throughout the party's existence, well into 1920.[86] As of February 1, 1920, there were twenty-three active party cells in Atkarsk Uezd with about 100 members and 700 sympathizers. Eight of the cells had been founded in 1918, eight in 1919, and seven in 1920. The oldest were the largest.[87] New cells appeared in Volsk villages in 1920 as well.[88] While the RCs may not have represented "a serious force at the national level," a confidential report

---

[80] TsDNISO, f. 151/95, op. 1, d. 35, ll. 1–53.

[81] Shestak, *Bol'sheviki i levye techeniia*, 33; Spirina, *Krakh*, 202; and Sagrad'ian, "Iz istorii," 110.

[82] RGASPI, f. 282, d. 2, ll. 72–73, 84, 90–91, and Suslov, *Sotsialisticheskie partii*, 38, 79.

[83] Shestak, *Bol'sheviki i levye techeniia*, 21; on military service see TsDNISO, f. 151/95, op. 2, d. 22.

[84] TsDNISO, f. 151/95, op. 1, d. 34, ll. 1–27.

[85] Sagrad'ian, "Iz istorii," 113; see also TsDNISO, f. 151/95, op. 1, d. 61, and op. 1, d. 97.

[86] TsDNISO, f. 151/95, op. 2, d. 40, l. 3.

[87] Ibid., f. 151/95, op. 1, d. 102, l. 1.

[88] Ibid., f. 151/95, op. 1, d. 97, l. 7.

from mid-1920 fears their strength in Saratov Province, especially in Saratov, Atkarsk, and Volsk.[89]

The Revolutionary Communists in Atkarsk

The Revolutionary Communists enjoyed their greatest support in At-karsk District, where the vulnerable Bolsheviks prevented RCs from entering the presidium of a congress of soviets in November 1918.[90] As we have seen, the Atkarsk Bolshevik organization declared the RC Party organization illegal, but the latter reacted bitterly, taking its case to the All-Russian Central Executive Committee.[91] When Denikin's forces placed Saratov under siege and the Communists sought accommodation with the "peasant Bolsheviks," the RCs fared better at local congresses.[92] However, the RCs most likely were underrepresented: the local organization boasted 800 members already in 1918, approximately the size of the Bolshevik organization a year later.[93]

Sources confirm the revival in Revolutionary Communist Party fortunes, but also that the Atkarsk Bolsheviks once again adopted a hard line toward their populist rivals.[94] An Atkarsk Bolshevik in August 1919 insisted the RCs were "nothing more and nothing less than a blockhead with eyes." Emphasizing the RCs' "lack of ideas," he acknowledged that the party "is needed by us until it fulfills all of our orders. When it stops fulfilling them, we'll throw them out on their ears."[95] In September the Atkarsk RC committee informed Saratov that "relations with the Bolsheviks were becoming worse and worse," in part owing to the Revolutionary Communists' uncovering of abuses in the local soviet.[96] Protesting the mean-spirited behavior of the "dishonest" local Bolsheviks, their arbitrary policies in the countryside, and the arrest of party members purportedly for no reason at all,[97] RCs refused to reveal the location of its party cells in the countryside or how many members

[89] Ibid., f. 151/95, op. 1, d. 83, ll. 2–3.

[90] Ibid., f. 151/95, op. 1, d. 32, l. 3.

[91] Ibid., f. 200, op. 1, d. 92, l. 1, and Antonov-Saratovskii, *Sovety*, 2: 424–25.

[92] *Izvestiia Atkarskogo Ispolnitel'nogo komiteta*, no. 238, July 1, 1919, 3, and no. 297, Sept.10, 1919, 3.

[93] That is, after "party week." TsDNISO, f. 200, op. 1, d. 43, l. 23.

[94] Ibid., f. 200, op. 1, d. 45, l. 111, and f. 27, op. 1, d. 18, l. 31.

[95] Ibid., f. 27, op. 1, d. 227, l. 45.

[96] Ibid., f. 151/95, op. 1, d. 48, l. 14; RGASPI, f. 282, op. 2, d. 12, l. 21. See also ll. 24 ob–26.

[97] GA RF, f. 9591, op. 1, d. 67 (the entire delo), and TsDNISO, f. 151/95, op. 2, d. 4, l. 48.

the party had.[98] The two parties continued to clash at congresses of soviets, when Bolsheviks ignored calls for proportional representation.[99] The RC uezd committee complained to the Center that "persecution . . . is constant." It insisted that elections to the village and volost soviets had been carried out under dubious circumstances, that Bolsheviks assailed them in the press and sought to limit their support at local congresses, and that the Cheka turned a blind eye to corruption, instead focusing its efforts on attacking the Revolutionary Communists.[100] Repression accounts for the RCs' poor showing at local congresses at the start of 1920, when they complained to Moscow about the Atkarsk Cheka's capricious encroachment upon them.[101]

In connection with serious internal threats to Soviet power and the Bolsheviks' need to compromise once again in mid-1920, the RCs' fortunes improved; they now accounted for a full third of the members of the local executive committee, and their deputies constituted almost half of those sent to a congress of soviets in Saratov, which the RCs' P. F. Sapozhnikov chaired.[102] With the "brilliant" victories of the Red Army, there was widespread belief among RCs that a period of peaceful development would begin, which would enable them to influence Bolshevik policies in the villages.[103] But complaints continued to be lodged regarding police harassment and Bolshevik attempts to discredit the RCs as "counterrevolutionary" and even "criminal" elements.[104] In August 1920 RCs demanded the Bolsheviks provide proof for their accusations that the RCs plotted to overthrow Soviet power, organized kulak elements in the countryside, and participated in other traitorous behavior.[105] Expressing their support for Soviet power, Atkarsk RCs insisted that they were not about to merge with other populist groups.[106]

The weakness of the Bolshevik Party in Atkarsk undoubtedly accounts for its hostility toward the Revolutionary Communists. If the Atkarsk Communist Party Organization continued to grow during 1920, many were "paper" Communists whose work in the countryside

[98] RGASPI, f. 282, op. 2, d. 21, l. 16; TsDNISO, f. 200, op. 1, d. 87, l. 14; and f. 151/95, op. 2, d. 30, l. 35.

[99] TsDNISO, f. 200, op. 1, d. 45, l. 103, and f. 151/95, op. 2, d. 30, ll. 4–4 ob, 10.

[100] Ibid., f. 27, op. 1, d. 634, ll. 103–4.

[101] Ibid., f. 27, op. 1, d. 635, l. 18.

[102] *Izvestiia Atkarskogo Soveta*, no. 30, Feb. 10, 1920, 1, and *Izvestiia Atkarskogo Ispolnitel'nogo komiteta*, no. 240, July 3, 1920, 4.

[103] RGASPI, f. 282, op. 2, d. 25, ll. 10–10 ob.

[104] For example, see TsDNISO, f. 151/95, op. 2, d. 41, l. 5; op. 2, d. 31, l. 3; op. 2, d. 32, l. 69; f. 200, op. 1, d. 204, ll. 8–9; f. 27, op. 1, d. 635, l. 1; RGASPI, f. 282, op. 1, d. 1, l. 32 ob; and d. 66, ll. 4, 8.

[105] TsDNISO, f. 151/95, op. 2, d. 33, l. 24.

[106] RGASPI, f. 282, op. 2, d. 46, ll. 8–9.

was deemed "very poor." Local Communists functioned without coordination. They bickered, lacked "consciousness,"[107] and faced a hostile peasantry whose attitudes toward Soviet power "were not particularly good."[108] The newly elected uezdkom began functioning in conditions marked by a "complete breakdown" of Soviet institutions and party organizations.[109]

In hindsight it appears that the improvement in RC fortunes in mid-1920 had much to do with their criticism of the SRs and Mensheviks,[110] and perhaps with the Cheka's manipulation of the situation. That October the local organization ratified the decision made at a national conference to join with the Bolsheviks into a single party.[111] Yet this did little to fortify Soviet power locally.[112]

Problems from Within

Serious problems beset the party from the onset, which had much to do with a confused identity and with serious disagreement over how to reconcile pronounced support for Soviet power with the peasantry's open hostility to specific Bolshevik policies. Shortly after Left SR renegades formed the Revolutionary Communist Party, five members of its Central Committee joined the Communists. Saratov RCs responded by insisting the party must endure *until it convinced the Bolsheviks to accept the entire class of toiling peasantry as an active participant in the building of socialism.*[113] But at the local level, too, some of the party's founding members switched allegiance to the Bolsheviks.[114] RCs continued to withdraw from the party, usually to become Bolsheviks, until the party merged with the Communist Party at the end of 1920. As a legal party, the RCs were also liable for mobilizations; during the summer of 1919 participation in such campaigns depleted the party's ranks and resulted in the collapse of local groups.[115] Moreover, the existence of two parties whose official names contained the word "Communist" bred so much confusion in Saratov Province that some Communists began calling themselves Bolsheviks once again.[116]

[107] TsDNISO, f. 200, op. 1, d. 126, ll. 1, 2 ob, 3.
[108] Ibid., f. 200, op. 1, d. 126, ll. 6–6 ob.
[109] Ibid., f. 200, op. 1, d. 135, l. 2.
[110] RGASPI, f. 282, op. 2, d. 25, l. 19, and d. 24, l. 15.
[111] TsDNISO, f. 200, op. 1, d. 126, l. 37.
[112] Ibid., f. 200, op. 1, d. 279, ll. 25–32.
[113] Ibid., f. 151/95, op. 1, d. 32, l. 1.
[114] See GA RF, f. 393, op. 3, d. 330, l. 57, and TsDNISO, f. 151/95, op. 1, d. 17, l. 8.
[115] See, for instance, TsDNISO, f. 151/95, op. 1, d. 98, ll. 4–4 ob.
[116] Sagrad'ian, "Iz istorii," 121.

Other problems plagued the RCs too. Party members ignored instructions, claiming lack of time because of their involvement in Soviet work, or disregarding being summoned by the Red Army.[117] Party members also refused to participate in village and volost soviets, observing that there was no one to tend their fields.[118] Some RCs got into trouble for hiding deserters.[119] The RCs likewise suffered from a decentralized organizational structure, which enabled local leaders to interpret general policies as they saw fit. The Bolsheviks observed strains within the local RC leadership and a decline in Sapozhnikov's authority.[120]

The most serious dilemma facing the RC Party, however, concerned its relationship with other populist groups, for the party's success during the second half of 1919 along with the Bolsheviks' vulnerability promoted dialogue among radical populist groups regarding merger. Four of the nine members of the RC Party's Central Committee who backed the union of all revolutionary socialist populist parties into a new party, the Revolutionary Socialist Party, were expelled from the committee.[121] Ustinov vehemently opposed union, arguing that a new party of this sort would turn into a third, anti-Bolshevik force. Insisting that the Revolution's development would compel populist groups eventually to adopt the RCs' program, the party majority eschewed any compromise platform in order to preserve the class and revolutionary nature of its program and draw others to it.[122] At a Revolutionary Communist congress in October 1919, the majority of delegates shot down proposals to unite with other populists, but only after some protested that force had been used to prevent delegates from attending who supported an anti-Ustinov, pro-merger point of view.[123] Following the congress, the Central Committee minority continued the dialogue on merger.[124] Although most local organizations opposed union, the Moscow and Penza committees backed the idea. RCs in Volsk reiterated that only the Bolsheviks and RCs represented real *revolutionary* parties, while their Atkarsk comrades likewise affirmed that they shared com-

---

[117] TsDNISO, f. 151/95, op. 1, d. 49, l. 47; op. 3, d. 4, l. 39; TsDNISO, f. 151/95, op. 1, d. 108, l. 1; and RGASPI, f. 282, op. 2, d. 3, l. 78.

[118] For example, see TsDNISO, f. 151/95, op. 2, d. 33, l. 19; op. 2, d. 33, l. 3; and op. 1, d. 93, l. 7.

[119] Ibid., f. 151/95, op. 2, d. 32, l. 54.

[120] Antonov-Saratovskii, *Sovety*, 2: 46–47. See also TsDNISO, f. 27, op. 1, d. 491, l. 149.

[121] TsDNISO, f. 151/95, op. 1, d. 67, l. 2; f. 151/95, op. 1, d. 47, l. 5, and RGASPI, f. 282, op. 2, d. 3, l. 94.

[122] TsDNISO, f. 151/95, op. 1, d. 47, l. 11. Some RCs supported the idea of the party's merging with other left populist groups. See op. 1, d. 60, l. 1.

[123] Ibid., f. 151/95, op. 1, d. 47, l. 9.

[124] Ibid., f. 151/95, op. 1, d. 67, l. 9.

mon ideals with the Bolsheviks.[125] But the fact that discussions about merger were held makes clear why Communists feared the Revolutionary Communists might one day link with other populist groups.

The merger that eventually came was of an altogether different sort, for serious ruptures within the party surfaced at its Fifth Party Congress in the spring of 1920. Struggling to sort out the historical process as it unfolded, the RCs' Sapozhnikov and Ustinov now took giant steps toward acknowledging the Bolsheviks' narrative of the Revolution. The party's acceptance of the authority of the new Third Communist International, and the Bolshevik victory over the Whites, provided the context that compelled both theorists to break with some long-held populist principles. Sapozhnikov now admitted the leading role of the proletariat in relation to other social groups. Seeking to explain why social revolution had taken place in "backward" Russia, he convinced himself that the dictatorship of the proletariat had evolved *logically*, that opposition to it was *reactionary*, and that it would *eventually* establish a dictatorship of *all* toilers. Similarly, Ustinov came to accept the historical necessity of the dictatorship of the proletariat, maintaining there was no longer a need for loyal opposition parties. Arguing as he had before that the proletarian state could serve as the basis for the eventual implementation of the populist ideal, he called upon his critics to put an end to their beliefs (now prejudices), which history had shown to be wrong.[126] Disbanding the congress despite the wishes of the majority, the party Central Committee clearly stood at a crossroads.[127]

Given the Central Committee's stand during the Fifth Congress, subsequent developments come as no surprise. The Second Comintern Congress in July 1920 ruled that only one Communist Party in each country could be represented in the Comintern. Attending the congress, Ustinov and Sapozhnikov declared their readiness to subordinate the party to the decisions of the Communist International. The RC Central Committee then issued a secret declaration to the Comintern, stating the party's willingness to march in a single revolutionary front with the Bolsheviks. It also spelled out the disagreements, based on theoretical differences, that had prevented union in the past, including the nature of the historical process, the character of the class struggle, the class basis of the socialist revolution, and the organization of power.[128] The Sixth Congress of the Revolutionary Communist Party in late September 1920

[125] The situation in Volsk is discussed in ibid., f. 151/95, op. 3, d. 4, l. 34; for Atkarsk, see op. 2, d. 32, l. 16.

[126] Spirina, *Krakh*, 196–200, and Shestak, *Bol'sheviki i levye tendentsii*, 28.

[127] TsDNISO, f. 151/95, op. 1, d. 102, l. 7, and f. 151/95, op. 3, d. 13, l. 12.

[128] Ibid., f. 151/95, op. 1, d. 87, l. 29, and f. 200, op. 1, d. 90, l. 33.

resolved to merge with the Bolsheviks. Monitoring these developments, the Cheka promoted the rift that had been growing within the RC Party in regard to merger.[129]

In seeing the writing on the wall, Saratov RC leaders such as Sapozhnikov had sought to rationalize the movement toward merger by drawing on the party's intellectual heritage. Once the decision had been taken to form a united Communist Party, local organizations complied.[130] For example, the Saratov Uezd organization accepted the Comintern decision, but only 18 of the organization's 160 members joined the Communists.[131] The chair of the Atkarsk RC committee remarked that owing to the strained relations with the Bolsheviks, the RCs had no choice but to merge. He hoped such a merger would curb the arbitrariness of local officials and improve Soviet rule. Others justified their behavior by insisting they had no time to think of personal convictions when there was such a need to struggle with the world bourgeoisie.[132]

The Communists' Relations with the Other Socialist Parties

The Bolsheviks proved to be much less accommodating to the other parties composing the potential "third force." After the formation of the Revolutionary Communist Party, the Left SRs no longer played a pivotal role in Saratov Province. Although Saratov Bolsheviks often viewed the RCs as Left SRs, the Cheka knew the difference and reported that no Left SR organizations existed locally in April 1920. A few months later, however, the political police legalized Left SR groups that supported Soviet power in towns where they could be kept under surveillance. When the Cheka identified Left SRs in Balashov who opposed Soviet power, its fear that all populist groups would merge only deepened.[133]

Offering a program that appealed to Russia's peasant majority, the Right SRs posed a threat to Soviet power throughout the Civil War, but because the party remained in the underground for most of the period, few documents shed light on its attempts to restore the Constituent Assembly. The elliptical sources offer only an incomplete mosaic of party life in the underground. For example, in 1918 poet Victor Shklovskii, an SR, took part in plans to overthrow Soviet power both in Saratov and in "small, single-storied" Atkarsk, where the waiter in a Soviet-run

---

[129] Ibid., f. 151/95, op. 1, d. 83, ll. 2–3.

[130] Ibid., f. 151/95, op. 1, d. 110, ll. 1, 3.

[131] Ibid., f. 151/95, op. 3, d. 13, l. 18, and *Materialy k 9-i uezdnoi konferentsii*, 6.

[132] RGASPI, f. 282, op. 1, d. 47, ll. 23–23 ob, and d. 23, ll. 1, 5, 6.

[133] GASO, f. 3310, op. 1, d. 1, ll. 1, 124 ob, and TsDNISO, f. 151/95, op. 1, d. 83, l. 2.

cafeteria "had not washed since the start of the imperialist war."[134] The Cheka documented the plans for an uprising and also the party's role in the May 1918 rebellion in Saratov, connecting local groups to party organizations in Moscow and Petrograd.[135]

In the aftermath of the May 1918 Saratov rebellion and the Ural Cossacks' temporary ejection of the Bolsheviks from the Urals, the SR Central Committee began planning a large-scale revolt against Bolshevik rule. Samara, located up the Volga from Saratov, temporarily became the center of the SRs' activities. Once the Whites threatened to take the Volga region, disconcerted SR Party leaders agreed in February 1919 to compromise with the Communists and briefly published, legally, their party organ, *Delo naroda* (The People's Affair). Although this period of cooperation proved to be short-lived, a minority group formed the Narod Party, which urged the SRs to recognize the temporary necessity of the dictatorship of the proletariat and to join the Red Army. Saratov Province's N. I. Rakitnikov, who had served as deputy minister of agriculture in the Provisional Government in 1917, belonged to the Narod Party, which now backed Soviet power.[136] But the Communist Party's Central Committee remained suspicious of the populists' earlier campaign on behalf of "soviets without Communists," directing local organizations to monitor all SR materials.

Indeed, the SRs stepped up their activities against the Bolsheviks in 1920 after the White threat receded; an underground Volga oblast committee issued leaflets and carried out party agitation, much to the chagrin of the local Cheka, which failed to infiltrate the committee. Urging workers not to take part in the Bolsheviks' "pseudo workers' organizations" and to be prepared to rise up against oppression, the underground Volga SR committee denounced the violence, repression, and arrests associated with Soviet power.[137] When the Bolsheviks took reprisals against workers from the Zhest plant for failing to participate in the May Day activities in 1920, the SRs came to the workers' defense, castigating the Bolsheviks' use of "force and deceit." The SRs also criticized populist splinter groups such as Narod for accommodating Soviet power.[138]

In mid-1920, the Cheka believed the SRs represented the single great-

---

[134] V. Shklovskii, *Sentimental'noe puteshestvie: Vospominaniia, 1917–1922* (Moscow, 1923), 208–11, 215.

[135] Shabanov and Makarov, *Gubcheka*, 74–81.

[136] See *ISS*, no. 260, Nov. 22, 1919, 2; *Krasnyi pakhar'* (Balashov), no. 231, Nov. 22, 1919, 1; and Brovkin *Behind the Front Lines*, 181–84.

[137] GASO, f. 3310, op. 1, d. 1, ll. 1, 124 ob, and RGASPI, f. 274, op. 1, d. 18, ll. 24–25.

[138] RGASPI, f. 274, op. 1, d. 18, ll. 26–26 ob, 28–28 ob. Also, GASO, f. 3310, op. 1, d. 1, l. 138.

est threat to Soviet power, fearing that Left SRs, RCs, and other populist groups would rejoin the "parent" organization to form a potent challenge to the Communist order. The SRs' platform offered an attractive alternative to that of the Communists. The SRs opposed labor conscription and grain requisitioning, disseminating literature that called for the establishment of peasant unions, whose purpose was to reject Communism. Leaflets issued by the regional SR committee demanded political equality for all citizens, an end to civil war, the right to the fruits of one's labor, restoration of the Constituent Assembly, and creation of volunteer units that would sweep the Communists from power.[139] Because of the SR danger, the Communist Party now denied them legal status and the right to participate in the soviets. At this time the Saratov Cheka legalized (but not in the uezd towns) the so-called Minority SRs, who recognized Soviet power. The Cheka intended to manipulate the group in order to have it clash with SRs and RCs.[140] Following a conference in September, SR leaders gravitated to Saratov, where they agitated against Soviet power. The political turmoil of March 1921 discussed in chapter 12 indicates the party met with success in these endeavors. Monitoring SR activities following the revolt, the Cheka arrested thirteen party leaders. Others fled the province.[141]

In banning the SR Party in June 1922 the Communist Party orchestrated the "Trial of the Right SRs," indicting the party for planning uprisings in Saratov Province in 1918 and for most other manifestations of discontent with Soviet power. The local press repeated the accusations in detail.[142] Despite the ensuing repression, a Saratov SR Party organization managed to put out at least one issue of a handwritten newspaper, *Delo Povolzh'ia* (The Volga Area Affair), which denied the allegations made at the show trial.[143] The coup de grace came the next summer when the Soviet government liquidated SR party organizations in Saratov Province.[144]

It is difficult to measure SR — and Menshevik — influence during the

---

[139] GASO, f. 521, op. 5, d. 11, ll. 13, 24–25 ob. Some representative SR brochures are Partiia sotsialistov-revoliutsionerov, *Mirskoi prigovor* (n.p., 1921) and *Chto dali bol'sheviki narodu* (n.p., 1921). The SRs later deemphasized the political character of the Green movement. See *Kak Tambovskie krest'iane boriatsiia za svobodu* (n.p., 1921), 11.

[140] TsDNISO, f. 151/95, op. 1, d. 83, ll. 2–3.

[141] GASO, f. 521, op. 1, d. 718, l. 58, d. 11, l. 41.

[142] N. V. Krylenko, *Za piat' let: 1918–1922 gg. Obvinitel'nye rechi po naibolee krupnym protsessam, zaslushannym v Moskovskom i verkhovnom revoliutsionnykh tribunalakh* (Moscow, 1923), 91, 132, 157; *ISS*, no. 129, June 10, 1922, 1; no. 132, June 14, 1922, 1; and *Sovetskaia derevnia*, no. 132, July 2, 1922, 2l. See also GASO, f. 3586, op. 1, d. 56, ll. 1–5, and TsDNISO, f. 44, op. 1, d. 3, l. 36.

[143] *Delo Povolzh'ia*, no. 1, Sept. 1922.

[144] TsDNISO, f. 151/95, op. 1, d. 116, ll. 3–6.

Civil War because of the ever-changing nature of the parties' relations with the Communists, which put them at times in the opposition, and at other times legalized their activities. Another reason is that many SRs and Mensheviks hid under the "nonparty" or unaffiliated rubric. This category often included the majority of deputies at local congresses in 1919 and 1920. As nonparty delegates or deputies they could question Bolshevik practices and present the views of hostile peasants or workers.[145] The number of complaints of this sort rose in 1920.[146] Be that as it may, the sources also suggest that a legitimate "nonparty" category was emerging, which had much to do with growing estrangement from the state.[147]

Although the Mensheviks fared poorly in local elections to the Constituent Assembly, they made something of a comeback among Saratov workers in the spring of 1918, for which the Bolsheviks expelled them from the soviet. Afterward, the party never became a mass phenomenon, yet it continued to pose a threat to Bolshevik rule, in part because the Mensheviks also offered a rival interpretation of the Revolution that often made more sense than the Communists' version. Viewing the October 1917 events as a stage in the bourgeois-democratic revolution, the Menshevik Party refused to take part in an armed struggle against the Bolsheviks, but found their neutrality difficult to sustain when the White threat intensified. Saratov Mensheviks remained divided over this issue in 1918, although the Right faction prevailed locally. The Bolsheviks became more tolerant of their Marxist rivals when the Mensheviks dropped their demand for restoration of the Constituent Assembly in October 1918, and when the outbreak of revolution in Germany convinced some Mensheviks that the Bolsheviks' understanding of the present contained some merit. The Bolsheviks now tolerated them but kept them under constant surveillance and often placed obstacles in their path. Saratov Communists, for instance, refused to circulate Menshevik newspapers in February 1919 after the party was temporarily legalized, and in April they arrested their Social Democratic comrades, an act that prompted the chair of the local committee, E. Abramovich, to inquire whether the party's legal status had been revoked.[148] The Mensheviks issued manifestoes against the Whites in mid-1919, while agitating on behalf of universal suffrage, free elections, freedom of the

---

[145] See, for example, GA RF, f. 393, op. 3, d. 331, ll. 19–19 ob; *Izvestiia Atkarskogo Ispolnitel'nogo komiteta*, no. 277, Aug. 15, 1919, 3; and GASO, f. 456, op. 1, d. 206, ll. 1, 3 ob, 4, 6, 8.

[146] *Izvestiia Khvalynskogo Soveta*, no. 169, Aug. 1, 1920, 1; also *Izvestiia Atkarskogo Soveta*, no. 29, Feb. 8, 1920, 1.

[147] Ransome, *Crisis in Russia*, 179.

[148] TsDNISO, f. 27, op. 1, d. 32, l. 7, and f. 151/95, op. 1, d. 50, l. 2.

press, and an end to the arbitrary actions of the Cheka.[149] As a result, the Communists insisted that the Mensheviks abetted the White cause and Allied intervention, arguing that the Menshevik press's silence about White terror facilitated it.[150]

Menshevik as well as anarchist activities took on new vigor at the end of 1919 as the groups engaged local Communists in public debate.[151] Several months later Mensheviks urged workers not to vote for Communists in local elections and agitated against labor conscription. The Cheka arrested a Menshevik named Naletov, who tried to sabotage a general citywide conference of workers and soldiers. Although no party organization existed at this time, individual Mensheviks protested against labor conscription in Saratov factories, often presenting themselves as unaffiliated workers. They enjoyed popularity among printers, whose union elected a Menshevik majority.

In early 1920 a local Menshevik Party organization emerged in Saratov, which ignored rulings of its central committee in adopting a policy of neutrality in regard to the Communists, and in calling upon like-minded party members elsewhere to join it. For this transgression the party's central committee expelled the Saratov organization in May.[152] Yet many Mensheviks shared the point of view of their Saratov comrades. Denouncing bureaucratic rule and utopian tendencies in the Communists' economic policy, the Mensheviks claimed they were not undermining Soviet power but merely seeking influence over the working class. Given the far-reaching opposition to Bolshevik rule, the Mensheviks believed the Bolsheviks would be compelled to co-opt the Menshevik/SR program or face certain defeat.[153] After the downfall of Denikin, however, the Communists no longer saw a need to court Menshevik support and responded accordingly.[154] The Cheka crackdown intensified following disturbances in Saratov in March 1921, when the Bolsheviks co-opted an initiative group charged with liq-

---

[149] The Menshevik Party remained divided. See Nicolaevsky Collection, RSDRP, box 2, folder 3, "Proekt osnovnykh platform." The Saratov Cheka ignored an amnesty declared in conjunction with the anniversary of the Revolution back in November. See Brovkin, *Dear Comrades,* 141.

[150] I. Vardin, *Protiv men'shevizma (RSDRP men'shevikov v revoliutsii)* (Moscow, 1924), 15, 36, 43.

[151] See, for example, *ISS,* no. 4, Jan. 6, 1920, 2, and no. 7, Jan. 11, 1920, 4.

[152] GASO, f. 3310, op. 1, d. 1, ll. 1–4, 7, 124, 137, 146.

[153] Nicolaevsky Collection, RSDRP, box 2, folder 5 ("Taktika RSDRP v Sovetskoi Rossii, priniata TsK 13 iiulia 1920 g.").

[154] L. I. Merzliakov, "Bol'sheviki i sotsialisticheskie partii v gody grazhdanskoi voiny," *Problemy politologii i politicheskoi istorii: Mezhvuzovskii sbornik nauchnykh trudov,* no. 3 (Saratov, 1994): 41.

uidating the local Menshevik organization.[155] A similar fate befell the Bund and Zionist groups that the Cheka had also kept under careful surveillance.[156]

As we saw in chapter 2, anarchist groups raised their head in Saratov in early 1918.[157] Later, at the end of 1919, Moscow anarchists appeared in town, where they joined together local groups in the Union of Anarchist-Syndicalists of Saratov, formed a club, opened a cafeteria and library, and debated Communists. Some anarchists called upon workers to boycott Communist Party membership drives, while others advocated the overthrow of Soviet power. As a result, the Cheka began to monitor anarchist activities more closely, especially among soldiers. In intercepting soldiers' correspondence, the Cheka learned that anarchist agitation against Soviet power and against the Civil War had struck a responsive chord: soldiers viewed the Communists as usurpers. Anarchist promises to put an end to combat appealed to local peasants, who began to bring their young sons to Saratov to join the anarchists, thinking they could thereby avoid the draft. Reading the soldiers' mail convinced the Cheka that the anarchists were preparing to strike against Soviet power in February 1920, that it was impossible to differentiate between loyal and anti-Soviet anarchists, and that a network of organizations functioned at the provincial level. Thus the Cheka was ready to pounce when anarchists sponsored a well-attended public meeting on February 26, at which speeches rang out against Soviet power and rumors spread about an anarchist uprising in Moscow. Detaining over one hundred people, the Cheka arrested all registered anarchists in town. In the Cheka's estimation, agitation among army units had assumed "colossal" proportions and local Communists were foolish for giving the "parasites," "criminals," "deserters," and "speculators" so much space in which to agitate against mobilization, labor conscription, and Soviet power.[158] In mid-1920 the local press carried coverage of a trial of eighteen local anarchists, one of whom was sentenced to death (the others were imprisoned or sent to the front).[159] Afterward the

---

[155] Vardin, *Protiv men'shevizma*, 48, 61; *Otchet Saratovskogo gubkoma*, 4; GASO, f. 521, op. 5, d. 11, l. 41; and TsDNISO, f. 151/95, op. 1, d. 118, l. 2, d. 117, ll. 12–15. For reports of terror against the Menshevik Party see Nicolaevsky Collection, RSDRP, box 22, folder 8, "Soveshchanie RSDRP."

[156] TsDNISO, f. 151/95, op. 1, d. 111, ll. 16, 17. For the Zionists see ibid., f. 3310, op. 1, d. 1, ll. 11, 124 ob.

[157] GASO, f. 1280, op. 1, d. 2920, l. 1, and d. 2922.

[158] RGASPI, f. 17, op. 12, d. 469, ll. 105–6; GASO, f. 3310, op. 1, d. 1, ll. 11, 19–25; and TsDNISO, f. 151/95, op. 1, d. 54, l. 10a.

[159] *ISS*, no. 133, June 17, 1920, 3, and no. 135, June 19, 1920, 3.

Cheka prevented an active organization from emerging; however, individual anarchists continued to agitate against the Communists.[160]

Following the March 1921 disturbances and the transition to the NEP, the Cheka repressed all other socialist parties, co-opting some of their members. In 1923 the local Menshevik and Bund organizations and the SRs liquidated themselves, as some of their members joined the Communists.[161] The purpose of these public rituals, of course, was to suggest an artificial unity in order to dilute further opposition.

Conclusion

Based on this investigation of the Revolutionary Communists in Saratov Province, it is hard to accept the assessment that the party was "little" and "exercised no political influence."[162] To repeat, the party's sustained commitment to Soviet power proved a decisive factor in keeping the province from falling to the Whites as a result of a rejection of Soviet power from within. This observation above all holds true for mid-1919, when Saratov came closest to shaking off Bolshevik power. Although critical of specific Bolshevik policies, the RCs did not back away from their conviction that all other considerations had to be subordinated to the survival of Soviet power. This tactical stance held sway over most party members, making Bolshevik policies more or less acceptable, especially when their brunt was softened by local activists and rank-and-file party members, or conveniently ignored when necessary or when possible. Under the spell of vague images of a utopian future, RC leaders prided themselves in their party's revolutionary pedigree and acceptance of revolutionary change.

The RCs did not cooperate with the Bolsheviks merely because they wanted to save their party from collapse, but because they believed that they ultimately could persuade the Bolsheviks to change their ways. As a result, the RC Party fought to preserve and strengthen its influence over the peasantry—and thereby over the Communists. The Bolsheviks' attitude toward the other socialist parties, however, reflected the overall strength of Soviet power at any given time; the evidence adduced here reinforces Anweiler's assertion that "in crises the loyalty or conditional support of these groups was valued, but when danger diminished, they were ignored."[163] Thus, each partner brought an element of insincerity

[160] GASO, f. 3310, op. 1, d. 1, ll. 124 ob, 168.
[161] TsDNISO, f. 151/95, op. 1, d. 117, ll. 12 ob–15, and d. 118, ll. 1, 2, 7. For the Bund see op. 1, d. 111, ll. 16, 17. For the SRs see f. 151/95, op. 1, d. 116, ll. 3–6.
[162] Schapiro, *Origins*, 180, 181.
[163] Anweiler, *The Soviets*, 231–32.

into the relationship, and this is especially true of the Communists. While the Communists "used" the Revolutionary Communists, it was not without some acquiescence on the part of the RCs. They criticized the Bolsheviks on many counts and, as a result, the relationship between the two parties had an inherent tension, the mirror image of which was the need each had for the other, especially when faced with military threat from White forces.

Let's return to the notion that societies not only predetermine how their subjects rebel against constraints but also co-opt strategies of dissent. Ironically, and perhaps because the Bolshevik hold on power remained precarious throughout the Civil War, the process of co-optation between them and their populist ally remained a two-way street. In seeking to marginalize and repress this other revolutionary voice, the Bolsheviks found themselves locked in a dialogue with the very Revolutionary Communists they sought to discredit. (In some respects it is paradoxical that the word co-optation assigns negative values, for the very success it implies in persuading others is usually considered desirable.[164]) From the time of the RCs' crystallization from radical populism, the party saw its main purpose as the need to convince the Communists to broaden their narrow dictatorship of the proletariat to include all the toiling masses. The Bolsheviks' change of heart in regard to the middle peasants in March 1919 (co-optation of their opponents' criticism?) convinced the RCs that they were beginning to influence their Bolshevik comrades. Yet by the time the military confrontations drew to a close and the Bolshevik leadership faced the prospects of rebuilding a ravaged country, the RCs had even less cause to break with the Bolsheviks over measures the former found disagreeable and the latter claimed were necessitated by circumstances. The Bolsheviks had fared well in the discursive struggle among those who remained committed to Soviet power (and at times won over the support of the mainstream SRs and Mensheviks as well). This is especially true because some Revolutionary Communists from the start had accepted an important part of the Bolsheviks' version of the revolutionary tale that reified the proletariat, and now that the Whites had been defeated the Bolshevik version seemed even more compelling. Those RCs who had a hard time accepting this backed merger with other populist groups. For the rest of the party members, merger with the Communists merely exonerated their behavior since mid-summer 1918. In turn, the Bolsheviks absorbed more than individual Revolutionary Communist Party members in late 1920. Read Lenin's speech at the Tenth Party Congress justifying the introduction of the New Economic Policy and the end of grain

---

[164] Graff, "Co-optation," 17.

requisitioning: his attitude toward the peasantry bears an uncanny resemblance to the peasant Bolsheviks' notion of *vlast' trudiashchikhsia*.

The documentation on the other socialist parties and anarchists is far less extensive, owing to the largely underground status of these groups. However, the issues remain more clear-cut: the Bolsheviks tolerated them when necessary, and repressed them when the Bolsheviks believed they had the upper hand.

Part Two

SOCIETY AND REVOLUTIONARY CULTURE

Six

A Community in Disarray, a Community in the Making

EARLIER, I SOUGHT to show how Russian society, pulling itself apart at the seams, gave birth to the Civil War. To add balance to this perspective, however, it is necessary to shift focus away from society and onto the consequences of the conflict itself, which became an historical actor in its own right by shaping individual destinies and constraining human agency. No matter how one defines community,[1] the experience of civil war, exacerbated by ideologically inspired political and social programs designed to reorder society, which appealed to some people, sundered traditional political and economic divisions and created new ones. Plunging Saratov into social chaos, civil war destroyed an administrative tradition that had been in place for more than a century. The result was disruption in the language of community that had regulated its social structure, primitivization of its infrastructure, brutalization of its population, and the *embedding* of these consequences in ways that constrained later Soviet history. Saratov during the

---

[1] The concept of community as an analytical tool has been defined in a variety of ways—administratively, geographically, economically, or even psychologically, that is, according to one's sense of belonging. See the debate over the concept in Alan Macfarlane, "Discussion: History, Anthropology and the Study of Communities," *Social History* 2, no. 2 (1977): 631–52; Craig J. Calhoun, "History, Anthropology and the Study of Communities: Some Problems with Macfarlane's Proposal," *Social History* 3, no. 3 (1978): 363–73; and idem., "Community: Toward a Variable Conceptualization for Comparative Research," *Social History* 5, no. 1 (1980): 105–29.

175

Civil War was a community in disarray, but also a community in the making.

The trauma the local population experienced has significance far beyond the confines of Saratov Province. As a "product of all sorts of social relations, which cut across particular locations in a multiplicity of ways,"[2] Saratov had fallen under assault between 1914 and 1922. Its boundaries changed and its population reconfigured, it was a different Saratov Province that emerged from the ordeal. Yet as Allan Pred argues, "it is through their intersection with the locally peculiar, the locally sedimented and contingent, the locally configured context, that more global structuring processes are given their forms and become perpetuated or transformed."[3] In other words, while the particular combinations discussed in this chapter are unique, they have condensed within them more general experiences that are larger than the local. That is why Saratov could be just about anywhere in Russia and anywhere in Russia could be in Saratov.

Place as a Reflection of Power Relations

The chronic revision of the province's borders during the Civil War suggests how relations of power and discipline are inscribed into the spatiality of social life. As the hostilities unfolded, the Center came to see Saratov as an indispensable source of grain for the Bolshevik-held heartland, and Tsaritsyn as the linchpin of Red Russia's besieged, vulnerable southeastern flank. For this reason, the Soviet government in 1919 broke off Tsaritsyn District from Saratov Province and joined it with territory from Astrakhan Province and the Don region to form Tsaritsyn Province. Sovnarkom also extended Saratov's borders beyond the left bank of the Volga that year to include Novouzensk Uezd and the city of Pokrovsk after Samara Province had become a focus of the anti-Soviet opposition. During 1921, the Saratov gubispolkom split large Novouzensk Uezd into Pokrovsk, Novouzensk, and Dergachevsk Districts. But the rash of rural-based anti-Soviet disturbances erupting at this time, as well as famine conditions, prevented local authorities from establishing the firm state apparatus in Saratov's left-bank holdings they so desired. Saratov officials likewise temporarily brought into existence a new uezd, Elansk, by carving off volosts from Atkarsk, Kamyshin, and Balashov. They also linked up the German-populated volosts of Kamyshin

---

[2] Felix Driver and Raphael Samuel, "Rethinking the Idea of Place," *History Workshop Journal* 39 (1995): vi.

[3] Pred, *Making Histories*, 15.

Uezd with the riparian counties of Novouzensk and Nikolaevsk (re-named Pugachevsk) Districts of Samara Province, and later with Pokrovsk, to constitute the autonomous Volga German Labor Commune (*Trudovaia kommuna nemtsev Povolzh'ia*).[4]

The addition of Novouzensk to the ten original districts of Saratov Province (map 2) and of Nikolaevsk to the German autonomous region, which spun in Saratov's orbit, created a vast agricultural zone capable of feeding an estimated fifty million people. This explains Saratov's importance from Moscow's perspective. When Lenin's government ushered in the New Economic Policy in 1921, Saratov Province comprised twelve uezds, with a total territory of 8,348,867 square desiatinas (35,222 sq. miles), excluding the autonomous German region: Atkarsk, Balashov, Elansk, Kamyshin, Khvalynsk, Kuznetsk, Petrovsk, Saratov, Serdobsk, Volsk, and the two trans-Volga districts of Dergachevsk and Novouzensk. Six of the ten right-bank uezds survived the Civil War without border changes (Volsk, Kuznetsk, Petrovsk, Saratov, Serdobsk, and Khvalynsk).[5] Politics thus reconfigured Saratov Province, as state-defined interests placed its traditional spatial parameters under assault.

Population Change as a Reflection of Power Relations

The fluidity of Saratov's borders during the Civil War makes it difficult to interpret and compare aggregate statistics on specific social indices, the more so because imperfections mar the data, none of which is totally reliable. Carried out without adequate preparation and in less than ideal circumstances, the censuses of 1916, 1917, 1920, and 1923 provide only approximate estimates of how the Civil War affected the population of Saratov Province. World War I, of course, had set into motion an array of disruptive demographic trends. In the 1915–22 period, natural population growth in Saratov Province (the relationship between births and deaths) amounted to 2.03 per thousand inhabitants, whereas in the immediate prewar period, 1912–14, it had been 16.85

[4] GASO, f. 521, op. 1, d. 163, l. 34; *Otchet Saratovskogo Gubernskogo Ispolnitel'nogo Komiteta*, 22; *Statisticheskii sbornik po Saratovskoi gubernii* (Saratov, 1923), 6; *ISS*, no. 170, Aug. 6, 1919, 3; V. Shiriaev, "Ob izmenenii granits uezdov Saratovskoi gubernii," *Biulleten' Saratovskogo gubernskogo Soveta narodnogo khoziaistva*, nos. 3–4 (14–15) (1919): 11; Kalashnikov, "Saratovskaia organizatsiia," 5; N. I. Lukov, *O napravlenii agronomicheskoi raboty po raionam Saratovskoi gubernii v sviazi s organizatsiei krest'ianskogo khoziaistva* (Volsk, n.d.), 5; and Iu. A. Poliakov, *Sovetskaia strana posle okonchaniia grazhdanskoi voiny: Territoriia i naselenie* (Moscow, 1986), 62.

[5] Novinskii, "Administrativnoe delenie," 6–7; A. F. Milovzorov, "Obshchaia ploshchad' gubernii i sostav zemel'nykh ugodii," in *Statisticheskii sbornik po Saratovskoi gubernii* (Saratov, 1923), 1.

2. Saratov Province after Border Changes at the End of the Civil War.

per thousand. The birthrate already began to fall in 1915, when it dipped 23 percent from the previous year's figures. It then declined more sharply than all-Russian averages: a further 25 percent in 1916 and 30 percent in 1917. During the same period, the deathrate actually declined by 40 percent—from 29.12 per thousand in 1914 to 17.47 per thousand in 1917. The lower birthrates explain the reduction in the deathrates, as infant mortality in Saratov was generally high. Saratov Province's natural growth rate registered 17.32 per thousand in 1914, but only 1.31 per thousand in 1917.[6]

New circumstances brought about by Civil War shaped the population's natural growth rates after 1917. Birthrates and deathrates for

[6] A. A. Mal'kov, *Estestvennoe dvizhenie naseleniia Saratovskoi gubernii za period 1914–1925 g.* (Saratov, 1926), 6–7, and GASO, f. 456, op. 1, d. 424, l. 62.

1918 are unavailable, because the new authorities forbade the Orthodox Church to continue its customary registration procedures but had
not yet assumed responsibility themselves for such activities. The flawed
data from 1919 bear the telltale signs of a province under siege. Those
from subsequent years become more satisfactory, as the process of state
building got underway. Between 1919 and 1921 the province registered
a negative natural growth rate of − 3.66 per thousand inhabitants. As
background, by 1917 an estimated 44–54 percent of the able-bodied
men in the villages had been drafted; their demobilization in 1918 led to
an immediate, short-term rise in the number of marriages. The birthrate
increased, climbing to 31.73 in 1919, 31.88 in 1920, and 33.3 in 1921.
Corresponding deathrates for this three-year period, however, were
33.76, 39.78, and 34.05, respectively, producing negative overall growth.
Deteriorating economic conditions during the Civil War — food shortages, physical and psychological stress, epidemic diseases (especially typhus and the world influenza epidemic of 1918–19), to say nothing of
war casualties and arbitrary revolutionary justice — all took their toll.
An increase in abortions also contributed to the negative growth rate.
Although the Soviet government first legalized abortion in 1920, the
procedure clearly was available before then. Data from the maternity
ward at the city's major hospital indicate that the proportion of abortions to live births rose from 19.66 percent in 1914 to 33.5 percent in
1918 and to 40.45 percent in 1920.

After the start of World War I the deathrate in Saratov Province was
higher in the towns than in the villages (table 6.1). The wrenching social
changes that took place between 1914 and 1921 also affected birthrates, which in the countryside fell below that of the cities. During this
seven-year period men suffered a higher deathrate than women in the
province. In 1920, the deathrate exceeded the birthrate by 24,483 (14,250
men and 10,233 women), reaching its peak during the first quarter of
1920, and especially in the cities, which lacked fuel and adequate food
reserves. In 1921 the deathrate in Saratov Province fell, despite the
onset of famine, because local authorities, now that the major military
operations were over, succeeded in temporarily bringing epidemic diseases under control. However, the cumulative effect of the country's
preceding miseries — in the guise of famine — now struck hard. In 1922
the province registered a negative growth of − 16.63 per thousand,
owing to the stunning deathrate of 43.37 per thousand, a situation
worse than that of European Russia as a whole, whose natural growth
rate was .91. In 1922, the number of deaths surpassed the number of
births by 44,509 and was higher among men (61 percent of the total),
higher in the urban areas, and higher in the non-black-earth districts of

TABLE 6.1

Deathrates and Birthrates in the Towns and Rural Areas of Saratov Province, 1913, 1920, 1921, and 1922, per 1,000 Inhabitants

		1913	*1920*	*1921*	*1922*
In towns	Deathrate	27.5	58.8	63.9	88.8
	Birthrate	34.0	32.4	33.9	23.4
In the countryside	Deathrate	28.9	36.6	29.1	37.2
	Birthrate	48.5	31.1	32.5	27.2

Source: A. G. Kovalevskii, "Rozhdaemost' i smertnost' naseleniia Saratovskoi gubernii v 1920–22 gg. i 1913 g.," in *Statisticheskii sbornik po Saratovskoi gubernii* (Saratov, 1923), 66.

Khvalynsk, Kuznetsk, Novouzensk, Dergachevsk, and Volsk. The actual deathrate was most likely even greater than the figures suggest.[7]

With the exception of Atkarsk and Serdobsk, the district towns in the province experienced a population loss of −20.29 per thousand inhabitants, whereas a slight gain of 1.82 was registered in the countryside (table 6.2). After the beginning of hostilities in 1914, the deathrate in the towns remained higher than that in the countryside, particularly among males, while the birthrate remained lower. Data for the city of Saratov indicate that the deathrate in 1917 had grown by 17.7 percent over the 1914 figure; in 1918 by 62.5 percent; in 1919 by 138.2 percent; and in 1920 by 108.9 percent.[8]

In evaluating data for the hard-hit cities, the complex ways in which the Civil War affected demographic trends are thrown into sharper relief. In isolating the effects of natural population movements brought about by the Revolution and Civil War, it appears that migration *to* Petrovsk and Balashov offset the negative natural growth rates there (table 6.3). In other towns a specific set of negative conditions relating to the war, climate, food supplies, and other considerations promoted out-migration, thereby aggravating decreases in the natural growth rate. These towns attracted refugees and evacuees, but the deathrate among the transient elements tended to be higher than that of the indigenous population. Located in a region that suffered the poorest harvests and

---

[7] A. G. Kovalevskii, "Rozhdaemost' i smertnost' naseleniia Saratovskoi gubernii v 1920–22 gg. i 1913 g.," in *Statisticheskii sbornik po Saratovskoi gubernii* (Saratov, 1923), 62–66. For marriages and divorces see N. A., "Dvizhenie naseleniia Saratovskoi gubernii (1920–1925 gg.)," *Administrativnaia zhizn'*, no. 18–19 (1925): 3–4, 18–19. Information on abortions can be found in *ISS*, no. 11, Jan. 16, 1921, 2.

[8] If figures for 1922 are used, Serdobsk's population fell as well. Deathrates are found in Poliakov, *Sovetskaia strana*, 107.

TABLE 6.2

Changes in Population in Saratov Province 1915–22, per 1,000 Inhabitants

Cities		Countryside	
Saratov	− 25.79	Khvalynsk	− 7.13
Balashov	− 24.56	Kamyshin	− 1.13
Khvalynsk	− 23.96	Volsk	+ 0.11
Petrovsk	− 23.34	Kuznetsk	+ 0.71
Kuznetsk	− 13.95	Serdobsk	+ 1.97
Volsk	− 11.97	Petrovsk	+ 3.18
Kamyshin	− 9.63	Saratov	+ 4.05
Serdobsk	− 7.69	Balashov	+ 4.49
Atkarsk	3.51	Atkarsk	+ 5.03
Totals	− 20.29		+ 1.82

Source: A. A. Mal'kov, *Estestvennoe dvizhenie naseleniia Saratovskoi gubernii za period 1914–1925 gg.* (Saratov, 1926), 27.

highest deathrates during the famine, Khvalynsk endured the greatest population loss.

Available population figures for the urban centers of Saratov Province exclude soldiers in local garrisons, who became an object of a special military census the results of which were not made public. Statistics tend to include suburbs, defined according to their economic relationship with the city and population density. To place the data in comparative perspective, it should be noted that Volga- and Ural-area towns in general grew faster than those in any other region in Russia between 1897 and 1917. Between 1917 and 1920 cities in the Volga and Ural regions experienced the lowest population decline of any part of the country, averaging 12 percent (populations in towns in the central industrial provinces fell by 28.1 percent and in the black-earth provinces by 17.1 percent). By 1923 — and owing to the famine of 1921–22 that ravaged the Volga — these trends had reversed themselves. Urban centers in the central industrial provinces underwent a 20.1 percent average growth in population after 1920, whereas in the Volga and Ural regions they endured a decline in population.[9] As the data in table 6.4 reveal, the urban population of Saratov Province dropped off by 7.7 percent, from 380,978 to 351,374. Although the percentage of the urban population that was female — 53–54 percent — remained relatively constant throughout the seven-year period, the percentage of women declined more sharply than that of men between 1920 and 1923 (by 9 percent),

[9] O. Kvitkin, "Naselenie gorodov Evropeiskoi chasti RSFSR po perepisiam 1897, 1917, 1920, 1923 g.," *Biulleten' tsentral'nogo statisticheskogo upravleniia*, no. 77 (Aug. 25, 1923): 18.

TABLE 6.3

Population Changes in Cities in Saratov Province during War, Revolution, and Civil War

City	% of Population Change 1913–23	% of Population Change Resulting from Negative Natural Growth Rate, 1915–22
Khvalynsk	−37.89	−14.69
Volsk	−36.43	−7.78
Kamyshin	−36.04	−5.82
Serdobsk	−26.98	−4.52
Saratov	−23.43	−15.24
Kuznetsk	−13.09	−8.99
Petrovsk	−9.48	−16.15
Balashov	−5.62	−15.81
Atkarsk	+5.25	+3.10
Average for province	−22.92	−12.56

Source: Mal'kov, *Estestvennoe dvizhenie naseleniia,* 31.

probably because demobilization of the Red Army brought many men home.

Related data help us understand how demographic trends after 1914 altered the ratio of men to women, especially in rural areas. With the start of hostilities in 1914, large numbers of local men were drafted and refugees poured into the province as defense-related industries and institutions of higher education were relocated to the Volga region, away from the vulnerable front. Migration out of the cities to the villages also started up. By 1917, there were approximately 1,174 women in Saratov city per 1,000 males, a figure that remained fairly constant through 1920. It fell slightly (to 1,137) by 1923 mostly as a result of the demobilization of the Red Army. The greatest discrepancy—i.e., the fewest men—is found in the 20–29 and over-60 age groups. In 1920 there were 1,239 women per every 1,000 men in the countryside; however, as in the cities, in the 20–29 age group this figure shoots up—in the villages, to 2,974. Taking the province as a whole, there were 1,232 women per 1,000 men in 1920 and 1,252 women per 1,000 men two years later.[10]

A comparison with Petrograd and several other Russian cities shows that Saratov's deathrate was lower than the national average before

[10] M. P. Romanov, *Materialy po statistike g. Saratova,* no. 1 (Saratov, 1921): vi–ix; V. Novinskii, "Naselenie Saratovskoi gubernii po dannym demograficheskoi professional'noi perepisi 1920 g.," in *Statisticheskii sbornik po Saratovskoi gubernii* (Saratov, 1923), 51; and Mal'kov, *Estestvennoe dvizhenie naseleniia,* 42.

TABLE 6.4

Population of Major Urban Centers in Saratov Province, According to the
1917, 1920, and 1923 Censuses

City	*1917*		*1920*		*1923*	
	Total	*Women*	*Total*	*Women*	*Total*	*Women*
Saratov	223,414	120,311	189,242	102,559	183,145	98,535
Atkarsk	13,208	7,043	16,457	8,766	14,581	7,632
Balashov	23,677	12,623	25,971	14,154	21,636	11,567
Volsk	38,870	21,203	33,996	18,450	25,802	14,226
Kamyshin	26,677	13,979	20,846	11,260	18,977	10,149
Kuznetsk	29,957	16,379	27,093	14,936	26,912	14,334
Novouzensk			14,290	7,764	15,218	8,008
Petrovsk	20,442	10,850	20,733	11,529	18,953	10,086
Serdobsk	10,441	5,943	12,231	6,732	11,546	6,147
Khvalynsk	20,120	11,173	20,119	11,451	14,604	8,056
Totals	406,806	219,504	380,978	207,601	351,374	188,740

Source: O. Kvitkin, "Naselenie gorodov Evropeiskoi chasti RSFSR po perepisiam 1897, 1917, 1920, 1923 g.," *Biulleten' tsentral'nogo statisticheskogo upravleniia*, no. 77 (August, 25, 1923), 10–11, 26–27.

1918, but afterward exceeded it until 1924. In Petrograd, the deathrate per thousand inhabitants was 22.9 in 1917; 46.7 in 1918; 77.1 in 1919; and 50.6 in 1920. Comparable figures for Saratov are 30.0 in 1915; 69.8 in 1919; and 61.2 in 1920. In 1922 it climbed to 81.5, more than double the national average of 38. The natural growth rate in a range of cities in 1920 puts Novgorod at −1.3 percent, Smolensk at −3.7 percent, Moscow at −13.3 percent, Ivanovo-Voznesensk at −13.5 percent, Petrograd at −30 percent, and Saratov at −31.5 percent.[11]

The national professional census of 1920 and the urban census of 1923 permit a tentative examination of transformations in the social and professional makeup of the cities as a result of civil war. The data reveal defining trends as well as different ways of establishing categories and of self-identification. According to the 1920 census, the population of Saratov Province was 3,070,109, of whom 85.2 percent lived in the

[11] V. Z. Drobizhev, "Estestvennoe dvizhenie naseleniia Sovetskoi Rossii v 1917–1920 gg.," in *Velikii Oktiabr': Istoriia, istoriografiia, istochnikovedenie* (Moscow, 1978), 53–58, and Stephen G. Wheatcroft, "Public Health in Russia during the War, Revolution and Famines, 1914–1923: Moscow, Petrograd and Saratov," paper presented at an International Conference on the History of Russian and Soviet Public Health, University of Toronto, May 7–10, 1986. For Moscow see Sakwa, *Soviet Communists in Power*, 34–35.

villages.[12] Just under half of the total urban population resided in Saratov. The populations of Balashov, Atkarsk, Petrovsk, Elansk, Khvalynsk, and Serdobsk Uezds were more than 90 percent rural. Population density was highest in Saratov (63.3 per square verst) and Kuznetsk (47.8) Districts, and lowest in the trans-Volga steppe districts of Novouzensk and Dergachevsk, 11.6 and 9.4, respectively.[13]

The border changes during the Civil War altered the province's ethnic balance, mainly by placing Saratov's Germans in an autonomous "commune." According to the 1897 census, 76.75 percent of the province's population was Russian; all Slavs combined made up 83.1 percent of the total. The most important minority nationalities were the Germans (6.92 percent), Mordva (5.15 percent), and Tatars (3.95 percent). In 1924 Russians composed 80 percent of the province's population, Ukrainians 6.5 percent, Mordva 5.2 percent, and Tatars 5 percent.[14]

A source listing Saratov's population as 191,996 in 1920 puts the Russian population at 165,204 or 86 percent. The largest minorities included Jews (11,209), Germans (5,994), Poles (2,687), Tatars (2,285), Ukrainians (920), Letts (632), and Lithuanians (610). Many of the minorities had been evacuated to Saratov after 1914: in 1920, 13,148 refugees were registered in the city.[15] Related figures from 1919 show that 900 foreigners, mostly male, had taken up residence in the city; almost all were refugees or prisoners of war. Slightly more than two-thirds of the foreigners were "wage laborers" and the overwhelming majority of them were employed in Soviet offices and enterprises.[16]

According to the occupational census of August 1920, the total working-age population (16–50 years old) in Saratov was 97,902 (53,786 women and 44,116 men), among whom 59,900 were employed (62 percent of the men, 38 percent of the women). The census listed fifty-five occupations; "unskilled labor" made up the largest group in Saratov (35,857). The greatest number of people were employed as clerks (5,342), tailors (2,844), stevedores and loaders (2,222), metal craftsmen

[12] *Otchet 9-go sozyva,* 273, and *Chislennost' naseleniia Saratovskoi gubernii po dannym demografichesko-professional'nykh perepisi 28 avgusta 1920 goda* (Saratov, 1921), x. See also GASO, f. 456, op. 1, d. 414, ll. 87, 182.

[13] Novinskii, "Naselenie Saratovskoi gubernii," 49.

[14] N. A. Troinitskii et al., eds., *Pervaia vseobshchaia perepis' naseleniia Rossiiskoi Imperii, 1897 god,* vol. 38, *Saratovskaia guberniia* (St. Petersburg, 1904), passim; *Naselenie gorodov Saratovskoi gubernii,* 12; Saratovskoe gubernskoe statisticheskoe biuro, *Statisticheskii spravochnik* (Saratov, 1924), 68–73; and Poliakov, *Sovetskaia strana,* 159, 167, 168, 172, 190. For the size of minority populations in 1921 see TsDNISO, f. 27, op. 2, d. 747, ll. 8–9 (for 1920 see f. 27, op. 2, d. 1424, l. 3).

[15] Novinskii, "Naselenie Saratovskoi gubernii," 27, 44–45, and *ISS,* no. 72, March 30, 1920, 3.

[16] GASO, f. 456, op. 1, d. 236, ll. 25–26.

(2,177), accountants (2,136), teachers (1,528), shoemakers (1,173), technicians (662), telegraph operators (626), and joiners (614). Among the professions employing many people, women accounted for 83 percent of the tailors (a major change from the prewar period), 68.1 percent of the teachers, and 58.7 percent of the clerks, while virtually all of the joiners, technicians, shoemakers, and skilled metalworkers were men.[17]

Comparative data on occupation from 1920 and 1923 record the impact of economic ruin at the end of 1920, famine, and changes brought about by the introduction of the New Economic Policy in 1921. On the eve of 1917, 53 percent of the city's population of 232,015 belonged to the working class (skilled and unskilled).[18] The 1920 census data suggest that the overall occupational profile changed most substantially in regard to the large percentage employed as white-collar workers (*sluzhashchie*), including officials. The size of the industrial proletariat in the city between 1920 and 1923 fell by 37.4 percent owing to the transfer of industry to self-finance after the inception of the NEP, which forced some enterprises to shut down and others to cut back on the number of workers they employed. The number of individuals working as custodians (*prislugi*) dwindled as a result of the closure of many enterprises; however, the number of household or personal servants jumped from 0 to 542 after the NEP began. Similarly, the number of privately employed individuals who hired others grew. Although the number of private businessmen without hired workers declined, this category now comprised a larger percentage of the total working-age population of Saratov than before, rising from 9.6 percent to 12.3 percent. In addition to the 63,336 adults engaged in various occupations, 5,049 others served in army and navy units quartered in Saratov; another 15,647 persons were registered as unemployed. Yet another measure of the tragedy of the 1920–23 period is the actual and percentage rise in the number of dependents in state institutions, who after the famine composed 16.9 percent of the city's population[19] (table 6.5).

Between 1920 and 1923 the percentage of officials employed in administration and the courts actually doubled, despite the decline in their total numbers. So did the percentage working as inventory-control personnel and in the security organs. The upturn in administrative, justice, and security organ personnel resulted from the explosion of antigovern-

---

[17] Romanov, *Materialy po statistike*, 9; for age breakdown among Saratov's population see GASO, f. 456, op. 1, d. 424, l. 62.

[18] I. N. Kokshaiskii, *Predvaritel'nye dannye perepisi naseleniia goroda Saratova i ego prigorodov* (Saratov, 1916), 15.

[19] GASO, f. 521, op. 1, d. 906, ll. 142–43.

TABLE 6.5
Occupations of Working Population of Saratov, 1920 and 1923

Social Groups	Number 1920	%	Number 1923	%	Change	%
1. Workers	26,165	30.1	16,387	25.9	−9778	−37.4
2. Custodians (prislugi)	4,002	4.6	3,326	5.3	−676	−16.9
3. Officials	31,297	36.0	19,842	31.3	−11,455	−36.6
4. Free professions	745	0.9	569	0.9	−176	−23.6
5. Private business-men with hired workers	39	0.0	188	0.3	+149	+382.1
6. Private business-men without hired workers	8,320	9.6	7,803	12.3	−517	−6.2
7. Employed family members	2,305	2.7	1,300	2.1	−1005	−43.6
8. Dependants in state institutions	8,639	9.9	10,718	16.9	+2079	+24.1
9. Others (renters, "déclassé" groups, those not listing source of existence)	5,368	6.2	3,203	5.0	−2165	−31
Totals	86,880	100.0	63,336	100.0	−23,554	−25.9

Source: V. K. Novinskii, "Sotsial'nyi i professional'nyi sostav naseleniia goroda Saratova," *Nizhnee Povolzh'e*, no. 1 (1924): 82; GASO, f. 521, op. 1, d. 906, l. 143; and *Naselenie gorodov Saratovskoi gubernii v 1923 g.* (Saratov, 1924), 16.

ment feelings in the city and countryside that occurred in the spring of 1921, as well as from precautions taken in connection with the introduction of the NEP. The situation differed in the district towns, where the decline in the percentage of those employed as workers and officials was even more striking: the drop-off amounted to 50 percent and 46.5 percent, respectively.[20]

Although the statistics adduced above obscure individual human geographies, they nonetheless make clear that politics and ideology shaped those geographies. Initially better off than the country at large, grain-producing Saratov, by civil war's end, had succumbed to the cumulative effect of the hostilities and harsh government policies. Professor A. A.

[20] V. K. Novinskii, "Sotsial'nyi i professional'nyi sostav naseleniia gor. Saratova," *Nizhnee Povolzh'e*, no. 1 (1924): 84.

Malkov, a local statistician, sharply criticized the regime's misguided, desperate economic policies for the negative population trends, arguing that although the 1919 harvest amounted to only 72.2 percent of the 1914 yield, it would have more than sufficed to feed Saratov's population. "War Communism," concluded Malkov, "accomplished what perhaps was necessary, but shipment of food products outside the province was a cruel thing for the local population."[21]

"It's a Rare Citizen of the Republic Who Has Not Felt Like a Refugee"

Daniel R. Brower has argued that the demographic impact of the Civil War on the Russian city led to a process of "homogenization" as the cities, purged of their transient rural elements, took on an even more defined urban character than before the war.[22] But I would qualify Brower's conclusion by calling attention to the endless influx of transient elements that took the place of drafted males and urban dwellers who sought refuge in the villages. War, civil war, and then famine gave rise to successive waves of refugees and prisoners of war and made it impossible to count them—let alone to assist them—adequately.[23] The elliptical statistics only permit crude quantitative representations of the problem; much more evocative is the assessment of a local demographer who wrote that "we have lived through so much these past seven years that it's a rare citizen of the Republic who has not felt like a refugee, at least for a short while."[24] Apart from efforts to repatriate prisoners of war and other foreigners, authorities had to cope with domestic refugees. Out-migration from cities to the countryside, and from cities in other parts of the country to towns in Saratov Province, further stretched a strained system of social services, as did the arrival of hordes of "Civil War refugees" fleeing the shifting fronts, and of prisoners of war freed or left behind by the Whites. Finally, the famine of 1921 sent swarms of starving people, mainly peasants, to the cities in search of food and relief.

A variety of overlapping and ineffective organizations, often depart-

[21] Mal'kov, *Estestvennoe dvizhenie naseleniia*, 9, 10, 17, and *Chislennost' naseleniia*, xxii–xxiv.

[22] Daniel R. Brower, " 'The City in Danger': The Civil War and the Russian Urban Population," in Diane P. Koenker, William G. Rosenberg, and Ronald G. Suny, eds., *Party, State, and Society in the Russian Civil War: Explorations in Social History* (Bloomington, 1989), 64 (hereafter cited as *Party, State, and Society*).

[23] See Peter Gatrell, *A Whole Empire Walking: Refugees in Russia during World War I* (Bloomington, 1999).

[24] A. A. Mal'kov, "Bezhenskoe dvizhenie v sviazi s golodom v Saratovskoi gubernii," *Saratovskii vestnik zdravookhraneniia*, no. 10 (1922): 31.

ments or subunits of the Saratov Soviet and later of the gubispolkom, bore responsibility for assisting the province's refugees, who numbered 154,000 in March 1918, 76,000 of whom were unable to work. Hard put to cope with the changing character of the refugee problem, the soviet admitted the position of refugees was becoming "unbearable" and that local peasants sought to drive them out of the villages, to which the majority of refugees had been sent to work.[25] With the end of the hostilities between Russia and the Central Powers in 1918, the authorities attempted to repatriate prisoners of war. Between June and October 1918, more than 23,644 foreigners were sent home, mainly to Austria and Germany. In the year after repatriation began, an estimated 70,000 inhabitants of Saratov Province who had been imprisoned or living abroad came home, while 35,000 prisoners of war and foreign refugees were repatriated. Demobilized soldiers returning home to Saratov after the Revolution had a trying time readjusting to civilian life. The able-bodied did not qualify for welfare, but high unemployment levels made it impossible at times to return to the workforce until the formation of the Red Army.[26] This predicament would repeat itself with the demobilization of the Red Army at Civil War's end, creating a volatile political climate for the Communist regime. Meanwhile, prisoners of war and refugees who sympathized with Soviet power often expressed willingness to serve in the Red Army, frequently because of their involvement with Russian women or because of the prospects of securing land in the countryside. They were transferred to Saratov to join one of several international regiments.[27]

Once the Civil War began in earnest, the refugee problem turned tragic, as local authorities resorted to harsh and violent measures that conflicted with their political ideals. In material terms, refugees residing in towns appear to have been worse off than their counterparts in the villages, because of growing unemployment and the high cost of living in the urban centers. A set of snapshots from 1918 depicts strikingly similar circumstances throughout the province. The Kamyshin Soviet lacked housing and resources to assist the hungry that showed up each day begging for food. The inhabitants of Serdobsk refused to provide housing for refugees or to sell them bread at fixed prices. When a typhoid epidemic broke out among refugees crowded into squalid barracks, the Kuznetsk Soviet seized property from the "bourgeoisie" and moved the refugees into it. The Saratov official responsible for refugees

---

[25] *Saratovskii Sovet*, 403; see also GASO, f. 456, op. 1, d. 22, l. 1; op. 1, d. 3, l. 44.

[26] GASO, f. 521, op. 2, d. 24, l. 26. See also f. 456, op. 1, d. 3, ll. 50, 55.

[27] *Plennyi i bezhenets* (Saratov), no. 1–2 (1918): 53–54, and *ISS*, no. 206 Sept. 18, 1919, 4.

and prisoners of war resigned in angry protest when force was used to drive up the Volga several thousand famished and diseased refugees who had set up camp on the riverbanks. Expelled from some volosts by the increasingly hostile rural population, the refugees and POWs demanded to be sent home. Some braved the unknown to make their way back home unofficially.[28]

After 1918 the problem of domestic "Civil War refugees" took on new prominence, as an influx of petit-bourgeois and working-class elements from Moscow, Petrograd, and other cities relocated to district towns in Saratov in search of food. They showed up in Atkarsk with fistfuls of inflated currency, which jacked up local prices and placed some goods beyond the reach of the local proletariat, prompting the newspaper to dismiss them all as spongers, Sybarites, and speculators! Refugees put a strain on the single bathhouse still operating in Petrovsk. The 3,000 elderly men and women from Moscow and Petrograd who arrived in Volsk in the summer of 1919 found themselves in a "horrible situation." At the time, Saratov anticipated the arrival of an estimated 50,000 sick and wounded refugees.[29] By mid-1919 Civil War refugees from the Don region and Caucasus began to turn up in the province, especially in Saratov and in Volsk, an attractive destination point because of its easy access by rail. With resources spread thin and Denikin moving up the Volga, it proved no longer possible to count the refugees systematically.[30] Nor was it an easy matter to classify them, as the boundaries between refugees and criminals blurred. By mid-1919 authorities called attention to the massive influx of "all sorts of vagrants, pick-pockets, fortune tellers, singers, people with talking parrots promising happiness, petty tradesmen, Chinese, etc."[31]

The complications associated with the presence of refugees carried political as well as social repercussions, and rarely positive ones. Take the example of the evacuation to Saratov in the spring of 1918 of the sizable Gelferikh-Sade Factory from Kharkov. Expecting an influx of 700 workers from Kharkov, Saratov authorities rejoiced to learn that only 70 had arrived with the factory, since they could draw the remaining workforce from among the local proletariat, thereby alleviating unemployment in the city. But the Kharkov evacuees included a large per-

---

[28] *Plennyi i bezhenets*, no. 3–4 (1918): 54–56; GA RF, f. 393, op. 3, d. 333, l. 15, and d. 334, ll. 93–94; and Rashitov, "Sovety," 303–4.

[29] TsDNISO, f. 27, op. 1, d. 57, l. 5.

[30] *Krasnaia kommuna* (Atkarsk), no. 72, Nov. 20, 1918, 4; *Izvestiia Atkarskogo uispolkoma*, no. 217, May 31, 1919, 3; *Rabochii i krest'ianin* (Volsk), no. 148, July 5, 1919, 2; *Kommuna* (Petrovsk), no. 3 (72), Jan. 16, 1919, 3; and *ISS*, no. 258, Nov. 20, 1919, 2.

[31] *ISS*, no. 133, June 25, 1919, 4.

centage of independent-minded "political" refugees, who refused to subordinate themselves to the soviet, and instead established their own "republic," a term that had become a metaphor for the voluntary nature of all power relationships. Similarly, political refugees from Poltava gave part of their property to local anarchists, who became embroiled in a showdown with the soviet and, at the end of the year, discord between Bolsheviks from Ukraine and their local comrades resulted in Moscow's intervention in Saratov's affairs.[32]

The third wave of refugees to invade the province comprised those escaping the disastrous harvest of 1921. In the spring of 1921 the first groups fleeing Siberia reached Balashov. Elsewhere thousands of desperate people, many of them German farmers, snaked through the major thoroughfares of towns and set up camp at railroad stations, docks, and shelters. The coming of winter forced them to stop wherever they happened to be. In Saratov, this was the so-called "Refugee Town" on the Volga, a breeding ground for cholera. With no single agency responsible for the refugees, authorities put them up in makeshift shelters. "One can say with certainty," reported Professor Malkov, "that it was impossible to imagine anything worse than these buildings, without windows, doors, stoves, plumbing, toilets, etc." But worse there was, as Malkov himself admitted: the situation in the uezd towns. Between January and July 1922, 9,405 more refugees showed up in Saratov, of whom 1,184 died. And no wonder, for in February, 82 percent of them had contracted some form of infectious disease.[33]

Housing "Citizens of the Republic"

Social life "is always contingent upon what is materially available within a given locality at a given time and upon the geography of intangible power relations existing at the moment."[34] Consideration of Saratov's housing problems during the Civil War illustrates this point. Despite the steady decline of the urban population during the Civil War, Saratov, along with other cities in the province, experienced a housing crisis that worsened as the city swelled with refugees and transient elements and became the center of military operations for the southeastern front. Funds were unavailable for construction of new buildings or repair of the existing physical plant, part of which came to be used as a source of firewood. Mobilizations and demobilizations, fuel and supply

[32] Ibid., no. 71, April 13, 1918, 3, and no. 82, April 26, 1918, 3. For refugees see GASO, f. 521, op. 2, d. 44.

[33] Mal'kov, "Bezhenskoe dvizhenie," 31–36.

[34] Pred, *Making Histories*, 10, 15.

crises, military skirmishes, fires, and far-reaching economic break-down—all affected the city's ability to house its inhabitants. So did class-oriented housing policies. Even a cursory examination of the housing crisis provides poignant insights into the fleeting, confusing, and at times contradictory nature of the regime's policies.

Throughout the Civil War the Saratov Soviet promoted a selective, inconsistent, often ineffective class policy in regard to housing, whose role in legitimating Soviet power is difficult to determine. In early 1918 the soviet lowered rents in an effort to ease the burden on the poor and undoubtedly to bolster its own support. This took place as a contentious debate erupted among Communists over abolishing the right to own property altogether. Calling for an end to private ownership of housing in towns with populations greater than 10,000, an August 1918 decree left it to the discretion of local soviets how to billet troops, relocate the poor, and provide space for institutions and officials.[35] Despite confiscations and resettlement programs, and often because of them, the appeal of private ownership ultimately prevailed: when the NEP restored the right to own property, former owners hastened to reclaim their past possessions.

By 1919, the Saratov Soviet felt compelled to redefine its own class-driven policies, not only because civil war conditions made it impossible to secure the necessary economic resources to solve the mounting housing problem, but also because of the tenuous nature of its support. Until then, the soviet seemed determined to revolutionize living arrangements. Its housing subdepartment, however, fell under fire virtually from the beginning for its inability to respond to all of the requests, complaints, and demands from groups, agencies, and private citizens alike, for repairmen, materials, fuel, lighting, garbage removal, or for cleaning communal toilet facilities. Expressing concern over the lack of fuel to see Saratov through the winter of 1918–19, a beleaguered official warned his comrades that despite military operations along the Volga, the soviet had to do something, "now that the battle between the proletariat and Capital has begun."[36]

The attempt to set up housing committees in 1918 to distribute living space, collect rents, and assume responsibility for maintenance soon turned into a more ambitious program of grassroots, revolutionary democracy, as the committees were entrusted with distributing food supplies and administering the rationing system. Housing units of at least one hundred persons selected committees from among the adult population, excluding former home owners, members of the clergy, police and

[35] Brower, "'The City in Danger'," 74–75.
[36] GASO, f. 521, op. 1, d. 95, l. 4.

Okhranka officials, and those "living now and before the revolution on the labors of others." The ispolkom divided the population into four categories that were to be considered in carrying out its housing policies: factory workers, "responsible workers" (Soviet officials), the remaining laboring population, and the "nonlaboring parasitic population." Workers, officials in Soviet institutions, and Communists retained their former accommodations. Responsible Soviet officials were offered appropriate housing near their place of employment, while the "parasitic" elements were resettled or forced to take in the city's lower classes. The link between power and privilege during a time of unimaginable want took on many forms; that preference in allocating housing was given to officials did not go unnoticed, and this undoubtedly helps explain how the new system co-opted some people and made enemies of others.[37]

Historians of the Civil War face the tough task of discriminating between the endless issuance of rules and resolutions and the actual effect they had. Regardless of the 1918 campaign to select housing committees, they appear to have fallen victim to mass inertia, hostility, and, by 1919, to the crushing weight of an emerging Soviet bureaucracy that mistrusted lower-level institutions of power, particularly when the front moved uncomfortably close to Saratov. The soviet's new Housing Department exonerated itself for not establishing elected housing councils for each street because of the expense, but also because they could become "breeding grounds for counterrevolution." This concern proved overriding, for the department argued that even though the (Communist) building managers could not cope with the many demands made on them, it made sense to spurn elections, which would "make it possible for various counterrevolutionary elements to infiltrate [the committees]."[38]

In the fall of 1919, the "housing question worsened each day" as the crisis reached an "unprecedented" level. While "immense chaos reigned" in the Housing Department, and the steady flood of transients and lack of repair work took its toll, the military authorities likewise were blamed, for units leaving the city had seized furniture and destroyed many buildings in which they had been quartered.[39] According to the ispolkom, soldiers housed in 250 of the best buildings in town ruined 198 of them. A similar fate befell the city of Pokrovsk.[40]

---

[37] Ibid., l. 12.

[38] *ISS*, no. 33, Feb. 12, 1919, 1.

[39] Ibid., no. 206, Sept. 18, 1919, 4; no. 217, Oct. 2, 1919, 3; and no. 222, Oct. 8, 1919, 1.

[40] *Otchet 9-go sozyva*, 198.

The breakdown in city services, and growing indifference and negligence toward one's work brought on by the long hours one had to spend grubbing for food and keeping oneself clean and warm, resulted in frequent fires in the city — 492 in 1920. As their number increased, the party came to blame criminal elements and "counterrevolutionaries" as the perpetrators.[41] A fire breaking out on the outskirts of town on July 31, 1920, a dry, windy day, fanned out in all directions, turning into an unmitigated disaster. Most firemen had been sent out of town to make hay or cut firewood as part of a program of mobilization of civilians, and those in town had little water with which to fight the fire. Blazing out of control for eight hours, "the horrible fire spread at a dizzying speed, street after street burned down. Within an hour a powerful sea of flame greedily devoured thousands of homes. [One could hear] the screams and moans of the unfortunate victims, the heartrending shouts and cries of children. People were searching, screaming, sobbing, running, bustling about."[42] When the ashes had settled, 1,819 buildings had been destroyed, which had housed 25,000 people — about one-eighth of the city's population! One report claimed that more than one hundred people had died in the fire, but other sources are reticent on this point, an uncomfortable taciturnity that suggests local officials sought to repress the tragic news. The overwhelming majority of those made homeless had no place to go and located housing on their own, and this meant crowding into already tight facilities.[43] Despite initial reports trumpeting the authorities' successes in administering to the fire's victims, one account admits to the pettiness and flagrant abuses in evidence as several individuals claimed rights to the same apartment and "each tried to receive it through personal contacts, bribes, or all sorts of subterfuge." The account rings true, for it parallels developments in other areas of everyday life and was prompted by the same hopeless competition for limited resources.[44]

Accounts in the Saratov press following the fire do not assign blame for it; however, in early 1921 Saratov's *Izvestiia* reported that the large number of fires breaking out in Saratov were caused not only by negligence, but also by enemies of Soviet power and criminal elements trying to hide evidence.[45] Whatever the fire's origins, authorities had placed

[41] Ibid., 207, and *ISS*, no. 45, Feb. 27, 1921, 1.

[42] *ISS*, no. 173, Aug. 3, 1920, 3.

[43] Ibid.; *Izvestiia Atkarskogo uispolkoma*, no. 112, Aug. 4, 1920, 1; *Serp i molot* (Serdobsk), no. 165 (449), Aug. 4, 1920, 1; and *Otchet 9-go sozyva*, 200.

[44] *ISS*, no. 291, Dec. 22, 1920, 2.

[45] *Izvestiia Khvalynskogo Soveta*, no. 150, July 10, 1920, 1, and no. 172, Aug. 5, 1920, 1. B. I. Il'in blames counterrevolutionaries for the fire. See his *Saratov: Istoricheskii ocherk* (Saratov, 1952), 128.

Saratov under martial law in May 1920 owing to a growing anti-Soviet mood in the province. In blaming the Whites, Soviet leaders probably sought to deflect attention from their own ill-advised policy of sending firemen out of town as part of the militarization of civilian labor, which undoubtedly was largely responsible for the extensive damage the fire caused.

When the Communal Housing Department (*Gubkommunotdel*) set up in the wake of the great fire got down to its "colossal" work, it concluded that the housing problem was the "most painful" one confronting the city, in which the level of crowding was "shocking" and "stunning."[46] Conditions made it next to impossible for Gubkommunotdel to effect significant improvement, however, as did "disturbing" attitudes among officials and the people over whom they ruled. Two examples will suffice to convey the nature of popular attitudes toward communal property, which did not augur well for the emerging social relations defining the new sense of community. Dismayed by his comrades' total lack of concern over the city's physical plant, a Communist named Burmistrov singled out the fate of a wooden structure that quartered an army unit in 1919. By the time the soldiers left, all of the building's windows had been broken. The refugees who replaced the soldiers stuffed filthy rags into the window frames. The building was in disrepair when they withdrew, prompting the "good citizens" living nearby to dismantle the house board by board. "And when I walked past the last time," observed an enraged Burmistrov, "I saw a huge ditch instead of a building and a heap of garbage and bricks."[47] The second example, from Babine's diary, reveals how the country's slide into degradation did not spare the "lights of learning." On New Year's eve, 1921, he took Dr. McElroy, a representative of the American Relief Administration, on a tour of the university, which included a visit to the university outhouse. "It is hard to imagine a man more disgusted than the doctor was," wrote Babine. "The frozen excrement was piled up eighteen inches and two feet high above what were supposed to be seats. The floors were covered with excrement and thick ice that made use of the place next to impossible."[48]

Throughout the Civil War—and to a large extent owing to an erratic policy of nationalization—no one shouldered responsibility for the city's physical plant. Various efforts to mobilize the inhabitants in order to clean the city only contributed to attitudes noted above. At the start

---

[46] *Otchet 9-go sozyva*, 194–98.
[47] TsDNISO, f. 27, op. 2, d. 74, l. 38.
[48] Raleigh, *A Russian Civil War Diary*, 195.

of the Civil War, Moscow had issued rulings on abolishing private property and on the municipalization of property; however, daily realities prevented the widespread takeover of property in the city, and much of it simply fell into neglect. Great "diversity" characterized the management of nonmunicipalized housing, to say nothing of that controlled by the authorities. Elsewhere in Saratov Province, only 6 to 12 percent of all housing had been municipalized — in Saratov the figure was 16.2 percent (2,215 buildings out of 13,651).[49] The ambiguous legacy of the class-oriented policies that had been in force and the equally ambiguous policies of the transition to the NEP continued to breed discord, conflict, enmity, and dissatisfaction.

In the aftermath of anti-Soviet disturbances in the spring of 1921, Gubkommunotdel showered its solicitude on the population to dispel the prevalent view that it had dealt ineffectively with the housing problem. Perhaps its most visionary move was to turn the once posh Evropa Hotel into the First Proletarian Home, a communal living and eating arrangement designed to house 150 workers and their families.[50] The soviet also pressed for the election of housing committees once again, but the population this time proved slow to respond. Moreover, former bourgeois homeowners and "enemies of Soviet power" agitated against the housing committees, sowing discord. At heart, though, was the by now all too familiar issue of control: Gubkommunotdel was to regulate the committees that were to be organized on a class principle with the help of the trade unions. The episode reveals not only the extent to which the population had made an art of living despite Soviet power, but also the degree to which it had come to mistrust the capricious authorities.[51] From Babine we learn that middle-class Saratov as late as November 1921 kept its lodgings "intentionally in a state of extreme neglect and dirt . . . in order to scare the Soviet house hunters away."[52]

As the Civil War and famine drew to a close, the housing shortage remained critical in Saratov as well as in the district towns, with the exception of Kuznetsk, Serdobsk, and Atkarsk, which fate had exempted from some of the direct destruction of civil war. Apart from the damage occurring during the May 1918 uprising in Saratov, the city had been spared shelling and other military destruction. Nonetheless, the city's physical plant endured enormous losses, which can be explained

---

[49] GASO, f. 521, op. 1, d. 906, l. 143; *Itogi perepisi*, 30; and *Otchet 9-go sozyva*, 198.
[50] *ISS*, no. 91, April 25, 1921, 3; no. 146, July 3, 1921, 1; no. 167, July 30, 1921, 2; and *Otchet 9-go sozyva*, 199–200.
[51] *ISS*, no. 153, July 12, 1921, 2.
[52] Raleigh, *A Russian Civil War Diary*, 190.

by the exhaustion of resources and by the fire of 1920. Even with the decline in population after 1920, the average number of inhabitants per apartment remained high, amounting to 5.09.[53] Reports from the end of the Civil War spotlight the horrible condition of many buildings as well as of army barracks.[54]

The Lost War on Economic Ruin

After thrashing the White armies in early 1920, the fatigued and drained Soviet republic devoted all of its energies to "peaceful construction," to attempts to address industrial collapse, transportation breakdown, shrinking rations, and a dying city. As one local newspaper put it, Red labor would defeat the remaining enemies: "hunger, cold, and typhus."[55] Newspaper headlines throughout the province declared war on economic ruin, filth, disease, and hunger, while feature articles addressed the need to restore industry, raise productivity, and mobilize labor armies at the rear. In practice, however, peacetime Soviet construction meant the launching of feverish, militaristic, and largely ineffective campaigns against a spate of economic and social problems. Peaceful construction signified conscription of civilians and "voluntary" campaigns of all sorts in an attempt to repair the physical destruction caused by civil war. As the authorities saw it, "the economic front, the battle against economic collapse — is the very same as the military front, but stretching across all of Soviet Russia."[56]

The Saratov party organization singled out transportation at the end of 1919 as "the most serious question of Soviet construction," for the breakdown of this vital concern had made it impossible to guarantee even meager rations for the city's population and army units, or to provide sufficient fuel. The local railroad journal noted numerous fires, recurring accidents, and the regularity with which clerks and repairmen shirked their responsibilities. In 1920 the party failed to restore rail transport or to retain the loyalties of railroad workers, whose mood became agitated. Their publication reported that the prospects of living through another winter without sufficient food and fuel had confused their "weak, unconscious comrades." Everyday forms of resistance such

---

[53] GASO, f. 456, op. 1, d. 912, ll. 16–17, 21, and V. Serebriakov, "Itogi perepisi gorodov i poselenii gorodskogo tipa Saratovskoi gub. 15-go marta 1923 g.," in *Statisticheskii sbornik po Saratovskoi gubernii* (Saratov, 1923), 84, 86, 87.

[54] *Otchet 9-go sozyva*, 198, 232; on Atkarsk see GASO, f. 456, op. 1, d. 355, l. 48. For the barracks see RGASPI, f. 17, op. 13, d. 869, ll. 40–40 ob.

[55] *Privolzhskii krasnyi put'*, no. 3–4 (March, 1920): 6.

[56] *ISS*, no. 129, Oct. 10, 1920, 2.

as absenteeism shot up. "As always," the journal recounted, "poisonous, foul counterrevolutionary creatures still living among us take advantage of an opportune moment for their malicious agitation. They use all possible occasions for their fiendish whispering."[57]

But it was more than the inability to pay workers that made them susceptible to anti-Communist agitation. By the end of 1920 the economic situation had entered a sharp downturn, which called into question more than at any other time the regime's guiding policies. Civil war conditions had shattered much of the city's infrastructure and ruined many of the amenities of urban life. The periodic shortage and at times total lack of fuel, electricity, and water exacerbated the bleak housing situation and promoted the spread of infectious diseases. By early 1921 the city's water filtration system was greatly overloaded, and lack of transportation kept garbage piled high. Eight of the city's bathhouses had been restored by the end of 1920, but could not be used owing to fuel shortages. Moreover, within the province the communications system, giving way to years of neglect and abuse, now deteriorated further as peasant bands destroyed telephone lines and interrupted postal service.[58] District executive committees throughout the province mobilized party members to agitate and cajole and to take part in campaigns to lay up stocks for the winter of 1920–21. As the urban masses became demoralized and captious, and as the Red Army units in the Saratov garrison quit their posts, party external language became desperately solicitous. Everything would be done, the propaganda apparatus screamed, to improve the workers' material conditions, to raise the masses' cultural level and consciousness, to curb bureaucratism, to strengthen the fighting capacity of the Red Army. There may not be much food to dole out, but according to a recent decree, the laboring population would receive it free. Lavish rhetorical solicitousness too often had been resorted to in the past to have a salutary effect now. Many people saw it for what it was: a sign of utter weakness. Throughout the Civil War many had become disillusioned with the transmogrification of Soviet socialism into "commissarocracy." Now that the military campaigns had died down, they came to resent the continuation of the state's economic policies known as War Communism. Their material condition had not improved as a result of the campaigns of 1920, and, as will be shown in chapter 12, they challenged Communist authority by espousing the original ideals of the Revolution.

---

[57] *Privolzhskii krasnyi put'*, no. 23–24 (Dec. 1919): 1; *Na transport*, no. 78, Sept. 3, 1920, 2; no. 115, Nov. 21, 1920, 2; and no. 130, Dec. 9, 1920, 2.
[58] *Otchet 9-go sozyva*, 203, 228–31, 265–67.

A Breeding Ground for Disease

The changes brought about by social strife had resulted in a progressive deterioration in city services, while shortages of all sorts weakened residents' ability to fight off disease and infection. Bad nutrition, lack of heat, soap, and water, physical exhaustion and stress, serious overcrowding, and interaction with hordes of refugees transformed Saratov into a natural breeding ground for illness and infectious disease, giving rise to one of the most cataclysmic public health crises in modern history. Chronic scarcities of medicines, bandages, and vaccines aggravated the situation. So did the attitudes and inadequacies of Saratov's medical personnel, most of whom harbored grievances against the regime. Moreover, their own physical and mental weariness and vulnerability to disease frequently made a mockery of their chosen mission.

General conditions of health deteriorated rapidly after 1917. Throughout the first half of 1918 various strains of typhus and cholera stalked the province, especially along the railroad lines and the banks of the Volga where refugees congregated. "The sanitary situation in the city is horrible," concluded the ispolkom. "The city is dirty. . . . Living quarters, both socialized and not, are in awful sanitary condition." Until measures were taken, both prophylactic and otherwise, the deathrate for cholera patients reached 60 percent of those infected. The open coffins that were part of church burials helped to transmit the disease. Later in the year when Red Army soldiers crowded field hospitals, an investigatory commission chastised personnel for the lack of basic hygiene, indifference, and hostility.[59] But the situation in the field hospitals did not improve: in 1919 army hospitals lacked firewood, clean linen, medicines, instruments, and food. They bred epidemics, contributing to the high desertion rate among Red Army draftees. Underscoring the anti-Soviet mood of the doctors and nursing staff that worked "not out of conscience, but out of fear and necessity," Bolshevik E. N. Bogdanova despaired over her inability to effect any improvements. Additionally, medical personnel frequently fell ill, and whenever the 4th Army passed through the city, health officials had to battle with the military authorities, who wanted to take part of the city's medical staff with them.[60]

That year, 1919, marked the apogee of military operations in the environs of Saratov and a qualitative and dramatic downturn in health and health care. The infectious disease rate almost doubled from 68.3

[59] *Vrachebno-sanitarnaia khronika Saratovskoi gubernii*, no. 4–5 (1918), 94–145; GA RF, f. 393, op. 3, d. 327, l. 34.

[60] Bogdanova, "Uchastie zhenshchiny," 72–75.

per thousand in 1918 to 122.2 per thousand in 1919 (and to 121.1 in 1920).[61] Reports from across the province emphasize how civil war conditions had taken their toll in a variety of ways. Lack of nutritious food, terrible hygienic conditions, and the virtual disappearance of milk from the market elevated the deathrate for children in Balashov. Typhus claimed the lives of ispolkom members in Atkarsk, of medical personnel in Balashov, and of soldiers in the Kuznetsk garrison, who had no soap. In Saratov pure chance helped decide the fate of the sick: which ward one ended up in, which doctor or feldsher one was assigned to, or which cook was on duty could make the difference between life and death.[62]

At the end of 1919 city authorities set up an emergency commission to treat the various forms of typhus, which were infecting roughly three thousand people in the province each week. Medical personnel introduced martial law in the hospitals. In-patient and out-patient treatment proved inadequate and all house calls were canceled, as disease spread more quickly than during the epidemic of 1892, and the incidence of infection jumped as material conditions worsened. Fewer members of the medical profession were available to treat the sick, owing to mobilization, death, and illness (40 percent of the medical personnel had fallen ill). Soap and disinfectants disappeared. Not wishing to patronize the filthy Soviet barbershops "out of respect for the typhus raging all around," Babine began cutting his own hair.[63] Lice and bedbugs spread typhus; typhoid fever was passed on through feces (recall Babine's description of the university outhouse). Not surprisingly, the dirty outlying regions such as Glebuchev ravine registered the highest infection rates, but the number of recorded cases likewise rose in the city's center owing to overcrowding and to the fact that the comparatively better-off townspeople turned to doctors who registered their patients. Deathrates for typhus range from 5.3 to 19.6 percent in 1919, averaging 13.8 percent (9.2 percent in Saratov city). Deathrates were highest along railroad routes and among refugees, prisoners of war, and Red Army men.[64]

[61] Mal'kov, *Estestvennoe dvizhenie naseleniia*, 16–17, and S. G. Wheatcroft, "Famine and Epidemic Crises in Russia, 1918–1922: The Case of Saratov," *Annales de démographie historique* (1983): 332–34.

[62] *Izvestiia Balashovskogo uispolkoma*, no. 25, Feb. 4, 1919, 2; no. 95, May 6, 1919, 2; *Izvestiia Atkarskogo uispolkoma*, no. 179, April 9, 1919, 1–2; no. 181, April 11, 1919, 1–2; GASO, f. 521, op. 1, d. 434, l. 344; and *ISS*, no. 199, Sept. 10, 1919, 2. See also TsDNISO, f. 81, op. 1, d. 6, l. 28.

[63] Raleigh, *A Russian Civil War Diary*, 152.

[64] *ISS*, no. 240, Oct. 29, 1919, 2; no. 288, Dec. 25, 1919, 3; no. 292, Dec. 30, 1919, 2–3; no. 8, Jan. 13, 1920, 4; no. 31, Feb. 10, 1920, 4; and Mal'kov, *Estestvennoe dvizhenie naseleniia*, 16–17.

TABLE 6.6
Morbidity Rates for Typhus and Related Diseases in Saratov Province

	1918	1919	1920	1921	1922
Typhus	7,693	152,911	129,054	20,932	61,079
Relapsing fever	576	21,380	37,150	19,875	47,655
Typhoid fever	6,422	17,209	20,267	14,450	7,670
Undetermined	1,110	9,044	16,185	8.043	6,908
Totals	16,071	200,544	202,656	63,290	123,312

Source: Mal'kov, *Estestvennoe dvizhenie naseleniia,* 16.

Despite the bitter low temperatures in early 1920, the arrival of evacuees from the Don region kept infection rates up (table 6.6). So did the
drudgery of daily life. The trains bringing in the sick were death trains.
One train leaving the Don with 450 infected passengers arrived with
only 359 still living. The city grew "dirtier and dirtier" as the incidence
of typhoid fever "increased to unprecedented levels." "Constant standing in bread and other lines" resulted in Babine's clothes being so in-
fested with lice that he had to make an evening ritual of picking them
off his body.[65] At one hospital all of the doctors took ill except for the
head physician. The epidemics did not spare the district towns,[66] and
related diseases struck the livestock population too. Cattle plague
(*chuma*) reached epizootic proportions by 1920, as veterinarians lamented the total lack of medicines.[67] By early 1921 the city's dumping
ground where diseased horses were brought for slaughter had turned
into a nightmare. With the coming of spring the unburned carcasses
strewn about threatened to contaminate the city's water supply.[68]

Paralleling related trends in administration, city and provincial-level
health departments now organized local health protection departments
under the direction of district soviets. When spring came, they launched
a "clean-up week" to deal with the squalor. In Saratov about half the
city's population during 1920 attended public lectures on sanitation. As
part of the campaign, Saratov's *Izvestiia* reported with some irony on
conditions in the First Communist Hospital, distinguished by filth, rudeness, and the pilfering of state property. The paper recommended seizing control of one hospital, and appointing a new staff from the chief
physician to the lowliest guard, in short, doing what was necessary to
set up a system that other hospitals could emulate. Such open windows

[65] Raleigh, *A Russian Civil War Diary,* 160.
[66] *ISS,* no. 27, Feb. 5, 1920, 3.
[67] GASO, f. 456, op. 1, d. 532, l. 4.
[68] TsDNISO, f. 27, op. 2, d. 310, l. 9.

on contemporary realities serve as a necessary antidote to the impersonal statistics. Although Saratov and the district towns were comparatively well off in terms of number of hospital beds per capita, they suffered from lack of doctors. Related figures regarding the number of first-aid stations and out-patient clinics available to the unscrubbed masses show dramatic improvement since 1917, but the conditions within the medical facilities, the lack of medicines, bandages, and sanitary conditions, belie the statistical evidence. The situation in the villages was indescribably worse. All in all, medical service during the Civil War was generally accessible and it was "free." But quality suffered and privilege determined access to scarce medicines and supplies; these defects led to bribery at all levels and a black market in doctors' private services.[69]

The incidence of venereal disease during the Civil War, particularly syphilis, also reached alarming proportions owing to sexual licentiousness and widespread prostitution. Measures taken by the soviet in 1918 to outlaw prostitution and to transform prostitutes into productive citizens merely drove the vice into the underground. Moreover, as the front moved in on Saratov the regime had little zeal or energy for dealing with the problem. Economic necessity forced many into prostitution, while the local garrison provided an eager clientele. When Saratov fell under siege in July 1919, *Izvestiia* exposed the goings-on in Lipki Park, which before the war was the promenade of the well to do. When the militia arrived to arrest the large number of prostitutes there and send them to dig trenches, sailors came to their rescue and got into a brawl with the militia. The peddling of sexual favors in Lipki violated the revolutionary sensibilities of Central Committee member E. M. Iaroslavskii, sent to Saratov to mobilize forces during the siege. "Go at any hour, but especially at 5–6 o'clock in the afternoon to Lipki Park," he wrote. "You'll find all of the benches and tables, all of the lanes and pathways occupied by the idle ranks of young people in sailor and Red Army uniforms, unmarried women and young people in elegant outfits, prostitutes and their souteneurs." When the weather got too cold to brave the elements, prostitutes moved inside to the city's grimy teahouses. By late 1920 Saratov's central clinic treated up to 10,000 cases of venereal disease a month.[70]

As living conditions declined, little could be done to prevent women, children, and men from bartering their bodies for something to eat or

---

[69] GASO, f. 521, op. 1, d. 556, ll. 1–2 ob; *ISS*, no. 86, April 20, 1920, 3; no. 87, April 21, 1920, 1; no. 82, April 15, 1921, 4; no. 230, Oct. 12, 1920, 3; and *Spravochnik Saratovskogo gubernskogo otdela zdravookhraneniia*, no. 1, *na 1921 g.* (Saratov, 1921).

[70] *ISS*, no. 153, July 17, 1919, 2, and no. 230, Oct. 12, 1920, 4.

for some sorely needed item such as a chunk of soap (so essential for warding off disease) or item of clothing. Following the explosion of popular rage against Soviet power in March 1921, authorities once again sought to "reeducate" prostitutes and send them to work. But famine and the realities of the NEP interfered with these plans. Local sources claim prostitution took on enormous dimensions and had become professionalized, with more than three hundred hookers openly working the city's "finest" streets, where the earliest "results of NEP" could be seen on display in the "richest shops."[71]

In sum, at the end of the Civil War the prospects for adequate health care had not improved. The streets had "been turned into garbage dumps," and now instead of typhus, health officials declared war on cholera, a partner to famine. By the summer of 1921 the incidence of infection again reached alarming proportions: in one month the city reported over two thousand cases, with a deathrate of 58 percent. The medical profession's ability to carry out mass-scale inoculations of the city's inhabitants kept the population from being decimated. A few months later the press's attention turned to the staggering number of famine victims and to the rising health costs and uncertainties of the transition to the New Economic Policy. Once again, typhus returned.[72] During the year, 14,903 "refugees from hunger" fled to Saratov, where 96 percent perished.[73] A description of sanitary conditions in Saratov in 1922 claims that "the contamination of living quarters has reached extraordinary levels; the destruction of property continues . . . and water pipes are constantly bursting; at the bazaars and in stores there is a bacchanalia of reselling . . . contaminated and adulterated food products."[74]

The Hope and Pride of the Revolutionary People

A Serdobsk newspaper with considerable irony called them "the hope and pride of the revolutionary people."[75] These were the tens of thousands of local children and the millions nationwide that war and revolu-

[71] Ibid., no. 205, Sept. 11, 1921, 4.

[72] Ibid., no. 75, April 6, 1921, 3; no. 138, June 24, 1921, 1; no. 144, July 1, 1921, 1; no. 235, Oct. 18, 1921, 3; and *Protokoly dvukh zasedanii 1-oi gorodskoi konferentsii sanitarnykh, zhilishchnykh i uchastkovykh vrachei i predstavitelei raionnykh sanitarnykh komitetov ot 8–10 sentiabria 1921 goda* (Saratov, 1921), 4. Also see GASO, f. 692, op. 1, d. 103, l. 74.

[73] Mal'kov, *Estestvennoe dvizhenie naseleniia,* 29.

[74] S. Mamushin, "Ocherednye zadachi sanitarnoi organizatsii v g. Saratove i gubernii," *Saratovskii vestnik zdravookhraneniia* 2, nos. 9–12 (1922): 59–60.

[75] *Serp i molot* (Serdobsk), no. 223, Oct. 20, 1920, 1.

tion, epidemics and famine, had left homeless, destitute, neglected. They were orphans, abandoned children, refugees, children sent from the starving capitals, mentally retarded waifs—Russia's *besprizornye*. At the mercy of an impoverished and, later, depleted social system, they were brutalized by poverty and disease, filth and neglect, undernourishment, substance addiction, and physical and sexual abuse. Whether jammed into children's homes or making their wily way in the unfriendly streets or criminal underground, the waifs left a mark on the Soviet society of their adulthood.

Enduring food shortages and terrible sanitary conditions from the beginning of the Civil War, the more than thirty children's homes in Saratov Province could not cope with the demands on their resources. Prominent leaders of the Saratov Soviet in February 1918 realized the city could not honor Petrograd's request to accept 50,000 of its children and tried to deflect those scheduled for arrival to the district towns, where they would be closer to food supplies. At the time Petrograd made the request, local authorities discussed how to deal with the large number of child beggars "who in the name of Christ ask for alms." Soviet leaders saw them as a product of bourgeois society and searched for appropriate ways to house and educate them. These were still the halcyon days of the new world, when utopian ideas and plans to chart the future were in abundant supply, and resources were ample enough to be confiscated from someone. Declaring June 16 a holiday for the children of the poor, the soviet arranged free tram rides for them to Monastery Suburb, where they were fed "at the expense of the revolutionary people."[76]

A year of civil war, however, had cheapened life, depleted resources, and trimmed ambitions. Authorities complained of their inability to accommodate the influx of scabietic homeless children, many of them refugees, who showed up in town without parents, relatives, or acquaintances. Saratov's children's homes needed more space: at year's end the city's eighteen homes served an estimated 1,300 children under age fifteen. The homes lacked sufficient heat, soap, medicine, and linens. Contagious diseases visited frequently. Conditions had brought about a qualitative change in the children's behavior—criminal tendencies and activities replaced the widespread begging of 1918, probably because resources had become scarcer. Their behavior may also have reflected a rejection of the regime's social policies. It certainly shows they did not lack agency: in order to claim a place in a children's home, many of the criminally inclined older children, "who have no desire to learn, to

[76] *ISS*, no. 13, Jan. 18, 1918, 2; no. 29, Feb. 20, 1918, 3; no. 33, Feb. 24, 1918, 4; and no. 117, June 16, 1918, 3.

work, or to take part in the daily chores of the children's homes," maintained they were fifteen or under. Refusing to follow instructions or to clean up after themselves, they hurled vulgar insults at their teachers. Almost all of them had ties with the criminal world, and many were well known as professional burglars and pickpockets. At night they victimized the more innocent waifs, subjecting them to beatings, mutilation, and rape.[77]

The number of children's homes appears to have fallen throughout 1919; with the defeat of the Whites in early 1920 more homes were opened, including homes for Latvian, Jewish, and retarded children, enabling the city to house some 1,800 children. A medical commission examined all those without documents testifying to their age, and sent to work about 100 waifs deemed fit for physical labor. Despite these measures, an estimated 300 unattended, hungry children had turned to the authorities for help and dozens of new children were showing up each day. What would we encounter if we were to peer into the broken windows of a few children's homes? There was enough vile food to keep them alive from a caloric point of view, but no heat, blankets, soap, or hot water. Some children had not bathed or changed their undergarments in five months. They suffered from scabies and lice. Schools had been shut down owing to lack of fuel. The paucity of adequate clothing and shoes often prevented them from taking part in activities planned on their behalf. Like the city itself, the homes were dingy, cheerless, overcrowded, in urgent need of repair, and staffed by unqualified personnel.[78] Although evidence does not allow an informed estimate of the number of homeless waifs in Saratov and its environs, their number rose throughout the Civil War.[79]

The situation in the district towns was no better than in Saratov. Calling children's home no. 2 "a house of tears," the Serdobsk newspaper took readers inside and introduced them to the hunger, cold, and high deathrate among these children under seven. Gangs of street urchins roamed from city to city, and authorities sometimes found it easier to escort them out of town than to help them. When a group of thirty-one children arrived in Serdobsk from Rtishchevo, local authorities fed and clothed them, but could not provide adequate supervision, as a result of which they took to the streets and got involved in criminal activity. "The political and educational sides of life don't interest them,"

---

[77] Ibid., no. 188, Aug. 27, 1919, 2; no. 288, Dec. 25, 1919, 2; and no. 35, Feb. 14, 1920, 3.

[78] Ibid., no. 37, Feb. 17, 1920, 3; no. 40, Feb. 20, 1920, 4; Dec. 19, 1920, 3; *Otchet 9-go sozyva*, 86; GASO, f. 456, op. 1, d. 386, l. 29; and d. 421, l. 7.

[79] See Alan Ball, "The Roots of *Besprizornost'* in Soviet Russia's First Decade," *Slavic Review* 51, no. 2 (1992): 247–70.

complained *Serp i molot* (Hammer and Sickle). "Many of them don't even know who Lenin, Trotsky, Kolchak, and Denikin are or what they stand for." In late 1920, conditions in Serdobsk's children's homes housed on the property of the once privileged landowners reflected the general crisis-level breakdown of the entire economy. There were no bathing facilities or bed and personal linens. Dressed in tattered rags too flimsy to wash, the children suffered from scabies, eczema, and parasitic illnesses. Observers could hear them scratching and crying all night. Fed foul food, they lacked milk altogether. And they shocked their appalled and helpless benefactors by their rudeness and cruelty.[80]

The homeless children's position deteriorated sharply in 1921, for the economic collapse continued, resulting in the closing of many homes. The famine of 1921–22 threw many besprizornye into the streets, too (figure 6.1).[81] By late summer 1921 only three homes still operated, and this at a time when hunger added legions of new besprizornye to the enormous number already at large. Alan Ball has concluded that "the famine played a greater role in depriving children of their homes than did any other cause."[82] In such horrid conditions officials responsible for social services could do little to help, although they eventually did open more homes, accommodating a mere six hundred.[83]

An Ambiguous Legacy

Economic ruin proved every bit as difficult to lick as the White armies. Industrial output in the Lower Volga region in 1921–22 amounted to just 30 percent of its prewar level. Six years of hostilities, of wartime production that exhausted supplies, machinery, and labor, and of ideologically inspired and circumstantially applied economic policies had shattered the state's infrastructure, depleted its resources, brutalized its people, and brought them to the brink of physical exhaustion and emotional despair. Shortages of everything except enmity, cynicism, and contempt had unleashed people's vileness and exposed their vulnerability. The fierce struggle to survive did not spare the regime itself, whose external language acknowledged the plight of the people. Then, in 1921, famine, the last chapter of the calamitous Civil War, seized hold of the city and province and kept the region locked in its grip until after the 1922 harvest was in and even later. As a result of a shrinking

---

[80] *Golos kommunizma*, no. 151 (188), June 21, 1919, 3; *Serp i molot*, no. 38 (237), Oct. 4, 1919, 4; and no. 223, Oct. 20, 1920, 1.

[81] For example, see GASO, f. 521, op. 3, d. 25, l. 180.

[82] Ball, "Roots," 255.

[83] GASO, f. 329, op. 1, d. 222, ll. 3 ob–4.

6.1 Homeless children being evacuated by rail. Courtesy Saratov Kraevedcheskii Museum, photo 10668.

sown area and the meager harvest of 1921, 68 percent of the province's population was starving by the spring of 1922.[84] Even at the beginning of 1923, approximately 30 percent of the province's population remained classified as hungry; scattered pockets of hungry villages could be found as late as 1925.[85]

The consequences require little commentary. According to the 1926 census, Russia's most accurate since 1897, the population stood at 147,028,000 instead of the 175,000,000 it would have been if it had not been for war, revolution, and civil war.[86] In Saratov Province, the decline in population between 1914 (3,075,689) and 1922 (2,642,034) came to 433,655, an overall downturn of 14 percent. However, when the lower birthrates are factored in (444,011), overall losses during this seven-year period amount to 877,666 people or 28.5 percent.[87]

Soviet policies had resulted in a large measure of deurbanization, created a transient problem of enormous proportion, militarized civilian life, ruined infrastructures, turned towns into breeding grounds for diseases, and victimized children. Redefining social space, government pol-

[84] Rogovitskii, "Deiatel'nost'," 75–77.

[85] GASO, f. 456, op. 1, d. 912, l. 64.

[86] W. G. Rosenberg, "Introduction: NEP Russia as a 'Transitional' Society," in *Russia in the Era of NEP: Explorations in Soviet Society and Culture*, ed. by Sheila Fitzpatrick, Alexander Rabinowitch, and Richard Stites (Bloomington, 1991), 6.

[87] Mal'kov, *Estestvennoe dvizhenie naseleniia*, 52.

icies transformed individuals into migrants, refugees, class enemies, the diseased, the hungry, and the malnourished. The historiography on Russian cities tends to argue that urban and family institutions demonstrated remarkable persistence to survive, despite the prevalent disintegration.[88] They did, but in battered, altered form, and this was bound to have social and political consequences. Whereas Moshe Lewin argues that a "'primitivization' of the whole social system" occurred,[89] I stress that it was not simply a matter of regression, but also of new structuring. As Robert Argenbright observed, "The new forms of social behavior were focused on the necessities of physical survival." People had little time for political involvement. This "led to estrangement from the state,"[90] contributing to the Bolsheviks' winning the Civil War.

The sheer enormity of the convulsion shattered the traditional community as a form of social relations and revealed the extent to which the state was ready to reconfigure social space. Here I have painted a broad brush portrait of the trauma; later chapters, in restoring agency to society, will look at how it affected cultural engineering, social identities, and collective actions. To understand this dynamic, however, I wish to emphasize that the Civil War simultaneously saw the brutalization and impoverishment of society as well as the extension of utopian dreams and mobilizing policies that met with modest success, particularly among heretofore marginalized groups and the new generation coming of age.

[88] Brower, "'The City in Danger'," 59, and Diane P. Koenker, "Introduction: Social and Demographic Change in the Civil War," in *Party, State, and Society*, 53.

[89] Moshe Lewin, "The Civil War: Dynamics and Legacy," in *Party, State, and Society*, 416.

[90] Robert Argenbright, "Bolsheviks, Baggers and Railroaders: Political Power and Social Space, 1917–1921," *Russian Review* 52, no. 4 (1993): 509. Narskii reaches similar conclusions. See *Zhizn' v katastrofe*, 561–66.

Seven

The Cultural Practices
of Provincial Communism

REVOLUTIONS ARE not only about politics and social upheaval, but also about cultural creation. Realizing that culture could be
a conservative force that got in the way of their modernizing project,
the Bolsheviks sought to establish hegemony in a Gramscian sense over
their subjects by implementing ideologically inspired cultural practices.[1]
In revolutionizing culture, however, they confronted a problem that
would vex subsequent generations of Soviet leaders and revolutionaries
everywhere: how to successfully employ the despotic power of the state
in order to reconfigure society without jeopardizing their position.

The Bolsheviks' belief that they had the moral right to rule, their
delusions of imminent world revolution, and the great sense of urgency
they felt in remaking society justified their use of coercion. Nevertheless,
they disagreed over how best to implement new cultural practices. Although some party members opposed the complete destruction of the
cultural past and instead sought to "proletarianize" it by making it
more accessible, others advocated sacking old forms in establishing con-

---

[1] While ideology is contested and open to revision, hegemony is seldom contested and
"does not appear to be ideological at all." Both ideology and hegemony find reflection in
the wielding of power, which appears in what the Comaroffs call the "agentive" mode
(Mann's despotic power, see chapter 3) and in the nonagentive mode (Mann's infrastructural power). Agentive or despotic power manifests itself in its ability to control the production and consumption of signs and objects, whereas nonagentive power appears to be
beyond human agency. Comaroff and Comaroff, *Ethnography*, 27–29.

trol over the production and consumption of cultural signs. Intellectuals and artists for whom the Revolution had turned Russian society into a vast social laboratory joined them in these ventures, which provided them with an opportunity to press their own agendas. The aspirations of many elements within the intelligentsia, after all, intersected nicely with the Bolsheviks' own political and social project.[2] As party leaders and intellectuals quarreled among themselves over how best to effect cultural change, practices immersed in everyday life continued to direct people's perceptions along more familiar, less revolutionary pathways, preventing a complete destruction of past culture. This dynamic only served to strengthen the revolutionary intelligentsia's belief in the critical importance of its own role in transforming Russian society. Ultimately, the Bolsheviks sacralized a new world privileging workers and at times peasants through their actions, their use of a system of signs and symbols, and through their construction of a heroic narrative of the revolutionary present that reflected new social hierarchies and forms of power and that helped invent a *Soviet* tradition.[3] While this narrative of integration — and exclusion — made it possible for later generations of Soviet leaders to co-opt and mobilize individuals and groups, the employment of the despotic power of the state kept cultural hegemony an elusive goal.

Proletarian Cultural Organizations

Revolutionary dreaming found expression in iconoclastic efforts to sweep away old cultural forms and to create new ones. In its hurried drive to reconstitute society, the Soviet government abolished titles, private property, and ranks. It fashioned new language, social hierarchies (and divisions), rituals and festivals, myths, and revolutionary morality. It modernized the alphabet, introduced calendar reform, and sought to make revolution itself a tradition. Revolutionary songs, party newspapers, slogans, pamphlets, brochures, elections, and festivals took on new meaning.[4] To have power meant to have control, even temporarily,

[2] Recent studies have underscored the complicated interaction between the empowering environment of revolution, utopian stirrings of Communists and intellectuals alike, Russian cultural practices, and the larger contemporary arena of Western and even American culture. See in particular Katerina Clark, *Petersburg: Crucible of Cultural Revolution* (Cambridge, Mass., 1995). Michael David-Fox also suggests how the Bolsheviks' initiatives often extended existing dreams among the intelligentsia. See his *Revolution of the Mind: Higher Learning among the Bolsheviks, 1918–1929* (Ithaca, 1997).

[3] See Eric Hobsbawm and Terence Ranger, eds., *The Invention of Tradition* (Cambridge, Eng., 1983), 1–12.

[4] See Stites, *Revolutionary Dreams*.

over "the articulation and deployment of outward manifestations of the new nation."[5]

Responsible locally for cultural affairs and educational policies, the Provincial Department of Public Education (*Gubotnarob*) nationalized the city's theaters and other cultural institutions in 1918, banning the staging of farces, comedies, and operettas that lacked a social message,[6] and prohibiting Saratov's movie theaters from showing films that portrayed workers or peasants in a critical light.[7] The department also launched a permanent opera company, and cultural-enlightenment circles run by teachers.[8] By mid-1919 the department boasted that it had opened 515 theatrical and musical clubs for workers and children, and that it had "proletarianized" the local conservatory, whose student body now comprised 44.5 percent workers (vs. 14 percent before the Revolution). At Civil War's end Gubotnarob supervised the activities of 55 art studios throughout the province, enrolling 5,200 students, most of whom came from worker and peasant backgrounds.[9]

But the institution most identified in public consciousness with cultural revolution was Proletkult, organized in October 1918 after numerous false starts. Proletkult (an acronym for proletarian cultural-educational organizations) aimed to awaken independent creative activity among the proletariat. Like many others, the Saratov branch had four sections: theater, music, literature, and art, each organized into studios. Without a common vision of what "proletarian culture" was or ought to be, local cultural activists battled to found a new cultural order, confirming Mally's argument that their struggle "was just as contestuous as the efforts to change the political and economic foundations of Soviet society."[10] They debated issues such as what could be learned from the culture of the past, how much autonomy proletarian organizations should have, and how to allot scarce resources.[11] Proletkult also expended considerable energy retaining its independence in face of pressure from Soviet and party organs to have Proletkult organizations merge

[5] Hunt, *Politics, Culture, and Class*, 53.

[6] Merkul'ov, "Pervye shagi," 175; GA RF, f. 393, op. 3, d. 327, l. 58; see also GASO, f. 494, op. 1, d. 9, ll. 5–6; f. 494, op. 1, d. 13, ll. 2–7; and f. 494, op. 1, d. 15, ll. 83–83 ob.

[7] *Khudozhestvennye izvestiia*, no. 6 (1918): 2, and *ISS*, no. 124, June 14, 1919, 3.

[8] See GASO, f. 494, op. 1, d. 40a, ll. 11–12, 76–78 ob, and f. 494, op. 1, d. 110, ll. 2–6.

[9] GASO, f. 456, op. 1, d. 532, ll. 23–23 ob; *Godovshchina*, 66–72; G. A. Malinin and Z. E. Gusakova, comps., *Kul'turnoe stroitel'stvo v Saratovskom Povolzh'e: Dokumenty i materialy*, part 1, *1917–1928 gg.* (Saratov, 1985), 220–21. See also GASO, f. 494, op. 1, d. 5, l. 19.

[10] See Lynn Mally, *Culture of the Future: The Proletkult Movement in Revolutionary Russia* (Berkeley, 1990), xviii.

[11] See for example *ISS*, no. 181, Sept. 4, 1918, 3.

7.1 First Saratov Provincial Proletkult Conference, 1918. Courtesy Saratov Kraevedcheskii Museum, photo 33169.

with subdepartments of adult education.[12] The latter tended to prevail because Proletkult groups received precious meeting space only when they agreed to subordinate themselves to Gubotnarob (figure 7.1).[13]

Believing that it was "building a new temple of culture" with "blood and steel,"[14] Proletkult set up people's theaters, choirs, musical ensembles, libraries, cafeterias, writing groups, and workers' clubs, some of which catered to minority nationalities. The workers' clubs staged drama productions, ran libraries, provided activities for children, and promoted adult literacy programs, which built on a well-developed tradition among the local intelligentsia of educating working-class adults. Material and human shortages, however, undercut Proletkult's attempts to spread literacy,[15] while its efforts to politicize club activities proved largely unsuccessful because they bored workers. The cafeteria it opened in the "People's Palace" in a government building in the city's

[12] GASO, f. 329, op. 1, d. 4a, l. 125. See also GASO, f. 494, op. 1, d. 5, l. 34.

[13] KG, no. 307, March 15, 1919, 3; GASO, f. 329, op. 1, d. 41, l. 140; Godovshchina, 64–65; and Vzmakhi, no. 1 (1919): 122–25.

[14] Vzmakhi, no. 2 (1920): 80.

[15] ISS, no. 135, June 27, 1919, 3; ISS, no. 136, June 28, 1919, 3. See also Malinin and Gusakova, Kul'turnoe stroitel'stvo, 222–23, and GASO, f. 329, op. 1, d. 4a, ll. 72–72 ob.

center, moreover, attracted more members of the bourgeoisie than workers because it was too far away from the workers' own neighborhoods.[16]

Fierce debate accompanied Proletkult's efforts to revolutionize the
theater. Its leading theatrical specialist, Platon Kerzhentsev, steered the
organization's utopian efforts to move theater from a professional to a
mass base and to blur the distinction between art and nonart, and the
relationship between life and the revolutionary process itself.[17] Vision-
aries gave priority to involving workers in theater, supporting the notion that it was not important if a troupe performed badly, as long as it
was made up of workers.[18] But the amateur actors failed to satisfy
viewers, proletarian or otherwise; professional actors remained in demand and, not surprisingly, worked only for money. Their views and
tastes predominated until 1920,[19] when theatrical repertoires were
"cleansed of the garbage that had dirtied the stage before the Revolution." "Control" over theaters amounted to the restoration of classical
repertoires and to a lesser extent to the introduction of "reformist"
trends. Enthusiasts thus maintained that revolution had *not* transformed the theater, that there remained a profound need for new, revolutionary playwrights and proletarian actors.[20]

In need of a system of signs and emblems to distinguish itself from
the past, to represent the principles of Soviet power, and to win over the
population's sympathies, the new regime sought out local artists.[21] The
Revolution, however, had intensified an embittered feud between "futurist" (a term used to describe experimental styles such as cubism, im-
pressionism, and abstract art) and realist artists: with the exception of
the futurists, most Russian artists opposed the Bolsheviks. Yet artists
representing different currents in the art world began to cooperate with
them — in part because they controlled rapidly dwindling resources and
employed a large number of artists. The soviet's Department of Art, the
Union of Artists (*Rabis*), and Proletkult fell into the hands of futurists.

---

[16] GASO, f. 329, op. 1, d. 4a, l. 51.

[17] Writing about his native Saratov, novelist Konstantin Fedin captures much of the
excitement of such experimentation in his *An Unusual Summer* (Moscow, 1950). For the
debates see Robert Russell, "The Arts and the Russian Civil War," *Journal of European
Studies* 20 (1990): 219–20; Clark, *Petersburg*, 124–26; and GASO, f. 494, op. 1, d. 110,
ll. 2–6.

[18] *Izvestiia Balashovskogo uispolkoma*, no. 104, May 16, 1919, 3.

[19] *ISS*, no. 97, May 11, 1919, 3.

[20] Ibid., no. 87, May 11, 1919, 3; no. 161, July 26, 1919, 2; no. 274, Dec. 2, 1920, 4;
no. 286, Dec. 16, 1920, 3; GASO, f. 521, op. 1, d. 543, ll. 3, 5 ob; and *Vzmakhi*, no. 2
(1920): 85–86.

[21] For similarities with the French Revolution see Maurice Agulhon, "Politics, Images,
and Symbols in Post-Revolutionary France," in *Rites of Power: Symbolism, Rituals, and
Politics since the Middle Ages*, ed. by Sean Wilentz (Philadelphia, 1985), 177.

Some well-known artists—A. Savinov, A. Karev, P. Utkin, and M. Kuznetsov—headed up studios at the Bogoliubovsk Art School, which remained the heart of local artistic life. In addition, Proletkult opened an art studio run by advocates of abstract art and tenaciously defended them when their activities drew protest from the Center.[22] Through posters and visual displays, V. Iustinskii and other local futurist artists depicted the heroic aspects of revolutionary victories with allegorical or neoclassical figures influenced by the French Revolution, or with images of the sun. The content was martial and satirical.[23] Over time images became more accessible and less abstract as mystical elements of traditional Russian folk art became fused with political ideology.[24]

Some authors credit Saratov artist Nikolai Andreevich Koloiarskii with designing the first hammer and sickle emblem in Russia, one of the most recognized symbols of the Revolution (figure 7.2). Koloiarskii had studied at Bogoliubovsk, after which he worked at the Faberge house in Petrograd, where he witnessed the early events of 1917 before returning to Saratov. In November Lebedev commissioned artists at Bogoliubovsk to fashion a new emblem symbolizing Soviet power. Combining allegorical and symbolic elements, Koloiarskii's first attempt at a new emblem depicted three crossed symbols of the social groups composing Soviet power locally, the hammer, sickle, and sword (representing soldiers). Under pressure to craft the new emblem as soon as possible, M. D. Iastrebova, the artist chosen to embroider the symbols, simplified the design—and Soviet power—by dropping the sword. In early December the hammer and sickle already hung above the entrance to the hall where the gubispolkom convened.[25]

Proletkult and the Saratov Soviet also erratically published several short-lived journals featuring proletarian writers.[26] However, the literary studio, headed up by a baker named V. M. Blinkov, remained the weakest of Proletkult's activities. Lack of paper and quality proletarian prose as well as opposition from the intelligentsia prevented these journals

[22] Lynn Mally, "Artists and the Proletarian Revolution," unpublished conference paper presented at the 1984 Seminar in Twentieth-Century Russian and Soviet Social History, 15. K. Petrov-Vodkin, a native of Khvalynsk who acquired national fame, became one of the first spokespersons for Soviet art. See Ulf Abel, "Icons and Soviet Art," in Claes Arvidson and Lars Erik Blomqvist, eds., *Symbols of Power: The Esthetics of Political Legitimation in the Soviet Union and Eastern Europe* (Stockholm, 1987), 150–57.

[23] Russell, "The Arts," 237.

[24] For representations of women see Victoria Bonnell, "The Representation of Women in Early Soviet Political Art," *Russian Review* 50, no. 3 (1991): 276–77, 287.

[25] G. N. Koloiarskii, unpublished manuscript, "Kto sozdal pervuiu emblemu 'serp i molot'." Figes and Kolonitskii present a different scenario in *Interpreting*, 61–62.

[26] The Soviet put out *Gornilo* in 1918, which featured party intellectuals rather than plebeian writers.

7.2 The first hammer and sickle emblem designed in Saratov, and perhaps in Russia, by N. A. Koloiarskii (the text reads "Provincial Executive Committee"). Courtesy Saratov Kraevedcheskii Museum.

from being issued regularly, despite *Izvestiia*'s insistence that there was a good deal of workers' writing to publish.[27] In early 1921 the local literary studio for workers died out.[28]

By October 1919, Proletkult had set up numerous workers' organizations, clubs, and studios for singing, drama, painting and sculpture, and

[27] *Vzmakhi*, no. 1 (1919). Opposition is discussed in *Vzmakhi*, no. 2 (1920): 88. The Pokrovsk branch of Proletkult put out *Literaturnoe tvorchestvo proletariata*, no. 1 (1919).

[28] *ISS*, no. 63, March 23, 1921, 3. By Civil War's end only two issues of *Vzmakhi* with small press runs had been published. See *Vzmakhi*, no. 2 (1920): 87. See also the situation concerning music in *ISS* no. 106, May 15, 1921, 2; the Union of Artists put out a short-lived publication, *Sarrabis*, no. 1, Aug. 1, 1921, and no. 2, Sept. 1, 1921.

writing,[29] yet it lacked personnel, equipment, and accommodations. Shortages of heated facilities during the winter of 1919–20 seriously curtailed Proletkult's activities. Moreover, its relations with the local party organization, which attempted to control the organization, deteriorated.[30] Just as the party tried to manage Proletkult, the latter sought to impose its authority over the plebeian classes whose talents it wanted to unleash but only in a prescribed way. Comprised of an intelligentsia divided among itself, but mostly ill-disposed toward a marketplace in culture, Proletkult, and not workers, played the leading role in promoting proletarian culture, and for this reason had limited success. Whether or not a revolution in workers' consciousness had resulted is difficult to say, for it proved easier to reject the politics of the past than its culture.[31] In addition, a contradiction existed between Proletkult's desire to free workers from the influence of bourgeois cultural authorities and its determination to control workers' culture. Proletkult's leaders needed a working-class following to justify their own autonomy, but they did not believe in autonomy for workers and, as a result, workers' organizations often criticized them.[32] Ultimately, the experiment reinforced this branch of the intelligentsia's belief in itself as a prime mover in the historical process and in determining popular tastes.

Staging the Revolution: Revolutionary Festivals and Monumental Art

Russian revolutionaries, like their French counterparts, manipulated space in their attempt to transfer sacrality from the old to the new. Preferring large, open spaces "without memory" to the civic space of the old hierarchies, French revolutionaries selected new locations for political activity, purging urban space of prerevolutionary monuments. Saratov revolutionaries similarly removed tsarist monuments and emblems, but seemed less interested in civic spaces without memory and more in emphasizing symbolic inversion: they held workers' festivals in the city center and housed Soviet institutions and workers' clubs in confiscated government and private buildings of the elite in the very heart of town.[33]

[29] *Khudozhestvennye izvestiia*, no. 8 (1918): 11.

[30] Mally, *Culture of the Future*, 211.

[31] James R. Von Geldern, *Bolshevik Festivals, 1917–1920* (Berkeley, 1993), 72.

[32] *Vzmakhi*, no. 2 (1920): 85–86, 90.

[33] Mona Ozouf, *Festivals and the French Revolution*, trans. by Alan Sheridan (Cambridge, Mass., 1988), 126–96. Clark makes a similar observation about how Russian mass spectacles differed from the French. See *Petersburg*, 128. For her discussion of mass spectacles in Petrograd, see *Petersburg*, chapter 5.

If public ceremonies can be examined as metaphors upon which are inscribed assumptions about politics and social relations that legitimate the new order,[34] the first festival staged by Saratov Communists on the anniversary of the February Revolution in 1918 taught them an important lesson. An estimated 10,000 workers and soldiers accompanied by an orchestra marched past a tribune on centrally located Theater Square through an alley of red banners and red flags depicting the hammer and sickle. Following an impassioned speech by Antonov, the armed participants snaked their way to German Street, where shots rang out that killed a Communist named Tsyrkin.[35] As a result, the party took measures to guarantee that future festivals would leave little room for spontaneity and popular initiative, thus subverting the role of festivals as a spontaneous and even legitimate cultural practice. Instead, their new purpose was to reinforce the party's public transcript. This already became evident in the party's celebration of May Day that year (figure 7.3). A new Soviet flag and anthem (the "International") debuted at the celebration, cast as a funeral service for Soviet power's first martyrs. Local artists prepared panels and posters for the festivities that depicted symbols associated with labor, revolution, and the union of workers and peasants.[36] To prevent any embarrassment, the gubispolkom had published a list of approved slogans beforehand, and took measures to guarantee that the demonstrators were unarmed, except for members of a revolutionary guard. Soviet leaders expected trouble: SRs and Mensheviks had agitated against the festivities, tapping worker anger over recent Soviet elections and bruised feelings concerning the Bolsheviks' antireligious policies.[37] As one observer recalled, the celebration "had an almost exclusively military and official character. The civilian population took no part in the ceremonies for the day, much as they had been advertised by the Bolshevik authorities."[38] The Bolsheviks had not anticipated another problem. Commissioned to decorate the tribune, the artist F. Konstantinov, who had recently returned from France, draped it with black material on which he painted Matisse-like nude female figures in revolutionary red. Offended leaders ordered the fantasy figures

---

[34] See "Teufelsdrockh's Dilemma: On Symbolism, Politics, and History," in *Rites of Power: Symbolism, Ritual, and Politics since the Middle Ages*, ed. by Sean Wilentz (Philadelphia, 1985), 3.

[35] *ISS*, no. 47, March 12, 1918, 2, and Berdintsev, "Epizody bor'by," 9–10.

[36] Koloiarskii, "Kto sozdal," 42.

[37] E. A. Speranskaia, "Materialy k istorii oformleniia pervykh revoliutsionnykh prazdnestv v Saratove i Nizhnem Novgorode," in *Agitatsionno-massovoe iskusstvo pervykh let Oktiabria: Materialy i issledovaniia* (Moscow, 1971), 137–39; GASO, f. 521, op. 1, d. 47, l. 10; *ISS*, no. 87, May 5, 1918, 1; and *KG*, no. 56, April 28, 1918, 2–3.

[38] Raleigh, *A Russian Civil War Diary*, 77.

7.3 Celebration, probably of May Day, 1918. Courtesy Gosudarstvennyi Arkhiv Saratovskoi Oblasti (GASO).

covered, setting up a commission under Antonov to oversee preparations for the October Revolution celebration.

Revolutionaries not only instituted new holidays, but also sought to obscure the past by making it difficult to observe traditional holidays whose values were antithetical to the Communist order. Thus, in 1918 Sovnarkom banned the Feast of the Birth of the Virgin Mary, declaring that all factories and workplaces must remain open. Workers at several factories ignored the ban altogether, however, as old-timers griped that they had to work on a holiday, yet were given a day off to hear Trotsky speak. When rumors circulated that the Bolsheviks had likewise outlawed the celebration of Christmas, some workers decided to take the day off anyway and to make up the lost time later, thereby forcing the soviet to close factories so that people could honor their tradition.[39]

After Lenin's call in April 1918 for a program of monumental propaganda, which involved the dismantling of monuments honoring Russia's tsars and the creation of new ones, the government published a list of individuals to whom monuments were to be built in the hopes many would be ready for the anniversary of the Revolution. Unfortunately,

[39] Sokolov Diary, Sept. 8, 1918; Jan. 4, 1919; and Jan. 7, 1919.

7.4 One of the many revolutionary monuments that did not survive. This one was located at the entrance to Saratov's Radishchev Museum. Courtesy Gosudarstvennyi Arkhiv Saratovskoi Oblasti (GASO).

sculpture remained "the most backward and most adulterated of all the arts in Russia";[40] many of the works commissioned locally were executed incompetently, and often made from materials that did not hold up well against the Russian winter (figure 7.4). Another more serious problem impeded the Communists' efforts: in designing banners, flags,

[40] John E. Bowlt, "Russian Sculpture and Lenin's Plan of Monument Propaganda," in *Art and Architecture in the Service of Politics*, ed. by Henry A. Millon and Linda Nochlin (Cambridge, Mass., 1978), 184.

and other decorations, Saratov futurists, as elsewhere in Russia, complained that the masses had trouble comprehending their art.[41] However, as Saratov Communists began to standardize their symbols and introduce greater planning into their festivals, Lenin became a widely used living symbol and sacred center, reinforced by monuments to past heroes, thus creating the myth of a revolutionary prehistory.[42] For example, Sevastianov's design of a revolutionary panel for October 1918 depicted a heap of ruins (the old world) over which towered a figure of Lenin surrounded by workers hoisting a red banner. Imposing portraits of Lenin, Trotsky, Rykov (a local son), Vasiliev-Iuzhin, and Antonov-Saratovskii decorated the city's center. Antonov's commission ordered new monuments to Radishchev and Chernyshevskii (both of whom had ties to Saratov), Marx, Engels, and peasant rebel Stenka Razin. The festivities accompanying the unveiling of monuments to Chernyshevskii and Radishchev provided free entertainment and refreshments, common features of prerevolutionary festivals.[43]

Throughout 1918, leaders in Saratov and the district towns also renamed streets and squares in honor of the Revolution, and likewise sought to introduce new practices into the villages. Saratov's Theater Square was now named after the Revolution. In Balashov, a commission selected names to honor revolutionary leaders, the new privileged classes, and revolutionary concepts.[44] In the countryside committees of the village poor orchestrated village festivals, where peasants assembled at former manor houses, now transformed into schools, libraries, and first-aid stations, or else at churches or cemeteries to sing revolutionary and popular songs, under the banner "Long live Soviet power!"

In 1919 the party staged festivals against the backdrop of a raging civil war, adding new ones to boost moral, such as Red Army Day, for which the government announced an amnesty for deserters, a practice that became part of later celebrations.[45] Observed on March 8, International Women's Day was subsumed by the larger issue of military conflict and the precarious nature of Soviet power. The official slogan for the celebration made clear what women's role should be — "everything for the Red Army and everything for the front." Under siege and

---

[41] Speranskaia, "Materialy k istorii," 135–37, 151–52; and KG, no. 288, Feb. 18, 1919, 2.

[42] Richard Stites, "Festival and Revolution: The Role of Public Spectacle in Russia, 1917–1918," in Essays on Revolutionary Culture and Stalinism: Selected Papers from the Third World Congress for Soviet and East European Studies, ed. by John W. Strong (Columbus, 1989), 18.

[43] Speranskaia, "Materialy k istorii," 139–42.

[44] Izvestiia Balashovskogo Soveta, no. 192, Oct. 1918, 3.

[45] GASO, f. 507, op. 1, d. 13, l. 33.

vulnerable, local leaders now avoided public marches in favor of entertainment; financially pinched, they recycled old decorations. The May Day celebration featured fireworks and satirical skits in which orators hailed workers, the world revolution, the union of workers and middle peasants, and the need to defeat Denikin, Kolchak, and Co.[46] The May Day celebration in Atkarsk included a mass public viewing of a film, "Labor and Capital," and a demonstration featuring children and the opening of an art exhibit, after which people were treated to refreshments. In some villages Communist cells showed movies and organized meetings.[47]

The 1919 anniversary of the October Revolution emphasized the common inversion encountered in public that the hired slave had become master of the land, that a dictatorship of the proletariat had been established, and that Soviet power had replaced that of the exploiting classes. *Izvestiia* underscored the "gains" of the Revolution: land, the eight-hour day, workers' control, nationalization of industry, and the extension of culture and a social security network to the poor. The Komsomol provided entertainment, seeking to enroll new members and convince them they had been worse off under capitalism. An amnesty freed 585 people and reduced the sentences of others.[48]

In January 1920 Soviet power commemorated its victory over the Whites, not as a joyous festivity for the masses, but as a celebration of victors, who participated in a meeting of the soviet. Dignitaries from Moscow and the commander of the southeastern front addressed the assembled, while party leaders explained that world capitalism had recognized its inability to defeat Soviet power and was forced to end its blockade, which the Reds blamed for the country's economic woes. The same tone reigned over the anniversary celebration of the February Revolution. The soviet organized meetings for workers and soldiers, but fewer workers and soldiers participated than had been expected, owing to growing worker hostility and grim living conditions compounded by the harsh winter.[49] Featuring agitation meetings at the

[46] *KG*, no. 337, April 27, 1919, 3; no. 338, April 29, 1919, 3; no. 339, May 3, 1–3; *Krasnyi kanun*, a one-day paper put out on April 30, 1919; *ISS*, no. 100, May 15, 1919, 1; and TsDNISO, f. 151/95, op. 1, d. 78, ll. 8–8 ob.

[47] TsDNISO, f. 200, op. 1, d. 52, l. 93, and *Izvestiia Atkarskogo uispolkoma*, no. 204, May 14, 1919, 4.

[48] TsDNISO, f. 27, op. 1, d. 61, l. 83; f. 28, op. 1, d. 1, l. 11; op. 1, d. 5, ll. 21–22; *ISS*, no. 246, Nov. 5, 1919, 3; no. 248, Nov. 7, 1919, 1, 3; RGASPI, f. 17, op. 12, d. 466, l. 115; and GASO, f. 521, op. 1, d. 353, ll. 1, 4–5 ob, 8, 16.

[49] *ISS*, no. 18, Jan. 13, 1920, 3; no. 14, Jan. 21, 1920, 1, and no. 14, Jan. 21, 1920, 1. See also *BSG*, no. 1, 1920, 1.

workplace and in army units followed by entertainment, the anniversary of the October Revolution reflected the party's fear of large public gatherings.[50]

Economic breakdown compelled the Soviet government in 1920 to mobilize the population for the "economic front," as a result of which "volunteer" workdays (*subbotniki*) usually accompanied holidays. The first mass Communist subbotnik in Saratov took place on May 10, 1919; many more were held in 1920. Yet worker indifference forced the party to use coercion to promote participation. In March 1920 only 34 workers out of 300 showed up for a workday at a major plant. Although the local press gave extensive coverage to the "national" subbotnik held on May 1, 1920, workers at the Zhest factory went out on strike to protest Bolshevik policies "that had led the country to ruin."[51] Between June 5 and September 18, 1920, the party sponsored twenty-six subbotniki and Sunday volunteer workdays (*voskresniki*) in Saratov, involving 71,346 individuals. Others had to be canceled because few volunteers attended. In Atkarsk "absolutely no one showed up" at one subbotnik. Moreover, many Communists shirked the subbotniki by scheduling party meetings and other functions for when the workday was to be held. Acknowledging that Communists served as poor models for others, the gubkom abolished obligatory subbotniki for party members and resolved to keep them to a minimum for others. Leaders admitted that subbotniki had become obligatory burdens and that participants were "paid" with extra rations.[52]

The evidence from Saratov supports Von Geldern's argument that "the mixed sources and tangled communication of festivals revealed the uncertainty and intricacy of revolutionary cultural processes." Although the party channeled enormous human and material resources into these public expressions of revolutionary power, a groundswell of anti-Soviet feelings prevented the soviet from observing the anniversary of the Revolution in March 1921. Discontent with Soviet power and famine kept

---

[50] TsDNISO, f. 27, op. 1, d. 758, l. 18; *ISS*, no. 254, Nov. 9, 1920, 3; and *Na transport*, no. 110, Nov. 16, 1920, 2.

[51] *ISS*, no. 72, March 30, 1920, 3; no. 97, May 4, 1920, 2; no. 100, May 7, 1920, 4; and no. 113, May 23, 1920, 3. William Chase takes too optimistic a view of the 1920 May Day subbotnik in his "Voluntarism, Mobilisation and Coercion: Subbotniki, 1919–1921," *Soviet Studies* 41, no. 1 (1989): 112–14, 120.

[52] TsDNISO, f. 27, op. 1, d. 1078, l. 22; d. 477, l. 2; f. 81, op. 1, d. 16, l. 9; f. 200, op. 1, d. 126, l. 5 ob; RGASPI, f. 17, op. 12, d. 469, l. 23; *Ocherki istorii Saratovskoi partiinoi organizatsii*, 2: 122, 146–47; Poliantsev, *Saratovskaia partiinaia organizatsiia*, 198. Also see TsDNISO, f. 81, op. 1, d. 26, ll. 25, 26, 32, 73; f. 81, op. 1, d. 45, ll. 8–18, 55–60; and f. 138, op. 1, d. 10, l. 36.

the anniversary of the Revolution in November 1921 "modest," with no demonstration and only a few decorations.[53]

In reading these events as the Revolution's own history in the making, it is clear that the Communists believed they had the moral authority to stifle mass spontaneity and initiative. Fearing unrest, they disarmed the population and interfered in artists' representations of the Revolution. Designed to affirm current policies, the festivals became as monologic as the party's evolving external language. Concealing dreary realities, the festivals offered entertainment, food, and drink, and when the latter was in short supply, public amnesties of deserters and criminals. However, these came with strings attached: political lectures, volunteer workdays, and agitation meetings at the workplace. The festivals sacralized the party leaders' understanding of the historical process in class terms, which showcased the working class in public life, but only according to norms prescribed in the party's public register. Because the party, with the involvement of some intellectuals, determined the form and content of public festivals, it is hard to gauge how they might have fired the imagination of their participants.

The Communists' Organizing Scheme or Master Fiction

Like political elites elsewhere, the Bolsheviks justified their existence and determined their actions in terms of a master fiction or collection of stories, ceremonies, insignias, and formalities that they invented in this revolutionary situation.[54] Verbal texts took on special significance not only because Marxism was an ideology of the text, but also because the contingencies of civil war constantly redefined the new Communist culture and because language can evoke images, make comparisons, deal with the past and future, and relate events that cannot be depicted in action.[55] This is to the historian's advantage, for most of the visual sources have not survived. The emerging foundation narrative of the local revolution became codified in a volume edited by Antonov that appeared in October 1918, *Godovshchina proletarskoi revoliutsii* (Anniversary of the Proletarian Revolution). Its authors represented the October Revolution in ways that ascribed power and legitimacy to themselves, recasting the past to confirm the policies of the revolutionary

[53] Von Geldern, *Bolshevik Festivals*, 208, and *ISS*, no. 253, Nov. 9, 1921, 2.

[54] Clifford Geertz, "Centers, Kings, and Charisma: Reflections on the Symbolics of Power," in *Rites of Power: Symbolism, Ritual, and Politics since the Middle Ages*, ed. by Sean Wilentz (Philadelphia, 1985), 15.

[55] Stanley J. Tambiah, *Culture, Thought, and Social Action: An Anthropological Perspective* (Cambridge, Mass., 1985), 53.

present, and writing the tsarist old into the revolutionary new with a minus sign. Essays authored by Antonov present a version of October 1917 and the soviet's policies in 1918 that later found reflection in the writings of Soviet historians — except when the revolutionary authors discussed their independence, or the Center's weakness or failure to manage the provinces.[56] This is important, because the identity of a place is bound up with the histories told of it, and with the history that turns out to be dominant:[57] a key element in establishing hegemony was Moscow's imposing a Center-defined narrative of the Revolution.

According to Antonov's version of October 1917, the Saratov Soviet "with indomitable, superhuman energy, in the Sturm und Drang of a merciless class war, defended the supreme power of the workers and their interests, laying in unbelievably difficult circumstances the foundation of a new, social[ist], communal life."[58] Accenting the heroic aspects of the struggle for a new world, he denounced the vileness of the opposition. His revolutionary narrative advocates death to the enemies of the Revolution as the soviet honored its first martyrs and expelled the Mensheviks from the ranks of the working class. The authors of *Godovshchina* expressed faith in their ability to overcome the enormous obstacles facing them. Reflecting the influence of the Left SRs and Revolutionary Communists in the province, the volume maintains that because the proletariat in Russia was small, it needed the middle peasants.

The Bolshevik public register competed in what Gamson calls an "issue arena," comprising five "framing devices" used to define political issues: metaphors, historical examples that teach lessons, catchphrases, depiction, and visual images such as posters and monuments. It also applied three "reasoning devices" to justify political action: causal analysis (the historical roots of a problem); consequences (effects); and appeals to principle (a set of moral claims).[59]

In metaphor the Revolution appeared as a powerful storm, survival as a heroic battle or struggle, opposition as conspiracy, and the socialist future as a bright light or as the sun. The second device, historical example, drew lessons from the French Revolution and Paris Commune, and from the anti-Soviet behavior of Capital and the Allied forces. The third framing device, catchphrases, included world revolution, dictator-

---

[56] Antonov's autobiographical publications aroused the ire of some of his comrades in arms when they appeared in the 1920s. The ill will had much to do with personality differences and with the need to rewrite the past in terms of a troubled present during the 1920s. See GASO, f. 3586, op. 1, d. 66, ll. 6–10; d. 77; and d. 78, ll. 1–26.

[57] Doreen Massey, "Places and Their Past," *History Workshop Journal* 39 (1995): 186.

[58] *Godovshchina*, 26.

[59] Gamson, "Political Discourse," 221–22, 242.

ship of the proletariat or of worker and peasant power, the shameful betrayal of the SRs and Mensheviks, the dark forces of the old world, and the republic of soviets. With the fourth device, the old world was depicted as a heap of ruins, those who died for the Revolution as martyrs and freedom fighters, restoration of the Constituent Assembly as the return of the capitalist yoke, Russia as being receptive to a faster pace of revolutionary change than the West, and proletarian art as a new form of battle with the bourgeoisie. Finally, visual images serving as a framing device were conveyed by attending a revolutionary play, viewing an agitation film, visiting a monument to revolutionary heroes, or participating in a revolutionary festival. The language of Bolshevism in *Godovshchina* and in newspapers is studded with binary images (labor/Capital, workers/bourgeoisie, life/death, freedom/slavery, victory/ death, bright future/dark past), and inversions (the hired slave has become the master of the land and runs the factories, the humble now vote while the bourgeoisie are excluded from Soviet power.) Some formulations were oxymoronic (e.g., "the battle for peace"); ideological language often concealed judgments. Examples would be how the terms *proletariat* and *bourgeoisie* were used and understood. Yet another feature was what Epstein calls ideological homonymy, when two ascribed words have little in common (revolutionary war [positive] vs. imperialist war [negative]).[60]

The party's external language also applied three reasoning devices: causal analysis (World War, Allied blockade and intervention, sabotage, White Terror); effects (economic ruin, suffering, Civil War, Red Terror); and appeals to principle (the need to sacrifice for a bright tomorrow and for the sake of world revolution). The Communists took accusations (over their use of violence), depicted them as something positive (struggle or battle), and correlated them to some positive term or higher cause (such as peace).[61]

Obsessed with the future of the Soviet project, the Communists' organizing scheme demonstrated a remarkable capacity to adapt to changing circumstances.[62] For example, when the bourgeoisie failed to overthrow Soviet power in 1919 (ostensibly because the population rallied to defend Soviet power), Communist external language transferred the threat to hunger, which now had that capability. Thus, Saratovites needed to sacrifice (an appeal to principle) in order to feed the starving

---

[60] Epstein, *After the Future*, 107, 122.

[61] Ibid., 126.

[62] For an interesting discussion of Bolshevik eschatology, see Igal Halfin, *From Darkness to Light: Class, Consciousness, and Salvation in Revolutionary Russia* (Pittsburgh, 2000), 39–84.

children of Petrograd.[63] Likewise, it extolled the virtues of the party's new accommodation of the middle peasant by emphasizing that "the union of workers and peasants will destroy the union of the landowners and bourgeoisie."[64] Party narratives denied that the peasants opposed Soviet power, insisting that only a few were counterrevolutionary. They maintained that the Paris Commune had fallen because it had no support outside Paris. The provinces had to mobilize; the choices were either a complete victory of the laboring masses over Capital, or a new slavery. Revolutionary discourse scripted in women, but retained patriarchal forms, appealing to women to help men gain consciousness, and masculinity, by recognizing the real threat and defending the Revolution. It inspired soldiers to become heroes while Red female workers stood behind them.[65] In place by 1919, the framing devices readily allowed for the substitution of new enemies in place of the old. For example, local headlines in mid-1920 now called for "Death to the Polish bourgeoisie."[66] Because the West supported Poland, party external language depicted the workers' struggle as a war of independence to preserve the country's national integrity. Normally, internationalism was favorably contrasted to patriotism, but the latter quality took on positive connotations when Russian workers were called upon to save the Revolution by defeating "capitalist" Poland.

The Communists' bumptious external language also venerated revolutionary martyrs (Rosa Luxembourg, Iakov Sverdlov, Bela Kun, and local leaders such as Tsyrkin), and desecrated revolutionary enemies (world capitalism, the bourgeoisie, Denikin, Wrangel, Kolchak, kulaks, capitalists—and even backwardness, dirt, and disease). Public language ascribed positive meaning to workers' clubs opened by Proletkult, children's homes, revolutionary festivals, amnesties, red flags, and an array of discriminatory social policies aimed at the bourgeoisie.

The Communists' application of ideological language liberated them from the need to provide any logical proof for their claims. Erasing the differences between ideas and reality, they created a unique phenomenon in which ideology became their only reality.[67] The impoverished public language of Communism emphasized distrust of the social other; a hierarchy of class, soviets, privileges, even of countries; coercion as the necessary means that justified the hoped-for ends; and centralization, that is, a national ideology as opposed to a parochial one. The

---

[63] Poliantsev, *Saratovskaia partiinaia organizatsiia*, 75–76, 86–87.

[64] *Iubileinyi sbornik Saratovskogo gubprodkomiteta. 7 noiabria 1917 g. (25 oktiabria), 7 noiabria 1919 g.* (Saratov, 1919), passim.

[65] GASO, f. 521, op. 3, d. 16, ll. 152–53; also see TsDNISO, f. 138, op. 1, d. 58, l. 7.

[66] *ISS*, no. 100, May 7, 1920, 1–2.

[67] Epstein, *After the Future*, 102–3, 118, 154, 155, 161.

party's sense of its historical mission found expression in claims that the October Revolution and survival of Soviet power were *inevitable*.[68] This made it easier to account for the country's exhaustion, the failure of revolution in the West, and the retreat that the introduction of the NEP symbolized, especially as rival versions of the Revolution continued to attract adherents. Communist philippic insisted Capitalism remained doomed, and would trigger a new war and world revolution. Still dependent upon the world economy, Russia had to live with Capitalism, a dying dog, but one that could still bite. Lacking a large social base for socialist construction (decode: having few workers), the party had to rely on the petite bourgeoisie or would otherwise have forfeited the proletariat too, because so many workers during the Civil War had lost their class identity.[69] In other words, the Communists justified a workers' revolution even without workers, or, as will be argued in chapter 11, even without the support of workers.

The Revolutionary Press as Weapon

The soviet's *Izvestiia* remained the most important means for disseminating the party's public face and its master fiction. Yet paper shortages affected *Izvestiia*'s format and kept its press run woefully small — approximately 10,000 — throughout the Civil War. Posting the paper at 100 places in the city, the Soviet canceled personal subscriptions in order to send copies to volost soviets and army units. There was another reason for the paper's deterioration: the number of skilled printers in Saratov had declined precipitously, and young, poorly trained workers replaced them.[70] In an effort to win over the peasantry in late 1920, the party launched a new paper, *Sovetskaia derevnia* (The Soviet Village), featuring articles on the reconstruction of the rural economy and cultural change.

By mid-1918 *Izvestiia* had already become transformed into a sanitized publication depicting with hostility anyone that did not back Soviet power. Seeking to promote class identity, and struggle, in accessible language, *Izvestiia*'s utopian vision provided readers a heretical subversion of the social world to counter the ordinary one, thereby helping to bring about what it depicted.[71] News about the transactions of the so-

---

[68] Von Geldern, *Revolutionary Festivals*, 177.

[69] *Plenum Saratovskogo gubkoma*, 29–30, 41.

[70] In the fall of 1919 the local office of ROSTA also began to put out a modest wall newspaper for posting, *Krasnaia Volga* (Red Volga). See Iakorev, "Iz opyta," 239, and Galagan, "Iz istorii," 79.

[71] See Bourdieu, *Language and Symbolic Power*, 128.

viet disappeared from its pages, mirroring the plenum's loss of power, which shifted to the executive committee. Reflecting party initiatives and priorities, "campaigns" were showcased. *Izvestiia* experimented with many rhetorical devices that would become standard features of the Soviet press such as depicting the party's interests as shared by the working class, peasantry, and Red Army soldiers as a whole.

The Bolsheviks quickly learned that it costs money to establish hegemony. In 1919, when there were no resources to put out both *Izvestiia* and the party paper, *Sotsial-demokrat*, renamed *Krasnaia gazeta* in 1918, the latter was "temporarily" dropped; it never appeared again for the duration of the Civil War. This decision also reflected the political realities of an emerging party-state, as the newspaper set the parameters of public discussion — and criticism — of Soviet power. For instance, an editorial in July 1919 complained that the paper carried virtually nothing about "that which is going on under our noses," and acknowledged that party newspapers were unpopular. To compensate for this, Soviet leaders instituted a flawed program of "everyone a correspondent" whereby "the worker himself and the peasant himself must be both reader and writer."[72] In early 1921, *Izvestiia* gave no indication that serious troubles lay ahead, except for the concern it now lavished on the working class. Following disturbances against Soviet power, the anxious paper spotlighted world revolution and steps taken to improve the lot of workers and to restore agriculture. No longer distributed free of charge, it went only to paid subscribers.

Similar metamorphoses came to the uezd papers, which changed titles frequently, mirroring the decline of the soviets and rise of the executive committees, and later, the party's growing solicitousness toward the peasantry. In 1919 the papers began to publish decrees, but provided little coverage of local government, feeding readers a monotonous diet of international revolution. The papers also printed "conversion" tales, such as the one written by the editor of the Balashov paper who had preached the Gospel in Siberia before 1917, later converted to Bolshevism, and found spiritual "peace and tranquility" serving the Revolution.[73] More local news began to appear in the district papers in 1920, yet they still made few references to the functioning of local government. On holidays and to commemorate special events, some of the papers were printed in red ink. The papers' tone was doggedly didactic. For example, the Volsk paper during "clean-up week" declared that "every dirty

[72] *ISS*, no. 155, July 19, 1919, 2; no. 161, July 26, 1919, 3; and *Rezoliutsii i tezisy*, 16–20.

[73] *Izvestiia Balashovskogo Soveta*, no. 171, Sept. 22, 1919, 1–2, and no. 172, Sept. 24, 1919, 1. See also Halfin, *From Darkness to Light*, passim.

person with lice is a counterrevolutionary!" By 1920 most uezd newspapers were better produced and even more moralizing in tone. Their
back page targeted female workers and the young. The papers spelled
out what steps authorities took to improve living conditions, giving
more attention to the "economic front," and admitting "shortcomings"
and "difficulties," which they blamed on circumstances.[74] In 1921 the
papers trumpeted the launching of the NEP.[75] Advertisements reap-
peared, but the papers' political tone did not change, suggesting the true
limitations of the accommodation that the NEP represented. The party
continued to promote public values that were not necessarily those of
its readers, who by now had undoubtedly become experienced at decod-
ing the official press. In effect, the party had created a new press that no
longer made political power public. The role of newspapers was less to
provide news than it was to educate the public in the spirit of the
party's master fiction.

The Production of Agitation and Propaganda

In shutting down the multiparty debate over Russian political life, the
Communists sought to make their new public transcript of the Revolution accessible to workers, peasants, and soldiers through propaganda
and agitation. Tied to party organs in Moscow, the soviet's Agitation
Department popularized the party's version of the Revolution, coordinating local activities to ensure some consistency in the construction
of a unified narrative. The department prepared propagandists, drew up
instructions for carrying out agitation work, determined which ideas
would be presented in public lectures, organized meetings, and sent representatives to the district towns, the Department of Adult Education,
and Proletkult. It likewise promoted the party's agenda by showing
short propaganda films (*agitki*) and playing recordings of Lenin's
speeches. In addition, the soviet set up ad hoc agitation courses to
which it instructed each village to send two literate peasants.[76]
  The Bolsheviks' obsession with counting how many leaflets and newspapers they issued, how many lectures and agitation meetings they held,
and how many people were at the receiving end of such initiatives reveals the modernist origins of their project aimed at reconfiguring society through the conscious application of rational principles. Reducing

[74] *Kommuna* (Petrovsk), *Izvestiia Atkarskogo uispolkoma*, *Rabochii i krest'ianin*
(Volsk), *Krasnyi pakhar'* and *Bor'ba* (Balashov).
  [75] *Kommunar* (Petrovsk), no. 96, Dec. 4, 1920, 1; *Rabochii i krest'ianin*, no. 79, April
10, 1920, 1; and *ISS*, no. 231, Oct. 10, 1922, 3.
  [76] Iakorev, "Iz opyta," 232–36, 240.

their efforts to narrow quantitative terms, they crunched out data not only to justify the existence of the propaganda and agitation organs and the cost of maintaining them, but also to document the need for more resources when the efforts failed. The precise nature of the figures raises doubts about their validity, but says much about the Bolsheviks' intent and worldview.

In connection with the White offensive, agitation meetings at the workplace in Saratov and district towns proclaimed the imminence of world revolution and the vanguard role the international working class would play in it. Utilizing standard tropes, propagandists gave public lectures on workers' politics and Soviet power, the Communist Party and petit-bourgeois democracy, the separation of church and state, labor production and discipline, the current tasks of Soviet power, economic policy, current events, and the party's policies toward the middle peasants.[77] Often meetings began with the singing of the "International," followed by political agitation and the performance of popular folk melodies. Groups of agitators also formed detachments known as "dozeners" to battle against desertion, hooliganism, drinking, and White Guard activities.[78] Further, drawing on earlier precedents, the department coordinated the efforts of five agitation trains and a river steamer, each equipped with a cinema, radio station, and printing press that brought their message to provincial Russia, making popular the agitki. The "October Revolution" frequented Saratov Province; the boat, Red Star, visited the area in September 1919, sponsoring meetings and lectures, and emphasizing the party's social programs for workers, invalids, refugees, and families of soldiers.[79]

The Agitation Department organized frequent "campaigns" to mobilize the population around a specific theme. It held "front week" February 1–8, 1919, mobilizing thousands of people to clean snow from railroad tracks. The department collected money and gifts for the front, distributed leaflets, put up posters, and held meetings. "Party week," in November 1919, aimed to draw new faces into the party.[80] Similarly, the department sponsored a Soviet propaganda day, when it put out larger press runs of the local paper, held programs for children and adults, and showed free movies.[81] It dispelled rumors hostile to Soviet power.[82] Lec-

[77] *KG*, no. 293, Feb. 25, 1919, 4.

[78] TsDNISO, f. 200, op. 1, d. 42, l. 4; f. 138, op. 1, d. 1a, l. 13; and f. 136, op. 1, d. 3, l. 6.

[79] Maksakova, *Agitpoezd*, 7, and Vas'kovskii, "Sovety," 290–95.

[80] Iakorev, "Iz opyta," 245–46; *ISS*, no. 256, Nov. 17, 1919, 3; no. 263, Nov. 25, 1919, 3; and no. 267, Nov. 30, 1919, 1.

[81] GASO, f. 521, op. 1, d. 349, ll. 1–2, and *ISS*, no. 198, Sept. 9, 1919, 3.

[82] For example, *KG*, no. 298, March 2, 1919, 1, and *ISS*, no. 243, Nov. 1, 1919, 1.

turers spoke on the programs of the political parties, the battle between labor and Capital, the proletariat and science, the revolutionary movement in the West and in Russia, the class struggle, the meaning of Communism, and on policies of the Soviet government from land and food to education and church-state relations, to the meaning of the revolution in Germany.[83]

The department stepped up its activities when fresh threats challenged Soviet power. Declaring war on "political" illiteracy during the January 1920 soviet election campaign, it devoted special attention to women and to countering the efforts of Mensheviks and anarchists to draw support. Lecturers focused on why world revolution no longer seemed to be in progress, the activities of Mensheviks and anarchists, and labor conscription.[84] Afterward "labor front week" was held in conjunction with the working out of an economic plan for the province and the militarization of industry, which involved one-person management in factories, and labor conscription, perhaps the best indication of worker hostility to volunteer workdays. Maintaining that economic recovery was as urgent as military victory, the party justified the use of force.

The party eventually concluded that agitation alienated workers, because it failed to address what concerned them most: food shortages and the stark absence of basic necessities.[85] Seeking refuge in nationalism, agitators now linked the ubiquitous shortages to the war with Poland.[86] They held public readings of N. Bukharin and E. Preobrazhenskii's *The ABC of Communism*, perhaps the most widely read political tract of the time.[87] One can imagine how listeners and readers reacted to the authors' optimistic prediction that the Communist utopia was just around the corner, for, despite the sustained efforts to shape public opinion, a mass rejection of Soviet power in March 1921 demonstrates that propaganda efforts fell short. Moreover, lack of funds forced the soviet to shut down the party school, just at the same time that the introduction of the NEP threw the Agitation Department into disarray. Unprepared for the introduction of the NEP, the gubkom did

---

[83] TsDNISO, f. 27, op. 1, d. 17, ll. 70–76.

[84] Ibid., f. 27, op. 1, d. 932, ll. 2 ob, 4.

[85] *Na strazhe revoliutsii*, 10–11; *ISS*, no. 48, Feb. 28, 1920, 1; and *Rabochii i krest'ianin*, no. 55, March 10, 1920, 2. For nonparticipation see *ISS*, no. 35, Feb. 14, 1920, 2; no. 22, Jan. 31, 1920, 2; and TsDNISO, f. 138, op. 1, d. 17, ll. 45–45 ob. In Atkarsk the party dropped all agitation. See ibid., f. 200, op. 1, d. 126, l. 5 ob.

[86] *Rezoliutsii i tezisy*, 7–10, 13–16; see TsDNISO, f. 136, op. 1, d. 55, l. 17. Also see V. V. Kurgaev, "Politiko-prosvetitel'naia rabota Saratovskoi partiinoi organizatsii (1921–1922 gg.)," in *Iz istorii sotsialisticheskogo stroitel'stva*, no. 9 (1979): 169–70.

[87] *Piat' let II-oi raionnoi organizatsii komsomola*, 10.

not work out any strategies to present the new policy to the population until late in the year.[88] By then, famine and the drying up of state subsidies resulted in the closing of many libraries, clubs, and reading huts.[89] Be that as it may, the Communists had acquired extensive experience in mobilizing resources to shape popular attitudes and in defining which strategies they would resort to in the future.

Building Socialism through Enlightenment

Because no class or group can hold state power for long without establishing control over ideological state apparatuses (e.g., religion, education, legality, cultural activities), revolutionaries often find themselves in a bitter struggle to make their ideology the ruling one by taking over these institutions, especially the state educational system.[90] Lenin understood this. So did local Communists, some of whom envisioned having the state rear the children of the bourgeoisie so that they would become devoted to the Revolution. Although the harsh conditions in which the Revolution unfolded greatly handicapped utopian plans to educate all children in a collective spirit as the basis for a socialist order, the Bolsheviks made literacy and the spread of "enlightenment" a top priority in order to facilitate the reception of their public language.[91]

Directed by S. K. Minina, school reorganization got underway in early 1918, when Gubotnarob was set up and placed in charge of all public and church schools. According to plans drawn up to reform the schools, primary education would last six years, starting at age 8, and secondary education five years. Education was made free and coeducational and attendance mandatory. Religious instruction was banned and a 1:25 teacher/pupil ratio was recommended. Owing to lack of school buildings, the government called for the utilization of church premises for instructional purposes. The curriculum abolished corporal punishment, mandatory homework, and examinations, while the state promised to provide children with hot breakfasts and medical examinations.

---

[88] TsDNISO, f. 81, op. 1, d. 31, l. 15; f. 136, op. 1, d. 55, l. 43; and f. 27, op. 2, d. 726, l. 29.

[89] Kurgaev, "Politiko-prosvetitel'naia rabota," 181.

[90] Louis Althusser, *Lenin and Philosophy and Other Essays* (New York, 1971), 142–47, 152, 157, 162, 185.

[91] See, for example, David-Fox, *Revolution of the Mind*, and Sheila Fitzpatrick, *The Commissariat of the Enlightenment: Soviet Organization of Education and the Arts under Lunacharsky, October 1917–1921* (Cambridge, Eng., 1970).

Gubotnarob also intended to expand the existing network of preschools and kindergartens.[92]

Teacher hostility, lack of resources, and civil war conditions, however, dashed hopes of implementing these designs. In June 1918, the All-Russian Teachers' Union split when a majority of delegates recognized the Bolshevik government, which had resolved to raise teachers' salaries. Whereas "internationalists" prevailed in Balashov and other towns,[93] most Saratov teachers remained hostile to the Bolsheviks, undermining change "at each step," and making it difficult for the Bolsheviks to take over the schools.[94] Moreover, an epidemic of school transfers took place as teachers left their positions, were drafted, or fled. By 1920 the financial crisis prevented Gubotnarob from paying teachers' salaries and put a stop to restoring school buildings, which were in short supply since the Red Army had confiscated over 40 percent of them already in 1918. Some departments in the districts opened new schools, but these were exceptions.[95]

In fact, civil war realities reduced the number of pupils engaged in serious schooling for much of the period. At the end of 1918 there were 60 primary schools with an enrollment of 18,377 in the city of Saratov, and 10 secondary schools with 7,502 pupils. A year later authorities reported a greater number of schools, but fewer pupils. The absentee rate soared that winter in particular, owing to shortages of clothing and shoes, and to illness. Despite the fact that shifts were introduced so that buildings could house more than one school, children took to the streets, where many "speculated" or engaged in crime.[96] The new government also gave all nationalities the right to open schools in their native tongue;[97] however, it proved difficult to find experienced minority teachers, and thereby to expand education opportunities among the minorities.[98] The Bolshevik authorities certainly took pride in claiming that

---

[92] *ISS*, no. 260, Nov. 22, 1919, 2; no. 274, Dec. 9, 1919, 3; no. 197, Sept. 7, 1919, 4; *Prosveshchenie*, no. 1 (1918): 78–84; and GASO, f. 521, op. 1, d. 136, l. 64.

[93] *ISS*, no. 43, Feb. 25, 1919, 3, and *Izvestiia Balashovskogo Soveta*, no. 191, Oct. 1918, 3.

[94] *ISS*, no. 156, Aug. 3, 1918, 3, and no. 157, Aug. 4, 1918, 3. The rift was never overcome in Serdobsk. See *Golos kommunista*, no. 134, May 31, 1919, 3, and *Serp i molot*, no. 7 (291), Jan. 21, 1920, 2.

[95] GASO, f. 456, op. 1, d. 51, l. 50 ob; f. 521, op. 1, d. 95, ll. 15, 23; and GA RF, f. 393, op. 3, d. 334, ll. 18–22.

[96] *Prosveshchenie*, no. 2 (1918): 88; GASO, f. 456, op. 1, d. 421, l. 3; d. 632, ll. 1–14; and *ISS*, no. 243, Nov. 1, 1919, 2.

[97] *Prosveshchenie*, no. 2 (1918): 123, and GASO, f. 521, op. 1, d. 136, l. 233.

[98] *ISS*, no. 156, July 15, 1921, 2, and *KG*, no. 306, March 14, 1919, 3.

more schools and pupils existed in 1921 than in 1917, yet these figures tell an incomplete story.[99]

This point is confirmed when Gubotnarob's efforts to extend its authority to the rest of the province are considered. Departments at the uezd level proved to be no more successful than authorities in Saratov: local reports from March 1919 provide a disheartening picture, especially for school-age children from other parts of the country who had resettled in Saratov Province.[100] In Kamyshin only 35 percent of school-age children attended school. Teachers fled Petrovsk as Soviet power was being set up. Schools everywhere remained in deplorable straits. A report on the secondary school in Petrovsk paints an appalling portrait of filth, neglect, and "complete chaos everywhere." Not even the Alexander Trade School, once the pride of Saratov Province, was spared the sharp decline in discipline or in its physical plant. Gubotnarob built some new schools in early 1919; to staff them it processed would-be teachers through two-week teacher education programs and hired teachers who had fled starving Petrograd.[101] As a result, the number of schools — but not of school buildings and not necessarily of pupils — rose in Saratov Province in 1920 (table 7.1). But accounts from 1920 repeat the litany of reproaches made earlier: teacher shortages, the poor preparation of those recruited, the low priority of education, economic ruin, and the continued existence of the "bourgeois high school" that graduated more "useless members of the intelligentsia."[102] Moreover, reports on what transpired inside the classroom note the total absence of teacher control, the teaching of pro-tsarist sentiments and religious instruction, and anti-Semitism.[103] That fall hunger drove many teachers to other provinces in search of food,[104] as a result of which Saratov had 30 percent fewer teachers than it needed.

The peasants' mistrust of teachers and lack of clear directives from the Center similarly obstructed efforts to create a new type of school.

---

[99] The figures are found in *Biulleten' Saratovskogo Gubotnaroba*, no. 23 (1921): 57.

[100] GASO, f. 329, op. 1, d. 98, l. 41.

[101] *ISS*, no. 50, March 5, 1919, 3; no. 205, Sept. 17, 1919, 3; no. 240, Oct. 29, 1919, 3–4; and *Kommuna*, no. 87, Nov. 2, 1920, 2.

[102] GASO, f. 456, op. 1, d. 384, ll. 37–39; *Serp i molot*, no. 212 (496), Oct. 1, 1920, 2; and *Materialy k XIII-mu*, 100–101. On the bourgeois high school see GASO, f. 521, op. 1, d. 136, ll. 119–20.

[103] *Narodnoe prosveshchenie*, no. 2, Nov. 1921, 11; *ISS*, no. 223, Oct. 9, 1919, 3. See also *Golos kommunista*, no. 70 (107), March 8, 1919, 2; no. 118, May 11, 1919, 4; GASO f. 359, op. 1, d. 39, l. 35 ob; and *Doklad Vol'skogo uezdnogo Ispolnitel'nogo komiteta Sovetov rabochikh, krest'ianskikh i krasnoarmeiskikh deputatov* (Volsk, 1919), 6–7.

[104] *Oktiabr'skaia revoliutsiia*, no. 15 (623), Feb. 11, 1921; *Biulleten' Saratovskogo Gubotnaroba*, no. 2–3, (1921): 13; and *Narodnoe prosveshchenie*, no. 2 (1921): 11.

TABLE 7.1
Number of Primary, Secondary, and Technical Schools in Saratov Province as
of April 1, 1920

	Primary Schools		Secondary Schools		Technical Schools	
Uezd	Number	Pupils	Number	Pupils	Number	Pupils
Atkarsk	380	36,683	9	1,747	1	149
Balashov	398	35,368	29	2,963	3	147
Volsk	285	16,605	12	1,687	3	306
Kamyshin	254	15,865	5	759	2	105
Kuznetsk	188	23,056	17	1,804	1	88
Novouzensk	381	39,833	29	3,982	12	665
Petrovsk	358	35,000	13	1,702	1	105
Pokrovsk	23	2,543	3	349	1	683
Saratov	243	22,826	11	1,115	3	375
Serdobsk	257	30,051	12	2,134	1	83
Khvalynsk	179	13,871	7	1,065	1	98

Source: GASO, f. 456, op. 1, d. 421, l. 6.

Peasants looked upon the intelligentsia with ill will, particularly teachers, whom they considered lazy and pampered, while urban gymnasium graduates preferred just about any job in the cities to a teaching position in a village. Despite the estrangement, peasants backed the idea of having local taxes support rural schools, but little could be effected in this regard without the involvement of Saratov, which found itself short of personnel and resources.[105]

Gubotnarob likewise gave top priority to "democratizing" the student body at Saratov University and at other local institutions of higher learning whose students and staff opposed Soviet power. Eight "colleges" existed in Saratov in January 1921, enrolling 13,582 pupils; Saratov University registered 9,732 of the students and the polytech another 1,154. The Soviet state financed the education of almost half of these students.[106] To change the composition of the student body, Gubotnarob opened general university courses to everyone, and set up schools for adults, and a People's University that elicited such an enthusiastic response that registration had to be shut down.[107] To prepare workers to enter Saratov University in 1920, Gubotnarob established a

---

[105] See, for example, GA RF, f. 393, op. 3, d. 330, l. 188.
[106] Romanov, *Materialy po statistike*, 13.
[107] *ISS*, no. 10, Jan. 15, 1919, 3, and GASO, f. 456, op. 1, d. 218, l. 14 ob.

"workers' department." At first the university faculty boycotted the classes; however, they eventually cooperated with Gubotnarob, but found it difficult to teach the ill-prepared students,[108] most of whom were members of the party or Komsomol or came from the ranks of the unemployed or unskilled workers. In 1921 the university's workers' department instructed 774 adult students and another 3,009 adults in basic literacy classes.[109]

The Communists' adult education program likewise included the ambitious goal of wiping out illiteracy among adults in three years; however, 12,000 teachers were needed to accomplish this, most of whom had to be found locally and put through three-week preparatory courses. In March 1920 Gubotnarob resolved to open literacy programs wherever 10 percent or more of the local population was illiterate.[110] In May 1920 in the city of Saratov, 22,112 adults, mostly women, were targeted for the program, which divided the city's population into three age groups, giving priority to the youngest cohort. Gubotnarob opened 194 "schools," making it the obligation of the literate to teach the illiterate and shaming the former into doing so when they failed to volunteer.[111] In an attempt to end illiteracy among the 5 to 10 percent of new draftees who could not read, the department and military authorities set up "schools" and a Red Army "university" in Saratov and similar programs in each district.[112]

Officials also carried out campaigns against illiteracy in the district towns, and to a lesser extent in villages in which the adult population was mostly illiterate. Making education available to the poor, however, was sometimes at odds with their own cultural values. For example, many of those who registered to attend the people's university in Volsk never bothered to show up.[113] Balashov authorities lamented that only

---

[108] GASO, f. 456, op. 1, d. 218, l. 11 ob; *ISS*, no. 54, March 6, 1920, 3; no. 85, April 18, 1920, 3; no. 158, July 17, 1921, 2.

[109] *ISS*, no. 242, Oct. 26, 1921, 2; no. 246, Oct. 30, 1921, 2; also Malinin and Gusakova, *Kul'turnoe stroitel'stvo*, 126–27.

[110] GASO, f. 456, op. 1, d. 297, l. 14, and *ISS*, no. 87, April 21, 1920, 3.

[111] *ISS*, no. 248, Oct. 31, 1920, 4, and *Biulleten' Saratovskogo gubernskogo otdela po rabote sredi zhenshchin*, no. 2, March 9, 1921, 1.

[112] GASO, f. 521, op. 1, d. 577, ll. 2–2 ob; *ISS*, no. 98, May 5, 1920, 3; no. 147, July 3, 1920, 4. See also Mark von Hagen, *Soldiers in the Proletarian Dictatorship: The Red Army and the Soviet Socialist State, 1917–1930* (Ithaca, 1990), 89–114.

[113] *Izvestiia Vol'skogo ispolkoma*, no. 35, Feb. 14, 1919, 4; no. 38, Feb. 18, 1919, 3–4; *Materialy k XIII-mu*, 105; *Izvestiia Ispolnitel'nogo komiteta Vol'skogo Soveta*, no. 93, April 29, 1919, 3–4; *KG*, no. 298, March 2, 1919, 3; and *Rabochii i krest'ianin*, no. 259, Nov. 19, 1919, 1.

14 of the main library's 1,304 users one day were workers.[114] Kamyshin peasants played cards all winter, yet claimed they had no time to study.[115] In Atkarsk cultural-educational circles cropped up like mushrooms after a spring rain, but they faded away just as quickly.[116] It was estimated that in 1921 one million people in the province remained illiterate, and this after approximately 125,000 had received basic literacy instruction. Gubotnarob now predicted it would take eight years to wipe out illiteracy altogether.[117]

The party's ambitious designs to establish hegemony over the educational system and to wipe out illiteracy illustrate how utopian plans interacted dialectically with civil war conditions and hostility to Soviet power to bring about only partial change. Although the party had not established hegemony over this important ideological state apparatus, it controlled resources and began the process of educating a new generation in a different spirit. In making education the right of the working class (and of those associated with the party) the Bolsheviks placed schooling at the center of its social program, telling the poor that acquisition of knowledge was essential to overcoming centuries of tsarist oppression. Arguably, this might be interpreted as a Pyrrhic victory of sorts that tied the party's hands, for it made it necessary to interpret or justify all *future* policies through a proletarian filter. This could prove detrimental to the party when workers' attitudes and experiences clashed with Bolshevism as it was practiced. Moreover, whereas literacy seemed to help establish cultural hegemony, the disparity between people's everyday realities and party external language might have served to undermine the integrity of the printed word,[118] or to make the literate and newly literate more susceptible to counterideologies.

The Clergy: "An Anti-Soviet Force of Ignorance and Superstition"

The Bolsheviks also believed that a materialistic worldview needed to replace religion in order to implement the party's cultural policies. At the time of the Revolution, Saratov was home to eighty-nine houses of worship including Orthodox, Old Believer, Catholic, and Protestant churches, several mosques, and one synagogue. The soviet's efforts to carry out the separation of church and state as well as to remove

---

[114] *Izvestiia Balashovskogo Soveta*, Jan. 1, 1919, 4.

[115] *Nabat*, no. 22, Feb. 23, 1919, 3.

[116] *Izvestiia Atkarskogo Ispolnitel'nogo komiteta*, no. 360, Nov. 29, 1919, 4.

[117] *ISS*, no. 246, Oct. 30, 1921, 2. Literacy levels are available in *Statisticheskii sbornik*, 53–56.

[118] Brooks makes this point in "Competing Modes," 79.

schools from church supervision turned many believers against the new order. Saratovites, mostly women, protested the Soviet government's separation of church and state, and again when they feared anarchists were about to abolish religion altogether. While some clergy pinned the blame for the attack on religion as the work of Russia's convenient "other," the Jews, the local Jewish clergy joined with their Orthodox counterparts to rebuke Soviet power. Orthodox clergymen visited mosques as well, proposing that Muslim believers join them in a protest march against the Soviet government's stand on religion.[119] As a result of these efforts a Committee of the United Churches of Saratov issued a strongly worded document against the act of separation, which it represented as the destruction of the church. It called upon believers serving in the armed forces to ignore orders to confiscate church property and upon parishioners to march on the soviet in the event clergymen were arrested or church property seized. Afterward, parishes petitioned the ispolkom not to interfere with the churches, arguing—by bestowing subversive meaning to official discourse—that they had been built through private donations and therefore "belonged to the people."[120] The Revolutionary Tribunal heard the cases of several outspoken clergymen and shot one as an example of what others could expect.[121]

Throughout 1918 and afterward, the local Communist press depicted nonprogressive elements of the clergy as a counterrevolutionary force of darkness and superstition, although local sources fell silent about other aspects of church-state relations after 1918. A case in point is the attention devoted to Father Platonov, who was tried by a local revolutionary tribunal. Platonov was depicted as a Black Hundredite fanatic opposed to the progressive "Union of the Rebirth of the Orthodox Clergy," which backed sweeping reforms within the church.[122] Later, the press covered the split between the patriarch and the so-called Living Church movement that embraced the Revolution and supported the Soviet government's drive to seize church wealth to be used to purchase relief for the starving population during the famine of 1921–22.[123] By this time the party realized the complexity of its own relationship to religion and how difficult its task was to wean the population from the church, so intimately connected to the private sphere. Believing mothers bore responsibility for this, its propaganda efforts now targeted the young.[124]

[119] *Saratovskii Sovet*, 356, 359; *ISS*, no. 27, Feb. 17, 1918, 2; and no. 29, Feb. 20, 1918, 1.

[120] GASO, f. 521, op. 1, d. 109, ll. 6–7 ob, 10–10 ob, 34.

[121] *Godovshchina*, 32.

[122] *ISS*, no. 8, Jan. 12, 1919, 3.

[123] See, for example, *ISS*, no. 172, July 30, 1922, 2.

[124] TsDNISO, f. 110, op. 1, d. 5, l. 25, and *Godovshchina*, 61–62.

Crime and Justice as Culture

The Bolsheviks redefined crime and criminals, making both issues central to their attempts at cultural creation. By casting crime and punishment in the idiom of class, they offered new explanations for crime's perpetration and gave preferential treatment in sentencing to workers. This, plus a growing reliance on informants and denunciation, made substantial room for abuse. Moreover, when public hostility to Soviet power seriously threatened it, the party meted out draconian sentences, demonstrating its willingness to marshal the punitive powers of the state to secure compliance.

The Bolsheviks initiated their application of ideology to the legal system in early 1918 when the soviet dismantled the tsarist judicial apparatus, establishing under Commissar of Justice P. A. Lebedev a hierarchy of people's courts, revolutionary tribunals, and investigative commissions. Although many Bolshevik leaders belonged to the bar, lawyers in general assailed the party's assumption of power. Short of trained jurists, the soviet had to leave most legal professionals in their place well into 1918. In April a provincial congress of commissars of justice who "sometimes turned out to be real criminals" elected judges regardless of their legal training. The soviet set up twelve local people's courts,[125] investigated illegal actions of local organs of Soviet power and decree violations, and supervised legal institutions. It had the right to appeal sentences except for those issued by the Cheka.[126]

The Cheka attempted to establish a new police system (militia), but it lacked reliable members during the entire Civil War, proving unable to cope with the rapidly growing crime wave associated with rampant lawlessness and with the party's making traditional economic activity illegal.[127] Owing to the rising lawlessness perpetrated by criminals and demobilized soldiers, citizens had formed civil vigilante organs in December 1917; however, the soviet soon outlawed them, appropriating all weapons from Saratovites, and establishing a new militia in May 1918. This involved purging all "counterrevolutionary and Black Hundred elements" from the organization and recruiting from among more "desirable" social groups. By February 1919 only 2 percent of the city's 990 militiamen had served earlier; the party utterly failed to recruit new members from among them. Many militiamen harbored hostility to-

---

[125] *KG*, no. 40, April 10, 1918, 2; *Khronika*, 250; *ISS*, no. 40, Feb. 20, 1919, 1; Eugene Huskey, "The Russian Bar and the Consolidation of Soviet Power," *Russian Review* 43, no. 2 (1984): 116–31.

[126] *Godovshchina*, 61–62.

[127] GASO, f. 521, op. 1, d. 619, ll. 42–43, and *Godovshchina*, 103–4.

ward the Bolshevik order, abused their power, or were guilty of theft, bribe taking, or drunkenness.[128] In 1919, 13 percent of the province's 4,702 militiamen were dismissed for criminal activity and negligence,[129] while others deserted their posts during the White offensive.[130] Despite the shortcomings, the government had no choice but to cut funds for local militias; by 1920 militiamen were poorly clothed and had few weapons at their disposal (figure 7.5).[131]

What data exist underscore the general lawlessness of the time. When criminal elements from elsewhere began operating in Saratov in 1918 the soviet resorted to "merciless terror" to curb the increasingly audacious crimes,[132] executing fifty-two "hardened criminals" who tried to escape from jail. Despite an acute rise in crime and violence, the city's prison population remained fairly constant during the Civil War because the city lacked adequate jail facilities.[133] In January 1921, 1,323 people were behind bars (of whom less than 1 percent were women). The vast majority served time for economic crimes — robbery, theft, speculation, etcetera,[134] which can be viewed as "ideological" or political, since the Bolsheviks had now made some traditional economic practices illegal.

The number of criminal cases registered by the militia inched up from 1,936 in 1917 to 2,093 in 1918, but then soared to 4,129 in 1919, and 5,388 in 1920. A similar dynamic attributed to the deterioration of the economy and frequent amnesties of recidivists occurred at the district level.[135] The number of criminal investigations carried out, however, did not keep up with the rising crime rate.[136] Crimes perpetrated by children likewise rose steadily during the Civil War, since adults often involved teenage children in speculation because they received lighter punishment if apprehended.[137] Theft and embezzlement attained massive proportions

[128] GASO, f. 456, op. 1, d. 145, l. 63; *ISS*, no. 45, Feb. 27, 1919, 2; and P. N. Sinitsyn, *Istoriia raboche-krest'ianskoi militsii po Saratovskoi gubernii* (Saratov, 1924), 11.

[129] GASO, f. 521, op. 2, d. 35, l. 1, and f. 521, op. 3, d. 15, ll. 52–53.

[130] Ibid., f. 456, op. 1, d. 225, l. 138; d. 145, l. 6; and d. 218, l. 80.

[131] Ibid., f. 456, op. 1, d. 271, l. 197, and f. 456, op. 1, d. 390, ll. 182–82 ob.

[132] *Godovshchina*, 32; also see *ISS*, no. 45, Feb. 27, 1919, 2.

[133] *ISS*, no. 54, March 11, 1919, 3; no. 134, June 26, 1919, 3; and GASO, f. 456, op. 1, d. 145, l. 68. See also *ISS*, no. 90, May 12, 1918, 1; no. 113, June 11, 1918, 1; no. 114, June 12, 1918, 2; and GA RF, f. 393, op. 3, d. 327, l. 155 ob.

[134] Romanov, *Materialy po statistike*, 28.

[135] *Otchet Saratovskogo gubkoma*, 48. Reports from Balashov suggest a stunning level of violent crime at the district level. GASO, f. 456, op. 1, d. 145, ll. 63, 77 ob, and GA RF, f. 393, op. 3, d. 327, l. 197. For Atkarsk see TsDNISO, f. 200, op. 1, d. 91, l. 90.

[136] *ISS*, no. 125, June 7, 1921, 2. Typical militia reports are found in GASO, f. 456, op. 1, d. 384, ll. 64–64 ob.

[137] *ISS*, no. 245, Oct. 30, 1921, 2, and no. 104, May 12, 1920, 3.

7.5 Saratov militia before their departure for the front in 1920. Courtesy Gosudarstvennyi Arkhiv Saratovskoi Oblasti (GASO).

as living conditions deteriorated.[138] Tougher sentencing did not deter people. In 1919, 54 percent of crimes were classified as "criminal," but the number shot up to 73 percent in 1920, owing to the serious crackdown on "speculation."[139] This trend continued in 1921,[140] but now the authorities explained these crimes as unwelcome consequences of the NEP and not of the brutalization of society that had come about during the Civil War.[141]

Revolutionary tribunals established in January 1918 to deal with anti-Soviet agitation and bribe taking contributed to the growing arbitrariness of the emerging legal system. The tribunals condemned people to death for violent crimes, for stealing and selling state property, for extracting illegal contributions from the peasantry, and for sabotaging rail transportation. They issued fines for speculation. They commuted some death sentences and amnestied others owing to their youth or when their crimes were not premeditated or when they discovered that some women sentenced to death were pregnant.[142] A tribunal could be humane when a worker was involved,[143] but frequently individuals were arrested without any formal accusations having been lodged against them. The profile of cases the revolutionary tribunals handled did not change significantly during the Civil War.[144]

The dreaded Cheka proved to be even more arbitrary than the revolutionary tribunals, and not even the Communists were spared the organ's suspicious gaze.[145] The soviet had established a precursor to the Cheka in February 1918, which became the Cheka in May under the direction of Ivan B. Genkin, who was later expelled from the party for swindling and forging documents. The political police arrested 1,450 people during the first eight months of 1918 and shot 64 of them. The branches set up in the uezd towns became more powerful when the local Cheka carried out Red Terror in 1918 after the attempt on Lenin's life, executing 94 "counterrevolutionaries" in the province, and seizing hostages from among the bourgeoisie.[146]

Despite a system of double subordination to the soviets and central

---

[138] Ibid., no. 220, Sept. 30, 1920, 1.

[139] *Otchet Saratovskogo gubkoma*, 53–59, 62, 64.

[140] Ibid., 48.

[141] For late 1921 see GASO, f. 456, op. 1, d. 619, ll. 21–21 ob; for 1922 see *ISS*, no. 78, April 5, 1922, 1.

[142] GASO, f. 507, op. 1, d. 13, l. 18, and f. 1817, op. 2, d. 46, ll. 34, 19–19 ob.

[143] Ibid., f. 524, op. 1, d. 1, ll. 24–25, and f. 507, op. 1, d. 13, l. 18.

[144] GA RF, f. 1025, op. 2, d. 33, ll. 26, 52–70, and in *ISS*, no. 62, March 17, 1920, 3–4, and GASO, f. 507, op. 1, d. 108, ll. 80–80 ob.

[145] Ransone, *Crisis in Russia*, 61.

[146] *KG*, no. 273, Jan. 31, 1919, 3, and *Godovshchina*, 104.

Cheka in Moscow the Saratov Cheka continued to clash with state organs, because it could resort to summary justice in the event of serious threats to Soviet power.[147] In May 1919, the Cheka established new district committees to replace those abolished by local soviets that feared the committees' arbitrary powers.[148] However, the new committees also quarreled with party organizations over the Cheka's use of torture.[149] Even the gubispolkom came to blows with the Cheka when it arrested some of the original Cheka leaders and their wives.[150] Relations between the Cheka and party organs improved only after Comrades Zhukov and Lobov assumed responsibility for the organization.[151]

Depicting Red Terror as elemental acts of self-protection in response to White Terror,[152] the Cheka in 1919 meted out many short prison sentences, reserving the death penalty for crimes such as hiding Whites, and often demonstrated leniency when working-class or peasant party members admitted their personal weaknesses, for instance, drinking.[153] But the Cheka resorted to the death penalty more frequently during the summer siege of 1919 and during a second wave of Red Terror aimed at the bourgeoisie in September 1919. It executed a gang of thieves terrorizing Novouzensk and Balashov Uezds, shot officers and students for attempting to create a volunteer army with ties to Moscow and Samara,[154] set up a network of concentration camps to deal with prisoners of war and deserters from Denikin's army,[155] and used convict labor to rebuild the devastated infrastructure.[156] Later that year, the Cheka executed thirteen Black Hundreds, tsarist policemen, generals, and "millionaires," and forty-seven members of a monarchical spy organization comprising landowners and bourgeoisie, "but not a single worker or peasant."[157]

---

[147] *ISS*, no. 240, Nov. 2, 1918, and GASO, f. 507, op. 1, d. 13, l. 45. See *Iz istorii Vserossiiskoi Chrezvychainoi komissii, 1917–1921 gg.: Sbornik dokumentov* (Moscow, 1958), 192–94.

[148] Ibid., f. 456, op. 1, d. 85, l. 1; GA RF, f. 393, op. 3, d. 330, l. 27; *Izvestiia Vol'skogo Ispolnitel'nogo komiteta*, no. 38, Feb. 18, 1919, 4; *Izvestiia Balashovskogo Soveta*, no. 122, June 7, 1919, 3; and George Leggett, *The Cheka: Lenin's Political Police* (London, 1981), 137.

[149] *ISS*, no. 286, Dec. 23, 1919, 2.

[150] GASO, f. 521, op. 2, d. 34, l. 125, and f. 456, op. 1, d. 158, l. 89. See also V. M. Chernov, ed., *Che-ka: Materialy po deiatel'nosti chrezvychainoi komissii (Izdanie tsentral'nogo biuro partii sotsialistov-revoliutsionerov)* (Berlin, 1922), 196–204.

[151] GASO, f. 521, op. 3, d. 15, l. 34.

[152] *ISS*, no. 196, Sept. 21, 1918, 2.

[153] GASO, f. 521, op. 1, d. 343, ll. 1–3 ob, 5–7, 9–10 ob.

[154] *ISS*, no. 146, July 10, 1919, 2, and no. 151, July 15, 1919, 3.

[155] GASO, f. 456, op. 1, d. 218, l. 4.

[156] Ibid., f. 456, op. 1, d. 218, l. 151.

[157] *ISS*, no. 225, Oct. 11, 1919, 2; no. 258, Nov. 20, 1919, 2; no. 259, Nov. 21, 1919, 1; see also *Otchet Saratovskogo gubkoma*, 43–45.

To control the spread of anti-Soviet materials, it registered all 915 type-writers in Saratov.[158]

Emphasizing the pan-European nature of the phenomenon, Holquist argues that tools of state forged during the Great War and a shift in politics "intersected to produce surveillance as an essential aspect of Russian politics" among Red and White forces alike.[159] As a result, the Cheka's use of informants increased exponentially as the Civil War progressed. Before mid-1919, the Cheka had 100 informers in the province, but by September it had informants in *all* institutions, factories, and cooperatives in Saratov, the districts, volosts, and villages, for a total of 600, "and recruitment continues." "The goal of our information gathering" reads one document "is to illuminate all aspects of life in the province *so that the commission knows how each citizen is living and thinking.*" At Civil War's end the Cheka relied on a total of 1,758 informants province-wide.[160] Moreover, the Cheka daily received testimonials from citizens, informing it of "counterrevolutionary" activity, theft, speculation, sabotage, and other crimes.[161] Another trend emerged as well. The Cheka applied its most brutal punishments when the Soviet state felt most threatened, doling out tough sentences when Saratov fell under siege in 1919, after which it eased up until 1921.[162] In the three-month period ending in November 1920, the Cheka sentenced only 3 individuals to be shot.[163] During the spring 1921 uprising (March 1–April 15), however, it sentenced 219 people to death and others to various prison terms.

Conclusion

In order to remake the world according to their ideological visions, the Communists applied moralistic force and despotic power to make their own interests appear as universal ones. They also imposed a new order over social space as reflected in festivals, for which the party's external language served as a script. Necessary changes in the party's master fiction found reflection in the festivals, whose form and content evolved throughout the Civil War, becoming more sterile. The party gave people time off from work to participate in festivals, but demanded volunteer

[158] GASO, f. 521, op. 1, d. 427, ll. 29–42 ob.

[159] Peter Holquist, "Anti-Soviet *Svodki* from the Civil War: Surveillance as a Shared Feature of Russian Political Culture," *Russian Review* 56, no. 3 (1997): 445.

[160] Italics mine. GASO, f. 521, op. 5, d. 11, ll. 37 ob–38, and f. 521, op. 5, d. 13, ll. 5–5 ob.

[161] Ibid., f. 521, op. 5, d. 13, ll. 5–8.

[162] See the data in ibid., f. 521, op. 5, d. 13, l. 6.

[163] Ibid., f. 521, op. 5, d. 11, l. 1.

labor. It granted amnesties, but prevented spontaneous demonstrations. It sacralized the working class, but turned many of its elements anti-Soviet. The result was a superficial conformity that was ritualistic and opportunistic.

The Communists presented their master fiction to the population through newspapers, propaganda efforts, visual arts, and other forms. During periods of vulnerability the party took additional measures to propagate its views, bombarding the population with leaflets, brochures, and agitation literature; however, these frenzied efforts only underscored how little cultural capital the Communists had at this point. Encountering great difficulty in making its external language hegemonic, the party resorted to an array of rhetorical devices in which ideology became the only acceptable reality. The specifics of the ever-changing narrative are less important than how it worked through the use of metaphors, catchphrases, reasoning devices, moral claims, and new ways of thinking. All of these elements underscored the battle of the new world against the old, the need to sacrifice, and the despicable nature of the opposition. The battle could be against Whites, Greens, the bourgeoisie, Poles, economic ruin, filth, or whatever. Obsessed with the future, the narrative exhorted. It instructed. It justified. It classified. It preached class hatred. It redefined crime and what constituted criminal behavior. It conflated anything other than Bolshevik normative behavior with counterrevolution. It changed constantly at the risk of subverting itself. However, the basic tone, approach, and structures did not, despite the introduction of the NEP (and this reveals that policy's real limitations). By the time the Civil War drew to a close, the master fiction proclaimed that the Communist victory and survival of the Soviet state were inevitable. The message this conveyed to the receiver was that resistance was not only improper, but also futile. In promising a glorious future, the Bolsheviks inscribed historically delayed gratification into their master fiction. The existence within the party of an internal language, however, worked subtly to weaken the power of its public face, for the private language continued to suggest other realities.

The Bolsheviks' belief that people achieved Bolshevik-style consciousness through text fueled the party's literacy programs, but one can only imagine how people targeted for Communist propaganda received it: peasants in the 1920s, after all, did not understand the vocabulary or syntax of Soviet newspapers broadcast by the Communist caste.[164] Far-reaching anti-Soviet attitudes at the end of the Civil War certainly dem-

---

[164] Regine Robin, "Popular Literature of the 1920s: Russian Peasants as Readers," in *Russia in the Era of NEP: Explorations in Soviet Society and Culture*, ed. by Sheila Fitzpatrick, Alexander Rabinowitch, and Richard Stites (Bloomington, 1991), 256.

onstrate that counterideologies continued to challenge the Communists' tenuous hold on power, despite the fact that rival ideologies had access to considerably less public space. Of course, the Cheka remained poised to strike in such cases. Arbitrary at its best, revolutionary justice did little to build support for Soviet power even though in its own peculiar way it served to combat the indiscriminate violence, breakdown, and anarchy characterizing the period. At its worst, the Cheka's crude use of informants and designs to know "how each citizen is living and breathing" revealed that even the privileged social classes could not be expected to monitor themselves and thus had to be placed in social and economic positions that were open to policing. This not only fortified the despotic power of the state, but also took it to a new level. Such cynical use of human capital and raw agentive power became part of Communist cultural practices that helped obscure the fact that the party had failed to establish cultural dominance, while its ideology continued to invite argument.

Eight

Narratives of Self and Other

Saratov's Bourgeoisie

POWERFUL ANTIBOURGEOIS attitudes, shaped by the sustained activities of Russia's revolutionary parties in political life before 1917, also framed Civil War politics. By 1917 the term "bourgeois" already revealed an anti-Western, perhaps even an anti-urban impulse, and was used loosely to mark all well-dressed people or property owners. Depicting the bourgeoisie as an insidious and even diabolical force invited repression against the social other, which did not necessarily contradict the way ordinary people understood the term "democracy."[1] Tapping these feelings of hostility toward the well-to-do, the Bolsheviks granted full citizenship only to "toilers" in the new Soviet Constitution of 1918, depriving the bourgeoisie, clergy, officers, landlords, etcetera of their former rights. Such an understanding of class had an obvious Marxian pedigree in its reference to one's socioeconomic position, but it also shows a reconfiguration in political discourse in which class became an organizing category to construct everyday realities.[2]

---

[1] Kolonitskii, "Antibourgeois Propaganda," 188–96.

[2] See Sheila Fitzpatrick, "Ascribing Class: The Construction of Social Identity in Soviet Russia," *Journal of Modern History* 65 (December 1993): 746, 770. Since the Bolsheviks reconfigured political discourse so that class became the organizing center for constructing social realities, I take issue with some of Fitzpatrick's remarks in "The Bolsheviks' Dilemma: Class, Culture, and Politics in Early Soviet Years, *Slavic Review* 47 (1988): 599–613.

In this chapter I first briefly sketch the Saratov Communists' discriminatory practices toward the local bourgeoisie. Because Russia had been a society in which there had been little reciprocity and trust and much dependence and exploitation, the widespread discrimination and violence unleashed against them during the Civil War by the Soviet government represented not only acts of opposition but also forms of inscription (you are different, "other"), and acts of authority. The raw wielding of power invested the period with meaning and gave it structure just as speech and revolutionary rhetoric did.[3] In turn, these measures invited resistance or self-serving compliance from the bourgeois other, which merely strengthened the Bolsheviks' original distrust of them. Proceeding descriptively rather than empirically, I then offer readings of the diaries and memoirs of seven members of the province's bourgeoisie, which in all but one instance the authors decided to compose *because* of the transformative power of the Revolution and of its self-actualizing discourse.[4] The authors constructed these personal narratives about themselves and their world not only to communicate but also to discover who they were, providing a sense of concreteness and individuality to the experiences of Saratov's ascribed class other. In focusing "on the politics of its construction," I confirm that, always political, experience is "already an interpretation and is in need of an interpretation."[5] Suggesting how human geographies become infused with politics and ideology, I reveal how members of Saratov's maligned bourgeoisie ordered their world and understood the experience of revolution and civil war. Whatever corporate identity the bourgeoisie might have had before the Revolution, their new sense of coherence derived in large part ex post facto as a result of Bolshevik repression, which created a sense of lived commonality. In this regard, "the bourgeoisie" was fashioned by the Revolution's hostility, as the threat Bolshevism posed to the group ironically formalized its inchoate sense of cohesion. The Communists' class-based politics constituted these authors as different kinds of subjects, whose narratives provide evidence of alternative

---

[3] Anne Norton, *Reflections on Political Identity* (Baltimore, 1988), 145.

[4] As a form of interpretation the narratives confirm that how we construct our lives "is subject to our intentions, to the interpretive conventions available to us, and to meanings imposed upon us by the usages of our culture and language." See Robert Folkenflik, *The Culture of Autobiography: Constructions of Self-Representation* (Stanford, 1993), 38. If experience is a subject's history, then language is the site of its enactment (Joan W. Scott, "Experience," in *Feminists Theorize the Political*, ed. by Judith Butler and Joan W. Scott [New York, 1992], 34).

[5] Scott, "Experience," 38. On diaries composed as a response to the Revolution, see Jochen Hellbeck, "Speaking Out: Languages of Affirmation and Dissent in Stalinist Russia, *Kritika* 1, no. 1 (2000): 71–96.

values, practices, and subjectivities that give the lie to the Communists' constructions of social worlds.

Defining the Bourgeoisie and Fleecing Them

In identifying "the bourgeoisie," the Bolsheviks drew from a body of people who occupied similar social positions and who had similar kinds of "capital," dispositions, and life choices. Who were they? A 1915 census that put the city's population at 232,015 included two "bourgeois" categories, a professional middle class, which constituted 15.5 percent of the population, and a commercial one, which constituted 9.8 percent of Saratov's inhabitants.[6] Although Soviet propaganda othered the entire "class," the Soviet government directed its most discriminatory policies at the wealthiest elements, who composed roughly 5 percent of the population:[7] necessity compelled the Bolsheviks to staff Soviet bureaucracies with the class other, just as it drove many members of the bourgeoisie, despite any hostility they harbored toward Soviet power, to find employment in state agencies, where they mediated between the regime and the people. There is no way of determining how many members of the bourgeoisie fled Saratov at the time; however, circumstantial evidence suggests it was mostly the nobility, wealthiest commercial families, and army officers that emigrated, while the vast majority of professionals and merchants stayed behind. Thus, the percentage of the population that could potentially be identified by the new authorities as the class enemy remained larger than the percentage of people the Communists actively discriminated against; the marker "bourgeois" remained more of a political and even moral projection than a tight sociological category.[8]

In 1918, the Saratov Soviet waged intermittent "class war" against the upper bourgeoisie. Ignoring Moscow's ban on such practices, the soviet levied a ten-million-ruble assessment on them, because of the collapse of the tax and financial system as well as the need to raise an army to ward off the Cossack threat. As word of the soviet's intentions leaked out, members of the bourgeoisie went into hiding, prompting the soviet

---

[6] Kokshaiskii, *Predvaritel'nye dannye perepisi*, 15.

[7] Antonov, "Avtobiografiia," Tsentral'nyi muzei revoliutsii, GIK, 30244/200.

[8] This point finds further illustration in how the Bolsheviks viewed the intelligentsia, the social stratum that provided the top leadership of all political parties. Communists conflated members of the intelligentsia who did not back the Bolshevik revolution with the bourgeoisie. See, for example, TsDNISO, f. 200, op. 1, d. 279, ll. 25–32.

to arrest thirty individuals.[9] Some district and volost soviets followed Saratov's example, in part because the Left SR program also called for the expropriation of the capitalist classes. The zealous leadership of the Petrovsk Soviet, for instance, confiscated all valuables from the "bourgeoisie and kulaks." The Kuznetsk Soviet levied a tax on the propertied elements, taking twenty-six hostages in the process. Fearing the requisitioning of their property, the Kamyshin bourgeoisie began to sell their possessions, a practice the Cheka soon banned. Both in Saratov and in the districts, individual circumstances, the nature of one's involvement in the Civil War, the attitudes of party bosses, the degree of financial crisis locally, and the vicissitudes of a class war that could be turned on and off with a bribe or valuable personal contact made Communist policies highly arbitrary.

Seeking to consecrate the new order with practices that symbolized the changing rules of political and social life,[10] in the fall of 1918 Saratov's rulers inaugurated a program of resettling workers into the bourgeoisie's quarters[11] and of moving the latter into "special" ones.[12] Although it is impossible to say how many members of Saratov's upper class — or proletarians — were resettled, the personal narratives examined here suggest that the practice clearly made property owners feel vulnerable. The Cheka carried out similar resettlement programs in the district towns; outcomes in each case depended upon the zealousness, indifference, or corruption of local officials. The underhanded Balashov Cheka registered bourgeois families but did not expel them from their quarters: "In a word, all of the offended bourgeoisie turn to it and find protection." Similarly, in Atkarsk the bourgeoisie deflected efforts to move them out of their homes. Petrovsk authorities, however, resettled its bourgeoisie into barracks, declaring that "now the bourgeoisie work for their grub." Kuznetsk Bolsheviks proved less eager to register the bourgeoisie, purportedly owing to lack of paper on which to print registration forms. Besides, they argued, "we have almost no bourgeoisie"

---

[9] *Saratovskii Sovet*, 433–34; V. P. Antonov-Saratovskii, "Vospominaniia o V. I. Lenine," *Voprosy istorii*, no. 4 (1955): 40–44; GASO, f. 456, op. 1, d. 84, l. 1; f. 456, op. 1, d. 172, ll. 27–28; and Sokolov diary, entry for April 22, 1918. See also, GASO, f. 456, op. 1, d. 8, ll. 70–70 ob.

[10] Wilentz, *Rites of Power*, passim.

[11] GA RF, f. 393, op. 2, d. 80, l. 58.

[12] GASO, f. 456, op. 1, d. 20, ll. 6–7. A participant in the events named Firfanov recalled that workers who rejected the rites of reversal were under "Menshevik influence." However, it is likely that they resisted resettlement out of fear of what would happen to them in the event the revolution was reversed. I. I. Fir'fanov, "Piat' let bor'by," in *V boiakh za diktatury proletariata (Sbornik vospominanii uchastnikov Oktiabria i grazhdanskoi voiny v Nizhnem Povolzh'e)* (Saratov, 1933), 31.

since, owing to the closeness of the front, they had already fled. The few remaining bourgeoisie were found "only among refugees."[13]

Saratov's upper classes also underwent periodic confiscations and requisitions of valuables, luxury items, and food surpluses—many of which were carried out illegally by those abusing the times, for instance, when soldiers at gunpoint snatched winter coats from passersby.[14] As part of the Red Terror introduced in 1918, some local soviets took members of the bourgeoisie hostage. For example, the Kamyshin Cheka forced 125 of them onto a barge docked in the Volga.[15] The Atkarsk Cheka subjected the local bourgeoisie to searches, arrest, and resettlement, taking a group of them hostage and shooting a large number of those seeking refuge in the villages.[16] Members of leading bourgeois families in Saratov also found themselves imprisoned on a Volga barge, tormented with the fear of execution.[17] But the Saratov Soviet preferred less drastic policies with symbolic value. For instance, in preparing for the anniversary of the October Revolution, it ordered the bourgeoisie to sweep the streets and private shop owners to decorate their premises with red banners.[18] Saratov's factory region in January 1919 called for the conscription of the bourgeoisie for unskilled labor as per the Soviet Constitution.[19] That March the soviet requisitioned private libraries,[20] and in the fall mobilized medical personnel, students, and various professionals when the Whites threatened the region.[21] Similarly, the Volsk Cheka ordered the local bourgeoisie, clergy, and "parasitic" element to dig trenches around the city.[22]

When White armies and discontent in the villages endangered Soviet power in 1919, it often lacked the resources to encroach further upon the bourgeoisie. Be that as it may, the Cheka took hostages during the 1919 siege and, when Denikin's bands burst into the region, the At-

---

[13] GA RF, f. 393, op. 3, d. 327, ll. 14 ob, 15 ob, 17. For Atkarsk, see Maksakova, *Agitpoezd*, 157.

[14] GASO, f. 456, op. 1, d. 25, l. 18.

[15] *Izvestiia Kamyshinskogo Soveta*, no. 87, Oct. 2, 1918, 1. Of the 234 people the Saratov Cheka shot in 1918, 39 were executed as a result of the application of Red Terror. See GASO, f. 521, op. 3, d. 5, l. 1.

[16] TsDNISO, f. 200, op. 1, d. 5, l. 30; *Protokoly i doklady VI-ogo*, 119–21; and Rashitov, "Sovety," 260–62.

[17] The taking of hostages was a national phenomenon. See Leonov, *Rozhdenie*, 227–31. The Balashov Cheka executed a large number of "counterrevolutionaries." See *Izvestiia Balashovskogo Soveta*, no. 199, Oct. 1918, 3; no. 4, Jan. 5, 1919, 1; and Rashitov, "Sovety," 260–62.

[18] GASO, f. 456, op. 1, d. 20, ll. 5a, 26, 27.

[19] TsDNISO, f. 136, op. 1, d. 9, l. 1.

[20] GASO, f. 456, op. 1, d. 172, ll. 29–30.

[21] TsDNISO, f. 200, op. 1, d. 209, l. 1.

[22] GA RF, f. 393, op. 3, d. 332, l. 6 ob, and *Saratovskii Sovet*, 635.

karsk Cheka threatened to execute members of the bourgeoisie in the event of an uprising against Soviet power.[23] A September 1919 decree issued by the Saratov Soviet called for the reregistration of the bourgeoisie, revealing that earlier efforts to do so had been in vain.[24] When 7,000 members of the class other were eventually registered, the soviet found that half of them worked in governmental agencies, a situation common throughout the province.[25] In other words, since the Bolsheviks needed their class enemy, the process of othering had practical limitations. Bolshevik external language nevertheless called for "merciless red terror" and the "complete liquidation of the bourgeoisie,"[26] thereby casting them as other kinds of subjects.

Saratov University

Throughout the Civil War the Bolsheviks had to contend with the covert antagonism of the small but influential university community, which the party depicted as an integral part of Saratov's bourgeoisie. Opening in 1909, the university had to draw its faculty from other universities. Moreover, during the war, the government evacuated Kiev University (and its students) to Saratov, as a result of which it is difficult to determine what sort of identity and corporate traditions might have existed.[27] Nevertheless, the faculty at Saratov University opposed the Bolshevik Revolution from the start, prompting a pro-Bolshevik student to complain that "there's not a single lecture where the Messrs. bourgeoisie fail to lash out against the soviets."[28] In particular, the professorate resented the Bolsheviks' encroachment on university autonomy and the fate of the Constituent Assembly.[29] To be sure, a handful of instructors, mainly pharmacists, supported the Bolshevik order. Dismissing this new department as the "least respected" academic unit, one observer suggests that it comprised mostly Jews.[30] This remark reveals how widespread anti-Semitism was among the Russian intelligentsia, and also how such ascription colored the professorate's own politics. In early 1918 Vice Rec-

[23] *Izvestiia Atkarskogo Voenno-revoliutsionnogo komiteta*, no. 256, July 22, 1919, 4.

[24] *ISS*, no. 228, Oct. 15, 1919, 2.

[25] TsDNISO, f. 27, op. 1, d. 230, l. 26. For Serdobsk see GA RF, f. 393, op. 3, d. 327, l. 258. For the role of the lower-middle strata in Soviet state building see Daniel Orlovsky, "State Building in the Civil War Era: The Role of the Lower-Middle Strata," in Koenker et al., eds., *Party, State, and Society*, 180–209.

[26] *ISS*, no. 216, Oct. 1, 1919, 2.

[27] V. A. Solomonov, *Imperatorskii Nikolaevskii Saratovskii Universitet (1909–1917)* (Saratov, 1999), 50–84, 179–86.

[28] *ISS*, no. 3, Jan. 5, 1918, 4.

[29] *Prosveshchenie*, no. 2 (1918): 10, and *Znamia revoliutsii*, no. 2 (94), Nov. 1, 1918, 2.

[30] Telberg Papers, "Pervye otkrytiia," 5–9.

tor V. V. Vorms petitioned the student body voluntarily to raise tuition by 100 percent to avoid turning to the new authorities for assistance, a request that the students endorsed.[31] Defying orders of the soviet prohibiting public meetings, the university's student council censured those few students that backed the Bolsheviks. However, fear of arrest and violent clashes with Red Guard units — as well as the widespread belief that Bolshevik power would collapse — dampened the students' determination to ostracize pro-Bolshevik students.[32]

Nevertheless, at the start of 1919, only 4 percent of the ten thousand students enrolled in Saratov's colleges belonged to the Communist student union.[33] Later efforts to build support among the student body by organizing nonparty conferences turned into forums for expressing enmity toward the Communists. Anarchism attracted more support among students in 1920 than Bolshevism, as it did among workers. Some faculty members and students, however, actually rallied behind the Soviet government during the war against Poland in 1920, reflecting the complexity of political loyalties at the time.[34]

By civil war's end the Bolsheviks had failed to establish control over higher education, but had made it financially dependent on the state. The university's physical plant — and human resources — were in terrible straits. The university had no heat or water or funds to pay its custodial staff. Corpses lay rotting in the pathology department. Going without pay for months, the starving professors succumbed to disease. Special parcels for university faculty distributed by the American Relief Administration helped keep their ranks from being decimated by starvation. Moreover, in March 1921 the Cheka incarcerated faculty members, including the university rector whose diary will be examined in this chapter.[35] The precarious existence of the Saratov professorate forced them to go out on strike in February 1922, a desperate measure the party linked to anti-Soviet conspiracies hatched among émigrés in Paris.[36]

Bourgeois Experiences: Readings

In analyzing the symbolic content and conceptual coherence of the types of experiences Saratov's upper middle class had during the Civil War, I

[31] *ISS*, no. 27, Feb. 17, 1918, 3.
[32] *Prosveshchenie*, no. 14 (1918): 3.
[33] *ISS*, no. 11, Jan. 16, 1919, 2. Later see TsDNISO, f. 27, op. 1, d. 489, l. 44.
[34] GASO, f. 3310, op. 1, d. 1, l. 11, and V. P. Miliutin, *Narodnoe khoziaistvo Sovetskoi Rossii (Kratkii ocherk organizatsii upravleniia i polozheniia promyshlennosti Sovetskoi Rossii)* (Moscow, 1920), 19–20.
[35] GASO, f. 521, op. 1, d. 705, ll. 1 ob–4 ob.
[36] *ISS*, no. 47, Feb. 26, 1922, 2.

work from the premise that it is "not individuals who have experience, but subjects who are constituted through experience."[37] The individuals whose narratives I examine had at least some autonomy within the changing yet hostile political climate that constrained them. Viewing their actions as individual solutions to problems posed by circumstances and by direct actions of the Communists helps us to comprehend the bourgeoisie's collective experience and how it gave rise to everyday perceptions. In making experience visible through use of autobiographical documentation, the historian cannot ignore the agency question of self-representation. Gazing back over his or her life, the memoirist knows the outcome, whereas this is not always the case with the diarist, whose personal account is less of an artistic form than the memoir. Yet both forms of personal narration privilege an identity that must be viewed within conventions of time and space.[38] In considering the relationship between experience and language, I thus take the fictional encodings of the factual for granted and instead focus on how the authors depict themselves. My interest is in revealing authorial intent, submerged voices, subtexts, and hidden meanings and less on circumstances documented elsewhere. In describing how things appeared to be, our authors often prescribe how things should have been; it is such thick "prescription" as well as the subjective, partisan nature of personal narratives that make them so valuable.[39]

MIKHAIL CHEVEKOV: A STAUNCH KADET, PERHAPS A MONARCHIST

Eighteen-year-old Mikhail Chevekov, a student in the seventh grade at the Khvalynsk Male Gymnasium, began keeping a diary on September 19, 1917, which falls silent in June 1918—either because Chevekov perished at the hands of the local Cheka or because he successfully managed to join his family, who had escaped to the Don region.[40] Born into a wealthy landowning family, Chevekov offers a unique look at life in the district town of Khvalynsk during the early months of Soviet power.

[37] Scott, "Experience," 24, 26.

[38] Sidonie Smith, *A Poetics of Women's Autobiography: Marginality and the Fictions of Self-Representation* (Bloomington, 1987), 4–5. Unlike historical narratives, which take place in collective time, personal narratives privilege the temporal framework of their authors' lives. At the intersection of history and fiction, they are an extension of fiction in that imagination gives life shape *before* experiences. Folkenflik, *The Culture of Autobiography*, 55; Susanna Egan, *Patterns of Experience in Autobiography* (Chapel Hill, 1984), x, 12.

[39] Unless otherwise indicated, all of the emphases found in the following discussion are mine.

[40] The Mikhail Chevekov Diary is found in the Khvalynsk Local Studies Museum.

As the Civil War unfolded, categories of identity changed, as did the meanings of the categories and the possibilities for perceiving the self. Yet Chevekov never doubts who he is or what he believes in and thus represents the archetypal opponent of the Bolshevik order. His diary entries reveal a responsible and observant young man torn between the sense of self-discovery and optimism of adolescence and the unnerving political realities. He enjoyed the brilliant autumn weather of 1917, but occasional flashes of melancholy and a sense of foreboding punctuate his life as a student, prompting him to begin keeping a diary. "Judging by the mood in the country," he wrote on September 19, "*we, that is, the intelligentsia and rich people*, will remain alive only until the end of the war, for when the war ends the soldiers will pour in from the front and will leave the cities nothing. There will be murder, robberies, arsons, and God knows what. . . . *There will be an awful civil war.*" He defines himself not only by class (rich) and by disposition (an *intelligent*), but also by political conviction. Dividing Russian society into two groups or parties, the party of disintegration (headed by Kerensky) and of order (Kornilov), he labels himself a "staunch Kadet," and *"in view of all the brutality of the soldiers and peasants, perhaps a monarchist."* Expecting nothing good to come of the Revolution, he wrote: "Things have gone so far that *you begin to envy the dead*, not knowing whether tomorrow you'll be alive or dead."[41] His uncertainty about the future is one of the most repeated refrains in the diary; his anticipation of civil war its most haunting prediction.

Politics also intruded upon Chevekov's life in the classroom. His fellow students were divided politically, and circumstances affected the school's very existence. When a military training school was relocated from Petrograd in October, the gymnasium building was placed at its disposal, as a result of which Chevekov had to attend school on shift.[42] The men's gymnasium now met at the trade school on an abbreviated schedule. Listing his classmates, Chevekov provides thumbnail characterizations of them — honest, cowardly, sensitive, bold, serious, righteous, and weak-willed — or pins labels on them such as "idiot" or "lush."[43] In so doing a submerged voice approves of the author's own positive qualities.

Chevekov's sense of doom grew as political life became more strained and the country slipped into anarchy. He expected some sort of uprising in town already on October 12. On October 28 peasants poisoned the livestock on his family's estate, including his beloved stallion. "How

---

[41] Chevekov Diary, entries for Oct. 5 and 26, 1917.

[42] Ibid., Oct. 1, 5, 21, and 26, 1917.

[43] Ibid., Oct. 5, 1917.

cruelly I erred [in my understanding of the] peasant before the revolution," he penned. "*Now I can't stand to look at him.*" By early November it no longer was safe to venture out into the streets at night. "You think only about one thing," he wrote on November 9, "will you be alive tomorrow or not." Chevekov makes no mention of the Bolsheviks until 1918, remaining silent about why local soldiers and revolutionaries tagged him as an enemy of the Revolution. The admission that his father carried out organizational work on behalf of the Kadets in preparing for the Constituent Assembly elections might help explain why Chevekov had to go into hiding to save his life. Pursued by a mob of soldiers, he sought refuge in the home of a peasant, where he hid on the stove "covered with junk." "If we find him, we'll bayonet him," he heard the soldiers say. His being saved by a peasant did not soften his views of that class.[44]

After Khvalynsk went Bolshevik on January 1, it was no longer safe to brave the streets of the town, which was under martial law. Indiscriminate gunfire and shootings continued for weeks. On January 10 Chevekov set off to free his father, arrested by the new authorities that also confiscated his mill and inventoried his property. His father was released a few days later, perhaps owing to public indignation, for crowds now gathered at the soviet building demanding that those imprisoned be freed. Although the soviet's forces opened fire onto the angry petitioners, Chevekov seemed convinced that they would "*soon overthrow the Bolshevik riffraff,*" for the townspeople continued to protest Bolshevik practices. Class lines were drawn sharply: Bolsheviks shut down the gymnasium and symbolically cut off the colorful buttons from the students' uniforms. "I was almost arrested," wrote our protagonist, and some of his classmates were. Making no secret of his political predilections, Chevekov visited one of his classmates in prison. A few days later he wrote that he had "four revolvers for the Bolsheviks."[45]

Trenchant observations offer a sense of the brutality of the time as the circle began to close in on Chevekov and his family. At the end of January he advised his father to go into hiding; the next day his farm, mills, and property were seized. Reduced to tears, his parents fled to the Don.[46] The escape proved to be well timed, for in early March the "Soviet of Poor Farm-Laborers and Dog Deputies" began to arrest local merchants, who were thrown into jail and tormented. Chevekov equates such acts of violence with how the war and Revolution affected his own family: in 1917, peasants seized 750 desiatinas of the family's land as

[44] Ibid., Nov. 14, Dec. 10, and Dec. 23, 1917.
[45] Ibid., Jan. 25, 27, 28, and 31, 1917.
[46] Ibid., Jan. 29, Jan. 30, and Feb. 1, 1918.

well as several homes and barns. Yet Chevekov continued to believe that an enraged populace would sweep away the Bolsheviks, and this perhaps explains why he did not try harder to slip away from Khvalynsk. He certainly intended to do so. On May 10 Chevekov wrote that he was going to leave town "for it's very, very dangerous here." The remaining entries do not reveal our protagonist's fate. Still in Khvalynsk at the end of May when the Red Guard wanted to take him hostage, he escaped by dressing as a woman. The next day he was searched. One of his last entries ("my involvement with the murder of the machinist Ivan Zubov came up again") laconically suggests Chevekov participated in anti-Bolshevik activities.[47]

There is some correspondence between how the Bolsheviks depicted the bourgeoisie and Chevekov's own self-representation. Separated from the people by wealth and education, he held the underclass in low regard. His own sense of moral superiority, tempered by youthful optimism, sustained the deep confidence he had that his value system would prevail. This inability to accept the possibility of failure not only drove him, but also made it impossible for him to make peace with, or consider being co-opted by, the emerging new order.

LISA DMITRIEVNA URIUPINA: MARTYR

"I Lisa Uriupina want to keep a diary. I'm twelve years old and I'm a student . . . of Mr. Shtokfish." Written on September 2, 1915, this unassuming entry marks the start of a multivolume diary that Lisa Uriupina kept throughout her life. Unfortunately, her cautious relatives destroyed ten notebooks covering the dark years of the Stalin Revolution and World War II, 1928–46. Another ten notebooks, however, chronicle the author's—and Stalin's—last years, providing an unusual glimpse into the life of a middle-aged provincial woman during a period about which we know surprisingly little.[48] While the other narrators focus outward on society, Lisa's account is more personal and self-revealing.

Living in a prestigious neighborhood in the city's center not far from the Volga, the Uriupina family belonged to Saratov's elite commercial middle class. Lisa and her brothers (Volodya, Kostya) and sister (Katya) attended Saratov's best schools. Her father, a determined, forceful individual with strong convictions, refused to acknowledge Soviet power,

---

[47] Ibid., May 31 and June 5, 1918.
[48] Lisa Uriupina, "Zhizn'," Sept. 2, 1915. The diary is in my possession, a gift of Mr. V. Gleizer, to whom I am indebted.

ever. Following the attack on the old elite during the Stalin Revolution, he became a *lishenets* or deprived one, spending the rest of his embittered days cursing the regime that had destroyed his world and his status in it. Ironically, he outlived his children, including Lisa, who died in 1953.

Lisa's diary opens a window onto the life of a fifteen-year-old girl, offering a poignant gender dimension to our sample by revealing the complexities of women's self-disclosure. As narrator, her concerns are those of a young woman of means coming to grips with her budding sexuality. On the pages of her diary we encounter the Revolution and Civil War only when they boldly intrude upon her everyday existence. Such a fragmentary view has its limitations in helping us understand political dynamics; however, it also has advantages as childhood innocence makes way for experience. Lisa accepts her parents' enmity toward the Bolsheviks, but seems open to the possibility that the new order will bring about greater social justice. She does not rule out the possibility of perfecting humankind, yet she does so in a sentimental, seemingly nonideological way. From the very first pages, Lisa casts herself in the most melancholic light: she is sad, anguished, moved by her own ennui. What is most remarkable about this script is that, from the perspective of 1946 or 1950, she grew into it: Lisa never expected real happiness to come her way, and it didn't. A prank she pulled on the last day of school in 1916 ironically came to serve as a metaphor for her life: "In my joy I added on all my notebooks to the word 'student' (*uchenitsa*) the letter 'm'," making it martyr (*muchenitsa*).[49] This is the point at which her sense of self is perhaps realized.

Lisa received an outstanding education at Saratov's women's gymnasium, where she excelled. She loved to draw, and did so with some ability, illustrating her diary. She wrote about her girlfriends (all blockheads), about going to the movies or taking in an opera. Keeping a diary was common among her classmates: after reading others' diaries, Lisa concluded that her own was "stupid and empty." Yet flashes of penetrating insight put Lisa in touch with her innermost promptings. "*I'm a strange person*," she wrote in October 1917, "*and cannot find myself an ideal. At first I elevate everyone and then dethrone them.*"[50]

The political turmoil of 1917 did not capture Lisa's attention until later in the year, perhaps because she and her classmates, and her older sister Katya, began to discover boys. Bedridden with food poisoning during the events of October, she wrote that "all of the time there was cannon fire and some other [shelling]. Some sort of Bolsheviks and so

[49] Ibid., May 25, 1916.
[50] Ibid., notebook 1.

on. They're shooting from the Old Cathedral at the city administration." She confided in her diary that she felt repulsed and anguished: "*Oh this political chaos!*" "*My soul is empty, there's no reason to live! There's nothing to look forward to.* And the sky is so gray and lusterless, and life seems the same as the clouds." An "uprising" on the last day of December kept her at home, as she reports that seventeen people were shot in Theater Square.[51]

Lisa's political consciousness developed during the first weeks of the new year, when a decree of mysterious origins wrongly ascribed to the Bolsheviks, regarding the "socialization of women," evoked an impassioned response from her: "*The accursed Bolsheviks! We poor women, we're not considered human!* This is the first time I'm speaking out against the Bolsheviks, up until now I was indifferent, but this is inconceivable. What a nightmare! Why am I not a man? *It's horrible to be a woman.*" Lisa ended her diatribe by expressing the feeling of many of her background that things would be better if the Germans conquered Russia and drove out the Bolsheviks.[52]

Despite her growing awareness of the political events swirling about her, the focus of Lisa's observations remained fixed on school dances, young officers and soldiers, new shoes and eyeglasses, and poetry. In dialogic engagement with her melancholy, Lisa focused on how she felt. Growing gender awareness prompted her to lament the status of women in Russia's patriarchal society. We also encounter an oblique anti-Semitic remark so typical of her social milieu, and the first reference to a young Red Army officer, Misha Rudnevskii, "a real child," who would become the love of her life (perhaps only vicariously) even though circumstances and Lisa's own misguided quest for an ideal tragically drove a wedge between them.[53]

Spending part of each summer at their dacha outside Volsk, the Uriupina family found itself there during the anti-Bolshevik uprising at the end of June 1918. "The White Guard triumphantly entered the city," wrote Lisa. "They were strewn with flowers." Misha Rudnevskii proved to be a regular visitor at the dacha but had to flee when the White Guard approached. Lisa remarks that Misha and her father "weren't let through to Ukraine" and that her father was now going to make another attempt via Moscow. Such cryptic statements make it impossible to divine what her father was up to and why he had taken in a young Red Army soldier. Such passages indicate that the soft lines of

[51] Ibid., entries for Oct. 24/25 (29), Nov. 10, Nov. 13, and Dec. 31, 1917.
[52] Ibid., notebooks 1 and 2; Feb. 13, 1918.
[53] Ibid., notebook 2; quote found in entry for June 10, 1918.

Civil War were drawn in mysterious ways and that survival dictated all sorts of compromises and creative adaptations.[54]

Civil war began to encroach upon her life after the Uriupinas returned to Saratov in September 1918 and had to rent out Volodya's room and the hall to a dermatologist. The gymnasium students had to steel themselves for consolidation of school buildings and coeducational classes. On the first day of classes Lisa noticed that all of the icons had been removed. "With whomever you speak," she wrote, "everyone complains about lines, bread [shortages], hunger, and that's it." While she admits that the plans presented to them for the ideal Bolshevik school—with free tuition, hot breakfasts, and revised curriculum— struck a responsive chord within her,[55] her political views hardened as life took on new difficulties. *The Bolsheviks have turned everything upside down and are helping themselves to everything,*" she wrote— and later crossed out. Things became more difficult at home. Her father was angry, her mother seriously ill. "There's little bread. Mama made a loaf, adulterated with potatoes. And that's our new bright life for you!!! Long live the new era! Hooray! Hooray! Hooray!"[56]

As Lisa came to appreciate irony, the Communist Party channeled the cynicism of the Lisas of Saratov into acts of public support for Soviet power: she and her classmates participated in the public celebration of the first—and subsequent—anniversaries of October. Finding the red bunting on public buildings distasteful, she acknowledged the insincerity of the cheers of Hooray that came from the participants.[57] When the Soviet authorities made students take part in mandatory gardening, she found the experience boring and vile.[58] Yet, suggesting the transformative power of revolution, Lisa appropriated the most prominent trope of Bolshevik public discourse, that of struggle. "I found an aim in life," she wrote. "That's struggle. . . . I notice that the more I struggle with something, the more energy, strength, and faith I have." "Yes, I'm drawn to freedom and to light."[59]

Despite confiding in her diary at the start of 1919 that a renewed interest in life and cheerier mood had taken hold of her, Lisa soon sunk once again into self-indulgent melancholy. Although she wrote little about them, her parents' disposition contributed to her anguish. Christ-

[54] Ibid., entries for July 28, Aug. 19, Aug. 24, and Sept. 2, 1918.

[55] Yet she doubted how strong the ideal was. Ibid., entries for Sept. 15, Sept. 21, and Oct. 10, 1918.

[56] Ibid., Oct. 21, 1918.

[57] Ibid., Nov. 8, 1918.

[58] Ibid., May 13, 1919.

[59] Ibid., entries for July 26 and Sept. 4, 1918.

mas dinner lacked all of the traditional foods, and the very sight of her modest sausage pie reduced her mother to tears. When her father took ill, Lisa accompanied him everywhere to deal with "the fuss regarding contributions" [from the bourgeoisie]. The bitter cold and lack of fuel shut down her school. Although attending the opera and being pre- scribed a pince-nez lightened her heart, she remained intensely unhappy. "*This foul mood will stay with me forever*," she wrote to her diary. And with great foresight she added: "*I'll never have a family*."[60] A bit later she told her diary, "it's as if all of life has been turned inside out. Noth- ing is familiar anymore."[61]

Lisa imbued her writing with a new melodramatic tone during the spring of 1919, when she wished for herself "suffering . . . and eternal, agonizing melancholy." Looking forward to graduating from the gym- nasium the next year and to pursuing her education at Saratov Univer- sity, she decided to live "for the sake of art or for love." Her days were filled with talk about young men.[62] But Lisa's diary becomes terse as life grows more difficult in the fall and winter of 1919–20. Turning seven- teen on October 20, 1919, made her think about her future plans as she articulated a desire to continue with her drawing or to study bookkeep- ing. Driven out of their school building in early December, a small group finished their studies in two rooms of a private apartment "at the Slavins"—about whom we will read later. Rumors to the effect that the students would be dispatched to the front as nurses tempered any plea- sure she received from going to the theater or to movies in early 1920.[63]

Lisa made her last entry on the Civil War on the final page of her third notebook; we are not to hear from her again until 1924. "I'll tell you one thing," she wrote on January 31, "I must thank fate that I am living during the Revolution. . . . I strive for total freedom, for light, for harmony in the world, for truth and beauty, for, in my view, beauty will save the world." She added, "and I strongly believe in this renewal and resurrection of people, although I don't know where it will come from, perhaps from the teachings of Jesus Christ."[64] Rereading her diary in 1941, a shattered Lisa added: "*No, I don't believe in anything, the world is hopeless*." The changes that took place in her life between 1920 and 1941 may well be typical of those members of the class other who could not find a place in the new society, but had nowhere else to go.

[60] Ibid., notebook 3, entries for January–April 1919.
[61] Ibid., May 5, 1919.
[62] Ibid., entries for May and June 1919.
[63] Ibid., entries for October–December 1919 and for January 1920.
[64] Ibid., Jan. 31, 1920.

A. A. MINKH: HOSTAGE OF THE PROLETARIAT

A member of one of Saratov's most prominent families and son of a leading student of local history, A. A. Minkh played a visible role in local public life as a city duma member and chair of a special commission on adult education. Like many members of the intelligentsia, he scorned the Bolsheviks, but found himself serving the new authorities in order to support his family. Taken hostage by the Cheka in the fall of 1918 and imprisoned on a Volga barge, Minkh fled Saratov in early 1919. Swallowed up by the émigré community, he returned to Saratov in 1929 to be reunited with his wife. Together, they somehow managed to escape to Europe where, in 1932, Minkh composed an account of his experience in Saratov between 1917 and 1919. Deposited in the Russian émigré library collection in Prague, Minkh's memoirs made their way back to the Soviet Union with the Red Army at the end of World War II, where they remained classified until 1990.[65]

Following a brief description of Saratov that emphasizes its rich cultural life, Minkh explicates his role in politics after February 1917, when he set up new militia to replace the tsarist police. Characterizing Bolshevik leaders Antonov and Vasiliev as mediocrities, third-rate lawyers, "blockheads," "zeroes," with self-important, impudent personalities, Minkh expresses alarm and concern for the future.[66] As October approaches he describes the growing anarchy and violence that had seized hold of the population, and how workers opposed the Constituent Assembly elections and weary soldiers demanded peace.[67]

Defending the city duma during the October Revolution, Minkh confirms the masses' hostility toward upper-class Saratov. They gave him an identity by making him a subject: a "bourgeois." Using this label to describe himself, Minkh depicts October as a major turning point that ushered in a period of oppression, terror, and bloodshed; but, he is quick to point out, that was not how he and his associates saw things at the time. Common to the memoirs and diaries is the widespread feeling that Bolshevik rule simply could not last.[68] Still, Minkh went into hiding for a brief period, and was later questioned. As churches prayed for the collapse of the Bolshevik usurpers and criminal elements terrorized the population, he became a deputy in the citizens' groups formed to battle

[65] GA RF, f. 5881, op. 2, d. 506 (A. A. Minkh, Otryvki iz vospominanii ochevidtsa g. Saratova, 1917–1919).
[66] Ibid., ll. 8, 11–14.
[67] Ibid., ll. 17–21 ob.
[68] Ibid., ll. 22 ob–25.

crime. In his view, Bolshevik rule became more despotic with the departure of local leaders, and owing to the impact of the frontoviki and Cheka.[69]

Convinced that Soviet power would fall, the intelligentsia tried not to cooperate with it; however, as Minkh confesses, "*We began to give in.*" Some members of his social milieu became Communist sympathizers and even party members. In May 1918 Minkh became a controller in a Soviet organization, Novomet, which confiscated all metal found in the Volga basin. He did so not only to get fed, but also to be "*among his own*" (the intelligentsia). Minkh used his position as a cover for his "real job," which was to search for food. With a ship at his disposal, he bribed its captain, leader of the Communist Party cell, and head of the port police. The ruse came to an end in late August when the Cheka arrested Minkh, clamping him into a dark, vermin-infested jail cell with Saratov's merchants and clergy, as well as with peasants involved in uprisings against Soviet power. After several days the prisoners were lined up against the prison wall, expecting to be shot. Instead, they were taken to a barge, a floating prison on the Volga, as "hostages of the proletariat."[70]

Many local "formers" — members of the bourgeoisie — found themselves imprisoned on the barge, approximately 300 in all. Some were detained for only a few days or few weeks, but a core of about 65 individuals, including Minkh, were held on the barge for several months, where the guards threatened them with shooting and subjected them to other indignities. For the hostages, it was a time of "*fear, grief, despair, tears, physical and mental torment, and shameless betrayal.*" Minkh's company included much of the local tsarist legal profession; State Duma member N. A. Lvov; the chair of the Public Executive Committee in 1917, N. I. Semenov; the head of the local zemstvo, A. D. Iumatov; as well as numerous Saratov merchants, and — a seemingly neutral remark that speaks volumes — "only one Jew." "In a word our barge was like Noah's ark — with all sorts and kinds of people."[71] But this was not the case: the hostages' pedigree had something in common in the Bolsheviks' cosmology.

Minkh's identity as a bourgeois hardened when he emerged as a leader among the hostages. Describing a scene of near hysteria as the fearful hostages cried and fervently prayed for deliverance, Minkh

---

[69] Ibid., ll. 27–28 ob.

[70] Ibid., ll. 29 ob–34 ob.

[71] Ibid., ll. 35–36 ob. This comment reinforces my argument that the hostility unleashed by the Revolution and as reflected in Bolshevik repressive practices created "the bourgeoisie."

writes that he and a few others tried to calm down their fellow victims. Minkh revealed his understanding of the social hierarchy by dividing the collective into four groups (legal professionals and officials, merchants and middle-class Saratovites, members of the militia and police, and peasants), each of which elected an elder and an assistant. Minkh chaired the council of elders and presented the rules they had drawn up to the Cheka's Kravchenko, who accepted them. But if anyone tried to jump overboard, Kravchenko threatened, Minkh and every tenth man would be shot. In this manner a routine of sorts was established, as Cheka officials interrogated the imprisoned and compiled data on their past lives and the extent of their wealth.[72]

Random acts of kindness or expressions of solidarity occasionally broke the tension of the otherwise terrible conditions of confinement. The guards changed daily, and some of them took pity on their captives. Minkh was able to smuggle out letters to his wife and she in to him. Sent into the city as part of a work brigade, Minkh was fed by the son of a peasant formerly employed by Minkh who happened to come across him. This type of generosity appears in many of the narratives. Minkh's guards turned a blind eye so that he could briefly embrace his wife, while shocked passersby respectfully removed their hats and caps when they saw the captives. On October 20, twenty-five hostages were taken away, leaving sixty-five on board, including Minkh, for whom life took a turn for the worse. His euphemistic diary entries suggest he suffered a nervous breakdown and was saved by the Pogovskiis, all of whom later perished.[73]

Even Minkh's release had an element of cruelty to it: thinking he was being taken out on deck to be shot, he and the remaining prisoners were set free. The Cheka's Kravchenko later confided that many people had clamored for Minkh's release, not only those who had worked with him in the educational establishment and Sunday school movement (including workers), but also the Chekist, Max Deich. The reason is all too familiar: Minkh's cousin, a doctor, treated Deich's ill wife and asked Deich to intervene on his cousin's behalf as payment.[74]

Despite being subjected to such humiliations, no one was killed on the Saratov barge, unlike the situation in Penza and Tsaritsyn. Returning to Novomet, Minkh felt compelled to leave when he was pressed into becoming a Communist Party sympathizer. Afterward he took a job with a food committee (*prodkom*), charged with seizing grain from the villages. Minkh wrote in coded language about this brief chapter in

[72] Ibid., ll. 37–41.
[73] Ibid., ll. 41 ob–44 ob.
[74] Ibid., l. 43 ob.

his life, but his very mentioning of it can be interpreted as part of his confession. Tipped off that he was slated to be arrested once again, he escaped from Saratov and settled abroad.[75]

Minkh's firsthand account thus contains a discourse of witness, interpretation, and confession. When the hostility of the masses in October 1917 gave him an identity by making him a subject, he used the marker "bourgeois" to describe himself. He consistently depicted himself, and the social group with whom he identified, however, as hapless victims who worked in Soviet agencies and even became party sympathizers in order to survive and provide for their families. Although he became a "hostage of the proletariat," he chose to underscore the many small acts of kindness on the part of representatives of the class in whose name he found himself locked on a Volga barge. These good deeds toward the class other serve to reinforce the social hierarchy overthrown by the Bolshevik authorities and to suggest that the Russian people were at heart kind and decent, if simple. Duped by the Bolsheviks, they needed the bourgeoisie to set Russia right. In the end, Minkh exonerates himself for the tough choices he felt compelled to make. He is an archetype of the bourgeois victim who was forced to collaborate with the system he hated in order to survive. In describing how the Bolsheviks treated him he justifies his fleeing Russia and accounts for his behavior as a hostage of the proletariat.

IVAN IAKOVLEVICH SLAVIN (1851–1930): VICTIM OF THE MOTHERLAND

A scion of an influential merchant family, Ivan Slavin graduated from the law faculty at St. Petersburg University, after which he became a luminary in local public affairs, elevated to the rank of hereditary nobility. A lawyer, judge, city duma deputy, and administrator, Slavin devotedly participated in Saratov's transformation from provincial capital to bustling commercial center. A moderate liberal by political persuasion, Slavin was resigned to the seeming inevitability of the powerful, impersonal revolutionary wave that swept across Russia. He never actively opposed Soviet power but saw himself and those of his class as victims of the motherland and carriers of Russia's spirituality. There is something in Slavin's images reminiscent of writings on saints' lives, which also constitute a central trope in Russian literature.[76]

---

[75] Ibid., ll. 45–45 ob. Left behind until 1929, Minkh's wife compiled a list of prominent Saratovites who perished at the hands of the Bolsheviks. See ibid., ll. 46–48.

[76] Recently declassified, fragments of Slavin's memoirs are stored in GASO. Here I ex-

Cruel, arbitrary, inescapable fate represents the most powerful historical force in Slavin's narrative. The author makes this point at the start
when he places the Red Terror of late summer 1918 into its local and
national context, noting the attempt on Lenin's life, the menacing activities of the Czechoslovaks on the Volga, and the rise of the anti-Soviet
Samara government. "Reprisals had to be taken against someone for all
of these misfortunes and failures," he nobly explains. Arrested after a
church service in September 1918, he found himself locked up in an
overcrowded prison cell with a large group of prominent Saratovites
he knew. Slavin also willingly describes the indignities he and his co-
prisoners endured from the ill-mannered Cheka agent, while an anti-
Semitic remark Slavin makes suggests he too linked the Jews with Soviet
power. "Crammed like sardines" in a can, 20–25 prisoners had to make
do with a cell fit for nine. "Thus began our monotone, monotonous
drudgery."[77] Or so he thought. Several days later the Cheka transferred
the hostages to the Volga barge.

Slavin inscribes virtue and lack thereof on the human body, which for
him became a marker of social standing. Thus, his description of the
Cheka official Beliaev, who cursed the prisoners and their god, emphasizes Beliaev's unsavory human and physical qualities. "Small, stocky,
well-fed on free bread, his figure reminded you of a bedbug that drank
up the last drop of human blood. His impudent mug was that of a
typical lackey; his shrill voice intended to frighten." Compare this characterization with that of fellow hostage Prince M., "whose exterior and
bearing . . . was very attractive and interesting. . . . [His] noble, well-
born features reminded you of the outward appearance and head of
Turgenev; a noble, lordly, portly figure, with soft, flowing movements
and gestures, an attractive voice—all of this set out and created a pleas-
ant, indelible impression."[78]

Both Minkh's and Slavin's accounts suggest the Cheka did not know
what to do with the hostages. Despite the verbal abuse they endured,
the foul food, and the overcrowded conditions, the Cheka allowed the
hostages to receive parcels from home, to read newspapers, to play
chess, and to join work brigades in the city. The Cheka first released the
doctors held on the barge, undoubtedly because their skills were sorely
needed to treat Red Army men. As other hostages were set free, how-

---

amine the personal account written in January 1919 of his arrest and imprisonment, along
with Minkh, on a Volga barge, published as "V plavuchei tiur'me (na barzhe)," with an
introduction and commentary by V. Mironov, *Volga*, no. 1 (1993): 169–75.

[77] Ibid., 170.

[78] Ibid., 171, 174.

ever, the Cheka deposited fresh ones, including those composing a Who's Who of the tsarist judicial system.[79]

Slavin relates two critical moments of despair for the hostages. The first came in September when a violent storm on the Volga pitched and tossed the aching barge about like a toy boat. The second moment came as winter set in and plans to heat the barge remained unimplemented. Slavin poignantly reveals how he understood the experience of being a hostage and the Revolution itself:

> We are living through a historical squall, a terrible historical storm, a revolutionary wave has engulfed us and is carrying us along. . . . Perhaps it will deposit us at a calm place where we will rest, or perhaps it will smash us against the rocks and cliffs and we'll perish. We are pitiful creatures, but the Motherland will remain. . . . And here we are — the last victims of our revolution. The Motherland undoubtedly needs these victims like it needs victims on a field of battle, in trenches, or in military hospitals. We will make peace with this terrible twist of fate. . . . Human experiences in most cases are spun from autosuggestion. We need to instill in ourselves that we are the salt of the earth, the bearers and representatives of her spiritual power. *A crude, brutal, physical, animal force hates us for this and is tormenting us for this.* Perhaps we'll come out of this storm whole and find solace in the pleasant recognition that the Motherland needs the sufferings we lived through.[80]

Slavin's resignation contrasts with Minkh's decision to leave his homeland. Yet those who stayed behind needed to find meaning in their anguish. Slavin and his co-hostages could not resist the elemental and animal-like revolutionary wave; he understood his suffering as the inevitable price that he and those of his circle had to pay for the life and privileges they had enjoyed before, and for their role as bearers of Russia's spirituality.

RECTOR VLADIMIR DMITRIEVICH ZERNOV: NOTES OF AN *OLD* INTELLIGENT

The memoirs of V. D. Zernov, physicist, accomplished violinist, and rector of Saratov University, 1918–21, differ in intent, tone, and content from the other personal accounts considered here, in part because he had a particular purpose in writing them, in part because he composed them during the Stalin years. Born in 1878 into a Moscow Uni-

---

[79] Ibid., 173–74.
[80] Ibid., 174.

versity anatomy professor's family, Zernov arrived in Saratov in 1909 as the youngest (thirty-one years old) of the original seven professors appointed to the newly opened university. Elected rector of the university in September 1918, he presided over the institution's steadfast attempts to maintain its intellectual integrity as civil war raged. The Cheka arrested Zernov and two of his colleagues in March 1921, following their public remarks that material life and a scientific understanding of it were compatible with religious beliefs. Transferred to Moscow after a month in Saratov's dank Prison No. 3, he was eventually set free, after which he was cautioned not to return to Saratov. Zernov remained in Moscow, continuing to lead a distinguished academic life. He wrote his reminiscences between 1944 and 1946 — the year he died — for his young grandson.[81]

Like most members of the professorate, Zernov was drawn to Russia's Kadet Party. However, he shuns discussion of politics and ideology in his reminiscences, not because such things interested him little but because he undoubtedly practiced a form of self-censorship so as not to jeopardize his family in any way. Apolitical and nonjudgmental, the memoir on the surface seems devoid of any political significance. Yet in peeling away the author's layer of caution the reader uncovers a circumspect, gentle, matter-of-fact depiction not only of how things used to be but also of how people used to act, which offers a powerful, seductive alternative to the new order. The author entitled his memoirs "Notes of an Old Intelligent" (they appear as "Notes of a Russian Intelligent" in published form). His use of "old" represents the key to understanding the document's power. Spinning webs of meaning from categories drawn from the past, Zernov finds the practices of Soviet power alien.

Zernov's account begins with his childhood, in which the basic ingredients of a "cultured" life already fall into place. Like other Russian intellectuals, Zernov welcomed the February Revolution, yet reacted *"as if in a fog and with some bewilderment."*[82] The remainder of his observations about 1917 avoids political issues, focusing sharply on university life. Zernov becomes cautiously informative once his term as rector begins in the fall of 1918. He now bore responsibility for coping with difficult economic straits and for preserving the institution's inde-

---

[81] I am indebted to V. A. Solomonov who provided me with a copy of Zernov's (then) unpublished memoirs. Most citations come from this version, entitled "Zapiski starogo intelligenta." Solomonov later published the reminiscences in the journal *Volga*. See V. D. Zernov, "Zapiski russkogo intelligenta," ed. by V. A. Solomonov, with introductory remarks by S. Borovikov, *Volga*, no. 7 (1993): 116–48; no. 8 (1993): 123–44; no. 9 (1993): 114–30; no. 10 (1993): 97–120; no. 11 (1993): 137–49; no. 2 (1994): 112–39; no. 3–4 (1994): 117–32; no. 5–6 (1994): 115–32; no. 7 (1994): 127–54.

[82] Zernov, "Zapiski," 427.

pendence as its academic council was forced to add representatives from the student body and soviet. The next year university elections were no longer secret, and the admissions policy was open. The episode that best sums up the impact of revolutionary change on the university's intellectual climate, however, concerns the time an inexperienced Cheka agent sent to monitor Zernov's lectures dropped a revolver while Zernov was lecturing.[83]

Describing the university's relationship with the local soviet as "correct," "like relations between great powers," Zernov paints a droll picture of his attempts to secure fuel to heat the university during the winters of 1919 and 1920. Equipped with new oil-burning furnaces, the buildings faced winter without heat owing to lack of oil reserves. As a result, many classes were canceled, and professors lectured in their fur coats and boots. Fuel was available the next winter, and Zernov secured it by offering the head of the local oil trust some sheet music that interested the musician-turned-bureaucrat and by plying local transportation workers with grain alcohol the university had secured for other purposes.[84] Although there was no money to pay university salaries, the faculty managed by bartering the precious grain alcohol supplies for necessities. Shortages gave rise to behavioral patterns that Soviet citizens would later resort to instinctively as an anticapitalist revolution forced them to resort to precapitalist forms of behavior.

Zernov's position targeted his family for the soviet's class-based policy of relocating the city's bourgeoisie. Soldiers arrived to relocate his family in September 1918. Seizing the family's belongings, they left each family member with a single plate and place setting. In restrained language, Zernov describes the soldiers' reaction to a cache of silver napkin rings they discovered. Disappointed by the smallness of the "bracelets," the puzzled soldiers left them for their owners. Such incidents involving the revolutionary masses found sprinkled throughout the document suggest a condescending rather than hostile attitude toward everyday people. For a month the family lived in a university laboratory until it moved in with a local merchant and former city duma member, Tikhonov, an ailing old man who was later executed. Whatever reluctance the Tikhonovs had to sharing their home was mollified by their restrained pleasure at welcoming a family of their own type. Meanwhile, Zernov managed to get back his family's confiscated belongings thanks to the intervention of a colleague who had operated on and saved the life of a local Bolshevik leader shot earlier in the year.[85]

[83] Ibid., 438, 442–44.
[84] Ibid., 439–42.
[85] Zernov, "Zapiski," *Volga*, no. 3–4 (1994): 128–29.

One episode Zernov relates provides a telling commentary on how the professors learned a valuable lesson from the social other. Some faculty members participated in a wood felling expedition organized by the soviet, which promised to store the wood until winter, when it would distribute it to those who supplied it. As the professors struggled to fell the thick hardwoods, a group of blacksmiths who had accompanied them rested. The blacksmiths explained that the soviet had no intention of distributing the wood, and if it did "they'll give it to us" (the workers). "They turned out to be more farsighted than we," remarked Zernov. Nonetheless, for the most part Zernov viewed the social other as childlike, uncultured, and dirty.

Zernov calls attention to the disgusting nature of public bathroom facilities, and especially of the underclass's toilet habits, to suggest the breakdown of civility. His son Mitya refused to use the facilities in the university hospital because the bathroom floor was covered with urine and feces. After Tikhonov was shot and his family moved out of the house Zernov inhabited, a group of soldiers were brought in. When Zernov found liquid oozing through the ceiling into his apartment below, he discovered that the soldiers had begun to relieve themselves on the floor so as not to have to go out into the cold to use the facilities in the yard at night. The unit's doctor responsible for sanitation moved them out, enabling Zernov to turn the flat into a dormitory for university faculty. However, a "simple" woman shared the Zernov's apartment. "She was a harmless person," he wrote, who sang in a church choir. When the Zernov family left for Moscow she purportedly bowed and thanked his wife for accepting her, reminding us that there was another side to the soviet's relocation policies.[86]

Zernov's public support of efforts to counter the new order's official atheism caused his political troubles in Saratov. Apart from challenging a Bolshevik agitator railing against religion, Zernov and other faculty twice spoke at the cathedral on the theme of religion and science. Afterward a threatening article denouncing them appeared in *Izvestiia*. Arrest came at the beginning of Lent, March 8, 1921, in the midst of worker unrest. Cheka agents deposited Zernov in Prison No. 3, where he "saw a mass of acquaintances," including Ia. Slavin and other members of the "upper" class. Zernov tersely describes the filth and the disgusting food, the slop bucket used as a toilet and an old man suffering from colitis, the spiteful prison guard.[87] The authorities relocated the prisoners to a concentration camp attached to the prison complex, where his colleague A. A. Bogomolets, sent to examine the prisoners,

[86] Ibid., 463–69.
[87] Zernov, "Zapiski," 482–90.

cleverly arranged for Zernov to meet with his wife, who was disguised as a nurse. Zernov learned that a commission had arrived from Moscow to ascertain why the local Cheka had carried out so many arrests. Interestingly, he insists that everyone related to the prisoners with great sympathy and respect. *"No one renounced us, as it later became fashionable to do."*[88]

The author's description of the authorities' efforts to move the prisoners to Moscow reads as an indictment of the new regime's incompetence and a testimonial to the prisoners' innocence. A convoy of five "boys" escorted twenty prisoners to the Saratov train station, arriving after the train to Moscow had already left. It took a full week to get to Moscow, and at one stop the train disembarked while Zernov and a few others were waiting for tea. When a cab driver in Moscow felt sorry for the aging Slavin and helped transport him to prison, Zernov warmly approved of how the Russian people *"often behaved in the old days."*[89]

Zernov found everything about Moscow better than in Saratov. Prisoners in the capital set up a "prison university," held church services, and declared a hunger strike to speed up examination of their cases. Following pro forma interrogations, the prisoners were set free. Zernov agreed to remain in Moscow after his release, which had come about owing to the intervention of friends and colleagues on his behalf. Commissar of Health N. A. Semashko told him bluntly "we can look after you here but cannot vouch for the provinces." Zernov took temporary shelter in a special home for members of the intelligentsia, where he was served excellent food "seven times a day," while much of provincial Russia was starving. His reference to "another Jew atheist" reveals that Zernov shared the prejudice of so many other Russian intellectuals who saw a Jewish cabal behind the Revolution.[90] In September 1921 he traveled to Saratov with great difficulty in order to gather family belongings; he succeeded thanks only to extensive bribery.[91]

While eschewing political commentary and any direct criticism of the new regime, Zernov's personal history makes a powerful political statement by casting the old world in a nostalgic light and the new as arbitrary, corrupt, uncultured, tough, incompetent, and, at its very worst, violent and atheist. It does so not by offering potent juxtapositions, but subtle, matter-of-fact comparisons, in which the tone of the narrative is as significant as its content. This particular life story reveals how the self-identity of its author—an *old* intelligent—is arguably more impor-

[88] Ibid., 491–92.
[89] Ibid., 493–96.
[90] Ibid., 511–16.
[91] Ibid., 523–25.

tant than what happened to him: Zernov enjoyed a distinguished career under the Soviet regime; however, his value system always remained outside it.

ALEXIS V. BABINE: MORALLY INDIGNANT WITNESS AND SURVIVOR

Fate cast a complicated and original lot for Alexis V. Babine, a Russian-born American who accepted a teaching appointment as instructor in English at Saratov University in September 1917 (figure 8.1). Babine kept a diary of his experiences in Saratov, where he remained until 1922, when he was able, with the help of the American Relief Administration (ARA), to return to the United States.[92] Born in Elatma, Riazan Province, in 1866, he received an excellent education at the local gymnasium and then in St. Petersburg. The young Babine disappeared to the United States following a psychologically shattering incident when he accidentally killed a friend. Babine earned an M.A. degree in American history at Cornell University, after which he worked as a librarian at Indiana University, at Stanford, and then at the Library of Congress. During his tenure in Washington he negotiated the purchase and transfer of the 80,000-volume library of the wealthy Siberian merchant, G. V. Iudin, which remains at the core of the Library of Congress's Russian collection. Following the events of 1905, Babine returned to Russia determined to fulfill a yearning he had harbored for years: to publish, in Russian, a history of the United States. His two-volume work was issued in St. Petersburg in 1912. In it, Babine revealed his strong sympathies for the American political system and for "Anglo-Saxon" culture.

Described by those who knew him as sober, methodical, efficient, orderly, proper, and, on occasion, stubborn, Babine was a gifted linguist and diligent, intelligent student. He had a sense of adventure and enjoyed indulging his interests. He was private, elusive, secretive, and above all a survivor. Despite nostalgic references in the diary to the autocracy, he was not a monarchist *tout court*; the chaos and horror of the Civil War merely made him long for a return to the old order. His fondness for pragmatic American compromise politics had made him critical of Russia's backwardness and "political immaturity." The moderate socialist elements did not appeal to him because their all but blind yearning for change had contributed, in his view, to the Bolshevik vic-

---

[92] His diaries and related materials are held at the Manuscript Division of the Library of Congress. I published and annotated the diaries in 1988. See Raleigh, *A Russian Civil War Diary*.

8.1 Alexis Babine in Saratov during the Civil War. Prints and Photographs Division, Library of Congress, 26536 3239, box 4.

tory. The middle-class liberals' inability to challenge the militant revolutionaries during the Civil War made him lose respect for them, too.

Babine described the zigzag course of the Russian Civil War with profound moral indignation, even though he "always diligently kept out of politics." Above all, the diary focuses not on political ideas and causes, but on grubbing for food and staying alive. As the Civil War progressed and hunger destroyed life as it had been known, commentary on politics disappears from the diary; the entries become pithy and appear less frequently. Writing for an American audience, Babine kept his diary in the expectation that it would be published someday. Disgusted with what he called the "backwardness and barbarity" of his native country, Babine could be a myopic observer, as he expressed longing for a return to the old regime that had become politically and morally bankrupt even in the eyes of Saratov's middle class. His hatred of leftist groups extended with little discrimination to everyone and everything that wanted to give Russia a fresh start. Babine was anti-Semitic and anti-Polish. He expressed contempt for the lower classes that had fallen victim to the seductive slogans flung at them from the political left. Readers of the diary encounter "ill-smelling peasants," the "rabble from nearby villages," the "blushing nobility and ignoble vulgar," and Babine's "unusually stupid maid."[93]

Even though Babine did not ponder the deep-lying causes of the Revolution or the political cosmology of the Russian masses, we learn from his diary how the class-oriented policies of the Bolsheviks transmogrified the world of the former privileged. We learn about the "physical and moral flabbiness of . . . [Russia's] Christian citizens."[94] "The Russian tendency to protest against oppression and all sorts of barbarity by refusing to do any work," he tells us, "is, to me, as touching as the Russian incapacity to do anything to eliminate injustice."[95] Astutely, Babine realized that the common people felt alienated from Saratov's nonrevolutionary middle class, which was *corrupted by self-indulgence and physical idleness, disarmed and unfamiliar with the use of arms, incapable of resisting force by their own exertions, discredited in the eyes of a deceived people.*[96] On this subject we get Babine at his best:

> The more I look at my learned university colleagues, the more I listen to their eloquent and animated or passionately subdued talks on the present state of affairs, the more disgusted I grow with their inability to do anything. . . . No rights whatsoever will or can they defend with their own

[93] Ibid., xvi.
[94] Alexis V. Babine Collection, 3239. Babine Diary, Oct. 27, 1917.
[95] Ibid., Dec. 1, 1917.
[96] Ibid., Nov. 18, 1917.

flabby hands: they would much rather hire stronger hands than to expose their precious selves to the risks of a contest. Their chief end is life itself, and only life — under any conditions.[97]

In describing them he is describing — or denying — himself. When he realizes this, he needs to reinterpret his social stratum's inability to dislodge the Communists. On November 7, 1918, he wrote: *"the real object of the Communist Party is to sweep out of its way everybody to whom the undeceived and awakened people might turn for guidance in their active protest against oppression, and thus to perpetuate its rule."*[98]

Babine's diary entries for 1918 provide rich detail about daily life in Saratov and in his hometown of Elatma. He depicts the anger and hostility of those opposed to Bolshevism; growing public violence and mob justice; popular rumors about Cossack intervention; his service as a night watchman. He confirms that the Mensheviks enjoyed support among railroad workers in the spring of 1918, and the confusion reigning in the city during the May 1918 uprising. The diary documents the deterioration in living standards (hunting for food had already made jobs secondary in 1918); the amazing growth of a black market; "bagmen" whose illicit activities kept people alive; and behavior in lines. In June Babine left for Elatma, where his brother Peter was "reluctant to get involved." In Elatma during the launching of the Red Terror, Babine recoiled at the execution of a handful of prominent citizens, including four of his former classmates. "They were all good, influential citizens, selected to die during a drunken orgy in a brothel by our present ex-murderer rulers, Lepniov and Aleshin, after an order from Moscow, as a warning to the dangerous bourgeoisie in connection with the attempt on Lenin's precious life."[99] Upon his return to Saratov he comments on the taking of hostages, but it is not important to Babine whether the rumors he repeats are true that the "conservatives" on the barge were beaten with iron chains and that the one who had expired from the cruelty happened to be insane.[100]

Military operations along the Volga and the resulting chaos disrupted life to such an extent by early 1919 that Saratov no longer comes alive on the pages of Babine's diary.[101] As living conditions declined further that year, he saw himself transformed into that other he so despised. In February 1920 Babine noted that the temperature in his room never went above 35 degrees F. Examining himself for body lice now became

[97] Ibid., Feb. 2, 1918.
[98] Ibid., Nov. 7, 1918.
[99] Ibid., Sept. 21, 1918.
[100] Ibid., Dec. 12, 1918.
[101] Ibid., March 18, 1919.

a daily ritual. When the party declared war on economic ruin, Babine found himself conscripted for woodcutting expeditions. Corroborating Zernov's remarks, Babine tells us that university professors were doing a brisk business in peddling alcohol assigned to them for research purposes.[102]

From this point on, the theme of survival frames the diary,[103] for Saratovites already foresaw a terrible famine in the making, a vision amplified when hungry German colonists began camping on the Volga.[104] Babine's knowledge of English fortunately secured him a coveted spot with the American Relief Administration. Focusing his indignation on the besotted behavior of ARA employees, Babine's diary becomes long on moral outrage and short on substance. But the job kept him alive and enabled him to escape. On November 18, 1922, Babine arrived in New York, never to return to his native Russia again.[105]

N. I. ARKHANGELSKII: A STORY OF CONVERSION

One of the founders of the Social-Democratic movement in Saratov, N. I. Arkhangelskii became a prominent newspaper figure, serving as editor of *Saratovskii vestnik* (Saratov Herald) in 1917. Sometime before 1917 he began to back G. Plekhanov's so-called *Edinstvo* (Unity) group, which favored the continuation of the war, placing the group to the right of Saratov's political center. Arkhangelskii sided with the city duma in October 1917; however, he afterward played no part in the anti-Bolshevik opposition. When the soviet shut down all non-Bolshevik newspapers in the following months, Arkhangelskii threw himself into "cultural" work, taking over responsibility for the uezd art subdepartment until he joined the provincial department in 1919. Ironically, losing his newspaper gave him time to keep a diary, which he began in November 1917.[106] In it he depicts himself as an intelligent dedicated to spreading enlightenment among Russian workers. Although his initial

---

[102] See ibid., entries for February–June, 1920.

[103] The one exception when Babine stops focusing on survival strategies occurs in June 1920, when a visiting British Labour Party delegation that included Bertrand Russell visited Saratov. The authorities enlisted Babine to prepare a translation of the official address issued for the visitors. Babine did his best to hint "with what blackguards and choice scoundrels they were dealing." Raleigh, *A Russian Civil War Diary*, 163–64.

[104] Babine Diary, entries for August 1920–August 1921.

[105] Raleigh, *A Russian Civil War Diary*, 188–226. Correspondence regarding Babine's escape from Russia is found in the Herbert Hoover Presidential Library (ARA, Personnel, Russian, Babine, A. V.).

[106] N. M. Arkhangelskii's diary is found in the manuscript division of the Saratov Oblast Local Studies Museum.

conflict with Bolshevism kept open the possibility that Soviet authorities would label him a class enemy, as the Civil War unfolded Arkhangelskii himself came to denounce the bourgeoisie and to express admiration for the Bolsheviks' selflessness. His approval of the Bolsheviks rises with their military victory over the Whites.

Focusing on political life in Saratov, Arkhangelskii sheds little light on the cultural experimentation in which he took part, but confirms the deep hostilities between Proletkult and other organizations. In writing about Proletkult's involvement in local theatrical life, he lashes out at Bassalygo, the organization's local theatrical specialist, a "petty, vain, talentless little actor" who relished intrigue, favoritism, and vengefulness. He expresses equal dissatisfaction with futurists and poets, all of whom "tried to appear as Communists."[107]

The author's entries corroborate the widespread anti-Bolshevik feelings among Saratov's middle class in late 1917. As public organizations and officials went on strike against the new authorities and city duma members congregated in the underground, "agitation against the Bolsheviks went hand in hand with growing anti-Semitism," which our author did not share. Careful to dissect the rampant rumors circulating at the time in order to be fair to the Bolsheviks, he describes an atmosphere of alarm created by their news blackout and by the activities of criminal elements dressed in soldiers' garb.[108] Reporting the news with caution, he seems more critical of Saratov's "ignorant inhabitants" who saw Jewish cabals everywhere than he does of the Bolsheviks. Equally contemptuous of the "gloomy, unintelligent faces" of the anarchists, almost all of whom "were still boys," the author substantiates the rise in Menshevik fortunes among workers and their reluctance to join the Red Army. But his focus remains fixed on the uninformed inhabitants of Saratov who now pinned their hopes for salvation "on the Germans and their 'order.'" Without assigning blame, he describes the incipient breakdown of economic life on the Volga, which speaks metaphorically of the larger economy as a whole. "*The picture is cheerless and at the same time alarming. The poor Volga! The poor country!*"[109]

The diary shows how quickly political apathy seized hold of many, becoming a critical factor in the Bolsheviks' "winning" the Civil War. The apartment in which his family lived turned out to be caught in crossfire during the uprising in May 1918. But children continued to play, his wife continued to bake a birthday cake, and all Arkhangelskii

---

[107] Ibid., May 6, 1918, Dec. 20 and 21, 1918, Jan. 20, 1919, Feb. 17, 1919, June 8, 1919, and July 15, 1919.

[108] Ibid., entries for November 1917 through January 1, 1918.

[109] Ibid., entries for Jan.–April 13, 1918.

wanted to do was "to eat and sleep." Once the "facts" of the uprising began to emerge, Arkhangelskii berated the SRs for issuing a leaflet to the town's population, deceptively informing them that the soviet had fallen and that power had passed into their hands. "The Bolsheviks apparently turned out to be stronger, smarter, and above all demonstrated greater determination and courage," he wrote. Explaining that the soldiers opposed the soviet's present makeup rather than Soviet power, he shares with us the sinister remark of a Red Army soldier who declared that "the bourgeoisie should not rejoice — they won't be better off [if we come to power]."[110]

Arkhangelskii's life became more complicated after the uprising as the Bolsheviks equated all of their socialist rivals with the enemy. Despite fabricated allegations against him in *Izvestiia*, he believed a terrible political void would exist if the Bolsheviks were overthrown "in which squabbling among the political parties would thrive once again with all of its terrible consequences." Revolution had so shaken the state's foundation that Russia would barely be able to construct them anew "by her own hands." "The gravity of the moment lies in this, and not in Bolshevism," he concluded.[111] Derisive of the bourgeoisie's reliance on "foreign bayonets," he foresaw that "no constituent assembly or its microcosm in the provinces, the city dumas, will help. *We are entering a phase of bloody conflagration — socialism or capitalism, there is no middle ground.*"[112] Arkhangelskii expressed no sympathy toward the bourgeoisie even as rumors spread that they would be massacred and as hundreds were arrested; he wrote nothing about the seizing of hostages. This is instructive: it was his self-perception that bestowed an identity upon him, not his social standing. Troubled by the "dark reaction" sweeping over the population, including the intelligentsia, he lamented the rising anti-Semitism and renewed interest in religion. Society's indifference toward political life continued throughout the bitter winter of 1918–19, when "*each person withdrew into his personal life and concern for a piece of bread.*"[113]

The diary entries from 1919 paint a graphic picture of the confusion and panic linked to the White offensive against Saratov, which aroused people's interests once again in all sorts of rumors of salvation.[114] He informs readers that he turned down an invitation to work for *Izvestiia* because he did not want to mingle with the large number of pseudo-

---

[110] Ibid., May 17–19, 1918.
[111] Ibid., May 20–June 22, 1918.
[112] Ibid., Aug. 31, 1918.
[113] Ibid., Dec. 25, 1918, Jan. 19, 1919, and Feb. 23, 1919.
[114] Ibid., entries for April, May, and June 1919.

Communists employed there and in other Soviet offices, who "compromise Communism with their behavior, creating for Soviet power thousands of petty, invisible enemies full of malice. *They serve as deadly microbes, invisibly eating away at the Soviet organism. . . . It's disgusting to see these pretenders and hypocrites. And it pains me on behalf of committed, honest, pure Communists.*"[115]

Arkhangelskii's position became more precarious when Saratov fell under siege and he experienced "tormenting moments of uncertainty" regarding whether or not he would be arrested. Pondering the role journalists would play if the bourgeoisie proved victorious, he concluded that journalists would "scratch their pens in defense of the bourgeoisie" and would be well paid "in rubles and dollars," as a result of which the press would assume a mercenary quality like never before. If the socialists won, the "press would be stifled at the first opportunity. There would be no place for me as a journalist. *I prefer to devote the remainder of my life to cultural-educational work.*" Lamenting that arrest would interrupt his educational work among workers, he enthused: "workers are such a generous, wonderful audience." His is a story of a calling.[116]

Arkhangelskii appreciated the transformative power of the civil war experience. Children outside his window now played "shooting" games, just as in his own time Arkhangelskii played "cholera" and "pogrom." Without assigning blame, he comments that "arguments over a piece of bread, over an extra cucumber" took place in his home at the dinner table. In general, he bemoaned the growth of a "petty, hungry, greedy, and egotistical tribe" of people. A chance encounter with Ivan Slavin offers a break from the overall gloom and points to the importance of personal attitudes in weathering the storm of civil war. Recently released from his second arrest, Slavin was "lively and did not despair," remarking ironically that he had been detained a second time "for sitting in Lipki Park with a group of old people." These episodes unfold against a backdrop of "full-scale evacuation" from Saratov, of searches and of the arrest of those elected to the Constituent Assembly. Fearing the violent consequences that would accompany a White victory, the moderate socialists now threw in their lot with the Bolsheviks who, they believed, would "outgrow their extremism."[117] This belief became stronger as the Civil War developed.

The remainder of the diary, which stops on March 5, 1920, offers a mosaic of the somber mood among Saratovites. A second wave of Red Terror in the fall of 1919 struck fear even among those far removed

---

[115] Ibid., July 16, 1919.
[116] Ibid., July 7, 1919.
[117] Ibid., July 16–Aug. 10, 1919.

from politics. Recounting a horrific report on the Cossacks' capture of Tambov, the author observed that *"everyone understood that there can be no waverings: you're either for or against the revolution."* His conversion was now complete: "To struggle half-naked, without supplies, without resources against bourgeois forces of the entire world—isn't that a miracle?"[118] Tersely recording a large Communist demonstration following a wave of new arrests in which participants demanded "Death to the bourgeoisie" and "Long live Red Terror," he condemns the bourgeoisie's conspicuous consumption during a time of want for others. Without passing judgment, he notes the arrest and execution of former liberals. And again, he juxtaposes descriptions of the emaciated, weary, cold, hungry, unbathed, lice-infested majority with the bourgeoisie, whose resources and cleverness spared them this fate.[119]

As the year drew to a close the population went without bread, fuel, and soap. Stricken with typhoid fever and influenza like much of the population, Arkhangelskii admits "it's a nightmare to live."[120] The author's final preoccupation focuses on daily existence, suggesting how important economic ruin ultimately was to the Bolshevik victory. "Everything's falling apart," he cried out on February 16, 1920. People went "for months" without bathing or changing their underwear. Half the city did without water. "Excrement is dumped into the yards or onto the streets. Toilets are broken. Faucets don't run. There's garbage and filth everywhere."[121] Envy and greed disrupted family life as conversation was reduced to discussions of how to obtain basic necessities.

Arkhangelskii differs from our other protagonists. He was not anti-Semitic. He was critical of religion and superstition and offended by Russia's backwardness. His is not a narrative of hostile witness or confession, but of conversion, not to Bolshevism, but to serving the people. In ascribing identity to others according to their behavior and beliefs he, as the archetype fellow traveler, reveals a disposition that is all too similar to that of the Bolsheviks. At the same time, he elevates himself above the Bolsheviks, who, in his view, represent yet another expression of the backward people he feels committed to serve.

Conclusion

Constructing personal narratives not only gave our authors a sense of being an eyewitness to history, but also enabled them to record a cultural history that otherwise might have been forgotten by official histor-

---

[118] Ibid., Sept. 29, 1919.
[119] Ibid., Sept. 30, Oct. 3, Oct. 25, and Oct. 26, 1919.
[120] See ibid., Nov. 7–30, 1919, Jan. 3, Jan. 1–11, 11–27, and March 1, 1920.
[121] Ibid., March 4, 1920.

ical memory. Although the authors' language at times seems innocent of intention, each carries a stance or position toward the world, and toward the author's place in it, thereby offering an interpretation. Thus we encounter a staunch Kadet, perhaps a monarchist; a martyr; a hostage of the proletariat; a victim of the motherland; a member of the *old* intelligentsia; a morally indignant witness; and an *intelligent* committed to enlightening the Russian people. Reflecting an impulse to order their authors' lives, these tropes reveal ideologies of individuality. They reveal how our protagonists dealt with the issue of historical agency and understood their social otherness, which they saw not only in terms of their wealth but also, and more importantly, in terms of their values. Although these are qualitative understandings, they enable us to imagine experiential context and grasp subjective meanings. They are a kind of ethnographical way of knowing. Young Chevekov accepted himself as rich and as a member of the intelligentsia, social markers separating him from the brutal masses. As such he had something to defend, and he did. Uriupina's schoolgirl melancholy underscored her feeling that the world had been turned inside out, despite her bland assurance that she was thankful to live through the Revolution. Ironically, what she initially resorted to as a conscious, romantic literary device — her suffering — may have subconsciously circumscribed her adulthood. The martyr metaphor created a virtual event and, critically for autobiography, a virtual life.[122] Depicting himself as a passive victim of Bolshevik class policies, Minkh exonerated his being co-opted into the new administrative structure. He joined it in order "to be among his own." A victim of fate, a resigned Slavin saw his class as the representative of Russia's spirituality. Zernov presented himself as the embodiment of values and human associations once common to the intelligentsia, but no longer appreciated in Stalin's Russia. A witness only, Babine absolved himself of any responsibility for the Bolsheviks' victory, reminding us that most people in his circumstances gave survival top priority. Unable fully to embrace Bolshevism yet critically disposed toward the "bourgeoisie," Arkhangelskii opted to side with the Russian people, ascribing otherness to those of his own social milieu much the way the Bolsheviks ascribed otherness to him.

Swept up by the interdeterminancies of civil war, the authors of our narratives shed refracted light on why the Bolsheviks prevailed. Minkh provocatively poses the question of responsibility but leaves it unanswered: his fleeing Russia speaks for itself. Arkhangelskii notes how circumstances worked in the Bolsheviks' favor, describing how the daily fight for survival made people politically apathetic and helpless, robbing

---

[122] Egan, *Patterns*, 19, 45.

them of political initiative. Representing the Revolution as a powerful wave, Slavin suggests that his class was overwhelmed by its elemental power and spontaneity. At the same time, he believed the Communists wished to tap into the intelligentsia's desire to heal the rift between themselves and the masses. While the Slavins of Saratov associate the masses with Bolshevism, they nonetheless leave open the possibility of reconciliation. All of the accounts except the diaries of Babine and Uriupina describe acts of kindness on the part of Russia's downtrodden toward the marked bourgeoisie. Ironically, several of our authors also benefited from the intervention of Communist leaders. These inconsistencies magnified social ambiguities, further scrambling categories of difference and otherness.

Believing Communist power would collapse, our authors, all of whom except for Arkhangelskii expressed anti-Semitism, depicted those in power as mediocrities (Minkh), and even in negative physical terms (Slavin). Zernov represented the everyday people in whose name the Revolution was made as childlike (a sentiment Lisa Uriupina shared), uncultured, and dirty. Babine scorned the lower classes. Chevekov too associated Bolshevism with Russia's underclasses, holding them in contempt for their savagery and darkness. Even Arkhangelskii understood the Bolshevik phenomenon as an expression of the backwardness of the people.

Everyday activities in which repetitiveness normally dominates gave way during the Civil War to ruptures and discontinuities, not only in the rules of behavior but also in the modes of interpretation deemed valid. The Civil War context subjected symbolic referents to practical reevaluation, as the Communists' class-based policies constituted these seven authors as different kinds of subjects. As such, they associated revolutionary power with the social other and found virtue — and *meaning* — in their own suffering and endurance. Two of the authors grounded their authority to write about themselves in their decision to flee Russia. Equally significant, as later pages in the diaries of Uriupina and Zernov make clear, is that some of those who stayed behind remained other without going anywhere.

Nine

Not Seeing Like a State

The Red Guard Assault on Capital

EVER SINCE the end of the Civil War, participants, political leaders, and historians have debated the nature and significance of the economic formation that prevailed between 1918 and March 1921, known subsequently as War Communism. In elucidating the term, the partisan and scholarly literatures either emphasize the role of ideology in implementing "communist" economic principles during civil war conditions, or downplay it, underscoring instead the emergency nature of the measures enacted.[1] Yet the lessons learned from this case study of Saratov are less about the new economic order itself than about the significance of *how* the Bolsheviks attempted to put it into practice.

In regard to industry, the Civil War started immediately after October 1917, when the Bolsheviks began to limit private property and the market, encouraging workers' control and nationalizing banks.[2] Economic

---

[1] See Silvana Malle, *The Economic Organization of War Communism, 1918–1921* (Cambridge, Eng., 1985), 1–28, and S. A. Pavliuchenkov, *Voennyi kommunizm v Rossii: Vlast' i massy* (Moscow, 1997), 16–44. Lars Lih proposes that the term War Communism be dropped altogether. "The Mystery of the *ABC*," *Slavic Review* 56, no. 1 (1997): 50–72.

[2] Pavliuchenkov also makes this point in *Voennyi kommunizm*, 23–24. So does Gimpel'son, *Formirovanie*, 96. Some writers maintain that the Bolsheviks were actually on the eve of introducing the NEP, not War Communism, before the summer 1918, but I encountered little evidence to support this claim. See D. A. Baevskii, *Ocherki po istorii khoziaistvennogo stroitel'stva perioda grazhdanskoi voiny* (Moscow, 1957), and more recently G. A. Bordiugov and V. A Kozlov, cited in Pavliuchenkov, *Voennyi kommunizm*, 28–29.

"localism" accompanied political localism, as Saratov Communists ignored the government's grain monopoly and fixed prices until August
1918. Similarly, local economic agencies, understaffed and often populated by specialists hostile to Soviet power, became locked in competition with central organs, and frequently battled against the separate
Red Army bureaucracy, too. Economic localism soon clashed with centralizing impulses against a background of various ideological legacies.
These included the tsarist wartime economic model in place since 1915
in which state intervention and control played a major role, and utopan
Marxist visions of a socialist economy, which presumed an inherent
hostility in class relations and the superiority of socialist principles.[3]
While there is no denying the logic of previous state policies in shaping
economic practices during the Civil War—the state's interference in the
agricultural market in 1915, the introduction of requisitioning in 1916,
the establishment of a grain monopoly and the first efforts at nationalization in 1917—Bolshevik ideology *transformed* practices of state intervention by increasing coercion and justifying punitive measures
owing to civil war circumstances. We see this manifested in the implementation of the food dictatorship and nationalization of industry in
1918; in the obligatory grain quota assessment or *razverstka* and co-
optation of the consumer cooperatives in 1919; and in the militarization
of labor and greater use of violence in the countryside in 1920.

Ultimately, the utopian and pragmatic measures known as War Communism strengthened the authoritarian streak in Russian political
culture. They had other results as well. The Bolsheviks created an economic order characterized by centralization, state ownership, compulsion, the extraction of surpluses, forced allocation of labor, and a
distribution system that rhetorically privileged the toiling classes. In political terms, the party's economic policies contributed to the consolidation of a one-party state and the repression of civil society as the population turned its attention to honing basic survival strategies. In
practical terms, the price of survival was the temporary replacement of
the money economy with barter, famine, and the entrenchment of a
black market and a system of privileges for party members.

Saratov's Economic Council (*Gubernskii Sovet narodnogo khoziaistva*)

Given the primacy of bread-and-butter economic issues in bringing the
Bolsheviks to power, the new Soviet government gave top priority to

---

[3] Jacques Sapir, "La guerre civile et l'économie de guerre du système soviétique," in
Cahiers du Monde russe 38, no. 1–2 (1997): 9–28.

creating an organ responsible for economic life, the Supreme Economic Council (*Sovnarkhoz*). The Saratov Soviet established a provincial economic council (*Gubsovnarkhoz* or *GSNKh*) in December 1917, which assumed the functions of the local zemstvos and of public organizations formed during the war, such as the war industry and supply committees. Initially, Gubsovnarkhoz included supply, distribution, production, and labor protection departments, but by 1919 the council oversaw the work of sixteen departments, many of which the national government had mandated. The economic councils sought to promote the socialist revolution in the cities and villages by replacing capitalist economic relations. Yet, as Remington has argued, "where revolutionaries seek to mobilize society as a means of building a new state, the result is likely to be self-defeating."[4]

Industrial breakdown in 1918 posed the most pressing problem for Gubsovnarkhoz, which had to exert tremendous energy to prevent workers from pilfering raw materials and machinery at factories abandoned by their owners. Cautiously navigating the rocky transition from workers' control or supervision over the workplace to centralization, its leaders claimed that they improvised because they received few instructions from the Center. The GSNKh resolved which industries to nationalize and how to improve transportation, becoming embroiled in interagency squabbles in the process. Perhaps the most tangled were its relationships with the Provincial Food Supply Commissariat (*Gubprodkom*) and with sundry central agencies and their local representatives. For instance, Gubsovnarkhoz's chemical industry department bore responsibility for manufacturing soap, but so did a national agency. "Parallelism" of this sort represented a systemic problem during the Civil War.[5] Whenever local policies clashed with central directives—which was frequent—Moscow denounced what it interpreted as manifestations of localism.

In time, the functions of local *sovnarkhozy* became more clearly defined: they compiled statistics on all economic activity, managed those

---

[4] Thomas F. Remington, *Building Socialism in Bolshevik Russia: Ideology and Industrial Organization, 1917–1921* (Pittsburgh, 1984), 13.

[5] *Biulleten' Saratovskogo gubernskogo Soveta narodnogo khoziaistva*, no. 1–2 (1919): 2–4; *Piatiletie Saratovskogo gubernskogo Soveta narodnogo khoziaistva (1917/18–1923 gg.) (Sbornik statei i vospominanii)* (Saratov, 1923), 13, 17, 19–21, 95, 106. See also V. G. Khodakov, "Iz istorii obrazovaniia i deiatel'nosti Saratovskogo gubernskogo Soveta narodnogo khoziaistva, 1917–1918 gg.," *Trudy Saratovskogo sel'skokhoziaistvennogo instituta*, no. 1 (1966): 69–72; T. K. Kozlova, "Znachenie pervogo Vserossiiskogo s"ezda sovnarkhozov dlia khoziaistvennogo stroitel'stva Povolzh'ia v 1917–1918 gg.," *Vestnik Moskovskogo universiteta, ist.-filol. seriia*, no. 4 (1957): 118–19. See also Samuel A. Oppenheim, "The Supreme Economic Council, 1917–1921," *Soviet Studies* 25, no. 1 (1973): 13, and Malle, *Economic Organization*, 202–92.

branches of industry not under the control of Moscow agencies, and supplied and distributed goods to the population. Although designed to function as a local branch of the Supreme Economic Council, Gubsovnarkhoz instead fell under the influence of the provincial executive committee, especially after Sovnarkhoz separated industries into those with national and those with local significance. Yet pragmatism as well as conflict colored the relationship between the local council and Moscow. Since industries managed by the Center had a greater chance of securing fuel to keep operating, Gubsovnarkhoz now tended to accept the Supreme Economic Council's involvement in what the former otherwise considered local affairs. The grim task of presiding over the closing of factories and mills, largely due to acute fuel shortages, caused the change of heart.[6]

The military threat defined Gubsovnarkhoz's activities in 1919 and afterward, as some of its departments worked exclusively for the Red Army, and eventually all of them did so to some degree. Military authorities appropriated fuel, raw materials, and personnel, causing alarming shortages for the civilian economy and heightening disagreements with the Center. Lack of fuel, for example, closed down all of Volsk's cement factories, which earlier had produced one-third of Russia's annual output. To cope with the problems, Gubsovnarkhoz turned a blind eye to black-market activities while it promoted water and wind power. It too resorted to coercion, even though Gubsovnarkhoz recognized that strategy's drawbacks. In addition, the dearth of raw materials forced factories to cease their operations, as when the province's 120 soap factories shut down. Despite the closures, Gubsovnarkhoz experienced a shortage of skilled workers, a problem it solved by releasing workers from military service and by conscripting civilians. Further, it introduced piecework and bonuses in order to motivate workers to produce more.[7] The nagging absence of Gubsovnarkhoz's presidium members owing to frequent mobilizations, however, further limited its effectiveness:[8] its full plenum, in which Communists predominated, had not met in eight months as of September 1919.[9]

It took most of 1918 for economic councils to emerge at the district level. When the first provincial conference of sovnarkhozy convened in

[6] "Saratovskii Gubsovnarkhoz i promyshlennost' Saratovskoi gubernii," *Narodnoe khoziaistvo*, no. 11–12 (Moscow, 1919): 96–97; *ISS*, no. 21, Jan. 28, 1919, 2; and no. 27, Feb. 5, 1919, 2.

[7] *Obzor deiatel'nosti Saratovskogo gubernskogo Soveta narodnogo khoziaistva za 1919 god* (Saratov, 1919), i–xii; GASO, f. 456, op. 1, d. 223, ll. 1–17, and d. 142, l. 16.

[8] GASO, f. 521, op. 1, d. 392, ll. 2, 8 ob, 9–10 ob, 24 ob, and *Plenum Soveta narodnogo khoziaistva. 28 sentiabria-5 oktiabria 1919 goda: Materialy.* (Saratov, 1920), 1–15.

[9] *ISS*, no. 214, Sept. 27, 1919, 2.

May 1918, only Atkarsk and Volsk boasted such councils, but even they did not assume broad responsibility for local economic life until later. Representing local ispolkomy and labor exchanges, delegates described the difficulties they had carrying out nationalization, dealing with lack of funds, raw materials, and competent staff members, and finding food supplies for the local population—problems they solved independently by relying on barter and exchange between districts and beyond, and on forms of inventive financing. With no funds to pay workers, the Volsk Sovnarkhoz levied a contribution on its bourgeoisie. Mostly, though, the delegates rejected "Red Guard assaults on capital," preferring less disruptive "creative work" to restore the economy.[10]

Gubsovnarkhoz failed to develop stable ties with the district economic councils, which involved themselves in territorial disputes as well as squabbles with other agencies, especially food-supply organs. Poorly staffed and chaotically organized, local sovnarkhozy initially tended to take over the responsibilities of the zemstvos until the councils' tasks were more clearly defined. Often the interests of individual staff members determined the activities of district sovnarkhozy, many of whose departments functioned only on paper. Although the councils employed many individuals hostile to Soviet power, their main problem remained lack of clearly defined jurisdiction between the sovnarkhozy and the local agencies of the chief industrial branch administrations (glavki), which represented a major centralizing trend in economic life. The resulting bickering at times even ended in the arrest of Moscow's representatives, often paralyzing work. As the glavki tried to assume control of large enterprises and shut down others, they met with resistance from uezd sovnarkhozy. For example, the Volsk economic council only reluctantly relinquished responsibility for its cement factories.[11] Typical, too, was the state of affairs in Khvalynsk, whose sovnarkhoz suffered from desperate financial crises and trouble holding onto staff as well as abuses of power and pilfering of "state" property.[12]

While the success of the province's sovnarkhozy varied considerably,

[10] ISS, no. 94, May 17, 1918, 3; KG, no. 73, May 29, 1918, 4; no. 74, May 30, 1918, 4; no. 76, June 1, 1918, 4; Izvestiia Atkarskogo uispolkoma, no. 150, Nov. 7, 1920, 3; Biulleten' Saratovskogo gubernskogo Soveta narodnogo khoziaistva, no. 11 (1918): 9–10; Doklad Vol'skogo uezdnogo Ispolnitel'nogo komiteta, 9–11; Rashitov, "Sovety," 140; and Piatiletie, 21.

[11] Biulleten' Saratovskogo gubernskogo Soveta narodnogo khoziaistva, no. 3–4 (1919): 8–10; GASO, f. 48, op. 5, d. 107, ll. 90–90 ob; Plenum Soveta narodnogo khoziaistva, 13; Piatiletie, 79–84; Malle, Economic Organization, 255–80; Remington, Building Socialism, 63–74; ISS, no. 58, March 11, 1920, 3; and TsDNISO, f. 200, op. 1, d. 42, l. 5.

[12] GASO, f. 48, op. 7, d. 50, ll. 3–5, 12–16 ob; d. 10, ll. 3–3 ob; d. 86, ll. 31–34 ob; d. 162, ll. 1 ob–2; d. 190, ll. 1–2 ob; d. 191, ll. 9–9 ob, 289–91 ob. See also Izvestiia Khvalynskogo Soveta, no. 144, July 2, 1910, 2; no. 217, Sept. 29, 1920, 2; and Oktiabr'skaia revoliutsiia, no. 241, Nov. 7, 1920, 5–6.

most remained unstable as they bickered with Gubsovnarkhoz, the Center, and even with local executive committees and military authorities.[13] Despite Gubsovnarkhoz's confident expectation in mid-1920 "of a sudden victorious breakthrough over economic ruin,"[14] famine conditions made such optimism short-lived. The transition to the NEP in such stark circumstances forced a rethinking of the local economic councils, whose structures were simplified once the number of enterprises under their supervision sharply diminished. As unemployment shot up in 1921 and state agencies had to finance themselves, district sovnarkhozy cut the number of their departments to the bare minimum, while the government replaced the councils with industrial trusts and representatives from the Center. In July 1921 Gubsovnarkhoz employed roughly 4,000 individuals, but by October 1922, the total number had been slashed to 1,292.[15]

Saratov Industry during the Civil War

Blaming the First World War and territorial losses associated with the Brest-Litovsk Peace for the industrial crisis that had engulfed Russia, delegates to the First All-Russian Congress of Sovnarkhozy believed that centralization and class-based policies would restore the economy.[16] The experience of civil war, however, proved otherwise, forcing the Soviet government to introduce the NEP in 1921. Consideration of industrial production in Saratov Province makes the need for the NEP abundantly clear. Although reliable figures are difficult to come by, the All-Russian Industrial Census of 1918, which lists only some local enterprises, reflects what other sources indicate was a widespread pattern. Only 52 percent of the enterprises functioned normally, 32 percent stood idle, and another 16 percent operated at less than full capacity. The lack of raw materials and fuel as well as the breakdown of machinery accounted for the closures and downturn.

The industrial census reveals the extent to which agriculture shaped the local economy. The largest number of enterprises (72 percent of the 895 counted), employing 5,429 workers (31 percent of the total examined), prepared foods, and of those, the majority processed grain (525).

---

[13] *Narodnoe khoziaistvo Nizhnego Povolzh'ia*, no. 2–3 (1920): 14–15.

[14] Ibid., no. 4 (1920): 3.

[15] GASO, f. 48, op. 5, d. 134, ll. 2–3 ob, 8; *Materialy k XIV-mu*, 100–106; *Otchet o deiatel'nosti Saratovskogo gubernskogo Soveta narodnogo khoziaistva za 1921–22 khoz. god: XII-mu gubernskomu s"ezdu Sovetov* (Saratov, 1922), 1–7; *Piatiletie*, 25–27; *Otchet Saratovskogo Gubernskogo Ispolnitel'nogo Komiteta*, 166–93.

[16] *Biulleten' Saratovskogo gubernskogo Soveta narodnogo khoziaistva*, no. 2–3 (1918): 4–5; no. 9 (1918): 6–7, and no. 11 (1918): 1, 4–5.

Food-processing industries accounted for 46 percent of the monetary turnover in industry. The second largest category of enterprises manufactured leather and fur products. Found mainly in Saratov and its suburbs, the province's 43 woodworks had a workforce of 1,496. In fourth place were the province's 29 printing presses, which employed 1,314 workers. The processing of stone and clay occupied fifth place. The 46 metallurgical plants, predominantly in Saratov Uezd, engaged in repair work and the production of tin items, machinery, and instruments, and had in their employ 1,862 workers. Fourteen factories with 592 workers produced various consumer goods. Fourteen chemical plants employed 270 workers, and 15 textile plants an additional 3,742. Most of the latter now stood idle.[17]

Small-scale production prevailed in Saratov Province. The average enterprise listed 19 workers; however, 336 or 45.8 percent employed five or less and 77 percent of them had fewer than 17 workers on the payroll. Only 9 factories boasted more than 250 workers. In addition to the 17,152 workers considered by the census, an additional 26,253 toiled in other enterprises. Of this number, 38.5 percent were also engaged in the food processing industries, mainly flour and grain processing. The next largest categories were involved in the production of wool, wood processing, printing, metalworking, and the manufacture of machinery and instruments.[18]

Civil War brought about the nationalization of industry, which began spontaneously following the October days. Before June 1918, when the state issued a decree on nationalization, soviets confiscated enterprises without any plan, often in the wake of their seizure by workers' organizations or Red Guard units. Afterward, nationalization was carried out more systematically as central bodies got involved in the process.[19] Although the Saratov Soviet decided each case individually, it tended to favor nationalization. Thus, it seized control of local banks and nationalized the Riazan-Urals rail line in 1917, local drugstores in February 1918, and afterward the city's flourmills and metallurgical plants. Ini-

---

[17] V. Novinskii, "Fabrichno-zavodskaia promyshlennost' Saratovskoi gubernii: Nekotorye itogi Vseros. prom. perepisi 1918 g. po Saratovskoi gubernii po dannym predvaritel'nogo podscheta," *Statisticheskii vestnik Saratovskogo gubernskogo statisticheskogo biuro*, no. 2 (1921): 1–12, 20. See also GA RF, f. 393, op. 3, d. 327, ll. 235–35 ob. For an insightful study of the impact of the Civil War on local statisticians, see Martine Mespoulet, "Les relations entre centre et régions au moment de la mise en place des bureaux statistiques des gubernii: L'exemple du *gubstatbjuro* de Saratov, 1918–1923," *Cahiers du Monde russe* 38, no. 4 (1997): 489–510.

[18] Novinskii, "Fabrichno-zavodskaia promyshlennost'," 6, 14.

[19] *Biulleten' Saratovskogo gubernskogo Soveta narodnogo khoziaistva*, no. 2–3 (1918): 1–4.

tially, nationalization did not amount to any substantive structural changes.[20] As of August 1918, 55 percent of the factories in the province, employing 61 percent of the workforce, had been nationalized (that is, confiscated), and the figure shot up to include all significant enterprises by 1920.[21] In some instances it proved difficult to carry out the measure. For example, the soviet requisitioned some printing presses for its own use but, owing to lack of pro-Bolshevik cadres, met with resistance in nationalizing the printing industry, which remained under Menshevik influence. It eventually settled for "partial nationalization," amounting to control over resources. The soviet also clashed with Gubsovnarkhoz on the issue of state takeover of industry, accusing the latter of nationalizing only those enterprises that turned a profit.[22]

Nationalization made it easier for the state to cope with shortages by retooling industry to meet the military's needs first, but this policy wreaked havoc on the rest of the economy. From January 1919 until March 1920 a special "Department of Military Procurement" drained all industrial goods produced in the province, introducing military discipline at the workplace as Saratov came to supply all Red Army operations in the region. This policy of "everything for the front" and "everyone to the front" exhausted raw material and fuel reserves, as a result of which living standards plummeted, driving some workers to the villages.[23] Military orders in the metallurgical industry, for example, accounted for 43 percent of all orders by 1919. When those for the militarized railroads and repair work on navy vessels are considered, it becomes clear that the metallurgical industry worked almost exclusively for the military authorities. In fact, the importance of equipping the Red Army contributed to a reevaluation of the role cottage industries played in the Soviet republic.

Cottage industries accounted for roughly 25 percent of Russia's industrial output by 1913; on the eve of war about 45,000 small-scale cottage industries operated in Saratov Province, with 75,000 workers. While many Bolsheviks saw no future for cottage industries under socialism, the party's ambiguous official position on them guaranteed loose interpretation of their role at the local level. During the national-

[20] Kozlova, "Znachenie," 119–21; Rashitov, "Sovety," 124; *ISS*, no. 27, Feb. 17, 1918, 2; S. A. Sokolov, "Organizatsiia upravleniia narodnym khoziaistvom v 1918 g. (Po materialam zheleznodorozhnogo i vodnogo transporta Povolzh'ia)," *Povolzhskii krai*, no. 4 (1975): 122–23, 125–26.

[21] Novinskii, "Fabrichno-zavodskaia promyshlennost'," 19–21.

[22] Baren, "Sostoianie poligraficheskogo proizvodstva v Saratovskoi gubernii i kak otrazilas' na nem natsionalizatsiia," *Ekonomicheskaia zhizn' Povolzh'ia: Sbornik statei*, no. 2 (Saratov, 1919): 9–10; and *Saratovskii Sovet*, 775.

[23] *Piatiletie*, 6–7, 13–14.

ization of factories, some cottage and small-scale industries were closed and their inventories requisitioned by local authorities. Others shut down owing to shortages of raw materials or fuel. But more often than not local sovnarkhozy promoted cottage industries, frequently coming into conflict with central agencies once the state sought to include them in the realm of state economic activity. Realizing that the flexible and adaptable cottage industries more readily fulfilled the needs of the moment, the state encouraged their revival, deciding at the Eighth Party Congress in March 1919 to use them to fill government orders and to involve them in the state's plans for distributing raw materials. Bukharin and Preobrazhenskii's *The ABC of Communism*, written in 1919, maintained that the state should support cottage industries with financial aid and place orders with them through a centralized system.[24] By late 1919, their number had grown rapidly, because of their adaptability and because half of the military's local orders now went to cottage industries.[25]

The decision taken at the Eighth Congress evoked much misunderstanding in Saratov, prompting Gubsovnarkhoz to create a special department, which was immediately bombarded with requests by individuals to have returned to them property that had been confiscated earlier. The legislation permitted the return of cottage industries to their original owners, as long as the small industries employed no more than five workers if mechanized, and ten workers if not. Subsequent legislation excluded the return to their owners of those cottage industries now run by the soviet, and also those involved in processing leather for the army, since independent cottage industries would have undermined the state's own monopoly in this area. It appears, however, that these restrictions were frequently ignored.[26]

The depopulation of the cities, availability of raw materials in the locales, needs of the military, complaints from below aimed at the failures of the state's goods exchange, and measures taken by local sovnarkhozy all contributed to the cottage industries' revival. It was not only factory workers who had lost jobs and workers from other provinces who had moved to the Volga region that were engaged in cottage

[24] N. Bukharin and E. Preobrazhenskii, *The ABC of Communism* (Ann Arbor, 1966), 273–78. Lih argues that the document is misunderstood ("The Mystery of the *ABC*," 50–72), but Bertrand M. Patenaude takes a different view in "Peasants into Russians: The Utopian Essence of War Communism," *Russian Review* 54, no. 4 (1995): 552–70.

[25] Malle, *Economic Organization*, 77–87; "Otdel metalla i metalloobrabatyvaiushchaia promyshlennost' v Saratovskoi gubernii (1917–1920 gg.)," *Ekonomicheskaia zhizn'*, no. 1–2 (1920): 11; and *Za dva goda*, 17, 27–28.

[26] GASO, f. 456, op. 1, d. 218, l. 86, and "Saratovskii Gubsovnarkhoz i promyshlennost'," 99.

industries, but also white-collar workers and needy peasants.[27] As of January 1919, Saratov Province was home to at least 12,761 cottage industries, mostly rural. More than 5,000 of them, largely grain mills and creameries, processed food; another 4,635 produced metal products. Later during the Civil War the number engaged in leather and textile production expanded. The figures adduced above do not include small-scale industries that peasants wished to keep hidden from the state, such as the brewing of illicit spirits and manufacturing of items they could exchange on the black market. Given the draft rates into the Red Army, it is safe to assume that much of this activity was feminized. While no information exists on the number of peasants legally engaged in such activities, in Khvalynsk 15 percent of all village households were occupied in cottage industries and in Volsk, 13 percent.[28] All in all, consideration of the revival of small-scale industries demonstrates the party's eclectic approach to the economy as well as the population's resiliency.

As noted, a significant percentage of those employed in cottage industries were Saratov workers who relocated to the district towns or back to their villages, especially during 1919–20, in search of food and work and in order to avoid the front lines of civil war. Records available for 89 factories employing 9,122 workers in January 1919 show that by January 1920 only half of the enterprises were still operating, and only 53 percent of the workers remained at their benches. The largest and smallest enterprises were affected most: half of those with more than 100 workers shut down, as did 77 percent of the small cottage industries. During the year the number of metalworkers fell by 74.3 percent, food-processing workers by 53 percent, and chemical industry workers by 44 percent. But a 28 percent increase was observed in the tanning industry, which manufactured items for the army.[29]

Even though military orders declined as a percentage of the total during the first half of 1920, the downward trends in production actually picked up momentum at Civil War's end. Of the 614 large mills processing grain in the province, just 40 percent were functioning; by 1921 virtually all of the large mills stood idle or else operated sporadically.[30] The creameries and oil presses endured a similar fate.[31] Saratov's lumber

[27] *ISS*, no. 262, Nov. 25, 1919, 3, and GASO, f. 456, op. 1, d. 385, ll. 9–10.

[28] Ozerskii, "Kustarnaia promyshlennost'," *Ekonomicheskaia zhizn' Povolzh'ia: Sbornik statei* (Saratov, 1919): 35–38.

[29] B. Gutman, "Dvizhenie zaniatoe rabochei sily i zarabotka v 1919 godu po gorodu Saratovu," *Biulleten' Saratovskogo gubernskogo statisticheskogo biuro*, no. 1 (1920): 11–23.

[30] V. Vasil'iev, "Mukomol'naia promyshlennost' v Saratovskoi gubernii," *Ekonomicheskaia zhizn'*, no. 1–2 (1920): 15.

[31] "Masloboinaia promyshlennost'," *Biulleten' Saratovskogo gubernskogo Soveta narodnogo khoziaistva*, no. 1–2 (1919): 4.

industry came to a standstill owing to lack of raw materials and workers; however, at the level of cottage industry it continued to expand.
The local chemical industry also came to a halt with the exception of
those enterprises filling military orders. Although the situation in the
metallurgical industry was more complex, the trend here too was downward, as is most clear when considering labor productivity.[32] Overall, by
the time the party launched the NEP two-thirds of all industrial enterprises in the province had shut down.[33]

Affecting both large-scale manufacturing and cottage industries, the
launching of the NEP forced all enterprises to readjust to market forces.
Lack of materials and credit, the inability to carry out repair work, and
famine conditions guaranteed that this transition would be painful. Following its introduction, only 70 (the largest and technologically most
sophisticated) of 1,142 enterprises in the province remained in Gubsovnarkhoz's hands. It rented the remaining ones, mainly to cooperative
trusts that joined together related industries territorially and, to a much
lesser extent than elsewhere in Russia, to private hands, including former owners. Praising the NEP as the only salvation for war-weary Russia,
Gubsovnarkhoz reported that industry slowly began to recover by the
end of 1922. Nevertheless, by 1923 industrial production in the province had reached no more than 25 percent of the prewar level.[34]

Feeding the Saratov Republic

Across Russia, provincial organs often proved reluctant to release resources because they feared the destabilizing consequences of food shortages. Contributing in its own way to the country's food crisis, this phe-

[32] "Saratovskii Gubsovnarkhoz i promyshlennost'," *Narodnoe khoziaistvo* (Moscow,
1919), 97; L. Epel', "Otchet khimicheskoi promyshlennosti v Saratovskoi gubernii za
period 1917–1920 gg.," *Ekonomicheskaia zhizn'*, no. 1–2 (1920): 11–14; regarding labor
productivity see *Mestnaia promyshlennost': Al'bom* (Saratov, 1926), 5.

[33] See *Piatiletie*, 6–9, 49–78; "Saratovskii Gubsovnarkhoz i promyshlennost'," 97–98;
Otchet o deiatel'nosti, 10–11, 188–92; R. G. Belousova, "K voprosu ob perestroike
promyshlennosti Nizhnego Povolzh'ia na nachalakh Nepa (1921–1923)," in *Istoriia partiinykh organizatsii Povolzh'ia: Mezhvuzovskii nauchnyi sbornik*, no. 3 (1974): 21; A. E.
Livshits, "Deiatel'nost' partiinykh organizatsii Povolzh'ia po osushchestvleniiu leninskikh
printsipov novoi ekonomicheskoi politiki v promyshlennosti (1921–1925 gg.)," in *Trudy
prepodavatelei istorii KPSS vuzov Povolzh'ia*, no. 1 (Saratov, 1971): 77–91; Telitsa,
"Sostoianie," 70; and "Otdel metalla," 10.

[34] However, labor productivity rose. See *Piatiletie*, 10, 14, 29–30, 66; *Otchet Prezidiuma Gorsoveta*, 5; *Sovetskaia derevnia*, no. 81, Dec. 25, 1921, 2; Belousova, "K
voprosu," 24–27; *Odinnadtsatyi gubernskii s"ezd Sovetov rabochikh, krest'ianskikh i
krasnoarmeiskikh deputatov Saratovskoi gubernii, 16–17 dekabria 1921 goda: Stenograficheskii otchet* (Saratov, 1921), 34–35.

nomenon emerged during World War I and became more pronounced during the dislocations of 1917. As civil war unfolded, provincial agencies struggled to satisfy both local and larger demands on food supplies. Calling for the establishment of new agencies charged with provisioning, the Saratov Soviet's food-supply apparatus dates to a December 1917 directive. From this measure emerged the Council of Food Supply Commissars, which functioned until mid-June 1918, when the Provincial Food Supply Commissariat (*Gubprodkom*) replaced it. Since the 1917 harvest had proven to be much smaller than average, Saratov Province began the new year with an estimated deficit of more than 12 million poods (a pood is equal to about 36.11 lbs.) of grain. As a result, the soviet issued new ration cards to the city's citizens,[35] and reduced the bread ration to ¾ pound of bread a day for those holding a proletarian or red card and to ½ pound for the "bourgeoisie." Food supply commissars banned the free sale of bread—a decree that the population simply ignored—and set up a department responsible for obtaining food, fodder, and manufactured goods.[36] Despite these measures, no bread whatsoever was issued on the anniversary of the February Revolution,[37] forcing the soviet to permit temporarily the free sale of grain. Afterward, it began to purchase grain from peasants—at market or "speculative" prices, "thereby preventing an uprising."[38] In the hope of securing more grain and curbing the erosion of its popular support, the soviet devised a network of goods exchange points, which provided peasants with essential items. Weeks later it reluctantly raised fixed prices on grain because the city remained in desperate need of it.[39] The situation at the district level was no better. For example, in order to ward off the threat of hunger and discourage the flood of traders who poured into the rich agricultural district from poorer regions, a congress of soviets in Balashov decreed food supplies the property of the entire district. Resolving to distribute them equitably, the congress ruled that "all those refusing to obey the decree will be handed over to the revolutionary courts as enemies of the people."[40]

Discord complicated the working out of a new supply apparatus, as the Bolsheviks had no choice but to employ former officials in its new

[35] *ISS*, no. 77, April 20, 1918, 3. For the severity of the local grain crisis see Figes, *Peasant Russia*, 84–101.

[36] *ISS*, no. 25, Feb. 1 (14), 1918, 3; no. 27, Feb. 17, 1918, 3; and no. 46, March 12, 1918, 4.

[37] *Saratovskii Sovet*, 340–41, and Rashitov, "Osnovnye," 24.

[38] Bogdanova, "Uchastie," 59–60.

[39] *ISS*, no. 48, March 15, 1918, 1; no. 77, April 20, 1918, 3; and no. 80, April 24, 1918, 3.

[40] *KG*, no. 24, March 22, 1918, 4.

agencies whose views continued to shape policy. For instance, the local zemstvo administration had argued that the Provisional Government's grain monopoly, based on the German model, was inappropriate for Russian conditions and should not be implemented.[41] These attitudes help account for the Saratov Soviet's refusal to comply with the government's grain policies until August 1918. Moreover, officials in the local food commissariats formed a union that claimed it stood "outside politics," denying any political motives behind its frequent conflicts with Soviet power.[42] Not surprisingly, the requisitions department created to "battle against speculation" became a lightning rod for complaints. A bias against "speculation" had existed already before the war, but the term became even more of a moral category during the conflict, and this made compliance with government policies obligatory, with or without economic incentives. Owing to the lack of clear boundaries among government bodies, confusion over trade policies, and requisitions, many disputes arose that came to the department's attention.[43]

Market prices for food items had shot up by as much as 600 to 1,000 percent between June 1917 and mid-1918, rising particularly sharply at the end of this period.[44] To cope with the food crisis and to combat localism, the Soviet government on May 27, 1918, set up its central organization responsible for supplying the population with food and goods, the Food Commissariat (*Narkomprod*), which evolved into the most powerful ministry after the War Commissariat. It proved difficult to introduce the government's grain monopoly in Saratov, however, owing to the intrusion of the Czechoslovak military units in mid-1918, the lack of manufactured goods that could be used in the goods exchange, and a flood of paper money. Moreover, the soviet, as mentioned, did not acknowledge the government's grain monopoly and fixed prices until August, attempting to convince the government to declare Saratov a food-consuming rather than food-producing province. Meanwhile, local agents sent to the capital for sorely needed goods that could be used to secure grain from the peasantry found Moscow offices unreceptive, since they had received little food from Saratov.[45]

[41] GASO, f. 403, op. 3, d. 206. For the Provisional Government's grain monopoly see Lars Lih, *Bread and Authority in Russia, 1914–1921* (Berkeley and Los Angeles, 1990), 32–105, and T. M. Kitanina, *Voina, khleb i revoliutsiia (Prodovol'stvennyi vopros v Rossii, 1914–oktiabr' 1917 g.)* (Leningrad, 1985), 62–254.

[42] Sokolov, "Bor'ba," 78–84.

[43] *Iubileinyi sbornik*, 109–11, and Lih, *Bread and Authority*, 55.

[44] *Biulleten' Saratovskogo gubernskogo komissariata po prodovol'stviiu*, no. 9, Dec. 1, 1918, 1–63.

[45] GASO, f. 521, op. 1, d. 201, l. 62 ob, and Iu. K. Strizhkov, *Prodovol'stvennye otriady v gody grazhdanskoi voiny i inostrannoi interventsii, 1917–1921 gg.* (Moscow, 1973), 54–66.

Comprising Left SRs, Bolsheviks, and even Right SRs and Mensheviks, Gubprodkom bore responsibility for supplying the local population and for shipping agricultural products to the Center. Its own publication paints a grim picture of the seemingly insurmountable tasks it
and the country faced, which it blamed on the incipient breakdown in
transport and loss of grain-growing regions to the Whites. While acknowledging the Center's need for bread, some of the Bolsheviks employed in Gubprodkom grieved over the interference of agents sent by
Moscow. They competed with organizations from the central consum-
ing provinces, as well as with railroad workers and the Red Army, both
of whom also harbored hopes of obtaining foodstuffs from Saratov,
breeding "parallelism" and "disorganization." At the end of July, Gubprodkom banned any independent procurement within the province by
Moscow agents or by local authorities if they fell outside the committee's purview.[46]

By the time the province's first food-supply congress convened in August 1918, the Bolsheviks *and* Left SRs within Gubprodkom fully
backed the food dictatorship, arguing that since free prices had failed to
provide basic necessities to local populations, it was time to introduce
fixed prices and to turn armed force against the much maligned "bagmen" or illicit private traders. Making no reference to ideological considerations, other speakers likewise saw government intervention as a
necessary step, as it had been in Germany and elsewhere, owing to the
lack of goods available for free trade. The congress banned private
trade, acknowledged the need for fixed prices (yet left unresolved who
should establish them), and concentrated the power to administer the
goods exchange in the hands of a special collegium. But Gubprodkom,
too, had to rely on those not always sympathetic to its mission. Instructors it sent to inventory peasant surpluses actually agitated the peasantry, causing angry disturbances. Although many of them were students
and former officers hostile to Bolshevik power, Gubprodkom needed to
employ their services simply because there was no one else to send.[47]

Ultimately, the new measures disappointed ordinary people, for they
had assumed it would become easier to live once the new harvest was
in. When the soviet set up checkpoints to intercept grain being brought
into the city, dumping into the streets whatever flour was confiscated,
"people despaired" and "cursed the authorities."[48] A month later the
soviet estimated that 20 percent of the population drew on their own

---

[46] *Izvestiia Saratovskogo gubernskogo prodovol'stvennogo komissariata* (hereafter,
ISGPK), no. 1, July 14, 1918, 13, 18; and no. 3, July 28, 1918, 10–17.

[47] *ISGPK*, no. 5, Aug. 11, 1918, 6, 14–15, and no. 6, Aug. 18, 1918, 7–16. See also
ISS, no. 159, Aug. 7, 1918, 4.

[48] Sokolov diary, entry for Aug. 14, 1918.

resources to obtain bread in order to avoid the long lines that snaked through the city.[49] Attempting to placate workers, it increased their rations and those for the families of Red Army soldiers.[50] The problem was that the working class, while cursing speculators, *had* to engage in speculation itself. Everyone did. The activities of local railroad workers particularly distressed authorities, for the rail workers used their access to transportation to speculate. Soviet leaders recognized that the modest bread rations had driven the workers to speculate; when it raised rations to one pound a day on October 1, "bagging" declined.[51] Another problem affecting food supplies was the piling up of freight trains at stations and stops totally unprepared to receive them. The resulting pilfering of food supplies by local inhabitants, railroad workers, and soldiers assumed "colossal proportions."[52]

As in other areas of life, economic localism characterized the setting up of a food-supply apparatus, which proved unable to meet the population's needs. Once local authorities failed to convince the Center that Saratov should be classified as a grain-consuming province owing to the severity of the local food crisis, Gubprodkom backed the food dictatorship, but had no intention of using raw force to make it work. Meanwhile, workers appropriated Bolshevik public language in regard to chastising speculators, yet ignored their own necessary participation in the black market. It could not be otherwise, for the entire population needed to involve itself in "illicit" trade in order to survive.

Rationing Socialism

At the end of 1918 the soviet registered the province's population in order to issue new rations cards to all adults between sixteen and fifty years old, according to a class principle that privileged workers and discriminated against the bourgeoisie.[53] In some locales the discourse on food as a political weapon lacked ideological bite — for instance, in Kamyshin and Balashov. As the Civil War progressed food distribution rules tended to be framed in harsh language hostile to the bourgeoisie;[54]

[49] *ISS*, no. 190, Sept. 14, 1918, 3.

[50] Ibid., no. 196, Sept. 21, 1918, 3.

[51] GASO, f. 521, op. 1, d. 139, ll. 323–26, and *ISS*, no. 192, Sept. 17, 1918, 2.

[52] *Trudy chetvertogo s"ezda*, 11.

[53] GA RF, f. 393, op. 3, d. 327, l. 138. The Provisional Government's rationing norms placed those engaged in physical labor in a privileged position, but this also appears to have been largely a symbolic measure.

[54] *ISGPK*, no. 13, Oct. 6, 1918, 18; *Krasnyi pakhar'*, no. 246, Dec. 10, 1919, 3; and Antonov-Saratovskii, *Sovety*, 2: 341–42. For Narkomprod's rationing scheme see S. A.

however, the class principle of doling out food proved to be largely symbolic, owing to a constant reclassification of professions and to the fact that many members of the bourgeoisie took jobs in the Soviet bureaucracy in order to obtain rations. McAuley has documented a similar phenomenon in Petrograd.[55] Furthermore, people viewed their jobs not only as a potential source of food but also as a source of materials to exchange for it, prompting the authorities to carry numerous resolutions against the pilfering of state property, a phenomenon involving the entire population and one that remained a legacy of the period.

Owing to shortages and rampant speculation, in January 1919 the Saratov Soviet allowed peasants to market all nonregulated products, as well as potatoes and butter, in the city. This measure merely legalized what the soviet had no real power to prevent. The soviet also urged cooperatives to open public cafeterias, which functioned for less than a year, becoming another casualty of the Civil War.[56] Ignoring specialists' advice and basic hygiene, the public cafeterias offered not "public feeding," but "public poisoning."[57]

A March 20, 1919, decree sought to end competition among the three agencies that supplied the town population with food and goods — the city supply committee (gorprodkom), civilian cooperatives, and workers' cooperatives — creating a single distribution organ, which it placed "in the hands of the proletariat."[58] Although the siege of 1919 prevented the new law from taking effect until October, it became clear that workers viewed the development with total indifference. Only 2 percent of the 105,945 eligible voters cast ballots for representatives to the Joint Consumer Society, and in some of the city's electoral regions no one at all showed up to vote! No one in Balashov did, either.[59]

When Saratov fell under siege in 1919, the Defense Council in charge of the city reduced rations by a quarter pound. While Moscow's representative on the council, Dronin, insisted upon this action, many local Bolsheviks expressed their opposition to cutting rations and took their message to the public.[60] Writing allegorically, the party newspaper di-

Chernomorets, *Organizatsiia prodovol'stvennogo snabzheniia v 1917–1920 gody: Gosudarstvenno-pravovye aspekty* (Saratov, 1986), 98–100.

[55] McAuley, *Bread and Justice*, 286–94.

[56] *KG*, no. 294, Feb. 26, 1919, 1, and GASO, f. 456, op. 1, d. 172, l. 1. See also *Iubileinyi sbornik*, 49–51.

[57] *Obzor deiatel'nosti Saratovskogo Otdeleniia*, 16. Babine temporarily took his meals at a public facility. See Raleigh, *A Russian Civil War Diary*, 122.

[58] *Iubileinyi sbornik*, 25–26.

[59] *ISS*, no. 222, Oct. 8, 1919, 2; no. 63, March 18, 1920, 3; and *Krasnyi pakhar'*, no. 256, Dec. 21, 1919, 1.

[60] GASO, f. 521, op. 1, d. 434, l. 239.

vulged that angry Astrakhan workers demanding free trade and larger rations had killed Communists; however, the paper did not mention that loyal troops turned their machine guns on workers, resulting in one of the darkest tragedies of the Civil War.[61] Acknowledging that Soviet power's inability to feed starving workers exhausted their patience,[62] the soviet met with representatives of factory committees and unions in order to block Dronin's design to reduce rations by another quarter pound.[63] In accounting for the efforts of local leaders not to cut rations, it must be noted that the encroaching front disrupted the flow of supplies in 1919, as a result of which grubbing for food now took precedence over all other urban activities. The soviet therefore gave top priority to restoring rations once the Red Army had driven the Whites from the province. Yet any improvements turned out to be short-lived; at the end of December lines of shivering, hungry people formed each morning at 5 A.M. in the hope of securing bread.[64] Ferment among fuming railroad workers over paltry rations assumed such proportions that the Cheka closely monitored their activities.[65] The collapse of the supply system also drove the Petrovsk Executive Committee to ignore central decrees and to encourage free trade.[66]

Militarily, the tide of events had shifted in favor of the Communists by 1920, but keeping oneself fed, and poorly at that, took time, resourcefulness, and luck. The events leading to the famine of 1921–22 got set into motion during the summer of 1920, as the supply crisis deteriorated further owing to the war with Poland. Deliveries began to fall sharply at this time, stopping altogether by autumn, as a result of which city authorities were forced to reduce the proletarian ration to $\frac{3}{8}$ pound of bread a day. For several days in October they issued no rations in order to supply the front. Now populated with many new faces, the executive committee expressed its resolve to provide for the hungry outside the province, and to take "the most stringent measures" to wipe out bagging.[67] Ironically, on December 4, 1920, Sovnarkom informed all provincial supply commissariats that they were to distribute food free of charge to the working population.[68]

---

[61] *KG*, no. 323, April 6, 1919, 2–3. For the Astrakhan tragedy see Brovkin, *Behind the Front Lines*, 82–85.

[62] *ISS*, no. 179, Aug. 16, 1919, 2.

[63] GASO, f. 521, op. 1, d. 288, l. 20.

[64] *ISS*, Oct. 26, 1919, 2, and no. 286, Dec. 23, 1919, 4.

[65] TsDNISO, f. 81, op. 1, d. 7, l. 74.

[66] Ibid., f. 521, op. 1, d. 434, l. 393.

[67] *ISS*, no. 234, Oct. 16, 1920, 3, and GASO, f. 521, op. 1, d. 469, l. 141.

[68] GASO, f. 523, op. 1, d. 30, l. 26.

Co-opting the Consumer Cooperatives

With government encouragement, the cooperative movement in Saratov underwent rapid expansion during World War I; by 1918, approximately 45 percent of all households belonged to credit co-ops, the least developed form, and by August 1918, the province boasted 684 consumer cooperatives.[69] Largely in the hands of the moderate socialist parties, they soon found themselves disbanded, their leaders under arrest. In April 1918 the soviet restored them and released their officials, only to attack them at the end of the year when a congress of cooperatives turned into a battleground between the Bolsheviks and their socialist rivals. Arguing that the cooperative movement must become part of the state structure in order to achieve Communist forms of production and distribution, the Bolsheviks deprived the co-ops of their financial independence. Early the next year the movement lost its journal; in mid-1919 the state took control of the cooperatives; in early 1920 the state collapsed the movement into a single consumer's society. Insofar as the cooperative movement had always been dependent on state support, the independence that it lost was more of a political issue than an economic one.

Concern over shortages of foodstuffs and other commodities as well as over political opposition motivated the Bolsheviks, who depicted as opponents those who did not agree that the state should look out for the interests of the working class.[70] In December 1918 Saratov's co-ops merged into two—a general civilian cooperative and a workers' cooperative—both served by a new publication, *Kooperativnaia mysl'* (Cooperative Thought).[71] Former cooperatives once catering to special constituencies now became part of the civilian cooperative.[72] In Bolshevik hands, the workers' cooperative council (*Sarrabsoiuz*) sought to shoulder a greater role in procuring and distributing goods received from the Food Supply Commissariat (figure 9.1). A prevailing refrain voiced at a regional congress in January 1919 was that of the strained relationship between the co-ops and food supply organs, which speakers contended could only be rectified by placing procurement in the hands of workers'

---

[69] *Kooperativnaia mysl'*, no. 1 (1918): 3–4; I. N. Kokshaiskii, *Kreditnaia kooperatsiia v Saratovskoi gubernii k nachalu 1918 g.* (Saratov, 1918), 4; GASO, f. 403, op. 3, d. 176, ll. 1–6; *Souiz potrebitel'nykh obshchestv Saratovskogo kraia. Ob"iasnitel'naia zapiska k smete na 1918 god* (Saratov, n.d.).

[70] S. V. Veselov, "Kooperatsiia Sovetskogo obshchestva v novom osveshchenii," *Voprosy istorii*, no. 9–10 (1991): 25–35.

[71] *Kooperativnaia mysl'*, no. 7 (38) (1919): 5, and *Biulleten' Saratovskogo gubernskogo Soveta narodnogo khoziaistva*, no. 11 (1918): 21–22.

[72] GASO, f. 403, op. 3, d. 182, ll. 15–16 ob.

9.1 Second Congress of representatives of Saratov's workers' cooperatives, 1919. Courtesy Saratov Kraevedcheskii Museum, photo 22408/80.

co-ops. Speakers also rebuked the Saratov Gubprodkom because it included "bourgeois elements."[73]

When representatives of the various groups met in October 1919 to discuss formation of a Joint Consumer Society and the ruling that all citizens must enroll in the new organs, non-Bolsheviks chided the element of compulsory membership, mourning the loss of the cooperatives' independence precisely because they "were democratic."[74] An emergency meeting of workers' cooperatives for the Saratov region called to discuss the merger split along party lines, as Mensheviks and SRs, appearing as "unaffiliated" representatives, fought stubbornly to retain the co-ops' independence, dismissing the Bolsheviks' bland assurances that "proletarian influence" would survive.[75] Despite the cooperatives' co-optation by the party-state, they remained staffed by large numbers of non-Bolsheviks, because the party had to employ people with knowl-

[73] *Kooperativnaia mysl'*, no. 6 (37), Feb. 9, 1919, 8–9.

[74] GASO, f. 403, op. 1. d. 57, ll. 78–84, and op. 8, d. 2, l. 5. See also TsDNISO, f. 138, op. 1, d. 33, l. 17.

[75] GASO, f. 403, op. 8, d. 2, ll. 30–42 ob.

edge and experience.[76] With the start of the NEP, the state cooperatives, at least on paper, represented the only competitor to private entrepreneurs and no longer served merely as distribution organs. But by the end of 1921, the local cooperatives devoted their energies almost exclusively to feeding starving Saratovites. Their staffs slashed, they spoke out against mandatory enrollment in cooperatives. Whether this was owing to their being understaffed or a reflection of the fact that non-Communists remained influential in them is impossible to say.[77]

A slightly different scenario played itself out at the district level, but the end result was the same as in Saratov. In general, it proved difficult to establish single consumer societies in the districts, due to lack of instructions or contradictory ones, money shortages, and the desire on the part of many to maintain independent co-ops. And it proved difficult to sustain them due to unfavorable circumstances caused by the collapse of rail transport, industrial breakdown, and shortages of goods to exchange. For instance, lack of staff, low pay, and frequent replacement of cadres crippled the cooperative movement in Petrovsk. So did the decree on *tovaroobmen*, the commodity exchange, to be discussed below, because leaders withdrew from the cooperatives to open small shops. Interference from local committees of the village poor (*kombedy*), which divided among themselves goods meant for exchange, posed another problem. Owing to the inevitability of paying market prices, Khvalynsk's population became largely indifferent to what was once a robust cooperative movement, with the exception of workers, for whom the co-op had become nothing more than a "ration shop."[78] Learning that goods sent to Volsk's cooperatives had not been distributed, Gubprodkom temporarily shut them down.[79] Such phenomena prompted one critic to insist that "state power must be based on the economy, and not the other way around . . . as the socialists say."[80]

The Crusade for Grain

Alienating the peasantry and contributing to the famine of 1921–22, the Soviet government in August 1918 launched its first annual grain

[76] Ibid., f. 403, op.1, d. 151, ll. 1–2 ob.

[77] See *Otchet Saratovskogo Gubernskogo Ispolnitel'nogo Komiteta*, 127–28; GASO, f. 403, op. 1, d. 151, ll. 21–24 ob; d. 205, ll. 1–11 ob; and f. 403, op. 1, d. 216, ll. 1–4.

[78] GASO, f. 403, op. 1, d. 29, ll. 72–73, 89–90; d. 79, ll. 1–3 ob; op. 3, d. 207, ll. 4–5 ob; op. 8, d. 2, ll. 2–7 ob; and d. 7, ll. 2–3.

[79] *Izvestiia Ispolnitel'nogo komiteta Vol'skogo Soveta*, no. 79, April 10, 1919, 1. See also GASO, f. 403, op. 8, d. 17, ll. 10–14, and d. 2, ll. 62–64.

[80] Ibid., f. 403, op. 1, d. 69, ll. 1–4 ob.

procurement program,[81] which continued into the spring of 1919 when peasants prepared for the spring sowing. Similar campaigns followed in 1919–20, 1920–21, and 1921–22. Red Russia's loss of major grain growing regions in the Kuban, Ukraine, and Siberia helped create the desperate situation many of the industrial cities faced in early 1918. Despite public depictions of the Revolution as a worker-peasant one, party internal language saw the peasantry as a petit-bourgeois and thus hostile force. This ideologically shaped characterization differed from the general urban frustration with the peasantry that extended across the political spectrum but was mediated by the SRs' popularity. For instance, the peasant's reluctance to hand over grain willingly as a sacrifice to the Revolution convinced some Bolsheviks of the soundness of launching the campaign to foment class war in the countryside (see chapter 10). Ideology thus transformed practices of state intervention by increasing coercion and justifying punitive measures. Because siding with the poor peasantry failed miserably, in the spring of 1919 the party embraced the middle peasant, no longer a sociological stratum but a label pinned on any peasant who was not a kulak — and a kulak was any peasant who did not turn over grain when the state had nothing to exchange for it.[82]

For purposes of collecting grain, Narkomprod divided the province into twenty-one regions, setting up one hundred goods exchange points along railroad lines and the Volga.[83] Estimating that Saratov had a surplus of 22,143,000 poods of grain and other farm products, the government, following earlier precedent and expectations, declared the province a food-producing one and levied 31,100,000 poods on it. Lenin unequivocally let local leaders know that he considered it an enormous scandal that Saratov had "surpluses" while the capitals went hungry. During the 1918–19 campaign the government procured 38.2 percent of its goal nationwide, and 44.2 percent in Saratov Province. The fourteen million poods collected in Saratov before the end of 1918 placed the province first in the country, accounting for one-fifth of all foodstuffs procured. At the end of the campaign in 1919 Saratov ranked fourth nationally, representing an essential source of food for the central industrial provinces.[84]

Figes rightly argues that the procurement was so low overall because

---

[81] S. A. Sokolov, "K voprosu ustanovleniia prodovol'stvennoi diktatury v 1918 godu," *Povolzhskii krai*, no. 6 (1970): 28–30; Strizhkov, *Prodovol'stvennye otriady*, 102–35; and Patenaude, "Peasants into Russians," 553–54.

[82] Lih, *Bread and Authority*, 138–66.

[83] *Iubileinyi sbornik*, 64.

[84] Iakovlev, "Komitety," 131–32; *Vtoroi god s golodom* (Moscow, 1919), xi; and Figes, *Russian Peasant*, 250.

of "the breakdown of the state infrastructure at every stage of the pro-curement process."[85] Problems bedeviled the campaign in Saratov from the start. Carrying out their own requisitioning, military units interfered in the state's operation. Shortages of employees in the procurement bodies, the parallelism of government organizations, destruction caused by the Whites in Serdobsk and elsewhere, transportation difficulties, as well as sundry decrees issued by uezd executive committees undermined the campaign.[86] That summer and fall approximately seventeen brigades of Narkomprod's so-called Food Army (*Prodarmiia*), comprising over 3,500 workers from Yaroslavl, Moscow, Petrograd, Ivanovo-Voznesensk, and other cities, participated in the government's procurement program in Saratov.[87] Despite instructions to take part in the procurement, most of them ended up speculating in grain, thereby sabotaging the system of fixed prices. Another difficulty surfaced when Lenin authorized work-ers' brigades and representatives from the Moscow Soviet, children's homes, and hospitals to acquire small amounts of grain for themselves.[88] Gubprodkom officials knocked Lenin's decision, maintaining that the impact of this flood of bagmen was "catastrophic," making "the contin-uation of state procurements according to plan impossible."[89] Apart from the Food Army, Narkomprod organized additional detachments with approximately 2,000 members, far fewer than some local authori-ties considered necessary to safeguard grain already procured.[90]

Specialists employed in Gubprodkom lashed out against government policies, at times managing to present their disapproval in specialized publications that circulated narrowly. Since Gubprodkom comprised both Bolsheviks and a larger cohort of non-Bolsheviks, this critical sen-timent toward state policies may have represented a strange hybrid of anti-Soviet feelings and party localism. In 1919 one of Gubprodkom's agents observed that lack of reliable data represented the principal

---

[85] Figes, *Russian Peasant*, 254; see also *Iubileinyi sbornik*, 72.

[86] *ISGPK*, no. 24, Dec. 31, 1918, 4–8. See also GASO, f. 521, op. 1, d. 139, l. 291; GA RF, f. 393, op. 3, d. 335, l. 129; GASO, f. 456, op. 1, d. 27, ll. 98–102; and Vas'kovskii, "Sovety," 29.

[87] S. V. Terekhin, "Prodovol'stvennaia zagotovka," *Trudy Saratovskogo ekonomich-eskogo instituta*, no. 4 (1954): 35–36, and Iakovlev, "Komitety," 150–51, 163.

[88] See Sokolov's tendentious account in "K voprosu," 26–32, 38–39, and in *Revoliuts-iia i khleb*, 81.

[89] GA RF, f. 1235, op. 93, d. 491, ll. 104–7. See also l. 122.

[90] Strizhkov, *Prodovol'stvennye otriady*, 135–41, 145–46. For a discussion of tension within the government over controlling the Prodarmiia see Alessandro Stanziani, "La ges-tion des approvisionnements et la restauration de las *gosudarstvennost'*. Le *Narkomprod*, l'armée et les paysans, 1918–1921," *Cahiers du Monde russe* 38, no. 1–2 (1997): 83–116.

shortcoming of the campaign.[91] Other sources echo this assessment, pointing out that the government assigned Saratov an exaggerated quota based on data from earlier harvests, and did not take into account surpluses seized by the Whites or Saratov's large refugee population.[92] Be that as it may, there is no denying that the 1918 harvest was an above-average one except in Tsaritsyn and Kamyshin, as a result of which government prices were higher than those on the black market until the end of the year.[93]

The conditions in which Gubprodkom carried out procurement varied widely across the province, but it conveniently blamed kulaks and the bourgeoisie for the procurement policy's failures.[94] One instructor sent to Atkarsk disapprovingly recalled that the "well-off" elements "lived like little landlords," heretofore untouched by requisitioning or the government's grain monopoly.[95] Gubprodkom usually censured military authorities for carrying out their own procurement and for interfering in its activities. For instance, the commander of the Elansk garrison fell under fire for defending free trade. Ill-disposed toward a workers' brigade from Petrograd as well as toward local Communists, he had both pummeled, prompting an investigative commission to conclude that "the [local] population is counterrevolutionary."[96] In Saratov Uezd, grain flowed into the collection points slowly because of the high prices on the black market. Kombedy proved ineffective, as "kulaks" sold their products to agents from Moscow and Petrograd.[97]

Exceeding expectations, between 60 and 80 percent of the procurement in 1918–19 flowed into delivery points in the fall of 1918, when government prices satisfied peasants and when goods were available for exchange.[98] Not surprisingly, there was a correlation between availability of manufactured goods and the peasantry's willingness to market agricultural products. Procurement points paid up to 60 percent of the cost of grain turned over in manufactured goods and the rest in paper money; moreover, those handing over grain early benefited as government prices fell on products submitted in December. Peasants initially received a higher percentage of payment in goods than was called for, thanks to the unexpected availability of manufactured items evacuated

[91] *Iubileinyi sbornik*, 101.

[92] D. B., "Prodovol'stvennaia kampaniia 1918–1919 gg. v Saratovskoi gubernii," *Ekonomicheskaia zhizn' Povolzh'ia: Sbornik statei* (Saratov, 1919), 24–26.

[93] *Biulleten' statisticheskoi sektsii gubernskogo zemskogo otdela*, no. 9 (1918): 1, 4.

[94] Ibid., no. 13, (1918): 7; no. 17 (1918): 10–11; and the entire no. 22 (1918) issue.

[95] GASO, f. 456, op. 1, d. 51, ll. 131–31 ob.

[96] Ibid., f. 456, d. 521, op. 1, d. 444, l. 53.

[97] *ISGPK*, no. 13, Oct. 6, 1918, 1–2.

[98] Ibid., no. 15, Oct. 20, 1918, 8.

from Tsaritsyn.[99] Goods continued to serve as the most desirable medium of exchange not only because inflation made the value of paper
money volatile, but also because the government based taxes on how
much money was in the villages. As a result, once the peasants satisfied
their monetary demands, they destroyed the receipts.

Between December 1918 and March 1919 the quantity of grain deliv-
ered fell five times, forcing Sovnarkhoz to launch obligatory delivery of
foodstuffs by quota (*razverstka*) in January. Lih sees this "quota assess-
ing" as an actual concession to the peasants, an attempt to work with
them rather than to divide the village as during the kombedy period,
and in contrast to the situation that would develop in 1920, because
most villages carried out grain levies, and assessed everyone equally,
rather than extracting compulsory taxes from the rich.[100] Yet while the
state's earlier procurement policies included cereals and fodder, the new
policy covered *all* major foodstuffs and the state continued to set goals
from above. Moreover, Narkomprod's food supply detachments expanded rapidly at this time as more than 1,500 individuals were dispatched to Saratov Province. In addition, in 1919 an emergency tax was
levied against "the kulak and speculating population," which, in failing
to bring in the desired revenues, drove another wedge between town
and country.[101]

Extending the procurement to include all foodstuffs evoked a hostile
reaction from the peasantry, who flooded Narkomprod with complaints
about the government's assessments and with denials that they had any
surpluses. In Petrovsk the government's food policies resulted in the
declaration of an emergency situation.[102] Between a rock and a hard
place, the Saratov Executive Committee overruled a central decree to
requisition pigs because it "would turn the population [even more]
against Soviet power."[103] The commissariat's efforts to tease out grain
by making offerings of salt and vegetable oil largely failed because of
their availability on the black market. Therefore, Narkomprod sent
food brigades to all the districts, which, despite their use of coercion,
failed to secure the surpluses they sought.[104] The rates of fulfillment

[99] Sokolov, *Revoliutsiia i khleb*, 34, 43, 56.

[100] Lars Lih, "Bolshevik *Razverstka* and War Communism," *Slavic Review* 45, no. 4
(1986): 676–79, 685–86; Figes, *Peasant Russia*, 91; and Sokolov, "Iz istorii," 10. Lih
maintains that razverstka laid the groundwork for the tax in kind introduced with the
NEP; however, I find it difficult to argue this point in view of the Bolsheviks' use of
coercion. See *Bread and Authority*, 199.

[101] GASO, f. 456, op. 1, d. 218, l. 16 ob.

[102] *Kommuna*, no. 10 (79), Feb. 9, 1919, 4.

[103] GASO, f. 456, op. 1, d. 172, l. 8.

[104] *Iubileinyi sbornik*, 21, 67–70; D. B., "Prodovol'stvennaia politika," 26; Sokolov, "Iz

ranged from a high of 61.5 percent in Balashov to 9 percent in Volsk and 2.1 percent in Khvalynsk, with a province-wide average of 31.3 percent.[105] The party blamed the slow delivery of goods despite their availability in the fall of 1919 on the "unacceptable social composition" of the brigades, and on the failures of local soviets that turned a blind eye to "speculation."[106] Internal language deconstructed the euphemism "unacceptable social composition" found in the press. The "poorly instructed" brigade sent to Kuznetsk represented a motley collection of criminals who drank heavily and carried out illegal searches, justifying their tactics by insisting the Revolution had put an end to private property![107] Peasants bombarded *Izvestiia* with letters of complaint, many of which were anonymous.[108] In response to the outpouring of anger, the party promised to purge local food supply organs of scoundrels.[109]

The exchange of manufactured goods for agricultural products served as the linchpin of procurement. Established by an April 2, 1918, decree, tovaroobmen became mandatory for Saratov and twelve other "grain producing" provinces.[110] This involved setting up a food monopoly, abolishing private trade and establishing fixed prices, creating central supply organs, and combating speculation.[111] Yet as of 1919 the program was only being slowly implemented in the locales, which often interpreted the decree to their own advantage. For instance, cooperatives were instructed to release goods only when peasants turned over grain; however, in some volosts goods were exchanged for products other than grain, or were distributed without grain being turned in at all. Peasants appear to have supported distribution on an individual rather than collective basis, but the government saw this as a mixed blessing, because it further marginalized the poorer elements hailed as its bastion of support in the countryside. Between August 1918 and August 1919, the actual exchange of grain for goods ranged from 31.6 percent to 46.7 percent of the total in most uezds. Even in those dis-

---

istorii," 25; Terekhin, "Prodovol'stvennaia zagotovka," 37; "Iz istorii bor'by prodovol'stvennykh otriadov rabochikh za khleb i ukreplenie Sovetskoi vlasti (1918–1920 gg.)," *Krasnyi arkhiv*, no. 4–5 (89–90) (1938): 114–15. See also GASO, f. 456, op. 1, d. 49, l. 328.

[105] GASO, f. 523, op. 1, d. 18, l. 116.

[106] See, for instance, *KG*, no. 295, Feb. 27, 1919, 1.

[107] GASO, f. 523, op. 1, d. 17, l. 178.

[108] *Golos kommuna*, no. 29 (66), Jan. 18, 1919, 4, and no. 92 (129), April 6, 1919, 4.

[109] GASO, f. 521, op. 1, d. 304, l. 2.

[110] See M. I. Davydov, "Gosudarstvennyi tovaroobmen mezhdu gorodom i derevnei v 1918–1921 gg.," *Istoricheskie zapiski* 108 (1982): 33–59.

[111] *Iubileinyi sbornik*, 13, 20, 29–35.

tricts achieving higher levels, tovaroobmen failed to meet the peasantry's real needs for manufactured items in virtually all areas.[112]

Unfavorable sowing conditions in the spring of 1919—cold weather,
lack of rain, shortages of seed and draft animals—affected spring sowing, as did opposition to government policies and the Whites' intrusion
into the province.[113] Nonetheless, the government's assessment in 1919
represented a 23 percent increase over the previous year. In May it abolished food supply commissariats at the uezd level, replacing them with
district (*raion*) supply committees; in July it extended its procurement
policies in Saratov to products heretofore outside the state's reach. An
August 5, 1919, decree made the release of manufactured goods conditional upon the peasantry's mandatory handing over of their last agricultural surpluses. However, the decree allowed for handicraft products
to be introduced into the goods exchange, in effect admitting that requisitioning worked only when the state had something to barter.[114]

Acknowledging that a black market in just about everything undermined state procurement efforts and that surpluses were found "even
among Communists," the party justified the use of force to carry out
requisitioning. It attacked "speculation" and discredited the activities of
rural executive committees, accusing village authorities of preventing
workers from inventorying agricultural surpluses and of "openly organizing sabotage." The press likewise rebuked village executive committees for refusing to collect the emergency tax levied on peasants, for
neglecting the fields of drafted peasants, for hiding deserters, and for
engaging in speculation. The paper complained daily of bagmen who
packed passenger trains, attacked food supply detachments, set up mar-
kets on the outskirts of the city, and openly peddled butter, eggs, and
coffee in Saratov.[115] In turning its spotlight of shame on illicit alcohol
production, the party justified repression by insisting that drunkenness
had become so ubiquitous that it involved "everyone, including women
and priests."[116] When the grain collecting campaign in the fall of 1919
began a month behind schedule, Gubprodkom and the Center took
measures to agitate the peasantry, setting the tone for the campaign by
justifying repression. As Mgeladze put it, "if the workers don't receive
bread, the revolution will perish."[117]

[112] Ibid., 115, 122.

[113] *Biulleten' statisticheskogo otdela Soveta narodnogo khoziaistva po prodovolstviiu*
(Saratov, 1918), 5, 7–8.

[114] *Iubileinyi sbornik*, 54–57, 104, 116, and Vas'kovskii, "Sovety," 265.

[115] *ISS*, no. 101, May 16, 1919, 1, and no. 126, June 17, 1919, 1.

[116] *ISS*, no. 128, June, 19, 1919, 1; no. 129, June 20, 1919, 1; and no. 182, Aug. 20,
1919, 1.

[117] Ibid., no. 204, Sept. 16, 1919, 3.

Repression, however, sparked disturbances throughout the country-side, as volost soviets declared their outright refusal even to consider the state's quotas, and peasants protested government targets, claiming they did not leave them or their livestock enough to survive on.[118] Some vol-osts in Volsk managed to avoid participating in the campaign altogether, as a result of which the authorities resolved to release goods for the commodity exchange only in locales that met 60 percent of their target goals.[119] Elsewhere delays resulted owing to lack of money with which to pay peasants and lags in processing grain, in part caused by the state's requisition of horses. A desperate *Izvestiia* opined that "there is not a worse enemy in the Soviet republic than the peasant that hides his surpluses. He is the murderer of the starving workers of the northern provinces."[120]

Meanwhile, Gubprodkom officials continued to maintain that the major problem during the first two campaigns had been errors in calcu-lating the size of the harvest. While estimates were based on an arithme-tic average of the best, worst, and average yields in recent years, they did not take into account the amount of land under cultivation, which already had begun to shrink. Hoping to introduce a corrective to the procedures, Gubprodkom prepared an agricultural census for the 1920–21 grain campaign; however, the Center ruled that the new quota should be based on the previous two years' calculations. Aware that local peas-ants, lacking seeds and draft animals, had begun to sow only for them-selves, Gubprodkom asserted that the 1920–21 campaign should be set at no more than twenty million poods, and that any armed force used to dislodge grain from the countryside should be in its hands. But the agency erred in thinking that more accurate figures pointing to lower output locally would result in reduced expectations from the Center. There is no denying the evidence: late snows in the spring of 1920, drought in April, and less land under cultivation "did not bode well."[121]

Despite the efforts of some Gubprodkom members to cushion the blow to Saratov, the local party organization and Cheka enforced Mos-cow's brutal policies. Admitting the "total failure" of moral pressure and agitation in motivating the peasantry, whose mood it described as "totally oppositional," party officials lamented the lack of armed force

---

[118] GASO, f. 521, op. 1, d. 360, l. 111, and *Izvestiia Atkarskogo ispolkoma*, no. 343, Nov. 5, 1919, 3.

[119] Antonov-Saratovskii, *Sovety*, 2: 358–59.

[120] See *ISS*, no. 209, Sept. 21, 1919, 2; no. 213, Sept. 26, 1919, 2; and no. 220, Oct. 5, 1919, 2. Quotation found in no. 227, Oct. 14, 1919, 3.

[121] F. Platonov, "Khlebnaia kampaniia 1919–20 g. i perspektivy predstoiashchei 1920–21 god v Saratovskoi gubernii," *Narodnoe khoziaistvo Nizhnego Povolzh'ia*, no. 2–3 (1920): 3–7.

at their disposal and the detachments' "low level of preparedness" — code language meaning that the detachments speculated or sympathized with the peasantry. Those in charge remained determined to apply "maximum pressure" in forcing peasants to relinquish their "surpluses."[122]

All of the pieces of a disaster had fallen into place once Saratov's party leaders gave priority to filling state quotas. Despite the unpropitious conditions and mediocre harvest, they felt pressured to requisition owing to the rupture in transport, which all but stopped the flow of grain from Siberia and the Caucasus to the Center. Collection figures from the previous year only complicated their dilemma. Between August 1919 and June 1920, Saratov peasants met only 25.7 percent of the quota assessment for agricultural products (but 176.5 percent of the groats procurement, and 243.5 percent of the fodder procurement).[123] Deliveries began to rise after martial law was introduced in the province in July 1920 and after the new district committees, which had replaced uezd committees, began to function. In October the Soviet government militarized requisitioning, resulting in widely applied repression.[124] The policy triggered peasant uprisings in some districts as well as concerns over lack of seed and impossibly low norms established for the amount of grain peasants were permitted to keep for their own needs.[125] Communists sent to the locales requisitioned 50 percent of the state's target by December, the overwhelming majority of which they shipped outside the province. A transportation breakdown on the railroads as well as a burgeoning strike movement complicated these efforts.[126] Although some rural areas were already suffering from starvation, the party insisted upon the correctness of its requisition policies.[127] In early 1921, Martynov, chair of the local Gubispolkom, informed Moscow that "repressive measures were carried out in the extreme." Regretting that he did not have adequate armed force at his disposal because of the appearance of armed bands, Martynov maintained that he needed additional units to raise requisitioning levels, requesting that food brigades be supplied with armored vehicles.[128] Extending the use of military measures to obtain grain contributed singularly to the receptiveness with which local peasants at least initially welcomed armed peasant bands. To counter "banditry" and the early signs of widespread hunger, the

---

[122] TsDNISO, f. 27, op. 1, d. 758, l. 4.

[123] *Narodnoe khoziaistvo Nizhnego Povolzh'ia*, no. 4 (1920): 16.

[124] RGASPI, f. 17, op. 12, d. 468, l. 38; *ISS*, no. 151, July 8, 1920, 3; and no. 293, Dec. 24, 1920, 4.

[125] GASO, f. 456, op. 1, d. 675, l. 14.

[126] TsDNISO, f. 81, op. 1, d. 30, l. 4.

[127] *ISS*, no. 278, Dec. 7, 1920, 2, and GASO, f. 456, op. 1, d. 633, ll. 1–3.

[128] GASO, f. 523, op. 1, d. 30, l. 66.

government pledged that it would end requisitioning after 75 percent(!) of its target had been collected.

Conclusion

In a recent study that seeks to answer the question why well-meaning plans to improve the human condition go awry and often tragically so, James C. Scott argues that they fail when they impose schematic visions, which do not do justice to complex interdependencies involving local, practical knowledge that often cannot be fully understood. Although Scott focuses on the Soviet collectivization scheme as an example of a fatally flawed vision, he could just as convincingly have considered the bold experimentation of War Communism, for the conditions Scott identifies as being necessary for carrying out the social engineering at the end of the 1920s already existed during the Civil War: a "high-modernist" ideology, the willingness to mobilize the authoritarian power of the state to achieve state-defined goals, a fragile civil society, and the leadership's attempt to impose administrative order on society. While accusing the dreamy intellectuals behind these episodes of hubris, Scott acknowledges that they were "animated by a genuine desire to improve the human condition."[129] Hence the tragedy. We need to ask, however, why the Bolsheviks later drew on the Civil War experience as a formative one not with lessons to avoid, but with lessons to emulate. I suspect their faith in the inevitability of the collapse of capitalism vouchsafed by ideology, a broad-based belief in reason and rationality, and the specific historical context compelled them to pursue their vision. But there was something else at play. Coercion had worked, although it turned people against the party and exacted a costly human toll. The Bolsheviks realized this problem, yet later needed to rely on the same measures to hold onto power while they tried to effect the changes that they believed would make coercion unnecessary in the long run.

Nowhere is the state's intention more apparent than in its approach to extending its control to the countryside. While tsarist wartime practices shaped Bolshevik Civil War policies, the breakdown of the state apparatus and the Soviet government's willingness to use coercion set the tone for future relations between the party-state and peasantry. The justification of force and violence reveals implicit assumptions about governance and about the peasantry that obscure the miserable mis-

---

[129] James C. Scott, *Seeing Like a State: How Certain Schemes to Improve the Human Condition Have Failed* (New Haven, 1998), 1–8, 147–79, 342–57. Quote found on 343.

calculations the party made about the harvest. The party would do whatever it deemed necessary to stay in power. Ultimately, repression shaped peasant strategies to ward off domination. The result was famine. The introduction of the NEP was made possible only after a massive social and political rejection of War Communism and upheaval on the part not only of the peasantry, but also of workers and elements in the party and state apparatus. It is to these groups that we now turn our attention.

Ten

Peasants in a Workers' Revolution

LONG BEFORE students of peasant studies observed that subaltern groups have a remarkable capacity to reject or reverse dominant ideologies and to create social spaces that challenge power relations, the Bolsheviks understood that hitching the village to the locomotive of revolution represented a daunting undertaking. Be that as it may, the ideological lens through which the party viewed the peasantry dictated policies that created unfavorable circumstances of the Bolsheviks' own making. As James Scott has shown, every subordinate group creates out of its situation a backstage discourse or "hidden transcript" representing a "critique of power spoken behind the back of the dominant." What is so striking about the party-state's interaction with the peasantry during the Civil War is that Saratov's smallholders not only expressed their hidden transcript through the arts of passive resistance, but ruptured the "political cordon sanitaire" by rising up against Soviet power and challenging the Bolshevik process of domination.[1] Local in significance, these uprisings nonetheless posed a potent threat to Soviet power, for they represented its rejection at the micro-level, demonstrating that the peasantry at no point in the Civil War accepted the government's use of armed intervention in the village. The peasantry went down in defeat, but it wrung concessions from the urban commissars whose attempts to reconfigure social relations in the villages failed more than any of their other efforts to recast society.

Ultimately, the civil war experience strengthened the internal mecha-

[1] Scott, *Domination*, xii–xiii, 5, 18–19.

nisms of cohesion in the villages. Ironically, this meant that many peasants became what Bolshevik ideology claimed they ought to be: smallholders with a "petit-bourgeois" mentality. In other words, owing to the state's rapacious policies, to social experimentation, to the rupture of market relations, and to the increase in savagery, frustration with communal land tenure was becoming a crucial element in many peasants' understanding of what it meant to be a peasant, even though the concept of "private" property does not appear to have been well developed in the villages before 1914. This merely served to reinforce the Bolsheviks' deep-rooted prejudice against the countryside, fashioning the right mindset for the party to intrude again upon the peasant world when the state felt powerful enough to do so.

More Land but Less Bread: The Ambiguous Land Settlement

Until mid-1918 peasant village autonomy flourished as the peasants finished the social revolution in the villages. Some villages reacted to the Bolshevik revolution with hostility and suspicion, but often these feelings temporarily melted away once the smallholders associated the party with the decree that placed all land at the peasants' disposal.[2] To fortify Soviet power, the Fourth Provincial Peasant Congress convened in May 1918, drawing 388 Left SR delegates and 129 Bolsheviks, and chaired by Left SR Ustinov.[3] Although complaints rang out that authorities admitted only pro-Soviet delegates, the conference's composition underscores the vitality of the Left SRs at the time. Indeed, in addressing the gathering, Antonov spoke of the "family of workers and peasants," a trope that acknowledged radical populism's importance for the local revolution.[4] If there was ever a period when the peasantry broadly sympathized with Soviet power, it was now, as a set of questionnaires sent to the volosts indicates.[5]

Nevertheless, reports made at the congress emphasize how the collapse of the old system had made the countryside anxious. Subjected to arbitrary requisitions, contributions, searches, and seizures of grain, many villages lacked reserves, money, equipment, and fuel to run mills,

---

[2] GA RF, f. 393, op. 2, d. 80, ll. 38–38 ob, 303; *Saratovskii Sovet*, 277, 279–80; *Golos truda*, no. 32, April 3, 1918, 2–4; A. G. Rybkov, *Sud'ba Saratovskoi derevni: Istoricheskii ocherk sela Teplovka* (Saratov, 1994), 46; and Gerasimenko and Sem'ianinov, *Sovetskaia vlast'*, 202–7.

[3] *Sotsial-Demokrat*, no. 101, Dec. 24, 1917, 4; no. 103, Dec. 30, 1917, 3; and Sagrad'ian, *O sushchestvovlenii*, 31–33.

[4] *Protokoly Saratovskogo gubernskogo s"ezda*, 79, 86–90, 103, 113.

[5] *ISS*, no. 104, May 31, 1918, 3, and GA RF, f. 393, op. 3, d. 338, l. 320.

schools, and medical facilities. The breakdown of the market drove peasant agents to Siberia and elsewhere in search of cereals. Speakers lamented the capriciousness of political authority, lack of instructions from Saratov and Moscow, the outrageous behavior of Red Guard units in rural areas, and the turmoil caused by the Czechoslovaks. They noted clashes between rich and poor, decried the problems associated with refugees, and questioned the fate of the Constituent Assembly. While they accepted the necessity of the grain monopoly, they wanted the state to control the production and distribution of factory goods so that peasant needs could be satisfied.[6]

But it was land reform that interested the peasant more than anything else; on this question contradictory currents surfaced at the congress as delegates passed resolutions heralding the end of private ownership, while also conceding many peasants' instinctive desire for it. Although the party declared the superiority of collective agriculture, it downplayed the contradiction between this view and that of the peasantry, who looked upon the land and what it produced as belonging to them. In reporting how land had been redistributed as per the law of February 1918, speakers observed that local congresses had distributed land to the volosts and villages according to the amount a family could work without hired labor. Because the so-called "labor norm" varied among villages, however, the congress instructed communities to inventory land and to count the population in order to make land redistribution more "egalitarian."[7]

Greatly shaped by the return of peasant soldiers, the revolution in the Saratov countryside liquidated landowners' estates and promoted a leveling process, as a result of which the number of farmers with no land or minimal holdings or with more than ten desiatinas was sharply reduced (table 10.1).[8] The quantity of land in peasant hands increased substantially, and the amount per adult male (not household) increased from one to two desiatinas, or by 100 percent, a greater gain than in neighboring provinces. According to the 1919 census, the number of households between 2 and 8 desiatinas rose from 11,124 to 16,728, while the sum total of larger households between 8 and 25 desiatinas dropped from

[6] *Protokoly Saratovskogo gubernskogo s"ezda,* 24, 28, 30, 32, 35–36, 43, 47, 49, 51, 77, 83, 104. On contributions, see GA RF, f. 393, op. 3, d. 336, ll. 31–32; d. 335, l. 18; d. 334, l. 79; f. 393, op. 2, d. 80, ll. 76, 85, 145; f. 1235, op. 93, d. 493, l. 38; GASO, f. 456, op. 1, d. 84, l. 2; d. 89, l. 7; d. 91, l. 4; and f. 521, op. 1, d. 181, l. 113.

[7] *Protokoly Saratovskogo gubernskogo s"ezda,* 21, 28–29, 36, 148–50, 152–57, and GASO, f. 456, op. 1, d. 51, l. 63.

[8] S. Pskovskii, "Agrarnyi vopros i perspektivy agrarnoi politiki v Saratovskoi gubernii," *Ekonomicheskaia zhizn' Povolzh'ia,* no. 1 (1919): 9–10, 20–21, and Figes, *Peasant Russia,* 101–31.

TABLE 10.1

Size of Peasant Farms in Saratov Province on the Right Bank of the Volga, 1917–24, in Percentages

Amount of land	1917	1919	1920	1921	1922	1923	1924
None	13.40	8.42	6.70	6.07	4.04	3.23	1.50
Up to 1 desiatina	4.68	3.84	5.80	8.54	11.38	6.96	6.50
1.1 to 2 des.	9.67	10.87	13.60	16.97	19.28	15.66	16.60
2.1 to 4 des.	18.81	27.03	31.30	33.32	31.67	32.32	34.70
4.1 to 6 des.	15.80	21.72	22.30	20.20	17.80	22.07	22.00
6.1 to 8 des.	12.20	14.64	11.70	9.40	8.47	11.13	10.80
8.1 to 10 des.	8.37	7.46	5.00	3.47	3.66	4.62	4.20
10.1 to 16 des.	12.00	5.49	3.30	2.01	2.93	3.47	3.20
16.1 des. or more	5.07	.53	.30	.20	.77	.54	.50

Source: A. Kovalevskii, "Differentsiia krest'ianstva Saratovskoi gubernii v period s 1917 po 1924 god (Po materialam Saratovskogo gubstatbiuro)," *Nizhnee Povolzh'e*, no. 4–5 (Saratov, 1924): 31.

4,389 to 1,845.[9] (The average household had 5.5 inhabitants and the average village comprised 130 households.)[10] Owing to the destruction of the Stolypin farms, the influx of refugees, and the return of workers from the towns, the overall number of households expanded, and this meant that the amount of land under cultivation initially rose, except in Petrovsk, which was ravaged by epidemic diseases and lacked seed, draft animals, and equipment.

Conflict accompanied land redistribution in Saratov, but it is difficult to generalize about it because the fault lines ran in complex ways. Kinship ties, past experiences, factions, networking, and other considerations could be as important as social standing. Further, the peasants' appropriation of the language of class struggle in settling old scores and in justifying their collective decision making merely served to obfuscate the social dynamic it purportedly explained.[11] Stolypin peasants who

[9] GASO, f. 521, op. 1, d. 906, ll. 1–2. Computations that factor in the left-bank districts result in a lower percentage of gain. See Sagrad'ian, *O sushchestvovlenii*, 103, and Kovalevskii, "Differentsiia," 31–32.

[10] N. A. Neipert, "Izmeneniia velichiny posevnoi ploshchadi," *Statisticheskii vestnik Saratovskogo gubernskogo statisticheskogo biuro*, no. 2 (1920/21): 22–24; Saratovskoe gubernskoe statisticheskoe biuro, *Statisticheskii spravochnik* (Saratov, 1924), 79; Kritsman et al., *Materialy po istorii agrarnoi revoliutsii v Rossii* (Moscow, 1929), 2: 324–63, xlvi–xlviii.

[11] Peasants are likely to be more radical at the level of ideology than in their behavior, "where they are more effectively constrained by the daily exercise of power." See James C. Scott, *Weapons of the Weak: Everyday Forms of Peasant Resistance* (New Haven, 1985), 331.

had withdrawn from the commune and taken their allotment of land, often without the sanction of the village, now had to be content with only the land they could work. Those who resisted endured the fate of the landlords. Similar friction occurred in Tatar villages.[12] Another conflict hard to sort out concerned church property and influence. Since anticlericalism could be found in the Russian village long before the Bolsheviks, it is not surprising that some villages seized church lands; however, such measures could also alienate peasants.[13] It appears that the main antagonisms actually occurred between villages and volosts; in general, the village remained a cohesive unit in which the dominant struggle took place between insiders and outsiders;[14] when threatened by an outside force, peasants showed solidarity.[15] Even party documents observe that there was no real class stratification in the villages, only the existence of a "disorganized poor."[16]

Despite the transfer of land into peasant hands, the total amount under cultivation fell precipitously between 1914 and 1921. Using the land farmed in 1914 as a base of 100 percent, we find that 95 percent of this total area was sown in 1916, 80 percent in 1917, 58 percent in 1920, and only 49 percent in 1921. Raging civil war and the peasantry's penchant for underreporting their activity in the hope of easing the burden of requisitioning made it difficult to compile reliable statistics. Nonetheless, the numbers indicate that the sown area declined and that peasants began to plant less wheat and to cultivate rye and other staples that proved hardier in drought years. They also endured a dramatic reduction in the number of farm animals at their disposal.[17] The sharp decrease of sown area in 1919 goaded the authorities into establishing sowing committees; however, famine conditions had already been cre-

---

[12] GASO, f. 521, op. 6, d. 1, ll. 87–87 ob, and *Izvestiia Kamyshinskogo Soveta*, no. 89, Oct. 4, 1918, 1.

[13] *Saratovskie eparkhial'nye vedomosti*, no. 16–18 (1918): 213–15; GA RF, f. 393, op. 3, d. 340, l. 214; and *Kommuna*, no. 2 (71), Jan. 12, 1919, 3.

[14] GA RF, f. 393, op. 3, d. 331, ll. 20–20 ob; op. 2, d. 80, ll. 35–35 ob; and TsDNISO, f. 151/95, op. 2, d. 3, ll. 15, 29.

[15] See *Saratovskie eparkhial'nye vedomosti*, no. 16–18 (1918): 212–13; GA RF, f. 393, op. 3, d. 340, ll. 267–68 ob; and d. 340, l. 163.

[16] RGASPI, f. 17, op. 5, d. 201, l. 6.

[17] The number of horses fell by 51.7 percent, cattle by 42 percent; sheep by 51.5 percent, pigs by 94.8 percent, camels by 50.5 percent, and goats by 62.9 percent. See GASO, f. 521, op. 1, d. 906, l. 7; Kalashnikov, "Saratovskaia organizatsiia kommunisticheskoi partii," 11, 36; Barminov, "Bor'ba," 140; N. Kuznetsov, "Ploshchad' poseva v 1919 g.," *Biulleten' Saratovskogo gubernskogo statisticheskogo biuro*, no. 1 (1920): 3–5; N. Lukov, "Sel'sko-khoziaistvo Saratovskoi gubernii s 1917 po 1924 g." *Kommunisticheskii put'*, no. 9 (34) (1923): 82; Neipert, "Izmeneniia," 25–27; and Mal'kov, *Estestvennoe dvizhenie naseleniia*, 10, 66–71.

10.1 Sun-scorched field in Serdobsk Uezd. Courtesy Saratov Kraevedcheskii Museum, photo 10397.

ated, and whenever peasant bands slipped into a district they disbanded the committees.[18] In the hardest hit famine areas, the amount of land plowed for the spring 1922 sowing ranged from 11.2 percent to 35.4 percent (figure 10.1).[19] While lack of farmhands, seed, equipment, draft animals, and the disorganization caused by land redistribution took their toll, requisitioning and shortages of manufactured goods for the countryside represented the major reasons for the cutbacks. The cause of the decline was the "mood of the peasantry," and this owed everything to Soviet policies in the countryside.[20]

The Committees of the Village Poor

The Bolshevik Party's decision on June 11, 1918, to establish committees of the village poor (*kombedy*) to promote social revolution in the villages, facilitate grain collection, and curb free trade marked a tragic turn in the party's course in the countryside. Before mid-1918 the villages had begun to form positive associations regarding the Commu-

[18] GASO, f. 456, op. 1, d. 635, ll. 2–5; f. 521, op. 1, d. 469, l. 41; *Izvestiia Atkarskogo Ispolnitel'nogo komiteta*, no. 281, Aug. 20, 1919, 3; *Rabochii i krest'ianin*, no. 64, March 23, 1910, 1; and *Sovetskaia derevnia*, no. 10, Jan. 30, 1921.

[19] *Biulleten' Saratovskogo gubernskogo statisticheskogo biuro*, no. 1 (1922): 17.

[20] GASO, f. 523, op. 1, d. 30, l. 77.

nists because of the seizure of estates and redistribution of land.[21] Combined with the introduction of the grain monopoly and food dictatorship in May and the first mobilizations into the Red Army, the party's resolve to manufacture class war in the villages represented the beginning of the end of the fleeting period of peasant self-rule.[22] These measures also exacerbated the rift between town and country, strained relations between the Bolsheviks and Left SRs, who opposed the committees, and eventually forced the Bolsheviks to reject their own policies.

Yet with the exception of a handful of militants, local Communists themselves balked at setting up kombedy not only because they had peasant disturbances and military threats with which to contend, but also because many of them disagreed with the premise for organizing the committees. As if anticipating the party's future strategy of accommodating the middle peasant, the soviet addressed its appeal for organizing kombedy to both poor *and* middle peasants, whose support it deemed essential, defining a kulak as someone who ran a cottage industry, used hired labor, or held others in debt.[23] Saratov Bolsheviks clearly did not wish to undermine their alliance with the Left SRs, and also worried that peasant hostility to the committees would destroy the "unity at the rear" and thereby enhance Right SR popularity.[24] As Left SR V. Trutovskii claimed, it was "obvious to anyone who had ever been in a village" that the Bolsheviks had erred in setting up kombedy.[25] Because prominent Saratov Communists agreed, the organization of kombedy got underway in earnest only after the arrival of outside agitators. By November they had established 831 kombedy, and by year's end an estimated 1,594, mostly in Atkarsk, Petrovsk, Balashov, Saratov, and Serdobsk. Elsewhere they emerged when the military threat receded; few were set up in frontline Khvalynsk and Volsk. As a sign of the confusing times, the committees continued to be formed even after the government liquidated them.[26]

The kombedy appealed mainly to in-migrants, agricultural laborers lacking land, craftsmen, and other marginalized groups. The mass of smallholders responded with malice, even violence, to the call to set up kombedy, refusing to do so or establishing them in a manner to serve

[21] For Saratov Uezd see GASO, f. 521, op. 1, d. 75, ll. 1–65.
[22] Figes, *Peasant Russia*, 71.
[23] GASO, f. 456, op. 1, d. 14, l. 9; (Petrovsk) GA RF, f. 393, op. 3, d. 335, l. 134 ob.
[24] See, for example, *Svobodnyi zemledelets*, no. 12, 1918, 13; GA RF, f. 393, op. 3, d. 335, l. 217 ob; *Kommuna* (Petrovsk), no. 18 (87), March 9, 1919, 4; Antonov-Saratovskii, *Sovety*, 1: 352; and A. Izmailovich, *Posleoktiabr'skie oshibky* (Moscow, 1918), 22.
[25] V. Trutovskii, *Kulaki, bednota i trudovoe krest'ianstvo* (Moscow, 1918), 3–14.
[26] GASO, f. 456, op. 1, d. 108, ll. 8–8 ob, and TsDNISO, f. 1837, op. 1, d. 3, l. 39.

their own needs.[27] In one case an entire village insisted it comprised nothing but poor peasants. Since everyone would have to enroll in the committee, the village saw no reason to create it. Similarly, some kombedy maintained their villages lacked kulaks.[28] Elsewhere, smallholders broke away from their poorer neighbors to set up separate volosts; the number of volosts in Balashov during this period shot up from forty to seventy! Often the smallholders gained control of the kombedy and used them to deflect state domination.[29] In other cases, village soviets refused to recognize the kombedy whose purpose, the villagers believed, was to inform workers' brigades who in the village had grain surpluses.[30] Moreover, the kombedy frequently came to blows with rural soviets when they tried to arrest villagers, confiscate property, or assess taxes.[31] Although the kombedy had the right to reelect soviets, this had not been their intended purpose. Ignoring directives, Petrovsk Communists disbanded rural soviets, transferring power to the kombedy. And a provincial party conference in December 1918 handed over power to the kombedy in an effort to attract the middle peasants to them, presaging the party's own changes in regard to the middle peasants in March 1919.[32]

Saratov party leaders as well as "non-Communist" officials negatively assessed the committees for "completely paralyzing" the Provincial Food Supply Committee. Twisting the Center's decrees to serve their own interests, the kombedy ignored directives, permitted grain to be shipped out of the province, and brewed samogon. Even the party's public language concluded that the kombedy triggered peasant uprisings, forcing the peasantry to lose faith in Soviet power and weakening the socialist element by making the peasant more self-sufficient.[33] Once the kombedy were recognized as failures, the party explained that "kulaks" had predominated in some or that the committees had not attracted the poor but "criminal elements, hooligans, drunks, robbers, and loafers." Further, the Center rebuked local authorities for interpret-

---

[27] GA RF, f. 393, op. 3, d. 328, l. 163; d. 340, ll. 198–98 ob; and f. 393, op. 3, d. 331, l. 85.

[28] Rashitov, "Sovety," 311, and GA RF, f. 393, op. 3, d. 340, ll. 68–68 ob, 70.

[29] GA RF, f. 393, op. 3, d. 327, l. 264; d. 335, ll. 187, 139, and 65. See also *Izvestiia g. Balashova*, no. 203, Oct. 1918, 3, and *Kommuna*, no. 18 (87), March 9, 1919, 2.

[30] TsDNISO, f. 27, op. 1, d. 18, ll. 5–7, and Sviatogorov, "1918 god," 70.

[31] GASO, f. 456, op. 1, d. 108, ll. 8–8 ob; d. 27, ll. 90–91; f. 521, op. 1, d. 139, ll. 334 ob–335; *Izvestiia Saratovskogo gubernskogo prodovol'stvennogo komissara*, no. 20, Dec. 1, 1918, 6. See also GA RF, f. 393, op. 3, d. 327, ll. 15–15 ob, 19, 22 ob; and Suslov, *Politicheskie partii*, 52.

[32] GA RF, f. 1235, op. 93, d. 484, l. 2; GASO, f. 456, op. 1, d. 22, l. 15, d. 47, l. 75 ob; TsDNISO, f. 27, op. 1, d. 1, l. 5; f. 200, op. 1, d. 1, ll. 1–3 ob; Antonov-Saratovskii, *Sovety*, 1: 372–73.

[33] *Iubileinyi sbornik*, 70–71.

ing its directives "bureaucratically."[34] But the decree to disband the kombedy pleased many Saratov Communists.[35] One from Petrovsk quipped that it was "to Lenin's credit" that he recognized his mistake in regard to the middle peasant.[36]

Rural Governance, Soviet Style

Volost soviets replaced the tsarist zemstvos in early 1918; soon their executive committees (*volispolkomy*) became the most important organizational form of Soviet power in the countryside.[37] Containing few Bolsheviks, the volispolkomy were in the hands of male peasants in the 30–45 age group.[38] In 1918 the volost soviets' most frequently discussed problems related to food supplies, refugees, redistribution of land, law and order, record keeping, repairs, and financial difficulties, problems that became exacerbated by the rise of military actions against the soviets and creation of the kombedy.[39] For example, the Bazarno-Karabulak Soviet banned the removal of grain from the volost and formed armed detachments to replace the militia, owing to "total anarchy, both in an economic and in a political sense." The Bolshe-Ekaterinovsk Soviet in Atkarsk coped with acute food shortages by sending emissaries to other provinces to purchase grain with money seized during the breakup of the landowners' estates. To curb crime and violence, it confiscated weapons from soldiers returning from the front. Instructing its representatives to a provincial peasant congress to "express complete faith in Soviet power," it called for the speedy socialization of land and for providing the village population with farm equipment "with the aim of sowing all fields." Following the congress, the volispolkom carried out the land transfer, but not without dissension.[40]

Whenever they sought to protect their own from the intrusions of

---

[34] TsDNISO, f. 27, op. 1, d. 18, ll. 30 ob-31; GA RF, f. 393, op. 3, d. 338, l. 81; and *Golos kommunista* (Serdobsk), no. 148 (185), June 18, 1919, 3. SRs challenged this reading. See *Kooperativnaia mysl'*, no. 9 (40), March 2, 1919, 5, and *ISGPK*, no. 20, Dec. 1, 1918, 6.

[35] *Saratovskii Sovet*, 735, and GA RF, f. 393, op. 3, d. 327, ll. 2–9.

[36] *Kommuna*, no. 18 (87), March 9, 1919, 2, 4.

[37] GA RF, f. 393, op. 2, d. 80, ll. 207–7 ob, and f. 393, op. 3, d. 330, ll. 217–27 ob.

[38] Ibid., f. 393, op. 3, d. 328, ll. 301–1 ob.

[39] Ibid., f. 393, op. 3, d. 328, l. 202; d. 340, l. 5; f. 393, op. 3, d. 338, ll. 177–95; f. 393, op. 3, d. 33, ll. 39–171; f. 393, op. 3, d. 336, ll. 109–24 ob; f. 393, op. 3, d. 338, ll. 198 ob–223 ob; f. 393, op. 3, d. 340, ll. 18–27; f. 393, op. 3, d. 333, l. 262; f. 393, op. 3, d. 328, ll. 41–52; f. 393, op. 3, d. 332, ll. 37–50; d. 338, ll. 107, 175; GASO, f. 471, op. 1, d. 3, ll. 7–18; and f. 521, op. 1, d. 69, ll. 4, 31 ob, 43–46 ob.

[40] GA RF, f. 393, op. 3, d. 338, ll. 107, 175; and d. 328, ll. 64–86.

Soviet power or protest the bullish behavior of party agents sent from the uezd towns, rural soviets provoked criticism from urban Communists for their narrow, local views.[41] Volost records reveal that peasants did seek ways to rebuff the state's intrusion into the village, yet did so without appearing to be oppositional. One volost soviet rejected the decree to end religious instruction in the schools, yet informed non-Orthodox pupils that they could skip such classes if they wished. A volost soviet in Volsk found it impossible to send an armed detachment to the town after it had fallen to the Whites "since the population of our volost is against forming an armed guard."[42] Another recruited men who had not fought in the war and who "received their freedom thanks to their comrades." Elsewhere, peasants drew lots to determine who would take part in the armed guard. One soviet declined to register males for the draft, because the peasants did not want "to arm themselves and go to war," and also avoided taking an inventory of horses "because the [local] population does not have any extra horses." The Mariinsk Volost Soviet did not elect a military commissar "owing to lack of candidates."[43]

The decision to liquidate the kombedy included provisions for new elections to village and volost soviets, which often were carried out under pressure from Communist Party cells and the disbanding kombedy, resulting in clashes, intimidation, the use of force, and the arrest of Revolutionary Communists (RCs).[44] For example, Communists and members of the kombedy got elected in Balashov, but in several villages "populated almost exclusively by kulaks" RCs won, and in others peasants chose "unworthy elements" so as "not to waste good people." In Volsk there were "excesses." In Kamyshin Communists prevailed only "in rare cases." In Kuznetsk "the elections went badly in several volosts; despite the presence of Communist cells, not a single Communist was elected." Mostly Communists and the poor were chosen in Petrovsk, undoubtedly thanks to coercion.[45] Given the fate of the kombedy, however, it is not surprising that some rural poor proved reluctant to get involved in the elections.

[41] Ibid., f. 393, op. 3, d. 333, l. 322; d. 331, ll. 18–18 ob and 91–91 ob; *Izvestiia Atkarskie*, no. 47, Sept. 1918, 4; and GASO, f. 521, op. 1, d. 69, l. 31 ob.

[42] GA RF, f. 393, op. 3, d. 332, ll. 150–50 ob, 154, 159, 286.

[43] Ibid., f. 393, op. 3, d. 33, l. 87; d. 340, ll. 27–27 ob; d. 336, l. 96 ob; d. 332, ll. 73–74 ob; and d. 337, ll. 2–2 ob. See also TsDNISO, f. 27, op. 1, d. 11, l. 1.

[44] *ISS*, no. 22, Jan. 30, 1919, 1–2; GA RF, f. 393, op. 3, d. 336, l. 86; op. 12, d. 33, l. 2; op. 3, d. 331, ll. 3, 4 ob; *Krasnaia kommuna*, no. 154, March 5, 1919, 3–4; TsDNISO, f. 200, op. 1, d. 55, ll. 23–27; f. 151/95, op. 2, d. 41, ll. 2–3; op. 2, d. 16, ll. 12–13; and op. 1, d. 48, ll. 17–20.

[45] *ISS*, no. 37, Feb. 16, 1919, 4.

Since many young peasants had been drafted, older male peasants espousing "nonparty" views once again populated the soviets. However, volost soviet assemblies fell under the control of their executive committees and party cells after the former were declared the highest authority at the volost level in December 1919. The volispolkomy were to be elected for six months by volost congresses of soviets and were to comprise three to six members. Designed to manage local affairs between volost congresses, the committees became more bureaucratized, and more Communist in membership as the number of Bolshevik representatives rose from 52.9 percent in the spring of 1919 to 66.7 percent that autumn.[46]

Despite the concentration of Communists in the volispolkomy, they did not always promote the interests of Soviet power,[47] displaying "Schwekian" forms of resistance. Balashov and Atkarsk authorities, for example, complained of the "criminal inactivity of the volost and village executive committees," of their avoiding collection of a special tax on the "bourgeois-kulak element in the villages." Ubiquitous samogon brewing fell under fire, as did speculation in grain, meat, "and everything that can be speculated in." Rural party cells flooded soviets with requests for help in rooting out these phenomena, but "the soviets absolutely ignore[d]" them, "thereby forcing the cells to fight independently, which always results in enormous misunderstandings and clashes with kulaks." Exhibiting a common resistance strategy of subordinates, one volost representative claimed he knew nothing of the tax, or of the separation of church and state, because he was "not a specialist." Elsewhere a Communist-dominated volispolkom was replaced, since "the old ispolkom was too rude and was unable to deal with the peasants." Whenever Communists fell under fire, the party explained these shortcomings by pinning the blame for them on those who joined the party "not in the interests of Soviet power, but in their own interest and even in the interests of the White Guard attacking Red Russia." That is, Soviet power was satisfactory and Communists honestly served it; those who did not were really not Communists, and therefore Soviet power was not to blame for the problems.[48]

Communists may have predominated numerically in the volost soviets, but they remained under siege. Complaints rang out in Atkarsk about "lack of experienced people," and about how local congresses of soviets made up of "kulaks" "threw aside their restraint," "badgering

---

[46] See GA RF, f. 393, op. 13, d. 618, ll. 8–11; GASO, f. 456, op. 1, d. 211, l. 1; and Figes, *Peasant Russia*, 206–23.

[47] GA RF, f. 393, op. 3, d. 331, ll. 21–21 ob.

[48] GASO, f. 456, op. 1, d. 205, l. 51.

Communists relentlessly." "The middle peasants were fooled and deceived by the kulaks and they too turned against the Communists." The Communists' opponents, however, did not want to serve in the volispolkomy, as a result of which many Communists were reelected.[49] In the fall 1922 elections, Communists captured about half of the seats in the volispolkomy, which functioned in isolation from the villages they purportedly served.

Even though the number of Communists elected at the volost level increased in 1919, party representation remained insignificant or nonexistent in village soviets, which, on average, comprised ten members representing seven hundred peasants. Developing in an ad hoc fashion, most village soviets did not get set up until late 1918 or early 1919, and initially did not mark a break from traditional forms of village governance. Not surprisingly, 97.7 percent of the soviets' members were male peasants; 86.3 percent did not belong to any (legal) party and only 10.2 percent classified themselves as Communists or sympathizers. Although the deputies manifested the educational backwardness of the countryside, they were better educated than their fellow villagers.[50] Some villages did not elect a single Communist in either the May or December 1919 elections;[51] one village elected to its soviet individuals who had taken part in anti-Soviet disturbances earlier.[52] Elsewhere, abysmally low voter turnout suggests widespread apathy.[53] In some Atkarsk villages voter turnout was minimal, whereas in others the entire or vast majority of the population voted, and often for RCs. Women participated in elections in some villages, but usually only when they served as heads of households.[54] The Volsk newspaper observed that "in essence, there are no village soviets," for "chairmen" had merely replaced elders.[55] In 1920–21, Communists complained that "White Guard elements and illiterate peasants" or kulaks controlled the soviets and removed Communists from them.[56] Yet after the Civil War ended demobilized soldiers constituted the majority of deputies in village soviets and volispolkomy, a development suggesting how the party ultimately gained influence

---

[49] *ISS*, no. 177, Aug. 14, 1919, 1, and GASO, f. 521, op. 1, d. 549, ll. 1–3.

[50] Figes, *Peasant Russia*, 206–23, and his "The Village and Volost Soviet Elections of 1919," *Soviet Studies* 40, no. 1, (1988): 21–24.

[51] *Kommuna*, no. 39 (108), June 22, 1919, 3; *ISS*, no. 287, Dec. 24, 1919, 4; and RGASPI, f. 17, op. 5, d. 200, l. 11.

[52] *KG*, no. 305, March 12, 1919, 4.

[53] GASO, f. 456, op. 1, d. 179, l. 22.

[54] TsDNISO, f. 200, op. 1, d. 66, ll. 1–11, 17–18, and f. 1837, op. 1, d. 1, l. 24.

[55] *Rabochii i krest'ianin*, no. 177, Aug. 8, 1919, 2.

[56] GASO, f. 456, op. 1, d. 413, ll. 16–16 ob; *Sovetskaia derevnia*, no. 7, Jan. 7, 1921, 4; and *Bor'ba*, no. 123, June 7, 1920, 2.

over the countryside. However, these soviets rarely met; their members were dispersed, and peasants remained indifferent to them. "Power" often was in the hands of the soviets' secretaries simply because they were literate.[57]

Examination of rural Communist Party cells reveals a similar pattern. In October 1917 not a single cell existed in Saratov's villages. In June 1918 the provincial party organization created a department for work in the villages, which formed cells in conjunction with the establishment of the kombedy. There were 191 cells at year's end. After the Eighth Party Congress launched the controversial policy of conciliation vis-à-vis the middle peasant, the department established new cells, often comprised of marginalized elements, including schoolteachers.[58] The party's decision in late 1918 to abolish the kombedy, restrict the activities of the Cheka, tolerate some forms of political pluralism, and accommodate the middle peasant, however, undermined the cells.[59] For example, the local press now lavished attention on the party's newfound friend in the countryside, the middle peasant, castigated capricious requisitions and levies, and admitted that the peasant had good cause to loathe Red commissars,[60] resulting in the collapse of many rural party cells.[61] Furthermore, with the defeat of the Whites at the end of 1919 a militant mood prevailed within the party, which, in desperate need of food, squeezed the villages even more, delivering "a new blow" to the countryside. At the same time, party reregistration caused a drop in the number of party members in rural areas by 30–35 percent and more.[62] While the peasantry understood the significance of the victory over the Whites, the party's policy of courting the peasantry when survival was at stake, followed by a new arrogance once the Whites went down in defeat, taught the peasants to mistrust their rulers.

Examples drawn from Atkarsk illustrate that party cells often had little interaction with village soviets in the hands of RCs. Government policies, the behavior of Red Army units, and populist propaganda caused villagers "to hate the Bolsheviks," whom they looked upon as

[57] *ISS*, no. 103, May 19, 1921, 1, and RGASPI, f. 17, op. 14, d. 658, l. 116 ob.

[58] TsDNISO, f. 27, op. 2, d. 867, l. 3, and RGASPI, f. 17, op. 6, d. 277, l. 8.

[59] *Izvestiia Balashovskogo uispolkoma*, no. 83, April 16, 1919, 2; and RGASPI, f. 17, op. 6, d. 277, l. 9.

[60] See *KG*, no. 317, March 30, 1919, 1; no. 334, April 24, 1919, 4; *ISS*, no. 85, April 24, 1919, 1; *Golos kommunista*, no. 120, May 15, 1919, 2; and no. 125, May 20, 1919, 2.

[61] Suslov, *Sotsialisticheskie partii*, 11–13; Starikov, *Demokraticheskaia revoliutsiia*, 113; TsDNISO, f. 27, op. 1, d. 989, l. 71; RGASPI, f. 17, op. 5, d. 77, l. 9; and *ISS*, no. 116, May 30, 1920, 3.

[62] *Novyi mir*, no. 2, Feb. 14, 1920, 3, and RGASPI, f. 17, op. 5, d. 27, l. 120.

robbers.[63] And no wonder. Identical in composition to the kombedy, the "arbitrary" and "totally confused" cells comprised shopkeepers, "kulaks," and many who joined the Communists "in order to escape punishment for their crimes." Communists in Berezovsk raped the wives of Red Army soldiers. Cell members at times got control of the best parcels of land during redistribution, although much of it remained unworked. There is abundant evidence documenting the party cells and executive committees' use of force, illegal requisitions, sending troops against peasants, apathy, incompetence, samogon production, and drunkenness.[64] Concluding that there were "no committed Communists in the district" and fearing an uprising, the party called for disbanding *all* local party cells, holding free elections to rural executive committees, redistributing land, and supplying the villages with basic necessities.[65] The party believed the peasants were better disposed toward them after the purge of 1919,[66] but more critical reports temper the sanguine, most likely exaggerated, ones.[67]

In Volsk peasants obstructed the election of kombedy, chastising Communist Party cells whose hard-drinking and freewheeling members interfered with rural soviets. In October 1919 the party recognized 38 village cells with 692 members, evaluating its work in the Volsk countryside as "poor": cells collapsed owing to repeated mobilizations; they conducted no work on communal farms and little among the rural youth. The cells also had to compete with the RCs. However, it is difficult to generalize, for as late as January 1920 not a single political meeting of any sort had been held since the start of the revolution in the village of Teplovka, located outside Volsk![68] Peasant ill will and frequent mobilizations kept party cells ineffectual throughout 1920, as soviets hid deserters and shunned labor conscription and other unpopular policies through foot-dragging and equivocating. Desperate party cell members began to echo peasant demands for manufactured goods needed in the

[63] TsDNISO, f. 200, op. 1, d. 16, l. 22 ob, 35–35 ob, 53–53 ob; f. 1837, op. 1, d. 2, l. 1 ob; d. 3, ll. 15–22; and RGASPI, f. 282, op. 1, d. 1, l. 31.

[64] GASO, f. 456, op. 1, d. 218, l. 103; TsDNISO, f. 200, op. 1, d. 358, l. 121; f. 200, op.1, d. 92, ll. 9–9 ob; f. 1837, op. 1, d. 5, l. 6; *Izvestiia g. Atkarska*, no. 47, Sept., 1918, 4; and Berelovich and Danilov, *Sovetskaia derevnia*, 1: 160.

[65] GASO, f. 456, op. 1, d. 218, l. 88.

[66] TsDNISO, f. 27, op. 1, d. 989, ll. 8–9; *ISS*, no. 6, Jan. 10, 1920, 3; no. 27, Feb. 5, 1920, 4; *Izvestiia Atkarskogo Ispolnitel'nogo komiteta*, no. 386, Dec. 27, 1919, 4.

[67] RGASPI, f. 17, op. 5, d. 201, ll. 5–5 ob, and *ISS*, no. 120, June 2, 1920, 2.

[68] TsDNISO, f. 27, op. 1, d. 989, l. 9; op. 11, d. 202, l. 41; *ISS*, no. 123, June 5, 1920, 3; *Rabochii i krest'ianin*, no. 13 (308), Jan. 18, 1919, 2; no. 97, May 4, 1919, 3; no. 99, May 7, 1919, 2; and no. 100, May 8, 1919, 2.

villages, or else urged unleashing the Cheka on the villages to root out populist influence. Large numbers withdrew from the party.[69]

Information from other uezds shows that party cells never got established on a solid foundation during the Civil War, because they lacked committed Communists and backed unpopular policies. Whatever attraction there might have been for marginalized village elements to accept symbolic incorporation into the Bolsheviks' dominant ideology was often countered by the pull of village cohesion that centered on rejecting Communism's intrusion. Peasant malevolence toward Soviet power found expression in the refrain "we'll all become Communists and there will be no one left to sow." Moreover, many of those who enrolled in the party had done so "for the wrong reasons,"[70] and their actions damaged the reputation of Soviet power. Only 5 percent of rural cell members were committed Communists; the rest were "tsarist stooges."[71] The further away from Saratov a village was situated, the more likely its governing bodies comprised peasants unreceptive to Soviet policies.[72] Disagreements over mobilizations and requisitions at times drove these cells into the underground.[73] In some villages, "kulaks" organized Communist cells (at times clashing with rival cells) in order to bend governmental policies in their favor. In such cases they withdrew from the party just as readily when demands were placed on them.[74] Viewing circumstances through the ideological lens of party discourse does not prevent us from imagining village realities. A report concludes that wherever party cells were "on top of the situation" peasants tended to be satisfied; elsewhere, however, they had to endure a "bacchanalia of dictators and petty tyrants, drunk with power."[75] Rural party cells were in a state of collapse by late 1920;[76] not a single party cell existed in one of the province's largest villages, Bazarnyi Karabulak. By Civil War's end, the party's grip on the countryside remained limited to the administrative functions of soviets, while the traditional village commune continued to regulate land and other important social relations. The vil-

---

[69] *Rabochii i krest'ianin*, no. 100, May 11, 1920, 2; no. 101, May 12, 1920, 1; no. 111, May 25, 1920, 2; no. 113, May 27, 1920, 2; no. 114; *Vlast' sovetov*, no. 189, Aug. 28, 1920, 2; and RGASPI, f. 17, op. 5, d. 27, l. 119.

[70] Suslov, *Sotsialisticheskie partii*, 14–15.

[71] RGASPI, f. 17, op. 5, d. 201, l. 6.

[72] *ISS*, no. 101, Aug. 31, 1919, 2.

[73] *Kommuna*, no. 39 (108), June 22, 1919, 3; *Golos kommunista*, no. 51 (88), Feb. 14, 1919, 3; no. 142, June 11, 1919, 3; TsDNISO, f. 27, op. 1, d. 989, l. 11; and GASO, f. 456, op. 1, d. 218, ll. 103 ob-104.

[74] TsDNISO, f. 27, op. 1, d. 46, l. 14, and Suslov, *Sotsialisticheskie partii*, 14–15.

[75] GASO, f. 456, op. 1, d. 218, l. 89, and Suslov, *Sotsialisticheskie partii*, 19.

[76] TsDNISO, f. 27, op. 1, d. 725, l. 2; *Serp i molot*, no. 200 (484), Sept. 17, 1920, 1; and *ISS*, no. 116, May 30, 1920, 3.

lages were divided into two unequal camps: a handful of Communists and a vast sea of nonparty peasants. No one made any effort to bridge the two. Believing that the "Jews in power" bore responsibility for the government's antivillage attitudes,[77] peasants retreated into their world of tradition in a furtive effort to survive, seeking to have the conflicts of urban Russia intrude as little as possible into their lives, except for the restoration of the old market nexus.

The Experiment with Collectivized Agriculture

During the Civil War the Communist Party promoted a variety of collective farming endeavors: communes (*kommuny*, not to be confused with the village mir) or collective farms (*kolkhozy*); artels; and in 1920, partnerships (*tovarishchestva*). Communist themselves did not always understand the differences among these various forms,[78] and the peasants distrusted all of them, particularly the communes, which were the most "socialistic" or "collective" and idealistic. Never comprising more than 4 percent of the arable land in the province, the collective experiment failed disastrously, deepening the peasantry's mistrust of Soviet power. Located on confiscated latifundia, church, and monastery lands plus allotment land of the poor, the farms tended to be small in size, with communes averaging 205 desiatinas and artels 123 desiatinas. In 1919 the average kolkhoz had 73 members and the artel 89 members; these numbers declined by 1921.[79] The first commune appeared in March 1918 and the first artels in September.[80] By September 1920 there were 70 communes and 298 artels in Saratov, with 5,585 and 25,758 members respectively.[81]

---

[77] TsDNISO, f. 27, op. 2, d. 310, l. 4; f. 27, op. 2, d. 43, l. 122; and *Serp i molot*, no. 80, July 7, 1922, 1.

[78] N. S. Vlasov, *Kolkhozy i kooperativy Saratovskoi gubernii* (Volsk, 1925), 8; P. F. Iakovlev, "Komitety derevenskoi bednoty v Saratovskoi gubernii," *Trudy Saratovskogo sel'skokhoziaistvennogo instituta* 10 (1957): 351–70; and B. N. Knipovich, *Ocherk deiatel'nosti Narodnogo Komissariata Zemledeliia za tri goda (1917–1920)* (n.p., 1920), 10–21.

[79] S. Pskovskii, *Kollektivizatsiia zemledeliia v Saratovskoi gubernii* (Saratov, 1919), 3, 4–5, 9, 13–14; Vlasov, *Kolkhozy*, 17; S. Pskovskii, "Kollektivizatsiia zemledeliia v Saratovskoi gubernii," *Ekonomicheskaia zhizn'*, no. 2 (Saratov, 1919): 33; and P. T. Gubenko, "Iz istorii sovkhoznogo stroitel'stva v pervye gody Sovetskoi vlasti (1917–1920 gg)," *Trudy Saratovskogo instituta mekhanizatsii sel. khoz.*, no. 12 (1958): 3–5.

[80] Rashitov, "Sovety," 336; "K istorii vozniknoveniia sel'sko-khoziaistvennykh kommun i artelei v SSSR (1918 g.)," *Krasnyi arkhiv*, no. 4 (101) (1940): 139; and "Sotsialisticheskie formy sel'skogo khoziaistva v 1918–1919 gg," *Krasnyi arkhiv*, no. 5 (96) (1939): 3–54.

[81] *Ekonomicheskaia zhizn'*, no. 1–2 (1920): 22.

Local peasants loathed the communes, in part because the first collective farmers were newcomers to the area, workers fleeing the cities, and refugees. For example, a collective venture in Balashov Uezd comprised over 600 people, mainly old party workers and their families from Petrograd and Moscow. Roughly one thousand female factory workers from Ivanovo-Voznesensk lived on a commune in Petrovsk. Party literature aimed at them emphasized that, as workers, they were more politically conscious than peasant farmers, a point that made them no more willing to accept the grim conditions of the collective.[82]

Poor leadership and the belief of those working on the farms that the fruits of their labors belonged to them and not to the state plagued the communes. The inability to adjust to communal life and bickering among women proved to be the two most important reasons for expelling individuals from them. Although some communal farms merged, more were liquidated, mainly due to internal squabbling.[83] The farms also fell under the influence of bureaucrats appointed by the Center, not all of whom supported Soviet power.[84] A study from 1920 emphasized the shortage of workers owing to mobilization and lack of plans, basic necessities, equipment, instructors, etcetera. Late planting and improper harvesting resulted in tremendous waste, as did lack of initiative. Poorly supplied, those on the collective farms often lived in awful conditions.[85]

Despite the notions of dreamy-eyed intellectuals, the peasantry rejected the collective principle, making their hostility toward the farms almost legendary.[86] Perhaps because of their power over the domestic sphere, peasant women were especially suspicious of collective efforts. Peasants spread an array of rumors about the communes' "true" intentions. Representing them as a sinful ploy to lead honest Orthodox folk astray, peasants repeated the refrain "We are for the Bolsheviks, but we don't want any communes," and "Long live the Bolsheviks and soviets. Beat the Communists!"[87] Peasants torched the buildings of one farm.[88] Some communal farmers had to go to their fields armed with rifles. By early 1920 local authorities recognized that the communes' enormous

---

[82] *Izvestiia g. Balashova*, no. 198, Oct. 1918, 3; *ISS*, no. 287, Dec. 24, 1918, 4; and TsDNISO, f. 27, op. 1, d. 993, ll. 1, 3.

[83] TsDNISO, f. 27, op. 1, d. 993, ll. 1, 3; *Kolkhozy*, 42; "Sotsialisticheskie formy," 17; and Pskovskii, "Kollektivizatsiia," 31.

[84] *ISS*, no. 122, June 12, 1919, 1.

[85] TsDNISO, f. 27, op. 1, d. 989, ll. 37, 39 ob, 54, and *ISS*, no. 149, July 13, 1919, 2.

[86] Vlasov, *Kolkhozy*, 41.

[87] *Izvestiia Serdobskogo Soveta*, no. 29, Aug. 16, 1919, 2; *Izvestiia Atkarska*, no. 283, Aug. 1919, 3; *ISS*, no. 149, July 13, 1919, 2; Suslov, *Politicheskie partii*, 15; Charles R. Buxton, *In a Russian Village* (London, 1922), 42–43.

[88] *Serp i molot*, no. 84, April 28, 1920, 1; *Golos Kommunista*, no. 138, June 5, 1919, 4; and "Sotsialisticheskie formy," 16.

failure had further alienated the peasantry,[89] who compared the poor performance of the communes with the former landlords' success.[90] In fact, the experience of the collective farmers turned some of them against collective ventures; demands from within to leave in order to set up private farms rose at this time.[91] Tapping the peasantry's antipathy toward the communes, peasant bandits destroyed them whenever they encountered the farms.[92]

"Communist Cells . . . Operate in What Is a Conquered Country"

Any definition of "peasant" must allow room for the dynamic interaction between the village and the outside world, the boundaries of which were pliable and frequently renegotiated. In determining the party's policies in the villages, the ideology of Bolshevism as well as a strain in Russian intellectual life that viewed the countryside in a negative light often blinded the Bolsheviks to this reality. In fact, the language they used in describing the peasantry bears some striking similarities to the language of colonialism.[93] Acting as if it expected the peasantry to have an intuitive understanding of what a Marxist revolution was all about, the party explained peasant hostility as the consequence of the "low cultural level" in the villages, "political illiteracy," and the "lure of private property." Depicting the villages as "disorganized" and the peasants as "poor and ignorant know-nothings" who did not read newspapers and who lacked "consciousness," Communists blamed the "darkness" of the village for the peasants' antipathy toward Soviet power, susceptibility to rumors, and failure to appreciate the imminence of world revolution.[94] They understood that the peasantry demonstrated little interest in Communism, seeking solace in the argument that economic ruin caused the peasantry's lack of enthusiasm. That is, if Communism had worked, the peasantry would have been all for it. These rhetorical strategies framed the party's efforts to take the political pulse of the countryside, a task made complicated by the party's own flip-flops in policy.

Ideology also drove the Bolsheviks to find political solutions to the peasants' reluctance to turn over bread without a goods exchange. Declaring the battle for bread a form of class war, the Communists used

[89] *Rabochii i krest'ianin*, no. 92, April 29, 1920, 2, and no. 83, April 18, 1920, 1.

[90] RGASPI, f. 17, op. 5, d. 201, ll. 66–66 ob.

[91] *ISS*, no. 151, July 15, 1919, 2, and Figes, *Peasant Russia*, 130.

[92] Vlasov, *Kolkhozy*, 26.

[93] See, for example, Comaroff and Comaroff, *Ethnography*, 42.

[94] *KG*, no. 103, July 15, 1918, 4, and *ISS*, no. 62, March 23, 1919, 3.

state power to force unfavorable rules of exchange on the peasants. Gouldner sees this as internal colonialism because the Bolsheviks linked periods of "peaceable" administration with periods of violence, "treating them as part of a single process of domination which one may alternately impose on another." Some historians have acknowledged that this experience "left a readiness for a militant, authoritarian voluntarism,"[95] while others see the roots of Stalinism in the antipeasant, antimarket prejudices of the Marxist intelligentsia.[96]

The grammar of social intercourse between the party-state and the peasantry revealed itself in peasant uprisings in 1918 and in the miserable failure of the kombedy. Naturally, the party expected that its new policy in the countryside in 1919 would change for the better its relations with the peasants. Cheka reports do document an improvement in peasant attitudes toward Soviet power in early 1919, but ironically, for the wrong reasons: lack of clarity in government decrees, the creative interpretation of them in the villages, and Saratov's incidental ties with the locales.[97] There were more sanguine reports, too, which Pavel Lebedev dismissed as the misguided strategy of incompetent instructors who often recounted that all was well. Admonishing the party to uphold its union with the middle peasants, he charged that the party's squeezing of the peasants with an iron fist had provoked the uprisings against Soviet power:[98]

> The peasantry is well-to-do, the prominent middle peasant prevails, the poor peasant as a separate group does not exist. There are a handful, but with rare exception they haven't the slightest influence on the rest. The burdens the peasantry has to bear — mobilization, obligation to provide transport, and so on — breed dissatisfaction, yet with a correct and clear explanation the peasantry accepts the situation and so far cannot, under any circumstances, be called counterrevolutionary. The activities of local Communist cells and volost executive committees comprised of them, however, give rise to real animosity. These cells operate in what is a *conquered country*, treating everyone as kulaks and counterrevolutionaries with requisitions, confiscations, and widespread robbery as well as all sorts of other violence.[99]

The subsequent unleashing of peasant anger against Soviet power reflects the veracity of Lebedev's report, but also that his remarks went

---

[95] Alvin W. Gouldner, "Stalinism: A Study of Internal Colonialism," in *Political Power and Social Theory: A Research Manual* (Greenwich, Conn., 1978), 216, 238. The quote is by Robert Tucker, cited in Gouldner, 212. See also Leonov, *Rozhdenie*, 183.

[96] See Aleksandr Tsipko, "O zonakh, zakrytykh dlia mysli," *Nauka i zhizn'* (November 1988): 45–55, and Andrea Graziosi, *The Great Soviet Peasant War: Bolsheviks and Peasants, 1917–1933* (Cambridge, Mass., 1996).

[97] TsDNISO, f. 27, op. 1, d. 38, l. 147, and *Vos'moi s"ezd*, 395.

[98] GA RF, f. 1235, op. 93, d. 493, ll. 44, 48, 48 ob, 49, 49 ob, 50, 50 ob.

[99] Emphasis added. GA RF, f. 393, op. 3, d. 327, l. 270, also ll. 117–18, 119 ob–20.

unheeded by the party,[100] which maintained that Denikin's excursion into the province had made the peasantry positively disposed toward Soviet power, that desertion and the production of samogon had abated, and that village communities now plowed the fields of Red Army soldiers.[101] Yet confidential reports observed that the peasants remained dissatisfied, sending non-Communist deputies to local congresses when they did not have the option of electing Revolutionary Communists. Moreover, peasants failed to comprehend why factories were not producing goods needed in the villages. Pointing to the eight-hour day as proof of the party's unfair policies, they excoriated workers who had fled to the villages with stolen factory goods to exchange for food.[102]

In 1919 forced requisitioning replaced the heretofore haphazard approach to obtaining grain deliveries, coinciding with Moscow's removal of local leaders and the appointment of Radus-Zenkovich, who saw no need to court the middle peasants, despite party rhetoric to the contrary. Discontent stemming from unfair quotas and from confiscations surfaced immediately, as a result of which punitive measures proved necessary to realize the state's objectives.[103] A commission concluded that the food supply organs demanded more than the peasants could afford to turn over and that estimates of surpluses had been too high. The Communists also blamed low collection levels on the failure of party propaganda, the peasant's oppositional mood, anti-Soviet agitation, the interference of rival agencies, and overall conditions. Nonetheless, Saratov leaders determined that coercion must be applied to confiscate grain from "kulaks."[104] Anticipating the consequences, one confidential report predicted that "the villages soon will be against Soviet power, or at least against that form found in the villages." In June the Cheka arrested or removed authorities in volosts where peasants supplied grain slowly, while troops and workers' brigades extracted grain from peasants.[105]

The most outrageous application of force involved an armed unit of the province's food supply committee under the command of N. A.

[100] TsDNISO, f. 27, op. 1, d. 103, l. 15; GA RF, f. 393, op. 3, d. 330, ll. 214–15; GASO, f. 456, op. 1, d. 218, ll. 91, 95 ob.

[101] *Izvestiia Atkarskogo Ispolnitel'nogo komiteta*, no. 370, Dec. 9, 1919, 4; *ISS*, no. 193, Sept. 3, 1919, 3; no. 209, Sept. 21, 1919, 3; no. 211, Sept. 24, 1919, 2; no. 235, Oct. 23, 1919, 3; no. 236, Oct. 24, 1919, 3. See GASO, f. 523, op. 4, d. 16, l. 17; TsDNISO, f. 27, op. 1, d. 199, ll. 29–31; and d. 236, l. 20.

[102] *Znamia revoliutsii*, no. 1, Sept. 5, 1919, 1; GASO, f. 456, op. 1, d. 206, ll. 1–8.

[103] Radus-Zen'kovich, *Stranitsy*, 37; GASO, f. 521, op. 1, d. 359, ll. 1–6; *ISS*, no. 196, Sept. 21, 1919, 3.

[104] GA RF, f. 9591, op. 1, d. 65, ll. 1–12; GASO, f. 456, op. 1, d. 218, ll. 16, 18; d. 157, l. 55; *ISS*, no. 135, June 27, 1919, 3; no. 203, Sept. 14, 1919, 4; and TsDNISO, f. 27, op. 1, d. 758, l. 4.

[105] GASO, f. 456, op. 1, d. 218, ll. 87–88; f. 521, op. 1, d. 550, ll. 1–3; GA RF, f. 1235, op. 13, d. 493, ll. 17–18, 22–23; and *Krasnyi pakhar'*, no. 250, Dec. 14, 1919, 3.

Cheremukhin in the summer of 1919, which violently struck out against desertion and the brewing of samogon in Balashov. Known in party circles for his "tact, experience . . . and devotion to the interests of the Revolution," Cheremukhin torched 283 households in the village of Malinovka. Applying "revolutionary justice," he confiscated "kulak property," levied contributions on entire villages that participated in anti-Soviet uprisings, and shot "active opponents of Soviet power, deserters, kulaks, and chronic brewers of moonshine." Between July and September his forces executed 139 people in an attempt to break the spirit of those opposed to Soviet decrees. Party members, non-Communists, and Red Army units protested Cheremukhin's repression, while RCs accused Cheremukhin of threatening party members and shooting them without justification.[106] But Radus-Zenkovich protected him from the Central Committee and Cheka, insisting that Cheremukhin's detachment was a model of discipline and restraint, and that he "did not use force at all."[107] This unsavory episode and others like it made it certain that local peasants would welcome armed peasant bands bent on overthrowing Bolshevik power, despite propaganda campaigns targeting the countryside,[108] and claims at the end of 1920 that the peasantry's mood was "better than a year ago."[109] Such rhetoric eschewed mention of the savage force used to fulfill requisitioning quotas, and lulled the party into a false sense of complacency just as peasant bands swept through the province. Moreover, despite its awareness of the mediocre harvest, lack of surpluses, and the peasantry's willingness to meet quotas when goods were available for exchange, the party's fateful decision to employ force to secure its quotas contributed to the famine of 1921–22.[110]

Peasants in the Red Army

Mandatory service in the army also turned the countryside against the Communists. As background, between November 1917 and April 1918 at least 1.8 million soldiers from the front inundated the garrisons of the Kazan Military District, Russia's largest, where circumstances compelled local authorities to carry out demobilization independently. The

---

[106] GASO, f. 521, op. 1, d. 445, ll. 4–6, 19–21, 59, 76, 85, 102; f. 521, op. 1, d. 445, ll. 60–61 ob, 63–63 ob, 67; and TsDNISO, f. 151/95, op. 2, d. 8, l. 17.

[107] See Pavliuchenkov, *Voennyi kommunizm*, 208–11, and Radus-Zen'kovich, *Stranitsy*, 39.

[108] TsDNISO, f. 27, op. 1, d. 993, ll. 17–18, and RGASPI, f. 17, op. 5, d. 123, ll. 2, 14–14 ob.

[109] *Oktiabr'skaia revoliutsiia*, no. 254, Dec. 8, 1920, 3.

[110] GASO, f. 521, op. 1, d. 470, ll. 43–43 ob, and *ISS*, no. 228, Oct. 9, 1920, 3.

Saratov Soviet was unusual in setting up a special department to demobilize its garrison, and to cobble together units to ward off the Cossack threat. Yet the process resulted in clashes with the troops, especially over the control of armaments, as evacuated soldiers deserted en masse. While soldiers played a decisive role in tipping the scales in favor of the Bolsheviks, the union of frontoviki likewise made demands on the soviets and took part in uprisings in several towns, including Saratov. Hard pressed to satisfy the recalcitrant troops, the soviet disbanded the union in March 1918.[111]

In early 1918 agents arrived from the Center to assist the soviet in setting up Red Army units, and at the end of May the government drafted males aged twenty-one to twenty-five. Fearing that mass conscription would turn the countryside against Soviet power, the local party committee mobilized volunteers and then workers, resolving to extend the draft to the uezds only if the political mood warranted it. Despite the press's reports that workers responded favorably to the summons, only 1,864 volunteers signed up, and plans to extend the draft outside the city had to be scrapped. When full-scale civil war forced the government to draft peasants at the same time that it implemented other unpopular measures, the number of peasant disturbances shot up.[112] Be that as it may, by late 1919 the Saratov Military Department had formed ninety-six units, drafting 178,089 males, mostly peasants (figure 10.2). The authorities also mobilized 13,519 horses and a large number of carts and harnesses from local peasants.[113]

Peasant war-weariness and hostility toward serving in the army fueled uprisings against Soviet power, resulting in desertion rates of immense proportions. In September 1918 two newly formed units of the "People's Army" refused to go to the front, while mutinies broke out in other units. In early 1919 half of the local reserve battalion in Atkarsk deserted and recently mobilized German peasants rose up in Privolnoe. Fresh recruits rioted in Petrovsk, where the Cheka introduced martial law and resorted to gunfire to save the life of the Bolshevik Kosterin. Owing to lack of resources, the party failed to sustain "cultural work"

---

[111] S. I. Ionenko, "Likvidatsiia staroi armii v tylovykh okrugakh, oktiabr' 1917 g.-aprel' 1918 g.: Po materialam Kazanskogo voennogo okruga" (candidate diss. Saratov State University, 1982), 89–113, 121, 133–36, 166–72, and GA RF, f. 393, op. 3, d. 327, l. 64.

[112] Although a fire destroyed many of the pertinent archival documents, I examined the incomplete doctoral dissertation of V. A. Katkov researched beforehand, hereafter cited as Katkov, "Dissertation." This information is taken from 87–98. See also *ISS*, no. 158, Aug. 6, 1918, 3; no. 159, Aug. 7, 1918, 1; *Izvestiia*, no. 180, Aug. 20, 1918; and *Krasnoarmeets*, no. 1, Oct. 4, 1918, 1–2.

[113] See Katkov, "Dissertation," 98, 132, 135, 248–53, and 254–56, and *ISS*, no. 44, Feb. 24, 1920, 3.

10.2 Soldiers of the Saratov garrison gathered outside their barracks. Courtesy Gosudarstvennyi Arkhiv Saratovskoi Oblasti (GASO).

in the units,[114] or to make good on the paper benefits extended to the families of those drafted (but it overruled a decision to withdraw wages from soldiers hospitalized with venereal disease).[115] Local military authorities arrested commanders for the unsanitary conditions in barracks and for slipshod leadership, yet party internal language acknowledged the "extremely serious situation" in connection with the terrible material conditions, political agitation of the Bolsheviks' opponents, and anger in the countryside over the levying of an extraordinary tax. When an estimated 25,000 troops arrived in Saratov in June without boots, uniforms, and food, they issued an ultimatum that they would seize what they needed from local warehouses. There was no one to stop them.[116]

Desertion rates skyrocketed in connection with the White offensive, and when Denikin approached Balashov, peasants welcomed him as a liberator. Local authorities now resolved to take "merciless measures" against deserters, sending special units to Balashov, Volsk, and Saratov Uezds to deal with the problem. They punished those who harbored deserters, carried out roundups to catch those who had fled their units, and offered a series of grace periods whereby soldiers who had gone AWOL could turn themselves in without being punished. As a report from Atkarsk put it, "candidly speaking, you can say that there aren't any volunteers in the uezd." In October the military authorities issued documents to those of draft age in an attempt to crack down further on desertion. By November, 63,349 deserters had either been caught or voluntarily returned to their units.[117]

The party applied the most uncompromising measures, including shooting, to the one in thirty deserters it considered dangerous. It targeted its propaganda at the mass of "politically unconscious" peasant-soldiers in an attempt to discredit the widespread belief that Soviet power did not take care of the families of its warriors.[118] Indeed, soldiers deserted because they were concerned about the fate of their loved ones, because of the terrible conditions in the ranks, and because of their

---

[114] *Izvestiia g. Atkarska*, no. 51, Sept. 1918, 2; GASO, f. 521, op. 1, d. 439, ll. 3–3 ob; d. 444, ll. 40, 49; f. 521, op. 6, d. 1, l. 102; TsDNISO, f. 200, op. 1, d. 52, l. 18 and d. 67, l. 2; and *Kommuna*, no. 9 (78), Feb. 6, 1919, 3.

[115] GA RF, f. 393, op. 3, d. 327, l. 142.

[116] GASO, f. 692, op. 1, d. 36, ll. 4, 12, 123, 163; f. 456, op. 1, d. 33, ll. 74–75; TsDNISO, f. 27, op. 1, d. 56, l. 7; and RGASPI, f. 17, op. 6, d. 277, l. 96.

[117] GASO, f. 521, op. 3, d. 15, l. 29; op. 1, d. 420, ll. 2–2 ob; op. 4, d. 2, l. 1; f. 21, op. 1, d. 574, ll. 3 ob–4; f. 521, op. 2, d. 34, l. 93; TsDNISO, f. 200, op. 1, d. 53, l. 95; f. 27, op. 1, d. 202, l. 15; and Radus-Zen'kovich, *Dva goda*, 11–13. For desertion rates throughout the Red Army see Brovkin, *Behind the Front Lines*, 146–47.

[118] GASO, f. 692, op. 1, d. 108, l. 613, also d. 32, ll. 67, 107, 339.

opposition to specific policies such as requisitioning and imposition of the extraordinary tax. The party publicly admitted that the failure of rural soviets to work the fields of Red Army men contributed to the problem, which peaked in August 1919. So too did the vile conditions in military hospitals.[119] The peasant soldier's return to the village at this time is understandable, for in Serdobsk peasants divided up the land of those drafted, explaining that they did so because soldiers' families could not farm it with their own labor.[120]

Related to desertion was the problem of "mutiny," the most publicized case of which involved F. K. Mironov, a Cossack who joined forces with the Reds, but mutinied in August 1919. Tried in Balashov, Mironov, who saw himself as an SR Maximalist and who wanted to launch a Worker-Peasant-Cossack Party, insisted his actions were aimed at saving Soviet power from Denikin. The local press's explanation of what had made Mironov go bad reflects disagreements within the party leadership on its basic policies. In reporting what had driven Mironov into the opposition, the authors of newspaper articles gave some credence to his beliefs by the very fact of mentioning them. A one-time Red hero, Mironov broke with the party over "the behavior of local Communists in the Don" (a euphemism for the party's brutal policy of "decossackization"), over requisitioning, and over the party's "proletarian" policies that alienated the village. Sentenced to death, Mironov later was pardoned and enrolled in the party.[121]

If in early 1920 some reports suggested that desertion was on the decline and measures taken to combat it effective, the rate began to climb again owing to the growing appeal of anarchism and once the authorities began to use military units as work brigades.[122] The antiwar agitation of a group of Moscow anarchists who had moved to Saratov assumed "colossal proportions," alarming the authorities, who noticed a major change in the peasant-soldier's correspondence, which depicted the Bolsheviks as usurpers.[123] A new flood of propaganda tried to convince the peasant that the military entanglements with the Whites *were* the peasants' business. And, in an effort to reduce recidivism, many

[119] *ISS*, no. 171, Aug. 7, 1919, 2; no. 174, Aug. 10, 1919, 1; see also no. 182, Aug. 20, 1919, 2; no. 184, Aug. 22, 1919, 4; GASO, f. 456, op. 1, d. 8, l. 182.

[120] *Izvestiia Serdobskogo Soveta*, no. 18, Aug. 3, 1919, 2.

[121] See, for instance, *ISS*, no. 225, Oct. 11, 1919, 1; no. 231, Oct. 18, 1919, 2; *Krasnyi pakhar'*, no. 201, Oct. 8, 1919, 2–3; and no. 202, Oct. 9, 1919, 2. On decossackization see Holquist, *Making War, Forging Revolution*, chapter 6.

[122] GASO, f. 692, op. 1, d. 78; f. 456, op. 1, d. 413, l. 4; d. 437, ll. 16, 22, 23; f. 521, op. 4, d. 3, l. 1; d. 7, l. 6.

[123] RGASPI, f. 17, op. 12, d. 469, ll. 105–6, and GASO, f. 3310, op. 1, d. 1, ll. 33–35 ob.

deserters, especially older ones, were placed in special guard units not likely to see combat.[124] Despite these measures, desertion soared once again in connection with the Green movement in 1920. All in all, between 1918 and 1920 the authorities identified 101,142 deserters, that is, *over half* of those drafted locally.[125]

Peasant Uprisings

Societies that employ force to extract surpluses from the villages are more vulnerable to revolt than others. Breaking out in mid-1918, and cresting in the Green movement of 1920–22, rebellions against Communist power represented attempts to restore an earlier, partially mythical, time before Soviet power. Although the data do not provide aggregate statistics on the extent of peasant disturbances, they do reveal how violent, widespread, and sustained they were. Lars Lih's view that before the summer of 1920 there were "few significant uprisings in the countryside under permanent Bolshevik control" is simply untenable.[126]

The Soviet government did plenty to drive the peasantry into the opposition as early as 1918. It mobilized peasant youth. It brought in hungry urban workers from the outside to wrench grain from the countryside. It created havoc when it set up the kombedy. It levied an extraordinary tax. It attacked religion. It subjected the peasantry to abuses of power that exceeded anything Saratov's rural inhabitants had experienced before. A confidential circular divulged euphemistically that a major reason for the uprisings was "the lack of tact in the actions of representatives of Soviet power." For example, agents of different Soviet bodies, independently of one another, "literally terrorized the population" of Novouzensk Uezd with their confiscations, requisitions, and use of force.[127]

Beginning in Saratov Uezd in May 1918, disturbances spread to Volsk, Khvalynsk, Serdobsk, Kuznetsk, Atkarsk, Petrovsk, and the German colonies, some fifty volosts in all.[128] Usually the discontent was manifested in the collective action of entire villages. Obsessed with conspiracy, the leadership of the Saratov Soviet depicted the uprisings as part of a chain of anti-Soviet activities caused by "kulaks" and organized by

[124] See GASO, f. 692, op. 1, d. 108, l. 614. See also f. 521, op. 2, d. 41, ll. 1–1 ob. For White propaganda see f. 521, op. 5, d. 5, ll. 2–3 ob.

[125] *ISS*, no. 60, March 14, 1920, 2.

[126] Lih, *Bread and Authority*, 192.

[127] GASO, f. 521, op. 6, d. 1, ll. 7–7 ob, and GA RF, f. 393, op. 3, d. 327, l. 278.

[128] GASO, f. 521, op. 6, d. 1, ll. 51–51 ob; *Godovshchina*, 29; *Na strazhe*, 7; and Suslov, *Sotsialisticheskie partii*, 61.

Right SRs and Mensheviks. Behind the rhetoric was the realization that the seven hundred students and others sent to inventory food supplies represented an army of anti-Soviet agitators. Often employing Hungarian and Latvian units for the purpose, the soviet brutally repressed disturbances, particularly when peasants killed Communists or government agents.[129] In Staraia Topovka, Kamyshin Uezd, Russian and German "kulaks" executed seventeen Communists, after which Red Army investigators shot eighteen leaders, including a priest.[130] They put to death thirty "counterrevolutionaries" in another village.[131] Protesting government policies, peasants in Serdobsk's Bakursk Volost demanded the reelection of the local soviet. When the chairman of the uezd ispolkom, Gubin, and police fired into the air to disperse the crowd of peasants and soldiers, it turned on the Communists, killing them. In retaliation, Red Army units gunned down fifty-eight "kulaks."[132]

In Saratov Uezd, peasant disorders broke out in May, July, September, and November 1918, as a result of grain seizures, squabbles over compiling inventories of grain and livestock, the activities of the kombedy, "counterrevolutionary" agitation, and discontent with Soviet power.[133] Given the mood in the villages, it did not take much to trigger revolt. Banning the sale of new potatoes at the bazaar proved enough to cause some peasants to riot.[134] The most publicized case took place in the large and prosperous village of Alekseevka, where enraged peasants killed and maimed soldiers and the chair of the land department, twelve people in all. Disbanding the local soviet, they destroyed party and military documents, as well as portraits of Lenin and Trotsky, which they replaced with icons. Punitive detachments arrested over 500 villagers, shooting 34 of them. They seized horses and weapons, and left behind a detachment of "no less than 50" to keep order. Less violent uprisings occurred elsewhere.[135]

Disorders flared up throughout 1919, often linked to the same sorts of abuses cited earlier as well as to rampant rumors that Soviet power teetered on the brink of collapse — which it did. Such rumors can be read as an elementary form of disguised resistance that allowed subordi-

[129] GA RF, f. 393, op. 3, d. 327, ll. 37, 40, 43; f. 1235, op. 93, d. 491, ll. 51, 52, 68; and *KG*, no. 139, Aug. 17, 1918, 3–4.

[130] *Izvestiia Kamyshinskogo Soveta*, no. 95, Oct. 11, 1918, 4.

[131] TsDNISO, f. 200, op. 1, d. 5, ll. 5–7.

[132] Ibid., f. 1328, op. 1, d. 49, l. 2–2 ob; GASO, f. 521, op. 6, d. 1, ll. 135–36; and *Golos kommunista*, no. 71 (108), March 9, 1919, 4.

[133] GA RF, f. 393, op. 3, d. 327, l. 255.

[134] Firfanov, "Piat' let bor'by," 31.

[135] GASO, f. 521, op. 5, d. 1, ll. 1–2 ob; op. 5, d. 2, ll. 1–1 ob; op. 6, d. 1, ll. 4, 5, 27, 28, 28 ob, 33–33 ob; and *ISGPK*, no. 23, Dec. 24, 1918, 25.

nates to express aspirations while avoiding individual responsibility.[136] Shortages of every imaginable kind also affected the peasant's mood,[137] promoting bribery and other survival tactics, and elevating the overall level of violence in everyday life.[138] Peasants openly voiced their opposition to the Communists at uezd congresses in early 1919; they demanded the reelection of ispolkomy, clashed with party cells, and blocked attempts to mobilize horses.[139] German farmers killed twenty-three workers from Volsk's cement factories sent to secure surpluses.[140] Wielding farm tools, angry peasants in a Khvalynsk village drove away an armed detachment, which later returned, replenished, to arrest fifteen, whose fate is unknown.[141] Irate peasants in Volsk urged villagers not to give up their surpluses and to protest the war and mobilization, ending their appeal with "down with the Communists."[142] Peasants rebelled in twenty-two volosts of Serdobsk; in Meshchersk they refused to nationalize mills and ignored Soviet decrees.[143] Peasants in the Atkarsk village of Kraishevo fell under the influence of an inebriated peasant, who called for butchering all Communists. When a soldier shot and killed him, peasants brutally murdered agent I. D. Golev and four soldiers, crushing their skulls and beating their bodies beyond recognition. Units arriving the next day arrested thirty-six peasants, who were taken to Saratov and shot, after which "calm" was restored. A secret report concluded that the behavior of local Communists had turned the villagers against the party.[144]

The sources reveal little about peasant attitudes toward the Whites, but it may not be true that the villages hated them even more than they did the Bolsheviks, since the approach of the Whites sometimes emboldened the peasantry. In June 1919 deserters in eleven villages surrounding Arkadak led by former officers and clergy rose up under the banner "down with the war and Communists." In Balashov Uezd peasants car-

---

[136] Scott, *Domination*, 148.

[137] TsDNISO, f. 27, op. 1, d. 199, l. 16 ob; *Serp i molot*, no. 9 (208), Aug. 30, 1919, 2; *ISS*, no. 183, Aug. 21, 1919, 2; no. 287, Dec. 24, 1919, 4; no. 145, July 1, 1920, 2–3; and Antonov-Saratovskii, *Sovety*, 1: 224.

[138] *Izvestiia g. Atkarska*, no. 38, Aug. 1918, 3, and GA RF, f. 393, op. 3, d. 330, l. 32.

[139] See *Krasnaia kommuna* (Atkarsk), no. 151, March 1, 1919, 3–4.

[140] *Izvestiia Ispolkoma Vol'skogo Soveta*, no. 77, April 6, 1919, 1.

[141] GASO, f. 521, op. 6, d. 1, ll. 128–28 ob. Also see GASO f. 456, op. 1, d. 218, l. 25.

[142] Ibid., f. 521, op. 4, d. 7, l. 3. Peasants made anti-Soviet appeals by cutting apart newspaper letters and reassembling them. See GA RF, f. 393, op. 3, d. 332, l. 14.

[143] A. S. Umnov, *Grazhdanskaia voina i srednee krest'ianstvo (1918–1920 gg.)* (Moscow, 1959), 111.

[144] GASO, f. 521, op. 6, d. 1, ll. 153–55; TsDNISO, f. 27, op. 2, d. 1424, l. 4; f. 200, op. 1, d. 67, ll. 5–6; RGASPI, f. 17, op. 5, d. 200, ll. 2–3 ob. See also GASO, f. 521, op. 6, d. 1, ll. 147–47 ob.

ried out reprisals against Communists and government agents. In the village of Pechanka, women rioted to protest the actions of a food brigade. In Saratov, disturbances broke out over mobilization and over religious issues, fueled by rumors that a local peasant had mustered an armed unit ready to overthrow Soviet power.[145] In a Kuznetsk village, peasants armed with pitchforks repelled an attempt to arrest "counterrevolutionary and kulak elements that had raised their heads in the town and uezd." Claiming they were so far away when they squeezed the triggers that they could not see at whom they had fired, soldiers and police shot more than twenty peasants, mainly women.[146]

In the fall of 1919 peasant bands called Greens made up of deserters poured into Balashov and Atkarsk from neighboring Voronezh and Tambov, openly promoting the armed overthrow of Soviet power. Communists went into hiding as village soviets and volispolkomy ceased to function and as deserters appeared in all districts. Special detachments, arriving to "pacify" the peasants, shot innocent folk and pillaged the villages. Local Communists dismissed the peasantry's grievances as "kulak" complaints nurtured by Revolutionary Communists.[147] As if addressing the question of the similarities between Bolshevik policies toward the countryside and colonialism, party instructors reminded agitators that "the countryside was not an occupied country of savages and we are not occupiers."[148] The instructors acknowledged that the food committee agents' outrageous behavior had angered the peasantry, who nonetheless were "revolutionary," "hard working," "conscious," and "responsive." "Everyone works without rest and is willing to give up everything . . . when they're spoken to as human beings"[149]

Throughout 1920 peasants expressed antipathy toward government agents, ignored rulings, or interpreted them in their own interests.[150] Rumors that Soviet power had been overthrown unleashed a flood of anti-Soviet feelings and actions.[151] Village clergy condemned Soviet power,[152] while peasants showed keen interest in private farming, arguing that the smarter and more hard-working peasant tended to be better

---

[145] GASO, f. 521, op. 3, d. 16, l. 147; f. 521, op. 6, d. 1, l. 82; and f. 521, op. 1, d. 444, l. 29.

[146] Ibid., f. 521, op. 1, d. 444, ll. 22–23.

[147] Ibid., f. 521, op. 3, d. 15, ll. 6–8.

[148] Ibid., f. 456, op. 1, d. 218, ll. 89–90 ob.

[149] TsDNISO, f. 27, op. 2, d. 43, l. 7, and f. 151/95, op. 2, d. 37, ll. 21–22.

[150] GASO, f. 502, op. 1, d. 14, ll. 106–7; TsDNISO, f. 200, op. 1, d. 68, ll. 116 ob–117; and *Serp i molot*, no. 10 (24), Jan. 25, 1920, 2.

[151] GASO, f. 456, op. 1, d. 413, ll. 6–16, and RGASPI, f. 17, op. 12, d. 471, ll. 156–56 ob.

[152] TsDNISO, f. 27, op. 2, d. 814, l. 54.

off.[153] Disturbances broke out in a Balashov village over grain policies, and when Communists requisitioned the house of the village priest.[154] The Cheka noted that Atkarsk peasants petitioned local draft boards to release them from military service on religious grounds. Citing a Soviet decree, peasants flooded local people's courts with appeals insisting it was their legal right not to serve in the army.[155] Under anarchist influence, they rose up in Volsk and Atkarsk to protest requisitioning, labor conscription, and—a reminder of the deep cultural divide separating village realities from party ideals—the appointment of women to political posts. Balashov peasants had amassed caches of illegal weapons, including machine guns, and maintained ties with Wrangel's units.[156] Riled by rumors that surpluses would be taken, peasants rebelled in the village of Voskresensk. The mood in Balakovo was "alarming" in January 1921, because of Soviet food policies.[157] It was precisely at this time that local authorities understood the grave threat the Green bands pouring into the province and the circulation of Tolstoyan (pacifist) literature in Serdobsk villages posed for Soviet power.[158]

"No, I Am Not a Kulak"

Saratov peasants also practiced more passive, time-honored forms of resistance as they sought ways to exploit and suborn Soviet institutions for their own ends. For instance, when the Bolsheviks resolved to confiscate the property of 1,305 peasant families in the villages of Alekseevka and Ataevka, Atkarsk Uezd, some of them fired off written appeals to the authorities, insisting they were wrongly accused of being kulaks. Whether or not they were kulaks, according to the objective and subjective criteria of Soviet power, is less interesting than the rhetorical strategies to which they resorted. The formulaic appeals begin with a description of the peasant household in question, number of mouths to feed, size of the farm, and amount of farm animals. The authors note how many sons or grandsons served in the Red Army, how many had perished, and how many family members for whatever reason proved unable to contribute to its livelihood. In other words, they depicted themselves as hardship cases. Insisting they did not turn a profit or en-

---

[153] *Rabochii i krest'ianin*, no. 58, March 14, 1920, 2.

[154] Balashov filial, GASO, f. 27, op. 1, d. 79, ll. 2–2 ob, 77.

[155] Berelovich and Danilov, *Sovetskaia derevnia*, 1: 253.

[156] GASO, f. 3310, op. 1, d. 1, l. 38, and Berelovich and Danilov, *Sovetskaia derevnia*, 1: 325.

[157] GASO, f. 456, op. 1, d. 400, l. 18, and f. 3387, op. 2, d. 1, ll. 6, 7.

[158] *Serp i molot*, no. 94, July 27, 1921, 2.

gage in any suspect business activity, the peasants claimed they handed over surpluses to the state and that the village soviet could vouch for them. A statement such as "I'm horrified" (or surprised, even humored or puzzled) "to find that I'm on a list of kulaks" was accompanied by a "humble" request to "remove this shameful label from me and strike me off the list." The local soviet appended a document of support to each appeal.

After compiling an inventory of their property, some of the petitioners utilized phrases such as "I've always lived poorly, even more poorly than others," "I've lived off my own labor all my life," or worked "with my own callused hands." Others "protested" their "unfair" inclusion on so "shameful" a list, requesting they be called "ordinary citizen." Placing himself somewhere between a poor and middle landholder, one peasant denied he was a kulak because he worked and did not employ (exploit) others. Many authors relied on this strategy, seeking to show that their holdings placed them in the average or even below average categories. Another peasant maintained that he found himself on the list because of mean-spirited, hypocritical people, who looked "only at the brick walls of his house and not at his modest means."[159]

These peasants used the language of Soviet power and the party's own definition of kulak to make a case for themselves, suggesting a shrewd historical agency. They eschewed lodging any other complaints against Soviet power. The village soviets' backing of the appeals indicates that the councils were in the hands of forces in the countryside that might just as easily have found themselves on the list. Moreover, the formulaic quality of the appeals reflects an element of coordination on the peasants' part. Finally, the peasant's own ascription of class was based on the premise that villagers who toiled in the fields and did not rely on hired labor could never be considered kulaks, for it was these qualities that separated the peasant from the world of the former landlord, whose land these "kulaks" had eagerly seized. In ceding the symbolic high ground to Communist values, then, the peasants implicitly critiqued the regime for violating the norms by which it claimed to rule.

Saratov's German Peasants

Saratov's major shopping and commercial street before the Revolution and again today is called German Street, a marker of how the province's German population was and is perceived. While a group of prosperous,

[159] GA RF, f. 9591, op. 1, d. 67, ll. 1–32.

respected urban German families had become fully integrated into the sea of Slavs surrounding them, on the eve of 1914 the majority of Volga Germans remained farmers and handicraftsmen, linked by the market to their larger surroundings, yet separated from the Slavic peasant majority by language, religion, culture, tradition, and economic vitality. During World War I, tsarist decrees threatened confiscation of both land and commercial enterprises, even expulsion to Siberia, as a result of which some Germans began to emigrate. Although the Kerensky government lifted the restrictions placed on the colonists, they saw autonomy as the answer to their problems. Bolshevism struck a responsive chord mostly among German prisoners of war united by the Union of German Socialists of the Volga Region. Other members of the union blamed the Bolsheviks for Russia's political stalemate, maintaining that the Germans' salvation lay in autonomy.[160]

Autonomy was achieved in the wake of a clash between the German village of Shental and the Russian village of Mikhailovka in early 1918 in which forty people met violent deaths.[161] Afterward, Sovnarkom established the Volga Commissariat for German Affairs (*Povolzhskii komissariat po nemetskim delam*) in April 1918, charging it with setting up Soviet power. To facilitate this goal, Moscow sent former prisoners of war to Saratov, including Ernst Reuter, destined to become mayor of West Berlin. But Saratov leaders reacted with hostility to the committee's efforts, resolving to hold elections to local soviets and to convene a congress in Saratov. The gathering's executive committee included a radical majority of Bolsheviks and Left SRs, who did not reflect the true mood in the German districts. Despite Saratov's distrust of the commissariat[162] and intraparty squabbles, the commissariat achieved its goal in October, following months of disturbances in the German communities

---

[160] See F. S. Serebriakov, *Nemetskaia kommuna na Volge, vozrozhdenie iugo-vostoka Rossii* (Moscow, 1922), 7–11; *KG*, no. 34, April 3, 1918, 4. James Long does not accept the argument that the German colonists prospered. See his "Agricultural Conditions in the German Colonies of Novouzensk District, Samara Province, 1861–1914," *Slavonic and East European Review* 57, no. 4 (1979): 531–51. The best general history of the colonies is Long's *From Privileged to Dispossessed: The Volga Germans, 1860–1917* (Lincoln, Neb., 1988). See also Gerhard Bonwetch, *Geschichte der deutschen Kolonien an der Wolga* (Stuttgart, 1919); P. I. Zinner, *Nemtsy Nizhnego Povolzh'ia: Istoricheskii ocherk* (Saratov, 1925); and Johannes Schleuning, *Die deutschen Kolonien im Wolgabiet* (Berlin, 1919). The colonies' relations with Germany during the period is discussed in Alfred Eisfeld, *Deutsche Kolonien an der Wolga 1917–1919 und das Deutsche Reich* (Weisbaden, 1985). For a distorted "Soviet" history of the colonies, see A. K. Airikh, "Trudiashchiesiia nemtsy Povolzh'ia v bor'be za Sovety," *Nizhnee Povolzh'e*, no. 5 (1933): 7–20.

[161] GASO, f. 521, op. 1, d. 181, ll. 41–41 ob.

[162] GA RF, f. 393, op. 3, d. 327, ll. 158–63 ob, 288a, 295.

triggered by the state's food policies. Maintaining that no "real" Soviet power existed in the German villages and that its soviets "were composed of kulaks," the government transferred all of the commissariat's affairs to the Labor Commune of the Volga German Oblast (*Trudovaia kommuna oblasti nemtsev Povolzh'ia*),[163] composed of land from Samara and Saratov Provinces—Novouzensk, Dergachevsk, and Pugachevsk, plus territory from Atkarsk and Kamyshin. (Pokrovsk did not formally become part of the commune until 1922.) Saratov's attempt to block the formation of the commune prompted the German Communists to enlist the help of the Center.[164]

All of these changes occurred against a backdrop of growing resentment toward Soviet power as the Germans reacted violently to requisitioning and mobilization. A major disorder broke out in September 1918, as a result of which thirty-six "colonists" were shot.[165] Another serious uprising over mobilization flared up in Privolnoe in January 1919, resulting in the execution of twenty-five colonists. The Saratov gubispolkom admitted that agitators sent to the Germans were unfamiliar with their traditions and terrorized them. As party activists saw things, the more "advanced" nature of German agriculture and lack of poor elements among the colonists—in other words, their very success—had gotten them into trouble.[166]

The Soviet government's policies prevented any improvement in its relations with German farmers, few of whom joined the Communist Party. Despite propaganda efforts and partial confiscation of property, Germans did not respond favorably to mobilization orders, perhaps, as one agitator recalled, because rumors had it that if the Bolsheviks won the Civil War they would expel the colonists to Germany. Moreover, the families of those serving in the Red Army often lost their land, at least temporarily, suggesting spite within the German villages toward those who complied with mobilization orders. Certainly the fact that not many knew Russian had something to do with the high desertion rates among Germans as well.[167] Large numbers also deserted from German

[163] Ibid., ll. 173, 175–76, 305.

[164] The commune's three German uezds were reconfigured into thirteen cantons (*raionnye*) in the fall of 1919. A. A. German, *Nemetskaia avtonomiia na Volge*, part 1, *Avtonomnaia oblast', 1918–1924* (Saratov, 1992), 67–69. Also see *Sbornik statisticheskikh svedenii po avtonomnoi sotsialisticheskoi sovetskoi respublike nemtsev Povolzh'ia, 1916–1924* (Pokrovsk, 1924), 7–8, 11–12.

[165] Berelovich and Danilov, *Sovetskaia derevnia*, 1: 85–86.

[166] *ISS*, no. 7, Jan. 11, 1919, 3; GA RF, f. 393, op. 3, d. 327, ll. 312–13; German, *Nemetskaia avtonomiia*, 35–38; A. A. German, ed., *Istoriia respubliki nemtsev Povolzh'ia v sobytiiakh, faktakh, dokumentakh* (Moscow, 1996), 150–54.

[167] Firfanov, "Piat' let bor'by," 34–35; GASO, f. 456, op. 1, d. 3, ll. 31–32; and German, *Nemetskaia avtonomiia*, 159–65.

10.3 Starving German peasants abandoning their homes. Courtesy Saratov Kraevedcheskii Museum, photo 10490.

units in the Red Army used to suppress rebellions in Russian villages.[168] The party's requisitioning policies created the most enmity, and German peasants responded in familiar ways: they fed their livestock more, cut back on the amount of land sowed, and fought back. A spate of violent reprisals against Communists broke out across the German territory, inviting the toughest of reprisals.[169] In 1920 disaster struck. A bad harvest accompanied the exhaustion of local reserves and reduction in sown area by 60 percent. Applying "extreme force" to acquire grain, the party nonetheless collected only 1.1 million poods from the oblast by January 1922, by which time 95 percent of the 452,000 Germans were classified as starving (figure 10.3).[170]

Conclusion

The Soviet state made it clear that the peasants could not have their land and farm it as they saw fit, too. The appearance of urban brigades

---

[168] German, *Nemetskaia avtonomiia*, 72–83, 85–89, 90, 176.

[169] GASO, f. 3310, op. 1, d. 1, ll. 14–15.

[170] Serebriakov, *Nemetskaia kommuna*, 11–15; see also the documents in German, *Istoriia respubliki*, 70, 159–65; and E. Gross, *Avtonomnaia sotsialisticheskaia sovetskaia respublika nemtsev Povolzh'ia* (Pokrovsk, 1926), 18–27.

determined to wrest grain from the villages undermined whatever trust the peasants might have had in the Communists. So did the collective farming ventures and kombedy. The party's attempt to establish communal ventures reinforced the belief that the Communists wanted to destroy the fabric of village life, replacing it with unfamiliar practices. An unmitigated disaster in the eyes of the very party that had placed such hopes in them, the kombedy failed to force an artificial split in the countryside, and strained relations between Moscow and Saratov, whose leaders reluctantly backed the endeavor. As a result of these confused efforts, the party extracted the food it needed in the short run, but at the cost of undermining the productive capacity of the villages in the long run, and of making the peasant wonder what the attraction of Bolshevik-style socialism might be.

The peasants defended their social space against the intrusions of the state by disguising what was, at heart, ideological insubordination. Thus, they expressed willingness to provide an economic base and recruits for the Red Army, but did everything they could to look out for their own welfare. They also deserted en masse. Similarly, peasants voiced their acceptance of "fixed prices" on agricultural products, as well as the expectation that the state would provide them with the products they required rather than with useless paper money. In fact, peasants believed the goods they produced were "sacred property" while fixed prices were akin to robbery. Why should they sell at fixed prices but buy at "speculative" ones?[171] In so using the dominant discourse, the peasants justified any manifestations of discontent as being caused by the party-state's breach of the contract. While some peasants were co-opted into the system, most rejected Communist rule as best they could. At times this meant rising up against the authorities and killing party members and government agents. For the most part, though, this was less a matter of rejecting party rulings than it was of using them with ends in mind that were alien to the system they elected not to accept: their use of the dominant social order sought to defeat its powers, "which they lacked the means to challenge; they escaped it without leaving it."[172]

The Communists understood this. Virtually all peasants reacted in anger to requisitioning of horses and farm surpluses when carried out arbitrarily, often remarking that they supported the Bolsheviks who had given them land and Soviet power, "but hated Communists" who plundered the countryside. To the party the clever peasant was a socialist

---

[171] *Kooperativnaia mysl'* no. 9 (40), March 2, 1919, 5.

[172] Michel de Certeau, *The Practice of Everyday Life*, trans. by Steven Rendall (Berkeley, 1984), xiii.

when it behooved him to be so, yet at other times an opponent of Soviet power, even a counterrevolutionary.[173] This represents the party's awareness that the peasants manipulated the dominant discourse and probably contributed to the party's willingness to use force.

If the Civil War was a process whereby a fractious society renegotiated its values, then government policies in the villages, ironically, strengthened the appeal of ownership of land at the expense of whatever collectivist principles might have existed. Largely alienated from power, the peasant withdrew into the local economy and everyday life. Survival had made it essential for the peasant to become more self-sufficient by the winter of 1918–19. The famine of 1921–22 furthered this trend, for it led to a reduction in the overall number of households, except for those of over three desiatinas.[174] By the end of the Civil War many peasants rejected communal land tenure even though during the Revolution they had clamored for egalitarian distribution.[175] In fact, village Communists also sought to set up farms at the expense of party work and were censured for hiring others — in other words, for behaving like "kulaks."[176] The allure of "private" property did not sit well with party militants, some of whom already by 1919 voiced regrets over the dissolution of the kombedy and the party's embrace of the middle peasant, which they believed strengthened forces inimical to socialism.[177] A similar phenomenon occurred when the party introduced the NEP. While the party majority welcomed the relief the NEP brought, a minority of militants declared battle against its "harmful influences."[178] As later Soviet history reveals, these two strands of thinking in regard to the countryside — accommodation vs. forced social reengineering — continued to plague the party throughout the 1920s.

---

[173] GA RF, f. 393, op. 3, d. 327, ll. 19, 165–66; GASO f. 456, op. 1, d. 218, l. 94; and *Krasnoarmeets*, no. 8, Nov. 24, 1918, 10.

[174] Kovalevskii, "Differentsiia," 32.

[175] Figes, *Peasant Russia*, 59.

[176] RGASPI, f. 17, op. 14, d. 658, l. 71 ob.

[177] TsDNISO, f. 151/95, op. 1, d. 43, l. 2, and *Kommuna*, no. 39 (108), June 22, 1919, 4.

[178] RGASPI, f. 17, op. 14, d. 658, l. 71 ob; see also TsDNISO, f. 28, op. 1, d. 46, l. 125.

Eleven

"Given His Class Position, a Worker Can Be Nothing but a Communist"

ALTHOUGH THE Bolsheviks understood and depicted the events of October 1917 as a workers' revolution, the Saratov proletariat soon became disaffected with and eventually alienated from the new party-state. Their worldview shaped by ideology, Bolsheviks interpreted workers' estrangement as the consequence of deurbanization during the Civil War, and not as a change in workers' attitudes, maintaining that the number of "real" proletarians (in effect, a metaphysical concept tautologically defined as a worker who supported the party) simply had declined. The social turmoil at this time undeniably reduced the size of Russia's working class and reconfigured its gender and age composition. Many workers perished; most who enrolled in the Communist Party left their factory benches to serve in the burgeoning state bureaucracy. Others had multiple identities, some of which were temporary, when they entered the Red Army, returned to the villages, or joined the ranks of the unemployed. Yet a substantial core of urban workers remained in the factories, and their attitudes toward the Bolsheviks were indeed transformed. While some historians maintain that class consciousness did not disappear during the Civil War, but migrated to the home, neighborhood, and other local units,[1] I argue in this chapter that working-class consciousness — ironically — also found expression in resistance to and circumvention of Bolshevik practices, both in the implicit language of symbolic activity such as labor absenteeism and foot dragging,

[1] For example, Koenker, "Urbanization and Deurbanization," 97–99.

and in more antagonistic ways.[2] A consciousness of interpreted experience, it gave some workers their own collective identities outside those the Bolsheviks created for them. To be sure, economic hardship galvanized workers during the Civil War; however, it would be misleading to reduce their discontent solely to material conditions or to their prior experiences at the workplace. Instead, we need to link it to their political conflict not with their purported class enemy, the bourgeoisie, but with the Bolsheviks,[3] whom workers blamed for their deteriorating economic situation, the rift within the democracy, political repression, and the betrayal of the promises of 1917.

A Profile of Saratov's Working Class

It is difficult to determine the changing size of Saratov's working class during the 1918–22 period because the data are incomplete, and because the economic downturn, lack of raw materials and fuels, and shutdowns forced many proletarians to switch jobs. Moreover, contemporary observers, particularly the Bolsheviks, interpreted the data tendentiously. Resorting to rhetorical flourishes to reconfigure the number and profile of Saratov workers, the party emphasized the lack of skilled, conscious proletarians who by definition backed Bolshevik power. For example, according to the 1916 census, roughly 25,000 working adults belonged to the "industrial proletariat," but with the rise of worker opposition to the emerging political order in 1918, the party began to put the number of politically "conscious" and reliable industrial workers at only 10,000.[4] However, between 1916 and 1920, as the city's overall population declined from 232,000 to 190,000, Saratov's working class declined at the same rate: it was only after the 1920 census that the ranks of the working class became depleted at a rate that surpassed that of other social groups.

The size of the city's industrial working class in 1920 was 26,165, a figure excluding 4,000 service-industry workers, many of whom were women (table 11.1). The largest categories of workers were unskilled workers (24.8 percent), metalworkers (16.2 percent), port workers (15.2 percent), railroad workers (6.9 percent), construction workers (5.8 per-

---

[2] Comaroff and Comaroff, *Ethnography*, 157.

[3] As Jacques Ranciere has argued, working-class consciousness was in part shaped by workers' dream of the bourgeois "other." See *The Nights of Labor: The Workers' Dream in Nineteenth-Century France* (Philadelphia, 1989). Gareth Stedman Jones has shaped my thinking on how politics produced consciousness; see *Language of Class: Studies in English Working-Class History, 1832–1982* (Cambridge, 1983).

[4] *Saratovskii rabochii*, no. 1, April 5, 1918, 6, and no. 2, April 17, 1918, 8.

TABLE 11.1
Size of Saratov's Working Class, 1920 and 1923, by Occupation

Occupation	1920				1923				Change 1920–23
	Male	Female	Total	% of Total	Male	Female	Total	% of Total	
Agricultural workers	400	99	499	2.0	121	34	155	.9	−69.1%
Metalworkers	4,189	59	4,248	16.2	3,230	44	3,274	20.0	−23.0
Woodworkers	852	10	862	3.3	712	41	753	4.6	−12.6
Printers	564	170	734	2.8	441	85	526	3.2	−28.3
Sewing industry workers	450	916	1,366	5.2	120	125	245	1.5	−82.1
Tanners	1,139	104	1,243	4.8	315	15	330	2.0	−73.4
Tobacco workers	4	157	161	.6	30	104	134	.8	−16.8
Food-processing industry workers	1,109	179	1,288	4.8	572	60	632	3.9	−50.9
Construction workers	1,516	4	1,520	5.8	1,003	3	1,006	6.1	−33.8
Railroad workers	1,697	97	1,794	6.9	1,140	34	1,174	7.2	−34.6
Water transport workers	1,357	30	1,387	5.3	818	3	821	5.0	−40.9
Stevedores, dockhands, drivers, porters, etc.	2,901	1,083	3,984	15.2	2,435	395	2,830	17.3	−28.9
Power plant workers	251	1	252	1.0	409	1	410	2.5	+62.7
Other industrial*	111	245	356	1.3	71	91	162	1.0	−54.5
Unskilled	3,694	2,777	6,471	24.8	2,405	1,530	3,935	24.0	−39.2
Totals	20,234	5,931	26,165	100.0	13,822	2,565	16,387	100.0	−38.1

*Textiles, toiletries, chemicals, glass, etc.
Source: Naseleniia gorodov Saratovskoi gubernii, 32–33, and Novinskii, "Sotsial'nyi i professional'nyi sostav," 83.

cent), and water transport workers (5.3 percent). Women constituted 22.6 percent of the workforce (29.3% when other workers not included in the census are considered) and were found mainly in the sewing industry, in the unskilled category, and in small factories. They also composed 23 percent of the printers in what had been a male-dominated industry, and a large percentage of port workers engaged in heavy labor. The austere economic situation at Civil War's end reduced the size of the working class between August 1920 and the start of 1923 to 16,387 or by 37.3 percent. Women were particularly vulnerable.

The data confirm that the number of skilled workers receded during the Civil War as their mean age rose. Approximately 70 percent of all employed workers of both genders fell into the 15–39 age range (the male/female breakdown is 65.7 percent and 87.8 percent). The largest cohort (16.1 percent) belonged to the 17–19 age group (13.5 percent of the working men and 27.1 percent of the working women). Unfortunately, no prewar figures exist for comparison. According to type of industry, the 25–39 age group predominated in the metallurgical, machine-building, and flour industries, the 30–50 age cohort in the wood-processing industry, and a much younger 25–29 age group in the textile and wool industries. In printing, it was the 15–19-year olds.[5] As we saw in chapter 9, roughly half of local enterprises had shut down by the end of 1919, and a second wave of closures occurred at civil war's end. But it must be emphasized that the younger workers and female workers came from working-class families, and that key industries taken over by central agencies continued to employ a highly skilled workforce.

The Widening Gap between Wages and Prices

Given the worsening economic situation throughout the Civil War, wages took on a new importance for all workers, closely entwined with the twin issues of unemployment and food supplies. During 1918, disagreements on how best to remunerate workers disrupted local party meetings, caused serious divisions among workers, and gave the moderate socialist opposition more grounds on which to criticize the Bolsheviks. Choosing to view national decrees as nothing more than general guidelines, Antonov favored abolishing the monetary system altogether and introducing a goods exchange, while F. T. Ivanov backed a leveling of wages and goods distribution, a view that ultimately prevailed among the city's Bolsheviks. Setting the monthly minimum at 250 rubles and the

[5] TsDNISO, f. 110, op. 1, d. 2, ll. 2–2 ob, and "Iz itogov," 33–37.

maximum at 400 rubles, local leaders limited factory owners' profits to no more than a worker's annual wage. But these utopian notions did not sit well with those very strata of workers the Bolsheviks insisted should be the most conscious, the skilled metalworkers, some of whom threatened to walk out if leveling were introduced. Local unions and the Gubsovnarkhoz also voiced objections. Moreover, the debate caused a rift between metalworkers and white-collar workers at these same enterprises. An arrogant Antonov insisted that Saratov need not fear losing skilled workers, since Russia's hungry industrial cities would supply them. Vocal support for Antonov as well as for his opponents reflects the diversity of views that prevailed among workers at this time.[6] Later that summer Saratov agreed to keep its wages in line with the Center's ruling, but urged Moscow to allow local soviets to establish norms within their provinces.[7]

Barter and the rationing of necessary items based on social class began to replace the traditional money economy already in late 1918, when the authorities divided the population into four categories for the purpose of goods distribution. Workers belonging to unions, factory committees, and Communist Party cells fell into category one, and Soviet officials into category two. The remaining laboring population composed category three, and the "non-laboring, parasitic population," category four. The robust growth in union membership meant that the vast majority of those who worked at all soon fell into the top category, thereby making the differentiation largely meaningless. A study of workers' family budgets shows that wages made up only 65 percent of a Saratov worker's family income; the remainder came from selling clothing and other objects, from moonlighting, and from illicitly manufacturing items in short supply. Food expenditures drained 82 percent of a worker's pay. Although Saratov workers were better off than those in Petrograd and Moscow, they remained most concerned about their own declining living standard.[8]

In early 1919, skilled workers in the metallurgical and wood processing industries received roughly three times what unskilled workers earned. The average monthly wage in January was 444 rubles; by April the figure had gone up 37 percent. As conditions deteriorated, a greater percentage of workers appear to have backed a leveling of wages, including those who earlier had opposed it.[9] Workers now spent half of

[6] *KG*, no. 111, July 16, 1918, 4; no. 116, July 21, 1918, 3; and *Saratovskii Sovet*, 446–47.

[7] Rashitov, "Sovety," 144–45; GA RF, f. 393, op. 3, d. 327, l. 28; and *ISS*, no. 159, Aug. 7, 1918, 3.

[8] *ISS*, no. 193, Sept. 3, 1919, 2.

[9] TsDNISO, f. 81, op. 1, d. 15, l. 77.

their income on food purchases through labor organizations, and much of the rest of their money on acquiring food and other necessities outside such channels.[10] While prices on some products, such as eggs, cooking oil, milk, and millet, did not fluctuate, those for potatoes, butter, sugar, and wheat flour shot up. In April, a worker paid 45 percent of an average monthly wage for a pound of butter, a dozen eggs, a kilo of oil, or a pound of sugar.[11]

During the Civil War, wages did not keep up with prices, despite a chaotic system of bonus pay through which some workers earned 2,000 percent premiums.[12] Between July 1917 and June 1918 prices for food staples rose between 231 and 983 percent, while the cost of essential items such as kerosene, candles, and soap rose less dramatically.[13] This situation changed in 1919, when agricultural goods tended to cost less than manufactured items, which had already begun to disappear. For example, the price of cabbage doubled in 1919, yet kerosene became 100 times more expensive. In 1914, prices differed little throughout the province, but by 1919 price differentials could be huge. Prices rose constantly throughout 1919, between 500 and 2,000 percent, except when those for agricultural products fell at harvest time and again at the start of winter before they began to spoil.[14] Wages went up by 280 percent in 1919, but the cost of ten basic food items by 947 percent.[15] In 1920 market prices for the same products tended to fluctuate widely among the province's urban centers, yet they tended to shoot up at even more exorbitant rates than earlier (table 11.2) — more than twenty times for a pound of black bread and roughly forty times for a pound of potatoes. In July a pound of white bread cost 200 rubles. At the time, salaries at the Zhest plant ranged from 1,168 rubles a month to 2,880, while factory administrators earned 4,600–5,200 rubles.[16]

The average working-class family had five members and 1.2 workers

---

[10] *ISS*, no. 11, Jan. 16, 1919, 2.

[11] B. G., "Dvizhenie zarabotnoi platy v Saratovskom raione (ianvar'–aprel' 1919 g.)," *Ekonomicheskaia zhizn' Povolzh'ia: Sbornik statei* (Saratov, 1919): 51–53.

[12] "Otdel metalla," 10; TsDNISO, f. 27, op. 1, d. 489, l. 68; RGASPI, f. 17, op. 12, d. 468, l. 34; and "Saratovskii Gubsovnarkhoz i promyshlennost'," 97.

[13] *Kooperativnaia mysl'*, no. 10 (41) (March 9, 1919): 3; *Biulleten' statisticheskogo otdela Saratovskogo gubernskogo komiteta po proizvodstvu*, no. 9, Dec. 1, 1918, 9–24.

[14] P. Kadiksov, "Rost vol'nykh tsen v g. Saratove v 1919 g.," *Biulleten' Saratovskogo gubernskogo statisticheskogo biuro*, no. 1 (1920): 28–30; idem, "Dvizhenie vol'nykh tsen na tovary v gorodakh Saratovskoi gubernii v 1919 godu," 30–36.

[15] Prices on sugar, milk, and white bread rose even more precipitously. Gutman, "Dvizhenie," 18–21, 23, and Kadiksov, "Rost," 24–27.

[16] GASO, f. 19, op. 36, d. 11, ll. 40–43, 46 ob; N. I. Rakitnikov, "Vol'nye tseny na 15 iiunia po Saratovskoi gubernii v rubliakh," *Biulleten' Saratovskogo gubernskogo statisticheskogo biuro*, no. 2 (1920): 13.

TABLE 11.2
Free Market Prices on Basic Food Items in Saratov, Jan. 1920–Jan. 1921

	Price in Rubles				
Item	1/1/20	4/1/20	7/1/20	10/1/20	1/1/21
black bread (lb.)	20	50	130	275	450
potatoes	7	20	35	100	275
sugar	800	1800	2500	3500	8000
meat	120	250	400	400	400
milk (bottle)	120	170	150	300	800
eggs (10)	30	60	40	100	400
salt (lb.)	120	200	300	250	300

Source: Romanov, Materialy po statistike, 14.

and was largest among the better-paid metalworkers (6.1) and lowest among textile workers (4.4). Only 20 percent had a second worker (compared with 40 percent in Moscow). Whereas before the war workers expended 44 percent of their earnings on food,[17] a study shows a 150 percent gap between wages and real expenditures in 1919 and 1920. Although famine conditions made it impossible to calculate the gap between wages and expenditures after 1921, it widened even more as essential items disappeared. The cost of basic necessities such as a winter coat, hat, or boots made them off limits for all but the most successful "speculators." A winter coat, for instance, cost 400,000 rubles and a pair of boots 100,000 rubles. Moreover, prices climbed by 10–20 percent in February, on the eve of massive worker unrest in the city.[18] Soaring inflation in the second half of the year raised a printer's pay to 500,000–600,000 rubles,[19] but prices rose accordingly as famine took its toll.

The Face of Unemployment

Production for the war effort and overall collapse of the economy threw many people out of work during the Civil War, while growing shortages of essentials drove some of them back to the villages. Although Saratov experienced much less deurbanization than cities in the Russian North or Central Industrial Region, in part owing to the influx of hungry

[17] G. Kagan, "Biudzhet Saratovskikh rabochikh," Nizhnee Povolzh'e, no. 7 (1924): 35–38.
[18] Romanov, Materialy, 17.
[19] Osipov, Saratovskaia partiinaia organizatsiia v gody vosstanovleniia, 45–47.

workers from those regions, the city's population nonetheless declined and its workers faced the threat of unemployment. The transition to the NEP in this famine zone initially did nothing to ease their hardships.

While the Bolsheviks inherited an economy in difficult straits, the demobilization of the Imperial Army and existence of large numbers of outsiders dwelling in the province exacerbated the situation. To cope with the problem, factory committees began laying off workers in January 1918, some of whom had been employed for as long as twenty years, and proposed that only one adult be allowed to work in a family of six. Faced with hordes of unemployed mill workers in April, the soviet determined that owners give them the equivalent of three-months' severance pay; however, when it became clear that the mill owners lacked such resources, the soviet nationalized the enterprises. The fact that the party's mass base was already eroding furthered its perceived need to take action, for the socialist opposition rebuked the Bolsheviks whenever possible. Moreover, the frontoviki drove workers from their benches in order to make room for themselves. Most frontoviki sought office work in what had become a glutted market, even though only 42 percent had been employed as clerks before the war. To alleviate the consequences of unemployment, the soviet planned a series of public works, opened free cafeterias, shortened the workday, established wage scales, and decreed that no more than two adults would be allowed to work in each family. It set up a department to deal with the problem and a labor exchange that registered 13,000 unemployed persons in the city, many of whom were unskilled or office workers. Statistics reveal the dislocation caused by the war: in 1918, Saratovites constituted 64.4 percent of the city's unemployed, but only 54 percent in 1919.[20]

Saratov's labor exchange registered 26,221 unemployed in late 1918, of whom 41.6 percent received work. Since 24,322 jobs had become vacant during the period, it is clear that the work pool and labor needs simply were at odds. Unskilled workers and office workers continued to make up almost half of all those without jobs.[21] However, this situation changed in 1919 as unemployed workers without skills disappeared to the villages and district towns. Figures for May 1919 provide another glimpse of the problem, which affected men and women similarly. That

[20] *Godovshchina*, 31; *Saratovskii Sovet*, 387–89, 445–46; *Saratovskii rabochii*, no. 2, April 17, 1918, 4–5; no. 3, May 1, 1918, 5; Rashitov, "Sovety," 142–43; *ISS*, no. 24, Jan. 31, 1918, 4; no. 25, Feb. 1 (14), 1918, 4; no. 37, March 1, 1918, 2; no. 38, March 2, 1918, 4; *Slovo proletarii*, no. 6, Jan. 27, 1918, 1; and "Deiatel'nost' kassy bezrabotnykh," *Statisticheskii vestnik*, no. 2 (Saratov, 1921): 53–55, 60–62.

[21] *ISS*, no. 160, Aug. 8, 1918, 1, and Surikov, "Rynok truda," *Ekonomicheskaia zhizn' Povolzh'ia: Sbornik statei* (Saratov, 1919): 41, 47.

month 7,009 unemployed registered with the labor exchange (3,827 men and 3,182 women); 4,790 were sent to work, of whom 93.4 percent stuck at it. More openings materialized for male workers. Among those remaining without employment were office workers, trade and industrial employees, medical-sanitation workers, sewing industry workers, and custodians and other unskilled workers.[22] While not as acute, the situation played itself out similarly in the district towns, where labor exchanges also appeared in 1918. In Balashov, a Petrograder opened a labor exchange, organizing a union of unemployed. When lack of resources prevented the town from implementing his plans to set up a public works program, it sent many of the unemployed to do field work. In Volsk the authorities opened a cafeteria for the unemployed, but some of those who had registered as such had done so merely in order to have more time for "speculation." Such survival strategies were common.[23]

Approximately 9,500 unemployed, mainly unskilled workers and clerical workers, registered in Saratov monthly between April and August 1919, and between 25,000 and 50,000 province-wide. As before, the demand for labor almost matched the number of those without work, but their skills did not meet their employers' needs. When Saratov fell under siege fewer registered with local labor exchanges, since large numbers had been mobilized to fortify the city. When they returned home in August, the number of those who registered tripled. A profile of the unemployed finds mainly adolescents, the old, those unfit for manual labor, those who had never worked before, déclassé elements, and women. In order to curtail the number on welfare, the soviet tried to place some of them in other professions. It dispatched unemployed refugees and workers from other provinces to do field work, yet had difficulty mobilizing the refugees who, "despite all measures and repression taken," refused to register.[24] By this point Moscow agencies controlled most local industries employing skilled workers, who remained less vulnerable to the threat of unemployment.

The high turnover rate that characterized the labor market in 1919 and 1920 assumed a female face in Saratov (but not necessarily in the rest of the province). In the second half of 1919, women, particularly those employed as clerks, made up between 61 percent and 76 percent of workers that registered with the labor exchange. Both the number of

---

[22] *ISS*, no. 45, Feb. 27, 1919, 1, and no. 138, July 1, 1919, 4.

[23] GASO, f. 456, op. 1, d. 49, l. 224, and *Izvestiia Vol'skogo uispolkoma*, no. 22, Jan. 30, 1919, 3–4.

[24] GASO, f. 901, op. 2, d. 12, ll. 2–4 ob, 25–26. For Saratov's welfare system, see "Deiatel'nost' kassy bezrabotnykh," 53–55, 60–62, and Romanov, *Materialy*, 19.

unemployed and the number of openings fell during 1920; however, by
midyear the city was short 6,000 workers on average, especially construction workers, "intellectual laborers," and other skilled workers,
who were most likely to be men. Between January 1 and August 1,
1920, 56,611 men and 38,070 women registered with local labor exchanges, of whom 81 percent of the men (45,898) and 74 percent of the
women (28,145) were sent to work, some of whom took up field work
on farms.[25]

Whereas some factories received (decent) Red Army rations, and
some (such as the vegetable oil presses and creameries) gave their employees goods they manufactured, other enterprises offered only low
wages, forcing workers to flee to the villages, while no new influx of
workers arrived from the central provinces. To keep workers in place
the party introduced labor conscription for public works projects. When
it began to mobilize workers by profession, however, many went into
hiding or else attempted to mask their professions to avoid compulsory
labor. By mid-1920 the economic downturn foreboded the tragedy that
was to come, prompting thousands of workers to disappear. Bombarded
by requests from the districts to help place or feed workers from other
provinces whose skills were not needed, Saratov sought permission
from Moscow to send them back where they had come from, since
locally there was "nothing with which to satisfy them."[26]

Consideration of the nature of unemployment in several uezds shows
that in Petrovsk 38 percent of the unemployed were office workers and
another 20 percent were other white-collar workers. Not peculiar to
Petrovsk, this phenomenon could be found across Russia as the "entire
intelligentsia and petit-bourgeois elements from young to old join[ed]
Soviet service," some out of need, some in order to receive an unemployment card in order to avoid being discriminated against as a member of the bourgeoisie. The flow of the intelligentsia from starving cities
in central Russia compounded the problem in Petrovsk, since 63 percent
of local requests for workers were for unskilled laborers. In August
1919 the town began to register workers in preparation for labor conscription, even though it believed it was "absurd" since there was no
one available locally to implement mandatory labor.[27] In Volsk roughly
two-thirds of local workers registered with the labor exchange in 1918,

[25] *ISS*, no. 193, Sept. 3, 1919, 3; no. 223, Oct. 9, 1919, 3–4; no. 275, Dec. 10, 1919, 4;
no. 35, Feb. 14, 1920, 2; no. 40, Feb. 20, 1920, 2; no. 79, April 7, 1920, 3; and no. 96,
May 1, 1920, 5.

[26] GASO, f. 901, op. 1, d. 63, ll. 1–3; d. 64, ll. 87, 89; and *ISS*, no. 219, Sept. 29, 1920,
3.

[27] GASO, f. 901, op. 2, d. 13, ll. 42–43 ob.

and the rate remained high throughout 1919.[28] Labor conscription during the second half of 1920 provided only 60 adults able to carry out heavy labor and another 347 suitable for light work.[29] In Kamyshin workers deserted from labor brigades until the introduction of repressive measures. According to a report from Baronsk, many of those who had registered as unemployed had land in the villages to which they had returned, a phenomenon that gave unemployment statistics new meaning.[30]

Ironically, at the start of 1921, when a blind optimism prevailed within the party that it would quickly mend the broken economy, Saratov projected a need for workers that would have to be met by importing laborers from elsewhere, drawing up a prioritized list of essential industries whose requirements would be met first.[31] Yet famine conditions and factory downsizing in connection with the NEP soon made such projections meaningless. In fact, in Saratov unemployment became a more serious problem after the Civil War had ended.

Labor Organizations during the Civil War

Complicating the Bolsheviks' dealings with their socialist rivals, debate over issues of labor policy rocked the party already in the weeks following the October Revolution.[32] The role trade unions would play in promoting workers' interests represented a politically sensitive issue, particularly since the Mensheviks backed independent trade unions. Organized according to the shop principle in 1917, Saratov's unions lacked ties with the rest of the province as well as with factory committees in Saratov itself, which played a more visible political role than unions in 1917 and immediately after the October Revolution. Inspired by a decree of November 1917, factory committees established "control" over many enterprises in early 1918, which amounted to seizure of the workplace and removal of owners. In effect, the committees began to run rather than supervise factory administrations, as a result of which the Bolsheviks realized that spontaneous industrial democracy could be-

---

[28] *Doklad Vol'skogo uezdnogo Ispolnitel'nogo komiteta,* 47.

[29] *Materialy k XIII Vol'skomu uezdnomu s"ezdu sovetov rabochikh, krest'ianskikh i krasnoarmeiskikh deputatov 12 dekabria 1920 g.* (Volsk, 1920), 91, 95–96.

[30] GASO, f. 901, op. 2, d. 13, ll. 101–2, and f. 901, op. 1, d. 63, ll. 1–3 ob, 16–18.

[31] Ibid., f. 901, op. 1, d. 65, ll. 9–9 ob, and *Pervyi s"ezd proizvodstvennogo soiuza zheleznodorozhnikov Riazansko-Ural'skoi zheleznoi dorogi, 11–13 oktiabria 1920 g.* (Saratov, 1920), 76.

[32] See Diane Koenker, "Labor Relations in Socialist Russia: Class Values and Production Values in the Printers' Union, 1917–1921," in *Making Workers Soviet: Power, Class and Identity,* ed. Lewis H. Siegelbaum and Ronald G. Suny (Ithaca, 1994), 159–93.

come a political handicap. The First Provincial Conference of Trade Unions, which opened on July 1, 1918, recognized factory committees as local cells of unions subordinate to sovnarkhozy and organized on the production principle. This reorganization of unions by industry had its opponents, especially among office workers who opposed wage level-ing.[33] Joining forces with the local sovnarkhoz to deal with matters of production, discipline, and wages, Saratov trade unions gradually be-came extensions of party organs while workers enrolled in them to ob-tain larger rations.

Only a handful of unions had existed in Saratov before 1917, but during that year many emerged spontaneously both by occupation and by industry. In January 1918 the Saratov Council of Unions (*Gubprof-sovet*) comprised 32 unions, many of which were local, with 30,000 workers. By year's end, 67 unions existed in the province with 89,878 members. Gubprofsovet succeeded in bringing them under its wing, re-organizing them according to the production principle in 1919–20.[34] Sources put union membership at 141,852 province-wide in early 1919, and 213,163 members a year later, a robust growth most of which oc-curred outside Saratov. During the period when localism prevailed some union leaders formed regional associations; however, in February 1919, Moscow shut down all bodies of this sort as part of its efforts to cen-tralize state administration. When the First Provincial Congress of Unions met that month, the 136 professional organizations operating province-wide were reorganized into branches of 26 national unions.[35]

Although Bolshevik representatives constituted a majority at the con-gress (figure 11.1), it turned into a rancorous debate on Soviet power when Mensheviks championed an "independent professional move-ment" that would function as "a government within a government." Insisting that unions should be free of government control since the government had become the employer, they reasoned that unions must create favorable conditions for reviving industry, for ending the civil war within the democracy, for restoring a free press, and for pressuring

---

[33] *ISS*, no. 29, Feb. 20, 1918; *KG*, no. 24, March 22, 1918, 4; *Biulleten' pravleniia torgovykh i promyshlennykh sluzhashchikh*, no. 2, Aug. 15, 1918, 1–3; and Gromov, "Vospominaniia," 7.

[34] *ISS*, no. 83, April 16, 1921, 3; "Professional'nye soiuzy Saratovskoi gubernii," 158, 161–62; and "Dvizhenie chlenov professional'nykh soiuzov Saratovskoi gubernii za 1919–1921 g.," *Biulleten' Saratovskogo gubernskogo statisticheskogo biuro*, no. 1 (1922): 29–30.

[35] Vysshii sovet narodnogo khoziaistva, *Dva goda diktatury proletariata* (Moscow, 1919), 16, 22–23; *Istoriia organizatsii Atkarskogo uezdnogo soiuza proizvodstva i ego rabota s 1918 po 1922 gg.* (Atkarsk, 1922).

11.1 Bolshevik Kirill Plaksin played one of the most important roles in bringing the local unions under party control. Courtesy Saratov Kraevedcheskii Museum, photo 22408/10.

the Communist Party to soften its policies toward the peasantry. While the majority carried Bolshevik resolutions, it could not prevent the Mensheviks from articulating their attractive alternative.[36] Menshevik orators likewise transformed a conference in Atkarsk into a forum for voicing their political ideas, and perhaps did so elsewhere as well.[37] When confronted with recalcitrant or fractured union leaderships, the party disbanded them, monitoring the election of new committees.[38]

Some unions defied co-optation by the party-state, representing work-

---

[36] "Professional'nye soiuzy," 161–63, and *ISS*, no. 44, Feb. 26, 1919, 2.

[37] *Izvestiia Atkarskogo uispolkoma*, no. 174, April 2, 1919, 4; no. 182, April 12, 1919, 4; Koenker, "Labor Relations," 181; and *Istoriia organizatsii Atkarskogo uezdnogo soiuza*, 9.

[38] *Kratkie ocherki iz istorii Soiuza rabochikh vodnogo transporta* (Volsk, 1923), 51.

ers' interests against the encroachments of Soviet power; the leaderships of some of the largest unions remained non-Bolshevik well into 1920. Moreover, Bolshevik domination of unions did not guarantee that their leaderships would embrace party directives:[39] in April 1918 the metal-workers' union spoke out against compulsory Red Guard service, and in July Saratov printers, like those elsewhere, bucked efforts to enroll them in a union that backed Soviet power.[40] In August groups within the union of water transport workers expressed hostility to the government.[41] Many workers tried to use the unions to voice their discontent with Soviet power or, what appears to have been more common, with economic conditions, which in turn represented an implicit critique of the system.[42] Another strategy was to ignore the unions altogether once their leaderships fell under party control. Thus Gubprofsovet "successfully" carried out mobilization for food brigades, but failed to enlist union members to battle against Wrangel.[43]

When Saratov fell under siege in May 1919, its unions ranged in size from 300 to approximately 12,000 members. The two largest, with over 10,000 members, were the railroad workers' union and the union of office workers. In the districts, unions were particularly conspicuous in Volsk, Kamyshin, and Balashov, with more than 7,000 members. With 2,030 members, the union of employees in Kamyshin was the largest.[44] Union membership dipped, however, as Kolchak's forces approached the Volga, for Saratov's unions had to offer up to 20 percent of their membership in a major mobilization drive. While rationing policies resulted in mandatory union membership during the Civil War, some unions expelled members for not paying their dues, a sign of indifference or taciturn protest.[45] Moreover, in contrast with the situation in 1917, when workers had the right to strike, Soviet unions and factory committees now arbitrated labor disputes that concerned individuals, rather than entire work collectives. During the first quarter of 1919, 313 labor conflicts were registered, involving only 1,212 workers out of a workforce of 69,908. In the spring of 1920, the vast majority of those lodging complaints did so over pay disputes and as a result of being fired.[46]

The union leadership's support in 1920 of centralization, discipline,

---

[39] See *Trudy chetvertogo s"ezda delegatov Riazansko-Ural'skoi zheleznoi dorogi.*
[40] *Saratovskii rabochii,* no. 2, April 17, 1918, 13, and *ISS,* no. 137, July 11, 1921, 3.
[41] *Kratkie ocherki,* 44.
[42] GASO, f. 2972, op. 3, d. 3, l. 11.
[43] TsDNISO, f. 27, op. 1, d. 489, l. 83.
[44] *ISS,* no. 115, June 3, 1919, 3, and no. 155, July 19, 3.
[45] GASO, f. 2972, op. 3, d. 2, l. 11.
[46] *ISS,* no. 83, April 16, 1920, 3.

and labor conscription in order to restore the economy further alienated them from workers. This coincided with a rise in the activities of the socialist opposition. When the Second Provincial Congress of Trade Unions convened in June 1920, the gathering provided an opportunity for those in favor of independent trade unions to speak up. Although the party dismissed this opposition as efforts by anarchist-syndicalists to represent the interests of "backward" workers, the leadership of some of the largest unions (food workers, leather workers, printers, artistic workers, metalworkers, and office workers) until recently had remained in the hands of non-Communists.[47] Turning into forums for criticizing hard living and work conditions, as well as the state's usurpation of the trade union movement, local congresses increasingly featured "unaffili-ated," and not Bolshevik, majorities.[48] The best example is that of the municipal employees' trade union, which boasted the largest provincial branch in Saratov. The Communists disbanded the union and arrested its leaders because they favored an independent union.[49] Afterward, party organizers of a congress of the railroad workers' union took pre-cautions to prevent it from turning into an anti-Soviet forum.

Tensions within the Communist Party over labor conscription and other controversial policies resulted in altercations over what role unions should play in the postwar environment, involving the so-called Workers' Opposition associated with A. G. Shliapnikov and the Demo-cratic Centralists, as well as Lenin and Trotsky. Strictly a party affair, the debate did not appeal to workers.[50] As such, it did not create any significant problems within the Saratov party organization, whose mem-bers overwhelmingly backed Lenin's position.[51] Be that as it may, in the weeks before labor protest swept across urban Russia in early 1921,

---

[47] *Biulleten' Gubprofsoveta*, no. 3 (1920): 1; "Professional'nye soiuzy," 164–65; *ISS*, no. 239, Oct. 28, 1919, 2; and *ISS*, no. 53, March 5, 1920, 3.

[48] *Trudy 3-go Saratovskogo s"ezda Narodnoi sviazi* (Saratov, 1920), especially 10, 12–15, 35.

[49] G. Aronson, "The Employees' Trade Union and the Struggle for Unity and Indepen-dence of the Workers' Trade Union Movement, 1917–1920," RSDRP, Nicolaevsky Col-lection, box 33, folder 7, 3–4.

[50] See Larry E. Holmes, "For the Revolution Redeemed: The Workers Opposition in the Bolshevik Party 1919–1921," *Carl Beck Papers in Russian and East European Studies*, no. 802 (February, 1990): 6–9.

[51] Neighborhood party organizations voted for the various platforms in February 1921. Lenin's drew 77 votes, Trotsky's 8, and Shliapnikov's none. Elsewhere in the province, Trotsky's and Shliapnikov's positions also attracted few adherents except in Kuznetsk, where Trotsky's platform was carried. See TsDNISO, f. 81, op. 1, d. 49, l. 8; *ISS*, no. 40, Feb. 22, 1921, 2; I. R. Pleve, *Iz istorii Saratovskikh profsoiuzov, 1917–1922 godov* (Sar-atov, 1985), 8. For the districts see *Serp i molot*, no. 30, Feb. 11, 1921, 1, 2; *Kommuna*, no. 16, March 2, 1921, 1; *Oktiabr'skaia revoliutsiia*, no. 13 (621), Feb. 6, 1921, 3; and *Vlast' sovetov*, Feb. 3, 1921, no. 23, 1.

party domination over the unions weakened. Reproaches generated at a meeting of Rabis, the union of artistic workers, drove a Communist observer to retort that during the entire existence of Soviet power he had not seen "a more disgraceful openly counterrevolutionary professional meeting."[52] In Kamyshin, workers elected non-Communists to the union board in March because they "hated Communists," who complained that "before the unions were obedient but now are against the Communists."[53] Thus, although the party co-opted the trade unions, many of them remained oppositional.

Factory Conditions and Attitudes toward Work

The collapse of the economy and policies linked to War Communism not only resulted in factory closures, unemployment, and confiscation followed by promotion of cottage industries, but also affected how people worked and what they did on the job. In addition to meager wages, workers labored in exchange for rations and scarce necessities. In order to survive, they turned to the black market and to other survival strategies such as pilfering at the workplace, absenteeism, and shirking responsibilities. To a far lesser extent than before, work defined how a worker perceived himself or herself, yet it did become another experience through which workers judged Soviet power. Although kinship ties, neighborhood, and other factors provided networks of significance for workers, the economic experience of Civil War left an indelible imprint on their individual and mass consciousness by shaping a culture of mutual dependence in conditions of utmost want.

Growing indifference toward work and a drop in labor discipline had manifested themselves already in 1918[54] as factories closed, were taken over by state authorities, or retooled to produce for the Civil War effort and factory committees took steps to alleviate the lot of work collectives, often violating rules drawn up by the soviet. The situation deteriorated in 1919, when shortages of fuel shut down factories. Owing to a lack of raw materials, many workers at Novaia Etna "got sick," continuing to receive their wages, while at Saratov Manufacturing workers proposed using factory territory to grow food.[55] If Kamyshin workers showed little interest in seizing local factories in 1918, they now were

[52] *ISS*, no. 54, March 10, 1921, 2, and no. 68, March 29, 1921, 4. Also see Pleve, *Iz istorii*, 11.

[53] RGASPI, f. 17, op. 12, d. 474, l. 58.

[54] *ISS*, no. 113, June 11, 1918, 3, and Rashitov, "Sovety," 294.

[55] For Novaia Etna see GASO, f. 2972, op. 3, d. 3, l. 18, and *KG*, no. 330, April 16, 1919, 3.

accused of not being concerned with anything except their own personal interests.[56] The province's falling under siege forced workers to hunt for food to supplement their token rations. That fall and winter proved to be the bleakest to date; however, they were but a prelude to the unimaginably grim conditions of 1920–21. To counter the growing popularity of anarchist and Menshevik propaganda in early 1920, the party began to acknowledge the terrible conditions in which workers toiled. It admitted, for example, that the Sotrudnik metallurgical plant lacked firewood and raw materials and had to put 35 percent of its workers on leave. Conditions tended to be better at enterprises filling military orders, but even they endured hardships. Workers at the University Workshop, which made parts for American boot-making machines, brought home better rations because they were the only ones in Russia able to provide this sorely needed product. Similarly, shortages of liquid fuels and the use of firewood had increased the demand for saws, and by summer 1919, the Zhest plant began to produce them, allowing those workers better compensation. Productivity shot up once piece rates were introduced; however, 35 percent of the workers took sick leave, and the absentee rate climbed.

By 1920 appalling conditions prevailed at most industrial enterprises in Saratov Province. The Kolesnikov plant, which repaired vessels for the military, needed fuel and workers, and also had to cope with broken-down machinery. Likewise short of fuel, the Levkovich tobacco plant employed 515 workers, virtually all women, and had tobacco to process, but the pilfering of tobacco "took on alarming levels" and 31 percent of its workers took sick leave. Almost all had damaged lungs and suffered from tuberculosis. Productivity plummeted and absenteeism soared among the 80 workers at the prosthesis workshop, who seemed "indifferent to bonuses and interested only in obtaining food." Unsanitary conditions and low productivity prevailed at the city's slaughterhouse and central laundry. Moreover, the rate of absenteeism in the metallurgical industry in early 1920 was 20 percent for workers and 5 percent for white-collar workers, with a rate of 36 percent at the Ozu plant.[57] Labor productivity also further declined, as the situation on the railroad lines — a critical industry placed under the military — indicates: by 1920 there were twice as many workers as before because productivity had fallen by 50 percent.[58] Awful conditions prevailed in Volsk's dank cement factories, whose workers inhabited subhuman bar-

---

[56] GA RF, f. 393, op. 3, d. 333, l. 17 ob, and *Nabat*, no. 42, April 16, 1919, 3.

[57] *ISS*, no. 45, Feb. 25, 1920, 2; no. 46, Feb. 26, 1920, 2; no. 85, April 18, 1920, 4; no. 90, April 24, 1920, 3; no. 95, April 30, 1920, 3; and "Otdel metalla," 10.

[58] *Privolzhskii krasnyi put'*, no. 1 (1920): 12.

racks. To make ends meet, they set about providing their own food. Elsewhere, workers in the filthy dairy toiled twelve hours a day "as before" the Revolution for low pay and no insurance.[59] Sometimes workers' desperate efforts turned tragic, as when railroad workers in Rtishchevo helped themselves to surrogate spirits leaking from a railroad car, which they peddled and consumed themselves. The alcohol poisoned hundreds, resulting in dozens of deaths.[60]

As part of the new emphasis on restoring the economy in 1920, the authorities took measures to improve factory finances, obtain fuel, mobilize unions, and introduce one-person management at the workplace. None of these measures brought more than temporary improvements and, in fact, conditions worsened in the course of 1920. The situation did not differ in the uezds.[61] By early 1921, absenteeism remained over 20 percent at Saratov factories. Where absenteeism was down, the number of workers taking sick leave was high. Moreover, poor nutrition, lack of heat, and unsanitary conditions took their toll: 1,500 of 24,000 workers examined at this time in Saratov were infected with tuberculosis.[62]

Workers in the Bolshevik Revolution

Pierre Bourdieu suggests looking at class as a social space or a potential state, consisting of economic, cultural, social, and symbolic capital. While collectives have economic and social bases, they are also symbolic constructions "oriented by the pursuit of individual and collective interests (and, first of all, by the pursuit of the specific interests of their spokesperson)."[63] As the spokesperson for the working class, the Bolshevik Party sought to impose its principles on the construction of reality, in the hopes that they would be appropriated into the overall cultural scheme. We can appreciate the situation in all its complexity: the Bolsheviks created workers who in turn created the Bolsheviks. Needing working-class support in order to justify and rationalize the dictatorship of the proletariat they claimed to have established, the Bolsheviks endowed workers with a symbolic capital that the party manipulated through its control over the language used to give meaning to the term

---

[59] *Izvestiia Ispolnitel'nogo komiteta Vol'skogo Soveta*, no. 78, April 9, 1919, 4; no. 52, March 6, 1919, 4; and no. 62, March 20, 1919, 4.

[60] *Serp i molot*, no. 19, Sept. 11, 1919, 2.

[61] Litvinenko, "Zavod 'Kommunist'," *Nizhnee Povolzh'e*, no. 5 (1933): 39–40.

[62] For example, see *ISS*, no. 67, March 27, 1921, 3; no. 69, March 30, 1921, 3; no. 74, April 5, 1921, 2; no. 80, April 13, 1921, 2; and no. 232, Oct. 14, 1921, 3.

[63] Pierre Bourdieu, "What Makes a Social Class? On the Theoretical and Practical Existence of Groups," *Berkeley Journal of Sociology* 32 (1987): 3–4, 9, 13–14.

"worker." Invoking class as a weapon of exclusion and inclusion in their efforts to reconfigure Russian culture, the Bolsheviks constructed a working-class identity through their rhetorical flourishes, rather than reflecting one. Once workers became symbols in party narratives they lost the autonomous voice they had exhibited in 1917, as the party came to substitute itself for them. Given the claims the party made about the working class, the new identity the party formulated for workers became something one attained through correct behavior, sort of like culture itself. Class had become a social-psychological and political projection in which any act of opposition to Soviet power brought symbolic expulsion from the ranks of the true proletariat and confinement to the ranks of inferior class "others." As Saratov's Lomov put it, "given his class position, a worker can be nothing but a Communist."[64]

The party viewed workers hierarchically: highly skilled members of the industrial proletariat represented the conscious, revolutionary vanguard that supported Soviet power. Unskilled laborers and women occupied the lowest levels of this pyramid of consciousness. But a problem surfaced as early as the spring of 1918, when Saratov's workers clashed with the soviet. Since the dictatorship of the proletariat represented the very embodiment of the Revolution, the party had to explain this opposition to its policies. It did so by denying workers agency, depicting dissatisfaction among skilled workers as temporary wavering caused by the deceptive propaganda practices of rival socialist parties, and opposition among unskilled and female workers as the result of their lack of consciousness and susceptibility to rival propaganda in conditions of scarcity. As the Civil War deepened, the Bolsheviks blamed the physical disappearance of the working class and Saratov's shortage of skilled industrial workers for labor conflicts, representing opposition as the work of counterrevolutionaries, saboteurs, and misguided peasant-workers.

The party saw the Russian worker as a "poor worker" compared with those in the "leading" nations. In view of the realities of tsarism and the legacy of serfdom, the Bolsheviks believed, things could not have been otherwise. Consequently, "to teach workers how to work" — that is, how to be sober and productive and how to appreciate Soviet power — represented one of the Bolsheviks' most urgent tasks.[65] A document the party made workers sign, "The Proletarian Oath," enumerates a worker's obligations to the Revolution. "I, a son of the toiling people . . . in full accord with my conviction and conscience . . . recognize and support Soviet power as the single spokesperson of the needs of the proletariat and poorest peasantry." According to the oath, a true

---

[64] TsDNISO, f. 136, op. 1, d. 9, l. 7.
[65] *ISS*, no. 88, May 8, 1918, 2.

worker had to join the ranks of the Red Army when drafted; fulfill all directives of Soviet power and its representatives at the workplace; exert himself accurately and consciously in order to raise productivity; put in a full day's work and overtime if needed; and respect materials, instruments, and state property.

This list can actually be read as a litany of problems with which the party had to cope, as the behavior of Saratov's workers during the siege of 1919 shows.[66] Party external language at this time maintained that agitational efforts positively affected "the more conscious working strata who are devoted to the revolution." However, "a most significant part of the toiling people, among whom are many partially literate or completely illiterate persons, remain outside our party work, remain indifferent, and sometimes even hostile to the worker-peasant revolution."[67] The party press also shamed male workers at the Zvezda metallurgical plant by contrasting their reception of "the pernicious influence of SRs and Mensheviks" with the purported loyalty of female workers who rejected such "rotten agitation."[68] In other words, the party saw labor opposition as proof of the immaturity of Russia's working class. Such a view not only justified coercion for a higher cause, but came dangerously close to the Mensheviks' argument that for this very reason Russia was ill-suited for social revolution.

Workers' Hidden Transcripts

Although we lack extensive sources that illuminate the party-state's interaction with the working class, the elliptical party documents present an advantage, for they are framed by the relationship of domination.[69] Since repression soon restricted the ability of workers to shape public life, we can examine their "hidden transcripts," which represent a critique of power behind its back. [70] Saratov workers expressed their consciousness in routine acts of resistance and circumvention: voting against Communist candidates and resolutions, abstaining from voting when elections lacked real choices, foot dragging, inertia, absenteeism,

---

[66] GASO, f. 471, op. 1, d. 1, l. 2.

[67] *ISS*, no. 171, Aug. 7, 1919, 2.

[68] Ibid., no. 209, Sept. 21, 1919, 3.

[69] William Sewell invites us to imagine a social universe in which "every social relationship is simultaneously constituted by meaning, by scarcity, and by power." I draw on this perspective here. See "Toward a Post-materialist Rhetoric for Labor History," in Lenard R. Berlanstein, ed., *Rethinking Labor History: Essays on Discourse and Class Analysis* (Urbana and Chicago, 1993), 33.

[70] Scott, *Domination*, xii–xiii.

pilfering, dissimulation, co-opting Soviet public language and practices and using them to their advantage, spreading rumors, and so on. Mapping out a dense cultural grid, these forms in which workers "spoke" reveal how they constructed their self-awareness in seeing things differently from the Bolsheviks. Class, then, amounted to the point of intersection between their material world and their understanding of everyday life.

Under conditions of cultural rupture, conformity with authority is still likely to occur, especially when force is used, but will tend to be self-serving or ritualistic and opportunistic compliance without commitment. Yet another strategy involves retreating from the alien larger society into smaller, parochial units (such as family or neighborhoods).[71] Be that as it may, when a subject population takes issue with the messages of those in power, the disenfranchised often unwittingly internalize alien cultural forms. An example would be workers accepting their special role in the Bolsheviks' social hierarchy, even though they opposed specific Bolshevik practices. Involving more than accommodation and resistance, these processes gave rise to complex webs of mutual dependence.[72]

Advancing their socioeconomic interests within the framework of Soviet power, workers promoted values that were more democratic and inclusive in a practical sense than those of the Bolsheviks. Although workers appear to have harbored resentment toward the bourgeoisie, they did not, for the most part, welcome the growing rift within the socialist camp that emerged after October 1917. As the moderate socialists criticized the nondemocratic turn Bolshevik power had taken and the soviets' loss of their independence, workers' attitudes remained volatile and the Bolsheviks' powerful majority in the soviet began to erode; groups that had traditionally supported the party called for an end to Bolshevik rule and the restoration of the Constituent Assembly. In April 1918, the Menshevik-Right SR bloc attracted strong backing in elections to the soviet in which the Bolsheviks won only a plurality.[73]

Bolshevik efforts to mobilize workers into the Red Guard caused further dissatisfaction, because workers saw such service as a burden and act of discrimination, not a privilege or obligation. Although the Red Guard had played a crucial role in the showdown back in October, only a handful of the 1,500 armed workers remained active in the organization at the start of 1918. The soviet's general mobilization of workers in

---

[71] Eckstein, "A Culturalist Theory," 797.

[72] Comaroff and Comaroff, *Ethnography*, 43, 176.

[73] *ISS*, no. 73, April 16, 1918, 3; no. 74, April 17, 1918, 3; no. 75, April 18, 1918, 3; *KG*, no. 46, April 17, 3; no. 49, April 20, 1918, 4; no. 52, April 24, 1918, 4; and Rashitov, "Sovety," 213–16.

January triggered bitter debate. Presaging what would become ever more vigorous opposition later, workers' groups resolved that service in the Red Guard would interfere with the efforts of factory committees and unions to establish control over factories.[74] In March metalworkers rejected the call for universal Red Guard service, voting to expel from their union individuals who did not subordinate themselves to it, in effect placing their authority higher than that of the soviet.[75] A soviet plenum overruled the executive committee's decree calling for general military training, and representatives of sixteen unions blasted it for continuing to see the decree as being "in the interests of the working class." Griping that the burden of paramilitary training had fallen unfairly on workers, the plenum majority called for universal service and an end to civil war.[76]

In the wake of the May 1918 uprising, worker collectives carried resolutions in support of the Soviet government and of paramilitary training, but workers' attitudes had not really changed. Lamented *Izvestiia*, "things always turn out to be just the opposite." For example, in July mill workers adopted resolutions backing Soviet power and agreed to military instruction; yet when it was time to begin, they voted down the call to arms by secret ballot. On July 30 the soviet heard a report that "the less conscious workers began to relate to it [the training] apathetically." The "less conscious" rubric, of course, is a moral projection: conscious workers were those who accepted the measure. According to the report, training went poorly in some neighborhoods, prompting the soviet "to take repressive measures to force workers in the face of the threatening danger to learn how to bear arms." In other words, the party knew what was best for them. The fact that factory committees and unions endorsed the soviet's actions suggests that many had already fallen under party control. Nonetheless, as an enticement to get workers to cooperate, the soviet in August declared it "desirable" to raise rations to a pound of bread per day. Workers, however, remained hostile to the training as well as to being called up to serve in the army.[77]

Conflicts over wages also caused considerable controversy within the working class and between it and the Bolshevik Party. Whenever workers questioned the soviet's policies, party leaders presented the challenge

[74] See GA RF, f. 7471, op. 1, d. 89, l. 6; *ISS*, no. 6, Jan. 10, 1918, 1; and no. 23, Jan. 20, 1918, 3.

[75] *KG*, no. 42, April 12, 1918, 4.

[76] *ISS*, no. 83, April 27, 1918, 1; Rashitov, "Sovety," 251; and *Saratovskii rabochii*, no. 2, April 17, 1918, 13.

[77] *ISS*, no. 136, July 10, 1918, 3; no. 159, Aug. 7, 1918, 3; no. 167, Aug. 2, 1919, 3; GA RF, f. 393, op. 3, d. 327, l. 49; *Saratovskii Sovet*, 601; and GASO, f. 692, op. 1, d. 64; f. 521, op. 5c, d. 12, ll. 2–3.

as a reflection of the workers' low consciousness. For instance, when the soviet raised tram fares that summer the number of passengers fell, necessitating a cut in tram workers' wages, who in turn threatened to strike. Maintaining that the workers' behavior "played into the hand of the counterrevolution," Bolsheviks harshly denounced the "drop of consciousness" and unwillingness of the tram workers to subordinate their interests "to those of the majority of workers and citizens of . . . Saratov." Such "shame tactics" failed to impress the industry's clerical workers, who carried a resolution in support of the Constituent Assembly.[78]

Subjected to factory closures and growing difficulties in eking out a living in an increasingly repressive political environment, workers expressed their discontent, which reflected a level of collective consciousness and action, in whatever ways they could. Although economic issues provided the venue for voicing dissatisfaction, workers' actions indicate that they understood economic life as contested political ground. They opposed one-party rule, the silencing of the opposition press, attempts to co-opt labor organs, and other repressive measures. Such opposition often amounted to demands for secret ballots during elections to factory committees, the soviet, and other organizations. Backing leveling policies, some workers resented those who received preferential treatment, yet the grim realities of everyday life drove all workers to find ways to manipulate the system to their own advantage, thereby creating an ironic form of mutual dependence. For their part, the Bolsheviks alternated between repression and solicitousness, depending upon how vulnerable they felt. Bolshevik "hidden transcripts," however, reveal a desire to control, manipulate, and repress. For instance, following a meeting of railroad workers in October 1918, party organs compiled a list of 114 individuals who needed to be "isolated" owing to their hostility to Soviet power, their counterrevolutionary activities, or their belonging to the Right SRs, Right Mensheviks, or "wrong" class.[79]

As the economy further unraveled and workers competed for scarce resources, they naturally put their own interests above those the Bolsheviks deemed fitting. Ignoring their union, Saratov's dockworkers used every possible stalling tactic to disregard the soviet's efforts to mobilize them to unload barges of firewood. As firewood disappeared from the city in late November 1918, barges laden with the commodity filled the Volga, and a good freeze would have sunk them. Unable to get the dockworkers to unload the barges, Commissar Mazlakh temporarily released "monks and members of the bourgeoisie" jailed during the Red Terror to begin the task; as it turned out, they "worked better than the

---

[78] *Saratovskii Sovet*, 584–85.
[79] TsDNISO, f. 81, op. 1, d. 2, ll. 2–4.

dockworkers." Concluding that the well-paid dockworkers had become accustomed to working for themselves, the soviet decided to use armed force if necessary and to deprive them of their rations.[80]

In March 1919, "counterrevolutionary agitation" and "the most foolish, ridiculous rumors" disrupted factory committee elections at Saratov's tobacco factories (with a largely female workforce). Left SR claims that no dictatorship of the proletariat existed, "but a dictatorship of one party" forced the local press to deny this was true. Swayed by charges workers made concerning unfair play, the ispolkom resisted the army's attempt to take over a local printing press, because it feared the consequences of its workers receiving larger rations and being made exempt from military service.[81] The ispolkom had reason to be anxious, for workers bombarded Bolshevik speakers with "veiled" questions regarding higher pay for "specialists."[82] The Cheka portrayed the local railroad depot as "a nest of counterrevolution," rebuking the 1,000 workers employed there for performing work in an intolerable manner. Few worker collectives in Saratov were as skilled as these, revealing that the party grossly overestimated its support within the working class. Threatening to strike, the workers grumbled about lack of food and shoes and also that their circumstances were reminiscent of those under the autocracy: the administration was satiated but not the workers. Indeed, drawing parallels between the autocracy and the Bolshevik dictatorship became a common feature of workers' oppositional discourse and was a way for them to create themselves as workers. Delegates at a Volga region conference of railroad workers also protested the Cheka's arrest of union members, which the delegates insisted further disrupted transport. It certainly curbed the number of strikes.[83]

Troubled by workers' withdrawal from public life, the soviet organized "unaffiliated" workers' conferences in September 1919 at which activists were instructed to identify, recruit, and co-opt sympathetic "non-party" workers attending the gatherings.[84] This phenomenon coincided with calls within the party "to permit free discussion of all problems, to permit the creation of free workers' organizations, and to restore democratic guarantees."[85] But herein lay the Bolsheviks' dilemma: the slightly more open political climate encouraged the opposition.

[80] *Saratovskii Sovet*, 667–69.

[81] *KG*, no. 308, March 16, 1919, 3; *ISS*, no. 10, Jan. 15, 1919, 2; and GASO, f. 521, op. 2, d. 34, l. 103.

[82] *ISS*, no. 167, Aug. 2, 1919, 3.

[83] TsDNISO, f. 27, op. 1, d. 76, l. 112, also *Privolzhskii krasnyi put'*, no. 6–7 (1919): 44–45, and no. 11–12 (1919): 6–7.

[84] *ISS*, no. 183, Aug. 21, 1919, 2–3, and RGASPI, f. 17, op. 84, d. 145, ll. 3–7.

[85] *ISS*, no. 215, Sept. 30, 1919, 4, and no. 216, Oct. 1, 1919, 4.

Mensheviks and SRs still found a sympathetic following among printers, tanners, and others. Under Menshevik influence, Saratov's printers'
union not only voted against Communist-backed initiatives, but also
rejected the Menshevik Central Committee's conciliatory stance. At a
meeting of unaffiliated "white-collar" workers, participants removed
from the agenda the election of a Communist Party cell, heckling Communist candidates.[86]

The winter of 1919–20 was the worst yet: the city lacked fuel and
electricity to heat and illuminate buildings, water pipes froze and burst,
poorly fed Saratovites succumbed to disease; factory inspectors deemed
the vast majority of workplaces "unsatisfactory." The defeat of the
Whites encouraged an intensification of civil war policies to address the
problem. A January 1920 decree, which built on earlier attempts to
militarize labor, obliged all citizens to provide their labor to the state.
Soon the local executive committee announced that the entire adult
population would restore the railroads and river fleet, clean up the city,
and sow.[87] In March the Soviet government extended labor bonuses and
decreed a labor ration (based on the type of work one did) that replaced
the class ration. It set up labor disciplinary courts to deal with absenteeism, instituted one-person management, and restructured unions to
raise productivity. These measures, as well as use of bourgeois specialists, piece-rate wages, and labor books to control movement, provoked
waves of unrest in Russia, uniting workers who otherwise had little in
common and once again showing how they created themselves as workers. In turn, labor disturbances ended a period of relaxation in the
party's tolerance of rival socialist parties, just as it gave rise to opposition groups within the Communist Party.[88]

The opacity of some sources makes it impossible to determine
whether traditional shop-floor subcultures continued to provide leadership to workers' efforts to circumvent government coercion. Be that as
it may, workers' collective actions speak volumes about their concerns.
A party inquiry into why workers at the Sotrudnik plant did not show
up to do mandatory work concluded that the party cell had actually
opposed the measures, ostensibly to protect workers. Even though railroads had been militarized, their workers had not received rations and
therefore set about to secure food on their own.[89] Another prototypical
response to the workers' economic dilemma was that of workers at Mill

---

[86] Ibid., no. 253, Nov. 14, 1919, 4, and no. 269, Dec. 3, 1919, 3.

[87] GASO, f. 456, op. 1, d. 336, l. 8, and S. I. Gusev, *Trudovye mobilizatsii i trudovye armii v Saratovskoi gubernii: Materialy k 9-mu s"ezdu R.K.P.* (N.P., 1920), passim.

[88] Jonathan Aves, *Workers against Lenin: Labour Protest and the Bolshevik Dictator-ship* (London, 1996), 2, 5–38.

[89] *ISS*, no. 274, Dec. 9, 1919, 3, and TsDNISO, f. 81, op. 1, d. 33, l. 83.

No. 4, who showed up for work, punched in, and then went about their real business of queuing in lines. Some did not even bother to make an appearance at all, except to receive their pay. A surprise check in February 1920 revealed that only 45 percent of the workforce was present.[90] When the military authorities carried out a search among leather workers in Bazarnyi Karabulak, they discovered widespread pilfering, but could not crack down on the problem because the local militia was implicated in the operations.[91] Such collective actions certainly reveal a community of economic interest.

In addition to the Menshevik activities already noted, anarchists won elections at the Zhest and Zvezda plants (and Revolutionary Communists at several others), got the upper hand in a public debate with Communists, and disrupted a worker–Red Army conference in March 1920.[92] Party internal language interpreted the rise of anarchist (and Menshevik) fortunes at this time as an expression of worker hostility toward the labor draft, which it viewed as a "new, no less shameful form of desertion."[93] This interpretation, of course, further justified the use of compulsion. Moreover, a provincial meeting of the Union of Employees (*Rabotuch*) split when a resolution carried accusing Communists of disruptive tactics. The leader of the unaffiliated faction, Vinogradov, called for an independent labor movement and freedom of the press. As *Izvestiia* muttered, these were "wolves in sheep's clothing," also known as "socialist traitors — Mensheviks and SRs."[94] Pressured to carry a resolution greeting Lenin and Trotsky, workers at Print Shop No. 2 voted "neither for nor against" the document.[95]

Many workers also did whatever they could to avoid participating in "volunteer" workdays (subbotniki) (figure 11.2). When Zhest factory workers and others refused to take part in the "volunteer" workday on May 1, 1920, the Cheka began to closely monitor the mood at all local metalworks. While Gubprofsovet called the Zhest workers' protest "a violation of proletarian union discipline and the greatest of crimes against the entire working class," the regional SR committee denounced the public "trial," using the opportunity to raise a stinging indictment of the Communists' broken promises, repression, and disastrous eco-

[90] *ISS*, no. 32, Feb. 11, 1920, 3.

[91] GASO, f. 692, op. 1, d. 78, ll. 32–33.

[92] *Novyi mir*, no. 2 (1920): 9; TsDNISO, f. 81, op. 1, d. 33, l. 19; f. 151/95, op. 1, d. 53, l. 15; *ISS*, no. 62, March 17, 1920, 3; and *Privolzhskii krasnyi put'*, no. 3–4 (1920): 13.

[93] S. I. Gusev, *Ocherednye voprosy khoziaistvennogo stroitel'stva (O tezisakh Ts. K. R. K. P.): Materialy k 9–mu s"ezdu R. K. P.* (Saratov, 1920), 3–9.

[94] *ISS*, no. 56, March 9, 1920, 3, and no. 99, May 6, 1920, 4.

[95] Ibid., no. 100, May 7, 1920, 4.

11.2 Cleaning rubble from the street and restoring tram transportation during a subbotnik in Saratov. Courtesy Gosudarstvennyi Arkhiv Saratovskoi Oblasti (GASO).

nomic policies.[96] According to the Cheka, the opposition socialist parties had begun agitating workers back in November; however, the frustrated political police failed to uncover the SR oblast committee that had planned to hold a congress in Saratov.[97] Denying the workers agency, confidential documents link the unrest to opposition parties. Thus, the mood at Zvezda was "explosive" because Mensheviks hiding behind the "nonparty" rubric controlled the factory union. Similarly, the atmosphere at the prosthesis workshop was "hostile" because its leadership was Menshevik; at the Nobel Warehouse Mensheviks agitated only because the Communist Party cell remained small.[98] Yet it was working-class rejection of Bolshevik policies and not the opposition parties that provoked the unrest, and this was something the party's ideological gaze could not see. Blaming the growing number of fires in

[96] RGASPI, f. 274, op. 1, d. 18. ll. 26–26 ob.
[97] TsDNISO, f. 136, op. 1, d. 43, l. 20, and f. 27, op. 1, d. 491, l. 149.
[98] GASO, f. 3310, op. 1, d. 1, ll. 2–7.

urban Russia on "spies and saboteurs," the government introduced martial law in twenty-four provinces on May 11, including Saratov.[99]

In this strained environment the party took no chances. In June the gubkom called upon secretaries of party cells to hold conferences of unaffiliated workers under the banner "everything for the front," instructing the secretaries not to let the elections run their course. Instead, they were to identify approved candidates in advance, and to promote their election so that workers would not become suspicious. But the party could no longer hoodwink the by now cynical proletariat. Workers in some unions refused to vote on resolutions presented by Communists, while a wave of "Italian" strikes or factory occupations broke out elsewhere. Mill workers went out in July, protesting reduced rations, the unfair and chaotic goods' distribution, and lack of firewood. The party acknowledged that female workers in the sewing industry toed the line only because they feared their union's leadership.[100] Workers' unrest stimulated "complete demoralization" in the 40,000–man garrison (which included 13,000 former deserters), as soldiers insulted party agitators, protested the lack of rations, and demanded a forum to air their grievances.[101]

By August a calamitous situation had developed, for the consequences of the bad harvest now became apparent to some just as a current of misguided optimism regarding the possibility of rapidly constructing a Communist economic order prevailed within the party. Daily fires broke out in the city and one destroyed much of it, exacerbating poor living conditions and agitating the political mood. Strikes and walkouts occurred at Saratov's mills, at the Zhest plant, and at other factories, prompting a spate of arrests and repression. In September railroad workers went out on strike to protest a reduction in rations and new pay scales. Arrests only made the situation worse, forcing the administration to accept the workers' demands.[102] Menshevik and SR agitation continued unabated as tensions within the Communist Party triggered debates over the future of unions and the role of workers in production. To prevent widespread abuses, the party took measures to regulate sick leave, and to cut down on the systematic theft of materials that had taken on "epidemic" proportions at Zhest and elsewhere. The Cheka sent several ringleaders to concentration camps, and resolved that "a small purge" was needed at Zvezda and a "removal of hooligan ele-

---

[99] Aves, *Workers against Lenin*, 33.

[100] TsDNISO, f. 136, op. 1, d. 36, l. 11, and f. 27, op. 1, d. 492, ll. 14, 81, 83, 100.

[101] GASO, f. 521, op. 2, d. 41, l. 2; TsDNISO, f. 27, op. 1, d. 758, l. 15; and RGASPI, f. 17, op. 13, d. 869, ll. 2–6.

[102] TsDNISO, f. 27, op. 1, d. 507, l. 7; d. 758, l. 17; f. 81, op. 1, d. 31, ll. 9, 13; GASO, f. 692, op. 1, d. 78; *Na transport*, no. 43, July 17, 1920, 2; and no. 99, Oct. 13, 1920, 2.

ments" at Zhest. In all, at the start of 1921 the Cheka took more than 300 Saratov workers hostage in order to break the opposition.[103] Although the ferment touched all strata of Saratov workers, it must be emphasized that the skilled metalworkers, railroad workers, and printers — the most "conscious" workers — demonstrated the most determined resistance.

Workers contested repression and the Communists' violation of fair play and workplace democracy. Threatening to strike in January 1921, Novaia Etna workers protested the arrest of several of their comrades on the eve of their departure to Moscow to participate in a congress.[104] In early February Novaia Etna workers discussed the increasingly controversial issue of unequal pay at a time when the authorities needed to reduce rations. As part of the defense establishment, the Novaia Etna workers had benefited from bonuses, substantial enough to get by on, as a result of which productivity rose slightly, since workers did not have to spend their time searching for food. Appealing for an end to the "chaotic" system of remuneration and for a leveling of wages and rations, workers at other factories deemed less vital griped that they worked as hard as their Novaia Etna comrades and were physically broken by the starvation rations. Challenging the Communists to resolve the dilemma, Novaia Etna workers proposed gradually raising the pay and rations of other workers, rather than decreasing their own.[105]

As material conditions deteriorated that winter and demobilized Red Army soldiers returned home, workers blamed the Bolshevik regime for their suffering. Lack of fuel and materials kept factories idle as rumors spread that authorities had beaten and arrested protesting workers, that Soviet power had been overthrown elsewhere, and that government cafeterias fed workers cats and dogs. More than a form of dissident expression, rumors functioned as light artillery in the arsenal of workers' resistance. At the end of February 1921, construction workers and sewing industry workers threatened to strike. A confidential report found discontent in all factories over diminishing food supplies, as workers called for equal rations and an end to shock workers who received more for greater output. Seething with discontent, railroad and other workers in Pokrovsk excoriated the Communists. The document concluded that the political mood was "satisfactory,"[106] but as we shall see in the next chapter, this was far from the case.

[103] TsDNISO, f. 81, op. 1, d. 28, l. 418; d. 31, ll. 24, 31; GASO, f. 521, op. 2, d. 45, ll. 21, 22; *ISS*, no. 284, Dec. 14, 1920, 3; A. V. Goncharov and V. N. Danilov, *Saratovskoe Povolzh'e v period grazhdanskoi voiny (1918–1921 gg.)* (Saratov, 2000), 151.

[104] TsDNISO, f. 44, op. 1, d. 5, ll. 75–75 ob.

[105] Ibid., f. 44, op. 1, d. 5, ll. 82–83.

[106] *ISS*, no. 6, Jan. 11, 1921, 5; no. 10, Jan. 15, 1921, 2; Pleve, *Iz istorii*, 13; TsDNISO, f. 138, op. 1, d. 38, l. 47.

Conclusion

While the Bolsheviks' construction of class lends itself to being grist in the postmodernists' mill, more traditional structural definitions of class based on the proletarian model that until recently predominated in studies of labor history make evident that the most conscious Saratov workers broke with the party that ruled in their name. While civil war reduced the size of the Saratov proletariat and reconfigured it, most workers were at danger of becoming declassed *after* the military hostilities had ended. The conscious, skilled worker vanguard constituting a bastion of support for the Bolshevik Party existed only symbolically in party narratives, for authentic workers, whose behavior deprived them of these virtues, proved reluctant to give up their autonomy. In a sense, their ambivalence, disillusion, apathy, and resistance strategies reflected a class consciousness forged in their efforts to retain an independent voice. Because the party saw worker opposition as an embarrassment, it found dim reflection in Bolshevik documents. While we might regret that the sources do not tell more, they suggest that workers, especially the skilled, demonstrated political consciousness in their resistance to forms of Bolshevik control.

There are many reasons why the workers' movement during the Civil War failed to change the nature of the regime. Repression played an important part. So did the Communists' colonizing the discourse and organizational practices of the labor movement.[107] Unions became extensions of the party, but only after much opposition. And when they did, they lost workers' interest. Workers' mass withdrawal from trade unions in 1921 once membership no longer was compulsory makes this clear. Further, Civil War conditions gave rise to competition over scarce resources and to a parochialism that not only kept workers divided, but also made a mockery of party internationalist language. The gap between wages and real expenses, ubiquitous scarcities, and widespread unemployment compelled them to perfect survival strategies and to retreat from political life. Thus, economic issues both determined their behavior and also limited their options: Bolshevik control of the food supply and the physical exhaustion of the population played vital roles in the party's surviving the ordeal of Civil War.

The new relations between workers and the party-state negotiated during the Civil War based on adaptation, resistance, and forms of circumvention reordered daily life by promoting workers' strategies of evasion, avoidance, selective participation, and hostility. Moreover, in reading workers' actions as symbols of their political mood, it becomes

---

[107] Sakwa, *Soviet Communists in Power*, 269.

clear that a rupture had occurred between them and the party-state. Workers' behavior undermined the party's representations of them in its public language, which workers manipulated to their own advantage. The result was a form of mutual dependency and perhaps the origin of the popular view that workers pretended to work and the party pretended to pay them. The long-term effect of revolutionary transformations tends to diverge from original intents and "resemble more the revolutionary condition of society."[108] In other words, many features of Soviet life that observers identify with later periods had already found expression between 1918 and 1922. Judging by studies of labor protest under Stalin, the identities workers constructed for themselves through the experience of civil war temporarily survived the loss of their own public political space.

---

[108] Eckstein, "A Culturalist Theory," 800.

Twelve

A Provincial Kronstadt, Another Tambov?

AFTER THEIR lunch break on March 3, 1921, workers in Saratov's railroad shops did not return to their benches, but instead rallied to discuss an anticipated further reduction in food rations. Assuming what the Cheka called an "agitated and disturbing character," the meeting quickly turned into a forum at which offended workers lashed out against Soviet power and the Communists. Led by a former Communist, the railroad workers debated resolutions recently carried by the Moscow proletariat, who had demanded a coalition government and independent labor organizations. The next day the strike spread to the metallurgical plants and to most other large factories, as Saratov workers elected representatives to an independent commission charged with evaluating the functioning of all economic organs. When it convened, the body called for the reelection of the soviets and immediate release of political prisoners. Coinciding with an epidemic of peasant disturbances in the province's angry villages that threatened to rival that of neighboring Tambov, a depressed mood in local garrisons, and mass discontent among the nonproletarian urban elements with Bolshevik power, the events of early 1921 represented a danger to the party that was arguably more formidable than that of the Whites.

The withering of food supplies along the Volga in early 1921 had triggered a crisis of unprecedented proportions, but one that has been lost in the historical shadow of the Kronstadt uprising.[1] While labor

[1] For a discussion of the Kronstadt uprising see Paul Avrich, *Kronstadt 1921* (New York, 1970) and Israel Getzler, *Kronstadt, 1917–1921* (Cambridge, Eng., 1983). For the

379

disturbances in Petrograd at this time are usually viewed as a prelude to the soldiers' revolt at Kronstadt, when Red fought Red, a conspiracy of silence among Soviet historians, and, until recently, a lack of documentation, have relegated to obscurity similar ferment in Moscow and perhaps most provincial capitals. The party announced the end of grain requisitioning not only in response to rural unrest, but also in response to the wave of industrial strikes—which the party represented as a work slowdown or *volynka*—in key urban centers.[2] The issues that inflamed workers were not new, nor were they solely economic in nature, but now that the Whites had been defeated they were more sharply defined. In Saratov, repressive measures, concessions, and famine conditions eventually diffused the political crisis caused by worker and peasant unrest, giving the Bolsheviks another chance to consolidate their hold over a spent society.

On the Eve

Although shaped by ideology and by an evolving code of reporting, confidential Cheka and party reports offer assessments of the mass mood rarely found in the Communists' more propagandistic public language. Significantly, the reports document the near universal anti-Bolshevik feelings the local population harbored by late 1920, when they intensified among people from all walks of life. As factory workers agitated against the Bolsheviks, productivity continued to fall at Saratov factories. Concluding that "the worst can be feared," one report spoke of growing SR popularity among "less developed" lumber industry workers, who were labeled "the most anti-Soviet." But the every-bit-as-real unrest at the city's metallurgical plants and in the railroad shops posed an even greater threat, for their workers represented the anointed "conscious" element that by definition should back Soviet power. As anonymous citizens demanded the Cheka put an end to the illicit peddling of goods, workers went out on strike in Pokrovsk. Support for the Communists eroded so much by January 1921 that the gubispolkom deemed it dangerous to reduce rations. Instead, it called for a verifica-

---

Tambov peasant uprising see Oliver Radkey, *The Unknown Civil War in Soviet Russia: A Study of the Green Movement in the Tambov Region, 1920–1921* (Stanford, 1976); Delano Dugarm, "Peasant Wars in Tambov Province," in *The Bolsheviks in Russian Society: The Revolution and Civil Wars*, ed. V. N. Brovkin (New Haven and London, 1997), 177–200; and S. A. Esikov and L. G. Protasov, "'Antonovshchina': Novye podkhody," *Voprosy istorii*, no. 6–7 (1992): 47–57.

[2] Aves, *Workers against Lenin*, 111–57.

tion of reserves in the hopes that the actual situation would turn out to be less grave than it appeared to be.[3]

Party internal language pinned the blame for the "unsatisfactory" mood on the ubiquitous shortages, rather than on the politics that caused them. Explaining worker unrest as a response to economic conditions and as one mediated by the rival socialist parties was a form of silencing the other, more overtly political, aspects of workers' discontent. While there is no denying the impact material considerations had on workers' consciousness, workers since 1918 had also pressed political agendas, calling for free elections and independent labor organizations. In locating politics only in the economic discontent of the masses, the party not only revealed its materialistic worldview, but likewise denied workers political consciousness, even agency. Moreover, party internal language similarly blamed food shortages and foul living conditions in the barracks for the local soldiers' unreliability, and implicated grain requisitioning, carried out "unintelligently and tactlessly," for the heady ferment in Saratov's villages, which welcomed armed bands (Greens). Their arrival triggered massive uprisings and disturbances everywhere; even in those districts into which the bandits had not yet made significant forays, peasants lashed out against Communists. Unrest caused by requisitioning swept across Atkarsk, for example, where peasants murdered fourteen party members in December 1920.[4]

Just days before worker disturbances broke out in Saratov, the gubispolkom confirmed that the masses were voicing open hostility to the Communists, but once again explained this in terms of unpopular economic programs. It acknowledged that many Communists had discredited themselves and the party by taking advantage of their positions for personal gain, and that some village party cells illegally appropriated grain for their own use. Finding ample evidence of SR influence in the villages, the authorities concluded that if the supply situation did not improve, Saratov could expect uprisings, which would imperil Soviet power locally, because the Cheka lacked agents (many had left for the Polish front), the Red Army could not be relied upon, and the militia was short of weapons.[5] Since October 1920 the Cheka had monitored the activities of "nonparty" SRs and Mensheviks employed in key Soviet agencies, arresting and executing the "ringleaders."[6] Such measures failed to prevent the excesses the authorities feared, however,

[3] GASO, f. 456, op. 1, d. 532, l. 16, and f. 3387, op. 2, d. 1, l. 6.

[4] Ibid., f. 456, op. 1, d. 675, ll. 111, 150, 179; f. 456, op. 1, d. 678, ll. 71, 76–77 ob, 212, 232 ob–234; f. 471, op. 1, d. 22, l. 1; and Berelovich and Danilov, *Sovetskaia derevnia*, 1: 281.

[5] GASO, f. 456, op. 1, d. 675, ll. 304–4 ob, also f. 456, op. 1, d. 678, l. 75 ob.

[6] Ibid., f. 456, op. 1, d. 630, l. 10.

precisely because mass discontent ran so deep and had taken on a political face.

Peasants in Revolt

Appearing in Saratov in 1920 from neighboring provinces, armed bands turned rural dissatisfaction into a potential jacquerie. The troops of A. P. Sapozhkov, who burst into Saratov's trans-Volga districts that summer, first raised the banner of revolt, just as thousands of peasant soldiers returned home. But it was the incursions of forces associated with A. S. Antonov, K. Vakulin, and Popov at the end of 1920 that prompted local Communists to claim that "all measures must be taken immediately or else Saratov Province in all respects will be lost to the Republic."[7] As Lenin remarked, this "counterrevolution is without doubt more dangerous than Denikin, Yudenich, and Kolchak taken together."[8]

The Communist Party (and some Western historians) have depicted the disparate groups of self-defined peasant revolutionaries or Greens as a "movement," endowing them with more coherence than existed. Nevertheless, the peasant bands did pose a threat to Soviet power. Although the party blamed the phenomenon on the machinations of SR leaders, they spotlighted its "spontaneous" character, later denying they had had anything to do with the affair, perhaps owing to its ultimate failure.[9] More than just a reaction to economic exploitation, the uprising protested lack of freedom in the economic realm and the Soviet system's use of coercion in the countryside. A more furious expression of the same sort of discontent unleashed by the peasantry back in 1918 and again in 1919, the series of peasant wars had a source as much in the prevailing ideology of revolution as outside it.

The SR Party might not have orchestrated the peasant revolt, but individual party members ardently participated in it, and SR values — including violence — provided the political frame for the peasant rebels' program.[10] Despite some differences in the demands of particular groups, the Greens did not oppose Soviet power, but rather the specific policies of War Communism and the arbitrary lording over them of "vampire-Communists, Jews, and commissar-usurpers." Seeking to put an end to "Bolshevik tyranny," the Greens advocated restoration of the Constitu-

---

[7] GASO, f. 521, op. 2, d. 41, l. 3.

[8] V. I. Lenin, *Polnoe sobranie sochinenii*, vol. 43 (Moscow, 1970), 24.

[9] See Partiia sotsialistov-revoliutsionerov, *Kak Tambovskie krest'iane boriatsia za svobodu* (n.p., 1921), 11.

[10] Seth Singleton, "The Tambov Revolt (1920–1921)," *Slavic Review* 25, no. 3 (1966): 502.

ent Assembly and a parliamentary government without monarchists. Their own external language as conveyed in their slogans said it all: "Rise up, working people, shed your yoke and resume free labor. Long live free trade, freedom, and government elected by the people." "Down with communes and Communist-robbers! Long live Soviet power!"[11]

The Greens struck a responsive chord in Saratov Province in part because of the activities of the Union of Toiling Peasants (*Soiuz trudovogo krest'ianstva*) promoted by the SR Party, which advocated the overthrow of the Communists and election of a new Constituent Assembly. It is clear why the Bolsheviks suspected the SRs of planning an armed uprising against Soviet power: literature issued by the party's regional committee — in effect, a competing public transcript — called for the political equality of all citizens regardless of class, an end to civil war, the right to the fruits of one's own labor, restoration of the Constituent Assembly, basic human freedoms, the socialization of land, partial denationalization of industry, national self-determination, the restoration of handicraft industry, and creation of volunteer partisan units that would sweep the Bolsheviks from power.[12] One SR pamphlet urged Communists to give up power, intoning that they had no friends among laboring people and remained in power thanks only to their monstrous use of terror. Dismissing the Communists' argument that the peasantry lacked consciousness, the document charged that it was their very consciousness of human freedom that prompted them to rise up with primitive farm instruments against the party's machine guns. The pamphlet challenged the party, "intoxicated with its bloody dictatorship," to notice that *"even the proletariat considers the party a usurper."*[13]

A former second lieutenant in the Red Army, A. P. Sapozhkov launched a revolt against Communist power in July 1920 in Buzuluk, and for two months maneuvered in the region. At the end of July his troops, some 1,000–1,200 strong, attacked Novouzensk, where Sapozhkov's slogans, "Down with requisitioning" and "Long live free trade," struck a responsive chord among local peasants, making clear that this was more a peasant rebellion than a military mutiny. Appropriating Communist Party discourse, Sapozhkov maintained that Moscow's misguided policies demonstrated that White Guards had actually penetrated *the Communist Party's* inner sanctum. When troops in the Novouzensk garrison fled under artillery attack from Sapozhkov's

---

[11] TsDNISO, f. 200, op. 1, d. 292, l. 1; GASO, f. 521, op. 1, d. 633, l. 4; and German, *Nemetskaia avtonomiia*, 96–100.

[12] GASO, f. 521, op. 5, d. 11, ll. 13, 24–25 ob. Representative SR brochures are *Mirskoi prigovor* (n.p., 1921) and *Chto dali bol'sheviki narodu* (n.p., 1921).

[13] Emphasis added. RGASPI, f. 17, op. 12, d. 473, l. 144.

"army of truth," the Novouzensk Revolutionary Committee arrested the family members of those fighting in his band. Although Red units defeated Sapozhkov in September 1920, a Green who had fought with him, Serov, moved on to Uralsk, where he mobilized the peasantry against Soviet power until his defeat in 1922.[14]

Antonov's units, which transformed Tambov into a hotbed of revolt, made their first surprise intrusion into Balashov District on October 5, 1920. Withdrawing after killing twenty-three Communists, they returned in January, an estimated 9,000 strong. The Greens drove the party organization into the underground and burned alive three requisitioning agents before moving on to Serdobsk. Antonov focused on recruiting demobilized Red Army soldiers in locales reeling from the excesses of requisitioning squads. He relied on SR spy rings that provided him with lists of Communists and with information about the strength of and mood in Red Army units.[15] After entering a village Antonov typically addressed the village assembly, demanding an end to Soviet power and restoration of the Constituent Assembly. Shooting Soviet officials and requisition squad workers, his bands replaced rural soviets with "councils of five" in the territories through which they moved.[16]

In labeling the peasant rebels "bandits," the party sought to reduce them to nothing more than a criminal element, thereby diverting attention from the political threat they posed. Ironically, the party fell victim to its own rhetorical strategies. At first Moscow failed to understand the danger posed by the "bandits," forbidding the provincial military censor from printing anti-Green literature. One reason local Communists underestimated the Greens' appeal was because some peasants hid Communists and food supply agents when the bands appeared.[17] Villagers, after all, could not always differentiate between the Greens' form of social protest and criminal bands that had proliferated during the Civil War. But this soon began to change, and when it did the party started to employ the term *eserobanditizm* (SR-banditry), which added a counterrevolutionary connotation to the "criminals'" actions. To be sure, some peasants continued to reject the Greens; however, most sympathized with them, especially when the bands seized grain reserves and

[14] GASO, f. 456, op. 1, d. 676, l. 130; f. 521, op. 5c, d. 9, ll. 2, 3, 17; E. Vasina, *Banditizm v Saratovskoi gubernii* (Saratov, 1928), 5–7; Berelovich and Danilov, *Sovetskaia derevnia*, 1: 281–82; R. A. Taubin, "Razgrom kulatskogo miatezha Sapozhkova," *Bor'ba klassov*, no. 12 (1934): 56–62; and Figes, *Peasant Russia*, 335–40.

[15] Vasina, *Banditizm*, 1–3.

[16] See, for example, GASO, f. 521, op. 5, d. 11, l. 26, and f. 456, op. 1, d. 675, l. 82.

[17] G. Vedeniapin, *Balashovskaia organizatsiia RKP v bor'be s banditizmom, 1920–1921 gg.* (Balashov, 1922), 6–7; Levinson, "Kontrrevoliutsiia," 87–88; and TsDNISO, f. 27, op. 1, d. 507, ll. 24–25.

distributed them among irate villagers. Even when the Greens committed "excesses," many peasants balked at welcoming Red Army soldiers. Consequently, the movement assumed "colossal proportions"[18] as peasant uprisings erupted in *every* district within the province and peasants rose up against Soviet power with whatever "weapons" they had.[19] Demobilized Red Army soldiers played a central role in the villages both in welcoming and rebuffing the Greens.[20]

Saratov Communists realized the gravity of the Green threat once Kirill Vakulin's bands arrived in January 1921. Capturing Kamyshin and Khvalynsk, they executed all local Communists who fell into their hands.[21] Defeated in April, Vakulin went into hiding, but shortly thereafter launched a second raid during which he killed many Communists before he himself perished. However, Popov replaced him and the bands occupied Khvalynsk again.[22] Another attack that took place in March 1921 under the command of Piatakov ignited the Volga German autonomous oblast. Rovnoe became the center of hostilities as the local population joined his units in executing more than 200 Communists and their families. Some German peasants hid Communists, but a broad swath of the German-populated districts rose up before the Red Army reclaimed the territory. In Markshtadt alone the Red Army shot 286 individuals accused of anti-Soviet behavior, sent hundreds more to concentration camps, and levied fines on entire villages. Later, Serov's bands made forays into the German territories well into 1922.[23]

The relative isolation of local communities and the subaltern nature of the peasant world made it unlikely that a peasant revolt triggered by one-time Red Army men would succeed without outside leadership and organization. Be that as it may, the Bolsheviks realized that the spate of uprisings that they represented as a bona fide movement could have tipped the scales against the party because of the potent ferment in the cities. Interrupting grain requisitioning and agricultural production, the Greens threatened Soviet rule because they killed Communists whenever they encountered them and exacerbated food shortages in the cities. The

[18] TsDNISO, f. 138, op. 1, d. 33, l. 246; GASO, f. 456, op. 1, d. 400, ll. 156, 222; and *Balashovskaia organizatsiia*, 5, 8, 12. See E. J. Hobsbawm's *Bandits*, rev. ed. (New York, 1981), and GASO, f. 521, op. 1, d. 716, l. 1 ob.

[19] GASO, f. 521, op. 1, d. 633, 1l. 2–3 ob, and TsDNISO, f. 27, op. 2. d. 43, l. 124.

[20] GASO, f. 521, op. 5, d. 11, ll. 17–17 ob.

[21] Vasina, *Banditizm*, 4–5; GASO, f. 456, op. 1, d. 676, l. 114; f. 456, op. 1, d. 678, l. 203.

[22] GASO, f. 521, op. 1, d. 610, ll. 1–14; f. 471, op. 1, d. 23, l. 8. For Popov's band see Berelovich and Danilov, *Sovetskaia derevnia*, 1: 393–94, 397, 408, 419.

[23] German, *Nemetskaia avtonomiia*, 100–113, 157; GASO, f. 456, op. 1, d. 678, l. 163. For more on Serov's bands see Berelovich and Danilov, *Sovetskaia derevnia*, 1: 523, 614, 621–22, 649, 674.

peasant bands executed an estimated 570 Saratov Communists and sympathizers, destroyed 41 collective farms, disbanded Soviet agencies, attacked grain-collecting stations, and seized enormous quantities of seed, agricultural products, and livestock.[24] Often the approach of the Greens abetted anti-Soviet forces in the towns, as in Atkarsk when Popov's bands called upon workers to strike.[25] After Vakulin's bands held Kamyshin in December 1920, officials absconded against a backdrop of chaos.[26] Owing to Antonov's presence in Balashov, Communists quit the party, got themselves thrown out, or else fled.[27] In other towns mobilized Communists demanded rations for their families under threat of turning in their party cards.[28]

While the local press reported that peasants opposed the Greens, party internal language admits that peasants in some districts remained hostile to Soviet power or largely indifferent. In Atkarsk, poor peasants and newcomers welcomed the armed bands, while the better-off strata of the peasantry harbored as much suspicion toward the peasant "other" as they did toward the Greens. The party sought to change the peasants' attitudes toward the Greens by offering the farmers seed, but they took advantage of the gesture to curse Soviet power for not being strong enough to deal with the bandits to begin with.[29] Nor did the introduction of the New Economic Policy (NEP) win over the peasantry, who at first refused to believe the government had replaced requisitioning with a less burdensome tax in kind (*prodnalog*) and who then complained bitterly that it initially differed little from requisitioning.[30]

Once it understood the potency of the Green threat, the party vigorously suppressed the movement, secretly setting up an organ at the national level and a Revolutionary Military Council (RMC) in Saratov to combat banditry on January 5, 1921. One of its first acts was to quell an uprising in the Mikhailov garrison in Elansk under the banners "Down with the Communists" and "Free Trade," which resulted in the

---

[24] E. J. Hobsbawm, "Peasants and Politics," *Journal of Peasant Studies* 1, no. 1 (1973): 3–22; B. M. Chigirinskii, "Bor'ba bol'shevikov Nizhnei Volgi protiv kulachestva kak sotsial'noi opory kontrrevoliutsii v pervye gody NEPa," in *Iz istorii partiinykh i komsomol'skikh organizatsii Povolzh'ia* (Volgograd, 1972), 88; and A. I. Strel'tsova, "Partiinaia organizatsiia Saratovskoi gubernii v bor'be za provedenie politiki partii v derevne v vostanovitel'nyi period (1921–1925 gody)" (candidate diss., Moscow State University, 1953), 47.

[25] TsDNISO, f. 200, op. 1, d. 277, ll. 1–2.

[26] GASO, f. 456, op. 1, d. 695, ll. 14–15, and f. 521, op. 1, d. 610, ll. 3–4, 12–14 ob.

[27] TsDNISO, f. 27, op. 2, d. 310, l. 16.

[28] Ibid., f. 27, op. 2, d. 318, l. 19.

[29] *VSG*, no. 11 (1921): 9, 21–23.

[30] GASO, f. 521, op. 1, d. 718, ll. 1–10; f. 456, op. 1, d. 678, l. 227; and *ISS*, no. 115, May 26, 1921, 2.

brutal deaths of twenty Communists. To counter the bands' appeal, the RMC took hostages in each volost of the inflamed district. The measure had the desired effect.[31] Warning that the entire province might fall to the Greens, the gubkom requested cavalry units from Moscow to deal with the bands.[32] In April the gubkom established revolutionary committees that assumed power in the districts, instructing special forces to take punitive measures. It also ordered local populations to return all grain by May 1 or face harsh reprisals.[33] Launching a propaganda campaign to inform the population that the NEP had replaced the rapacious requisitioning with a tax in kind, the party emphasized the threats posed by the bandits as it paid homage to the memory of Communists slain by them.[34] Its public register depicted the Greens as a composite of all of the party's enemies, linking the movement to an SR-Kadet plot hatched in Paris responsible for Kronstadt and other disturbances.[35] Local party subordinates appropriated the stock interpretation found in external language, probably because doing so made them less responsible for events over which they had little control.[36] Although the party's demonization and composite projection had made the Greens into a more coherent movement than it actually was, the threat the peasant-soldier and peasant insurgents posed forced Communist leaders to put an end to the economic policies of War Communism. So did workers' unrest, whose contribution to this reversal of policy is much less appreciated.

The Strikes of March

The decision at the beginning of March 1921 to cut the already meager rations in order to stretch reserves until August would have forced the city's population of 182,000 to supplement official rations with food obtained elsewhere — or starve. After the soviet approved the measure on March 3, the supply organs prepared to reduce daily norms by approximately ¼ pound of bread. This represents the catalyst, but not the cause, of the labor unrest.[37] Beginning on March 3, the strike spread the

---

[31] GASO f. 456, op. 1, d. 675, ll. 19, 82–83, 109.

[32] Ibid., f. 521, op. 2, d. 41, l. 3.

[33] ISS, no. 73, April 3, 1921, 1, and German, *Nemetskaia avtonomiia*, 109.

[34] ISS, March 24, 1921, 1; see also *Serp i molot* and *Kommuna* for March–April 1921; GASO, f. 471, op. 1, d. 17, l. 25. Saratov's *Izvestiia* carried lurid reports of Green outrages against women, children, and government officials. See ISS, no. 83, April 16, 1921, 5–6; and no. 79, April 12, 1921, 4.

[35] See, for example, ISS, no. 54, March 10, 1921, 1, and Vasina, *Banditizm*, 5–7.

[36] GASO, f. 521, op. 1, d. 633, l. 4.

[37] The norms are found in ISS, no. 49, March 4, 1921, 1.

next day to the metallurgical plants and other large factories, as workers and nonworkers sent representatives to the railroad shops. While the turmoil touched all strata of the proletariat, male and female alike, the initiative for the disturbances came from the skilled stratum that the Communists normally deemed the most conscious. At these gatherings, workers tongue-lashed the Communists. The alarmed gubkom agreed to permit the setting up of a commission that would reexamine the activities of all economic organs and the Cheka, so discredited in the popular view. During the next two days, however, the assemblies held at factories to elect delegates to the commission bitterly denounced the Communists. Be that as it may, the elections temporarily diffused workers' anger, which did not escalate beyond the strike. As Saratov's proletariat awaited the commission's report, the unrest spilled over into Pokrovsk.

The election results represent the clearest statement yet regarding workers' attitudes at this time: the commission comprised 270 members, "less than ten" of whom were Communists. When the body convened, it called for open elections to the soviet and for the freeing of political prisoners. While the gubkom reported to the Center that some worker delegates quit the commission because they trusted Soviet organs, it appears more likely that they withdrew because they feared reprisals. Indeed, the Cheka made every effort to manipulate the situation, as party members sought to convince workers that the party served their true interests. Despite the pressure and intimidation, the 150 commission members who continued their deliberations believed a *political* solution offered the best answer to putting an end to workers' economic distress. Rejecting a resolution proposed by the gubkom on the supply situation, the workers' delegates once again demanded the freeing of political prisoners, new elections to the soviets and to all labor organizations, independent unions, and freedom of speech, the press, and assembly.

Under fire, the gubkom resolved to shut down the commission before it could issue a public statement calling for free elections and independent labor organizations. Admitting "shortcomings" in the functioning of state economic organs, the gubkom stressed the "counterrevolutionary" and "hooligan" nature of the commission despite its "healthy core." The accompanying measures it took make clear that the party committee expected workers to protest the dissolution of their elected representatives. It set up a Provincial Revolutionary Committee (*gubrevkom*), which introduced martial law both in the city and the garrison. It arrested the ringleaders of the workers' movement, "not less than 200, the majority of whom were workers," as well as "counterrevolutionaries" in Pokrovsk. It mobilized all party members to guard the gubkom and neighborhood party committees. As the local party organization secretly reported to Moscow, the *"all but general strike was liquidated after tremendous efforts on the part of the entire party and Soviet apparatus."*[38]

Sweeping through the ranks of local officialdom, Saratov University, and the free professions, the police crackdown depressed the workers' movement and activities of the rival socialist parties. In all, the Cheka handled 557 cases in March 1921, the majority of which were classified as "counterrevolutionary." It sentenced 219 people to death and others to various prison terms. It also expanded its network of informants throughout the province to 1,758 individuals. Most were party members, but others had been forcibly recruited. (The Cheka admitted the difficulty it had in convincing workers to inform on their comrades, in part because the "systematic plundering" of materials was so widespread, among both workers and managers alike.) The next month the Cheka shot another 62 individuals and sentenced 205 more to jail.[39]

Following the wave of repression, railroad workers and dockworkers and some printers refused to resume work. Although threats and intimidation as well as a spirited campaign extolling the virtues of the NEP eventually had their desired effect, intermittent strikes and other forms of worker protest continued sporadically throughout 1921. Reassuring Moscow that the workers' movement was "beginning to die down," the gubkom correspondence depicts worker discontent as being economic in nature. One report admits that the strike wave had assumed a political character, but blames the Mensheviks for this, thereby further denying workers political consciousness. Singling out the influence of Mensheviks at two print shops whose workers carried resolutions calling for the restoration of the Constituent Assembly, the gubkom declared its intention to hold a show trial "in order to discredit the Mensheviks."[40]

Initially making only vague reference to worker unrest in Saratov, *Izvestiia* appealed to workers and citizens to discount counterrevolutionary agitation against Soviet power triggered by food shortages. Blaming the crisis on capitalism and the war, on bandit activity, and on the enemies of the working class—the bourgeoisie and their hirelings, that is, the moderate socialists—the paper opined that the causes of the current situation were obvious "to all thinking and honest people." Re-

[38] (Emphasis added.) TsDNISO, f. 27, op. 2, d. 43, ll. 75, 76, 94, 124, 136. Also see RGASPI, f. 17, op. 13, d. 869, l. 4; f. 17, op. 13, d. 867, l. 3; GASO, f. 520, op. 1, d. 633, l. 4; and Antonov-Saratovskii, *Sovety*, 2: 176–80.

[39] GASO, f. 521, op. 5, d. 11, ll. 37–38, and f. 521, op. 5, d. 18, ll. 1–2.

[40] Ibid., f. 521, op. 1, d. 633, l. 4.

luctant to describe the workers' disturbances as a "strike" because of the word's political connotation, the newspaper insisted it was not one. "But it wasn't work either." Its depiction of a debate among workers over whether or not the October Revolution was premature (the Menshevik position) dismissed their discontent as "simply the voice of the workers' hungry stomach," yet allowed for the possibility that agitators had stirred them up.

The language found in *Izvestiia*, much like the party's internal language, contained judgments that present as natural certain characteristics of Russia's key social groups. It denied any political motives behind the labor ferment and exonerated workers of their actions by suggesting that agency belonged to others. The paper gave full coverage to the "traitorous" Kronstadt uprising and to the introduction of the NEP, alluding to the unrest in Saratov in cryptic language. Calling upon readers to remain vigilant, *Izvestiia* maintained that the events of the past few days "are a wonderful lesson for those who thought that the battle with the enemies of the revolution and working class is already over." *Izvestiia* also dismissed reports in émigré papers and over the Paris radio about uprisings in Russia, including one in Saratov that established an anti-Bolshevik republic. The paper blamed the rumors on a "White-SR plot against Soviet power."[41] Throughout March the newspaper referred only obliquely to internal party debates, consoling readers with the admission that, despite the class nature of grain requisitioning, the party had made "a number of mistakes." Reporting that the investigation into the Cheka's activities revealed no abuses, the newspaper affirmed that the refrain "Down with the Communists" was still unfairly heard at factories. *Izvestiia* also had to comment when local printers did not show up for work, resulting in the paper's not being issued.

On March 22 *Izvestiia* announced that the Saratov Revkom would rule until further notice. It mobilized all able-bodied adults to clean the city and fell timber, perhaps to keep them occupied and under surveillance. It banned all public gatherings, classified strike activity as counterrevolution, and extended an amnesty to peasant bands if they gave themselves up before April 5. The committee also removed all obstacles to the free sale and trade of seed and grain. Pinning the blame for the party's failures on class "others" who had infiltrated the party, *Izvestiia* informed readers that the Cheka had executed six people, several of

---

[41] *ISS*, no. 50, March 5, 1921, 1; no. 51, March 6, 1921, 1–2; no. 52, March 8, 1921, 1; no. 53, March 9, 1921, 1; no. 54, March 10, 1921, 1; no. 55, March 11, 1921, 1; no. 56, March 12, 1921, 2; no. 57, March 15, 1921, 1; no. 62, March 22, 1921, 1; no. 66, March 26, 1921, 1; and no. 77, April 9, 1921, 4.

whom were former police agents that later joined the Communist Party, which they had then discredited by taking bribes.[42]

In offering a public explanation of the March events, the Bolsheviks insisted that SR and Menshevik counterrevolutionaries had tapped the petit-bourgeois spontaneity of Saratov workers, imputing to the participants a preindustrial or undeveloped consciousness. The Bolsheviks admitted the workers' terrible economic straits, concluding that the party's inability to satisfy workers made them hostile to the Communists.[43] Thus, party public interpretations of the March events deny their incredibly important political significance. They deny that Saratov's most skilled workers played a crucial role in the strikes, which the party insisted were a work slowdown or volynka. To be sure, to do otherwise would have repudiated the party's own sense of legitimacy as the victors of October 1917 and the Civil War. However, these statements were not so much a conscious act of denial as a reflection of how local leaders often appropriated external language to explain events that they could not control but for which they might be held responsible. Some party leaders realized the political side of the discontent.

"All of Saratov Has Turned into One Big Uprising"

Government surveillance of the army's and general population's correspondence has a long history in Russia, but became institutionalized during World War I, at a time when the powers involved in the conflict stepped up their efforts to gather information about the mood of the population in their respective countries. Holquist emphasizes that the desire to generate such information was more important than the material itself, that the purpose of surveillance was "to act on people and change them." The Bolsheviks, naturally, adopted this political practice in their efforts to manage and remodel the population, extending their surveillance to correspondence, telegrams, telephone conversations, and radio broadcasts. In August 1920 the government transferred surveillance of general correspondence to the Cheka. By this time, the surveillance organs intercepted virtually all mail that passed through the post, employing thousands of specialists as well as a large support staff. Twice a month they prepared "top secret" reports (*svodki*) for an elite

[42] *ISS*, no. 59, March 17, 1921, 1; no. 61, March 20, 1921, 1–3; no. 62, March 22, 1921, 3; no. 63, March 23, 1921, 1; and no. 68, March 29, 1921, 4. The examples on workers' life are found in no. 57, March 15, 1921, 2; no. 58, March 16, 1921, 1; no. 59, March 17, 1921, 1; and no. 69, March 30, 1921, 3.

[43] *ISS*, no. 74, April 5, 1921, 3, and no. 78, April 10, 1921, 3. See also *Sovetskaia derevnia*, no. 40, June 19, 1921, 1.

stratum of party leaders, comprising approximately eighty individuals or fewer, on the mood of the population.[44]

The Cheka's report on the mass mood in Saratov during March 1921 includes excerpts from approximately 400 private letters of Saratov's citizens.[45] Among other things, passages document, in visceral language, the workers' uprising, the arrest of the commission elected by workers, and the startling success of the Greens. Collectively, these letters help explain why the Communist authorities took such desperate measures to crush the uprising. "There's terrible unrest in Saratov. There are strikes everywhere and people aren't working." "Life is awful. Railroad workers are striking, but don't know how to link up with Petrograd workers in order to strike together." "There are uprisings all around Saratov." "All of Saratov has turned into one big uprising." "Now the question is not only about food, but also about the release of the commission we elected to inspect Soviet agencies, which was arrested." "The Communists will soon fall, there are strikes everywhere." "There are disturbances across Saratov Province, and near Saratov Antonov's, Vakulin's and Popov's bands are operating. If Communists fall into their hands, they kill them."

The correspondence also serves as a testimonial to the population's despair over the appalling living conditions. "You can say that the people here are famished and broken. They drag whatever they can to the bazaar, sell it, and eat it up. Everyone is embittered. . . . Thus, instead of freedom, equality, and brotherhood, we have just the opposite. Everywhere there's mud, filth, and every imaginable abomination." "It's terrible here in the children's shelter. The boys fight and I cry each day. . . . It's very cold in the shelter and we're hungry." "In Saratov they're feeding us cats and dogs." "Here in the rear we've had three and a half years of Soviet power and nothing has changed for the better, in fact things have gotten worse. . . . The commissars . . . live best of all." The despair even affected party members. "I quit the party because I believe it is necessary to carry out free trade in the country, and nothing good will come of Communism."

The public's awareness of Bolshevik repression contributed to the

---

[44] Holquist, "Information," 417, 421–22, 434, 443; V. S. Izmozik, "Perliustratsiia v pervye gody Sovetskoi vlasti," *Voprosy istorii*, no. 8 (1995): 27–31; Irina Davidian, "Voennaia tsenzura v Rossii v gody grazhdanskoi voiny," *Cahiers du Monde russe* 38, no. 1–2 (1997): 118–21. See also I. Davidian and V. A. Kozlov, "Chastnye pis'ma epokhi grazhdanskoi voiny: Po materialam voennoi tsenzury," *Neizvestnaia Rossiia XX vek* (Moscow, 1992), 2: 200–252; Vladlen S. Izmozik, "Voices from the Twenties: Private Correspondence Intercepted by the OGPU," *Russian Review* 55, no. 2 (1996): 287–308; and Berelovich and Danilov, *Sovetskaia derevnia*, 1: 7–12.

[45] The quoted material is found in GASO, f. 521, op. 2, d. 45, ll. 1–23 ob.

feelings of hopelessness. "Here they're taking hostages, they're SRs, and the majority are shot." "All of the prisons are overflowing. They've arrested about thirty professors alone, and they're treating them terribly. Yesterday the medical students met to discuss the professors' arrests, but they dispersed them with lashes." "There have been a large number of arrests of the professorate, old officers, peasants." "The number of arrests is growing in Saratov. Several university professors were arrested. The average inhabitant sits quietly and only curses the Communists, but is so cowardly that when he reads the papers that are posted, his face takes on a loyal expression as if he might see a Bolshevik who might suspect him of disloyalty."

The excerpts make clear that Bolshevik practices already shaped how people thought they could express themselves, and that the censors even monitored Cheka operatives. "There's lots of news, but I can't write; the censor wouldn't let the letter through." "I'm telling you that if you are going to write me such indiscreet letters and thereby place you and me into the devil knows what sort of predicament, I'll not answer you. I hide your letters in fear." "I write often, but probably there's a delay at the post office and censor's." "As regards my convictions, you can pick up on them from the sixth line in my first letter. Don't forget that [they] . . . vigilantly monitor correspondence." "I serve in the Cheka and very often have to go out on raids and roundups all night long without sleeping. Each night we go to arrest the bourgeoisie, priests, and others. The Saratov Extraord. Comm. [Cheka] operates at full steam, each night dragging off 100 people to prison. There's a lot of news, but I can't write about it."

The documents reveal that citizens, for whatever reason, squealed on others, at times appropriating the language of Bolshevism toward their own ends. "To the staff member on duty. Comrade! I request that you send a militia officer to search the private apartment of speculators. . . . I request that you requisition their clothing, which is bourgeois." Finally, the letters expose the widespread activities of the black market, suggesting that the intelligentsia fared better than workers. "Almost all of the intelligentsia . . . are carrying out sabotage. Some speculate and those in power live well and have lots of things. But the workers living on their own labor . . . are cold and hungry [and] couldn't have shoes or clothing." "I was at Alesha's. She's really speculating well." "A third-year medical student . . . heads up an outpatient clinic and the main drugstore in Saratov. I was at her place today and she gave me [baking] soda. Mama, write and let me know what you need. I can get hold of anything." "My son-in-law works in the Utilization [scrap yard] Department, and heads up the distribution of bread and feeds himself generously. . . . And the other landlord brings meat home from the slaughterhouse non-stop. Thus, some suffer from overeating, while others are starving."

The Political Mood after March

Despite the steps the regime took to cope with popular discontent, the wave of anger directed against the Communists raged throughout 1921 against a backdrop of growing starvation and continued havoc wreaked by peasant bands.[46] Reports from May, for instance, address the "catastrophic situation in the district towns" and in the villages where despondent parents abandoned their children, who besieged volost and village soviets in search of food. The anti-Soviet mood in the trans-Volga districts provided fertile soil for the Greens, while in others shortages prompted peasants to flee the province. Although the peasants voiced approval of the new tax in kind, they did not believe the Soviet government would implement it. Worker disturbances continued to flare up in Pokrovsk, while railroad workers in Krasnyi Kut and elsewhere engaged in "Italian strikes," that is, seizure of the workplace. Some Saratov workers threatened to strike, while absenteeism among railroad workers shot up to 50 percent.[47]

Growing hunger depressed the popular mood in June, when absenteeism and desertion reached "colossal" proportions, especially on the rail lines. In Pokrovsk it was as high as 70 percent. At Saratov's metallurgical plants, Novaia Etna and Boiler Factory No. 1, workers called for searches among Communists, whom they suspected of hoarding food. The next month lumber industry workers and haulers refused to go to work, making a host of economic demands. "Counterrevolutionary" agitation was on the rise among water transport workers, whose popular refrain, "if you can't provide bread, then stop governing," struck a responsive chord. Workers also voiced anger with Soviet officials that took advantage of the new economic climate to get rich at the expense of the toiling people. Work stoppages and absenteeism remained common and workers continued to organize political meetings, yet party documents deny that strikes broke out, once again defining away these everyday forms of resistance. The Cheka arrested thirteen SRs that month, noting that the Kadet Party tried to reorganize at the provincial level. As rumors spread that Soviet power would soon collapse under the onslaught of another foreign intervention that would bring Mil-

[46] TsDNISO, f. 27, op. 2, d. 44, l. 137, and GASO, f. 521, op. 4, d. 9, l. 1.

[47] GASO, f. 521, op.1, d. 643, ll. 4–5; d. 718, ll. 19, 30; f. 456, op. 1, d. 663, ll. 101, 106, 118; and RGASPI, f. 17, op. 13, d. 867, ll. 1–3.

iukov to power,[48] the Communists expanded their army of informants in order to crush the activities of underground political parties and to assess the mood of the population.[49] Workers at Novaia Etna and the tram yards refused to go to work in late 1921. Cheka reports for the remainder of 1921 and for 1922 characterize the mood in the city as even "worse" owing to the growth in prices on the free market in conjunction with massive layoffs at Saratov factories.[50] As before, Cheka reports linked discontent to bread-and-butter issues, thereby discrediting workers' political agendas, and maintaining that if the acknowledged personal failures of individual Communists could be rectified, the party would once again become synonymous with Soviet power.[51]

Famine: The Last Chapter of Civil War

Although climatic conditions contributed to the famine that held the Saratov region tightly in its grip until late 1923, it is hard not to agree with James Long, who blames politics as the primary factor contributing to the calamity.[52] Some contemporaries reasoned that peasants placed less land under cultivation in response to official food supply policies, especially after 1919, when the government extended requisitioning from field crops to virtually everything produced. Other observers emphasized that the state's mobilization of horses and the peasantry's lack of farm implements, material inputs, and seed played a key role in reducing the amount of land they worked. Unfortunately, the summer 1920 harvest proved to be disastrously small, while that winter's planting was sharply curtailed. When food brigades launched their determined drive to meet state quotas in October 1920, the peasants made the mistake of thinking that nothing would be taken from them if they had little. Before the campaign ended, food brigades had collected almost 90 percent of the province's assessment.

It is doubtful that Moscow knowingly allowed the famine to develop, but it ignored local reports until late spring 1921, when mass discontent

---

[48] GASO, f. 521, op. 1, d. 643, ll. 8–8 ob, 11; f. 521, op. 5, d. 11, ll. 39–41 ob; and f. 521, op. 1, d. 716, ll. 1–1 ob.

[49] RGASPI, f. 17, op. 13, d. 867, l. 86.

[50] GASO, f. 521, op. 1, d. 643, ll. 13–16 ob.

[51] TsDNISO, f. 27, op. 2, d. 826, ll. 39, 42, 63, 78.

[52] James W. Long, "The Volga Germans and the Famine of 1921," *Russian Review* 51, no. 4 (1992): 510. Markus Wehner also blames politics for the extent of the disaster. See "Golod 1921–1922 gg. v Samarskoi gubernii i reaktsiia Sovetskogo pravitel'stva," *Cahiers du Monde russe* 38, no. 1–2 (1997): 223–42. Some contemporary sources did so implicitly, too. See I. Korsakov, *Golod v Sovetskoi Rossii i ego prichiny* (Iuriev, 1922), 3–12.

and chilling detail on the magnitude of the potential human suffering put an end to any doubts about the gravity of the crisis along the Volga. Ignoring orders from Moscow, the gubispolkom ended requisitioning and chided the Center for not heeding local warnings. Although the gubispolkom allowed the free sale of seed, it remained in short supply, and this undermined the sowing campaign, as did the incursions of peasant bands and the unusual lack of precipitation and hot weather.[53] After the famine had claimed its first victims, the Soviet government agreed to accept foreign relief. Soliciting help from abroad must be seen as an act of desperation; fear of the possibility of renewed political intervention colored all of the Bolsheviks' subsequent dealings with foreign agents.[54]

The emergence of government and semi-independent agencies to administer famine relief dates to July 1921, when the government chartered a relief committee, whose members included a large number of prominent figures who were hostile to the Bolsheviks. Days later, however, the party created a rival government relief agency, *Pomgol* (*Komitet pomoshchi golodaiushshim*), and shortly thereafter disbanded the "counterrevolutionary" relief committee. A branch of the national relief committee functioned in Saratov until October, when the gubispolkom replaced it with the Provincial Commission to Help the Starving (*Gubernskaia komissiia pomoshchi golodaiushchim*), which extended branches to the uezds and volosts. The government also set up peasant mutual assistance committees, freed the trans-Volga and hardest hit uezds from the new tax in kind introduced by the NEP, allocated seed to the province,[55] and churned out propaganda materials to mobilize the countryside.[56] A special committee extended relief to the province's Communist Party members, who bombarded the party organization with requests for food, money, and clothing.[57] Reflecting all of the shortcomings of ruling political institutions at the time, the organizations created to combat famine were marred by widespread pilfering of food, sloppy record keeping, poor work habits, and other abuses.[58]

The most controversial famine relief measures concerned the govern-

[53] GASO, f. 456, op. 1, d. 630, ll. 4–7; Long, "The Volga Germans," 511–19, and *ISS*, no. 107, May 17, 1921, 1. For a comparison of Saratov and Petrograd during the famine see Christopher Williams, "The 1921 Russian Famine: Centre and Periphery Responses," *Revolutionary Russia* 6, no. 2 (1993): 277–314.

[54] Charles M. Edmondson, "The Politics of Hunger: The Soviet Response to Famine, 1921," *Soviet Studies* 29, no. 4 (1977): 509–12.

[55] *Otchet Prezidiuma Gorsoveta*, 4–5, 8.

[56] See, for example, GASO, f. 608, op. 1, d. 1, l. 62.

[57] TsDNISO, f. 27, op. 2, d. 1631, ll. 1–58.

[58] GASO, f. 608, op. 1, d. 1, ll. 111, 174 ob, and f. 608, op. 1, d. 13, ll. 15–17 ob, 109.

ment's confiscation of church valuables, ostensibly to pay for famine relief. Roslof's study of the government's policies toward Orthodoxy at this time confirms long-held suspicions that it encouraged factionalism and feuding within the church in order to control it. In particular, the government sought to undermine the church by encouraging dissident voices from within, particularly the so-called Living Church movement, which hoped to work out a modus operandi with the Soviet state. The behind-the-scenes manipulation fostered a bitter split in Saratov between the forces of the Living Church, which had adherents in the city, and the regular parishes that supported Patriarch Tikhon, resulting in the arrest of the local bishop, Dosifei.[59] Against this backdrop, the confiscation of church valuables proved to be a messy affair, while related campaigns to get the population to part with its valuables proved unimpressive.[60]

Once the government allowed the establishment of state and semi-independent agencies to administer relief in the summer of 1921, it could no longer maintain its silence about the tragedy.[61] Local newspapers now published frank exposes of the extent and nature of the disaster. Saratov's *Izvestiia* blamed it on problems inherited from the Old Regime, in particular the war, the ruin associated with it, and counterrevolution. The paper, however, soon began to stress the spontaneity of the calamity, casting the famine as a phenomenon that could not have been foreseen.[62] Acknowledging the impact of the drought and the country's backwardness, party internal language also ascribed blame to the 1920–21 requisitioning campaign.[63] As Comrade Merenchenko put it, the campaign took everything, "not only grain surpluses, but the most essential things (seed grain and fodder), and this is why we're starving." He likewise expressed the exasperation of many local Communists with Moscow's reaction. "I don't know if there was an order from the Center to take everything from the peasant down to the last

---

[59] Edward A. Roslof, "The Renovationist Movement in the Russian Orthodox Church, 1922–1946," (Ph.D. diss., University of North Carolina, 1994); *ISS*, no. 35, Feb. 22, 1922, 1; no. 141, June, 1922, 2; no. 154, July 1922, 3; *Chernaia godina*, no. 1 (1922): 30–34; TsDNISO, f. 27, op. 3, d. 923, l. 66 ob; RGASPI, f. 17, op. 14, d. 658, l. 71.

[60] TsDNISO, f. 138, op. 1, d. 53, l. 61, and f. 27, op. 2, d. 801, l. 2.

[61] Edmondson, "Politics of Hunger," 513–15; A. A. Mal'kov, "Golod v Saratovskoi gubernii v 1921–22 godu," *Saratovskii vestnik zdravookhraneniia*, no. 11 (1922): 37; and *Chernaia godina*, no. 1 (1922): 27, 34–35.

[62] *ISS*, no. 166, July 27, 1921, 2; no. 171, Aug. 2, 1921, 1; and "Russian Agriculture and the Revolution," 48, 55, 69–70.

[63] See, for instance, V. D. Chenykaev, "Golod i rol' obshchestvennogo vracha v bor'be s nim. Doklad s"ezdu uzdravov i sanvrachei 14 oktiabria 1921 g.," *Saratovskii vestnik zdravookhraneniia* 2, no. 9–12 (1922): 49.

kernel or if this was undertaken independently by local organs of power."[64]

Saratov Province experienced a greater need for food and seed than any other region in the country. Between October 1921 and June 1922, the number of people starving rose from 893,325 or 28 percent of the population to 2,070,560 or 68 percent, of whom just under half were children (910,000).[65] Conditions, of course, varied widely across the province (table 12.1). At the high end of the range stood Novouzensk Uezd, where as of April 1922, 99 percent of the population was classified as starving, and at the low end Serdobsk, where 16 percent of the inhabitants went without food. As of April, the state fed 173,573 of the starving Saratovites, and foreign relief agencies 626,349. This meant that roughly 60 percent of those classified as starving still received no relief. Moreover, the rations doled out to the needy usually amounted to only one-fifth of an individual's caloric needs. However, by mid-1922, international organizations handed out 1.5 million meals a day in Saratov Province. Of this number, the American Relief Administration (ARA) contributed over one million rations daily.[66]

ARA and the Save the Children Fund entrusted to the Norwegian explorer, Dr. F. Nansen, began setting up operations in Saratov in September 1921. The British branch of the Save the Children Fund, led by Lawrence Webster, coordinated the fund's operation in Saratov. Within months the Vatican, the German Red Cross, and other organizations had also sent representatives to the province. ARA concentrated its efforts in the hardest hit trans-Volga uezds and in Saratov, while the British focused their attention on the right bank of the Volga (figure 12.1). By January 1922, ARA fed 64 percent of the province's starving children, provided significant amounts of medicine and clothing, and made it possible for Americans to sponsor Russian families.[67] Although many

[64] GASO, f. 456, op. 1, d. 531, ll. 10, 12–16, and RGASPI, f. 17, op. 13, d. 869, l. 5.

[65] GASO, f. 521, op. 1, d. 619, l. 47 ob. See related figures in *ISS*, no. 245, Oct. 29, 1921, 1, and no. 28, Feb. 4, 1922, 1; *Sovetskaia derevnia*, no. 80, Dec. 22, 1921, 2; and *Chernaia godina*, no. 2 (1922): 24. See also L. I. Lubny-Gertsyk, *Dvizhenie naseleniia na territorii SSSR za vremia mirovoi voiny i revoliutsii* (Moscow, 1926), 27.

[66] *ISS*, no. 81, April 9, 1922, 1; Mal'kov, "Golod," 43–46; Wheatcroft, "Famine and Epidemic Crises," 345; Harold H. Fisher, *The Famine in Soviet Russia, 1919–1923: The Operations of the American Relief Administration* (Freeport, NY: 1971, reprint of 1927 edition), 556–57; and Narodnyi komissariat po prodovol'stviiu, *God bor'by s golodom: Uchastie narodnogo komissariata po prodovol'stviiu v dele pomoshchi golodaiushchim* (Moscow, 1922), 1, 7–10, 13, 30–33.

[67] *ISS*, no. 216, Sept. 24, 1921, 2; no. 228, Oct. 9, 1921, 2; no. 229, Oct. 11, 1921, 3; no. 253, Nov. 15, 1921, 2; no. 280, Dec. 10, 1921, 2; no. 286, Dec. 17, 1921, 1; no. 26, Feb. 2, 1922, 1; and *Sovetskaia derevnia*, no. 93, Feb. 5, 1922, 2. See also, GASO, f. 608, op. 1, d. 1, l. 288.

TABLE 12.1
Percentage of Saratov Province's Population Classified as Starving as of April 1922, by District

District	Percent
Novouzensk	99%
Pokrovsk	97%
Saratov	88%
Dergachevsk	87%
Kamyshin	80%
Volsk	75%
Khvalynsk	70%
Balashov	53%
Kuznetsk	47%
Elansk	33%
Petrovsk	23%
Atkarsk	21%
Serdobsk	16%

Source: ISS, no. 81, April 9, 1922, p. 1.

peasants expressed doubts that someone would give them something for nothing, they soon began to say that ARA "must be sent from God" (figure 12.2). Others asked to be taken to America, or complained about ARA's political neutrality.[68]

The political dimension of relief only exacerbated the poor cooperation ARA representatives encountered on the part of Soviet agencies, which refused to provide ARA with information on seeded area, local crops, and related issues. ARA files are full of charges and counter-charges regarding breaches of the so-called Riga Agreement that regulated relief measures. The breakdown of transportation, rivalries between Soviet agencies, pilfering of supplies, difficulty of keeping accurate statistics, and suspicion of local Communists also complicated ARA's tasks. So did anti-ARA propaganda carried out by Communists.[69] Moreover, as the administration's activities began to wind down in late 1922, the Cheka placed on trial several Russians employed by ARA, whom it accused of stealing and depicted as class enemies.[70] While acknowledging the efforts of some Soviet officials, ARA's John P. Gregg,

[68] Hoover Institute, ARA, box 100, Saratov Reports, no. 1, 1921–22, Bi-Monthly Report Enclosure no. 61 (John P. Gregg, 5); see also ARA, Russian Operations, box 71.

[69] Hoover Institute, ARA, box 100, Saratov Reports no. 1, 1921–22, 1, 6–7. All of these problems and complaints are also discussed in the report of John P. Gregg, found in ARA, Russian Operations, box 99, especially 85–100. See also GASO, f. 521, op. 1, d. 480, l. 69, and German, *Nemetskaia avtonomiia*, 138–39.

[70] *ISS*, no. 203, Sept. 7, 1922, 3, and no. 204, Sept. 8, 1922, 1.

12.1 The arrival of representatives from the British Save the Children
Fund being welcomed by Politburo designee Birman. Courtesy Saratov
Kraevedcheskii Museum, photo 10698.

who headed up the Saratov operations, castigated the treatment ARA
received from Soviet officials and blamed Moscow for setting the hostile
tone.[71]

Gregg had a point. Because the Soviet government distrusted ARA
and other foreign agencies, it sought to monitor their activities, appointing representatives to all foreign relief organizations. The Politburo designated Birman as its plenipotentiary in Saratov. As he put it, "We
know that this foreign mission arrived not only to feed, but also to
carry out a definite counterrevolutionary policy." Instructing them to

[71] Gregg Report, ARA, 96.

12.2 Food line at an ARA kitchen in Saratov Province. Courtesy Saratov Kraevedcheskii Museum, photo 10642.

pass themselves off as non-Communist officials, Birman assigned agents to district party committees whose purpose was to spy on ARA's activities and prevent scandals. Uezd executive and party committees, however, sometimes exposed the true identity of the emissaries or dealt directly with ARA, prompting Birman to quip that "all of our stupidities" are known abroad. Demanding that Birman's emissaries observe party dictates, local Communists complained that his men organized drinking bouts with the foreigners, lived with them, and shared their food. In justifying the "fraternization" policy, Birman insisted that "for diplomatic reasons it's necessary to accept an entire array of otherwise impermissible things such as drinking bouts and a little something else" — carousing with prostitutes, an issue not discussed in ARA documentation.[72]

The famine caused another wave of refugees to roll across Saratov Province, and they contributed to the outbreaks of water-borne, food-borne, and air-borne epidemic diseases, which often accompany starvation. Cholera epidemics broke out in the city in mid-1921, and a typhus epidemic hit that winter. Between January and June 1921, 9,405 refu-

[72] TsDNISO, f. 27, op. 2, d. 801, ll. 3–4, 12–13 ob.

12.3 Victims of the famine. Courtesy Saratov Kraevedcheskii Museum, photo 10453.

gees passed through the city, where they lived in indescribably squalid conditions in makeshift barracks along the Volga. Documenting 1,184 deaths among them from cholera, typhus, and starvation,[73] local health authorities between July 1921 and January 1922 evacuated 45,427 refugees from the province.[74]

Descriptions of the famine add a macabre dimension to the mind-numbing statistics (figure 12.3).[75] Following violent anti-Soviet uprisings in the German colonies, hordes of colonists congregated in Saratov along the riverfront, where they contributed to the rapid spread of cholera, but the only assistance the local authorities could provide was to remove the dead bodies.[76] In the hard-hit areas peasants were known to dig their own graves, fearing no one would be left to bury them. Some German families resorted to self-immolation to spare themselves an ag-

---

[73] Mal'kov, "Bezhenskoe dvizhenie," 31–32, 34–36.

[74] Wheatcroft, "Famine," 347.

[75] For example, see GASO, f. 456, op. 1, d. 661, ll, 8, 11; f. 456, op. 1, d. 971, l. 8; f. 471, op. 1, d. 23, ll. 9–11; f. 471, op. 1, d. 26, ll. 97–97 ob; and f. 608, op. 1, d. 13, l. 140.

[76] Ibid., f. 456, op. 1, d. 629, ll. 1–2; f. 456, op. 1, d. 634, ll. 1–3; and *ISS*, no. 155, July 14, 1921, 2.

onizing death. Cannibalism took on such levels in certain districts that people were afraid to bury their dead in public and posted guards over fresh graves.[77] In Khvalynsk cases of famine-related murder and suicide were reported.[78] It is hard to imagine more wretched conditions than those existing in children's homes in the trans-Volga uezds, where children were dying because local relief agencies had nothing to dole out: under the new rules on self-financing that accompanied the NEP, the homes were left without heat, electricity, medicine, and adequate staff.[79] In stark contrast, with the introduction of the NEP, some fancy shops sold exotic cakes and individuals "squandered millions" on games of lotto and roulette, and on fancy foods.[80] In February 1922 the gubispolkom resolved to put an end to these "contradictions of the NEP."[81]

Misinformation as well as the party's perception of the Germans as "aliens" played roles in the famine's development in the Volga German oblast.[82] Ignoring the harbingers of hunger, a well-armed detachment of more than 500 Tula workers began to seize grain from the local peasants when they stopped marketing it, wreaking havoc on the local economy and discrediting Soviet power. A German pastor recorded how Tula workers whipped and tortured those suspected of hiding grain, and beat mothers who begged the workers not to take their last reserves from their hungry children. Dismissing appeals from local party organizations as manifestations of localism, Moscow relentlessly pursued its policy of force, which resulted in a warm reception for Vakulin's and Piatakov's bands. In March 1921 peasants in revolt held a large part of the oblast, where Soviet power hung by a thread. Because the Center deprived the oblast of state support of any kind, famine raged in the oblast well into 1925, entailing out-migration and the usual horrors: children with swollen bellies, feeding on surrogates, cannibalism, disease, and death.[83]

A government commission sent to assess the situation concluded that Narkomprod's policies had brought enormous political and economic

[77] Ia. A. Volin, "Uzhasy goloda i liudoedstva v Rossii v 1921–22, gg." (Kazan, 1922), unpublished manuscript, Hoover Archive, 14–26; Sovetskaia derevnia, no. 85, Jan. 8, 1922, 4; no. 102, March 9, 1922, 2; and Chernaia godina, no. 2 (1922): 25.

[78] Sovetskaia derevnia, no. 55, Sept. 25, 1921, 2.

[79] GASO, f. 456, op. 1, d. 913, ll. 4–5. See also Otchet Saratovskogo Uezdnogo Ispolnitel'nogo Komiteta, 28–30.

[80] Chenykaev, "Golod i rol'," 50.

[81] GASO, f. 456, op. 1, d. 729, l, 4, and f. 521, op. 1, d. 619, l. 15.

[82] Long, "The Volga Germans," 515.

[83] German, Nemetskaia avtonomiia, 93–97, 102–4, 114; Gross, Avtonomnaia, 20–22; N. N., "The Hardships of Our Co-Religionists in the German Volga Colonies," 9–14; Hoover Institute Archive, ARA, container 99, appendix 1b to report "The Civil War in Saratov Guberniia and Region of the Volga."

harm to the German oblast, and that the members of the food brigades, who did not know the language or customs of the population, committed outrageous crimes. Nonetheless, Narkomprod resolved to carry out the new tax in kind, thereby falling victim to the stereotype according to which all Volga Germans were prosperous. Meanwhile, a mass exodus got underway of those settlers with nothing to sow or eat. Despite this, by January 1922, 96.9 of the population was starving. ARA, Nansen's Save the Children Fund, several other foreign organizations, and Soviet agencies fed roughly 91 percent of the oblast's population by mid-1922. Despite their mistrust of the foreigners, the secret police found no evidence that they carried out anti-Soviet activities.[84]

Without the generous support of foreign relief agencies, especially of ARA, the famine would have claimed hundreds of thousands of additional lives in Saratov Province. In 1922 the number of deaths in the province surpassed the number of births by 44,509, but the actual death rate was higher. By January 1923, 28.5 percent of the population of Dergachevsk, 18.5 percent in Novouzensk, and 18.5 percent in Khvalynsk had perished since the start of the famine. Arkadii German's calculations put famine losses in the Volga German oblast, perhaps the hardest hit, at not less than 150,000 people, or almost one-third of the inhabitants. The famine also caused a loss in the annual birth cohort of as much as 43 percent. There were other demographic consequences as well. Between July 1921 and January 1922, local authorities evacuated 104,645 individuals from the province, while tens of thousands of others took flight. Another 70,000 fled the Volga German region or were evacuated.[85] But how do we measure the effect of malnutrition on those who survived, especially the children?

The Long Road to Recovery

To what extent did the introduction of the NEP salve the festering wounds of local society? Despite the hostility of some of its members to this "pact with the devil," once the Communist Party agreed to the measure, it expended considerable efforts in rationalizing it to the public, which had a positive impact.[86] Nevertheless, famine conditions negated in the short run the salutary effects of the introduction of the tax in kind and free trade. Although the NEP provided the opportunity for

---

[84] German, *Nemetskaia avtonomiia*, 114–15, 119–23, 129, 132–37, 159–65.

[85] Ibid., 178. Early estimates placed the figure at 10 percent or 48,000 people. See Long, "The Volga Germans," 523; Wheatcroft, "Famine," 339, 347; and GASO, f. 456, op. 1, d. 912, ll. 59.

[86] See, for example, GASO, f. 456, op. 1, d. 675, ll. 230–30 ob.

economic recovery, Saratov had to pass through a dark period when some benefited from the new conditions while most people fought in desperation to stave off starvation. This was not the only consequence of the NEP to discredit it. Insolvent enterprises and bloated government agencies threw large numbers of workers and officials into the streets in 1921 and 1922, a practice that especially affected young proletarians and female workers. While transportation breakdowns and lack of raw materials stalled efforts to raise productivity,[87] low-paid workers found that their wages were not even enough to cover the mandatory deductions now taken for rent, rations, union dues, and utilities.[88] The NEP also compromised the Communist Party and its affiliate organizations. Many members took advantage of the situation to acquire property or else slipped away from Saratov as the going got tough.[89] Once bankrupt enterprises released large numbers of youth, the party had a hard time maintaining the Komsomol.[90] The market itself caused another problem, because in a situation of want it attracted those who had access to goods. The result was "enormous, systematic pilfering" at the workplace by non-Communists and Communists alike. It assumed such alarming proportions that the Cheka set up a secret department to combat it and what it viewed as the accompanying underground activities of "counterrevolutionary" parties. Finally, there was the question of politics. Workers initially welcomed the introduction of free trade, but they had mixed feelings about the NEP's failure to effect a political loosening up.[91] By July 1922 the party carried out virtually no party work at private enterprises; only 8 percent of the 3,000 workers at Saratov Manufacturing were Communists, and only 3 of the city's 300 printers.[92]

In the countryside, Saratov peasants remained suspicious of the Soviet government's replacing requisitioning with a tax in kind, believing the reintroduction of the former was only a matter of time (a feeling shared by some local party officials as well) or that the tax would be even more onerous. Further, the NEP initially proved to be irrelevant to many peasants because of the famine. True, the authorities did end requisi-

---

[87] *ISS*, no. 163, July 23, 1921, 1; no. 282, Dec. 13, 1921, 2; no. 24, Jan. 31, 1922, 2; no. 35, Feb. 12, 1922, 2; no. 123, June 2, 1922, 2; GASO, f. 521, op. 5, d. 11, ll. 48–49; and TsDNISO, f. 136, op. 1, d. 81, l. 1.

[88] TsDNISO, f. 27, op. 2, d. 801, l. 5.

[89] Ibid., f. 27, op. 2, d. 801, ll. 6 ob, 7, 10–10 ob. See also f. 27, op. 2, d. 729, ll. 52–53; f. 27, op. 2, d. 826, l. 39; f. 44, op. 1, d. 1, l. 41; and *Serp i molot* (Serdobsk), no. 181, Dec. 8, 1921, 2.

[90] TsDNISO, f. 27, op. 2, d. 801, ll. 3–3 ob.

[91] GASO, f. 521, op. 1, d. 718, ll. 55, 62 ob.

[92] TsDNISO, f. 27, op. 2, d. 824, l. 30; f. 27, op. 2, d. 801, ll. 41–42; *ISS*, no. 107, May 13, 1922, 2.

TABLE 12.2

Number of Needy Peasant Households Suffering from Conditions Other Than
Famine as of Jan. 1, 1923

Condition of Household	Number of Households
Without land	37,363
With a disastrous harvest	38,000
Suffering from natural disasters	10,000
Without horses	153,289
Without any livestock	99,038

Source: GASO, f. 456, op. 1, d. 912, l. 59.

tioning and permitted the free sale of seed and then of all goods, but
many peasants had already been sentenced to starvation. Ironically,
party reports indicate that the "poor elements" of the countryside, upon
which the Bolsheviks had relied earlier, remained the most hostile to
Soviet power. Left without seed and livestock, they sowed the land
under terrible conditions, often pulling the plows themselves.[93]

Meanwhile, overly optimistic reports maintaining that the famine had
ended by mid-1922 resulted in the premature termination of famine
relief,[94] as a result of which it would take years of concentrated effort
and renewed famine assistance in addition to good harvests to bring
about a recovery (table 12.2). Because the below-average 1922 harvest
did not justify the hopes placed upon it, in January 1923, 30 percent of
the population of Saratov Province remained classified as starving. Although the amount of land under cultivation rose by 12 percent and the
size of livestock herds by 35 percent, the sown area represented only 56
percent of the 1914 level and livestock herds 60 percent of the prewar
number. With the further demobilization of the Red Army, the ranks of
the unemployed swelled throughout 1923. The province was now home
to 55,000 refugees, 25,325 invalids, 17,170 unemployed, 70,000 homeless waifs, and 15,255 children in state homes.[95] Conditions of hunger
and unemployment fed the growing criminal underworld, which the
Cheka feared would turn political.[96] Nineteen twenty-four proved to be

[93] TsDNISO, f. 27, op. 2, d. 801, ll. 9–10 ob; f. 27, op. 2, d. 330, ll. 11–20; and
RGASPI, f. 17, op. 14, d. 658, l. 71.

[94] TsDNISO, f. 27, op. 2, d. 801, l. 59; Charles M. Edmondson, "An Inquiry into the
Termination of Soviet Famine Relief Programmes and the Renewal of Grain Export,
1922–23," *Soviet Studies* 33, no. 3 (1981): 370–71. Edmondson dispels the accusation
that the Soviet government had falsified harvest estimates and statistics, 382.

[95] GASO, f. 456, op. 1, d. 912, ll. 59, 62a; f. 521, op. 1, d. 908, ll. 1–3; and f. 521, op.
1, d. 906, l. 22.

[96] GASO, f. 540, op. 1, d. 1, ll. 1–3.

another drought year, as a result of which the amount of land under cultivation receded once again, and the province produced far less than it needed.[97] Thus the NEP brought no significant economic improvement to Saratov before the mid-1920s, suggesting that our understanding of the policy is in need of revision.

Conclusion

This case study of Saratov demonstrates that the political crisis the party faced in early 1921 was more far-reaching and systemic than heretofore believed. Despite Communist Party explanations to the contrary, worker unrest of early 1921 represented an enormous threat to Soviet power because "the all but general strike" involved almost the entire workforce, which comprised numerous strata of proletarians normally divided by different interests. Moreover, the explosion of discontent took place as the Saratov countryside tried to shed itself of Soviet power and as worker disturbances, the true extent of which has yet to be appreciated, broke out elsewhere in Russia. United in their hostility to the harshness associated with the militarization of labor, the co-optation of worker organizations, and an acute supply crisis, skilled, "conscious" workers led the Saratov strike movement. Dismissing worker demands for a constituent assembly and worker democracy as nothing more than the hollow slogans of Mensheviks and SRs, the Communists failed to see that the labor unrest had little to do with these parties per se, and had everything to do with the political and socioeconomic promises of 1917 concerning free elections, independent trade unions, and freedom of speech, the press, and assembly. Political consciousness builds on past experience. Workers had much more consciousness than party discourse allowed, and they manifested it in their desperate opposition to Bolshevik rule.

In depicting worker and peasant hostility as nothing more than anger over their economic conditions, party public language maintained that setting the economy right would bolster its authority. Although the party's private language fell under the influence of this discursive strategy as well, it at times acknowledged that the cause of worker discontent was not an either/or situation and that there was also a political side to the unrest. This explains why the Communists banned other political parties and sought to smooth over the deep divisions the unrest had caused within the party itself. Confidential Cheka reports make clear, however, that the hostile and expectant attitudes of Saratovites

[97] Strel'tsova, "Partiinaia organizatsiia," 174.

changed little by mid-1922. Coercion and the suppression of the rival socialist parties merely guaranteed that the mass mood would remain one of estrangement or ambivalence. Besides, the concessions ushered in by the NEP had the potential to make some people's positions worse in the short run. In benefiting peasants and certain other groups, the concessions gave the impression that the Leninists had fallen under the influence of their rivals' programs. This took the edge off the opposition, since so many seemed eager to have order reimposed, but it also gave the Bolsheviks good cause to be vigilant. There was another reason, however, why violence did not start up again: not only coercion and concessions defined this period, but starvation. While acute supply problems may have been the catalyst that caused workers to revolt, hunger ironically may also have been the reason the Bolsheviks were able to stay in power at this critical juncture. The Bolsheviks had survived the Civil War, but had not won it.

Conclusion

DEVOTED TO decentering and to broadening the agenda of standard narratives of the Russian Civil War, this book investigates how political events, ideologically inspired social engineering, and cultural creation played themselves out at the local level during circumstances of sustained crisis and emergency in a country with an authoritarian political culture. In bringing to life the experiences of various social groups during the Civil War, I suggest how the tragedy shaped and confined later chapters in Soviet history. Most importantly, I conclude that the Soviet 1920s contained no real alternatives to a Stalinist-like system. Distancing myself from authors who pin the blame for this on ideology alone, I complicate our understanding of this central issue in Soviet history by considering the interplay of ideology, circumstances, Russia's backwardness, the country's political traditions and culture, and other factors during a prolonged period of social and political turmoil beginning with the Great War.

To do so, I first spotlight the enormous importance of language. Taking poetic license, we might say that the Bolsheviks not only fought their way to power, but also talked themselves into it, both literally and figuratively. Examination of the external (public) and internal (secretive) languages of Bolshevism reveals how the party understood its historical mission and the world about it. Bolshevik external language already in 1918 depicted the "heroic" present as a revolutionary dictatorship of the proletariat and, when convenient, the peasantry, under relentless siege by conspiratorial counterrevolutionaries. As a centralized party-state began to assert itself against manifestations of localism, its external language, despite frequent fissures, became more authoritative and monologic, eventually allowing room only for affirmation. While Bolshevik external language had the capacity to transform human relationships and to help bring into existence that which it represented, it was likewise referential and responsive. One of its practices became a lasting legacy of the Civil War: it need but mention real, potential, or imagined struggles in order to justify policies made in the name of discipline (or to account for shortages). To deal with the obvious discrepancies between social realities and their depiction in party external language, the Bolsheviks designed various rhetorical strategies. For example, they pinned labels on their enemies, denied or disputed rival claims, and determined social and political identity — class — through behavior. Whenever the party fell under siege, its external register even acknowledged its helplessness, thereby often undermining that language by discounting earlier versions of it. Thus, control of the written word contributed to the party's victory in the Civil War, but it paradoxically also served to erode the Communists' credibility.

Analysis of party internal language further shows that the Bolsheviks had unconditional faith in their historical mission and confidently believed that they had the "moral authority" to rule, both of which enabled them to rationalize their use of force. Mistrusting the autonomy of those very social groups in whose name it governed, the party leadership remained determined to rule without mass support. Meanwhile, party cadres learned how to observe the forms and formalities of both languages and their variants as they evolved. Once localism came under fire by Moscow, internal language became the medium through which debates over control, localism, and virtually all other controversial issues took place. Matters relegated to internal language continued to bleed through into the external language throughout the period, however, and that is why the leadership sought to rein in minority views within the party itself.

In mapping the course of the Civil War, we also need to factor in the role of a prolonged period of warfare, and all that it entails, in the process of state formation. World War I inaugurated a century of revolutionary explosions and of ideologically fueled, and often vindictive, politics. The anarchy and violence that characterized the era beginning in 1914 influenced how the revolutionary state would serve as an instrument of restructuring. In order to stay in power and to safeguard the state, the Soviet government tapped its "despotic" power, the willingness to govern without negotiation with society, creating the illusion that state and society (minus its class enemies) were one. Bolshevik despotic power had much to do with the tsarist autocratic tradition, but also with political and social processes in which the state interacted, let loose during the fury of the 1914–22 period. Above all, the dynamic and contested relationship between centers and peripheries (e.g., between Moscow and Saratov, between Saratov and the district towns, between the district towns and volosts, between the volosts and villages, etc.) not only rendered the Bolshevik Party even less monolithic than previously believed, but also makes more understandable its reliance on repression.

Local identities could serve as a form of political capital; however, the manifestations within the Communist Party of "localism" did not represent the possibility of a more democratic form of Bolshevism. I argue this for two reasons. First, Bolshevism as practiced was the product of the processes noted above, which affected more than the Bolsheviks: this period in general bode ill for the development of democratic politics within any political movement in Russia. Second, party internal language generated in Saratov reflected the perception that the reason for the transformation of the "democratic" soviets from revolutionary organs into pillars of the state bureaucracy lay in the shortcomings of those social groups in whose name the party ruled. In this regard, most Bolshevik leaders were in agreement. All told, the fate of the soviets makes evident that popular participation in public life became a casualty of civil war; the complex processes by which the Leninists helped to destroy democratic values arguably damaged socialist ones as well. In sum, the rupture between party hyperbole regarding, and the actual practices of, Soviet "democracy," already at this time scrambled the distinctions between what constituted the authoritative, the authentic, and the real.

Although the party-state that emerged by 1921 in some respects represented a radical extension of the past rather than a revolutionary break with it, ideology transformed the Bolshevik state's practices, thereby constituting a foundational moment in the evolution of Russian political culture. Subject to constant development and elaboration, political culture evolves gradually, a process that appeals especially to the young and socially marginal. Even though it had little space for democratic politics, Bolshevik rule insisted upon popular participation and assent and thereby marked a real rupture with the past by involving workers, peasants, women, youth, and minorities in public life. Drawing elements of the formerly disenfranchised into the Soviet party-state, the Bolsheviks periodically purged some of them, and frequently forgave others breaches of discipline, which the party leaders presented as another consequence of a low cultural level. Because periods of radical change carry considerable baggage from the prerevolutionary period, these individuals drew their idea of what constituted acceptable behavior among officials from what they had experienced under the autocracy. They likewise drew it from the public behavior of party commissars, many of whom succumbed to the corrupting influences of power. The conditions of the time endowed these new models with unsavory features. Instead of allowing the democratic potential of Russian political culture to develop, civil war conditions resulted in curtailment of democracy within the party, the use of force to achieve political objectives, and reliance on a plebeian population for support, thereby spinning a tangled web of dependence, mistrust, and exploitation. In attempting to redefine what constituted a public sphere and civic behavior in a Russia rent by social strife, the Communist Party internalized alien cultural forms just as the population over whom it ruled did.

The 1914–22 period constrained the democratic capacity of Russian political culture, but it continued to coexist along with other forms of authoritarianism. For instance, in co-opting their socialist rivals' strategies of dissent, the Bolsheviks internalized some of their rivals' ideas, while others survived in the underground. One of the most revealing finds in the archives is the critical role played by the Revolutionary Communists in Saratov, whose support for Soviet power and willingness to work with the Bolsheviks kept the province from falling to the Whites. In providing compelling evidence of a broader political spectrum than current historiography allowed, this study modifies the prevailing binary of Red vs. White. True, the Bolsheviks' strategy of co-opting their populist partner became a characteristic practice during the Civil War and an essential element of the formative experience for all involved. In seeking to marginalize and repress this other revolutionary voice, however, the Bolsheviks found themselves locked in a dialogue with the Revolutionary Communist discourse it sought to discredit. The same is the case in regard to its relationship with the Mensheviks and SRs. Manipulating the dominant discourse in which politics were played out, the Bolsheviks often presented their rivals' ideas as their own. This enabled the Bolsheviks, in a controlled environment, to make a case against the further independent existence of these parties. Moreover, although the Communists succeeded in co-opting or driving into the underground their socialist — and nonsocialist — opponents, the ideas and political impulses they represented survived as forms of otherness. The Civil War thus bequeathed a syncretistic culture combining different forms of belief and practice. Attempts made in subsequent decades of Soviet history at social engineering would generate both fresh support for, and new hostility to, the system.

Part Two of this book underscores the extent to which the Civil War experience reconfigured Saratov as a set of social relations by sundering traditional political, social, and economic divisions and creating new ones. In plunging Saratov into social chaos, the Civil War destroyed an administrative tradition long in the making, as place became a reflection of power relations. The brutalization of Saratov's population, breakdown of the economic infrastructure, and fierce struggle to survive generated many negative practices as well as attitudes of indifference toward public property, and estrangement from the state. Some of these became embedded in ways that constrained later Soviet history. Despite the relentless chaos of the time, the local shaped more global structuring processes and forms: it bears repeating that while the events described in this book are unique to Saratov, they have condensed within them more general experiences that could be just about anywhere in European Russia.

Bolshevik cultural policies and practices did not ease estrangement from the state because the party's application of coercion (despotic or agentive power) to bring about cultural hegemony made it an elusive goal. The party swept away old cultural forms and established control over the production and consumption of cultural signs, but the result was superficial conformity that was ritualistic and opportunistic. This is especially true as practices immersed in everyday life, such as illicit economic activity, the observance of religious rites, or old school curricula, continued to direct perceptions along more familiar, less revolutionary, pathways. Nevertheless, the Communists constructed a narrative of the Revolution that reflected new social hierarchies and forms of power in which ideology became the only acceptable reality. By the end of the Civil War, the Bolsheviks' version of the revolutionary tale insisted that the Communist victory had been inevitable, thereby conveying the message that resistance was both improper and futile. Moreover, the Bolsheviks inscribed historically delayed gratification into their narrative in promising a glorious future. Placing literacy at the center of their social programs, they told the downtrodden that acquisition of knowledge would help them overcome centuries of tsarist oppression. The disparity between everyday realities and Bolshevik propaganda, however, probably not only discredited party propaganda, but also might have undermined the integrity of the printed word or made the newly literate more susceptible to counterideologies. Because the appeal of the latter continued, the Cheka placed informants in all institutions to monitor public life; even rank-and-file Bolsheviks could not be expected to police themselves. This was more than a modernist proclivity to know what one's subjects thought—it represented an inherent distrust, not only of society, but also of its own cadres, and became an integral part of Communist cultural practices that helped obscure the fact that the party had failed to establish cultural hegemony while its ideology remained contested.

These points become more obvious when I consider the importance of social and cultural identities in shaping the total experience of revolution and civil war. Personal narratives authored by members of Saratov's bourgeoisie disclose how the class other ordered their world and understood the experience of civil war, and how politics and ideology infuse human geographies. The discrimination and violence unleashed against the bourgeoisie invited resistance or self-serving compliance from them, which in turn strengthened the Bolsheviks' original distrust of this sorely needed but maligned social group. Many members of Saratov's bourgeoisie became Soviet civil servants of one kind or another, affecting the practices of Soviet power in ways that have not yet been fully appreciated. Recording a cultural history that otherwise might have been forgotten by official historical memory, the personal narratives they left behind disclose that their authors understood their social otherness not in terms of their privilege, but in terms of their values and beliefs. They associated revolutionary power with the social other, in this case, the plebeian population or Jew, finding meaning in their own suffering and fortitude. Many of those who did not flee Russia remained other without going anywhere.

The Bolshevik state's social and economic policies likewise reconfigured the identities of society's lower elements. While Bolshevik attempts to create a new economic order exposed their belief in an inherent hostility in class relations and in the superiority of socialist principles and methods, they also reflected a tsarist economic model in place since 1915 in which state intervention and control played major roles. Bolshevik ideology transformed practices of state intervention, however, by increasing coercion and justifying punitive measures, as the party took whatever steps its leadership deemed necessary to stay in power. The party's economic policies, for instance, contributed to the consolidation of the one-party state and the repression of civil society, thereby strengthening the authoritarian streak in Russian political culture. At the same time, people honed basic survival strategies, becoming further alienated from Soviet-style public life. The Bolsheviks later drew on the Civil War experience as a formative one not with lessons to avoid, but with lessons to emulate, in part because coercion had kept them in power. True, it turned people against the party and exacted a costly human toll. Yet, the Bolsheviks needed to rely on the same measures to hold onto power while they tried to effect the changes that they believed would make coercion unnecessary in the long run. And this ultimately helped to doom the Soviet modernization project.

The state's intentions are most apparent in its approach to controlling and transforming social relations in the countryside. The ideological lens through which the party viewed the peasantry dictated policies that ignored the peasants' aspirations and multiple social identities. The hidden transcripts of the Saratov peasantry expressed not only their adeptness at the arts of passive resistance, but also their willingness to defend their social space by rising up against what they saw as Communist tyranny. Some showed their skill at manipulating the dominant discourse to justify their actions as being caused by the party-state's breach of the social contract. In the process, the peasantry succeeded in wringing concessions from the Bolsheviks, but only temporarily, since the two strands of thinking within the party regarding the countryside—accommodation vs. forced social engineering—continued to coexist. Moreover, the civil war experience ironically strengthened the cohesion of village social life. The state's rapacious policies had made ownership of land a major element in many peasants' understanding of what it meant to be a peasant, since survival had made it necessary for the peasant to become more self-sufficient. This merely served to reinforce deep-rooted Bolshevik prejudices against the peasantry, who also remained other within the system that outwardly assimilated them. In so doing, they weakened its powers that they lacked the power to change.

The Communists' relationship with the working class was no less problematic, for it too developed a form of consciousness that found expression in resistance to and circumvention of many Bolshevik practices. This consciousness of interpreted experience gave them collective identities outside the one the Bolsheviks created for them of the conscious, skilled worker vanguard constituting a bastion of support for the party. Some authentic workers proved reluctant to give up their autonomy. Using the vocabulary and symbols of the Revolution to their advantage whenever possible, they resisted repression and the Bolsheviks' colonization of the discourse and organizational practices of the labor movement. These strategies reflected a class consciousness, expressed as efforts to retain an independent voice. Further, Bolshevik economic policies gave rise to competition over scarce resources and to a parochialism that made a mockery of party internationalist language. Necessity likewise forced workers to sharpen basic survival strategies and to withdraw from public life, and this, also, shaped later Soviet history. The new relations between workers and the party-state negotiated during the Civil War based on adaptation, resistance, and forms of circumvention reordered daily life by promoting workers' strategies of evasion, avoidance, selective participation, and even hostility. Such behavior undermined the party's representations of them in public language, which workers manipulated to their advantage, thereby creating an unusual form of mutual dependency.

In early 1921, both the active and more passive forms of resistance among workers, peasants, and town dwellers created the gravest crisis to date for local authorities, who resorted to unprecedented ferocity to crush the opposition. In depicting worker and peasant hostility as nothing more than anger over their economic conditions, the party maintained that restoring the economy would bolster its authority. To play it safe, the Communists banned other political parties and sought to smooth over the deep divisions the unrest had caused within the Communist Party itself. But none of this changed the hostile and expectant attitudes of Saratovites, or overcame their alienation from the state. The Bolsheviks had defeated the Whites and Poles and had repressed and co-opted the other socialist parties, providing an element of stability simply by eliminating alternatives in an environment in which people clamored for the reimposition of law and order. Lenin's party, however, remained at odds with much of society, fragmented as it was. The Bolsheviks had not negotiated a settlement with it, but merely established military dom-ination over it. They fought and survived this war against society with coercion, concessions, and famine. While they did not consciously cause mass starvation, they took advantage of its tendency to rob people of initiative to stay in power. This concluding chapter in the Civil War reveals the Bolsheviks' greatest dilemma: they could not hold on to power and permit dissent to legitimize itself, yet by not allowing oppo-sition to legitimize itself, they in the long run planted the seeds of their own destruction.

To conclude, this study of Bolshevism in power reveals that it became closed to real alternatives. A basic pattern of governing had taken root that combined elements of violence, mobilization, and control of human resources with co-optation, rewards, concessions, and strategies of inte-gration. A basic pattern of being governed emerged as well, finding ex-pression in adaptation and dependency, but also in superficial and/or opportunistic conformity, forms of otherness, circumvention, evasion, and, rarely, open hostility. The NEP, which did not bring recovery to Saratov Province until the mid-1920s, represented nothing more than what party leaders said it did: a temporary retreat in the party's project for social transformation; had it been allowed to develop unfettered, it would have threatened the party-state's monopoly on public life. The Civil War proved to be a formative experience in that it had created a kind of foundation on which the future was built, shaped by multiple, independent processes that developed at different paces, affecting each other in unpredictable ways. Many of the features of the Soviet system we associate with the Stalin era and afterward were already clearly ad-umbrated, practiced, and even embedded during the 1914–22 period. They reflected familiar elements of Russian political culture, but also new forms shaped by ideology, circumstances, situations, people, and chance, and forged in the fire of civil war.

Bibliographical Essay

I HAVE COMPILED a selected bibliography of works cited in this book, which readers can consult by visiting the Princeton University Press web page at *www.pupress.princeton.edu*. This bibliography is not a complete listing of all of works and sources that I have drawn upon while researching and writing my book, but it does indicate the range of materials that have informed the study.

I launched the project during a six-month stint in Moscow and St. Petersburg in 1986, when I obtained limited access for the first time to Soviet archives. This was before foreign researchers could consult archival inventories or visit repositories without special permission. During my stay I worked in what is today *Gosudarstvennyi Arkhiv Rossiiskoi Federatsii* (The State Archive of the Russian Federation, or GA RF), where I benefited most from collection (*fond*, or f.) 130 (The Council of Peoples Commissars); f. 393 (People's Commissariat of Internal Affairs); and f. 1235 (The All-Russian Central Executive Committee). I also used the collection of the Supreme Court of the RSFSR (f. 1005), and the personal papers of V. P. Antonov (f. 7471) and A. Minkh (found in f. 5881). The GA RF materials are particularly valuable in detailing the spread of Soviet power in 1918, but are much less useful in illuminating subsequent years of the Civil War. Later, after the sweeping changes brought about by the Gorbachev Revolution, I returned to GA RF to tap recently declassified material, especially f. 9591 (Collections of the Petit-Bourgeois Parties).

Glasnost made it possible for me in 1990 to visit Saratov, a city closed to foreigners since before World War II. The unrestricted access I received there to *Gosudarstvennyi Arkhiv Saratovskoi Oblasti* (The State Archive of Saratov Oblast, GASO)[1] forced me to reconceptualize

---

[1] See the outdated but still helpful two-volume published guide to GASO, *Kratkii spravochnik: Spisok fondov Gosudarstvennogo Arkhiva Saratovskoi Oblasti i ego filialov v gg. Balakove, Balashove, Vol'ske, Pugacheve* (Saratov, 1984).

the book and to turn it into a more ambitious study. Although a fire in the archive in the mid-1970s destroyed part of its holdings, including material on the military aspects of the Civil War, GASO houses the most important documentation on the period. Between 1990 and 2000, I visited Saratov ten times, where I utilized twenty-six collections in GASO and over four hundred archival units (*dela*) containing tens of thousands of sheets (*listy*). Especially helpful were f. 329 (Saratov Provincial Department of Public Education); f. 456 (Saratov Provincial Administrative Department of the Soviet's Gubispolkom); f. 521 (Executive Committee of the Saratov Soviet); f. 523 (Saratov Provincial Food Supply Committee); f. 692 (Saratov Provincial Military Commissariat); and f. 3310 (Saratov Provincial Cheka). The contrast between secret reports found in the archive and coverage of these events in the local press intrigued me from the start and became a key interpretive frame for my book. In 1999 the staff at GASO assured me that I had exhausted all of the archive's holdings on the Civil War, including newly declassified materials. The kindheartedness and professionalism of GASO's staff compensated for the poor quality of many documents surviving the Civil War, when officials, out of necessity, often wrote (or typed with faded ribbons) on the back of documents because paper was in short supply. Moreover, during my early visits to Saratov xeroxing and microfilming were not available, as a result of which I hired over forty student scribes to copy information for me.

The collapse of the Soviet Union also opened the long-sealed holdings of the Communist Party archives, both in Saratov and in Moscow. I spent several summers working in the party archive in Saratov, today known as the *Tsentr Dokumentatsii Noveishei Istorii Saratovskoi Oblasti* (Center for Documentation of the Contemporary History of Saratov Oblast, TsDNISO).[2] Here I combed the collections of the Saratov gubkom (f. 27), the Saratov Komsomol gubkom (f. 28), the Left SR and Revolutionary Communist Parties (f. 151/95), and f. 1328 (Party Court of the Saratov Provincial Organization). I also made strategic forays into the collections of the Saratov city neighborhood party committees, the Atkarsk Uezd committee (f. 200), and representative party cells and factions at factories and in professional organizations. In all, I consulted eleven collections and more than four hundred dela, which shed light on the Communist Party as well as on its socialist allies, and without which I would have been unable to imagine the experiences of local Communists during 1917–22.

---

[2] No guide was available at the time, but a basic one has since been compiled: *Tsentr Dokumentatsii Noveishei Istorii Saratovskoi Oblasti: Kratkii spravochnik-spisok fondov* (Saratov, 1998).

After familiarizing myself with the abundant holdings in Saratov, I decided to concentrate my efforts on using local depositories rather than on working in the *Rossiiskii Gosudarstvennyi Arkhiv Ekonomiki* (Russian State Archive of the Economy), which largely duplicates what is available locally. However, I did profit from working in the former Communist Party archive in Moscow, *Rossiiskii Gosudarstvennyi Arkhiv Sotsial'no-politicheskoi Istorii* (Russian State Archive of Social-Political History, RGASPI), where I drew from f. 17 (Central Committee of the Bolshevik Party). I also studied the collections of the central committees of the SRs, Mensheviks, Left SRs, and Revolutionary Communists, and the personal papers of V. A. Radus-Zenkovich (f. 605).

I likewise benefited from conducting research in other repositories in Saratov and elsewhere. In the Saratov Local Studies (Kraevedcheskii) Museum, I obtained access to unpublished memoirs, particularly those of N. I. Arkhangelskii, and to the museum's photograph collection. In the Khvalynsk Local Studies Museum I secured a copy of the unpublished diary of Mikhail Chevekov. The Balashov Local Studies Museum provided me with photographs and with materials on the Solonin affair, discussed in chapters 3 and 4. I examined rare contemporary provincial publications, often unavailable elsewhere, as well as dissertations defended locally, at the Saratov University Research Library. Unpublished materials held in the private collections of G. Mishin, V. V. Gleizer, S. V. Katkov, V. A. Solomonov, and V. N. Semenov were also put at my disposal and proved invaluable for my study. At the Central Museum of the Revolution in Moscow I duplicated photographs and looked at the personal papers of V. P. Antonov (Saratovskii). At the Hoover Institution I analyzed the papers of the American Relief Administration's Russian Operations concerning Saratov and also the (then) unprocessed collection of the SR Party in the Nicolaevsky Collection. The Library of Congress's Manuscript Division holds the papers of Alexis Babine and of George Gustav Telberg, which I read.

In the course of my research I realized that it was necessary to familiarize myself with what branches of GASO located in Balakovo, Balashov, Engels, Pugachev, and Volsk have to offer. A visit to the archive in Balashov revealed a goldmine of documentation, but convinced me that working at the micro-level would add detail—and years—to my project but not necessarily affect my conclusions. Still, such collections are one of the best kept secrets of the Russian archival system. (The major reason for this is that the national commission that approves dissertations will not allow someone to defend a work based on documentation at the district level, although this restriction is likely to be lifted.) Fortunately, Saratov historian Arkady A. German made full use of the Civil War materials in the branch archive in Engels in researching his two-volume history of the Volga Germans, volume 1 of which I drew upon extensively.[3]

It took perseverance, luck, and a sense of humor to obtain access to newspapers published in Saratov Province during the Civil War. No depository library holds complete runs of any of these papers, as a result of which I was forced to read them out of chronological order and over a long period in libraries and archives in Moscow, Leningrad/St. Petersburg, and Saratov. The unexpected short- and long-term closing of major Russian libraries, owing to leaky roofs, fires, and other mishaps, only complicated my efforts to tap this source, so essential to determining how the Bolsheviks depicted the revolution and civil war in process. Most important to my study were *Izvestiia Saratovskogo Soveta* (ISS), the local Communist Party newspaper; *Krasnaia gazeta* (KG), the local Izvestiias issued in the district towns;[4] and the episodic newspaper put out by the Revolutionary Communists, *Znamia revoliutsii*.

The more than twenty-five local journals and bulletins published during the Civil War also constitute an essential source for my study. Representative examples that proved to be particularly important are *Biulleten' Saratovskogo statisticheskogo biuro*; *Biulleten' Saratovskogo gubkoma*; *Ekonomicheskaia zhizn' Povolzh'ia*; *Kooperativnaia mysl'*; *Na transport*; *Novyi mir*; *Saratovskii vestnik zdravookhraneniia*; *Prosveshchenie*; *Statisticheskii vestnik*; and *Vzmakhi*.

Published documentary materials—minutes and protocols of national party conferences and congresses, brochures put out by the Left SRs and SRs, and document collections on soviets, the Cheka, economic activity, the army, etcetera—further enriched my study. Saratov historians published document collections during the Soviet period such as *Saratovskaia partiinaia organizatsiia v gody grazhdanskoi voiny: Dokumenty i materialy, 1918–1920 gg.* (N. Poliantsev et al., eds., Saratov, 1958), but this and other Soviet-era compilations suffer from a tendentious selection process. More useful are document collections that went to press before Stalinist orthodoxy seized hold of the historical profession, such as M. F. Vladimirskii's *Organizatsiia sovetskoi vlasti na mestakh* (Moscow, 1921), and the two volumes edited by V. P. Antonov-Saratovskii, *Sovety v epokhu voennogo kommunizma: Sbornik dokumentov* (Moscow, 1928, 1929). Despite their shortcomings, the published protocols of the Saratov Soviet also proved to be a necessary

---

[3] *Nemetskaia avtonomiia na Volge, 1918–1941*, vol. 1, *Avtonomnaia oblast', 1918–1924* (Saratov, 1992).

[4] These papers changed titles frequently during the Civil War. Complete publication information is found in A. A. Iudina and Z. I. Stepanidina, *Spisok Saratovskikh periodicheskikh izdanii, 1917 (noiabr')–1967*, part 2, *Gazety* (Saratov, 1971).

source (V. P. Antonov-Saratovskii, ed., *Saratovskii Sovet rabochikh deputatov, 1917–1918: Sbornik dokumentov* [Moscow and Leningrad, 1931]). I profited most, however, from documentary evidence issued in Saratov during the Civil War itself such as *Itogi perepisi naseleniia g. Saratova i ego prigorodov 28 avgusta 1920 g. po uchastkam militsii i kvartalam* (Saratov, 1921); *Iubileinyi sbornik Saratovskogo gubprodkoma. 7 noiabria 1917 g. (25 oktiabria), 7 noiabria 1919. g* (Saratov, 1919); and *Obzor deiatel'nosti Saratovskogo gubernskogo Soveta narodnogo khoziaistva za 1919 god* (Saratov, 1919). Various *otchety* (reports) were likewise indispensable. Some representative examples are *Otchet Novouzenskogo soveta soldatskikh, rabochikh i krest'ianskikh deputatov* (Novouzensk, 1918) and *Otchet Prezidiuma Gorsoveta i Gubispolkoma* (Saratov, 1921). Finally, the protocols of and resolutions carried by local conferences, congresses, and meetings also enhanced this study. Examples are *Plenum Saratovskogo gubkoma RKP (Doklady i rezoliutsii)* (Saratov, 1921); *Rezoliutsii VIII s"ezda sovetov Saratovskoi gubernii* (Saratov, 1921); *Protokoly i doklady VI-ogo Atkarskogo uezdnogo s"ezda sovetov R.K.iK.D. 15–19 dekabria 1918 g.* (Atkarsk, 1918); *Trudy I-go oblastnogo s"ezda rabochei kooperatsii Saratovskogo kraia* (Saratov, 1919); and *Vtoroi Saratovskii gubernskii s"ezd kommunisticheskogo soiuza molodezhi, 11–14 fevralia 1920 g. (Rezoliutsii i tezisy, priniatye s"ezdom)* (Saratov, 1920).

My fortuitous access to unpublished memoirs found in official repositories and in private hands suggests that the provinces contain a wealth of largely untapped sources for the study of Soviet history. As chapter 8 indicates, this project benefited greatly from both unpublished and rare published memoirs, which proved key in my documenting the experiences of Saratov's bourgeoisie during the Civil War. Among Bolshevik memoirs, the most revealing are those brought out during the event or in the 1920s. Edited by V. P. Antonov-Saratovskii, *Godovshchina sotsial'noi revoliutsii v Saratove* (Saratov, 1918) helped to establish an official version of the local revolution. Memoir collections issued on the fifth anniversary of the Revolution also are illuminating: *Piatiletie Saratovskogo gubernskogo soveta narodnogo khoziaistva (1917/18–1923 gg.): Sbornik statei i vospominanii* (Saratov, 1923), and *Piat' let proletarskoi bor'by, 1917–1922* (Saratov, 1922).

Soviet secondary literature on the subject proved useful in that I came to question most of its tenets. More so than in their treatment of 1917, Soviet historians patently falsified the history of the Civil War, undoubtedly because the party's mass base had eroded during the ordeal and the archives are choking with materials that document opposition to Bolshevik rule. The best works put out at the local level, by F. A. Rashitov and G. A. Gerasimenko, deal with 1917–18; only a handful of studies even treat the 1919–22 period. Since the collapse of the Soviet Union, however, Russian historians from both the older and younger generations have broken out of old paradigms. I have in mind works by E. G. Gimpel'son, *Formirovanie Sovetskoi politicheskoi sistemy, 1917–1923 gg.* (Moscow, 1995), and S. A. Pavliuchenkov, *Voennyi kommunizm v Rossii: Vlast' i massy* (Moscow, 1997).

The limited Western scholarship on the Russian Civil War tends to focus on military concerns, Allied intervention, and politics at the top. There are exceptions that have influenced my work. Orlando Figes authored *Peasant Russia, Civil War: The Volga Countryside in Revolution (1917–1921)* (Oxford, 1989), but he was unable to work in Saratov archives and, as I mention in chapter 5, did not know about the important Revolutionary Communist Party. Vladimir N. Brovkin's *Behind the Front Lines of the Civil War: Political Parties and Social Movements in Russia, 1918–1922* (Princeton, 1994) contains some critical insights; however, it is marred by a polemic style and selective treatment of topics. Also important to my study are the articles and forthcoming book of Peter I. Holquist, *Making War, Forging Revolution: Russia's Don Territory during Total War and Revolution, 1914–1921* (Harvard).

My work is likewise informed by scholarship on the French Revolution. In particular, I benefited from reading Keith M. Baker, *Inventing the French Revolution: Essays on French Political Culture in the Eighteenth Century* (New York, 1990); François Furet, *Interpreting the French Revolution* (New York and London, 1981); Lynn Hunt, *Politics, Culture, and Class in the French Revolution* (Berkeley, 1984); and Mona Ozouf, *Festivals and the French Revolution* (Cambridge, Mass., 1988).

Among the works that have shaped my thinking about the historical process itself are Louis Althusser, *Lenin and Philosophy and Other Essays* (New York, 1971); Lenard R. Berlanstein, ed., *Rethinking Labor History: Essays on Discourse and Class Analysis* (Urbana, 1993); Pierre Bourdieu, *Language and Symbolic Power* (Cambridge, Mass., 1991); Michel de Certeau, *The Practice of Everyday Life* (Berkeley, 1984); John and Jean Comaroff, *Ethnography and the Historical Imagination* (Boulder, 1992); Harry Eckstein, "A Culturalist Theory of Political Change," *American Political Science Review* 82, no. 3 (1988): 789–804; Susanna Egan, *Patterns of Experience in Autobiography* (Chapel Hill, 1984); Mikhail N. Epstein, *After the Future: The Paradoxes of Postmodernism* (Amherst, Mass., 1995); William A. Gamson, "Political Discourse and Collective Action," *International Social Movement Research: A Historical Annual* 1 (1988): 219–44; Anthony Giddens, *A Contemporary Critique of Historical Materialism*, vol. 2, *The Nation-State and Violence* (Oxford, Eng., 1985); Gerald Graff, "Co-optation," in *The New Historicism*, ed. by H. Aram Veeser (New York, 1989),

168–81; Michael Mann, "The Autonomous Power of the State: Its Origins, Mechanisms and Results," in *States in History*, ed. by John A. Hall (Oxford, Eng., 1986): 109–36; Allan Pred, *Making Histories and Constructing Human Geographies: The Local Transformation of Practice, Power Relations, and Consciousness* (Boulder, 1990); Robert D. Putnam, *Making Democracy Work: Civic Traditions in Modern Italy* (Princeton, 1993); James C. Scott, *Domination and the Arts of Resistance: Hidden Transcripts* (New Haven, 1990), *Seeing Like a State: How Certain Schemes to Improve the Human Condition Have Failed* (New Haven, 1998), and *Weapons of the Weak: Everyday Forms of Peasant Resistance* (New Haven, 1985); Joan W. Scott, "Experience," in *Feminists Theorize the Political*, ed. by Judith Butler and Joan W. Scott (New York, 1992), 22–40; and Edward W. Soja, *Postmodern Geographies: The Reassertion of Space in Critical Social Theory* (London, 1989).

Index